FILMS FOR, BY AND ABOUT WOMEN

by
Kaye Sullivan

The Scarecrow Press, Inc.
Metuchen, N.J., & London
1980

Library of Congress Cataloging in Publication Data

Sullivan, Kaye, 1921-
    Films for, by, and about women.

    Bibliography: p.
    Includes indexes.
    1. Women in moving-pictures--Dictionaries.
2. Women in the motion pictures industry--Dictionaries.
3. Women moving-picture producers and directors--
Dictionaries. 4. Moving-pictures--Catalogs.
I. Title.
PN1995.9.W6S95   791.43'09'09352042   79-26830
ISBN 0-8108-1279-7

CONTENTS

FOREWORD

My aim is twofold. First, I want to assist women and men
wishing to explore the changing and diverse roles women assume in
society. The films annotated herein provide, I believe, a historical
view of sex roles--a view that allows a better perspective on the relationship between being human and being a woman or a man. Sec-
ondly, I want to present women filmmakers and identify the genre
of films made by each one. Along with credits, running time, date
and availability, I have included a brief description of film content.
Many of these descriptions were taken from distributors' catalogs;
others I prepared from notes taken as I viewed the films.

Historically, women have been involved in all aspects of filmmaking, but they have not been given recognition or proper credit
for their efforts. I hope my work will correct this to some extent.
In the past decade, women have begun to appear in significant numbers as producers, directors, writers, editors, and cinematographers. Included among the filmmakers in this book are producers, directors, and screenwriters. Not mentioned are women editors and
cinematographers. I am happy to see that the objective of these
women filmmakers is to depart from the customary depiction of
women as sex objects, hookers or doormats, and to show women as
strongminded, independent and vital. Furthermore, I believe the
technical quality of these films is superb and getting better all the
time.

I have tried to give the user of this book as many rental
sources as possible. However, on some very recent films, there
is only one source for sale/rental. When I found more than one
title for a particular film, I cross-referenced in order to facilitate
a search. Rental fees were omitted because they fluctuate.

My search was done mostly from reference materials available in the Evergreen State College Library, Olympia, Washington. I have not included film distributor catalogs in the bibliography section, so the distributors in the Directory section should be considered part of the bibliography.

Many descriptions of the films included in this publication originally appeared in the University of California Extension Media Center publication, Films 1977-1978, a comprehensive bulletin describing over 4,000 films in dynamic areas of national interest. They are used here by permission.

I would like to dedicate this book to all women, to share my efforts with those wishing to broaden their knowledge through films about women, and with those who wish as well to understand historically the contribution women have made in filmmaking. I also dedicate this book to those filmmakers who wish to know what areas are lacking films, in order that they may expand their work to such areas.

Kaye Sullivan
Fall 1978

USER'S GUIDE

If you know the title of the film, refer to the main section of this book where films are arranged alphabetically by title, word by word. Foreign titles are interfiled alphabetically as spelled but initial articles have been ignored. For example, L'Avventura is listed in the "A" section (not in the "L" section).

Abbreviations used are "m" running time in minutes; "B" black/white; "C" color; "C/B" color/black and white; "r" release date; "si" silent; "n.d." no date; "p" producer; "d" director; "p/d" producer/director; and "s.w." screenwriter. Initials following a quote you will read as those of the person or source quoted.

Directly following each film title in the main section, you will find indicated the running time, whether color or black and white (or both), production or release date (or no date). Following the date, there will be a format identification. Films are mostly 16mm. If the medium is not 16mm, you will find a format identification indicating the medium (SLIDES, VIDEO, 8MM, or FILM-STRIP). Following that, if it is a foreign film, the language used as well as whether English subtitles are used is indicated. If the film is dubbed rather than subtitled, this will be noted.

At the end of each film description, you will find symbols (separated by semicolons) for the producer, sales outlet(s), and rental outlet(s). Should you find only one symbol, it means that the producer is also the sales and rental distributor. In these cases, I have not located another source of distribution. To find the source go to the List of Symbols (Appendix A) and locate the code(s) which you have found. They are listed alphabetically, followed by the identification of each one. Next, go to the Directory (Appendix B) where you will find an address for the source. For your convenience, I have tried to list

vii

as many rental sources as possible located throughout the United States. Address changes, corporate name changes and changes in distributorship are up-to-date at the time of publication of this book.

The Directory section lists names and addresses of filmmakers, as well as distributors, in alphabetical order. However, in case of a corporate name such as "William Greaves Productions, Inc.," you will find it listed as "Greaves, William, Productions, Inc."

If you do not know the title of a film, refer to the Subject Index section, where titles are listed under appropriate categories.

Finally, for those of you interested in women filmmakers and titles of films made by each, I have included an Index of Women Filmmakers. It lists alphabetically the names of filmmakers with titles of their films listed in alphabetical order. The main section of the book will tell you whether the filmmaker directed, produced, wrote, performed or shared in these functions.

FILMS FOR, BY AND
ABOUT WOMEN

A TO B (36m C 1971)
Depicts a teen-age girl making the transition from the role of
a girl ruled by the adult establishment to that of a free woman
among her peer group of drug and rock music enthusiasts. p. Nell
Cox; TL; EMC.

ABEL GANCE: HIER ET DEMAIN see ABEL GANCE: YESTER-
DAY AND TOMORROW

ABEL GANCE: YESTERDAY AND TOMORROW (28m C 1968)
Documentary on the contributions made to the motion picture industry by Abel Gance, French director. Shows his aesthetic and
technical inventions. By Nelly Kaplan; MGH.

ABORTION (40m C 1971 reel/cassette)
Explores the abortion issue in a discussion session by several
women. They discuss their abortion experiences, as well as the
moral, social, and legal implications of abortion. By Constance
Beeson; MMRC.

ABORTION (30m B 1971)
A strong film about the need for women to gain the right to control their bodies. Portrays the horror of U. S. drug experimentation
on Third World and white women in the South, in ghettos, and in
Puerto Rico. BWFC; IE.

ABORTION (28m C 1975 VIDEO)
As a way of helping people understand the decisions women have
to make in coping with pregnancy, six women candidly discuss their
experiences. Abortion is seen as a clear choice, the only alternative and the least awful alternative. Not all questions are answered,
but a good case study of the dilemmas of six women is presented.
NOWP; CREOU.

ABORTION AND STERILIZATION; Human Sexuality Series (29m C
1972 VIDEO)
Describes emotional reactions of individuals who have undergone
vasectomies and abortions as delineated in a workshop led by ob-
stetrician-gynecologist Ronald Pion, M. D. The new menstrual aspiration abortion technique is demonstrated and compared with standard methods. UHAWAII, KHETTV; PTL.

ABORTION AND THE LAW (54m B   1965)
Summarizes the attitudes and legal aspects of abortion in England, Sweden, Poland, Chile, Mexico and Japan, as well as in the
U. S.   Includes opposing viewpoints of lawyers, physicians and clergymen.   Includes interviews with young women who have undergone
abortions which were illegal at the time this film was made.
CBSTV; CAROUSEL; AIMS, BYU, EMC, FSU.

ABORTION AT WILL IN THE FIRST TWELVE WEEKS (57m B
1969)
Shows advocates and opponents of legalized abortion as they dispute whether or not a woman has a right to terminate her pregnancy
during the first three months.   NET, IU; BU, EMC, IU, UILL.

ABORTION: PUBLIC ISSUE OR PRIVATE MATTER? (25m C 1971)
Is abortion the decision of the pregnant woman alone?   Or must
her family, the church and society as a whole participate?   This
film covers many sides of this issue.   Both pro- and anti-activists
in the Washington, D. C. area speak out with conviction on the effects of abortion.   The legal aspects of providing abortions are described in light of the Supreme Court decision.   WRCTV; FI; EMC,
MSU, OKSU, PAS, UILL, UU.

ABOUT A TAPESTRY (10m C 1972)
Hermann Hesse's own words used to describe a tapestry he
owned.   By Isa Hesse; FIFWF.

ABOUT CONCEPTION AND CONTRACEPTION (11m C 1974)
Designed for use by professionally trained personnel of Family
Planning Agencies and by experienced teachers in high school and
college.   Very clear, animated drawings illustrate how conception
occurs and how the various birth control devices, surgical methods,
and the pill function in preventing conception.   The film has no narration but does need commentary by the presenter.   Ideally suited
for illiterate or semi-illiterate audiences, for audiences where the
English language proves to be a handicap, and for teaching situations
where the presenter wants to illustrate contraception techniques while
accompanying this illustration with his/her own interpretation.
NFBC; PERENNIAL.

ABOUT PUBERTY AND REPRODUCTION (12m C 1975)
Meant to be used with special audiences who need tailor-made
explanations, either in simple language, sign language, foreign language or in carefully selected terminology.   For that purpose the
film is silent and consists of animated, stylized illustrations of the
external and internal changes which occur in boys and girls at puberty.   A brief outline of pregnancy and childbirth is included at the
end of the film.   The instructor has to do the talking, while the
film provides all the visual and graphical materials desired for a
comprehensive presentation.   Also available in Spanish.   NFBC;
PERENNIAL.

ABOUT SEX (23m   C   1972)
   Has a delicate blend of beauty, humor, and earnestness that
characterizes young people. In a frank and natural tone, it explores
sexual attitudes and feelings and separates fact from fiction. Provides straightforward information about pregnancy, contraception,
venereal disease, abortion, homosexuality, masturbation, and related topics. With text. TEXFM.

ABOUT V. D. (14m   C   1975)
   Meant to be used with special audiences who need tailor-made
explanations, either in simple language, sign language, foreign language or in carefully selected terminology. For that purpose, the
film is silent and composed of stylized, animated drawings depicting
the transmission, symptoms, and effects of syphilis and gonorrhea.
The instructor has the benefit of doing the talking, while the film
provides all the visual materials desired for a clear presentation.
Also available in Spanish. NFBC; PERENNIAL.

ABSTRACT-EXPRESSIONIST MOVIE (5m   C   si   1974)
   A film made without a camera. Brush strokes made directly
on the film move in a tempo suggesting an objective correlative for
"action painting. " d. Pat Sloane; NLC.

ABSTRACTION (8m   C   1971)
   "Interpretation of abstract form as found in the combination of
the nude body, landscape and object. " R. S.   By Rosalind Schneider;
FCOOP, VRI.

ACCOMPLISHED WOMEN (26m   C   1974)
   Focuses on women speaking on a wide range of topics from politics to personal feelings, all pointing to a new attitude and image
women have about themselves. They are Katherine Graham, past
President of Washington Post Co. ; Dr. Virginia Apgar, leading spe-
cialist in problems in newborn infants; La Donna Harris, founder of
Americans for Indian Opportunity; Shirley Chisholm, U. S. Congresswoman; Nikki Giovanni, major American poet; and Helen Reddy, pop-
singer. By Charles Braverman; FI; MSU.

ACROBATS OF GOD BY MARTHA GRAHAM (22m   C   1969)
   A satirical dance comedy about dancers and their teacher, the
choreographer. It is Miss Graham's fanfare for dance as an art,
"a celebration of the trials, tribulations, discipline, denials, glories
and delights of a dancer's world. " By John Houseman; PF; UILL.

ACT OF CONTRITION (4m   B   n. d.)
   Provides an introduction to discussion about women's sexuality,
and their relationship to the church. Captures the confusion and
guilt created by the conflict between natural responsiveness and
church patriarchal morality. By Diane Graham; WFC; IRISF.

ACTOR (54m   C   1968)
   Lively examination of stage actors, their "mystique, " their
motivations and their traditions by leading English actors, directors

and playwrights.   Actress Joan Plowright discusses male domination
of the theatre.   Narrated by Alec Guinness.   ABCTV; ABFI; EMC,
UILL.

ACTOR WORKS, AN (A SCENE FROM "THE TROJAN WOMAN")
   (20m   C   1970)
   Viveca Lindfors, distinguished star of stage and screen, shows
how she taps her own resources of memory, imagination and skill
in order to identify with and ultimately become Queen Hecuba in
The Trojan Woman.   Opening in the privacy of her home, she con-
fides her feelings before setting off for the day's job.   The film
then picks her up at the studio as she starts her mental-emotional-
physical warm-up.   Through close-ups, it then progresses with her
through the infinitely demanding process of transforming herself into
Queen Hecuba mourning for her murdered grandchild.   FPDB/STPL;
PHOENIX; UILL.

ACTRESS, THE (90m   B   1953)
   Semi-biography of Ruth Gordon.   d. George Cukor; s. w. Ruth
Gordon; MGM; FL

ACTUATE I, ACTUATE II, ACTUATE III (15m   C   1974)
   Cinematic choreography, cine dancers affected by techniques
peculiar to the motion picture camera.   d. D. Samatowicz; NLC.

ADAM'S RIB (101m   B   1949)
   The interest in this exceptionally witty comedy is less related
to whether lawyer-husband Spencer Tracy or lawyer-wife Katharine
Hepburn will win the court case they're battling, but rather in
watching the on-going battle of the sexes they conduct both in and
out of court.   p. Lawrence Weingarten; d. George Cukor; s. w. Ruth
Gordon, Garson Kanin; MGM; FL

ADAM'S RIB; Girls and Women Series (30m   B   1971)
   Woman's role in society has traditionally been limited to positions of lesser importance, based on physical differences.   Yet how
much of this difference is inborn and how much is influenced by
socialization and education?   A children's drama group improvises
a typical family scene, followed by discussion on the improvisation
and the children's elaboration of their concepts of adult roles.
UMITV; PAS.

ADAPTING TO PARENTHOOD (20m   C   1975)
   Focuses on parenthood.   A number of new parents speak of their
initial problems--sleeplessness, crying babies, interfering grandparents, frustration and guilt at not feeling the serenity they had anticipated.   p. /d. Alvin Fiering; POLYMORPH; UM.

ADJUSTING TO AMPUTATION (13m   C   1976)
   Three youngsters in their late teens, adjusting to the loss of a
limb, share their problems, frustrations, and hopes.   They are presented to the viewer as realistic but successful coping models.
d. /p. Patricia Rambasek, SCC; HSCC.

ADMITTANCE, THE (43m B   1968)
Study of the reactions of members of a family confronted by
the severe mental illness of one of its members.   Illustrates the
problems of arranging mental hospital admittance for an urgent case.
d. /p. Patricia Watson; NFBC.

ADOLESCENCE (22m B 1967)
Poignant description of the ballet world.   Shows devotion of
Sonia Petrovna (14-year-old student) and Madame Egorova (a great
dancer at age 84).   NAVC; EC, UILL.

ADOLESCENCE: CRISES OR OPPORTUNITY (13m   C   1973)
Presents a sensitive look at the common problems of growing
up.   An adolescent's sometimes difficult search for identity is
seen through the thoughts and experiences of a teen-age girl and the
comments of a psychiatrist, Dr. Donald Muhich.   The habitual desire to please "others" (especially parents) brings confusion and depression.   Dr. Muhich emphasizes that much of the emotional turmoil of adolescents as they separate from their families is a normal
and even necessary part of maturing.   He points out the important
role of older friends, pastors, and others who can help the adolescent ease into the wider experiences of maturity.   FFAIR.

ADVENTURES OF AN *, THE (10m   C   1957)
"Man, " represented by an asterisk symbol (*), is introduced as
a baby enjoying the visual excitement of the world about him.   As
he grows, his ability to see and enjoy life becomes lessened.   He
emerges as an adult who is unable to see and feel freely.   Through
the eyes of his own child, however, he is able to rediscover the
world of life and beauty. "--Hubley Filmography.   SBI; FI, UC, USC.

ADVENTURES OF PRINCE ACHMED (65m C/B n.d.)
This first full-length animated film in the history of cinema tells
of the love of a poor tailor for a beautiful princess and the battle
between the white spirits of the magic lamp and the mythical and
monstrous djins and afreets.   Taken from The Arabian Nights.   Silent with music score.   By Lotte Reiniger; CEA.

ADVERTISEMENT (17m C n.d.)
"Turned-on Berkeley boy sells us his life.   Who is he: kid
waking up on the floor of his mother's house, revolutionary in the
street, golden-haired angel. "--CCC.   By Harriet Rohmer/Bret
Rohmer; CCC.

ADVICE FOR ASPIRING DOCTORS (29m C n.d. VIDEO)
Two Third World women doctors talk about their careers and
give advice to aspiring doctors.   KQEDTV.

ADVOCATES: ON ABORTION AT WILL IN THE FIRST 12 WEEKS
see ABORTION AT WILL IN THE FIRST 12 WEEKS

AFFAIR TO REMEMBER, AN see LOVE AFFAIR, OR THE CASE
OF THE MISSING SWITCHBOARD OPERATOR

AFFINITIES (5m   C   1972)
Beethoven's variations on Mozart's "la ci darem la Mano" synthesized by computer.   A ballet of squares and octagons in many forms,
exhibiting a variety of geometric and sometimes sensuous interactions.   By Lillian Schwartz; LPL

AFGHAN WOMEN; Faces of Change Series (17m   C   1975)
Afghan women live separated from public life in keeping with
conservative Islamic tradition.   The film follows their daily routine,
demonstrating their limited, yet influential roles.   By Nancy Dupree/
Judith Von Daler; AUIS; WER; EMC, IU, MSU, UILL, UK.

AFRICAN HERITAGE SERIES   see   MARRIAGE OF AMEY AND
ADISA, THE

AFTER THE VOTE (22m   B   1971)
"Serious and comic picture of the effects of sex role stereo-
types.   Professor Ron Lambert, a Canadian psychologist, and Ti-
Grace Atkinson provide the perspective. "--Odeon.   By Bonnie Kreps;
ODEON; EMC.

AFTER THE VOTE: NOTES FROM DOWN UNDER   see   AFTER
THE VOTE

AFTER THE VOTE: REPORTS FROM DOWN UNDER   see   AFTER
THE VOTE

AGING; Developmental Psychology Today Series (20m   C   1973)
Shows that there are many patterns of aging and that many widely-
believed negative stereotypes about the aged are untrue.   Two major
sociological theories describing the relationship between the aged individual and society, the Activity Theory and Disengagement Theory,
are discussed by Dr. Vern Bergston.   CRM; IU, MSU.

AGING: THE SEARCH FOR ETERNAL YOUTH (23m   C   1974)
The phenomenon of aging is examined by looking at the ways in
which different people cope.   Dr. Robert Butler, psychiatrist, believes there will be a new militance among the aging, stemming
from overemphasis on youth culture.   Sculptress Louise Nevelson,
still young at 70, illustrates the help of philosophy and creativity.
Dr. Ivan Popov's health spa in Nassau, called "Renaissance" is
visited by the camera, and the various forms of his "revitalization
therapy" demonstrated.   HL; DA; UILL.

AGNES DE MILLE; FALL RIVER LEGEND (11m   C   1972)
Presents excerpts from Agnes De Mille's ballet.   Based on the
story of Lizzie Borden, who was tried and acquitted for the murder
of her father and stepmother.   The setting is in the reconstructed
New England village of Sturbridge, Massachusetts.   Dancers from
the American Theatre perform the roles which include mime as
well as dancing.   GPI/GWWP; PARACO; UILL.

AID TO FAMILIES WITH DEPENDENT CHILDREN, INTAKE INTER-

VIEW; Studies in Interviewing Series (Pt. I, 17m; Pt. II, 17m;
Pt. III, 19m; Pt. IV, 19m; B 1965)
Four training films designed to stimulate questions and discussion on the subject of interviewing. Shows how the interviewer's
skills, values, and attitudes affect the interview and determine its
success. USC; EMC.

AIN'T NOBODY'S BUSINESS (54m C 1977)
Features six female prostitutes, as well as a male member of
the vice squad, Margo St. James. Includes footage from the First
World Meeting of Prostitutes. Filmed in the homes of prostitutes
by the all-women crew of Barrett-Pages Mountain Moving Picture
Company. d. Sally Barrett-Page; TPL

ALADDIN (15m B n. d.)
An animated film based on live shadow play. The Arabian
Nights story of a poor tailor, a genie, the Caliph's daughter and a
sorcerer. By Lotte Reiniger; CEA.

ALAE (5m C 1975)
For the first time, birds from the real world were optically
scanned, the sequence was fed into the computer to reappear as
completely new images in flight. By Lillian Schwartz; LPL

ALBUM (5m C 1976)
Growing up female in the nuclear family and surviving with a
sense of humor intact is the story of this charming, brightly-colored
family album of pop-deco drawings. The subject's feelings towards
her mother and father, and the abrupt censorship of her first innocent awakening are rendered with warmth and sparkle. By Linda
Heller; SB.

ALEXANDER AND THE CAR WITH A MISSING HEADLIGHT (13m
C 1967)
Story of a little boy's adventures with an old car. Adapted from
book by same title. By Cynthia Freitag; WESTON.

ALI: FEAR EATS THE SOUL (94m C 1974)
Loneliness brings together a 60-year-old German cleaning woman
and a Black Moroccan immigrant-worker. The film is not a study
in racial prejudice nor is it a tender love story, but a test of their
love for one another as they confront prejudices and hostility. Ger-
man/subtitled. d. Rainer Werner Fassbinder; NYF.

ALICE ADAMS (99m B 1935)
In a tragic-comic vein, the film explores the frustrations and
loneliness of a small town girl (Katharine Hepburn) from a not-so-
well-to-do family in the 30's as she struggles to be accepted by her
more aristocratic peers. Adapted from the novel by Booth Tarking-
ton. d. George Stevens; RKO; FL

ALICE DOESN'T LIVE HERE ANYMORE (112m C 1977)
A story of a woman who buries her aspirations to be a pop

singer at the insistence of her crude and insensitive husband. When
her husband dies in a road accident she takes off on a desperate
journey to fulfill her dreams, encountering misadventures and frustration at almost every turn of the road. Some of the film was improvised by Ellen Burstyn from her own experiences. Ms. Burstyn
stars in this film. A good documentary-style movie about the conflicts of today's woman. d. Martin Scorsese; WSA; SWANK.

ALICE NEEL, COLLECTOR OF SOULS (38m C 1977)
    Profile of the 76-year-old portrait painter who spent most of
her early life in poverty, rejected by the art establishment.
CINE16.

ALICE'S WORLD (26m C n. d.)
    The history of photography has harbored many strange and
poignant careers but few have been more poignant than that of Alice
Austen (1882-1952). Helen Hayes narrates this portrait of the photographer extraordinaire who, in the heyday of her career, produced thousands of pictures depicting life at the turn of the century.
Featured are over 125 historic photos that bring us back a lost era.
WNETTV.

ALICIA (75m C Scope 1976)
    Features Alicia Alonso, a prima ballerina among contemporary
ballerinas. Combines biographical and performance sequences.
Alicia discusses her history in ballet. Shows a glimpse of her
early life and includes parts of Giselle, The Black Swan, Grand Pa
de Quatre, and Carmen. d. Victor Casaus; Cuban Film Institute;
TFC.

ALKSANDE PAR see LOVING COUPLES

ALL ABOUT EVE (130m B 1950)
    The penetrating story of an older actress near the end of her
fabulous career, doing battle with a calculating, treacherous newcomer, is shown with wit and unfailing candor employing sharp and
sardonic dialogue. d. Joseph L. Mankiewics; FOX; FL

ALL COME TO LOOK FOR AMERICA (4m C n. d.)
    Using a series of beautiful color photographs and the kinesthetic
animation technique popularized by Dan McLaughlin, Arthur Liosett,
and Charles Braverman, the filmmaker has produced a kaleidoscopic
review of American history. Comparable in style to Braverman's
American Time Capsule, only in this instance the film has a more
romantic and positive philosophy. By Kathy Strickland; CFS.

ALL KINDS OF PEOPLE (28m C 1972)
    Shows the wide range of jobs available with the telephone com-
pany. Although a propaganda film for the telephone company, it
does show women working in many unusual areas. VA; NYTC.

ALL MY BABIES (55m B 1953)
    Portrait of a midwife's extraordinary character seen as she

delivers babies and gives prenatal care.   George Stoney's classic
documentary filmed in Georgia.   Owing to its on-camera delivery
sequence, the film is restricted.   CMC; BYU, EMC.

ALL OF US STRONGER (9m   C   1976)
   Women doing karate, tell about their self-defense experiences
and how they are realizing their own power.   KART; SB, IE.

ALL OUR VOICES (31m   C   1975)
   Informative film on the understanding of bi-lingual bi-cultural
education.   Shows how educators are incorporating this concept into
the educational system in Illinois.   Sponsored by Illinois Office of
Education.   By Claudine Jordan; BESC.

ALL OUT (27m   C   n. d.)
   A shocking statement of man's inhumanity to man.   The film
shows how some people's lack of love and dignity will permit them
to go to any length for money.   Using a television game show as a
symbol of modern life, this biting satire probes the psyche of the
greedy.   By Nan Martin/Bob Hastings; MG.

ALL THESE WOMEN (80m   C   1964   Swedish/subtitled)
   Mocks the pompous world of a concert cellist and his many
critics, censors, and mistresses.   Cornelius, one critic, proposes
that he write the biography of Felix, the cellist.   In exchange, the
cellist must play the critic's musical compositions.   Bergman's slapstick humor pokes fun at the snobbish pretensions of drawing room
art.   d. Ingmar Bergman; JANUS.

ALMIRA (20m   B   n. d.)
   "A cine-dance film ... evocative of a woman's terror in break-
ing away from conventional form: an initiation. "   N. L. K.   By
Nancy Larue Kendall; CCC, FCOOP.

AM I WIFE, MOTHER ... OR ME (31m   C   1976)
   Edited version of I Love You, Goodbye.   UU.
   See   I LOVE YOU, GOODBYE

AMAZING COLOSSAL MAN, THE (6m   C   1964)
   "Story, papier-mâché characters, sets, animation, camera work,
editing and sound created by 12 children (ages 6-12) at the Yellow
Ball Workshop. "--Y. A.   d. Yvonne Anderson; FCOOP.

AMAZING EQUAL PAY SHOW, THE (50m   C   1977)
   A political burlesque in seven tableau.   Incorporates elements
from the musical, the horror film and the crazy comedy.   Examines
the question of equal pay, women's participation in unions, and the
wider problem of the status of women's work under capitalism.
Shows how the British Equal Pay Act of 1970 does little to improve
women's wages or working conditions.   LWFG in collaboration with
the Women's Street Theatre Group.   WMM.

AMELIA EARHART (26m   B   1965)
   Using rare documentary footage, the film portrays the personal

life and history-making deeds of Amelia Earhart. CBSTV; IE; ASFI, MMA.

AMERICAN CHARACTER, THE (Series) see AUNT ARIE

AMERICAN MEMOIR SERIES see HISTORY

AMERICAN MYTH (9m C n.d.)
"Hand-drawn capsule of American life. A political, sociological heavy."--CCC. By Priscilla Humay-Witek; CCC.

AMERICAN PARADE: WE THE WOMEN, THE see WE THE WOMEN

AMERICAN RADIATOR (10m B si 1970)
"A cryptically sensuous first film with secret affinities for Georgia O'Keeffe.... It demonstrates that formal time, in film, is as plastic as light, or space."--Hollis Frampton. By Marcia Steinbrecher; FCOOP.

AMERICAN TRAGEDY, AN (96m B 1931)
Adapted from Theodore Dreiser classic about a weak-willed young man who falls in love with a rich girl but is unable to disentangle himself from a factory girl he seduced. d. Joseph Von Sternberg; UNIVE.

AMERICAN WOMAN, THE (15m C n.d.)
Presents the official story of the 23-million member Council of Women. Includes historic coverage of American women leaders and the activities of 29 organizations making up the NCW. KLEINW.

AMERICAN WOMAN IN THE 20TH CENTURY (58m B 1964)
Surveys the changing role of the American woman in the 20th century from Gibson Girl through the Flapper, Rosie the Riveter and up to the women of the sixties who shaped and reflected the sexual and social mores of our time. WOLPER; UAA.

AMERICAN WOMAN IN THE TWENTIETH CENTURY, THE (50m B n.d.)
Presents fast-moving calvalcade of the American woman, from Gibson Girl to Rosie the Riveter, finally emerging from the shelter of the Victorian Era to become the captive goddess of today's suburbs. METROM; FI; NIU, UMIS.

AMERICAN WOMAN--PARTNERS IN RESEARCH (14m C 1960)
Uses a coffee percolator to illustrate how women can help in the design of their future household items by appraising the style and simplicity of proposed products. CORGLW; HWP.

AMERICAN WOMAN, THE: PORTRAITS OF COURAGE (53m C 1977)
This drama-documentary highlights the careers of 10 American women who fought courageously to establish, preserve and expand

the liberties we now enjoy.   Describes the heroism of the Revolution and the battles against slavery, racism, sexism and exploitation of labor.   Offers tribute to the famous and not-so-famous women who helped shape our destiny.   Sybil Ludington, Deborah Sampson, Abigail Adams, Elizabeth Cady Stanton, Susan B. Anthony, Belva Lockwood, Harriet Tubman, Sojourner Truth, "Mother" Mary Harris Jones, Rosa Parks and others.   Based on Anne Grant's "Our North American Foremothers."   Also available in two parts.   p. Gaby Monet; d. Hobert Deubel; ABCTV; CUNLIM; MGH, UW, UC.

AMERICAN WOMAN'S SEARCH FOR EQUALITY (C 1973 SFS)
Women are a majority in America but their impact on national affairs and policies has been disproportionately small.   Individually and collectively women are mounting a concerted drive against discrimination.   Interviews reveal how women from all walks of life view their current status.   KPL

AMERICAN WOMEN: TWO HUNDRED YEARS OF AUTHENTIC
FASHION (C n. d.   SFS)
Designed to help students discover how fashions have reflected political and social events of the past 290 years.   Guide included. BUTP.

AMERICANS: 1776, THE (28m C 1976)
Depicts the life of the everyday person during the time of the Revolution.   Shows crafts, ways of life, and the differences of attitudes among the many different types of peoples in the colonies. d. /p. Helen J. Secondari; HFHA.

AMERICA'S CRISES SERIES see PARENTS

AMERICA'S FIRST GREAT LADY (POCAHONTAS) (27m B n. d.)
Tells of the Indian maiden, Pocahontas, who saved Captain John Smith from death at the hands of her tribe and fell in love with him.   When Smith was believed lost at sea, she was released from captivity by John Rolfe, the tobacco planter.   He captured her heart and married her.   IDEAL; UKEN.

AMPUMARATA see FINNISH FRUSTRATIONS

ANAÏS NIN, PTS. I and II (50m n. d.   VIDEO)
Part I is a personal interview wherein Anaïs talks about the importance of internal changes which the women's movement has generated in women.   She speaks about social roles, competition vs. collectivity and American men.   In Part II, she speaks in front of a large audience about the intimate nature of human creativity.   RF.

ANAÏS OBSERVED (68m C 1974)
A portrait of Anaïs Nin.   This film conveys her fundamental femininity, her strength as an artist, the delicacy of her prose, and the wisdom and serenity of her being.   (Also see A PAINTER'S JOURNAL.) By Robert Snyder; GP, CANTOR.

ANCIENT ART OF PERU (15m C 1960)
    Presents an introduction to the art of the main cultures of pre-
Columbian Peru. Shows ruins and choice objects dug out by
archaeologists reviving the achievements of 3,000 years of Peru-
vian civilization. By Penelope Strouth; FIM.

ANCIENT FOOTPATH (20m C 1960)
    Documents the migration of the Mixtec Indians in Southern Mex-
ico (1100-1300 A.D.) through an Indian boy's dream. The people
and places are authentically Mixtec as is the final plume dance performed at the archaeological site, Monte Alban, in Oaxaca. By
Madeline Tourtelot; GP.

... AND ANOTHER MOTHER FOR PEACE (28m B 1971)
    Beginning with cinéma-vérité footage of draft protestors and
anti-war demonstrators, this earnest film moves on to present four
moving portraits of families who were touched by the Vietnam "in-
cursion"--families who were enduring personal tragedies while Washington policy-makers were awaiting some Mystic Light at the End of
the Tunnel... Narration by Paul Stewart. d. Samuel Spewack;
KP.

... AND EVERYTHING NICE (20m C 1974)
    Norma Adams explains the purpose and function of a women's
liberation organization. The narrative follows a married woman in
her mid-30's whose sudden awakening brings her to a consciousness-
raising group in a "NOW" Center. She decides to get a job and
does not choose any radical options. The narrative is intercut with
Gloria Steinem who interprets the action and intellectualizes about
the issues involved. By Norma Adams; BFA; EMC. IU, OSU, PAS,
UKEN, UM.

AND I DON'T MEAN MAYBE (25m B 1974)
    A taut suspenseful drama on the initiation-into-manhood theme
using four characters and set in and around a cabin in Death Valley.
A springboard for discussion of male group behavior, masculinity,
ritual violence, and aggression. By Mark Griffiths; WOMBAT.

"AND IT IS PART OF ME" (9m C n.d.)
    Introduces Natalie Hammon who has turned a barren hill-top
into a beautiful Japanese garden, in which she tells of her philosophy. Accompanied by koto music. By Elda Hartley; HARTLEY.

AND NOW MIGUEL (95m C 1966)
    About child growth and family life in Spanish-speaking families.
Of a boy yearning for the day when he will become a man like his
father. Based on a book by Joseph Krumgold. UNIVE; CINE, CVE,
CW.

AND ON THE SIXTH DAY (6m B n.d.)
    Three basic socio-religious problems affecting our society are
powerfully depicted in this film through quasi-documentary technique
with no solution offered by the filmmaker. The first part addresses

the question of aloneness and lack of help from others, the second
part looks at abortion, and the third part covers prejudice. The
effect is to arouse the emotions and tempers of the audience and
stimulate discussion. By Christine Hornisher, UCLA student; CFS.

AND THEN THERE WERE ... (3m C 1973)
    "Mosaic cutout technique of animation using thousands of squares
of paper to compose a forest and the events which take place there.
Nature destroys and refurbishes itself; man destroys."--L. K.   By
Linda Klosky; KLOSKY.

... AND THEY LIVED HAPPILY EVER AFTER (12m C 1975)
    Examines the expectations of women in marriage.   Provocative
interviews intercut with advertising reveal why their impressions of
marriage have little to do with reality.   The film becomes a moving
comment on cultural manipulation.   d. Kathleen Shannon; p. NFBC;
EDC, EMC.

AND WHO ARE YOU?; Choice: Challenge for Modern Women Series
    (30m B 1966)
    Hubert S. Coffey and Marya Mannes discuss discovery of one's
inner self and the possible conflicts in maintaining one's individuality.
EMC; UMIS.

AND WOMEN MUST WEEP (26m C 1972)
    Dramatizes the events which occurred in Princeton, Indiana, in
1956-57 during a wildcat strike.   Narrated from a woman's point of
view.   Depicts the increasingly violent acts such as bombings and
the near-fatal shooting of an infant which were a result of disagree-
ments within the union over the legality of the strike.   Concludes
with a discussion of right to work legislation.   CENTRON; NRW; IU.

AND YOU ACT LIKE ONE TOO (24m B 1976)
    Deals with a young mother who has her first extra-marital af-
fair on the day of her 13th birthday.   d. /p. Susan Seidelman;
SEIDELMAN.

ANDEAN WOMEN; Faces of Change Series (19m C 1975)
    Film views Andean peasant women's daily life.   These women
carry much of the responsibility for family survival; yet, paradoxically, their world is dominated by men.   AUFS; WER; EMC, MSU,
UILL, UK.

ANDREA ACTING OUT (12m C 1974)
    "Study of the filmmaker's 10-year-old daughter which reveals
the fantasy dream life of a child.   The film explores the subtle
changes that have begun to take place as she matures."--R. S.   By
Rosalind Schneider; SCHNEIDER.

ANDY WARHOL (53m C 1973)
    Warhol talks with de Antonio, Barbara Rose and others.   Foot-
age from his films: Trash, Chelsea Girls, Heat, and Women in
Revolt.   By Lana Tse Pink Jokel; BP.

ANDY WARHOL: MENKEN (20m C si n.d.)
"A long day in the life of pop artist Andy Warhol. "--M. M.
Marie Menken; GP; FCOOP.

ANGEL BLUE SWEET WINGS (4m C 1968)
Celebration of love in animated collage. By Chick Strand; SB.

ANGELA--LIKE IT IS (60m B 1970)
Presents Angela Davis, who speaks from prison shortly after
her arrest in December, 1970, on charges of conspiracy to commit
murder. Includes a panel discussion with attorney Margaret Burn-
ham, editor Joe Walker of "Mohammed Speaks," and Charlene
Mitchell of the Angela Davis Defense Committee. AMDOC.

ANGELA DAVIS: PORTRAIT OF A REVOLUTIONARY (60m B
1972)
A moving documentary with footage of UCLA and the women's
house of detention in New York. Angela Davis' strength, courage
and her willingness to talk openly about ideas provides the kind of
role model that women rarely see and always need. d. Yolunde
Du Luart; NYF.

ANGELUS (15m C n.d.)
The aged of the world have lost their beauty to the eye--but the
souls inside them remain filled with hopes and memories, struggling
against the loneliness and separation forced upon them by a youth-
oriented society. Angelus is, on the surface, a look at a group of
elderly women in their day-to-day existence: going to church, working, or simply dreaming of that which is no longer. The story of
these ancient lives is told in images rather than words: the pictures
which emerge are those of sentenced isolation. Only memories of
those who touched their lives for but an instant fill the void: a husband killed in war, a brother who passed away, all remain in the
mind as they were once in life. Angelus gives us a rare opportunity
to see the world as these women do; to empathize with these lives
which represent our destiny. p. Mafilm Studios, Budapest;
CAROUSEL.

ANGIE (11m C 1972)
Angie describes with pride the love her family shares but ques-
tions the prejudice she sees around her toward Mexican Americans.
She discusses her philosophy for changing society; BFA; BU.

ANIMALS ARE CRYING, THE (15m C n.d.)
Presents the problem of over-population of cats and dogs in
America. By Mary Jo Smith; LCA.

ANIMALS OF THE DESERT (12m C 1967)
A closeup view of animals in their natural surroundings. By
Geraldine Byers, Justin Byers; BFA.

ANIMALS RUNNING (20m B 1974)
"A continuous stream of animals from bison to splinters of

fishes casting a hypnotic spell. "--Freude Bartlett.   By Anne Severson; SB.

ANN: A PORTRAIT (24m   C   1971)
A unique modern dancer, Ann Halprin integrates her art and personal life so fully one becomes the other.   An impressionistic film.
By Constance Beeson; AFI; TL.

ANN RUTLEDGE (33m   B   1956)
Film portrays Lincoln as a young lawyer, as a member of the legislature, the political atmosphere of the period, his physical and mental deterioration after death of Ann Rutledge, and his subsequent rehabilitation.   MGH; EMC, UM.

ANNA (21m   C   n.d.)
Anna Webster is a middle-aged housewife who discovers that her husband (Harry) is seeing another woman.   To her dismay, Anna finds that Harry's girl friend is young and attractive, and Harry clearly adores her.   Everything about their relationship has an ominous air of permanence.   Shaken by the thought that her marriage actually may be in danger, Anna at first reacts with bitterness. Later she tries to provoke a reaction from Harry--anything that might give her hope.   Anna is surprised to receive an invitation to tea from Harry's girl friend.   p. Church Television and Radio Centre in England; GPN.

ANNA KARENINA (42m   B   1935)
An abridged version of the Tolstoy novel, showing Czarist Russian society of the late 19th century.   Describes the ill-fated romance of Anna Karenina with Count Vronsky and the inevitable tragedy resulting from the defiance of convention.   MGM; ed. by TFC; FI; IU, UILL.

ANNA ROSENBERG (28m   B   1952)
Presents Anna Rosenberg, Ass't. Secretary of Defense and the first woman in the defense department, who discusses manpower in the armed forces with Martha Roundtree (moderator), Doris Fleeson, Yates McDaniel, Lawrence Spivak and William White.   From "Meet the Press."   NBCTV.

ANNA SOKOLOW DIRECTS ODES (37m   B   1972)
"Words can lie, but not movement ... " Anna Sokolow tells her students.   Filmed while she was artist-in-residence at Ohio State University in 1966.   She is shown sharing her philosophy and dance techniques with students.   Film ends with a performance to the accompaniment of Edgard Varèse's "Poeme Electrique."   Includes an unusual sequence photographed with kaleidoscopic lens.   OHSU; UILL.

ANNE HUTCHINSON, PTS. I, II; Profiles in Courage Series (9m   B   1965)
Shows Ann Hutchinson's fight for religious tolerance and freedom of conscience in Puritan New England.   SAUDEK; IQF; OKSU, PAS, UG, UILL, UIO.

ANNE OF A THOUSAND DAYS (146m   C   1970)
Portrays Anne Boleyn (Genevieve Bujold) and Henry VIII (Richard Burton) in the love affair that led to the schism between England and the Roman Catholic Church.   d. Charles Jarrott; s. w. Bridget Boland; UNIVE; CINE, CVE, CWF, TWY.

ANNE SEXTON; Poetry Series (30m   B   1966)
An introduction to Anne Sexton and a view of her poetry.   Includes her reading "Her Kind, " "Self in 1953, " "Those Times, " "Little Girl, " "My String Bean, " "My Lovely Woman, " and "Live. " NET, IU; BU, UILL.

ANOTHER PILGRIM (42m   B   1968)
Explores the relationship of two people and their one-day affair that ends in a dual suicide, using as a basis a kabbalah legend about a sorceress seducing men into the eternal life through death. By Elaine Summers.   SUMMRS.

ANSELMO (4m   C   1968)
Expert optical printing combined with a loving concern for the subject which lends a spiritual quality to this documentary of a street musician in a small Mexican town.   A hymn to the magic of tubas and life spirits is expressed in music.   By Chick Strand; SB.

ANTI-WOMEN'S LIBERATION; Woman Series (29m   C   1974   VIDEO)
Midge Decter (author of The New Chastity, and Literary Editor of Saturday Review World) and Lucianne Goldberg (co-author of Purr, Baby Purr, and national chairperson and co-founder of the Pussycat League) tell why they became concerned about the negative influence of "The Movement" on America's women.   WNEDTV; PTL.

ANTONIA: A PORTRAIT OF A WOMAN (58m   C   1973)
Portrait of Antonia Brico, history's first woman conductor, who, in 1930 at the age of 28, became the first woman to conduct the Berlin Philharmonic Orchestra, then considered the world's finest. By Judy Collins, Jill Godmilow; PHOENIX; EMC, ISU, PAS, UIO, UM.

ANY EMPTY SPACE (35m   B   n. d.)
An intimate cinéma-vérité study of theatre students who begin without any previous training, work diligently for eight weeks, and become a successful Mime Troupe under the direction of Bud Meyer, Theatre Department, Northwestern University.   The film follows the evolution of the group from initial orientation to the first performance.   Emphasis is placed on the process of building a "spirit of company, " and the kinds of mental and physical disciplines demanded by the art form.   By Mary Ann Childers, Victoria Hamburg, and John Pease.   NWUFL.

ANYTHING THEY WANT TO BE; Sex-Role Stereotyping in Schools, a Series (7m   C   1974)
Explores sex-role stereotypes in intellectual and career-oriented activities.   Covers both elementary and high school events, illus-

trating two themes: the low level of competence expected of girls
in both academic and vocational problem-solving tasks, and the
subtle manner in which girls' career aspirations are channeled.   By
Gloria Golden/Lisa Hunter; FWLERD; EMC, UW.

ANYTHING YOU WANT TO BE (9m B 1971)
   Expresses the conflicts of a teenage girl who is growing up
with the notion that "you can be anything you want to be. " She
discovers that this is on the collision course with reality ... the
reality of society's prescribed feminine roles and restricted career
opportunities.   By Liane Brandon; ECCW; UM, UW.

APARTMENT, THE (125m B 1960)
   The Apartment spins dizzily around the business hour shenani-
gans of a handful of overly lusty executives and the willing cooperation of junior executive Jack Lemmon who lends his apartment to his
bosses for that purpose.   Lemmon is hopeful of being promoted.
Funny, but acid, in that modern business men's methods are often
inhumane in pursuit of the immoral.   d. Billy Wilder; UAS.

APOTHEOSIS (5m C 1972)
   "Apotheosis, which is developed from images made in the radia-
tion treatment of human cancer, is the most beautiful and the most
subtly textured work in computer-animation I have seen. "--Roger
Greenspun, New York Times.   Also available in video cassette.
By Lillian Schwartz/Ken Knowlton; LPL

APOTHEOSIS (25m C n. d.)
   Closeup of John and Yoko in a medieval-looking village.   Camera in a balloon. ...   By Yoko and John Ono; GENESIS.

APPALACHIAN SPRING (32m B 1959)
   Full-length Martha Graham ballet--one of her outstanding works.
The dance tells in lyric terms of the couple's wedding day, the build-
ing of their home, their celebration, the sermon, the blessing.   The
day ends and the young couple begin their life together.   EMC; BYU,
PHOENIX, UILL, UM.

AQUARIANS AND ANTIQUARIANS (3m B 1972)
   A walk through downtown New York City and Lincoln Center.
By Patricia Sloane; WAF.

AQUATENNIAL (34m B si 1974)
   A series of 22 black and white still photos shot at a parade.
By Linda Klosky.   KLOSKY.

ARABESQUE (7m B 1965)
   The sense of estrangement felt by a high school girl is docu-
mented in a series of vignettes that follow a day in her life.   By
Nancy Linde; YFD.

ARABESQUE FOR KENNETH ANGER (4m C n. d.)
   "Animated observations" of the intricate tile and stonework of

the famous Alhambra, an Islamic palace.   Music by Teiji Ito.   By
Marie Menken; FCOOP.

ARE YOU LISTENING SERIES see WOMEN IN MANAGEMENT;
    WOMEN IN MIDDLE MANAGEMENT; MEN AND WOMEN IN
    MANAGEMENT

ARE YOU READY FOR SEX?--VALUES AND DECISION-MAKING
    (25m   C   1976)
    A combination of dramatic scenes and discussion to stimulate
classroom discussion of sexual values and decision-making.   d.
Sheri Gillette Espar; p. S. G. Espar, Henry Mayer; PERENNIAL.

ARE YOU THE ONE? (24m   C   1969)
    Drama illustrating that marital success is largely determined
by the partners' compatibility.   Doug and Marilyn, college students,
found conflict continually arising between them over important issues such as the role of women after marriage, child rearing, and
general interests.   Finally the parting.   BYU; EMC.

ARETHA FRANKLIN, SOUL SINGER (25m   C   1969)
    Profile of a leading vocalist and exponent of soul music who be-
gan her career in the choir of her father's church.   Documents rehearsals as well as intimate sessions with friends and advisors.
Includes a brief survey of the development of soul music.   ABCTV;
MGH; UILL, UM.

ARROWS (4m   C   n. d.)
    A playful, erotic, funny film by a woman about a man.   By
Barbara Scharres; CENTER.

ART IN AMERICA (Pt. I), THE BEGINNINGS; Americana Series,
    No. 19 (25m   C   1976)
    Traces the history of creative work done by the Indians, Es-
kimos and Hawaiians.   Also depicts the influence of the Spanish in
the New World during the 16th century, followed by 17th-century
British influence.   Artists discussed: Singleton Copley, Benjamin
West, Gilbert Stuart, Charles Wilson Peale, John Turnbull, Edward
Savage, and others.   By Irene Zmurkevych; HANDEL.

ART IN AMERICA (Pt. II), HUDSON RIVER SCHOOL TO DADA;
    Americana Series, No. 20 (25m   C   1976)
    Presents an overview of the art history of the U. S. in the early
19th century.   Reflects romantic realism, nature, and a new freedom in the landscape paintings of the Hudson River School.   Concludes with the development of the Dada Movement in this country.
By Irene Zmurkevych; HANDEL.

ART IN AMERICA (Pt. III), THE TWENTIETH CENTURY; Ameri-
    cana Series, No. 21 (25m   C   1976)
    An overview of art history of the U. S. in the 20th century.
Analyzes the works of early modernists as well as those who established themselves later in pop art, assemblage, optical, minimal,

junk and video art.   Survey also made of Black, Chicano and Asian
artists.   By Irene Zmurkevych; HANDEL.

ART IN AMERICA (Pt. IV), BLACK ARTISTS OF THE U. S. A. ;
   Americana Series, No. 23 (25m   C   1977)
   Documents the contributions of Black painters and sculptors,
and the cross-currents of influence with the establishment art.   Beginning with the Colonial period, Black artists created intricate
wrought iron, cabinetry, pottery and voodoo masks.   Joshua John-
ston painted portraits of the post-Revolutionary U. S.   Sculptress Edmonia Lewis' works were symbolic of the oppressed people.   Henry
Ossawa Tanner lived in Paris, dealt chiefly with biblical themes.
Over 40 artists and their works from all periods are touched upon
in the course of this film.   By Irene Zmurkevych; HANDEL.

ART OF AGE (27m   C   1971)
   Positive aspects of aging.   How the philosophy that one is "under the obligation to live as long as one is living" underlines the
fulfilling and productive lives of four elderly citizens--a retired
mailman, a woman artist, a former businessman, and a lady with
an incurable bone disease.   Activities, hobbies, and relationships.
PARACO; OSU, USC.

ART OF LOTTE REINIGER, THE (14m   C   1975)
   A fascinating record of Lotte Reiniger on her films--a pioneer
in the development of animated films.   CEA; ABFL

ART OF MARIE COSINDAS (29m   C/B   1960)
   Presents Marie Cosindas' (Polaroid photographer) color photographs along with comments by museum visitors, art critics, and
former subjects.   Shows her discussing her work with others, creating a still life, and working on two portraits.   Includes one of
her experimental film clips.   IU; PAS.

ART OF MEDITATION, THE (28m   C   1972)
   Presents Alan Watts who gives advice on means of meditation
by using nature photography and natural sounds.   By Elda Hartley;
HARTLEY.

ART PROFILE: BARBARA WEISBERGER (28m   C   1971   VIDEO)
   An intimate portrait of Barbara Weisberger, founder and artistic director of the Pennsylvania Ballet Company of Philadelphia,
filmed on location at the studio, on tour, and at an experimental
dance presentation.   WHYYTV; PTL.

ART UNDERFOOT (6m   C   1971)
   Shows how a young woman finds art in the streets of New York
City by making wax "rubbings" (which she later paints with bold
graphic designs) from the patterns on manhole covers.   Ends with
her doing a "rubbing" of the Brooklyn Bridge, where she says she
would like to do the whole world.   From "The Great American
Dream Machine. "   IU; EMC.

ARTHUR AND LILLIE (30m   C   1976)
A film about Arthur and Lillie Mayer, 89 and 86 and both in-
defatigably young, living a creative old age.   Arthur Mayer's recollections of the great days of Hollywood showmanship and publicity
stunts fills in an important perspective on film history.   One gets
from the film the sense of two lives that have remained marvelously
open--open to fresh ideas and new experiences.   Lillie was among
the first suffragettes.   PF; EMC, VFL

ARTISTS IN AMERICA SERIES see BARBARA LINDEN; MARY
PRITCHARD; ROBERTA FLACK

ARTS CIRCUS, THE (4m   C   n. d.)
A vividly colorful film in which weird beings emerge from the
screen to cavort.   By Kathy Rose; CFS.

AS LONG AS THE RIVERS RUN (62m   C   1971)
A documentary showing confrontations between Native Americans
and game authorities over fishing rights in Washington State.   Reviews historical background, treaties and recent court decisions.
Emphasizes the strength and equal part of Native American women
in this struggle.   By Carol Burns; IMPF.

ASCENT (30m   C   1970)
Climb of the rock walls of Yosemite's El Capitan, demonstrating
technique, equipment and safety.   By Virginia Bauer Duncan.
KQEDTV; FW.

ASH WEDNESDAY (99m   C   1973)
Trying to regain her lost youth, a fat, baggy, middle-aged
housewife (Elizabeth Taylor) enters a clinic in Italy where complete
plastic surgery (body sculpture) is performed.   She emerges a
gorgeous 35-year-old.   Co-scripted by Ruth Gordon; d. Larry
Peerce; PARAMOUNT; FL

ASPIRATION ABORTION WITHOUT CERVICAL DILATION (12m   C
1972)
Discussion of pre-abortion counseling and importance of patient's
mental attitude.   Step-by-step photography of aspiration abortion
technique.   PAS.

ASPIRATIONS (10m   C   n. d.)
A unique blending of fantasy and reality against a background of
popular music images of womanhood.   This startling film frankly
explores the longings and terrors of becoming a woman in our society.   By Peri Muldofsky; YFD.

ASSAULT ON THE EIFFEL TOWER (25m   B   n. d.)
Details the ascent of the Eiffel Tower by four French alpinists,
without elevator or stairs.   Highlights the pursuit of gendarmes and
the mountaineers gaining the summit of the famed landmark.   d.
Jacqueline Jacoupy; FIN; CFS.

ASSERTIVE TRAINING FOR WOMEN, PT. I (17m   C   1973)
Ten vignettes deal with simple interpersonal situations--borrow-
ing class notes, refusing dates, seeing a physician, as well as with
more complex situations involving parents.   Designed as a stimulus
for group discussion and role playing.   APGA; MS, OSU, UKEN,
UM, UMIS.

ASSERTIVE TRAINING FOR WOMEN, PT. II (18m   C   1973)
Eleven vignettes begin with simple interpersonal situations--
someone cutting into line, dealing with a demanding employer, being
asked to canvass for charity.   Concludes with a series of more
complex situations involving a passive husband, a flirtatious man, a
highly opinionated man, etc.   APGA; MSU, OSU, UIO, UKEN, UM,
UMIS, UW.

AT LAND (15m   B   si   1945)
"A poetic self-revelation transcends itself in the intense odyssey of a seeker after personal identity throughout the hazards and
challenges presented by the world; the sense of danger, the thrill,
of spanning magical sensations, the conflict between naked impulse
and its consummation, the suspense of the search, all these modu-
late a particular emotional adventure."--Parker Tyler.   By Maya
Deren; GP.

AT MY MOTHER'S HOUSE (6m   C   si   n.d.)
A still life dedicated to Vermeer and filmmaker's mother.   By
Naomi Levine; FCOOP.

AT 99: A PORTRAIT OF LOUISE TANDY MURCH (24m   C   1974)
Early in the film we meet Tandy Murch surrounded by her
large family celebrating her 99th birthday.   Here she is the center
of attention, and cameras to record the historic moment are everywhere.   After the event, we get to know Louise in her most usual
daily life.   She lives in a house she has occupied for 68 years.
She comments "I am alone a lot, but I am never lonely."   By
Deepa Mehta Saltzman; ECCW; UILL, UM.

ATHZUR (3m   C   1974)
A color structural/animation film.   A woman's growth as a human being.   By Terry Sheehy; SHEEHY.

ATTENTION MUST BE PAID; Insight Series (27m   C   1973)
Shows how a group of Senior citizens finds new meaning and
hope in their lives as, one by one, they are drawn into the loving
world of a cancer-stricken Mr. Cahn.   Illustrates the healing and
enriching power of love.   KIESER; PAULST; MG.

ATTICA (90m   C   1974)
This documentary is a detailed probe by a young woman director into that rebellion at Attica Prison in September 1971 which
left 39 dead and hundreds wounded.   Interviews with inmates form
the base of the movie.   Along with interviews, the movie contains

footage of the McKay Commission hearings and film of the actual
assault itself.   By Cinda Firestone; TFC; EMC.

AUCASSIN AND NICOLETTE (16m   C   1975)
Animated creation of a 13th-century French ballad.   Written in
Renaissance-style and played on instruments of the period by the
Huggett family.   d. Lotte Reiniger; p. Guy Glover; NFBC; EMC.

AUNT ARIE; American Character, The (Series) (18m   C   1975)
This is an excursion into the living history of a passing generation.   Aunt Arie, high on her farm in the Blue Ridge Mountains
in North Carolina, tells her story in the rich idiom of Appalachia.
One can recognize the roots of our cultural heritage and compare
and evaluate the contrasting life-styles that helped form the American character.   Eliott Wiggins and the Foxfire staff; EBEC, IU.

AUNT CLARA (28m   C   1967)
An interview with the 93-year-old frontier artist, "Aunt Clara"
McDonald Williamson, whose late in life hobby resulted in an im-
pressive collection of "primitive" paintings.   As Aunt Clara relates
her homespun philosophy about art and life, the camera views her
paintings which portray scenes of her childhood in the little town of
Iredell, Texas.   Provides a colorful record of the simple country
life and times of the early West.   ABCTV; MGH; UILL.

AUNT HARRIET (18m   C   n. d.)
Helen Mason and her boy friend can't get married until they
find a home.   They decide the flat in which 79-year-old Aunt Harriet lives would be ideal and they begin making plans to find a
place for Aunt Harriet.   The doctor recommends a home that spe-
cializes in "people like Aunt Harriet. "   The Masons, who have long
viewed Aunt Harriet as an eccentric relative to be tolerated on
special holidays, think the idea a perfect solution to the problem.
If only Aunt Harriet would cooperate. . . .   GPN.

AUNTIE MAME (143m   C   1958)
Recreating her stage performance, Rosalind Russell plays the
high-living Mame whose mad-cap life takes on a new complication:
a 10-year-old nephew.   d. Morton da Cost; WSA; BF, CINE.

AUTOBIOGRAPHY OF A WOMAN (20m   C   n. d.)
This film makes visual all the hidden brutal and repressive
forces that have kept women (especially in middle class) in their
place--at the same time giving more positive future direction.   By
Barbara Dills, Alex Little, Jean Weinberg; IRISF.

AUTOBIOGRAPHY OF MISS JANE DUBOIS, THE (162m   B   1977
VIDEO)
An in-depth interview with a 32-year-old Black woman.   Through
Jane's lively and open discussions we find out what life is like for
poor, urban, Black women.   Jane Dubois has raised two children
of her own, acquired an equivalency diploma and begun college.
While working as a teacher's aid she also has to cope with the New

York welfare bureaucracy. This videotape is edited thematically
into 12 chapters: each presents a different aspect of Jane's character. By Alan Hertzberg; IE.

AUTOBIOGRAPHY OF MISS JANE PITTMAN, THE (116m C 1974)
    Acclaimed adaptation of Ernest Gaines' novel about the tenacity
and courage of a Black woman from her childhood as a slave to her
march for civil rights at the age of 110. d. John Korty; LCA; BF,
CINE, CWF, EMC, MGH, ROA, SELECT, SWANK, UM, UU,
WHOLFC.

AUTOPSY, THE (5m C 1972)
    A powerful exploration of the possibilities of death. Can be
used as a discussion guide in medical schools and in counseling
professions dealing with older people and people facing death. A
good experimental film for students in film study. By Royanne
Rosenberg; SB.

AUTOPSY OF A QUEEN (28m C 1974)
    Documentary of Virginia City, Nevada in the late 1800's. Fea-
tures a brief animated historical sketch followed by scenes of the
frontier life: a silver mine tour, wild-West shoot-outs and gambling.
The sound explores the confronting philosophies of the right and the
left, the young and the old. By Patricia Amlin; AMLIN.

AVES: MAGNIFICENT FRIGATE BIRD, GREAT FLAMINGO (23m
    C 1973)
    Forms of frigate bird and flamingo in flight. By Nancy Graves,
VRI.

L'AVVENTURA (145m B 1961 Italian/subtitled)
    A party of wealthy society people go on a yachting holiday off
the coast of Sicily. Among them is Anna, involved with Sandro,
an architect corrupted by easy success. They stop to explore a
barren island and a storm comes up. Anna is found missing and
some of the party remain behind to search for her. Although Claudia, Anna's confidante, at first blames Sandro for Anna's possible
suicide, she falls in love with Sandro in the resulting vacuum.
The lovers return to the hotel to rejoin their society friends. Then
Claudia wakes up one night to find Sandro missing, only to find him
sprawled on the couch with a girl. Sandro breaks down. Moved
by compassion and despair, Claudia forgives him as a grey dawn
breaks. A provocative statement on modern society. d. Michelangelo Antonioni; JANUS.

BABY IS BORN, A (23m C 1975)
    A literal photographic record of an actual hospital delivery, this
film tells the real story of the birth of a young couple's first child.
The husband takes on a meaningful supportive role throughout the
birth process. Shows a post-natal visit where the obstetrician
counsels on future pregnancy planning as well as on birth control.

Also available in Spanish.   By Henry Mayer, M. D. , Sherri Gillette
Espar; PERENNIAL.

BACK STREET (100m   B   1921)
Contrasting the social situation where marriage is a public affair and love a private matter with a situation where the separation
of lovers is deliberate and considered normal.   An original and incisive statement on the place of women in American society.   The
first screen version of Fannie Hurst's melodrama.   d. John N.
Stahl; UNIVE.

BACK TO SCHOOL, BACK TO WORK (20m   C   1973)
Examines the common forms of opposition faced by wives and
mothers who wish to return to school or work.   Divided into ten
vignettes; the projector may be stopped at indicated intervals for
discussion.   Depicts opposition from female friends as well as husbands.   Guide book available.   d. Joan Pearlman; APGA; EMC.

BAGATELLE FOR WILLARD MAAS (5m   C   n. d.)
"New version of the now famous film made for her husband,
the poet and filmmaker.   Returning from the Brussels Fair, she
shot this at Versailles and the Louvre. "--Charles Boultenhouse.
By Marie Menken; FCOOP.

BAGGAGE (22m   B   1969)
A lyrical parable on the mental burdens of a young girl.   Played
by renowned Japanese mime, Mamako Yoneyama.   An unusual catalyst for discussion.   p. Alexander Neel; PARACO, VFI; UILL.

BALI TODAY (17m   C   1968)
Margaret Mead's commentary on the religion, art, and culture
of Bali.   Shows the daily routines of the villagers and their remarkable devotion to artistic endeavor and harmony in life and art.
Wedding ceremonies and ritual in cremation shows.   By Elda Hartley, HARTLEY; EMC.

BALINESE FAMILY; Character Formation in Different Culture Series
(17m   B   1951)
Portrays how a Balinese father and mother treat their three
youngest children--the lap baby, knee baby, and child nurse.   Shows
the father giving the baby his breast, the behavior of the knee baby
during the lap baby's absence, and the difficulties the small child
has in caring for the younger baby.   p. Gregory Batson and Margaret
Mead.   NYU; EMC.

BALL OF FIRE (111m   B   1941)
An encyclopedist completing an entry on contemporary slang decides to study the vocabulary of a night club singer, Sugarpuss
O'Shea.   Before he knows it, he and his six eccentric colleagues
find themselves involved over their heads with a girl on the lam
from notorious gangsters Duke Pastrami and Joe Lilac.   d. Howard
Hawks; GOLDWYN; ABFL

BALLAD OF JOSIE (102m   C   1968   Reg. /Scope)
A widow starts a sheep ranch in Wyoming, setting off a war
with the cattlemen and a woman's suffrage movement.   d. Andrew V.
McLaglen; UNIVE.

BALLAD OF THE IRON HORSE, THE (29m   C   1970)
Shows the importance of rail transportation and points out that
railroads have opened up and expanded every nation in the world today.   By Helen Jean Rogers, John Secondari; LCA.

BALLERINA (78m   B   1953   (dubbed))
Violette Verdy, the prima ballerina for the New York Ballet,
plays the ballerina heroine in The Tale of Nicole.   The heroine is
a young dancer on the eve of her first triumph.   The success of
her performance is disturbed by three suiters.   Nicole plays with
the possibilities of all three lovers but finally discovers the substance of her life in her audience, the theatre and the dance itself.
d. Simon Schiffrin; IVY.

BALLET ADAGIO (10m   C   1951)
An exquisite presentation of the ballet Spring Water--danced by
David and Anna Marie Holmes.   Norman McLaren uses slow motion
to increase the viewer's perception of ballistic movement and to
heighten the aesthetic and emotional response.   Special lighting
focuses attention on the dances and sharpens the three-dimensional
effect.   By Norman McLaren, NFBC; PF; UILL.

BALLET BY DEGAS (11m   C   1951)
Presents the paintings of Degas: "The Ballet Class, " "Corphyee
Resting, " and "Ballerina and Lady with the Fan" (from the Phila-
delphia Museum of Art); and "On Stage, " "Dancers Practicing at the
Bar, " and "Pink and Green" (from the Metropolitan Museum of Art).
ABFI; UILL.

BALLET'S GOLDEN AGE (1830-1846); Cultural Heritage Series (10m
C   1957)
Uses rare prints to visualize the exquisite loveliness of the ro-
mantic period of ballet and some of its celebrated ballerinas.   Quo-
tations from letters and reviews of the period re-create the interest
and excitement of the art and pay tribute to the talents of Marie
Taglioni, Fanny Ellsler, Charlotta Grisi, Lucille Grahn, and others.
WALA; COR; UILL.

BAOBAB: PORTRAITS OF A TREE (53m   C   1972)
Shows a century-old Baobab tree and explains its important role
in the lives of African wildlife.   Includes scenes of bushbabies, fruit
bats, elephants, hornbills.   By Joan Root/Alan Root; MGH; EMC,
UILL.

BARBARA (13m   B   n. d.)
The film came about after hearing a newscaster state that a
quiet mother of four got up in the middle of the night and shot her
four children, her husband, and herself.   Her first reaction was

shock--what would make someone do that? Her second, almost immediate thought, was to recall the fantasies she had resulting from
a sense of despair she felt in a situation. ... A brutal but a real
look at feelings many women repress. By Diane P. Graham; IRISF.

BARBARA HEPWORTH (31m B 1967)
     Barbara Hepworth narrates, in part, this study of her art and
of her philosophy. Analyzes the emotional qualities of shapes and
textures, the power of subtle analogies in form, the depth of her
own feeling of the unity of man and his landscapes. Works in progress and completed are shown. BBCTV; TL; UILL.

BARBARA LINDEN; Artists in America Series (29m C 1970)
     Portrait of Barbara Linden, uniquely talented theatre director
in Boston, who has established an exciting new experiment in children's theatre. Includes excerpt from her production "Creation. "
WGBHTV; IU; PAS.

BARBARA'S BLINDNESS (17m B 1965)
     The main source of the film seems to be an old grade-school
morality movie on the appreciation of eyesight. Stars a golden-
haired Mary who finds herself temporarily blind and a leaden-voiced
narrator who finds himself our unwitting straight-man. The film is
re-edited and intercut with other stock footage to create an object
lesson on the nature of vision. By Joyce Wieland/Betty Ferguson;
FCOOP.

BAREFOOT DOCTORS OF RURAL CHINA, THE (52m C 1975)
     The film presents a unique and intimate view of life in the
Chinese countryside. Examines China's innovative efforts to provide adequate health care services for its agrarian population of
over 600, 000, 000 people. Focuses on training and activities of the
"barefoot doctors" in both Western and Chinese medical techniques.
It shows the importance of women in their current family-planning
campaign. By Diane Li; CDFL

BARNETT THE CHILD (48m C 1971)
     Follows a young Swedish couple who are having their first child
and presents a complete account of the conception, gestation, and
delivery of the child. Animation explains the menstrual cycle and
conception. Actual photographs that trace the step by step development of the fetus are intercut with sequences that show the prenatal
care and training of the mother. Includes a summary of the en-
lightened job-leave and medical benefits for pregnant women in
Sweden. Shows in detail midwife assisted delivery with the father
present. Concludes with the baby's first physical examination and
a brief description of postnatal care. Swedish production with
British narrator. IFB; EMC.

BARRETTS OF WIMPOLE STREET (111m B 1934)
     A bedridden poetess recuperates when she falls in love and is
able to leave her father's tyranny. Based on the lives of Elizabeth
Barrett and Robert Browning. d. Sidney Franklin; MGM; FL

BARRIER BEACH (20m   C   1971)
"Unique photographic study of the changes in a barrier beach over a period of a year. "--ACL   By Mary Hill; PARACO.

BASKER'S TRADE: MALVINA REYNOLDS (29m   C   n. d.   VIDEO)
Malvina performs in the style of basker, or street musician. Her songs include: "No Hole in My Head, " "The Little Red Hen, " "The Money Crop, " and "God Bless the Grass. "   KQEDTV.

BASKET BUILDER (12m   C   1974)
Features a basketbuilder who lived in the Virginia Blue Ridge Mountains.   Describes how he split logs, cut them to size and wove baskets.   Depicts the basketmaker reminiscing about his life in the mountains until he was forced to move to the lowlands when the government established the Shenandoah National Park.   By Lucy Ann Kerry; BRF.

BATHING BABIES IN THREE CULTURES (9m   B   1954)
Comparative study of the interplay of mother and child in three different settings--the Sepik River in New Guinea, a modern American bathroom, and a mountain village in Bali.   By Margaret Mead/ Gregory Bateson; EMC.

BATIK REDISCOVERED (9m   C   1966)
Illustrates batik, a wax and dye resist method of textile decoration, which began in Persia or India around the 12th century.   Shows multi-color and single color processes of both traditional and modern batik.   By Juanita Haines/Frank Bach; BFA.

BATTERED WOMEN: VIOLENCE BEHIND CLOSED DOORS (21m   C   1976)
Close-up look at women who are trapped with violent men and the social pressures that bind them in abusive relationships.   JGMF; UW, UM.

BATTLE OF THE VILLA FIORITA (111m   C   1969)
Maureen O'Hara is the quiet respected member of a fashionable circle of British art and music enthusiasts.   She marries and lives sedately with her husband and two children until a famed Italian composer, Rossano Brazzi, comes to town.   She finds herself magnetically drawn to him and he to her.   She faces the moment of truth on the last day of the festival--she departs with the stranger, leaving her husband to explain to the children.   d. Delmer Davis; CINE, TWY.

BAYMEN--OUR WATERS ARE DYING (29m   C   1976)
Documentary portrait of the baymen, clam diggers of Eastern Long Island, who are the major suppliers of shellfish in this country.   Delineates their traditional way of life from beginning to the present which is threatened with extinction by water pollution. d. /p. Anne Belle; BELLE.

BE SOMEBODY (2m   C   n. d.)
Provides a glimpse at the obsession for constant change in

women's fashions and anatomy in general to keep pace with current
trends. "A sharp phenomenological pan on the Barbie Doll inter-
changeability of Madison Avenue's image of women. "--UCLA Bruin.
By Elena Erenberg; CFS.

BEATRICE TRUM HUNTER'S NATURAL FOODS (60m   C   1973
    VIDEO)
    Beatrice Trum Hunter, author of The Natural Foods Cookbook
and The Natural Foods Primer, draws on her 20 years of experience
working with natural foods.   She covers everything from growing
bean sprouts to making a nutritious party pizza.   She shows how to
fortify common foods to increase their value.   WGBHTV; PTL.

BEAUTY KNOWS NO PAIN (25m   C   1972)
    Presents a jaundiced view of the Kilgore College Rangerettes in
Texas.   It is possible to see this film as a "straight" presentation of
the cheerleaders' education, but a knowing eye will appreciate the
irony and ambiguity of paramilitary values applied to the (unliberated)
aspirations of young women.   d. Elliott Erwitt; BM; BU, EMC, PAS,
VFL

BECKY SHARP (67m   B   1935)
    Becky, the ruthless lady of 19th-century balls and parlors, takes
society by storm.   She marries for money, exposes the hypocrisy
of moralizing matrons, and crashes through the restrictions that tied
less determined women.   Becky Sharp's (Miriam Hopkins) brash independence makes her a prototype.   Based on William Thackeray's
Vanity Fair in Becky Sharp.   d. Rouben Mamoulian; RKO; IVY.

BECOMING (13m   B   1969)
    Explores the changing identity of modern women.   Portrays the
complexity of her role in various settings--at home, at work, at
leisure, and at different stages of the life cycle.   OSU.

BED AND SOFA (72m   B   si   1927   Russian/subtitled)
    A masterpiece of the silent screen made after the Russian Revo-
lution.   Tells the story of a wife in relation to husband and lover,
the women in relation to each other, and all three in relation to
their daily work-lives.   One of the few films that show honestly a
woman's position and options in a man's world.   d. Abraham Room;
ABFI, KP.

BEDROOM, THE (10m   C   1971)
    "Takes a bedroom and brings it to life. Beginning with the rugs
on the floor, objects are animated in most amusing fashion. "--FIM.
By Anna-Lena Keating; FIM.

BEFORE PREGNANCY; Pregnancy and Childbirth Series (9m   C
    1977)
    Stresses the importance of having a baby as the result of a
positive decision on the part of both parents.   The physical health
of prospective parents is discussed and pre-pregnancy testing is detailed.   Preparing for the future baby's surroundings is highlighted.
CRAF; IFB.

BEGINNINGS OF A LONG AND REAL REVOLUTION, THE (90m
   C/B n. d. SLIDES)
   Two hundred historical slides with prerecorded script on the
women's movement. NOW.

BEGINNING OF LIFE, THE (26m C 1975)
   Presents the actual cell development of human life in all its
beauty and biological precision. Films through electron microscope,
the formation of living human egg and sperm cells in the body, fertilization, cell division, initial growth to heartbeat, all in the
healthy body. p. CINESC; PF; UILL.

BEGONE DULL CARE (9m C 1949)
   A lively interpretation of jazz in fluid lines and colors. The
film is organized into three parts, each with its own distinctive
tempo, movement, and artistic interpretation. The most famous
abstract film produced to date using the scratch-and-paint on film
technique. By Evelyn Lambert/Norman McLaren. NFBC; BYU;
CFS.

BEHAVIOR IN BUSINESS SERIES see PRODUCTIVITY AND THE
   SELF-FULFILLING PROPHECY: THE PYGMALION EFFECT;
   TRANSACTIONAL ANALYSIS

BEHIND THE VEIL (50m C 1971)
   Documentary of a harem life in eastern Arabia. The Crown
Prince of Dubui is taking a wife. The film witnesses ritual of the
wedding preparation, religious men, tribal dances, food preparation,
the race of the most-prized Arabian steeds, etc. We see remarkable happenings with the so-called genteel sex: women carrying on
business transactions in a bank, learning to read and write. We
see the bride discarding the veil after the wedding night. By Eve
Arnold; IMPF.

BEING A PRISONER (28m C 1975)
   A glimpse into the lives and circumstances of the women who
are incarcerated at one prison in New Jersey. Made with the assistance of the women themselves. A sympathetic film asking for
more understanding of these largely ignored people in prison.
d. /p. Suzanne Jasper; KFPC.

BEING A WOMAN SERIES see DO I REALLY WANT A CHILD

BEING DIFFERENT; What Do You Think Series (11m B 1957)
   Shows how a 14-year-old boy is laughed at by his friends when
he starts a butterfly collection. Asks whether the boy should conform to the opinions of his friends or pursue his own interests.
By Julia Murphy; NFBC.

BEING IN LOVE (30m B 1963)
   Dramatic meeting between two brothers, one of whom is plan-
ning to divorce his wife to marry a woman he met in business. Dr.
Marie Piers discusses the possibilities for success of such a second

marriage and explains normal and pathological attachments and attractions. She comments on the interconnection between mind and
body as well as the varying love needs of individuals.   IU; EMC.

BEING ME (13m B 1969)
Documents a creative dance class of nine Black and white girls
(ages eight to thirteen) conducted by Hilda Mullin at the Pasadena
Art Museum.   No formal instruction is given.   Each child follows
her own body rhythm, not one that is prescribed or superimposed.
Ms. Mullin believes that movement forms the matrix from which the
child organizes and experiences herself and that it is this medium
that gives the child an ability to integrate her experience as she
grows.   EMC; UILL, UU.

BELLE CEREBRALE, LA (THE DREAMER) (14m C 1972)
Technically a stunning male fantasy about the nature of woman
that is worth viewing in the spirit of knowing one's enemy.   An
artist's model sits naked and passive in a gangland hideout while
off-screen two men discuss a number of violent incidents.   She has
an erotic dream in which she dances frantically to rock music, then
appears to have orgasm during a shoot-out.   French production, in
English.   d. Peter Foldes; FI; EMC.

BELLE DAME SANS MERCI, LA (4m C 1973)
An old woman growing blind and deaf remembers her life.   By
Alexis Rafael Krasilovsky; RAFAEL.

BELLE OF THE NINETIES (76m B 1934)
"Amid the lithographic Police Gazette settings of the Sensation
House in New Orleans, Ruby Carter (Mae West) rules the sporting
world with queenly insolence.   As she herself sagely observes, 'It
is better to be looked over than to be overlooked, ' and her ser-
pentine gowns, hayloft coiffure and hour-glass figure insure her
against neglect. "--A. Senwald, New York Times.   She has a healthy
admiration for a good man and Tiger Kid fills the bill--she fights
those that conspire to separate them.   d. Leo McCarey; s. w. Mae
West; PARAMOUNT; UNIVE.

BELLS ARE RINGING (127m C 1960 Reg. /Scope)
Delightful yarn about a timid dreary girl who works for a telephone answering service and simply can't keep from taking a deep
personal interest in all the clients.   d. Vincente Minelli; s. w. Betty
Comden; MGM; FI.

BELLS OF ATLANTIS (10m C 1953)
A beautiful and rare film experience based on Anaïs Nin's prose-
poem "The House of Incest. "   Commentary and performance by Ms.
Nin evokes the watery depths of the lost continent, Atlantis.   It's
a lyrical journey into the depths of a dream of another life in another time.   p. Ian Hugo; FIM.

BEN-HUR (129m B 1926 si/with music)
The monumental battle at sea and the chariot race; claimed by

some as two of the most expertly filmed action-spectacle sequences
ever photographed.   d. Fred Niblo; s. w. June Mathis; MGM; FI.

BERKELEY 12-1 (5m   B   n. d.)
   Filmed clashes with the police during the battle for People's
Park.   By Donna Deitch; CCC.

BERNADETTE DEVLIN (30m   B   1972)
   The last appearance of Ms. Devlin in the U. S. during her tour
early in 1971.   Makes a strong plea for the poor and working people
of all nations to unite against oppressive living conditions.   AMDOC.

BETTER BY CHOICE ... THAN BY CHANCE (11m   C   n. d.)
   The central message of this film is that if young people are
given an opportunity to openly learn about and discuss the facts of
human sexuality, unplanned pregnancies can be avoided.   Presents
an overview of the facts of contraception and reproduction.   Discusses the points young men and women must consider before em-
barking on a sexual relationship.   p. Cincinnati Adolescent Clinic;
PIC.

BETTY BOOP SCANDALS (72m   B   1974)
   Ten animated classics dated from 1928-34 are united to present
Fleischer's best productions in "The Betty Boop Scandal. "   Fleischer
projected the spirit of the 30's in intense, hard-edged animation.
The value of this film extends beyond the liberated antics of the
heroine.   Betty Boop can be rediscovered by audiences across the
nation as a landmark in screen animation and a vivid evocation of
our past.   By Max Fleischer; music by Cab Calloway; IVY.

BETTY CARTER ... WHAT'S NEW; Interface Series (29m   C   1975
   VIDEO)
   Jazz vocalist Betty Carter, who has worked with many of the
great jazz artists including Ray Charles, talks about her work and
the state of the music business.   She sings "What's New, " "Just
Friends, " and "I Didn't Know What Time It Was. "   WETA; PTL.

BETTY REID (29m   C   n. d.   VIDEO)
   Bay area Third World songwriter sings in concert about her ex-
periences of being a woman with a Third World background.
KQEDTV.

BETTY TELLS HER STORY (20m   B   1972)
   Basically a monologue, this cinéma-vérité exercise demonstrates
the value of repetition without becoming redundant.   Betty tells her
story of a beautiful expensive dress and the fate that befell it.   Then
she tells it again.   By Liane Brandon; CININC; UM.

BETWEEN MAN AND WOMAN (33m   C   n. d.)
   Filmed interview with Dr. Everett L. Shostrum and Mr. Howard Miller of ABC-TV Chicago.   The film depicts the various marital roles people play in a relationship between husband and wife such
as--the "Mother-Son" relationship, the "Daddy-Doll" relationship,

the "Bitch-Nice Guy" relationship, the "Master-Servant" relationship, the "Hawks" and the "Doves." Adapted from book with same title. PFL

BEWARE THE RAPIST (20m C 1977)
How to be aware of rape situations. DAVPS.

BEYOND BLACK AND WHITE (32m C 1975)
The psychological, sociological and historical origins of prejudice against minorities and women are clarified for front line supervisors and other levels of management. The most frequently occurring and most sensitive problems regarding minorities and women are covered in dramatic vignettes which provide positive and realistic answers. By Max Miller; AVANFI; MM; UM.

BEYOND SHELTER: HOUSING FOR THE ELDERLY (25m C 1976)
Discusses housing and support facilities for old people. Denmark is chosen as the model for the type of planning so badly needed in North America. Advocates independent living as opposed to confinement and isolation in institutions. d. Ronald H. Blumer; p. Dr. G. Rosenberg; FILOAG

BEYOND THE BEAUTY MYTH (29m C 1975 VIDEO)
Biologist and author Deborah Chase, author of The No-Nonsense Beauty Book speaks about the weak FDA regulations of the cosmetic industry and how manufacturers exploit women selling useless, expensive, and sometimes harmful products. WNEDTV; PTL.

BIAS (A FOUR-LETTER WORD) (22m C 1976)
Examines universally accepted attitudes that our so-called civilized society not only accepts but encourages. Among the many forms of bias considered are sexism, racism, age group and occupational stereotypes, and even negative self-image. p. Claire Menken/Shepard Menken; d. S. Menken; s. w. Roz Lieberman/Jack Lieberman; MALIBU.

BIG BOB KUHN (14m C n. d.)
A thought-provoking documentary about a 12-year-old boy talking about his feminist mother. Shows the things he does in life, talks about what he has learned and is learning about marriage, child custody, divorce, the nuclear family, what he looks up to in a man, and how he views himself and the future. By Sarah Kuhn; SARSAKU.

BIG HENRY AND THE POLKA DOT KID (33m C 1977)
A young orphan is taken in by his aunt and uncle. Ultimately, through saving the life of a blind old dog, he teaches his uncle that "being practical" is not the only thing in life. Based on the story "Luke Baldwin's Vow" by Morley Callaghan, and featuring Ned Beatty, Estelle Parsons, and Chris Barnes. p. Linda Gottlieb; d. Richard Marquand; LCA.

BIG NUMBERS ... LITTLE NUMBERS (11m   C   n. d.)
Shows use of scientific notation (exponents based on 10).   By
Katherine Cornwell, Bruce Cornwell; BFA.

BIG TOWN (25m   C   1973)
A study of two segments of society in Scarsdale, N. Y. :   the
upper middle class and those of the lower middle class as they com-
mute to work.   The upper middle class is the target of barbed
satire.   By Claudia Weill/Eliot Noyes; TEXFM; EMC.

BIGAMIST, THE (80m   B   1953)
Explores the dilemmas of male/female relationships during the
50's in America.   One wife (Joan Fontaine) is an ambitious career
woman; the other (Ida Lupino) is a warm motherly waitress.   Together they present the polarized roles society defines for women.
Between them stands the husbands they both love.   The film questions the institution of marriage and the social stereotypes that con-
fuse and constrict the needs of men and women.   d. Ida Lupino;
FMI; IVY.

BILL OF RIGHTS IN ACTION: WOMEN'S RIGHTS, THE (23m   C
1974)
An open-ended film regarding whether women should be allowed
to compete in men's athletic events.   A high school girl wants to
enter the men's swim meet.   Her attorney says the state by-laws
which prohibit this are unconstitutional because the 14th Amendment
guarantees equal protection regardless of race or sex--or are they?
d. Bernard Wilets; BFA; OSU, UK, UM, USC, UWY.

BILLIE JEAN KING (22m   C   1973)
Profile of Billie Jean King, professional tennis player and the
first woman in any sport to win over $100, 000 in the first full year
of the women's tour.   Included is a match in which she is over-
whelmingly defeated by young Chris Evert.   TELES.

BILLIE JEAN KING'S TENNIS FOR EVERYONE (13-10m segments
C   n. d.)
Filmed program developed by Billie Jean King covers fundamentals of tennis playing for the weekend amateur.   Sophisticated
strategies for the professional are included.   p. Barbara Chamber-
lain, Tom McHugh; NTFLMA; ABFL

BING BANG BOOM (24m   B   1969)
A novel approach to teaching music to children filmed in a
Toronto classroom.   Composer-conductor R. Murray Schafer has
seventh grade students listen to all sounds around them and even in
them.   From such basics, children develop quite spontaneously an
awareness of rhythm and musical phrasing.   They then go on to try
their own composition.   By Joan Henson; NFBC.

BIOFEED BACK (10m   C   1973)
"Drugless, mind-over-matter treatment for medical problems
... "--L. T.   By Lois Tupper; CMC.

BIOGRAPHY OF SUSAN B. ANTHONY (19m B 1951)
Covers Ms. Anthony's campaign for women suffrage. Washington, D. C. Public Library.

BIOGRAPHY SERIES see GRACE KELLY; HELEN KELLER; MADAME CHIANG KAI-SHEK; QUEEN ELIZABETH II

BIRD (1m C n. d.)
An animated one-minute flight. By Sharon Hennessey; CCC; SB.

BIRD LADY VS. THE GALLOPING GONADS (1m B 1976)
Subtitled "A Spring Fantasy," Bird Lady's white line on black background richly sprouts blossoms. It bursts with pantheistic fertility. Human forms irresistibly fly, change and mix with plants, animals, birds, arrows, hands, phalluses and hungry suns as everything comes joyfully together in mirthful mythic warmth. By Josie Ramstad; SB.

BIRD'S LIFE, A (9m C 1975)
An animated creation of a woman trying to free herself from the domestic prison of her family. Overwhelmed by her overbearing family and never-ending chores, the woman seeks entertainment at a Hypnotism Act. Instead she finds she can really fly. Helpless and distraught, father and son pester the mysterious hypnotist for her return. When that fails, he mesmerizes them to rejoin her in a flight of their own. The extent of their bondage is not clear until the ironic twist of the ending which finds her once more serving her airborne family in a tree. This film offers a sobering birds-eye view of an important issue: alternative careers for today's women. Story by Milos Macourek; d. Macourek Dubrava; animation by Vera Maresova, Jaroslav Doubrava, Joseph Hekrdla; ABFL

BIRDS OF THE GALAPAGOS (15m C 1970)
Shows the unique birds found in the Galapagos Islands. By Elda Hartley; HARTLEY; PARACO.

BIRTH (72m B 1968)
Warm, candid cinéma-vérité documentary of a young couple who are about to have their first baby. Follows the couple through their daily life--to work, to natural childbirth class, and to her prenatal examination. Reveals the couple's hopes and expectations about parenthood and family. Includes Debbie's labor and delivery with Bruce helping. Documents the universal experience without being overly clinical. Affirms the synthesis of sex and love. By Evelyn Barron/Arthur Barron; IU; EMC.

BIRTH AND DEATH see BIRTH; DEATH

BIRTH CONTROL (60m B 1966)
A comprehensive look at the legal, medical, moral, and social aspects of the birth control issue in the U. S. Reporters interview people who use the services of birth control clinics, administrators

of private clinics, federal and state officials, and public health administrators.   Birth control clinics and their problems are examined in various cities.   IU; EMC.

BIRTH CONTROL AND THE LAW (51m   B   1962)
Discussed from both legal and moral standpoint is whether birth control services and information should be tax-supported.   Varying viewpoints are examined here, with the controversial issue centered around Chicago's Cook County Hospital.   Also reported is the dispute in New Haven, Connecticut where a clinic of the Planned Parenthood Federation was closed by police.   CBSTV; CAROUSEL; ASFL

BIRTH CONTROL, HOW? (32m   B   1965)
Examines the social and religious implications of birth control pills and family planning.   David Brinkley interviews Dr. John Rock (developer of the first oral contraceptive) and Reverend John O'Brien. NBCTV; FL

BIRTH CONTROL: THE CHOICES (25m   C   1976)
Several women are filmed as they discuss reasons why they do not want to become pregnant.   Each voices her particular needs and specifications for birth control.   All agree no one method is right for everyone and a doctor should be consulted regarding this.   All forms of birth control devices are shown and discussed.   A physician and counselor recount the advantages and disadvantages of each. d. John Irvin; CFP; LCA.

BIRTH CONTROL: THE CHOICES (25m   C   1976)
Presents the uses, limitations and side effects of the usual methods of birth control, as well as tubal ligation, vasectomy and abortion.   A physician, birth control counselor, young persons who relate their experiences, and animation are used to explore the choices.   d. Chris Burrill; CF.

BIRTH FILM, THE (35m   C   1974)
Wife/husband team of movement lawyers decide to have their second baby at home.   Film explains why.   Photography of the pregnant mother showering and the birth is beautiful and immediate. However, the obvious material well-being of these middle class folk may inhibit the majority of women from identifying with the film. By Susan Kleckner/Kritin Booth Glen; NYF.

BIRTH OF A FAMILY (24m   C   1975)
Designed for couples or single women to demonstrate preparation for childbirth.   We see one couple attending a class on childbirth preparation in order to secure accurate information and to make themselves physically as well as psychologically ready for the event.   The scenes of class instruction are juxtaposed with scenes of the actual birth, early labor, transition, the full emergence of the baby and the placenta.   The film clearly demonstrates the relationship between careful preparation and actual delivery. CATFSH.

BIRTH OF APHRODITE (13m C 1971)
Uses unique experimental distortion techniques to re-create the Greek myth of Aphrodite: her long gestation in the sea, her birth amidst sea foam, and her final ascent to the heavens. AUSLANDER; EMC.

BIRTH OF THE BIG MAMOO (6m C 1974)
Inside the Mamoo a cell is born. Struck by sperm it begins to metamorphize into a worm. The Mamoo swallows an apple, offered to it by a serpent. The worm bores its way into the apple and emerges a butterfly. The butterfly's fluttering causes the Mamoo to rise and change into a blimp-cloud. The butterfly curls up into an egg. A bird snatches the egg from the cloud and carries it to its nest where it sits on it and knits. The egg hatches into the tree of life. The tree changes into a womb from where the little Mamoo emerges. d. Jody Silver; NLC.

BIRTH WITHOUT VIOLENCE (21m B 1975)
A stunning no-narration film on Frederick Leboyer's history-making method of minimizing the birth trauma. Filmed in a serene dimly-lit delivery room. Shows Leboyer's relaxed massaging, bathing and stroking of the vulnerable neonate. The baby's facial expressions, body movements and behavior are strikingly photographed. p. Frederick Leboyer; NYF.

BIT WITH KNIT, A (15-30m series C 1974 VIDEO)
A series designed exclusively to help one work with easy-care knit fabrics. Rita Barker, home economist, introduces methods and procedures that will enable one to make beautiful knit garments. WSWPTV; PTL.

BITTER VINTAGE SERIES see ROSE ARGOFF

BLACK GIRL (60m B 1965 French/subtitled)
A rare, stark and frighfening portrait of the exploitation of an African girl who is virtually enslaved by a middle-class French family as their servant. d. Ousman Sembene; NYF.

BLACK GIRL (107m C 1972)
Realistic and sensitive dramatization of a Black girl growing up in America. Explores strengths and struggles of three generations of women in her family. d. Ossie Davis; CINEREL; SWANK

BLACK HIGH SCHOOL GIRLS (30m C n.d.)
"As far as our principal is concerned, Washington High School really doesn't have a problem.... If you say: 'How come we can't have Negro girls on the Varsity cheerleaders? ... You know, have anything to do with government?"--interviewee. By Martha Stuart/ David Ruskin; STUARTM.

BLACK JACK'S FAMILY (53m B 1972)
Black Jack is the name of the youngest of four children. The film describes the family life-style. The mother has four children

from two previous marriages.   During the course of the film she
marries Brow, with whom she is living at the beginning of the film.
They live in fairly open style and consider themselves political radicals.   d. William Dorker/David Millholland; GVHOOD.

BLACK JOURNAL SERIES   see   BLACK WOMAN, THE

BLACK MODERN ART (22m   C   1976)
    Profiles three Black American artists, their work and their
artistic philosophies.   Shows Dana Chandler working with brightly
colored bold images dealing with the major theme of Black American
consciousness.   Sculptor Valerie Maynard speaks of herself as a
purveyor of social themes and emotions.   Painter and poet Leroy
Clarke works in bright, primitive, often surrealistic images.   He
speaks of his opposition to any force which tends to dehumanize or
destroy life.   p. Fundacion Juan March; d. Juan A Ruiz-Anchia;
TFC.

BLACK P. STONE (30m   C   1971)
    "The Black Stone Rangers, now the Black P. Stone Nation, is
certainly thought of as a problem in Chicago.   We want to get to
know them as people."--M. S.   By Martha Stuart/David Ruskin;
STUARTM.

BLACK PANTHERS: A REPORT (26m   C   1968)
    Explores the goals and dynamism of the Black Panthers.   The
film cuts back and forth among key figures in the Black Power Movement.   No answers are given nor are any judgments made.   By
Agnes Varda; GP.

BLACK PUDDING (7m   C   1970)
    A Black comedy surrealistic cartoon film reminiscent of the
world of odyssey; with caricatures fornicating and excreting as they
go.   By Nancy Edell; CFS.

BLACK WINDOWS (11m   B   n. d.)
    Tells how some churches are trying to bridge the generation
gap.   By Hannah Roman/Joseph Roman; CENTER.

BLACK WOMAN, THE; Black Journal Series (52m   B   1971)
    Poetess Nikki Giovanni, singer Lena Horne, Bibi Amina (wife
of Le Roi Jones), and other Black women discuss role of Black wom-
en in contemporary society and the problems they confront.   Discusses relationship of Black women to Black men, Black women to
white society, and Black women to the liberation struggle.   d. Stan
Lathan; IU; AIMS, EMC, MSU, PAS, UILL, UM, WSU.

BLACK WOMAN SPEAKS TO WHITE WOMANHOOD (15m   B   n. d.
    SLIDE TAPE)
    Text is from a poem by a Black woman proudly and emotionally
speaking of the past and present relationship between women of her
people and white women.   Ends with a plea for sisterhood to fight
the oppression of all women.   ONR.

BLACK WOMEN IN THE MEDIA (30m   C   n. d.   VIDEO)
     The Bayview-Hunters Point Community College presents awards
and citations to Bay Area women in the media.   KQEDTV.

BLESSINGS OF LOVE (9m   C   1971)
     Discusses courtship, marriage and old age showing moments of
humor, sadness and tenderness.   TRNKAJ; ABFL

BLONDE VENUS (97m   B   1932)
     Marlene Dietrich plays a devoted wife who takes a job in a night
club to raise money for her husband's terminal illness.   Bachelor
playboy (Cary Grant) befriends her and gives her money out of concern and affection.   The husband misunderstands and throws his
wife out.   d. Joseph Von Sternberg; PARAMOUNT, rel. by UNIVE;
UNIVE, TWY, CVE.

BLOOD AND SAND (75m   B   si   1922)
     A classic, based on the novel by Vincente Blasco Ibáñez, about
a bullfighter who falls in love with a beautiful girl and forsakes his
wife.   Things go wrong for him and he loses his concentration in
the bullring with disastrous results.   d. Fred Niblo; s. w. June
Mathis; PARAMOUNT; BF, CVE.

BLOSSOMS IN THE DUST (99m   B   1941)
     Life story of Edna Gladney whose work for orphaned and illegiti-
mate children in Texas serves as a model of humanitarian concern.
d. Mervyn LeRoy; MGM; FL

BLOT, THE (100m   B   si   1972)
     Deals with a topic, seldom, if ever, given much attention; that
of "genteel" poverty and the stubborn pride which keeps a certain
class of people starving rather than accept charity.   w/Clair Windsor.   d. Lois Weber; WARFB/WEBERP; MMA.

BLOW FOR BLOW (COUP POUR COUP) (89m   C   1972   French/
     subtitled)
     Women workers occupy a mill and garment factory and sequester
the boss until their demands for better working conditions are
granted.   A fictionalized reconstruction of various actual strikes
that occurred in France in 1968, the film represents collective efforts of a professional film crew, a few actors and actresses and
about 60 women workers who had participated in the strike.   p. /d.
Marin Karmitz; TFC, IE.

BLOW-UP (110m   C   1966)
     A young arrogant photographer in London stumbles onto a scene
in a park.   The woman he photographs seeks him out to obtain the
film he shot of her.   His response is one of curiosity, nothing more.
He seduces her and tricks her in order to keep the film.   Finding
among the shots a detail of a hand holding a gun, he is unable to
comprehend what he has, unable to connect with the reality of the
situation.   Every character in this film has a hollowness.   Women
are treated as sex objects, men are portrayed as empty and irre-

sponsible. Antonioni successfully creates a set of symbols depicting the alienation of modern life. d. Michelangelo Antonioni; MGM; FI.

BLUE ANGEL, THE (94m B 1929 German/subtitled)
Emil Jannings stars as Professor Rath, a stern middle-aged high school teacher whose infatuation with Lola, a sultry cabaret singer, leads to his dismissal, humiliation, madness and death. With piercing irony, Sternberg focuses on the way in which passion that at first humanizes Rath gradually destroys him. Based on the novel Unrat, by Heinrich Mann. d. Josef Von Sternberg; BF, CFS, CWF, FI, MGH, SELECT, SWANK, WHOLFC.

BLUE DASHIKI (14m B 1969)
Follows the adventures of a young boy as he tries to earn money in order to buy a dashiki that he has seen in a local African import shop. By Maclovia Rodriguez; EBEC.

BLUE LIGHT, THE (90m B si 1932)
Based on an old legend of the Italian Dolomites. Leni Riefenstahl produced, directed and starred in this story of a wild mountain girl believed by villagers to be a witch. She meets her death leading a young man to great treasure. By Leni Riefenstahl; FIN; BLACKHAWK.

BLUE VEIL, THE (114m B 1951)
Presents the experiences of a war widow who becomes a governess first to make a living, later to serve those she loves. Stars Jane Wyman, Charles Laughton and Joan Blondell. Adapted from a story by Francois Campaux. p. Jerry Wald/Norman Frasna; d. Curtis Bernhardt; RKO; BF.

BLUEBERRIES FOR SAL (9m C 1967)
Story of a little girl who meets a bear while picking blueberries with her mother. Adapted from story by same title by Robert McCloskey. By Cynthia Freitag; WESTON.

BLUEFIN RODEO (10m C 1963)
A film of the Annual Classic of Big Game Anglers. The film takes you out to sea to witness the duels between men and fish. By Margaret Perry; CORNELL.

BLUENOSE SHORE (18m C 1969)
Story of the Bluenose schooner of Nova Scotia that excelled for years in yachting contests. Shows recreational activities on the coast of Nova Scotia. By Margaret Perry; BU.

BOB AND CAROL AND TED AND ALICE (104m C 1969)
A sophisticated satire exploring the relationship between two young married couples who start off as "just friends" and become involved in something else. d. Paul Mazursky; COLUMBIA; SWANK.

BOB THOMPSON (25m C n.d.)
Portrait of Bob Thompson, a Black American artist. By Dorothy Beskind; BESKIND.

BODY, THE; Human Sexuality Series (28m   C   1972   VIDEO)
A discussion of concepts of the body and an explanation of male
and female sexual and reproductive anatomy.   Interviewed is plastic
surgeon Robert Flowers, M. D. , who introduces the use of sexual
vocabulary.   UHAWAII/KHETTV; PTL.

BONDING BIRTH EXPERIENCE, THE (20m   C   1976)
The birth of a family's third child is depicted from the onset of
labor through postpartum at home.   Illustrates concepts of family-
bonding, positive birth experience, and consumer choices in health
care.   d. Gay Courter; p. Philip Courter; PARENTP.

BONHEUR, LE (85m   C   1965   French/subtitled)
A poetic and sensuous hymn to the happy life ... the story of
one man in love with two women.   p. /d. Agnes Varda; JANUS.

BORAN HERDSMEN; Faces of Change Series (17m   C   1974)
Portrays the life-style, culture, daily and seasonal activities of
the Boran herdsman of North Kenya.   Shows the society's dependence on cattle and the necessity for water.   Depicts how the cattle
are cared for, moved to water, and inoculated by the government.
Records how climate conditions have forced the society to accept
farming.   AUFS; WER; IU.

BORAN WOMEN; Faces of Change Series (18m   C   1975)
Examines the contradictions in the lives of Boran women of
Northern Kenya as they maintain their traditional role in a herding
culture and at the same time are exposed to education and other
aspects of modernization.   By Judith Von Daler/Nancy Dupree;
AUFS; WER; EMC, IU, MSU, UK.

BORIS GODOUNOV (105m   C   1954   Russian/subtitled)
Story of Boris Godounov, a 16th-century Czar, who has ascended
to the throne by murdering a young prince.   Godounov is conscience-
stricken, a fact which is used by enemies to devise an elaborate
plan to gain the throne.   Director Stroyeva has emphasized the use
of common people as commentators on central characters' actions.
One of the finest opera films ever made.   p. /d. Vera Stroyeva;
s. w. Stroyeva/N. Golovanov; ABFL

BORN YESTERDAY (103m   B   1951)
Judy Holliday plays the dumb-blonde girl friend of millionaire
junkman Broderick Crawford.   Crawford hires scholarly William
Holden to "culture" his girl friend, with the dumb-blonde ending up
too smart for Crawford's own good.   Based on play by Garson
Kanin.   d.   George Cukor; COLUMBIA; ABFI, BF, TWY.

BOTH/AND (25m   C   n. d.)
In this landmark film on bisexuality, a group of nude people
discuss how they came to bisexuality and their experiences.   Interspersed are scenes of group sexual activity.   By Laird Sutton;
MMRC.

BOTTLE BABIES (26m C 1976)
Babies in the Third World are dying because their mothers feed
them Western-style baby food. Those that do not die are drawn into the vicious cycle of malnutrition and disease that will leave them
physically and intellectually stunted for life. Rather than breast-
feed their babies, these mothers are influenced by the widespread
advertising (in all languages and dialects) of large Western companies such as Borden's, Bristol-Myers, and Nestle. The film explores the alarming increase of what has become known as the
"lactogen syndrome" or commerciogenic malnutrition. TFC; UILL,
UW.

BOURBON IN SUBURBIA (27m C n. d.)
Statistics tell us that alcoholism is the most widespread disease
in the nation. The saddest and most difficult to reach victim of
this illness is the American housewife. This sensitive and realistic
film is a psychological probe of America's most destructive and
widespread social problem. By Anne Francis/Marie Windsor; MGH.

BOWL OF CHERRIES (8m B 1965)
"Texture, color, and mystery of life comes alive through a
young girl's dissection of a vegetable garden. "--YFD. By Susan
Whyne; YFD.

BOWL, THEATRE, GARDEN, MARBLE GAME (7m C n. d.)
A selection of visual surprises including four animated anecdotes.
By Susan Pitt Kraning; CCC.

BOX, THE (5m C 1967)
"Live action changes to animation in a man's odyssey into a
dream-like scientific land. "--M. C. By Maureen Cellwood; CELL-
WOOD.

BOYS WITH LONG HAIR (30m C n. d.)
"I mean to be serious about it, long hair is something very
much a hassle. "--M. S. By Martha Stuart/David Ruskin; STUARTM.

BRAND NEW LIFE, A (72m C 1974)
Drama about a happily married 40-year-old woman with a ful-
filling career who discovers that she is pregnant for the first time.
Realistically depicts the dilemma facing the couple over whether to
have the child, since both are reluctant to alter their satisfying
life-styles. In the end, the woman decides that she wants the baby.
She and her husband are both happy with the decision. Features
Cloris Leachman and Martin Balsam; d. Sam O'Steen; LCA; EMC,
TWY.

BRANDENBURG CONCERTO NO. IV (11m B 1963)
Presents a performance by the Ohio State University Dance
Group of Bach's "Brandenburg Concerto No. IV" as choreographed
by Ruth Currier and Doris Humphrey. OHSU; UILL.

BREAK AND ENTER (30m   B   n. d.)
About tenants' rights in New York.   New York City has been
boarding up a number of buildings, throwing people out to make way
for urban renewal.   People in these buildings (mostly poor minority
members) refused to be moved.   Operation Move-In starts with four
families and ends with 150 families occupying 38 buildings.   The
women are strong leaders--very articulate and determined to win.
TWN.

BREAKFAST DANCE (6m   B   n. d.)
Portrays a woman serving breakfast to her family.   You see
her feelings about her role in a slow-motion dance-like portrayal.
A surprise ending packs a wallop.   By David Wilson, UCLA.

BREAKING OUT OF THE DOLL'S HOUSE (32m   C   1976)
Edited version of A Doll's House.   UILL.   See A DOLL'S
HOUSE.

BREAKTHROUGH (30m   B   n. d.   VIDEO)
The search for identity is the focal point in activities for inter-
action--including dance, communication of feelings, movement training, fantasy, etc.   By Constance Beeson; IE.

BREAST CANCER (23m   C   1976   ed.)
The new and open attitude toward breast cancer is bringing
about some important changes in the discovery and treatment of
that disease.   Step-by-step instructions are given on how every woman should give herself an examination.   p. Lucille Clark; d. C. E.
Rickey; KABCTV; ABFI.

BREAST SELF-EXAMINATION: A PLAN FOR SURVIVAL--A LIFE-
TIME HABIT (10m   C   1974)
A straightforward explanation of how--and why--women should
examine their breasts regularly.   By Dolores E. Fiedler, M. D.
MIC/FPP; UK, WAYSU.

BREATHLESS (89m   B   1959   French/subtitled)
A young American girl, Pat (who hawks Herald Tribunes on the
streets of Paris) and a Humphrey Bogart parody, Michel (who steals
cars, kills cops, borrows money he'll never return) team up to go
nowhere.   But you'll never see two people go nowhere so quickly
and with such determination.   d. Jean-Luc Godard; CORINF.

BRIDE AND GROOM   see   FOLLY

BRIDE WORE RED, THE (93m   B   1937)
A cabaret girl (Joan Crawford) is given two weeks in the Tyrol
with high society.   She hopes the time will never end and tries for
love with a millionaire playboy.   When her identity is discovered
she loses the society man but still has the love of the village postman.   From Ferene Molnar's unpublished play, "The Girl from
Trieste. "   d. Dorothy Arzner; s. w. Tess Slesinger/Bradbury Foote;
MGM; FI.

BRIDGES-GO-ROUND (4m C 1958)
A unique study among experimental films; a study of the patterns made by bridges in space, their massive power, and the particular quality of motion that is given to bridges when moving in relation to them. By Shirley Clarke; SB, CCC.

BRIEF ENCOUNTER (99m B 1946)
A very British, low-key and poignant story of romance between two middle-aged people, both married to others. An ordinary middle-class housewife and mother meets a similarly conventional doctor. Casual acquaintance turns to romance to the surprise and shock of both. With Celia Johnson and Trevor Howard. d. David Lean; s. w. Noel Coward; WRS.

BRINGING UP BABY (100m B 1938)
The orderly life of a staid paleontologist is upset by a very wealthy, very confusing and confused young lady (Katharine Hepburn). Rapid-fire dialogue, zany story, wacky characterizations plus the Hawks' fun kind of direction make this one of the most enduring examples of screwball comedy. Features the song "I Can't Give You Anything But Love. " Based on short story by Hager Wilde. d. Howard Hawks; RKO; FL

BRINK, THE (40m B n. d.)
A film metaphor, based on a poem by Ruth Weiss. Compares the actualization of a human being to the metamorphosis of a caterpillar into a butterfly. Direction and narration by Ruth Weiss. CCC.

BRINK OF LIFE (100m B 1957 Swedish/subtitled)
Studies the grief of two women who have been denied the birth of their babies--one by miscarriage and the other in sacrifice for the mother's life. A third woman not wanting her illegitimate child, witnesses their suffering and is moved to accept a commitment to her child's birth. Bergman is severely simple in his analysis of the irony of circumstances and human tribulations. d. Ingmar Bergman; JANUS.

BROADWAY CRAZY QUILT (15m C 1974)
"Experimental film of colored lights inspired by the construction of American patch work quilts. "--K. N. By Kristina Nordstrom; NORDSTROM.

BRONTË SISTERS (19m C 1970)
Eric Portman describes details of the lives of the Brontë family and examines the personality of each sister. Scenes depict people casually strolling in 19th-century dress in the somber beauty of the Yorkshire landscape which appears much as it did then. Poems read are: "Often Rebuked, " "Charlotte's Letters, " (by Emily), and "Self-Communication" (by Anne). IFB; BU, BY, EMC, UILL, UU.

BRONZE ZOO, THE (16m C 1973)
Shows the entire process of creating a bronze zoo as done by contemporary sculptor, Shay Reiger. By Sonya Friedman; TEXFM.

BROTHER CARL (97m B 1971 Swedish/subtitled)
Tells a story, linear in form, about real people stripped down
to their imaginary psychology. d. Susan Sontag; NYF.

BUDDHISM, MAN AND NATURE (14m C 1968)
Alan Watts discusses the Buddhist concept of man as a part of
nature. Photographs and scenes of Chinese and Japanese paintings
show the harmony of Buddhist philosophy with nature and illustrate
the influence Buddhism has had on Chinese and Japanese art. By
Elda Hartley; HARTLEY.

"BUENOS DIAS, COMPANERAS": WOMEN IN CUBA (58m C 1975)
An intimate look at the lives of four Cuban women of entirely
different circumstances. The film investigates how some of the
women of Cuba have adapted to the Revolution and made it their
Revolution. It shows how the Revolution has_affected the structure
of Cuban society; its aims, its attitudes, its view of work and study,
and its male and female roles. Particularly "machismo." d. Aviva
Slesin; p. Vivienne Leebosh; PHOENIX.

BUILDING AN ORGANIZATION see ORGANIZING FOR POWER:
THE ALINSKY APPROACH

BUILDING BELIEF, PT. I (28m C n.d.)
Dorothy Heathcote's objective here is to encourage an understanding of the words "A nation is as strong as the spirit of the
people who make it." She and the children share their first day in
a hard and barren land, each identifying with a particular settler.
Together they question, list strengths, and share their "memories."
Developing these memories into a chronicle broadens scope and lifts
diction in the writing of their history. NWUFL.

BUILDING BELIEF, PT. II (29m C n.d.)
Continuing her work with the same group of youngsters, Dorothy Heathcote poses three moral dilemmas, using drama to evoke
focus and feeling. First, she abdicates her leadership role, leaving the group on their own to divide the land. Then, assuming the
role of an old woman, who is hurt and angry because they have left
her no place to live, she pushes them to take account of the community's elderly. Finally, she asks them to face the death of a
young man mauled by a lion. NWUFL.

BULLFIGHT (9m C 1955)
Integrates a stark dance with dramatic footage from a bullfight
in Spain. By Shirley Clarke; MOMA.

BUNNY; Social Seminar Series (16m C 1971)
A typical junior at UCLA. Casual drug usage is just one aspect of her life. EMC.

BURDEN THEY CARRY, THE (28m B 1973)
Only recently recognized is the universal need to be able to
speak freely about sex. Dr. Bergstrom-Wahlan, a Swedish educator,
shows how she handles the subject with each age group. NFBC; FL

BUS STOP (96m   C   1956)
 Don Murray is as subtle as a cub as he woos Marilyn Monroe.
He had come to the big city to rope a wife and, like it or not,
Marilyn Monroe is chosen.   Monroe, as a target of the young cow-
boy's ardor, is perfectly delightful as the "chantoosie" from the
Ozarks who sings in the local cafe.   d. Joshua Logan; FOX; ABFL

BUSH MAMA (90m   B   n. d.)
 An impressionistic portrait of the changing consciousness of a
Black woman living on welfare in the Los Angeles ghetto.   She is
trying to raise her young daughter alone after her man is imprisoned for a crime he didn't commit.   A sensitive and powerful
portrait of urban Black America as seen through the eyes of a
strong, proud Black woman.   By Haile Gerima; TFC.

BUSING: A ROUGH RIDE IN SOUTHIE (29m   C   1976)
 Examines court-ordered busing in Boston and focuses on the
tense situation in South Boston.   Traces the effect busing has had
on three families.   The complexities of busing are expressed in
the attitudes of these families and in their honest discussion of
this issue.   p. /d. Ellen Boyce/Sam Kauffmann; KAUBOY.

BUSY KNITTER: PT. I, THE (10/30m   series B   1965   VIDEO)
 Elizabeth Zimmerman shows complete construction of a sweater.
WMVSTV; PTL.

BUSY KNITTER: PT. II, THE (13/29m   series B   1967   VIDEO)
 Elizabeth Zimmerman shows how to make a Scandinavian type
of sweater.   WMVSTV; PTL.

... BUT WHAT IF THE DREAM COMES TRUE? (52m   C   1971)
 Revealing portrait of the goals and problems of an upper-class
family whose dreams of an affluence in the exclusive suburb of
Birmingham, Michigan are realized.   Examines with insight the dis-
tinctly different pressures on each member of the family.   Shows
that pursuit of "the American dream" may mean an exchange of material problems for psychological ones.   CBSTV; CAROUSEL; BU,
EMC, UILL, UM.

BUTTERFIELD 8 (109m   C   Reg. /Scope   1960)
 High-priced model Glorie (Elizabeth Taylor) is a beautiful, tempestuous, but wanton woman whose lucrative job allows her to pattern her life to suit her changing desires.   Ever-searching for love,
she meets Harvey (the married man for whom she is willing to
change her ways) who deserts her.   d. Daniel Mann; MGM; FL

BUTTON, BUTTON (13m   C   1969)
 A documentary which includes interviews with button makers,
button wearers, and button collectors.   Uses these interviews, together with scenes of animated buttons, to present a view of the
U. S. today.   By Suzanne E. Bauman.   BAUMSZ.

BY THEMSELVES (34m   B   1977)
 Portrait of three single women--one divorced. one widowed, and

one unmarried--who discuss solitude, careers, and personal encounters. A documentary that captures the satisfactions and frustrations of a professional woman alone. Barbara, the divorced
woman, is a law professor working in a traditionally male profession. She and her parents analyze her divorce. She speaks ar-
ticulately about controlling her own life, feeling lonely, and coping.
Although she treasures her independence, she misses a caring relationship. Betsy is a widowed 40-year-old graduate student who
lives with three elementary school teachers and feels locked into
an all-female world. She comments on the difficulty of meeting men
in unforced settings, and of the pain of always returning home alone.
EMC.

CABBAGE (9m C n. d.)
    "I like to film ordinary things I do and see everyday because
film makes it so easy to see the immense cosmic fearsomeness
and beauty of everything. While watching film, I can abandon myself to the event. I don't find that so easy to do in the kitchen in
the morning. I still don't understand that part. "--D. W. By
Dorothy Wiley; CCC.

CABINET, THE (14m C 1972)
    Cabinet full of toys and memorabilia that come alive to recreate
half-remembered childhood. By Suzanne E. Bauman; CAROUSEL.

CACTUS FLOWER (102m C 1969)
    Goldie Hawn plays the kooky blonde who entraps a playboy-
dentist, long a confirmed bachelor, but one who pretends to be a
family man. To keep Goldie from getting serious and to protect
his status, he convinces his prim, plain nurse to pose as his wife.
The sudden blooming of this long unnoticed "cactus flower" into an
attractive woman causes hilarious confusion. A comedy based on
a Broadway hit by Abe Burrows. d. Gene Saks; p. M. J. Frankovich;
s. w. A. L. Diamond; COLUMBIA; WHOLFC.

CAESAREAN BIRTH EXPERIENCE, THE (25m C 1976)
    Two emergency caesarean sections are followed with com-
mentary by the parents, obstetrician, pediatrician, and anesthesi-
ologist. Other mothers discuss the emotional and physical impact
of their caesarean births. d. Gay Courter; p. Philip Courter;
PARENTP.

CAESAREAN SECTIONS (11m C 1967)
    Illustrates surgical techniques used in various types of caesar-
ean sections. Technical, for medical students and medical personnel. UNWORLD; BU.

CAFETERIA OR HOW ARE YOU GOING TO KEEP HER DOWN ON
    THE FARM AFTER SHE'S SEEN PARIS TWICE? (1m C/B n. d.)
    "Diane feeds calves imagination and granola to see life's possi-
bilities from many viewpoints while tap dancing with a marble
bear. "--CCC. By Judith Wardwell; MOSHE; SB.

CAIDA, LA see FALL, THE

CALIPH STORK (10m   B   1930's)
An animated film based on live shadow play.   The Caliph of
Bagdad is turned into a stork by his wicked uncle, but soon has
revenge.   By Lotte Reiniger; BBCTV; CEA, MGH.

CALL ME MAMA (14m   C   1977)
In this frank autobiography, Miriam Weinstein, a 30-year-old
mother with an 18-month-old son, talks of her responsibilities, feelings and perceptions of herself as mother.   In documentary scenes
of everyday life we see Eli act demanding and willful, refuse to
share toys and play "nicely" with a little girl, and generally be
exasperating.   The film raises many questions: Is there a "right"
or "best" way to raise your child? Is it possible, by taking one's
responsibility too seriously and trying too hard, to make mothering
more of a chore than it need be?   What is the effect of vastly differing infant personalities on the mother and her sense of accomplish?   A useful film for starting a discussion of what is involved
in being a parent, the expectations and realities.   p. /d. Miriam
Weinstein; POLYMORPH.

CAMERA MASSAGE (6m   B   1968)
"Media is the massage.   Film is the meditation.   Massage is
done by the camera and lights.   Meditation is recorded on the film
camera, massage on a girl "--T. I. By Takahiko Iimura; CCC.

CAMERA WOMAN (7m   B   1969)
Dynamic sequence of a woman shooting on location.   Made for
a KQED-TV Women's Program.   By Emiko Omori; OMORI.

CAMINO REAL (3m   C   si   1972)
A look at bubbling water.   "Dreams: to have the courage to
make something useless (to sleep fiercely) endlessly. "--M. E.   By
Martha Edelheit; EDELHEIT.

CAMPAIGN (20m   C   1973)
Documentary of the campaign for the office of state senator.
Cathy O'Neill, a young woman emerges from the role of housewife
and amateur to battle an encumbent.   Although she loses the race
by one percent, her near-victory is an encouraging sign in a district
where a woman has never been a political candidate.   Volunteers
acquire skills of organization, fund raising, publicity and persuasion.
By Joan Churchill, James Kennedy; CF; EMC, UM.

CAN ANYBODY HEAR THE BIRDS (10m   B   n. d.)
Filmed in three adjacent seasons.   This film explores, with
wonder, the relationship of sculpture to human beings and nature.
Harpsichord music on accompanying tape.   By Anne Kish; CCC.

CARAVAN (22m   B   1974)
A theatre director at work during a rehearsal of an autobiographical play about a woman filmmaker.   During a group discussion, she

explores her difficulties as a women in the arts.   By Mary Jane
Soule/Joan Barkhausen; FF.

CAREERS AND BABIES (20m   C   1977)
    Decisions concerning careers and babies are complex.   Each
woman must work out her own schedule, priorities, and values.
The film shows four women who have reacted individually to this
common question.   The women speak for themselves and tell us of
their feelings and the choices they have made for themselves.   This
film will allow the audience to form and refine their own opinions,
to compare possibilities, and to reach personally meaningful conclu-
sions.   p. Alvin Fiering; d. Georgia Morris; POLYMORPH.

CAREERS FOR NOW SERIES   see   NEW ENTREPRENEUR

CAREERS IN THE 70'S SERIES   see   WOMEN IN CAREERS

CARING MORE THAN A DAY (20m   C   1972)
    Mainly through interviews with the Chairman of the group (Doro-
thy Pitman Hughes, a Black woman), we learn of the philosophy and
establishment of a Community Day Care Center.   Ms. Hughes is a
vocal, dynamic Black woman whose disillusionment with the public
care available was such that she was inspired to do something about
it.   Shows community organizing, finding a suitable building, reno-
vating it, and finally, the opening of the center.   A good film for
groups considering such a service.   By Richard Oretzky, National
Council of Churches; ORETZKY.

CARMEN (10m   B   1933)
    An animated film based on live shadow play.   Based on themes
from Bizet's Carmen--ending with a humorous treatment of the bullfight.   By Lotte Reiniger; BBCTV; MGH, CEA.

CARNAL KNOWLEDGE (96m   C   1971)
    A study of people trying to exist by the rules of a changing
world.   A penetrating look at our changing sexual attitudes.   Controversial, perhaps, but Carnal Knowledge has become one of those
films that remains an effective "document of our times."   Written
by Jules Feiffer, with Jack Nicholson, Ann-Margret.   d. Mike
Nichols, EMBASSY; ABFI, BF.

CAROL (22m   C   1977)
    Filmed story of Carol Anthony--a successful sculptress.   Carol
herself expresses the final moment: "My buds are opening, I'm
just starting to see something in my work and I want to be there
for the blooming."   The story of a fulfilled person, both as artist
and human being.   p./d. George W. George, Geoffrey D. Nypom-
mik, Keith W. Rouse; PHOENIX.

CAROLINE (28m   B   n.d.)
    To the public, she is the pleasant, never-ruffled handler of
everyone's complaints at the office.   But, behind her calm exterior,
the film reveals doubts about her personal life--the domestic world
of husband and child.   MGH.

CARROLL BAKER AS HARLOW (13m B 1965)
    Actress Carroll Baker discusses the life of Jean Harlow and
her forthcoming interpretation of Jean Harlow in a biographical film.
Carroll Baker is transformed through makeup and hairstyling techniques into an amazing likeness of Jean Harlow. p. TURMOS;
PARAMOUNT; ABFL

CASA DEL ANGEL, LA see END OF INNOCENCE

CASE OF SUICIDE (30m B 1968)
    Study of a 17-year-old wife and mother who committed suicide.
Examines the causes of her action, interviews those close to her,
and discusses what could have been done to help her. TL; EMC.

CASE OF THE ELEVATOR DUCK, THE (16m C 1974)
    Introduces an imaginative 11-year-old "Detective" who lives in
a high-rise city housing project. Describes how he finds a pet duck,
forbidden in the apartment building, and depicts his efforts to find
the owner. Based on a book by Polly Berrien Berrends. By Linda
Gottlieb/Joan Silver; LCA.

CAT BALLOU (96m C 1965)
    Jane Fonda appears in the title role as the frontier lady of
propriety who, when her father is murdered by a hired killer and
his ranch seized, turns outlaw with a vengeance. d. Elliot Silver-
stein; COLUMBIA; ABFI, BF, CINE, CWF.

CATECHIST, THE (20m C n.d.)
    Presents the story of the conversion of Joanne Kitagawa, one
of the first of the native African lay missionaries and teachers.
ASFL

CATFOOD (13m C 1968)
    Shown is a cat devouring fish after fish. The imagery is con-
sistent throughout. Includes shot of the fish, the cat eating, his
paw clawing another fish, etc. d. Joyce Wieland; FCOOP.

CATHERINE THE GREAT (93m B 1934 (dubbed))
    A lavish, historical drama closely following the actual life of
the Russian Czarina who is portrayed by Elizabeth Bergner. Bergner's Czarina, surrounded by the pomp of Russian Imperial Court,
is sympathetically presented as a woman whose destiny was mis-
directed by rigid marital customs. d. Paul Czinner; p. Alexander
Korda; ABFI, BF, IVY, KP.

CATHERINE THE GREAT (26m C 1976)
    Based on historical research, Catherine the Great, portrayed
by Zoe Caldwell, is interviewed by Patrick Watson. Interview begins with Watson reading a list of Catherine's lovers as she smiles.
After a brief discussion on the subject, Catherine speaks of her
rise from a princess to become the empress of Russia. The subject of her marriage is raised. Catherine points out, as Peter's
bride, it was not possible to produce an heir. Consequently, Peter's
mother encouraged her to take a lover. Catherine spoke of her

superb job of public relations which helped her ascendancy to power after Peter's death. The interview situation in the film vividly illustrates Catherine's skillful use of femininity to seduce her interviewer away from uncomfortable questions.   p. McConnell Advertising in cooperation with LCA; LCA.

CATHERINE WOOD MARSHALL; Person to Person Series (17m   B 1955)
     An interview with Catherine Wood Marshall, author of A Man Called Peter.   Presents a discussion of her biography of her husband, Peter Marshall, a Presbyterian minister and Chaplain of the Senate until his death in 1949.   Mrs. Marshall and her son Peter describe their activities.   Mrs. Marshall escorts a tour of her home in Washington, D. C.   CBSTV.

CATS AND DOGS (23m   B   1973)
     Explores the relationship between a man and woman in a series of episodes which reveals much about them and about their attitudes toward each other.   She is concerned with understanding and developing a deeper relationship.   He is impatient with her intellectualizing the situation.   After a final quarrel, she leaves.   They meet again, but there seems little chance of a new understanding between them.   A good discussion film on marriage and interpersonal relationship.   By Paul Gurian; VFI, PARACO.

CATSUP (3m   C   1966)
     Shows a number of cats as they come out of bright colored bags and a box, play with a wind-up toy frog, and then return to their places.   By Tana Hoban; TEXFM.

CATUOR (4m   C   1970)
     Combines animated design with jazz accompaniment in a play on the French word, "quator."   Features a cat who can multiply himself while conjuring up musical acrobats.   By Judith Klein; NFBC; SFD.

CAVALCADE OF AMERICA SERIES   see   SKIPPER'S LADY: DUTY FIRST

CAYUGA RUN--HUDSON RIVER DIARY: BOOK I (18m   C   1967)
     A profoundly sentimental journey on a train from New York to Poughkeepsie.   By Storm De Hirsch; CC.

CEILING, THE (40m   B   1962   Czech/subtitled)
     About a fashion model who sets herself a low ceiling of attainment and settles for an easy life rather than reaching for something more fruitful.   Her awareness of her predicament is heightened through the contrast between her beautiful figure and the disillusioned face she can't help noticing as she passes store windows in the night.   By Vera Chytilova; IMPF.

CELEBRATING A CENTURY (28m   C   1976-77)
     Story of the building of an American international exposition.

Gives historical background of international expositions and considers the impact of the Philadelphia Centennial of 1876 on the nation and the world.   The re-creation of the Philadelphia Centennial at the Smithsonian Institution is the primary picture source for the film.   Narrated by James Whitmore.   d. /p. Karen Loveland; SMITHS.

CELEBRATION AT BIG SUR (82m   C   1971)
     Folk-rock music festival benefit with Joan Baez, Steven Stills, Neil Young, Joni Mitchell, David Crosby, John Sebastian, Graham Nash and Dorothy Morrison.   Filmed at the Esalen Institute.   By Johanna Demetrakas, Baird Bryant; FI; MGH.

CELEBRATION IN FRESH POWDER; Insight Series (27m   C   n. d.)
     More and more, young women of today are able to decide for themselves whether or not to have an abortion.   Increasingly, abortions are performed by bona fide physicians without the aura of dirt, disease and dishonesty.   Thus, abortion becomes a moral question rather than a legal one.   This film presents a timely and sympathetic exploration of the unwanted pregnancy.   Young people need to know all the available options and their consequences.   By Candace Clark and Lynne Marta; MG.

CELS (6m   C   n. d.)
     A series of animated vignettes.   Doors open and close revealing thoughts in the form of film experiences.   By Suzan Pitt Kraning; CCC.

CENTAUR (10m   C   1973)
     The poetry of the horse and its rider.   The camera reveals details of hoof movement and pace, as they dance upon the earth and sand, canter through the woods, or soar over the jumps.   By Susan Gibbard; NFBC; PF.

CENTRAL PARK CONSPIRACY (15m   B   n. d.)
     Youth and the establishment are contrasted as a rock group takes over quiet Central Park.   The generation gap is explored in a series of vignettes that illustrate the conflicting pastimes of young and old.   By Terry Motlik; YFD.

CHAIM SOUTINE (28m   C   1970)
     Presents the life and times of painter Chaim Soutine, from his childhood in Russia to his death in wartime Paris.   Illustrates his works and those of his intimates, including Modigliani.   Features interviews with friends, painters and collectors who explore his character and painting techniques.   By Rita J. Morrison; MGH.

CHAIRS (5m   C   1971)
     "Chairs behave like people. "--Cinema Femina.   By Maria Lassnig; FCOOP.

CHAIRY TALE, A (10m   C   1957)
     A fairy tale with no narration.   This film is a kind of a simple

ballet, a pas de deux, of a youth and a common kitchen chair.   The
young man tries to sit in a chair, but the chair refuses to be sat
upon.   The ensuing struggle, first for mastery and then for understanding, forms the story.   By Evelyn Lambart/Norman McLaren;
IFB; ASU, BU.

CHALLENGE FOR CHANGE PROGRAM   see   ENCOUNTER AT
    KWACHA HOUSE--HALIFAX; ENCOUNTER WITH SAUL ALIN-
    SKY, I: CYC TORONTO; ENCOUNTER WITH SAUL ALINSKY,
    II: RAMA INDIAN RESERVE; EXTENSIONS OF THE FAMILY;
    LIKE THE TREES; LITTLE BURGUNDY; MOTHERS ARE PEO-
    PLE; ORGANIZING FOR POWER: THE ALINSKY APPROACH
    SERIES; POW WOW AT DUCK LAKE; THEY APPRECIATE YOU
    MORE; TIGER ON A TIGHT LEASH; WOULD I EVER LIKE TO
    WORK

CHANGING; Social Seminar Series (31m   C   1971)
    Follows a young family seeking to create an alternate life-style
that stresses openness and spontaneity, and includes use of marijuana.   Shows mother and father coping with changing relationships
with children, friends, employer and each other.   NAVC, EMC.

CHANGING IMAGES: CONFRONTING CAREER STEREOTYPES; Sex-
    Role Stereotyping Schools, A Series (16m   B   1975)
    Reveals the influence of sex-role stereotypes in the career ex-
pectations of elementary school children.   Shows how a skillful and
sensitive teacher leads her culturally diverse class of third and
fourth graders through a five-week project designed to identify; challenge, and begin to change the stereotyped beliefs held by boys and
girls.   p. Gloria Golden; EMC.

CHANGING MOTHERHOOD; Woman Series (29m   C   1975   VIDEO)
    Sociologist Jessie Bernard talks about the changing role of moth-
erhood in the U. S.   WNEDTV; PTL.

CHANT D'AMOUR, UN (20m   B   si   1948)
    A silent work on homosexual love in prison, blending the in-
mates' frustrated reality with their explicit fantasies.   "As in his
novel 'Our Lady of the Flowers' ... the lines between fantasy and
reality are kept in constant flux. "--Ron Epple, Media and Methods.
d. Jean Genet; GP; IE.

CHARACTER FORMATION IN DIFFERENT CULTURE SERIES   see
    BALINESE FAMILY

CHARLES DARDEN: CONDUCTOR (14m   C   1972)
    "Charles Darden, young Black music teacher, founder and con-
ductor of the Berkeley Free Orchestra, apprentice to Seiji Ozawa,
talks about being Black, about his career, the role of music in today's society, about working with children... "--BFA.   By Sue
Lederer; BFA.

CHARLIE COMPANY (9m   C   n. d.)
    A surrealistic cartoon using visual imagery similar to her film
Black Pudding.   By Nancy Edell; CFS.

CHARLIE DOZES OFF AND THE DOG BOTHERS HIM (3m   C/B
    1973)
    A visual poem about sleep and wakefulness.   By Alexis Rafael
Krasilovsky; RAFAEL.

CHARLIE'S DREAM (3m   C   1972)
    Visual poem about dreaming.   By Alexis Rafael Krasilovsky;
RAFAEL.

CHEAP THRILLS (10m   C   n. d.)
    Students at Antioch-Columbia build an inflatable house.   They
collapse it, rebuild it, and engage in play inside it.   The event was
created for the film, which is the filmmaker's first.   By Victoria
Rouse; CCC.

CHEN: WOMEN'S AUXILIARY CORPS (15m   C   n. d.)
    Shows women being inducted into the army from the recruiting
base.   Depicts their training, and the role that they eventually play
in the Israel Defense Force.   ALDEN.

CHICAGO MATERNITY CENTER STORY, THE (60m   B   1977)
    A group of mothers tell why the patient-centered, low-cost,
preventative care delivered by the 78-year-old Chicago Maternity
Center was worth fighting for.   Shows a moving presentation of a
difficult home delivery.   Provides a historical analysis of health
care in America and shows why modern medicine rejects the Center's approach in favor of high-profit hospital-based care.   Mothers
confront the Center's Board of Directors as the mothers fight to
keep the Center open but it is soon closed after the new hospital is
built.   The struggle for good health care goes on.   SFN.

CHICKEN SOUP (14m   B   n. d.)
    Bubba Anna, a Jewish grandmother in the Bronx, gives a highly
verbal demonstration of how to make chicken soup.   With help from
her husband Willie, Anna Schecter cleans, plucks, singes, boils and
stirs her way through what becomes a celebration of life.   A fond
and often funny glimpse into a vanishing life-style.   By Ken Schneider; CAROUSEL.

CHIKAMATSU MONOGATARI see CRUCIFIED LOVERS, THE

CHILD, THE; PT. I (29m   C   1975)
    Documents the development of the infant during the first two
months after birth.   Details the care, handling, feeding and the
ordinary day-to-day routines of parenting.   Shows a brief sequence
of the actual delivery.   d. Robert Humble; p. Colin Low, Tom Daly;
NFBC; MGH.

CHILD, THE; PT. II (28m   C   1975)
Documents the development of the infant during the second to the 14th month after birth.   d. Robert Humble: p. Colin Low, Tom Daly; NFBC; MGH.

CHILD, THE; PT. III (28m   C   1975)
Documents the development of the infant during the 12th to 24th month period after birth.   d. Robert Humble; p. Colin Low, Tom Daly; NFBC; MGH.

CHILD OF DANCE (9m   C   1970)
"Charming film about children and dance: the children, aged four to six, are members of Virginia Tanner's famous Creative Dance Studio at the University of Utah."--FL   By Judith Hallet, Stanley Hallet; FIM.

CHILDBIRTH (17m   C   n. d.)
An extraordinary, warm documentary chronicling the birth of a baby.   Captures the interaction between husband and wife during parent preparation classes.   Includes labor and delivery (with the husband present) and caring for the baby during rooming-in.   Manages to convey information while retaining a sense of the humanity and humor of the people involved.   A shortened version of "Not Me Alone."   p. /d. Alvin Fiering; POLYMORPH.

CHILDBIRTH, PT. I; Women Series (29m   C   1974   VIDEO)
Ms. Doris Haire, medical writer and organizer of family maternity workshops, and Dr. Mortimer Rosen, an obstetrician with special interest in problems of the newborn, discuss the high incidence of deaths and neurological impairments among American babies.   WNEDTV; PTL.

CHILDBIRTH, PT. II; Women Series (29m   C   1974)
Dr. Sumner J. Yaffe, a pediatrician, and Ms. Doris Haire, author: "The Cultural Warping of Childbirth" and other publications on maternity care, express the hope that educating women and obstetricians to the dangers of drugs will reduce the frequency of birth injuries and infant deaths.   WNEDTV; PTL.

CHILDCARE: PEOPLE'S LIBERATION (20m   B   1970)
A good beginning film on child care.   Starts from women's isolation with their children and moves to the community day care center.   Shows the ways that parents and children can develop new relationships with their peers and each other.   It is implicitly, though not overtly, anti-sexist and anti-racist.   Presents the problems of working mothers and the pitfalls of corporate child care.   By Bonnie Friedman/Karen Mitnick; SFN, TWN.

CHILDREN AS PEOPLE (28m   B   1977)
Allows observation of children in alternative education--spontaneous events, shared activities, group and individual projects. Children progress at their own pace with teachers offering guidance and resources rather than direction and discipline.   Learning ma-

terials are varied and flexible.   Commentary by John Holt, author
of "How Children Fail," "The Underachieving School," etc.   p. Alvin Fiering; d. Werner Bundschuh; POLYMORPH.

CHILDREN IN PERIL (24m   C   1972)
Considers the plight of the battered child and the battering parent in humanistic and realistic terms.   Points out that parental
cruelty toward children and infants stems from "end-of-the-rope"
situations--crises such as parental quarrel or job failure.   Lay
therapists, trained for emergency help and follow-up, are shown in
action backed by foster-parent support.   Examines newer approaches
in helping the battered child.   ABCTV; XEROX; UW.

CHILDREN MAKE MOVIES (11m   C   1963)
Shows a group of children ages five to twelve, as they make a
"scratch film" using a small straight pin and felt-tip pens for color-
ing.   Presents a film made by the children.   It is a spontaneous
creation of city of blocks built by a group of children of many races
and creeds.   By Dee Dee Halleck; MGH.

CHILDREN OF CHANGE (31m   B   1960)
Dramatizes the special stresses and strains placed on children
whose mothers work outside the home, and on the mothers themselves.   Shows the educational values and contributions to mental
and emotional health of day care centers for young children.   Somewhat dated in format but content still valid.   IFB; BU, EMC, PAS,
WSU.

CHILDREN OF DIVORCE (37m   C   1976)
Examines the consequences and feelings of the real victims of
divorce--the children.   They are bewildered at events they do not
understand, guiltily feeling they are at fault, and suffering a sense
of rejection by the parent who leaves.   This study of the impact of
divorce on children reveals the necessity for parents to bury their
hostilities and to provide children with access to both parents.   Examines custody, child support laws and social agencies such as Big
Brother and Parents Without Partners.   d. Mike Gavin; NBCTV; FI.

CHILDREN OF PARADISE (188m   B   1946   French/subtitled)
It's a sumptuous dream vision of 19th-century Paris.   It's about
love, the theatre, mime, the spoken word, street people, aristo-
crats, murderers, thieves, and saints.   It is bawdy, flamboyant,
delicate, touching and always artfully romantic.   James Agee says
"it's the highest kind of slum-glamour romanticism about theatre
people and criminals done with strong poetic feeling...." d. Marcel
Carne; FI.

CHILDREN OF THE NORTHLIGHTS (20m   C   1976)
Author-illustrators Ingri and Edgar Parin d'Aulaire, through
method of color lithography involving the use of stones, show scenes
of the production of their latest book, home movies, and many of
their drawings.   d. Jane Morrison; WESTON.

CHILDREN OF THE REVOLUTION (30m B n. d.)
Through impressions filmed in infant day care centers, nurseries, schools and work places, Cuban young people and adults are
seen in the process of defining themselves and the shape of their
Socialist Society.   By Jane Sellers; TWN.

CHILDREN OF THE SUN; First American Series (10m C 1960)
Depicts, through animation, the happy child from healthy birth
to seven years of age.   The unhappy under-privileged youngsters of
the world, of whom three out of four are under-fed, are then contrasted.   Faith Hubley/John Hubley; UNICEF; FL

CHILDREN'S HOUR, THE (107m B 1962)
The film presents an essentially sympathetic (as opposed to political) view of the lesbian dilemma and in this way will fail as a
film for self-affirmation.   Portrays the struggle of a lesbian as an
isolated person without the possibility of community.   Adapted from
a play by Lillian Hellman.   d. William Wyler; UAS.

CHILDREN'S SCHOOL, THE (17m B 1969)
A moment in an experimental school for children.   By Deborah
Dickson-Macagno; DICKSON.

CHINA COMMUNE (35m C n. d.)
Takes an intimate look into the way of life and institutions of
the Kwang Li People's Commune, Peoples Republic of China.   Introduces the commune system of administration, its division of labor, and its various forms of political education.   Depicts workers
and students, visits a family in their home, travels to a city, village and marketplace and views an operation by acupuncture.   Shows
that much progress has been made, and that personal incentive plays
a major role.   By Peggy Printz; WESTLC.

CHINA: MODERNIZATION THROUGH HUMAN POWER (17m C
    1967)
Traces the gradual mechanization of the economy of China from
agriculture to heavy industry.   Pictures the position of women in the
Chinese labor force.   Deals with China's traditional export industry.
Asahi TV; WSU.

CHINAMOON (15m C 1975)
Chinamoon takes place in a brothel--a timeless, nameless
brothel.   Experimental and impressionistic in technique, the movie
centers around the formally ritualized world of a room inhabited by
four prostitutes.   They are depicted with tenderness and sensitivity;
not as sex objects, but tragically, as tired, sexually depleted wom-
en.   The finale of the film is a pagan chorus, in song and rite.
Having shown the use of women's bodies which destroys their souls,
a ritual murder of the men who have come in contact with them
takes place.   By Barbara Linkevitch; SB.

CHINATOWN (131m C 1974 Reg. /Scope)
Set in seedy Southern California of the 1930's, Chinatown rever-

berates with the subtle eroticism of the love affair between Dunaway
and Nicholson. As in the film-noir detective movies it styles itself
after, the mood is pervasive, ominous and shadowy in this highly
complex tale of values corrupted by greed and the lust for power.
d. Roman Polanski; PARAMOUNT; FI.

CHINESE FARM WIFE; Faces of Change Series (17m C 1975)
    Portrait of a Taiwanese woman whose husband is a salaried
factory worker. Shows that she is a full participant in farming and
community activities in addition to her role in supervising the children's education and managing the household. AUFS; WER; EMC,
IU, MSU, UK.

CHIPMUNK AND HIS BIRD FRIENDS (10m C 1967 rev.)
    Shows the relative size of various birds, their color patterns
and their feeding habits. By Marian Evans; BFA.

CHISHOLM--PURSUING THE DREAM (42m C 1974)
    Documentary about Shirley Chisholm along the campaign trail for
the 1972 presidential nomination. Includes interviews, speeches
about the Black Panthers, talking to school children and campaigning
in Spanish on the street. She knew she would not win but chose to
pursue the American dream for those who have been left out, as a
catalyst for women, Blacks, the poor and the young. She inspired
many who never took an interest in politics before. By Tom Werner,
Bob Denby; FREDF; NLC, UM.

CHOICE: CHALLENGE FOR MODERN WOMEN SERIES see AND
    WHO ARE YOU?; ATTITUDES OF AND ABOUT AMERICAN WOM-
    EN IN THE MID-60's; FAMILY AFFAIR, THE; IS PERSONAL
    GROWTH SELFISH?; MARRIAGE OR MIRAGE; PRINCIPLE THAT
    COUNTS, THE; TIME OF YOUR LIFE, THE; UNLONELY WOM-
    EN, THE; WAGES OF WORK; WHAT IS A WOMAN?; WHAT IS
    THE SHAPE OF TOMORROW?; WHERE DOES ALL THE MONEY
    GO?; WHO WANTS FREEDOM?

CHRISTIAN MYSTICISM AND THE MONASTIC LIFE (20m C 1976)
    Filmed in the great Catholic and Protestant monasteries of
Europe and America. Attempts to give the viewer the feeling of
the mystical experience through the use of music and nature photography. d./p. Elda Hartley; HARTLEY.

CHRISTOPHER STRONG (77m B 1933)
    Lady Cynthia, daredevil pilot, falls in love with a married man
and promises to give up flying after one final trip. s.w. Zoe Akins;
d. Dorothy Arzner; RKO; FI.

CHRISTO'S VALLEY CURTAIN (28m C n.d.)
    Tells the story of Greek artist Christo who hangs his famous
curtain in a Colorado valley with a team of engineers, ironmakers
and students. By Ellen Gifford, Maysles Brothers; MAYSLES.

CINDERELLA (10m B 1922)
    A fairy tale in silhouette animation based on live shadow play.

A charming version of the best known fairy tale of all.   By Lotte
Reiniger; BBCTV; CEA, MGH.

CIRCLE OF LIFE SERIES   see   TO BE A MAN; TO BE A PAR-
     ENT; TO BE A PERSON; TO BE A WOMAN; TO BE GROWING
     OLDER; TO BE IN LOVE; TO BE MARRIED

CIRCLES I (7m   C   1971)
     A computer generated abstract film.   Circles revolve in, around,
and through each other.   They float off like loosened coils and evolve
into whirling spheres.   The pale color of the circles multiplying into brilliant hues against a stark musical accompaniment evokes the
sound of endlessly bouncing springs.   By Doris Chase; FCOOP;
CFS.

CIRCLES I, VARIATION II (7m   C   1972)
     Film's imagery is identical with CIRCLE I.   However, this film
uses a music score that is more melodic and thus gives the film a
much more melodic quality.   By Doris Chase; CFS.

CIRCLES II (14m   C   1972)
     "Dance/sculpture film that explores new dimensions in color and
space ... develops like a fugue with dancers moving through themes
that are repeated with variation and multiplication."--D. C.   By Doris
Chase; PERSPECTIVE.

CIRCLES II, VARIATION II (8m   C   1973)
     "Uses dancers, the Mary Staton Dance Ensemble of Seattle ...
primarily as elements in a rich semi-abstract movie in which post-
production work is almost as important as the lovely rolling and
dancing with circles (sculptures by Doris Chase) that takes place in
front of the camera ... colorized into soft monochromatic pastels..."
--Roger Greenspun, New York Times.   By Doris Chase; PERSPEC-
TIVE.

CITIES ARE FOR PEOPLE (30m   C   n. d.)
     "Documentary about pollution, urban clutter and prejudice in the
desert playground of Las Vegas."--M. G.   By Mollie Gregory;
TFEL

CITY LIMITS (29m   C   1971)
     Presents Jane Jacobs, author on urban affairs, examining prob-
lems of cities, and the effects of the automobile, high-rise buildings
and apathy on and toward urban development.   Asserts that the citizens of cities can themselves solve their problems.   NFBC; PAR-
ACO.

CITY THAT WENT TOO FAR, THE (20m   C   1976)
     Traces the cause and effect of New York's financial crises.
d. Mary Manilla; p. PENN; MTP.

CITY TREE, A (9m   C   1973)
     A city tree tells its sad story in verse: it can't touch other

trees, it is surrounded by dogs, asphalt and noise.   Lyrical and
moving.   By Barbara Kay Kerans; PARACO.

CITY TRIP, A (3m C 1972)
    Urban school children imagine and create a fantasy-interpretation
of their urban environment with animated cut-out shapes, improvised sound effects and music.   Sponsored by Walker Art Center
and Urban Arts of Minneapolis, Minnesota.   d. Suzan Pitt Kraning;
CCC, SB.

CIVIL RIGHTS RETROSPECTIVE; Profile: Political Wife Interface
    Series (30m C 1975 VIDEO)
    An appraisal of the civil rights movement through interviews
with Andrew Young, former Executive Secretary of the Southern
Christian Leadership Conference, Floyd McKissick, former Executive Director of CORE, and Ella Baker, one of the founders of
SCLC and a pioneer in the civil rights movement.   Includes a profile of Roscoe Dellums, wife of Representative Ronald V. Dellums
(D-Ca.), which examines the pressures and conflicts faced by the
political wife in Washington politics.   p. WETATV; PTL.

CLARITY (16m C 1976)
    Examines male-female role playing and how it is influenced by
imaging (the process of intellectual conceptualizing).   MGH.

CLASSICAL LITERATURE SERIES see WUTHERING HEIGHTS

CLEO FROM 5 to 7 (90m B 1962 French/subtitled)
    Cleo goes to the doctor to find out for sure if she is dying--
as foretold by a card reader--but she must wait from 5 until 7 for
the results of the test.   Life flashes by Cleo: the Parisian pop
singer, the spoiled child.   A young soldier, Antoine, well acquainted
with fear and presence of death helps change Cleo into a thoughtful,
compassionate woman.   d. Agnes Varda; CORINF.

CLICK CLOCK (3m B n. d.)
    "Animated television footage. "--P. S.   By Patricia Sloane; WAF.

CLOISTER, THE (19m n. d.)
    Documents a woman's experience inside the New York City
House of Detention for women.   It seeks to communicate the universal reality of individual violation.   The film is a bare, stripped,
through-line of experience presented without any contexts for escape.   From a screenplay by Andrea Dworkin.   p. /d. Gretchen
Langheld; FCOOP.

CLORAE AND ALBIE (36m C 1975)
    Documentary on how two courageous women cope with their
daily problems positively and with a lively spirit.   Albie, broke but
unbroken, is putting herself through college with any job she can get;
fixing up her apartment with scraps and imagination to look great.
She is determined to get her life together no matter how hard it is
to do it alone.   Clorae is a young mother, divorced, raising three

children on her own, working nights so she can go to high school
during the day, and using every opportunity to make life work for
herself and children.   Sponsored by National Institute of Education;
EDC; UW.

CLOSE-UP--FIRE! (58m   C   1973)
    Examines the seeming failure of business and government to pro-
tect the public properly from fire hazards in some consumer products
and in transportation and housing.   By Pamela Hill; PHOENIX.

CLOVEN HORIZON (10m   C   n. d.)
    View of the remarkable crayon paintings by Sundaravalli, daugh-
ter of a South Indian goldsmith.   By Kantilal Rathod; FIM.

CLUB, THE (5m   C   1975)
    As animated phalluses drift absent-mindedly about, the panning
camera catches them in characteristically clubby activities: reading
newspapers, smoking cigars, doing push-ups.   Plays with stereo-
typical images of the male through humor and visual shock.   A
spoof on male bonding.   d. George Giffin; SB.

COCKABOODY (9m   C   1974)
    A charming film about early childhood in which the two Hubley
daughters at ages three and five explore their home environment
from bathroom to bedroom.   They engage in fantasy and fun, and
in the process reveal many characteristics of early child behavior
including sibling rivalry.   The daughters' actual tape-recorded
voices were used for the soundtrack and the animation is done in a
clear, outline-figure style.   By Faith Hubley/John Hubley; PF; CWU,
FI, FIM, VFL

COLETTE (30m   B   1953   French/subtitled)
    Presents, through flashback technique, the life story of the
famous author and actress, Colette.   Shows how many events influenced the writing of her 50 books.   Uses still pictures and photography to portray her life's experiences.   Narration by Colette.
JACF; ABFI, IU, PAS.

COLLAGE (6m   C   1975)
    A swift assortment of moving images.   Filmed from a color
television monitor that was computer-controlled.   By Lillian
Schwartz; LPL

COLLUSION: CHAPTER EIGHT (24m   B   1973)
    Follows "Alice In Wonderland, " who is reaching forty, as she
goes through a series of puzzling and embarrassing encounters as
a result of the conflicting demands placed on women in present day
society.   By Milena Jelinek; RONIN.

COLOR OF RITUAL, THE--THE COLOR OF THOUGHT (26m   C
    1968)
    Trilogy consisting of Divinations, Shaman, and Peyote Queen.
"Multiple voyages into buried continents of the self, exploring ...

areas of no-time, new space. All three are interrelated and best
experienced together. "--S. D. H.   By Storm De Hirsch; FCOOP.

COLOR RHAPSODIE (7m   C   n. d.)
    An abstract film visually interpreting Liszt's "Hungarian Rhap-
sody No. 2. " By Mary Ellen Bute; CFS.

COLORS ALL AROUND US (7m   C   1974)
    Introduces the three primary colors to young children.   By
Shirley Gweyneth Miller; PARACO.

COLORS: RED, GREEN, BLUE, PURPLE (4m   C   si   n. d.)
    "Alternating frames in pure color. "--P. S.   By Patricia Sloane;
WAF.

COLUMBUS AND ISABELLA; You Are There Series (22m   C   1972)
    Many myths surround Columbus's difficulty in getting Spain to
support his voyage to prove that he could reach lands in the East
by sailing west.   Isabella's personality and character, as well as
Columbus's somewhat arrogant ways, are some of the factors relating to the famous decision that led to the discovery of the New
World.   CBSTV; BFA.

COME BACK CHARLESTON BLUE (101m   C   1972)
    A merry cops-and-robbers chase through Harlem in search of
the legendary Charleston Blue, a slain 30's gangster who appears to
have come back to life.   The film is Black and human.   It is a
comedy; like real comedy it isn't one-sided.   s. w. Peggy Elliot;
d. Mark Warren; WSA; CWF, TWY.

COMEDY IN SIX UNNATURAL ACTS, A (20m   C   1975)
    A loving satire on various stereotypes of lesbians including such
favorites as "wallflower, child molester, stompin' dyke, and seduc-
tress. "   d. Jan Oxenberg; OXENBERG.

COMFORTS OF HOME (40m   C   1974)
    Based on Flannery O'Conner's short story about the relationships
between a mother, her son, and a young girl.   By Leonard Upson,
Jerome Shore; PHOENIX.

COMING ATTRACTIONS (77m   C   1970)
    "... looks backward into memories and forward into the future
of Francis Francine, an elegantly dowdy transvestite of, and indeed
beyond, a certain age. "--Roger Greenspun, New York Times.   By
Beverly Conrad, Tony Conrad; FCOOP.

COMING OUT (30m   C   1973)
    A documentary on Gay Liberation Weekend in New York City.
Features a parade from Greenwich Village to a "Gay-In" at Central
Park with participants being interviewed.   By Ken Geist; GP.

COMING OUT (11m   B   1973)
    "First film of this Berkeley Lesbian Feminist Collective, show-

ing the problems and fears as well as joys and triumphs of coming out. "--BLFFC; BLFFC.

COMING TO KNOW (10m B 1976)

Two women discuss the development of their identities as lesbians, from early fantasies to first experiences. Feminist politics
played a significant role in their coming out. Their discussion is
warm and comfortable as they share their stories by the fireplace
and meditate together in the woods. By Marie Ashton; MMRC, SB.

COMMUNITY CORNER (15m C 1976 VIDEO)

A good introduction to the People's Food System: Shows how
volunteers run a small San Francisco food co-op, providing nutritional organic foods at low cost. Everyone chips in--running the
cash register, cutting cheese, carrying baskets of food, etc. Shows
people working together to meet their basic needs. IP; IE.

COMMUTERS (5m C n. d.)

A brief, subtle, and ultimately devastating look at those who
daily ride the trains to, and from, a wealthy New York suburb. By
Claudia Weill, Eli Noyes; NLC.

COMPAÑERAS AND COMPAÑEROS (80m C 1970)

Political documentary filmed in Cuba showing young Cubans'
daily lives--attending class, working, holding meetings, dancing and
singing. By Barbara Stone, Adolfas Mekas, David Stone; MFLMC.

COMPARISON SERIES see THREE GRANDMOTHERS

COMPUTER SAID, THE (2m C n. d.)

"Comedy set to a much edited version of a Bell Telephone record. ... [A] computer learns to speak, to sing and to engage in the
pursuit of happiness, in this case wooing a female computer who is
musically inclined. "--CCC. By Jan Baross; ABFI; CCC.

COMPUTERS (10m C 1970)

Describes the major components of a modern computer and explains how the binary number system is useful in computer technology. By Ellen Landweber, Victor Landweber; BFA.

CONCERTS ON FILM SERIES see MARIAN ANDERSON

CONEY ISLAND OF THE MIND (8m C 1973)

"A trip into the destructive unconscious: Ego, Super Ego, and
Id, through the rooms of Sisyphus, Ixion, and Tantalus, Brutalizer
and victim, and the last room, Eye of Ultimate Silence. "--S. G.
By Sylvianna Goldsmith; GOLDSMITH.

CONFESSION (75m C n. d.)

This romantic film focuses on a group of young people, several
filmmakers included, at a town on Japan's Inland Sea. With depth
(but no plot) we see the relationships of the people develop. Influences from many other countries are evident in the film, though

the tone of it is still very Japanese and reflects the culture of modern Japan.   Two reels, either one may be shown first.   By Nobuhiko Ohbayashi; CCC.

CONFLICT AND AWARENESS SERIES see HOMOSEXUALITY--WHAT ABOUT McBRIDE; I ONLY WANT YOU TO BE HAPPY

CONFLICT WITHIN, THE (SERIES) see FAILING MARRIAGE, THE

CONGRESSWOMAN BELLA ABZUG (29m   C   1976   VIDEO)
    Moderator Sandra Elkins discusses women in politics with Congresswoman Bella Abzug.   In her three years in Congress Representative Abzug has fought for legislation for women, which includes the recently-passed laws eliminating discrimination against women who apply for credit, a flexible hours bill, and a proposed Social Security benefit for homemakers.   KNEDTV; PTL.

CONNECTION, THE (102m   B   1961)
    Based on Jack Gelber's play about eight junkies waiting for a fix in Greenwich Village loft, this film is more than just a slice of funk-city life.   It's a gut-level assault on complacent middle-class voyeurs, a live theatre experience calculated to provoke, to break down the proscenium barrier.   By Shirley Clarke; NYF.

CONRACK (107m   C   1973   Reg. /Scope)
    An idealistic teacher comes to teach on a small island off the South Carolina coast.   The island is untouched by modern technology and education, and is populated by poor Black people.   The teacher finds that his unorthodox methods do not sit well with the superintendent whose commitment to tradition exceeds his commitment to education.   d. Martin Ritt; co-sw. Harriet Frank; Fox; FI.

CONSCIOUSNESS-RAISING GROUPS (29m   C   1974   VIDEO)
    Claudia Dreifus (an outspoken advocate of women's liberation and author) and Judy Sullivan (an art historian, feminist and author) discuss a frequently misunderstood aspect of the Women's Movement --the consciousness-raising group.   They explain its purpose and how to begin one.   WNEDTV; PTL.

CONTEMPORARY FILMS ITSELF (16m   B   n.d.)
    "A semi-documentary, cinema-erudite-film-expose of corporation life and death, shot on location in Woodstock, New York, and at McGraw-Hill. "--D. T.   By Doris Tourmarkine; FCOOP.

CONTINUING RESPONSIBILITY, A see ORGANIZING FOR POWER: THE ALINSKY APPROACH

CONTINUOUS WOMAN, THE (25m   C   1974)
    A positive film about strengths and alternatives of women through the eyes of five women who recognize their own strengths--a Black school teacher, a lesbian clinical psychologist, and three generations of white middle-class women.   A good film for lecture or discussion when you want to discuss sex roles in a non-threatening way.   By Darlene Marvey; TCWFC.

CONTRACEPTION (23m   C   1973)
Explains the advantages and disadvantages and comparative effectiveness of currently available contraceptives.   The various kinds
of contraceptives shown are: condoms, diaphragms, IUD's and oral
contraceptives.   WILEY.

CONVERSATION WITH BETTY FRIEDAN, A; Woman Series (29m
C   1974   VIDEO)
Betty Friedan has been in the forefront of the Women's Movement since her book, The Feminine Mystique, was published in 1963.
She predicts new horizons for political action by the movement in
areas such as housing, economics, credit, aging, etc.   Moderator
is Sandra Elkin.   WNEDTV; PTL.

CONVERSATION WITH ELEANOR ROOSEVELT, A (30m   B   1958)
Mrs. Roosevelt talks with William Atwood, editor of Look Magazine, about political obligations of the citizen: about the practical
mechanics of politics, her opinion of her husband's achievements
and mistakes, the present day challenge, and her hopes for the future.   NBCTV; FI; UM.

CONVERSATION WITH GOLDA MEIR, A (27m   C   1973)
Features Israel's Prime Minister, Golda Meir, talking about the
meaning of Israel to its own people, to those Jews who live in other
countries, and the responsibility of the Jewish nation to the world at
large.   ADL.

CONVERSATION WITH INGRID BERGMAN, A (59m   B   1967)
Presents an interview with Ingrid Bergman in which she discusses her childhood ambition to be an actress.   Highlights her appearances in plays, and roles in movies.   Relates her opinions on
the differences among audiences, and directors, and presents an
actress's approach to different media.   NET, IU.

CONVERSATION WITH VIVECA LINDFORS, A; Woman Series (29m
C   1974   VIDEO)
Actress Viveca Lindfors reflects on her stage and screen career,
her life, marriage, and her exposure to the plights and challenges
of women today.   She does this while reading and preparing for production of her own one-woman show, "I Am a Woman. "   WNEDTV;
PTL.

COOK COUNTY INTERNS (30m   C   1972)
"The people you are about to meet are residents and interns at
Cook County Hospital in Chicago.   You may have heard about them
as part of the debate over how to improve health care in this country. "--M. S.   By Martha Stuart/David Ruskin; STUARTM.

COOL PLATES/HOT CAR (19m   C   1975)
Film alerts recruits and patrol officers to commercial auto
theft procedures and "modus operandi. "   Discusses arrest and investigation procedures with emphasis on the "VIN"--Vehicle Identification Number.   Shows auto registration fraud attempt.   d. Bill
Brose; p. Patricia Brose; WBPL

COOL WORLD, THE (90m B 1964)
Tells the story of Duke, a Black adolescent who aspires to the leadership of his gang, The Royal Pythons. The Cool World was the first full-length film ever shot in Harlem. The camera captures the sidewalk ambience with the constant movement of people, the slang-studded repartee, the wide-eyed children and the sniffing dogs--expressing perfectly the repressed tensions created by lives lived with limited options. By Shirley Clarke; ZPH.

CO-OPTATION OF THE WOMEN'S MOVEMENT IN ADVERTISING
(B/C n. d.   30 slides)
Women's images in advertising. WRP.

COPLAND PORTRAIT (29m C 1976)
Intimate portrait of America's most acclaimed composer, Aaron Copland, offering insights and reflections on American musical history. p. Frieda Lee Mock, Terry Sanders; d. Terry Sanders; NAVC.

COQUILLE ET LE CLERGYMEN, LA see SEASHELL AND THE CLERGYMAN, THE

CORETTA SCOTT KING, CIVIL RIGHTS LEADER; Face the Nation Series, No. 37 (30m B 1969)
An interview with Coretta Scott King. CBSTV; HIS.

CORITA'S ICEMAN BAR (6m B n. d.)
"Places, people, and past events in a Southwestern town are recalled in a collage of rapidly edited images. "--E. A. B.   By Eleanor Anderson Boyer; CENTER.

CORONATION OF QUEEN OF ENGLAND (5m B n. d.)
Presents the three-hour ceremony of the crowning of the eighth Queen and 55th monarch of the British Empire. WSA; OKSU.

CORTEGE OF EAGLES BY MARTHA GRAHAM (35m C 1969)
A dance-drama set in ancient Troy at the time of its fall to Greece. Miss Graham portrays the bereaved Queen Hecuba, who, when faced with the inevitable consequences of the violent times, is driven to terrible violence herself. Musical backgrounds, artistic scenery and elegant costumes complement the general stage picture. By John Houseman; PF; UILL.

COSAS DE MI VIDA (23m C 1976)
Focuses on the details of the life of Anselmo Aguascalientes, born into poverty and orphaned at age seven, a musician in a small Mexican town. There's a sense of sadness in the middle-class values he has developed even though much of his struggle has been for the sake of his 10 children. His pride in their musical accomplishments is apparent, but also his obsession with acquiring the accoutrements of middle-class life: stereo, television, refrigerator, etc. Along with his possessions Anselmo has a modern-style mistress in whom he is more interested than he is in his wife. The latter is seen cooking and washing, locked into the traditional modes

of female behavior, almost untouched by her husband's socioeconomic behavior.   p. /d. Chick Strand; IE.

COSMETIC SURGERY; Woman Series (29m C 1975 VIDEO)
    Plastic surgeon Zahide Prono discusses the myth and realities
of cosmetic surgery, including the techniques used for breast en-
largement, face lifts, and reduction surgery for breasts, thighs and
buttocks.   He explains what this type of surgery can accomplish and
how long it lasts: Sandra Elkins, interviewer. WNEDTV; PTL.

COULD TELL A WHOLE LOT, BUT AIN'T NO USE TO TELLIN' IT
    (28m C n. d.)
    "Affectionate study of Rebecca Thomas, a 102-year-old woman
in Altoona, Pennsylvania.   Describes vividly her bout with smallpox,
working in a drugstore where she "leeched, cupped, and bled" people who were ill, working in an animal rendering plant, Garfield's
election, the Spanish-American War and the Johnstown Flood. "--
L. J. M.   By Lisa J. Marshall; WPSXTV; MARSHALL.

COUP POUR COUP see BLOW FOR BLOW

COUPLES (9m C n. d.)
    "A woman's tragic love affair. "--Cinema Femina.   By Maria
Lassnig; LASSNIG.

COUPLES IN INDIA (30m C n. d.)
    Young couples discuss changing life styles, birth control and
parenting.   Made for World Population Year.   By Martha Stuart/
David Ruskin; STUARTM.

COURTSHIP AND MARRIAGE (60m B 1961)
    Examines courting customs in Sicily, Iran, Canada, India and
Southwest India.   Matchmaking and chaperoning are part of the customs in Sicily, while in Iran a man courts a woman he has never
seen.   In Canada, the young people are free to regulate their own
behavior; in India everything is arranged by the families.   NFBC;
CORNELL, EMC, PAS.

COVER GIRL (107m B 1944 French/subtitled)
    An exhilarating fantasy about a Brooklyn singer who reaches
the height of her career.   d. Claude Chabrol; COLUMBIA; KP,
SWANK.

COVER GIRL: NEW FACE IN FOCUS (28m C 1968)
    A "model of the year" contest winner comes to New York to be
trained for a career in the fashion world.   Unconscious ironies abound
and consciousness is unmistakably raised.   By Frances McLaughlin;
NOX; NASHH; MTP.

COWS (3m C 1972)
    Handpainted film about woman's relation to the media and cows
at the McNulty Dairy Farm.   By Alexis Rafael Krasilovsky; RA-
FAEL.

CRAIG'S WIFE (75m B 1936)
    Rosalind Russell plays Harriet Craig, a woman desperate for
material security for which she gives up everything else. d. Dorothy Arzner; COLUMBIA; KP, SWANK.

CREATIVE CRAFT--A SERIES see HOW TO MAKE A LINOLEUM
    BLOCK PRINT; HOW TO MAKE A MASK; HOW TO MAKE A
    PUPPET; HOW TO MAKE A STENCIL PRINT; HOW TO MAKE
    PAPIER-MACHE ANIMALS; HOW TO MAKE POTATO PRINTS

CREATIVE DRAMA: THE FIRST STEPS (29m C n. d.)
    Experience in creative dramatics helps children to form the
habit of independent thinking and of organizing ideas as they build
with others toward a common objective. The children develop a
sharpening awareness of sense impression, freeing them to express
ideas and feelings in movement and speech. This helps them to
grow in understanding people. By Rita Criste, Winifred Ward;
NWUFL.

CREATIVE PARENTHOOD (30m C n. d.)
    A group of parents discuss the ways they have shared parenting
to avoid stifling roles. By Martha Stuart, Ivan Carry; STUARTM.

CREATIVE PERSONS SERIES see WELTHY FISHER

CREATURES, LES (102m B 1966 Scope French/subtitled)
    The camera eye focuses on the mysterious island in Britanny
where the goings-on are, to put it mildly, strange. Allegory, science fiction, and a heady dose of the supernatural all bubble mer-
rily in the Varda stew. Its elements, though bizarre, are close
enough to the familiar to shake us. d. Agnes Varda; NYF.

CREDIT-ABILITY GAP, THE; Woman Series (29m C 1974 VIDEO)
    Married, single and divorced women face the same barrier--
their sex--when attempting to obtain credit, mortgages and loans in
America today. Nancy Polikoff of the Center for Women's Policy
Studies discusses the problems that women have obtaining credit,
loans, mortgages, etc. WNEDTV; PTL.

CRIES AND WHISPERS (95m C 1972)
    Focuses directly on the oppression and isolation of women and
their response to it among themselves. It also raises a number of
class questions without ever resolving them. The sisters in this
film respond to their confinement with both a mystical lesbian love
and cruel self-abuse, as if they feared closeness more than any
other conceivable terror. d. Ingmar Bergman; JANUS.

CRIME OF INNOCENCE, A (27m C n. d.)
    Examines a society that is embarrassed by mental retardation.
Peter Carling rents a house in a middle-class suburb and moves in
with eight mentally retarded young men. He wants them to learn
about accepting responsibility, division of tasks and community living. The homeowners are up in arms; fear and ignorance are the

motivators.   An important film for anyone working with mentally
and physically handicapped persons.   By Lynn Carlin, Martin Sheen;
MGH.

CRIMINAL MAN SERIES   see   SEXUALITY AND CRIME

CRISIS: WOMEN IN HIGHER EDUCATION (30m   C   1972)
    Covers a wide range of speakers and concerned women who
raise questions and voice opinions about this national problem.   By
Dr. Konnilyn Feig; UMAINE.

CROCUS (7m   C   1971)
    Using cut-out animation, the filmmaker depicts a man and a
woman making love.   Their free-floating fantasies: birds, vegetables, fish and flowers pass serenely overhead and into the night
sky of contentment.   By Suzan Pitt Kraning; SB, CCC, FCOOP,
NLC.

CROW BOY (13m   C   1971)
    Story about a shy Japanese boy who can imitate the sounds of
the wild.   Adapted from book by same title by Taro Yashima.   By
Cynthia Freitag; WESTON.

CROWD, THE (93m   B   si   1928)
    A key work of King Vidor's social cinema.   The film is built
like a Dreiser novel of small details piled upon one another to make
the portrait of one person whose very individuality makes him the
mirror of us all.   d. King Vidor; MGM; FL

CRUCIFIED LOVERS, THE (CHIKAMATSU MONOGATARI) (100m   B
    1955   Japanese/subtitled)
    Set in 17th-century feudal Japan, a gentle scrollmaker and his
master's wife fall in love.   The two are soon discovered and attempt
to flee--only to be hunted down by the lord's retainers.   d. Kenji
Mizoguchi; CVI, NLC.

CRUISE, THE (8m   C   1967)
    "People and numbers and chance.   Set on board a cruise ship,
symbolic of our present democratic systems of government.   Everything functions correctly until an antisocial passenger begins to violate the rules, resulting in gradual breakdown of established patterns."--Hubley Filmography.   By Faith Hubley, John Hubley; PF.

CRY OF PAIN, A (15m   C   1977)
    A touching film about families in distress and what can be done
to help them.   Candid interviews with abusive parents reveal that
they are ordinary people from all walks of life who are re-enacting
their own tragic childhoods.   Some of the approaches described in
the film are: crisis nurseries, temporary shelters, foster homes
for children, hot line communications systems, Parents Anonymous
and therapy groups for parents.   d. John S. Allen; p. Leonora Pirret Hudson; MMM.

CRYSTAL LEE JORDAN (16m C 1974)
The film follows Crystal Lee Jordan--wife, mother, and blue-collar worker--in her attempt to establish a union in the J. P. Stevens textile mills in Roanoke Rapids, N. C. Ms. Jordan was dismissed by J. P. Stevens after having spent 17 of her 34 years laboring as a mill hand. We see her husband and children participating in the activities with pride. By Joan Fiore, KERATV; IU.

CULTURAL HERITAGE SERIES see BALLET'S GOLDEN AGE
(1830-1846)

CULTURAL INFLUENCES; Human Sexuality Series (28m C 1972
VIDEO)
Guests from India, Japan, China, Korea, Samoa and Nicaragua discuss sexual practices common in their cultures and explore differing attitudes toward virginity, premarital sex, homosexuality, illegitimacy and the "double standard. " UHAWAII, KHETTV; PTL.

CUMMINGTON STORY, THE; American Scene, The (Series) (22m
B 1945)
Portrays the experiences of a refugee family in a New England town, their differences as newcomers, and their later acceptance as newcomers into the community. d. Helen Grayson; p. USOWIO; NAVC.

CUMULUS NIMBUS (6m B 1973)
Lyrically photographed and edited, this sensitive film deals with the erotic wish of a young woman who is wondering if she is gay. By Virginia Giritlian; SB.

CURIOUS CASE OF VITAMIN E (29m B 1975 VIDEO)
Stimulating and probing documentary about the "wonder drug" that is said to prevent old age, stimulate the sex drive, and protect the human body from the hazards of smoking and smog. Examines virtually all general-interest aspects of Vitamin E--including possible relationships to wound-healing, sex, aging, air pollution, and the prevention and cure of disease. Tells what foods contain Vitamin E, how much is needed in the diet, and what progress has been made in the treatment of Vitamin E deficiency in human beings. Features Adelle Davis, author and lecturer in nutrition. EMC.

CYCLES (10m C 1971)
A mysterious and dynamic visualization of a woman's rape, and her subsequent return to the womb. By Linda Jassim; CFS, NLC.

DADDY DON'T BE SILLY: A CASE FOR EQUAL RIGHTS (27m C
1975)
Featuring Bill Moyer, this documentary was made after Congress passed the Equal Rights Amendment but before ratification by the States. The title was taken from Moyer's daughter's response to his question whether she should become a doctor or nurse. The

incident became a symbol for the cultural attitudes that foster discrimination against women, attitudes the Amendment would correct.
Debate in Maine reveals fears that ERA may lead to "unnatural
equality" of the sexes.   Includes an interview with Judge Burnita
Matthews.   Presents opinions of men and women both in favor of
and opposed to the proposed amendment.   NET, IU; UILL.

DAILY LIFE IN CHINA'S COMMUNES (40m   C   n. d.)
    An authoritative and comprehensive look at daily life in China's
communes, where the vast majority of China's population lives.
Focuses on communal areas located in Kiangsi, Honan, and Hopei
provinces.   Examines in detail the social, cultural and political aspects of life in the communes--including childcare, birth control,
housing, education, medical care, local and state planning, and rural
forms of proletarian culture.   By Gael Cohany; TFC.

DAISIES (74m   C   1966)
    A free-wheeling, slapstick, almost psychedelic happening about
two girls, both named Mary, in a relentless search for "kicks. "
Its humor, exuberance, and closing dedication suggest that it is not
making a simple moral judgment.   It is really an elegy to the absurd.   Based on a story by Vera Chytilova, Ester Krumbachova,
and Pavel Juracek; d. Vera Chytilova; ABFL

DAISY MILLER (91m   C   1974)
    Tale of a free-spirited young rich American coquette touring
Europe with her permissive mother and bratty little brother.   She
scandalizes her compatriots by kicking over the traces of hypocritical society dominated by snobs and cynics.   The world of lost
Americans abroad (some weakened by too much alien culture, others
penalized for their ignorance) is skillfully re-created in this adaptation of the Henry James novella.   d. Peter Bogdanovich; PARA-
MOUNT; FL

DAN BASEN (12m   C   1970)
    The painter at work shortly before his death.   By Robin Lloyd;
FCOOP.

DANCE (3m   C   n. d.)
    "East meets West up in the air. "--CCC.   By Mako Idemitsu;
CCC.

DANCE--ANNA SOKOLOW'S "ROOMS"; U. S. A. Series (30m   B
    1966)
    A complete performance of Rooms, one of the most influential
ballets in American dance.   Created in 1954 by Anna Sokolow, its
theme is the tragic isolation of man in the jazz age.   The individual
dances are entitled "Escape, " "Going, " "Desire, " and "Panic. "
Solos are performed by Zeva Cohen, Jack Moore and Jeff Duncan.
Musical score by Kenyon Hopkins.   NET, IU; UILL.

DANCE CLASS (9m   C   1971)
    Traces the development of the modern dance.   Features Martha

Graham, the brilliant pioneer of modern dance. Shows the Toronto
Dance Theatre in classes taught by Peter Randazzo and in rehearsal
of an original ballet. d. Joan Henson; NFBC; ABFL

DANCE DEMONSTRATION see TECHNIQUES OF CONTEMPORARY
    DANCE

DANCE--ECHOES OF JAZZ; U. S. A. Series (30m   B   1966)
    Traces the development of the jazz dance from tap dancing
through the orchestrated jazz of the thirties to the abstract and symbolic music of the sixties.   Features such dancers as Honi Coles,
Paula Kelly, Buzz Miller, Mary Hinkson, Michel Harty, and John
Butler.   NET, IU; IU.

DANCE ELEVEN (8m   C   1975)
    Cynthia Anderson, of the Joffrey Ballet, dances a duet with her
own image reproduced electronically to create effects of reinforce-
ment and rhythmic repetition in motion.   By Doris Chase; ABFL

DANCE FIVE (5m   C   1975)
    Brilliant dancer/choreographer Kei Takai dances against a video-
synthesized version of a large kinetic sculpture which is incorporated
into the visual image by multiple solarization.   The catlike movements of the dancer as he moves down the labyrinth of arches is
accompanied by music composed and performed by Timmy Thompson.
By Doris Chase; ABFL

DANCE--FOUR PIONEERS; U. S. A. Series (29m   B   1965)
    Introduces the four major choreographers (Martha Graham, Doris
Humphrey, Charles Weidman, and Hanya Holm) who revolted against
the conventions of ballet to produce American modern dance.   Film
clips and still photographs taken in 1934 show the dancers and their
teachers during the beginning days of Mount Bennington College.   By
means of quotations from recorded speeches made at various times,
each choreographer explains his or her view of the meaning dance
should have within the arts.   Closes with a full production of Doris
Humphrey's "Passacaglia" by the American Dance Theatre at Lincoln
Center in 1965.   NET, IU; UILL.

DANCE, GIRL, DANCE (89m   B   1940)
    A rare combination in this film--a film directed by a woman
that deals explicitly with women and the images held of them by men.
Maureen O'Hara and Lucille Ball play aspiring dancers, with Ball successful through burlesque and O'Hara intent on ballet.   In a truly un-
precedented monologue at the film's climax, O'Hara makes explicit
the undercurrent issues of male fantasy and the abuse of art.   p.
Harry E. Edington, Erich Rommer; d. Dorothy Arzner; s. w. Tess
Slesinger/Frank Davis; RKO; FL

DANCE--IN SEARCH OF LOVERS; U. S. A. Series (30m   B   1966)
    Shows how a new dance--"Lovers, " musical score by Ned
Rorem--is created through months of effort and prepared for opening night before an audience.   Choreographer Glen Tetley is seen at

his first session with three members of his quartet, with his set
designer Willa Kim, and at rehearsaL   Examines the professional
careers and private lives of the three dancers--Mary Hinkson,
Carmen de Lavallade, and Scott Douglas.   NET; IU; UILL.

DANCE IN THE SUN (6m   B   1953)
   "Two renditions--one in the rehearsal hall, the other on a
beach--of the same dance (edited together)"--MOMA.   By Shirley
Clarke; MOMA.

DANCE--NEW YORK CITY BALLET; U. S. A. Series (30m   B   1965)
   Four pas de deux by George Balanchine, co-founder and choreographer of the New York City Ballet, are introduced by star members of his company--Jacques D'Ambroise, Suzanne Farrell, Melis-
sa Hayden, Patricia McBride, Arthur Mitchell and Edward Vilella.
The performance, prefaced by Balanchine's comments on his philosophy of dance, includes "Tarantelle," "Meditation," and excerpts
from Agon and Pas de Deux.   NET, IU; UILL.

DANCE NINE (4m   C   1975)
   Gus Solomons, Jr., dances a duet with a sculptural form created by the video device--the Rutt/Etra Synthesizer.   The sculpture
appears in detail, then in silhouette, against colored backgrounds,
as the dancer's interactions blend with the jazz score of George
Kleinsinger.   The effect is one of liquidity, transforming the screen
into half-real, half-abstract designs with striking three-dimensional
qualities.   By Doris Chase; ABFL

DANCE SEVEN (8m   C   1975)
   Marnee Morris, of the New York City Ballet, dances with video
effects of feedback and de-beaming for added visual excitement.
Clear images give way to color separations which fragment the
dancer's movements, then alternate with views which simultaneously
juxtapose her entire figure with close-ups of her face.   Genji Ito's
music alternates between classical and impressionistic as "moving
paintings" evolve dramatically.   By Doris Chase; ABFL

DANCER'S WORLD (33m   B   1957)
   Martha Graham, noted choreographer and modern dancer, discusses the dancer as creative artist.   She explains the dancer's
craft simply and clearly as members of her company illustrate her
theories in a beautifully executed dance.   Choreographed by Ms.
Graham especially for the film.   Included are most of the movements and basic techniques required by a modern dancer.   Concludes
with excerpts from the company's repertoire.   WQUED; KROLL:
EMC, PHOENIX, OKSU, UILL, UMIS, UU, WAYSU, WISSU.

DANCING PROPHET (25m   C   1970)
   A film in honor of Ruth St. Denis, "the mother of modern
dance."   Traces the steps in her artistic thought and development.
By Edmund Penney.   PF; UILL, USC.

DARIA AND DENNIS (10m   C   1972)
Recorded wedding of Daria Halprin and Dennis Hopper.   By
Constance Beeson; BEESON.

DARING AMERICAN SERIES   see   MISSION TO MALAYA

DARLING (122m   B   1965)
A cinderella girl of the jet set, Diana Scott adorns magazine
covers on newsstands throughout Europe.   Relating her story to a
woman's journal, she reveals in passionate clichés how a lowly
fashion model became an Italian Princess.   d. John Schlesinger;
AVCO; ABFI, BF.

DARWIN AND THE GALAPAGOS (15m   C   1971)
Explains that the Galapagos Islands are dramatic examples of
the delicate balance that exists between organisms and their environment.   Shows the unique species found here and examines how it
was that a visit here gave Darwin the proof for his theory of evolution.   By Elda Hartley; HARTLEY.

DATE WITH DIZZY (11m   B   1956)
A satire on the production of a TV commercial in the Hubley
studio, bringing together the talents of Dizzy Gillespie and his Quin-
tet who improvise a musical soundtrack and John Hubley who draws
the pictures to advertise an "instant rope ladder."   By Faith Hubley,
John Hubley; SBI; FIM.

DATELINE ISRAEL, 1973 Series   see   CONVERSATION WITH GOLDA
MEIR, A; SPY BY A MARRIAGE, A

DARIO DE ROSA MARIA, EL (7m   B   1976)
A young Puerto Rican woman starts out with romantic thoughts
about a handsome man who seems to be her dream.   When she goes
out with him, however, his rough manners disappoint her.   Her
thoughts then turn to a rich man who has been paying her many at-
tentions, her boss at work.   He is a perfect gentleman, soft-spoken,
well-dressed, and seductive.   He invites her out and she accepts.
The ensuing plot lays bare her boss's evil intentions, but Rosa
Maria proves herself courageous and determined.   Finally, with the
happy ending, she has learned that surface appearances can fool
you.   She discovers for herself the right path to follow.   By Isabel
Castellano; WMM.

DAUGHTER, THE (86m   C   1973)
An interracial love story set in present-day Copenhagen, this
bold but tender film treats many contemporary themes--racism,
narcotics, lesbianism--with understanding and honesty.   d. Mac
Ahlberg; PRU; FL

DAVID AND LISA (94m   B   1962)
Portrays with great sensitivity and perception the very special

relationship which develops between two emotionally disturbed teen-
agers.   s. w. Eleanor Perry; d. Frank Perry; CONTINENTAL; TWY.

DAVID: OFF AND ON (42m C 1973)
    Documentary filming of the filmmaker's brother David.   The
lens divides Davis into a hundred hues for us to look at one by one.
In his first 21 years he has been a school boy, an alcoholic, a
heroin addict, a convict, a mental patient, a resident of purgatory
and hell.   No fiction, no disguises and no apologies; nothing is
softened except love and understanding.   d. Martha Coolidge; p.
Doro Bachrach.   EMC; FI.

DAVID WHEELER THEATRE COMPANY OF BOSTON (8m C 1975)
    The camera follows David Wheeler from his home, to his office
at Boston University, to the rehearsal of a new play.   He discusses
why he has remained in Boston while great theatre is supposedly
done in New York and how being in Boston has permitted him an
artistic freedom unknown in New York City.   Includes scenes from
"Medal of Honor Rag. "   Photographers--Joan Weidman, Claudia
Weill; p. /d. Joyce Chopra; MCA.

DAY CARE: CHILDREN'S LIBERATION (15m B 1971)
    The establishment of a cooperative neighborhood day care center
in New York's Upper West Side proved a liberating experience for
children and fathers as well as mothers.   TWN.

DAY CARE TODAY (27m C 1972)
    A model presentation of three show-case day care centers: a
community-oriented infant care center, a factory center for the children of employees, and a university teacher training center.   Although all three are operated in different ways, the general impression in each case is of children being well cared for and given interesting learning environments.   A hope of tomorrow rather than
the reality of today.   p. Alvin Fiering; d. Miriam Weinstein;
POLYMORPH; EMC, IU, UU.

DAY IN THE LIFE OF BONNIE CONSOLO, A (16m C 1975)
    Shows the daily routine of a woman born without arms--including
shopping, driving her car, and caring for her home and two healthy
children--as she relates her philosophy of life and the values that
have led her to struggle to overcome her handicap.   INSPRO; BARR;
EMC, NIU, UILL, UM, UMIS.

DAY OF FREEDOM: OUR ARMY (17m B 1935)
    Documentary about the Wehrmacht made for Hitler's Minister
of Defense, General Von Blomberg.   By Leni Riefenstahl; FIM.

DAY OF PLANE HUNTING (20m B n. d.)
    Footage of the crucial role Vietnamese women play in the strug-
gle against U. S. imperialism.   Women are shown participating in
production, education, combat; and the cooperative way in which they
carry out their daily lives.   Vietnamese translation.   TWN.

DAY OF THE LOCUST, THE (120m   C   1975)
Examines human frailty in the world of Hollywood (circa 1938)
and finds the subculture town to be the pit of all that is false, degenerate and loveless in our society.   The savage accuracy of its
satire and its surrealistic portrayal of sexual degeneracy makes the
movie both a pertinent and disturbing work of film art.   Appropriate
to the author's apocolyptic vision, this epic uses Hollywood sleazi-
ness as a metaphor for decline of the West.   Judith Crist says this
"... reaches to the very heart of what is the matter with the American dream." Based on the novel by Nathanael West.   d. John
Schlesinger; PARAMOUNT; FI.

DAY OF WRATH (98m   B   1943   Danish/subtitled)
Setting is in a small 17th-century Danish town, and is essentially a dream of conscience and guilt.   An old woman suspected of
witchcraft is arrested by town authorities, tortured into admitting
guilt and burned.   Before her death, however, she indicates that
the town parson's young wife had learned the secrets of witchcraft
from her mother.   The parson's wife becomes obsessed with the
suspicion with which she is regarded and this, combined with her
feelings of guilt at having been unfaithful to her husband, leads her
to believe she is indeed a witch.   Based on play Anne Pedersdotter,
by Wiers Jensen.   d. Carl T. Dreyer; ACB; CORINF.

DAY OFF, A (30m   C   1973)
Two men meet by accident and take a day off to drink, talk and
seek adventure in the manner they might have done when they were
in school.   Both have experienced troubled relationships with women,
both are lonely men harboring strong sexist attitudes.   They are
unable to relate to each other as true friends.   Provides opportunity to discuss themes like "money as a basis of some human relationships"; the hostile, dwarfing, indifferent and oppressing environment of the city; and male chauvinist exploitive behavior.   By
Robert McKeo; UM.

DAY WE SEIZED THE STREETS OF OAKLAND, THE (12m   B   1968)
Shows student attempt to close down the Oakland Induction Center
in October 1967 to protest U. S. involvement in Vietnam.   Traces the
five-day predawn confrontation with the police culminating in a brief
victory as students occupy downtown Oakland.   By Patricia Amlin;
CCC.

DAY WE WON'T FORGET, A (28m   C   1976)
Explores the devastating effects of the Teton Dam break and resulting flood on June 5, 1976, in Southeastern Idaho.   Residents
are seen in massive cleanup and rebuilding tasks trying to bring
order out of chaos.   Why wasn't a strong warning issued?   Nine
people died and 887 farms and 773 homes were destroyed.   The
public seems to have gotten the word only as the dam broke.   p. /d.
Judith Hallet, Diane Orr; KUTV.

DEAD BIRDS (83m   C   1963)
Intensive two-year ethnographic study documents the way of life

of the Dani, a people dwelling in the mountains of western New
Guinea.   The Dani base their values on an elaborate system of
intertribal warfare and revenge.   Clans engage in formal battles
and are constantly on guard against raiding parties.   When a warrior is killed, the victors celebrate and the victims plan revenge.
There's no thought in the Dani world of wars ever ending; without
them there would be no way to satisfy the ghosts of the dead.
Wars also keep a sort of terrible harmony in life that otherwise
would be dull.   PHOENIX; EMC.

DEADLY IS THE FEMALE see GUN CRAZY

DEATH (43m B 1968)
     Shows Albro Pearsall, a 52-year-old terminal cancer patient,
through his last days at Calvary Hospital in the Bronx.   Raises
many questions relating to the communication with the dying and the
metaphysical relationship of death to the human person.   By Evelyn
Barron, Arthur Barron; IU; EMC.

DEBORAH SAMPSON: A WOMAN IN THE REVOLUTION (16m C
     1976)
     A story about a freedom fighter in the Revolutionary army un-
like all the others.   A woman, Deborah Sampson, enlisted in the
Continental Army under the assumed name of Robert Shurtlieff.
She fought at Tarrytown and Yorktown.   Wounded twice, she tended
to the wounds herself to avoid discovery of her sex.   Finally, suc-
cumbing to a malignant fever, medical treatment allowed her true
identity to be discovered.   GREENF; BFA.

DECIDING TO ORGANIZE see ORGANIZING FOR POWER: THE
     ALINSKY APPROACH

DEEP BLUE WORLD (7m C 1973)
     Filmed underwater adventure fantasy with brilliant use of orig-
inal film techniques.   By Sylvia Dees, Ken Randolph; PF.

DENISE LEVERTOV AND CHARLES OLSON; Poetry Series (30m B
     1966)
     Introduces the personalities and works of Denise Levertov and
Charles Olson through their readings and approaches to poetry.   In
her home Levertov talks about herself and methods of work.   She
reads "Life at War," "Losing Track," "The Ache of Marriage," and
"Two Angels."   Olson, at home, describes and analyzes his concept
of open verse composition.   He recites his poems including "Letter
27 Maximums to Dog Town," and "The Librarian."   NET, IU; BU,
UILL.

DESIGN IN MOVEMENT: THE HAND IS MEANT TO FEEL (15m
     B n.d.)
     "Study of design vocabulary of touch and movement rather than
of vision."--C. F.   By Patricia Wright; CF.

DESIGNING WOMEN (29/29m series C 1969 VIDEO)
     Series emphasizes fabric selection, line, form and color.   Anne

Darlington, television producer and home economist, is the instructor.   Contact Public Television Library for description of individual
films in the series.   MCFPB; PTL.

DESIREE ALONE (29m   C   n. d.)
Portrays a woman living on an isolated farm whose only means
of livelihood is collecting bloodsuckers and selling them to the local druggist.   She uses this money for her own pleasure and escape.
A brooding, melancholy study of loneliness and the fantasies it
spawns.   FI; VFL

DESTROY, SHE SAID (100m   B   1969   French/subtitled)
A hypnotic and haunting film about five alienated people isolated
in an unworldly hotel.   Enmeshed in a ritualistic power game, they
inexorably assume interchangeable personalities as each acts out his
own ambiguous charade.   "It is tender, human, and physically eloquent. "--The New Yorker.   d. Margeurite Duras; GP; FL

DESTRY RIDES AGAIN (82m   B   1939)
Based on Max Brand's novel.   A famous western farce with
Marlene Dietrich playing the role of the saloon-girl, Frenchy.   d.
George Marshall; UNIVE; CVE, UNIVE.

DEVELOPMENTAL PSYCHOLOGY TODAY SERIES see AGING;
CHILD, THE (PTS. I, II, III); PRENATAL DEVELOPMENT;
SEX ROLE DEVELOPMENT

DEVIL IS A WOMAN, THE (80m   B   1935)
Archetypical picture of woman as seductress/witch and man as
helpless/innocent.   Dietrich plays a young woman at a fiesta who attracts a young man for whom she bears nothing but contempt.   He,
aware of the tragedy of the situation, nevertheless cannot extricate
himself from his infatuation.   With Marlene Dietrich, Cesar Romero.
d. Joseph Von Sternberg, PARAMOUNT; MMA.

DEWEY CANYON III (34m   B   1971)
Filmed anti-war activities staged in Washington, D. C. during
the week of April 1971.   Made for Vietnam Veterans Against War.
By Deidre English, David Davis, Aly Sujo and Steve Talbot; CFS.

DIANE (27m   C   1969)
A frank and sympathetic portrait of a young woman from South
Dakota, who is trying to make it as an actress and model in New
York.   With ironic humor, she describes the frustrations and loneli-
ness that confront young people in New York struggling to create
their own lives in their own ways.   By Mary Feldhaus-Weber; WFF;
ODEON.

DIANE, THE ZEBRA WOMAN (24m   B   1962)
"Grade Z home movie. "--Sheldon Rochlin.   By Diane Rochlin,
Sheldon Ronchlin; FCOOP.

DIARY OF A CHAMBERMAID (81m   B   1946)
Celeste (Paulette Goddard) becomes a maid in a Provincial

French house.   Her subservient position makes her vulnerable to
the dark intrigues of the small town.   Preyed upon by the local
men, she struggles for her liberation.   d. Jean Renoir, film made in
U. S.   IVY.

DIARY OF A MAD HOUSEWIFE (94m   C   1970)
The disintegration of marriage and resulting fragmentation of
the individual is the subject of this film.   A status-conscious lawyer
drives his wife to infidelity by the demands he places on her.   d.
Frank Perry; s. w. Eleanor Perry; UNIVE; CINE, CVE, CWF,
SWANK, TWY, UNIVE.

DIARY OF A RAPE (82m   C   1976)
A spine-tingling drama that deals with a situation that can occur all too easily these days.   No one has the right to take something that doesn't belong to him, and "Diary of a Rape" is the engrossing story of what happened when one man attempted it.   d.
Richard Campbell; GRPI; TWY.

DIARY OF A SCHIZOPHRENIC GIRL (108m   C   1968   Italian/sub-
    titled)
A true story of a rare case of schizophrenia treated successfully by a female Swiss analyst using a method called "symbolic
realization."   This method consisted of reconstructing the 18-year-
old girl patient's personality, starting back with early childhood and
re-living, one by one, every emotional stage of her young life.
The film revolves around three women: the mother, still young,
attractive, vain and selfish, who rejects her daughter at birth because pregnancy had interfered with her plans; the daughter, who,
since childhood, suffered from lack of maternal love, a lack which
propels her toward insanity; and the analyst, a woman of extraordinary understanding who has to stand up against the girl's family
and hospital authorities who oppose her methods.   d. Nelo Risi;
HCW.

DIARY OF ANNE FRANK (150m   B   1959   Reg. /Scope)
Documents based on the diary of a Jewish girl before she was
killed in a Nazi concentration camp.   Written during the two years
of hiding in an Amsterdam attic, her diary records the alarms,
quarrels, reconciliations, and mutual discomfort of eight frightened
people.   d. George Stevens; co-scripted by Frances Goodrich; FOX;
FL

DIARY OF CONNIE McGREGOR (28m   B   1963)
Documents a student nurse's experience in a chronic disease
hospital   Stresses the contributions and responsibilities of nursing
both physically and psychologically.   Reveals the personal satisfaction and gratification of nursing.   NYUCM.

DICHOTOMY (7m   C   n. d.)
In this confrontive film, the everyday activities of a young
male couple at the University of Rochester are contrasted with stri-
dent anti-homosexual speeches and obscene phone calls (recreated).

The two men go for a walk, shop and study while in the soundtrack vehement condemnations of homosexuality are made by a minister, a therapist and several men and women.   By Marshall Goldman; MMRC.

DICK AND JANE AS VICTIMS (25m   C/B   n. d.   150 slides w/cassette tape)
Based on the book of the same name, this slide-tape show extensively documents sex role stereotyping in children's readers. Activity in boys is contrasted with passivity in girls in this survey of 134 widely used elementary school books.   WOWL

DIFFERENT WITH DIGNITY (13m   C   1974)
Five sharp satirical vignettes show masculine and feminine "role playing" in our society.   Each situation examines a clash between gender-related roles "inborn?"   What happens when a man or woman breaks out of the gender role society expects?   What has been the effect of the "women's liberation movement?"   PAULST; MG; UILL.

DIG: A JOURNEY INTO THE EARTH (25m   C   n. d.)
A scientifically accurate introduction to earth science for children is presented as a lively adventure story in which a boy and his dog take an unexpected trip through geological time with a talking rock as their guide.   This popular film was intended to make earth science an enjoyable experience for children age 7-12, but grownups "dig" it, too.   Also available in three parts.   By Faith Hubley, John Hubley; FIM.

DIG WE MUST (10m   B   n. d.)
"Improvisational dramatic satire.   A surreal artist attempts to overcome Con Edison and find his inner light. "--L. I.   By Louva Elizabeth Irvine; FCOOP.

DIONE (6m   C   1973)
Fantasy shots of a pregnant woman wandering on an island. Merged with actual scenes of her natural childbirth.   By Constance Beeson; BEESON.

DIRT (4m   C   1971)
"A woman is dragged, struggling, with increasing violence, across dirt.   The motion, energy and way of filming came largely from my need to personally deal with the actions on news of the violence in the riots of the 1960's... "--A. G.   By Amy Greenfield; GREENFIELD.

DIRTY BOOKS (17m   C   1973)
A humorous drama of a young woman with no sexual experience who is a professional writer of pornographic novels.   Bored with her typewriter and her squalid New York apartment she considers accepting a strange job in California, visits her parents, seeks boyfriend's advice.   Although her situation is treated lightly, the film suggests that sexual revolution will not in itself end a woman's

sense of inadequacy or search for happiness.   By Linda Feferman;
NLC.

DISAPPEARANCE OF SUE, THE (3m   C   1972)
   "A whimsical pixillated story of a lady in a black coat disappearing, via a soda-cracker ritual in the park and a floral experience in the famous Como Park Conservatory."--K. L.   By Kathleen
Laughlin; SB.

DISCOVERING THE ARTS OF BALI (15m   C   1974)
   Shown are art works ranging from temple carvings and paintings
to weaving, tie-dying, batik, dancing, puppetry and story telling.
By Diana Colson; COLSON.

DISCUSSION OF SHIRLEY JACKSON'S THE LOTTERY, THE (10m
   C   1909)
   Scenes from the companion film The Lottery, are used to illustrate a discussion of the meaning and purpose of Shirley Jackson's
tale of ritual sacrifice in a small American town.   Raises questions
about communal violence, scapegoats in American society and the
blind adherence to society.   EBEC; UL

DISPOSSESSED, THE (33m   C/sepia   1970)
   In 1970, the Pit River Indians reoccupied a small part of their
ancestral lands in Northern California.   Pacific Gas & Electric Co.
had them arrested for "trespassing."   Music by Buffy Sainte-Marie
and Talbert Wilson.   With reference book.   By Maia Sortor, George
Ballis; CCC.

DIVINATIONS (6m   C   1964)
   Feelings of secrecy and excitement pervade this film made with
experimental techniques such as negative images, underexposure and
individually etched frames.   By Storm De Hirsch; CCC.

DIVINE COMEDY, THE (12m   C/B   1971)
   "Purgatorio in video transfer."--A. R. K.   By Alexis Rafael
Krasilovsky; RAFAEL.

DIVINE MIRACLE, THE (6m   C   1973)
   Animation and live action are interwoven in painstaking celestial
mechanics, combining the intricacies of the optical printer with a
"divine" sense of humor.   The vivid graphics of Catholic devotional
postcards (Jesus, Raphaelite Angels and sunsets streaming in techni-
color piety) delicately hover between satire and childlike awe as the
Second Coming comes, and then goes.   By Daina Krumins; CCC, SB.

DIVORCE, PT. I (20m   C   1975)
   Focuses on emotional issues, issues with family and friends,
and issues relating to starting new relationships.   Vignettes are
used to examine problems of personal identity and the stigma of
divorce.   Central issues include regaining confidence, channeling
the energy of anger and guilt, coping with the emotionality of divorce, and letting go.   Issues with family and friends revolve

around confronting faulty assumptions and stereotypes, and dealing
with guilt-inducing statements; problems which friends have in ad-
dressing the recently divorced and of inviting them to parties; the
issues of new relationships, including the fear of getting involved;
uncertainty about current single world protocol; and excitement of
new opportunities.   Tries to help the viewer construct the thoughts
and behaviors necessary for a constructive divorce.   APGA, UM.

DIVORCE, PT. II (20m   C   1975)
    Focuses on the intertwined issues relating to ex-spouse and
problems of children.   These include handling the feelings of being
a single parent, communicating with the former spouse during and
after divorce, handling the emotions of the children, and relating to
the former spouse's new boyfriend or girlfriend.   Discusses such issues as: How does a person handle violations in visitation rights
and child support payments?   How does one confront stereotypes
ascribed to children of divorced families?   What can parents do to
make divorce easy on the children?   What are the father's rights
in taking custody of the children?   APGA, UM.

DIVORCE, AMERICAN STYLE (109m   C   1967)
    A clever satire on the institutions of marriage and divorce in
this country.   It centers on a 17-year marriage in its dissolving
stages.   The wife reaps the material benefits and reduces husband
to near poverty.   Husband (Van Dyke) befriends another "Sunday
father" and victim of alimony drain, who is desperately seeking a
new husband for his ex-wife.   In this way he can free himself of
the payments and marry his pregnant girl friend.   But first, a husband must be found for Van Dyke's ex-wife, and an amiably inane
car salesman is drawn into the machinations.   Based on a story by
Robert Kaufman.   d. Bud Yorkin; p. Norman Lear; COLUMBIA;
ABFI, BF, CINE, FC, WCF, WEL, WHOLFC.

DIVORCE: FOR BETTER OR WORSE (49m   C   1977)
    An ABC news closeup on the plight of divorcees and divorcing
couples and the many forces that work upon or victimize the divorced person.   Among the areas explored in this film are lawyers
and the law, marriage and sex counseling, and the displaced home-
maker.   Focuses on actual case histories to show why there are
desperate needs for legal reform, stricter regulation of counselors
and therapists, and greater public awareness of the financial and
emotional problems facing divorced persons.   By James Benjamin;
ABCTV; MGH.

DIVORCE INSURANCE; Woman Series (29m   C   1974   VIDEO)
    An insurance plan to protect marriages from the financial burden
of divorce and child support is the discussion by Diana Du Broff, a
New York City matrimonial lawyer and creator of "divorce insurance. "   KNEDTV; PTL.

DO BLONDES HAVE MORE FUN? (2m   C   n. d.)
    Split screen images are used so you see a lot of dazzling maga-
zine ad blondes at once.   Final shot is a Black child staring at the

camera, creating a sudden sense of media's impact on our image of women. FCOOP.

DO I REALLY WANT A CHILD; Being a Woman Series (28m C 1976)

Two successful professional people, Vicky and her husband Jim, are unexpectedly faced with the fact that she, at 40, is going to have a baby. Vicky goes through considerable soul searching. The film ends without a solution. Cloris Leachman and Martin Balsam, who play husband and wife with total conviction, convey the weight of this problem which faces many couples today. TEI; LCA; UMIS.

DO I REALLY WANT TO DIE? (31m C n. d. subtitled)

A number of people who thought about and attempted suicide speak in frank and penetrating way of their behavior and feelings and the events leading up to the suicide attempt. The film deals not just with suicide, but the ways in which we all at times feel isolated and alone, fearful and temporarily without hope. The film is useful in discussing personal mood swings, what influences our behavior and feelings, what upsets us, and what can be done by family and friends to help those who begin to withdraw into themselves. And, finally, the film helps clarify issues relating to life cycles, the goals we set for ourselves and the crises we have to cope with as part of the aging process. It lends itself to discussion of what we want from life, from others, and how we can improve our relationships. p. /d. Fons Grasveld; POLYMORPH.

DR. DOLITTLE SERIES (A TRIP TO AFRICA; IN CANNIBAL LAND; THE LIONS'S DEN) (10m ea B 1928)

Animated films based on live shadow play. Three tales of exploration in darkest Africa, based on Hugh Lofting's famous Dr. Dolittle series. By Lotte Reiniger; CEA.

DOCTOR GLAS (83m B 1969 Danish/subtitled)

An alienated old man aimlessly wanders through Stockholm and bitterly recollects his youth and the crucial moments of his life. Filtering the story entirely through the protagonist's point of view, Zetterling dramatizes Glas's multifold consciousness in rapid flashes of memory, dream, and daydream. Based on the novel by Hjalmar Soderberg. d. Mai Zetterling; FOX; FL.

DOCTORS' WIVES (100m C 1971)

A striking portrait of contemporary America. Doctors who know everyone's secrets except those of their wives and wives who have everything but husbands form the basis of this story from the novel by Frank G. Slaughter. The film centers on the lives of five physicians running a plush clinic in a wealthy community and their spouses, all of whom are friends. With the murder of Dyan Cannon as the first of a series of crises, the personal and professional lives of these vivid characters are dramatically intertwined, with sometimes tragic consequences. d. George Schaeffer; p. M. J. Frankovich; COLUMBIA; WHOLFC.

DODSWORTH (101m B   1936)
Explores the problems faced by an aging married couple.   Upon
retiring, wealthy industrialist Dodsworth (Walter Huston) takes his
wife on a European vacation.   Once there, however, she becomes
obsessed with the loss of her youth and throws herself into several
flirtations.   Dodsworth finds himself crushed by the very years of
leisure he has looked forward to all his life.   Adapted from the
Sinclair Lewis novel. d. William Wyler; GOLDWYN; ABFL

DOES ANYBODY NEED ME ANYMORE? (29m   C   1975)
A dramatization of the effects of new values and changing life-
styles of middle-age women and their families, starring Maureen
Stapleton and Paul Sorvino.   LCA; CWU; UMIS.

DOLCE FESTA, LA (31m   C   1977)
Captures the warmth of a people celebrating a tradition.   All
who come to this annual festival in the Lower Eastside of Manhattan, Mulberry Street, once the center of Italian-American settle-
ments, enjoy themselves as Little Italy prepares one of the grand-
est, most elaborate San Gennaro Feasts in the country.   This is a
film about the creation of this festival.   The once tiny neighborhood
gathering now attracts over 2, 000, 000 devotees, tourists and festival
lovers.   d. Kathleen Dowdy.   CECROPIA.

DOLL, THE (7m   C/B   1974)
"Young woman fantasizes that she is nothing in this psychic
struggle for identity. "--C. B.   By Constance Beeson; BEESON.

DOLLARS (114m   C   1971)
A fast comedy thriller about the robbery of a Hamburg bank.
Warren Beatty is the brains while Goldie Hawn is the brainless ac-
complice.   Together they stage a phony bomb scare that gets them
into the safe deposit vault to switch money of several criminals.
This all leads to a sequence of chases with comic suspense and
amusing plot twists.   p. M. J. Frankovich; d. Richard Brooks;
COLUMBIA; WHOLFC.

DOLL'S HOUSE, A (109m   C   r1974)
Joseph Losey's production offers an authentic portrayal of 19th-
century society and values, while revealing the striking relevance
of Ibsen's theme today.   Jane Fonda plays Nora, a rich version of
most women--most women except for those who have developed a
new consciousness.   Finally, Nora awakens to an awareness that
she must take the first step toward becoming a whole person.
Based on Henrik Ibsen's 1879 play A Doll's House.   p. Joseph
Losey; CBSTV; ABFI, BF, EMC, LCA, MGH, SELECT, TWY,
WHOLFC.

DOLL'S HOUSE, THE (17m   B   1969)
Dramatizes an adaptation of Katherine Mansfield's story.   Presents class bitterness and intolerance as seen through the society of
a child's world.   By Sonia Gorelik-Carson; SLFP.

DOLL'S HOUSE, A; Pt. I, DESTRUCTION OF ILLUSION (33m   C
   1968)
   Scenes from Henrik Ibsen's play A Doll's House.   Nora appears
to live a pleasant, easy life with her executive husband and three
children.   As the play develops, her illusions about herself and
family are shattered.   Deeply shocked, she walks out, slamming
the door on her doll house.   Professor Norris Houghton comments.
EMC; ASU, BU, BYU, IU, PAS, UC, UILL, UIO, UMIS, UWY.

DOLL'S HOUSE, A; Pt. II, IBSEN'S THEMES (28m   C   1968)
   From Ibsen's play A Doll's House, Professor Norris Houghton
examines recurring themes: which of Nora's illusions about herself and family are shattered?   Has she betrayed her duty to her
family and herself?   What elements of an apparently idyllic life
cannot be trusted?   EMC; ASU, BU, BYU, IU, PAS, UC, UILL,
UIO, UMIS, UWY.

DOMESTIC TRANQUILITY (7m   B   1973)
   By accident, a wife and mother cleaning a closet shelf encounters her own long-buried ambition to be an artist.   Painfully
she faces the children, her husband's freedom "to work" at home,
and her own neglected desires.   By Harriet Krieger; WMM.

DONKEY SKIN (PEAU D'ANE) (90m   C   1971   French/subtitled)
   A renowned French fairy tale in which the King loses his beautiful wife.   He vows not to remarry until he has found a woman as
beautiful as she.   Unfortunately there is one person that fulfills
this requirement--his daughter, the Princess.   With the aid of her
Fairy Godmother, the Princess escapes her father's designs.
Cloaked by the skin of an enchanted donkey, she hides in the forest
where she eventually encounters a neighboring Prince and her own
happiness.   d. Jacques Demy; p. Mag Bodard; JANUS.

DONNA AND GAIL: A STUDY IN FRIENDSHIP (49m   B   1968)
   A case study of the loneliness of two post-high-school girls in
a large city who form a friendship out of desperation.   In sharing
an apartment, problems arise because of an emotional attachment
and differences in personality.   A trained counselor-observer tells
the story and gives an insightful interpretation of the motives for an
establishment of such a friendship as well as personality patterns
which cause it to dissolve.   NFBC; MGH; EMC.

DON'T GIVE UP ON ME (29m   C   1976)
   Barbara, mother of two small children, is accused of abusive
behavior and is in danger of having her baby taken from her by the
courts.   Included along with re-created scenes from this adapted
case history (police intervention, neighbor criticism, courtroom pro-
ceedings, counseling sessions) are several scenes from an actual
counseling workshop involving child-abusive parents charged with intensely emotional insights into the reason behind their actions.   Presents a view of the child abuse problem from the desperate parent's
point-of-view.   MTROLA; UW, UMIS.

DOODLERS, THE (5m C 1976)
"Miss Nose and her troupe of doodlers, who are themselves
doodlers in many media, sit down to a tea party laced with corn-
starch. This is a whacky film whose creator envisions her drawings coming to life: rebelling, socializing, and engaging in the art
of animation themselves."--Karen Cooper, Film Forum. By Kathy
Rose; SB.

DOONESBURY SPECIAL (26m C 1977)
A humorous yet uncompromising view of our changing patterns
and lifestyles. Shows us that transition and process are part of the
natural condition--that we must reconcile what is valuable from the
past with the exigencies of the future. Using the animation technique, the Hubleys have effectively captured the essential spirit of
Walden Commune and its inhabitants. By Faith Hubley, John Hubley; PF.

DOROTHEA LANGE: THE CLOSER FOR ME (30m B 1966)
Dorothea Lange, photographer-artist, her personality and her
work. Includes her photographs during the depression, World War
II, and the growth of urban sprawl in contemporary California. She
believes that the world is not being truly photographed today. Her
proposal of a new photographic project involving the cities of America is the subject. NET, IU; CWU, EMC, NIU, PAS, UIO, UM.

DOROTHEA LANGE: UNDER THE TREES (30m B 1965)
Dorothea Lange, her photographs and philosophy. As she prepares for a one-woman exhibition of her work, she comments on the
reasons and emotions that moved her to photograph particular scenes.
A memorial to her and to the despair and hope of the 1930's which
she documented in photographs. NET, IU; BU, EMC, NIU, PAS,
UIO, UM.

DOROTHY HEATHCOTE TALKS TO TEACHERS, PT. 1 (30m C
1973)
In a teacher's workshop, Mrs. Heathcote, England's outstanding
drama educator, explores the theory of improvised drama as a
teaching tool for all classroom teachers. She analyzes her unique
process, explaining and illustrating techniques for developing materials, the uses of drama elements and the segmenting of ideas to
achieve dramatic focus. NWUFL; NIU, UILL.

DOROTHY HEATHCOTE TALKS TO TEACHERS, PT. II (30m C
1973)
Drama in the classroom continues with the discussion of techniques developed by Mrs. Heathcote. "Questioning," "Storyline,"
"Universals," and "Brotherhoods" are examined. Drama is related
to developing language and social skills while teaching subject material. Mrs. Heathcote's educative process is based on total involvement that ultimately modifies behavior. NWUFL; NIU, UILL.

DOUBLE DAY, THE (56m C 1975)
An informative and thought provoking documentary on the lives of

working women in Latin America.   The women (from all levels of
society) describe their situations (common to women everywhere) in
which they work both in the home and out.   They discuss their
struggles for equality in work situations, and their family relationships; their values, and the effects of society on them.   Reveals
their increasing awareness.   Also available is a Spanish version.
d. Helena Solberg-Ladd; FILM PROJECT; TFC, UM.

DOUBLE DAY'S WORK, A
    Edited version of DOUBLE DAY, THE (q. v.).   From: IE.

DOUBLE INDEMNITY (107m   B   1944)
    An insurance agent and a greedy blonde connive to bump off her
husband and collect the proceeds.   The insurance company closes
in as their relationship disintegrates.   Based on James Cain's
novel.   d. Billy Wilder; PARAMOUNT; CVE, UNIVE.

DREAM LIFE (LA VIE REVEE) (90m   C   1971)
    Story of a friendship between two women who struggle to liberate
themselves from the image of the "ideal man. "   The major premise
of this film is role reversal--a step towards liberation.   The filmmaker wanted to show that great friendships exist between women,
so that for a time at least, they don't need men.   She is primarily
interested in the individual's subconscious and how it relates to the
conscious mind.   By Mireille Dansereau; FAROUN, NLC.

DREAM RISING (10m   C   1975)
    Computer-generated animation.   "Dream flickers and time's
womb conceives, back beyond and beyond. "--V. C. M.   By Vicky
Chaet Meyer; MEYER.

DREAM STUDY (7m   C   n. d.)
    A body portrait of a young woman in relation to nature and to
herself by means of superimpositions.   A sensuous abstraction.
By Rosalind Schneider; FCOOP.

DREAM WIFE (99m   B   1953)
    A plain American man, played by Cary Grant, firmly believes
a woman should place her man before her career.   Therefore, when
he finds his fiancee is more interested in business than in him, he
looks for another, more subservient woman.   He finds a Near Eastern princess trained in the art of serving men.   The excitement of
this lighthearted film begins when she arrives in New York with her
dowry of goats.   d. Sidney Sheldon; MGM; FI.

DREAMER, THE see BELLE CEREBRALE, LA

DREAMS AND ASHES (7m   B   n. d.)
    A moody psychodrama in which the levels of reality and fantasy
shift back and forth to depict the sexual frustration of a lonely young
spinster.   By Joan Kasich; CFS.

DREAMS ARE (10m   C   n. d.)
    "Paintings, drawings and photography with an original musical

soundtrack, and quotes from Emerson, Bergson, and e. e. cummings are used to portray the strange quality of dreams. "--CCC. By Carol Fox; CCC.

DRESSING BY DESIGN SERIES (No. 1--SILHOUETTE, 24m; No. 2--
    LINE, 29m; No. 3--TEXTURE, 30m; No. 4--COLOR, 24m;
    No. 5--COLOR AND WARDROBE, 29m; 1968)
    A condensed five-part television course given by University of
California at Berkeley Consumer Sciences program.   Designed to
teach women to see themselves objectively and to create wardrobes
that project their individuality.   Write to EMC for description and
cost for each part of the series.

DRIPPING WATER (11m   B   1969)
    You see nothing but a crystal white plate and water dripping into
the plate from the ceiling.   You hear the sound of the water dripping.   The usual reaction is "Oh, what is it, anyhow?   Just a plate
with water dripping into it. "   Filmmakers' contention is that that re-
mark has no love--for the world, for anything.   By Joyce Wieland,
Michael Snow; FCOOP.

DRIPS IN STRIPS (3m   C   si   1961)
    "Spattered paint responding to gravity, forming its own patterns
and combinations of color. "--M. M.   By Marie Menken; FCOOP.

DROWNING MOON (1m   B   1975)
    A short poem written by filmmaker's uncle during her childhood
is illustrated in a vision of bright nocturnal memory: the rippling
reflection of moon on water as it is crossed by the fluttering flight
of a moth.   By Mary Beams; SB.

DUE TO YA YA (10m   C   1971)
    Portrait of a filmmaker's grandmother.   "A look into the pri-
vate world and special memories of an 86-year-old Greek immigrant.   Set in a tiny New England mill town near the seacoast. "--
CCC.   By Kit Carson; CCC.

DUET FOR CANNIBALS (105m   B   1969   Swedish/subtitled)
    A psychological comedy-drama about the strange influence an ex-
iled German leader and his wife exercise over a young Swedish
couple who came under their spell.   ". . . a visually spare, cerebral
comedy about a former revolutionary living in exile with his wife,
and about the bizarre games they play to disguise their impotency.
It's an amazingly mature and controlled movie to come from someone whose only previous experience has been thinking about movies,
but who apparently has been thinking well. "--Vincent Canby, New
York Times.   By Susan Sontag; GP.

DUOS--COMBINATIONS FOR A PORTRAIT (11m   B   n. d.   sound on
    tape)
    Filmed spontaneously, Duos is a portrait of two college room-
mates.   The accompanying taped sound-collage acts as a mirror to
the action on the screen.   By Anne Kish; CCC.

DWIGHTIANA (4m   C   1959)
A charming and frivolous animation.   By Marie Menken; FCOOP.

DYKETACTICS (4m   C   1974)
The first lesbian lovemaking film made by a lesbian.   A short,
gentle statement of women loving women.   By Barbara Hammer,
Christine Saxon, Poe Asher; SB; MMRC, IE.

DYLAN THOMAS: THE WORLD I BREATHE (60m   B   1968)
The life and the work of poet Dylan Thomas.   Available with
filmmaker appearance only.   By Perry Miller Adato; PMA.

E. E. O. C.   (38m   C   1970)
Story takes an informal and systematic look at the machinery of
the Equal Employment Opportunity Commission.   Shows how it serves
both the minority community and women.   The film dramatically illustrates typical violations of Title VII of the Civil Rights Act.   Narrated by Ruby Dee.   WGPL

EACH CHILD LOVED (39m   C   1971)
Explores one woman's experience, thoughts and feelings before,
during, and after her abortion.   The film does not deal with moral
and intellectual issues.   PP.

EAMES AT MOMA (10m   C   1973)
"A film reportage of the Museum of Modern Art Exhibition of
all of Charles Eames' furniture.   Includes interviews with Charles
and Ray Eames and Eliot Noyes, architect."--P. M. A.   d. Perry
Miller Adato; ADATO.

EAMES CELEBRATION: SEVERAL WORLDS OF CHARLES AND
RAY, AN (90m   C   1977)
Profiles Charles and Ray Eames, a creative couple renowned
for their design work in architecture, filmmaking, science, communications, painting and furniture design.   Includes a number of
excerpts from their films, views of major exhibits, a visit to their
unique home in California, and comments by colleagues on their
achievements in communicating ideas through design.   p. Perry
Miller Adato; IU.

EARLY EXPRESSIONISTS (15m   C   n. d.)
"Two- to four-year-old children recording their spontaneous and
rhythmic movements with various art media."--MGH.   By Joyce
Brooke; MGH.

EARLY WORDS (22m   C   1972)
Shows a child of 22 months interacting with his mother and beginning to talk.   Freeze frames and narration isolate and emphasize
the relationships between environmental objects and the actions and
utterances of the child.   Informative and concise production.   WILEY;
EMC.

EARTHMOTHER (28m   C   1974)
A portrait of a woman who runs a Christian rehabilitation home
for ex-convicts and her relationship with two men who came to the
home after their release from prison.   A document of the power of
faith itself to change people's lives.   d. Martin I Ostrow; p. Alfred
R. Shands III; ASP.

ECONOMICS AND THE AMERICAN WOMAN; Woman Series (29m   C
    1974   VIDEO)
Elizabeth Forsling Harris, feminist, states that the contribution
that women make to the nation's economy is grossly underrated.
WNEDTV; PTL.

EDDIE (27m   C   n. d.)
Discovery that a newborn infant is mentally retarded is a numb-
ing experience for parents.   This film tells how a young couple reacts to the sad news that their first son was born with a genetic
defect.   By Ellen Geer, Don Stroud; MG; MGH.

EDITH HAMILTON (30m   B   1960)
Edith Hamilton speaks of ways in which the Greek civilization
was unique in the history of the world, the fundamentals of Greek
philosophy, and the reasons for the fall of Greece.   FI; UC.

EDNA ST. VINCENT MILLAY: MILLAY AT STEEPLETOP (25m   C
    1976)
Millay's sister reminisces about life with Edna at her New York
country estate, Steepletop.   FFHL

EFFECTS OF GAMMA RAYS ON MAN-IN-THE-MOON MARIGOLDS
    (101m   C   1972)
A rapacious, embittered widow (Joanne Woodward) has two teen-
age daughters: Ruth, outgoing like her cynical slob mother and
sensitive Matilda who finds solace from the madness of her home
life in the world of science.   The girls develop defense mechanisms
to keep themselves from being overexposed (like the gamma rays
on marigolds) to their mother's influence.   d. Paul Newman; FOX;
FL

EGG AND THE EYE, THE (25m   C   1968)
A unique and striking survey of art history from cave paintings,
through the Renaissance, to present day "op" and "pop. " Includes
viewpoints on art from Plato, Seneca, Da Vinci, and Harold Rosenberg, New York critic.   By Edie Brown Eisenberg, Jeffrey Brown;
CAROUSEL.

EGGS (10m   C   1971)
This film about human ecological problems and the future of
planet Earth is an excellent opener for discussion of some of today's most vital issues.   It offers an optimistic outlook for finding
the answers to such questions as: What will be the quality of life
in the future?   Will we have a choice when it comes to population
control?   Who will do the planning if we don't?   By Faith Hubley,
John Hubley; FIM.

EGGS AND ELEVATORS (4m B 1974)
"Comedy of a woman cracking up, flipping out. "--Freude Bartlett. By Ellen Gifford; SB.

EGGS AND MARROW BONE (4m C n. d.)
A thoroughly professional stylized cartoon adaptation of this
Welsh ballad, capturing all of its wry sick humor. Folk-singing
narration by Dave Zeitlin. A U. C. L. A. animation workshop film.
By Carol Roe, Ralph Hart; CFS.

EIGHTY MILLION WOMEN WANT? see WHAT 80 MILLION WOM-
EN WANT

81 BACON (6m B n. d.)
A film about what happens to a young man when he tries to
speak to the other passengers on a bus. By Virginia Giritlian; CCC.

EL GHORBA see PASSENGERS, THE

ELASTICITY (22m C 1976)
This highly stylized autobiographical film employs sounds and
images from the American collective unconscious (much of it derived from Hollywood filmmaking) to create a dream-collage. Made
to express Strand's most personal preoccupations. Expands upon
the surrealistic independent filmmaking pioneered by Maya Deren in
the 1940's and 1950's. By Chick Strand; SB.

ELEANOR AND FRANKLIN: THE EARLY YEARS (103m B 1975)
Story of Franklin and Eleanor from their childhood to Franklin's
entering the world of politics. It is also a touching and poignant
love story. d. Daniel Petrie; TALPAR; LUC; BF.

ELEANOR AND FRANKLIN: THE RISE TO LEADERSHIP (103m B
1975)
The second half of the story of Eleanor and Franklin continues
where the early years left off. "Rise to Leadership" follows
F. D. R. 's emergence as an astute politician and his years as President. Tells of his painful bout with polio, a secret love affair and
its effect on his marriage to Eleanor, and eventually his death.
Daniel Petrie; TALPAR; LUC; BF.

ELEANOR ROOSEVELT (26m B 1965)
Uses rare shot-at-the-time footage to portray the personal life
and history-making deeds of Eleanor Roosevelt. WOLPER; SEF;
OKSU.

ELEANOR ROOSEVELT; Wisdom Series (30m B 1958)
Mrs. Roosevelt speaks with William Atwood, senior editor of
Look, about the political obligations of a citizen, the practical
analysis of politics, her husband's greatest achievements and mis-
takes, and her hopes for the future. NBCTV; FI; EMC, PAS.

ELEANOR ROOSEVELT BIOGRAPHY (28m C 1963)
Traces the life of Eleanor Roosevelt, an august fighter for

human rights. Presents her childhood and explains that she was a
shy, unattractive little girl, ill at ease in the social whirl of her
prominent family. WOLPER; AFL CIO.

ELEANOR ROOSEVELT STORY, THE (90m B 1965)
    An Academy Award documentary on the life of Eleanor Roose-
velt. It tells the story of "an unhappy little girl in a lost family
in a vanished world" who became the First Lady of the Century. It
is also a story of American history, spanning the country's transition from the relatively placid 19th century to the turbulent times
of today. Mrs. Roosevelt's life, itself a moving drama, is made
more so by the poetry of Archibald MacLeish's script. d. Richard
Kaplan; p. Sidney Glazier; LANDAU; ABFI, TWY.

ELEANOR ROOSEVELT WE REMEMBER, THE (30m B 1963)
    Helen Gahagen Douglas, author of the book The Eleanor Roose-
velt We Remember, observes the first anniversary of the death of
Eleanor Roosevelt with the recorded voices of John F. Kennedy,
Adlai Stevenson and Mrs. Roosevelt herself. NBCTV; NAAJS.

ELECTRONICS: AN INTRODUCTION (9m C 1972)
    Follows the development of electronic devices--a conductor, an
electric light bulb, a diode vacuum tube, an amplifier and the
transistor. Concludes with a brief survey of electronic applications.
By Ellen Landweber, Victor Landweber; BFA.

ELEGY FOR MY SISTER (10m C 1972)
    "Slow-motion suspension tone poem filmed at Jones Beach upon
the passing of my Sister Jane. Edited in the camera. "--L. E. L
By Louva Elizabeth Irvine; FCOOP.

ELEMENT (13m B si 1973)
    "The female person in motion--nude and covered with wet, black
claylike mud. Exploration of a single human being falling into,
sliding along and rising out of this glistening substance over and
over summons up specific sensations from a very primitive and
visceral part of the human being. "--A. G. By Amy Greenfield;
GREENFIELD.

ELIZABETH: THE QUEEN WHO SHAPED AN AGE; Western Civiliza-
        tion: Majesty and Madness Series, The (26m C 1971)
    Recreates the personality of Queen Elizabeth who ascended the
throne of England and transformed a bankrupt land into the most
powerful nation on earth. Depicts how she faced the pressure of
plots and intrigues to fence with politicians and ambassadors to gain
precious time for England. Shows how the determination of Elizabeth shaped her own age and history of the West for centuries.
LCA; BU, IU, OKSU, UC, USC, UM, UMIS.

ELUSIVE GEISHA, THE (25m C r1976)
    Follows a geisha's typical day through the preparation (makeup,
costume, etc.) to the actual re-enactment of a teahouse scene where
the geishas entertain Japanese businessmen. Places in perspective

the geisha's role in the social and cultural structure of Japan.
d. /p. Frank Heimans; PARACO.

EMERGENCY: THE LIVING THEATRE (28m C 1969)
     Inside the Living Theatre.   By Gwen Brown; QP.

EMERGING WOMAN, THE (40m B 1974)
     A history of American women and their struggle.   Using old
film clips, engravings, photographs and newsreels, the film explores the varied economic, social and cultural experiences of wom-
en.   Shows how they felt about their condition and how their sex,
race and class often determined their priorities.   Includes parts on
working women, Black women (both slave and free), women in the
labor movement and suffragettes.   d. Melanie Maholick, Lorraine
Gray, Roberta Haber, Helena Solberg-Ladd; FIM; UIO, UM, UK,
UW.

EMMA BELLE SWEET (15m B 1962)
     Tells the story of a Golden Key Award teacher who brought the
real meaning of good teaching to everyone.   Miss Sweet was the
teacher who was the influence on Dr. Ralph Bunch during his forma-
tive years.   NEA; UU, UWY.

EMOTIONAL DEVELOPMENT: AGGRESSION (19m C 1973)
     Are we killer apes?   Or do we learn to aggress?   A nursery
school provides the arena for exploring these questions on film.
p. Barbara Jampel; CRM; MGH.

EMOTIONS AND PHYSIOLOGY OF THE MATURE WOMAN (31m C
     n. d.)
     Discusses the nature of middle-age for women and how they cope
with biological and psychological stresses undergone during this
period.   (p. unknown); WAYSU.

EMPTY NEST, THE (20m C 1973)
     Discusses the threat of extinction of one of nature's most fas-
cinating birds, the osprey or fish hawk.   Since 1950, 90 percent of
these birds have disappeared due to the lingering effects of hard
pesticides.   Provides an informative study of the osprey's courtship, rearing of the young, and flight patterns and habits.   It explains the significance of the food chain in perpetuating the deadly
consequences of pesticides in the environment.   By Judy Kress;
LCA.

ENCOUNTER (9m C si 1967)
     "A conflict, a struggle for possession, within one woman or be-
tween two women ... this psychic story is told in terms of a
dance. "--A. G.   By Amy Greenfield; FCOOP

ENCOUNTER AT KWACHA HOUSE--HALIFAX; Challenge for Change
     Program (17m B 1967)
     A group of Black and white youths gather at an inter-racial
club in Halifax to discuss issues of vital concern to them: discrim-

ination in employment and housing, the limitations of education for
Blacks, the kind of protest action that is taking place in the United
States and what it might accomplish in Halifax.   By Bonnie Klein;
NFBC.

ENCOUNTER WITH SAUL ALINSKY, PT. I: CYC TORONTO; Chal-
    lenge for Change Program (29m   B   1967)
    Documents a lively confrontation between Saul Alinsky, profes-
sional activist from United States whose efforts are directed toward
organizing the poor, and several members of the Company of Young
Canadians.   In what the C. Y. C. members and he say about the
means and the costs of securing social change, there is expressed
the dilemma, the doubts and the challenge facing all socially engaged people.   By Bonnie Klein; NFBC.

ENCOUNTER WITH SAUL ALINSKY, PT. II: RAMA INDIAN RE-
    SERVE; Challenge for Change Program (32m   B   1967)
    A provocative film in which young, articulate Indians test their
inherent, tolerant philosophy against the more pragmatic ideas of
Saul Alinsky.   The Indians argue for a revision of the hundred-year-
old Indian Act by peaceful persuasion.   Alinsky advocates more direct development of power to bring about the changes they seek.
By Bonnie Klein; NFBC.

END OF AUGUST AT THE HOTEL OZONE (87m   B   1967   Czech/
    subtitled)
    A stunning film about the last nine women left alive by nuclear
war. . Compelling in its authenticity, less science fiction than stark
realism.   Provides some feminist insight, one of which is that wom-
en who have escaped socialization can be as strong and daring as
men without being self-conscious about it.   By Jan Schmidt; NLC.

END OF INNOCENCE (76m   B   1957   Spanish/subtitled)
    The story concerns a 16-year-old girl (Elsa Daniel), whose emo-
tional growth has been stifled by a puritanical mother.   When the
girl falls in love with a youth who seduces her, she is unable to
overcome the intense guilt which haunts her.   Original title: La
Casa del Angel.   Based on a novel by Beatriz Guido; d. Leopold
Torre Nilsson; ABFL

END OF THE ART WORLD, THE (40m   C   1972)
    Uses film techniques to demonstrate correspondences of visual
arts with and without movement.   By Alexis Rafael Krasilovsky;
VRL

END OF THE GAME, THE (28m   C   1976)
    A microscopically detailed view of the interdependence of ani-
mal life in natural jungle habitat.   Filmed in Zaire, Kenya and
Tanzania.   d. Robin Lehman; p. Robin Lehman, C. Wilbur; PHOE-
NIX.

END OF THE ROAD (110m   C   1970)
    Director Ava Kian's private vision of an America that has

flipped out; a gun-crazy country torn by madness on many levels.
One of the more chilling episodes among fictional treatments of a
woman's life and love.   Adapted from John Barth's novel by same
title.   Rated X.   d. Aram Avakion; HCW.

ENGLAND OF ELIZABETH (26m   C   1961)
    Uses artifacts of the period to indicate how the growth of the
maritime fleet; the personality and influence of Elizabeth I; and the
songs, sonnets, plays, and other writings of authors like Shakespeare all help to convey the power, prestige, and spirit of the
England of Elizabeth.   Depicts 16th-century England through views
of the little-changing countryside, art treasures, maps of explorers,
books and architecture.   Recalls Tudor history, the Reformation,
Caxton's printing press and the first printed book, Drake's voyage
around the world, and the defeat of the Spanish Armada.   Presents
portraits of personalities of the period.   Shows Shakespeare's home
at Stratford on Avon and reviews his early life, his marriage and
his successes in London.   BTF; IFB; UILL.

ENIGMA (4m   C   1972)
    "Lines and rectangles are the geometric shapes basic to Enigma,
a computer graphics film full of subliminal and persistent image effects.   In a staccato rhythm, the film builds to a climax by in-
stantly replacing one set of shapes with another, each set either
changing in composition and color or remaining for a moment to vibrate strobiscopically and then change."--The Booklist.   p. Lillian
Schwartz, Ken Knowlton; LPL.

EQUAL RIGHTS AMENDMENT, PT. I; Woman's Series (29m   C
    1974   VIDEO)
    Ann Scott, head of the Washington, D. C. legislative office of
the National Organization for Women, and Karen DeCrow, lawyer and
author of Sexist Justice, maintain the ERA will have powerful economic and psychological impact.   Moderator Sandra Elkins.   WNEDTV;
PTL.

EQUAL RIGHTS AMENDMENT, PT. II; Woman's Series (29m   C
    1974   VIDEO)
    Two opponents of the Equal Rights Amendment, Phyllis Schlafly
and Geline Williams, discuss their objections to the ERA and tell
why they feel it is unnecessary and may be harmful.   WNEDTV;
PTL.

EQUAL RIGHTS FOR WOMEN: A SPECIAL REPORT FOR INDUS-
    TRY (20m   C   1973)
    Title VII of the Federal Civil Rights Act prohibits discrimina-
tion in private employment based on sex.   This act has revolu-
tionized the working women's rights.   This film presents case
studies in which women have lodged complaints against companies
for sex discrimination.   Points up the fact that unless a company
takes a progressive stand regarding women employees, it can become the victim of expensive law suits.   Bureau of Business Practice; UILL, UM.

ERA AND THE AMERICAN WAY (26m   C   1974)
    This film is an impartial statement of the terms of the Equal
Rights Amendment.   An always lively and sometimes very funny
document of responses by the "person in the street" when asked if
they want the ERA passed.   These responses constitute the soundtrack of the film while the visual images switch back and forth
from the American way of life as it is now to photographs of life
at the turn of the century.   A good film to spark discussion about
ERA and on the legal position of women generally.   p. Nevada
League of Women Voters; Molly Gregory; TFEI, SB.

ERICA (24/15m series   C   1972)
    Textile designer, retailer, best-selling author and international
authority on needlepoint, Erica Wilson, offers instruction in needle-
craft.   Write PTL for individual program titles.   WGBHTV; PTL.

EROSION (11m   C   1968)
    Explains the erosion process, showing such areas as the Colo-
rado Plateau.   Geraldine Byers, Justin Byers; BFA.

ESCAPE TO NOWHERE (25m   C   1968)
    A 16-year-old girl talks about the role drugs play in her life.
She is lonely, confused and unfulfilled.   The film suggests that
drugs made her this way.   Designed to open communication chan-
nels between parents and children, teachers and students.   PROART;
EMC.

ESKIMO ARTIST KENOJUAK (20m   C   1964)
    Kenojuak is an artist and sculptor who is also wife and mother,
and who makes her drawings when she is free of the duties of trail
or camp.   Here is a strange world where, in the deepening Arctic
twilight, the snow, the sky, the very air seem to throng with
shadows.   The thoughts of the woman are spoken as commentary
for the film and add to our understanding of the images she creates. ...   "Many are the thoughts that rush over me, like the wings
of birds out of darkness."   So her pictures appear, like many winged
birds, wavering shadows on the snow.   NFBC; MGH; OSU, PAS, UM,
USC, WAYSU.

ESPECIALLY FOR FATHERS (12m   C   1962)
    Shows the important role of the father in supporting his wife in
labor.   The couple in this study have trained for a "participating
childbirth."   Their portrayal is natural, convincing and interesting.
Directed to nursing students, medical students and hospital orientation for expectant parents.   SJDAED; EMC.

ESTHER DANCES HELEN KELLER (10m   C   n. d.)
    Introduces Anne and Paul Barlin (highly regarded for their cre-
ative dance for the elementary school student) who present one of
their young student's dance interpretation of Helen Keller's awakening to the outside world.   Provides an example of how one student
put movement concepts into practice.   By Anne Barlin, Paul Barlin;
SLFP.

EUGENE (24m   B   1971)
    Character study of a young retarded man and his family.   By
Marian Siegel; SIEGELM.

EVA (105m   B   1962)
    Tyvian Ones (Stanley Baker), a Welshman who has acquired a
reputation for his novels about coal mines, meets and falls in love
with Eva (Jeanne Moreau), a high-priced prostitute with a cold cynical outlook on life.   Despite her exterior, she is constantly anguished.   Eva needs a man who can protect her, and since Tyvian
is himself weak and dependent, she treats him cruelly.   Despite
Tyvian's humiliation by Eva and the death of his wife as a result
of his relationship with Eva, he continually returns to the woman.
Based on the novel by James Hadley Chase.   d. Joseph Losey;
ABFL.

EVA HESSE (15m   C   n. d.)
    "Visit to the studio of the sculptor Eva Hesse, who died in
1970 after a brief but brilliant career ... shows Eva at work, and
explores the materials she employed and the objects she surrounded
herself with. "--Program, "Women Artists As Filmmakers Festival, "
NYC.   By Dorothy Beskind; BESKIND.

EVA PERON (23m   B   1963)
    Highlights the life of Eva Peron, an obscure actress who rose
to become the wife of the Argentine dictator Juan Peron.   Uses
newsreel footage to show the forces and events which brought the
Perons together.   Emphasizes the constant struggle for power, recording how Eva built a strong and loyal group of followers.   Ends
with Eva's death in 1952.   WOLPER; STERLTV; IU.

EVA ... WAS EVERYTHING BUT LEGAL (93m   C   n. d.   Swedish/
    dubbed)
    Eva, a foster child in the home of an elderly couple, lived a
lonely life.   All but rejected by her foster parents and the inhabitants of the small Swedish town, Eva becomes easy prey for a
prominent middle-aged man who notices her voluptuous physical development.   Finding what she believes to be an easy way to give
and receive love, Eva soon finds her double life causing a scandal
that shatters the small town with lurid details of adultery and guilt,
leading to a sensational trial of all the men involved.   d. Torgny
Wickman; WSA.

EVERGLADES, THE (7m   C   1973)
    A plea for preservation of the delicate eco-system of the Ever-
glades--its shallow water, grassland, sloughs and bird and marine
life.   By Naomi Armstrong, Leslie Armstrong; PARACO.

EVERY DAY'S A HOLIDAY (79m   B   1938)
    A saga of Peaches O'Day who picks up spare pennies by selling
the Brooklyn Bridge to turn of the century suckers.   She dodges a
police warrant by posing as Mlle. Fifi, the musical rage of Paree,
and keeps her theatrical franchise by electing Edmund Lowe mayor

over villainous Lloyd Nolan.   In the background, vaguely discernible
over West's undulating hips, are many other comic stays.   d. A.
Edward Sutherland; s. w. Mae West; Emanuel Cohen Production;
PARAMOUNT; UNIVE.

EVERY GIRL SHOULD BE MARRIED (84m B 1948)
A young store clerk decides she wishes to marry a doctor and
sets about "trapping her man with great diligence and forthrightness."
Based on a story by Eleanor Harris.   s. w. Don Hartman, Stephen
Morehouse; d. /p. Don Hartman; RKO; FL

EVERY SECOND CAR (28m B 1955)
Six experts in automotive safety point out that, although driver
education is important, preventive engineering can reduce traffic
fatalities by 60 percent with minimum expense to car buyers.   Experimental crashes under controlled conditions are shown.   By Patricia Watson; NFBC; EBEC.

EVERYBODY RIDES THE CAROUSEL, PT. I, II, III (24m ea. pt.
C 1976)
This animated film invites the viewer along on eight "rides"
through the human life cycle.   The eight stages of life are described
by psychologist Erik Erickson.   p. Faith Hubley, John Hubley; PF.

EVERYTHING A WOMAN COULD WANT (26m B n. d.   VIDEO)
Half vérité-documentary and half symbolic montage.   Shows
three women who have rejected what they had and tried to find what
they really wanted.   By Shera Thompson, Shelly Surpin; THOMSURP.

EVE'S MIND; Girls and Women Series (30m B 1971)
Panel of women discuss feminine psychology, touching on problems and potentials of four ages and stages.   UMITV; PAS, UM.

EXACT CHANGE (6m C n. d.)
Man comes to New York City and interacts solely with vending
machines.   Very sad, with noise of coins forming the soundtrack.
By Vicki Polon, Michael Bortman; POLON.

EXCEPT THE PEOPLE (20m C 1971)
A study of the separate worlds and social problems of the various ethnic groups who live in several blocks on the Lower East Side
of New York City.   By Abigail Child, Jonathan Child; TL.

EXCURSION (5m C si n. d.)
No commentary provided.   By Marie Menken; FCOOP.

EXCUSE, THE (16m C 1975)
A sensitive portrait of the American poet Ruth Stone as both a
woman and an artist.   Shot in and around the poet's farmhouse in
Vermont, the film intercuts readings of her poems with scenes of
her everyday activities during which she reminisces about her past
and discusses the present.   She recollects the origins of her poetic
creativity in childhood and talks of her feelings now, as a widowed

mother with three daughters.   But her reminiscences return continually to her dead husband, Walter, also a noted poet.   The
poems she reads expand on her recollections and also indicate the
ways by which the poet deepens, through her art, her understanding
of her experiences. p. /d. Sidney Wolinsky; exec. p. Hyman Wolinsky; EMC.

EXILES, THE (72m B 1961)
    Dramatic documentary of the problems encountered by American
Indians living in our urban areas and caught between two conflicting
cultures.   d. Kent Mackenzie; MGH; UL

EXPANDING UNIVERSE OF SCULPTURE (15m C 1970)
    Portrays the amazing range of what modern art is including in
the concept of sculpture: proceeds outward from the familiarity of
Alex Calder's mobiles and stabiles through the use of plastics,
acids, metals, scrap, and light.   Eventually arrives at Doris Chase's
movable sculptures with dancers inside in an on-stage performance.
By Elda Hartley; HARTLEY; UL

EXPERIMENT IN MEDITATION (18m C 1971)
    "Zooming in on the rose becomes a figure of vision for the act
of meditation; in and out, and back again for a closer, more inspec-
tive, introspective look. "--Casey Charness.   By Storm De Hirsch;
FCOOP.

EXPERIMENTS IN FILM: WOMEN (85m C/B 1974)
    A showcase for women artists.   A distillation of the finest film-
works presented in New York City in 1974.   Conceived by feminist
Jodie Lowe, it is not a feminist-political program.   See individual
titles: PLUMBLINE; BIRTH OF THE BIG MAMOO, THE; ROAD
TO A MOUSE; PAINTING; RETICULATIONS; WATERS DREAM;
ORDINARY DAYS; ACTUATE, ACTUATE II, ACTUATE III; AB-
STRACT EXPRESSIONIST MOVE.   NLC.

EXPLORING THE CRAFTS: POTTERY (10/29m ea.   B   1967
    VIDEO)
    This is a series of programs which introduces and demonstrates
the basic techniques of working with pottery.   Preparing the clay,
forming, decorating and finishing are all covered in the ten lessons.
An outline of very basic tools is presented, but the most important
tools are the potter's own hands.   The instructor, Mrs. Vivika
Heino, encourages the beginner's expression of creativity.   Write
to PTL for individual titles.   NHMETV; PTL.

EXPLORING THE CRAFTS: SILK SCREEN PRINTING (6/29m ea.
    B   1968   VIDEO)
    Mrs. Ellen Eppelsheimer, member of the New Hampshire
League of Arts and Crafts, former president of the New Hampshire
Hand Printers Guild, and art columnist for the Concord Monitor, in-
troduces the basics of silkscreen printing.   Emphasis is on work
that can be done along with the programs in a classroom atmosphere.
Write to PTL for individual program titles.   NHMETV; PTL.

EXPLORING THE CRAFTS: WEAVING (8/29m ea. B 1968
   VIDEO)
   Mrs. Lilly Hoffman, a professional weaver and teacher of the
craft, provides basic instruction in weaving. The series includes
an explanation of the terms, the preparation of the loom, an actual
demonstration of weaves, and a display of finished work. Write to
PTL for individual program titles. NHMETV; PTL.

EXTENSIONS OF THE FAMILY; Challenge for Change Series (14m
   C n. d.)
   A self-selected "family of 13" buys a house in a large western
city and shares responsibilities. Originally, four adults held the
mortgage. Since the film was made, two of the original members
have moved and new arrangements have been made to share equitably
with other people who have joined the group. This is a continuing
experiment with "alternatives" to the prevailing nuclear family structure. By Kathleen Shannon, Len Chatwin; NFBC; EMC.

EYE MUSIC IN RED MAJOR (4m C si n. d.)
   "Study in light based on persistence of vision and enhancement
from eye fatigue. "--M. M. By Marie Menken; FCOOP.

EYE OF THE STORM, THE (26m C 1969)
   A documentary account of Mrs. Jane Elliott's innovative and
successful attempt to introduce her third grade class in rural Iowa
to the realities of prejudice. Color of the eyes was the criterion
of superiority. Each child spent one day as the oppressed and one
day as the oppressor. The results of the experience were striking
for the children and presented important implications for their classroom and for the country in relationship to the realities of prejudice
as it operates in society; XEROX; EMC.

EZRA JACK KEATS (17m C 1970)
   Filmed interview with well-known illustrator of children's books.
Concludes with a discussion of his book A Letter to Amy. By
Cynthia Freitag; WESTON.

FABLE OF HE AND SHE (11m C 1973)
   This animated fable by Eliot Noyes, Jr. gently challenges stereotyped and sexist thinking and celebrates the joys of individual self-
expression. LCA; CWU, UILL, UIO.

FABULOUS TEMPLES OF THAILAND, THE (10m C 1974)
   Brief introduction to Thai history and culture with a focus on
the exotic Buddhist temples. By Diana Colson; PARACO.

FACE OF SWEDEN: THE EXPRESSIVE SOCIETY, THE (29m B
   1963)
   Focuses on actress Ingrid Thulin and producer-director Ingmar
Bergman. Ms. Thulin comments on the acting profession in Sweden.
Presents background to the development of Bergman. Includes

scenes from his work Winter Light in which Ms. Thulin played the leading female role. IU.

FACE THE NATION SERIES see CORETTA SCOTT KING, CIVIL RIGHTS LEADER; PRIME MINISTER GOLDA MEIR, ISRAEL

FACES (130m B 1968)
Widely praised drama noted for its starkly realistic depiction of marital disintegration and infidelity and its portrayal of the everyday banality and emptiness of contemporary upper middle-class life. Critically acclaimed as a courageous description of an American middle-aged couple during the height of the "youth era," and considered one of the most important films of the 1960's. d. John Cassavetes; CONTINENTAL; BF; EMC, FIF, SELECT, WRS.

FACES OF CHANGE SERIES see AFGHAN WOMEN; ANDEAN WOMEN; BORAN HERDSMAN; BORAN WOMEN; CHINESE FARM WIFE, A; THREE ISLAND WOMEN; VIRACOCHA; WOMEN IN A CHANGING WORLD

FACES OF WOMEN (10m C 1972)
Animated film on series of portraits of a number of women Foldes has known. Each face becomes what he sees behind it, and returns to normal. By Peter Foldes; VFI, FL

FACTORY (56m B 1972)
Cinéma-vérité study of blue-collar workers and their economic and psychological plight. Captures the sights and noise of a New York wedding-ring factory. Interviews workers who express feelings of futility and intercuts factory scenes with glimpses of management sales meetings and cocktail parties. A stark powerful record. By Evelyn Barron, Arthur Barron; FL; EMC.

FAILING MARRIAGE, THE; Conflict Within, The (Series) (20m C 1977)
Examines various aspects of communication in a disintegrating marriage. Written, directed and produced by two psychiatrists. By Alan L. Summers; SUMMERS.

FALL, THE (86m B 1961 Spanish/subtitled)
Story centers around an innocent young girl who has been raised in a repressive environment. The girl (Elsa Daniel) becomes a boarder in a house inhabited by a nervous, asthmatic woman and her four perverse children. There, the girl has her first romantic encounters: with a prudish lawyer and with the children's eccentric uncle. The film stresses the explosive nature of virginal emotions in his depiction of the girl's unusual and tragic affairs. Original title: La Caida. Based on a novel by Beatriz Guido. d. Leopold Torre Nilsson; ABFL

FALLEN ANGELS (29m C 1972 VIDEO)
A harrowing study of problems of alcoholism among women. Former alcoholics offer graphic testimony describing their long ordeal with the bottle. KDINTV; PTL.

FALLING STAR (12m C n. d.)
    An animated Indian legend of fecundity taken from Hyemohost
Storm's "Seven Arrows, " and created with Storm's assistance.   By
Kay Miles, Susan Norton; VQ; IE.

FAMILIES: ALIKE AND DIFFERENT (15m C 1976)
    Introductory film in a cross-cultural series depicting basic as-
pects of family life--with the same three families in all five films.
d. Jane Treiman, George Quilkin, James Kennedy; CF.

FAMILY, THE; Social Seminar Series (30m B 1971)
    Captures elements of well-adjusted household interaction that
show the effects on family members' growth and development.
Shows relaxed situations of the white, active, middle-class family,
as well as those with potential conflict.   NAVC; EMC.

FAMILY AFFAIR, THE; Choice: Challenge for Modern Women
    Series (31m B 1955)
    Story of a family whose relationships are strained to the break-
ing point by an adolescent son's defiance which brings to the surface the husband's smoldering resentment against the wife's domination.   Presents typical interviews in a family service agency and
shows how troubled families may be helped to see their difficulties
more clearly and take constructive action.   IFB; EMC, UMIS.

FAMILY ALBUM (10m C 1973)
    Four members of a family separated by divorce discuss how
this separation has affected their lives.   Their reaction provides insight into reasons for marital disintegration.   Still photographs supply a history of the family through 18 years of marriage.   IU

FAMILY: LIFESTYLES OF THE FUTURE; Towards the Year 2000
    Series (22m C 1972)
    Margaret Mead discusses stresses on the contemporary, iso-
lated nuclear family, and the growth of alternative, communal living
groups.   Visits three types of communes.   DA; EMC, CWU, PAS,
UILL.

FAMILY LIVING PROGRAM SERIES see LOVING; TEEN-AGE
    PREGNANCY

FAMILY PLANNING; Human Sexuality Series (28m C 1972 VIDEO)
    Obstetrician-gynecologist Ronald Pion, M. D. , conducts workshop
on methods of contraception.   Detailed descriptions of contraceptive
devices and a discussion dealing with psychological concerns about
contraception are presented.   UHAWAII/KHETTV; PTL.

FAMILY PLANNING; Nine to Get Ready Series (29m B 1965)
    Discusses various aspects of family planning including the popu-
lation explosion and approaches to individual family planning.   Tells
about agencies which are available to assist in family planning.
Features Dr. J. Robert Bragonier and Leta Powell Drake.   KUONTV;
UNEBR.

FAMILY PLANNING (10m   C   1968)
Explores the definite advantages of planning the number of children a couple wish to have.   Although the film states that there is
an acceptable method of family planning for everyone, it does not
recommend or discuss specific birth control devices.   Also available
in Spanish.   KUONTV; UMIS.

FAMILY PLANNING AND SEX EDUCATION--A SERIES see LOVE
IS A PLANNED FAMILY; METHODS OF FAMILY PLANNING;
PURPOSES OF FAMILY PLANNING

FAMILY PLANNING--CHILDREN BY CHOICE (14m   C   1973)
Focuses on family planning from a medical and sociological
standpoint.   Poses questions about family planning and explores the
effect of children on relationships.   Discusses the responsibilities
of child rearing.   DUNLF; AMEDFL.

FAMILY PLANNING: MORE THAN A METHOD (28m   B   1971)
Shows how paraprofessionals can handle an emotional problem
successfully with a personal approach.   By Phyllis Chunlund Johnson; PP.

FAMILY TREE (15m   C   1949)
Describes the settlement of Canada, covering the period from
the days of European explorers to the driving of the last spike in
the Canadian Pacific Railroad Line and the come-on for the settlers
to the prairies.   By Evelyn Lambart; NFBC.

FANNIE BELL CHAPMAN: GOSPEL SINGER (42m   C   1975)
Fannie Bell Chapman (surrounded by her family and friends in
Centreville, Mississippi) is the leader of gospel singing, praying,
and faith healing in her area.   Fannie is a great motivating force
in all their lives.   Her daughter joins her in singing throughout the
film.   Fannie talks about her original music and how she gets the
inspiration.   The words and the music just come to her, from
where she does not know.   The film is full of music, philosophy,
and spirit of this simple Southern Black woman whose life is dedicated to her view of God.   By Bill Ferris, Judy Peiser, Bobby
Taylor.   e. Judy Peiser; CFSF.

FAR CRY FROM YESTERDAY, A (20m   C   1975)
Fifty-two percent of all 13- to 19-year-olds in the U. S. have
had sexual intercourse, but only 10 percent of these sexually active
young people use reliable birth control.   Sixty-one percent of the
boys and 70 percent of the girls currently having intercourse believe the girl who becomes pregnant should have the baby and raise
it, either married or unmarried, helped by her boyfriend or not.
The film tells the story of two of these teen-agers who accept an
unplanned pregnancy because "they have such a beautiful thing going, "
without seriously considering the consequences.   The film traces
those consequences, the near tragic results of their decision; the
deterioration of their loving relationship and destruction of their
lifestyles as the newborn baby demands constant care, responsibil-

ity, planning--in short, becomes "a terrible burden." PPTUC;
PERENNIAL.

FARENTHOLD: A TEXAS CHRONICLE (32m C 1974 r1976)
     Based on the 1974 Texas gubernatorial campaign of Frances
"Sissy" Farenthold, this documentary chronicles the important
events in Farenthold's political career. Still photographs and newsreel footage document her history as a reform politician. Interviews with her and others sharpen this portrait of a unique political
figure, whose career reflects the emergence of women in the political arena. d. Estelle Changas; p. Estelle Changas, Kay Loveland; CHANGAS.

FAREWELL TO BIRDIE McKEEVER (25m B 1959)
     Birdie, the receptionist, creates consternation when it's dis-
covered she can barely type. The firm's executives are putting off
the unpleasant task of firing her when she announces her marriage.
She is given a check and a farewell gift only to hear that her sister
has been hired to take over. Birdie's sister is unskilled but cur-
vaceous. She is welcomed and told how little work she would need
to do. RSP; EMC.

FASHION: THE SECOND SKIN; Towards the Year 2000 Series (22m
     C 1971)
     Designer Rudi Gernreich and China Machado, senior fashion
editor of Harper's Bazaar, predict and discuss future fashion trends,
including the unisex style, increasing nudity, the antifashion movement, and the application of sophisticated technology to clothes design and manufacture. Takes a light humorous approach to the subject. DA; EMC, UL

FASTER PUSSYCAT, KILL KILL! (71m B 1966)
     A story of a new breed of superwomen emerging out of the
ruthlessness of our times. Three go-go girls wildly dance the wa-
tusi before the leers, the jeers, and lecherous come-ons of their
drooling all-male audience. Outside the microcosmic bar they embark on a wild, violent and deadly journey of vengeance on all men.
A bizarre mixture of humor, horror, satire and social significance.
d. Russ Meyer; MEYER; RONIN.

FAT FEET (20m C/B 1966)
     An erotic portrait of people in the city using animation on
pixilation. By Yvonne Anderson; YBW; FCOOP.

FATHER OF THE BRIDE (92m B 1950)
     Devoted father rebels when his daughter tells him she wants to
marry. The feeling continues until after "the modest wedding" father will be paying for long into the future. Based on novel by Edward Streeter. d. Vincente Minnelli; co-scripted by Frances Goodrich; MGM; FI.

FATHOM (90m C Scope 1967)
     Wearing the shortest of skirts and the lowest of necklines, super-

heroine sky-diver joins the search of NATO agents for a nuclear
trigger device mechanism, which, if found by the enemy, would of
course destroy the world.   d. Leslie H. Martinson; FOX; FL

FEAR (7m   B   1973)
A young woman is saved from rape by a latent anger harbored
from her employer's decision to deny her promotion because she is
a woman, a metaphorical rape she doesn't resist.   However, the
appearance of a real rapist triggers her latent rage.   Although he
has a gun, she fights him, chases him, and manages to hold him until police arrive.   d. Jean Shaw; WMM.

FEAR WOMAN (27m   C   1971)
Examines the social texture of Ghana where women have eco-
nomic power and are rapidly achieving political and social power.
Included are three interviews with a business woman, a Supreme
Court Judge and a tribal chief, each offering provocative comments
on the role of women in emerging nations.   By Elspeth MacDougall;
MGH; CWU, OSU, UILL, UM.

FEATHERS IS A (BIRD) IF IT IS A BIRD (5m   B   n.d.)
An imaginative animated film, using bits of dreams and breakfast time family fantasies about birds and flying.   By Pamela Ram-
sing; CCC.

FEELING GOOD (25m   C   n.d.)
In several settings, men share their boyhood experiences and
feelings today about self-sexuality.   They focus on significant mas-
turbatory experiences, the pleasurable parts of their bodies, and
having a unique, self-focused experience.   One person sums it up
as "feeling good about masturbation enabled me to feel good with
others."   By Laird Sutton; MMRC.

FEELS OF BLUE (6m   C   1969)
"Fragmented lake landscape; willows, rain, sun, and snow ...
with multiple electronic-concrete sound overlays, light love and
humor."--Bob Liikala.   By Isabelle Liikala; FCOOP.

FELICIA (13m   B   1972)
A 15-year-old Black girl's quiet inquiry into her life in a
segregated community.   Filmed in her home, school, and neighborhood in Watts, in the spring of 1965, shortly before the area was
devastated by riots.   Expresses her own observations and feelings
about elements of her daily life.   BFA; EMC, BU.

FEMALE HOMOSEXUALITY; Woman Series (29m   C   1975   VIDEO)
Author-editor Barbara Love discusses her lesbianism and so-
ciety's impact on female homosexuality.   Sandra Elkin, moderator.
WNEDTV; PTL.

FEMALE SEXUALITY (16m   C   n.d.   VIDEO)
Members of the women's re-entry program at Diablo Valley College discuss women's rights as sexual beings, the myths, the facts,

the relatively new research in sexual dysfunction, sex therapy, and the role of communications in breaking down stereotypes.   KQEDTV.

FEMALE SEXUALITY, PT. I; Woman Series (29m C 1974 VIDEO)
    Barbara Seaman, author of Free and Female and Mary Jane Sherfey author of The Nature and Evolution of Female Sexuality, discuss female sexuality.   WNEDTV; PTL.

FEMALE SEXUALITY, PT. II (29m C 1974 VIDEO)
    Sexual unresponsiveness and its treatment is the topic when psychiatrist and sex therapist Dr. Singer Helen Kaplan and sex researcher Shere Hite, author of Sexual Honesty by Women for Women, join Sandra Elkins, moderator, in a discussion of female sexual dysfunctions.   WNEDTV; PTL.

FEMINIST PARTY STREETWALKS, THE (6m B 1972)
    "Flo Kennedy and the Feminist Party demonstrate against the whiteout of Shirley Chisholm, and racism and discrimination against women by the media."--Herstory.   By Marian Hunter, Patricia Bertozzi; HERSTORY.

FEMINIST THERAPY; Woman Series (29m C 1975 VIDEO)
    The relatively new field of feminist therapy, a form of psychotherapy which developed out of the women's movement, is discussed by feminist therapist Pauline Bart and program moderator Sandra Elkin. WNEDTV; PTL.

FEMME DU GANGES, LA see WOMAN OF THE GANGES

FEMMES SAVANTES, LES see LEARNED LADIES

FETAL ALCOHOL SYNDROME (13m C 1976)
    Examines the severe form of retardation known as "fetal alcohol syndrome." Attributed to alcoholism in the mother, this form of retardation is recognizable at birth--undersized babies with narrow slit-like eyes with drooping lids.   Examines the development of these children and the consequences of "fetal alcohol syndrome." Fetal damage is permanent and one-half of the babies born of alcoholic mothers are affected.   d. William B. Hill; NBCTV; FI; CWU, UW.

FIANCEE DU PIRATE, LA see VERY CURIOUS GIRL, A

FIBERGLASS RP BATHROOMS AT HABITAT (6m C 1967)
    Describes construction of bathrooms of reinforced plastic, which were used in habitat '67 at Expo '67 in Montreal.   By Sally MacDonald.   CRAF for FIBERC; FIBERC.

FIFTH STREET WOMEN'S BUILDING FILM (15m B 1971)
    Made for one of the 100 women who took over an abandoned city-owned building in New York City to establish a service center for all women.   Despite negotiations with the city and growing support, they were evicted by the police.   By Jane Lurie; LURIE.

FIFTY-ONE PERCENT (30m C 1971)
This film stimulates managers and supervisors to provide additional opportunities and more equitable treatment for women in business and industry. It is a dramatic documentary about three wom-
en: a manager, a secretary and a professional. Their experiences
are the catalysts through which are exposed the prevailing opinions
regarding working women in most companies. d. Dick Feldman;
p. Robert Drucker & Co. ; DRUCKER; SSF; EMC; MSU, UW.

FIGHTING BACK (24m C n. d.)
When a woman is being raped, even if her mind tells her to
fight back, often her body will not listen. Women are socialized
not to be aggressive and not defend themselves. A female martial
arts teacher instructs a class of women how to physically defend
themselves. New York City police offer some advice to women who
are attacked, and New York Women Against Rape discuss the psychological effects of being raped. IU.

FILM FOR MY SON (28m C 1975)
"The Filmmaker records her son on film so that one day he
might see himself as she experienced him. The film is also about
the intermingling of memories which their relationship evokes from
her: principally, her childhood in rural Yugoslavia during World
War II and her early fears of motherhood. It is a film which en-
compasses a paradox: made to record the moment, while ruminating
upon the illusive nature of our most previous experiences. There
are intimate scenes between mother and child which speak to the
universality of this relationship as well as the specifics of Stefan's
four-year-old life on Manhattan's Upper West Side and Nadja's memories of Eastern Europe and a war she cannot forget. "--Karen
Cooper, Film Forum. By Nadja Tesich-Savage; SB.

FILM GENERATION AND DANCE, THE (60m C 1969)
"Four filmmakers--Shirley Clarke, Ed Emshwiller, Hilary Harris and Norman McLaren--talk about dance and film. Excerpts
from their films or entire films trace their development and major
achievements. "--P. M. A. By Perry Miller Adato, Jac Venza;
ADATO.

FINAL HOURS OF JOAN OF ARC, THE; You Are There Series
(26m B 1956)
Uses a dramatized "on-the-scene" news type of interviewing and
documentary reporting to present the story of the trial of Joan of
Arc and how she was burned at the stake for refusing to deny the
story she had told. Portrays various attitudes of the day. CBSTV;
MGH; IU.

FINAL PERFORMANCE OF SARAH BERNHARDT, THE; You Are
There Series (28m B 1955)
Presents a high point in the history of the American theatre as
one of the world's greatest actresses defies the approach of death
to go on to the stage once more to say goodbye to the public.
CBSTV; ISU, UILL, UKEN.

FINE FEATHERS (5m   C   1968)
    In this cut-out color cartoon two quarrelsome birds get the urge
to change their plumage.   A bluejay wants to be decked out in the
green of cedar, and a loon in the burnished red of oak leaves.
Neither bird had reckoned on the consequences of vanity.   Along
comes a gust of wind, and both learn to their consternation that
their natural, well-anchored feathers made much better protection.
By Evelyn Lambart; NFBC; BM.

FINE TIMES AT OUR HOUSE (27m   C   1972)
    "Music of the last generation of the fast-fading mountain culture
of pre-Foxfire Appalachia. "--L. A. T.   By Lois Ann Tupper, Maureen
McCue; WFC; IRISF.

FINNEGANS WAKE (97m   B   1965)
    Based on James Joyce's book Passages from Finnegans Wake.
The film achieves the innocent effect of the great dream novel; it
touches myth, touches the collective unconscious.   By Mary Ellen
Bute; EVERGREEN; GP.

FINNISH FRUSTRATIONS (AMPUMARATA) (8m   B   1974   Finnish/
    subtitled)
    The film is an indictment of the sexual inequality in Finnish
society, dramatized through a young girl's dance-hall encounter.
p. Eila Kaarresalo-Kasari; FCOOP.

FIREARMS (7m   B   n. d.)
    "A universal soldier discovers who he is really fighting. "--
M. H.   By Marjorie Heins; FCOOP.

FIREFLY (4m   B   n. d.)
    Abstraction on a Black dancer, Carie Mae Weems.   Companion
piece to the film Woman.   Original Arp sound by Niel Murphy.   By
Constance Beeson; BEESON.

FIRST AMERICAN SERIES see   CHILDREN OF THE SUN

FIRST LADY OF THE WORLD, THE (53m   B   1962)
    Presents highlights from the life of Eleanor Roosevelt, including
her years as wife of the President, her activities during World War
II and her work with the United Nations after the war.   p. HEARST;
BCGFLM.

FIRST LADY OF THE WORLD: ELEANOR ROOSEVELT; History
    Makers, The (Series) (25m   B   1974)
    Old family photographs and early newsreel footage illustrate
Eleanor Roosevelt's recounting of her early childhood marred by the
deaths of her mother, brother, and father.   She learned in her
early years that she liked social work during which time she met
her husband, F. D. R. , and married him.   The film tells how her
strong-willed mother-in-law and husband stifled Eleanor from developing strengths of her own.   In 1921, F. D. R. was stricken with
polio.   That shattering blow began a new life for Eleanor.   She

became an outspoken civil rights advocate.   Following her husband's
death, she became a world figure in her own right.   Concludes with
Adlai Stevenson's eulogy of her.   PARACO; CWU, UILL.

FIRST MOVING PICTURE SHOW (7m C 1973)
    Describes how a little clay man stumbles over his ability to
draw.   Shows that after drawing more pictures than he can hold, he
hangs his drawings on his clothesline and by pulling the line faster
and faster, the drawings became "The First Moving Picture Show."
By Nancy Faye Karkowsky; PHOENIX.

FIRST THERE WAS SARAH (25m C 1971)
    The film tells us the history of women employed by Western
Electric.   The first woman hired, more than 100 years ago, was
Sarah Adlum.   Covers the cross-section of skilled and unskilled
jobs held by today's 70, 000 female employees, their benefits and
opportunities.   Reveals, however, the scant representation of women
in top management positions.   d. Ted Lowry; WESTEC.

FISHES IN SCREAMING WATER (6m C 1969)
    "Stars George cat, with music composed and performed by his
brother, Mamacat."--P. C.   By Pola Chapell, FCOOP.

FITTING IN (21m C 1977)
    Focuses on two individuals--Mildred with three grown children
raised while she was in a wheelchair and recently starting a new
career, and Roy, a mechanical engineer suddenly afflicted by a
crippling nerve disease and returning to work after a two-and-a-
half year struggle.   Mildred and Roy have resolved complex emotional problems as they moved from being totally disabled to being
contributing members of the community.   They have carefully prepared both themselves and their environments to accept their physical limitations.   Reflects the changing view of the handicapped as
full participants in American society.   The expanded guarantees to
education, jobs and access to public spaces (as set forth in HEW
504 enacted in June 1977) will enable the disabled to participate in
all aspects of life.   This film will help prepare both the able-
bodied and the disabled to accept their increased responsibility as
well as the increased opportunities.   p. Peter Feinstein; d. Miriam
Weinstein; POLYMORPH.

FIVE (5m B 1967)
    Theatre piece composed of stills of a young man in different
costumes and always playing a trumpet.   Created for dancer Elizabeth Harris.   By Constance Beeson, Ronald Chase; BEESON.

FIVE ARTISTS BILLBOBBILLBILLBOB (70m C 1971)
    A portrait of five sculptors, painters and filmmakers and their
friends and families.   Filmed in Marin County, California, the camera follows the group into the studio, at parties, galleries, fishing,
etc.   Sound track is a mixture of comments and music by the artists and personal impressions of friends.   By Dorothy Wiley, Gunvor Nelson; CCC.

FIVE EASY PIECES (100m   C   1970)
Jack Nicholson plays Robert Eroica Dupea, a man fleeing from
his heritage and family, his personal failures, and ultimately himself.   Involved in this life is a dewy-eyed "cracker" waitress who
goes through a greal deal of pain to please him; however, in the
end she is abandoned like a puppy at a gas station.   d. Bob Rafel-
son; p.   B. Rafelson/Richard Wechler; s. w. Adrian Joyce; RBC,
SWANK.

FIVE FACES OF MADAME KY, THE (55m   C   1967)
Shows the effects of the war on the country, the people and the
leaders of South Vietnam.   Develops around the premier and Madame
Ky.   Presents Madame Ky as she is seen by the world as the First
Lady of South Vietnam, as she is to her husband, to her children,
to the women of South Vietnam and as a woman to herself.
BAILYB; AVED.

FIVE PORTRAITS (41m   C   n. d.)
"Studies of five people in Kentucky's criminal justice system:
a juvenile delinquent, a police chief, a circuit judge, a jailor, a
felon.   Made for the Kentucky Crime Commission. "--N. C.   By
Nell Cox; COX.

FIVE STAR EGO (4m   B   n. d.)
A satirical comment on the relative inhumanity of military gen-
erals who casually sacrifice their troops in exchange for another
star on their caps.   In this film the troops are represented by eggs.
The satirical comment develops through the process of stop motion/
live action animation.   By Hanna Roman; MFCF; CFS.

5 X MARILYN (14m   B   1973)
A sad and sexy memorial to Marilyn Monroe.   The combined
repetition of Monroe's melancholy voice singing "I'm Through with
Love" and of the grainy, fragile image gives this film the rare
poignancy of a beautifully spoken elegy.   A strong comment on a
society which values physical beauty above all else.   By Bruce Conner; SB.

FLAME IN THE WIND (122m   C   1971)
Presents the story of a young man's conflict within himself as
he faces a choice between organized religion and what he believes
to be the true way of salvation.   p. /d. Katherine Stenholm; UF.

FLASHETTES, THE (20m   C   1977)
Shows how a community project helps its young Black female
members develop self-confidence and self-respect.   The founder/
coach tells how he started the club and shows how he works with
the girls.   By Bonnie Friedman; LPF; NDF.

FLICKERS (20m   B   n. d.)
"The inauguration of Nixon and various counter-inaugurations, in-
terviews with different kinds of people. "--N. T. S.   By Nadja Tesich-
Savage; TESICH.

FLICKORNA see GIRLS, THE

FLIMFLY (1m C n. d.)
"A lyrical song to the joys of childhood. "--Freude Bartlett.
By Judith Wardwell; CCC.

FLORENCE LUSCOMBE, SUFFRAGIST (29m C 1975 VIDEO)
    Early days of women's rights movement are recalled by 88-
year-old Florence H. Luscombe.   When she was graduated from
M. I. T. in 1909, the only Americans who were not allowed to vote
were criminals, the insane and women, she says.   WNEDTV; PTL.

FLOWER SHOW, THE (Series) (14/29m ea.   C 1973 VIDEO)
    Designed to introduce a new hobby, to stimulate an appreciation
and love of nature as an inexpensive source of beauty, and to teach
the skills and joys of flower arranging.   The Flower Show was written by and features Mrs. Amalie Adler Ascher, a prominent Baltimore flower arranger, teacher and author.   Mrs. Ascher takes the
viewer through a step-by-step construction process, explaining terms
and methods, as she makes at least one arrangement on each program.   Write to PTL for individual program titles.   MCFPB; PTL.

FOCUS (3m C/B si 1973)
    "Black and white movement, disorienting up and down, quiets
to a stable viewpoint of slow jerking movement in a playground.
The movement becomes less multidirectional until finally a face on
the merry-go-round suddenly changes to real-life color and real-life
speed, grounded by the staring of a child. "--M. H.   By Martha
Haslanger; HASLANGER.

FOG PUMAS (25m C 1967)
    A lyrical fantasy populated by an imaginative assortment of hu-
man beings, creatures, places and events.   Widely hailed as an
artistic masterpiece.   By Gunvor Nelson, Dorothy Wiley; SB, CCC.

FOLIMAGE (14m C n. d.)
    Leaf images, multiple patterns, endless color harmonies and
movements: A dancer, a young girl, lovers; interesting technique.
By Madeline Tourtelot; GP.

FOLKSONG FANTASY (7m C 1951)
    A puppet film.   By Alma Duncan; NFBC.

FOLKSONG PATCHWORK (Series) (3/29m ea.   C 1971 VIDEO)
    A series of musical specials with folksinger Cynthia Gooding.
Described by the San Francisco Chronicle as having "one of the
deepest, richest contralto voices that has ever melted a microphone, "
Miss Gooding creates lasting images for the eye, ear and mind in
Folksong Patchwork.   The series is presented in a changing set of
three-dimensional patterns of authentic patchwork quilt motifs.   Individual program topics are 1) Tradition songs about traditional attitudes toward the place of women in society; 2) A "musical autobiography"--songs of Gooding's childhood, youth and professional

experiences; 3) A musical illustration of the elements of the folk-song.   MAETEL; PTL.

FOLLOW THE READER (15m   C   1976)
Uses music and humor to help students in expanding their use of language as a medium of communication to enrich their intellectual, social and emotional involvement in the world.   By Suzanne Bauman; BAUMSZ.

FOLLY (3m   C   1972)
Sometimes called "Bride and Groom, " Folly makes a tart, short and sweet statement on the nature of repetition as part of the human condition--with special reference to women.   By Freude Bartlett; CCC; SB.

FOOD FOR THOUGHT; Woman Series (29m   C   1975   VIDEO)
Nutrition experts Dr. Eleanor Williams and Maruka Fernandez discuss the world food crisis and American nutritional crisis.   An uneven distribution of resources and land has left two-thirds of the world ill-fed while synthetic food, technology, waste and poor eating habits have turned the United States into a land of the over-fed and under-nourished.   WNEDTV; PTL.

FOOD FOR YOUTH (Series) (10/27-28m ea.   C   1974   VIDEO)
A series on nutrition and meal planning, covering basic facts about nutrition, balanced diets, caloric intake, eating environments and how eating habits affect the individual--especially the child.   The series is aimed primarily at school food service personnel, but also communicates information about nutrition to parents, teachers and administrators.   George R. Kerr, M. D. , a pediatrician and Assistant Professor of Nutrition at Harvard University's School of Public Health, is the series host.   Special pricing arrangements apply to this series.   Write to PTL regarding pricing as well as individual program titles.   USDAES; PTL.

FOOD PRESERVING (Series) (10/29m ea.   C   1975   VIDEO)
A series on the techniques and materials used in preserving foods by canning, drying, pickling, freezing, and making jams and jellies.   Instructor Margaret Meador works with a variety of fruits, vegetables and meats and gives detailed directions and demonstrations for each method.   The emphasis is on safety in preparation and on economy.   Write to PTL for individual program titles.   WSWPTV; PTL.

FOOL THERE WAS, A (75m   B   si   1914)
The original super-seductress who gave the word "vamp" to the English language.   As the evil woman who lures a good man to his destruction, Theda Bara became famous overnight.   d. Frank Powell; FOX; BF.

FOOTLIGHTS (11m   C   1974)
"A young tap dancer is very nervous about performing.   The ghost of a woman performer comes back and tells her it's okay to

be a woman and to be successful. "--Freude Bartlett.   By Virginia
Giritlian; SB.

FOOTPRINTS OF THE MAYAN GODS (29m C 1969)

Discusses reasons for the decline and fall of civilizations.   Contrasts the ancient Mayan architectural splendors with the simplicity
of the modern life and the religion of the present descendents of the
Mayans.   Filmed at the ruins of Copan, Tikal, Palenque, Bonampak, Uxmal, Tulum and Chichen-Itza.   By Elda Hartley, Joseph
Campbell; HARTLEY.

FOR BETTER OR WORSE (7m B 1973)

Professional by day and domestic by night, a newlywed pediatrician finds herself working a double shift even though her husband cooked elegant meals for her during their pre-marital romance.   Eventually he reforms after he reads Ms. magazine, and
he agrees to share the housework.   It could be argued that this arrangement still leaves her with a job-and-a-half.   Even though
equality isn't achieved, they at least learned to be flexible.   d.
Judith Shaw Acuna; WMM.

FOR LOVE OF A WOMAN; Men and Women of Our Times Series
    (15m B n. d.)

Tells the story of the Duke of Windsor, who gave up a kingdom
for a woman.   FOX; STAR.

FOR TOMORROW WE SHALL DIET (24m C 1976)

A number of threads are interwoven in exploring this complex
subject.   A young woman sets out to lose 20 pounds; discovers the
need to change eating habits, dangers of fad diets, relation of
calories to energy output, proper nutrition and exercise.   d. Bill
Haugse; CF.

FORBIDDEN PLAYGROUND, THE (11m B n. d.)

"Dance film photographed in a modern playground, with documentary sequences of NASA astronauts. "--M. H.   By Maxine Haleff;
FCOOP.

FOREIGN AFFAIR, A (116m B 1948)

Marlene Dietrich plays a former Nazi who claims women can
have no politics but has a good thing going in occupied Berlin as
the darling of the servicemen who patronize the off-limits nightclub
where she is the star performer.   She is an engaging black-
marketeer protected by an American officer, but her secure world
tumbles when it is invaded by Jean Arthur, a member of the Congressional investigating committee who decides the military is covering up.   d. Billy Wilder; PARAMOUNT; UNIVE rel. ; TWY,
UNIVE.

49-'17 (79m B si 1917)

An action Western with many innovations.   Created by one of
the two pioneer women directors in the silent era.   The title is derived from its being the 49th Universal production in the year 1917.
d. Ruth Anne Baldwin; UNIVE; KP.

FOUR FAMILIES, PTS. I & II (61m B 1961)
On-the-spot comparison of family life in India, France, Japan and Canada with anthropologist Margaret Mead discussing how the upbringing of children contributes to a distinctive national character. MGH; BU, OKSU, PURDUE, UILL, UW.

FOUR LADIES ON STAGE (15m B n. d.)
Shows four topless dancers working in Times Square explaining their philosophy about life and work. By Janet Foreman; FOREMAN.

FOUR PLUS TWO (4m B si 1971)
A film poem that explores the delicate and mystical relationship a young girl develops for her horse. By Pat Saunders; FCOOP.

FOUR SQUARE (18m C si 1971)
"Designed for simultaneous projection by four projectors on four screens arranged in a square, enclosing the audience ... basically a film about red, the space and time... "--B. D. /T. C. By Beverly Conrad, Tony Conrad; FCOOP.

4 X 8 = 16 (3m C n. d.)
A whimsical entertaining psychedelic dada film using multiple imagery, not in superimposition, but in simultaneous projection on individual areas of the screen. Accompanied by folk-rock music track. By Christina Hornisher; CFS.

FOUR WOMEN (5m C 1970)
Dancers from the Harlem Preparatory School interpret Nina Simone's song about Black women. Filmed in counterpoint with images of women in the community. By Ilanga Witt; YFD.

FOUR WOMEN ARTISTS (2/18m ea. C 1975 SFS)
The theory behind the work of four major contemporary artists. Shown are sculptures of Nevelson and Marisol, and paintings of O'Keeffe and Frankenthaler. EDC.

FOUR YOUNG WOMEN (20m C 1974)
Explores the attitudes, motivations, and feelings of four young women of different races and ages who, for a number of reasons, have had or are planning to have abortions. Presents abortion as a personal experience without judgments. Includes interviews with the women's friends, husbands, and parents. Concludes with doctor's explanation of the medical procedures involved in an abortion. PERENNIAL; EMC, MSU.

FOUR YOUNG WOMEN: ON ABORTION (15m C 1975)
Four women tell of their reasons for deciding to have an abortion and their reactions to the experience itself. The interviews are followed by one with a doctor, who explains the various modern surgical procedures used in these operations. SEESAW; PERENNIAL; UILL.

FOURTEEN (7m C 1974)
"Quick images of an ingenue, the filmmaker's daughter, Kim

Beeson. "--C. B.   Sound by Niel Murphy.   By Constance Beeson;
BEESON.

FOX, THE (110m   C   1968)
    Misses Dennis and Heywood, longing for harmony and private
fulfillment, isolate themselves on a remote chicken farm in rural
Canada.   A fox was destroying their livelihood until a wanderer appears and kills the fox.   But his brusque male presence in the uneasy nest of the women shatters their delicate relationship.   He
precipitates one toward full-hearted physical union, the other toward
frenzy and death.   Based on D. H. Lawrence novella.   d. Mark
Rydell; WSA.

FRAGILE EGOS (35m   C   1969)
    Portrait of a fiftyish woman who has been in and out of mental
hospitals since her teens, focusing on her struggle to find a place
for herself in the community while she works as a secretary at the
hospital in which she was formerly a patient.   Shows her working,
talking with her boss, conferring with her psychiatrist, and interacting with friends.   Deals with the difficulties of interpersonal relationships and how one influences others in order to be liked.
Avoids suggesting interpretation.   Designed to provoke questions.
IU; EMC.

FRANCES FLAHERTY: HIDDEN AND SEEKING (56m   B   1971)
    Documentary of the late wife of filmmaker Robert Flaherty.
She had been living on their farm for 20 years since the death of
her husband, and had been active in civic affairs.   She never lost
the poetic vision, keen eye for beauty and simple truth inspired by
Robert.   The camera observes Mrs. Flaherty in her daily routine
allowing her personality and ideas to reveal themselves.   MGH; UM.

FRANKENSTEIN IN A FISHBOWL (43m   C   1973)
    Revealing and sometimes gruesome documentary on plastic
surgery, showing why two middle-aged women, one poor and the
other rich, endure extreme pain in order to rejuvenate their appearance.   Includes graphic scenes of the surgeries and the post
operative condition of the two women, and suggests that their deeper
problems will not be solved by surgical means.   Provocative comment on a culture that discriminates against aging or unattractive
women.   d. Barry Pollack; TL; EMC, UM.

FREAKS (30m   C   n. d.)
    "I guess the value of living in a commune is not only to be
able to trade, [and] share laughter ... but to be able to share experiences. "--interview by Martha Stuart, David Ruskin; STUARTM.

FREE TO BE ... YOU AND ME (42m   C   1974)
    Invites viewers to discover a fascinating world of endless vari-
ety where all of us have the right to be ourselves.   Many famous
people involved in skits, songs and stories, to bring across the message relating to such matters as friendship and cooperation, life-
goals and social roles for individual fulfillment, self-reliance and
independence.   A mini-course in self-awareness.   MGH; ROA, UM.

FREE TO CHOOSE (17m   C   1974)
Explores the new realities of the contemporary woman, and encourages choice of work and life-style based on interests and skills
rather than on traditional male-female roles.   Focuses on various
people speaking about themselves in non-traditional roles.   FFAIR;
UILL.

FREE WOMAN, A (100m   C   1972   German/subtitled)
A story of one woman, Elisabeth, who has gone through a divorce and is fighting for the custody of her child.   She is now free--
free in a world in which relationships between men and women are
beginning to undergo such profound, often devastating change.   A
remarkable detailing of the emancipation of a young woman.   A film
that mirrors the subordination of women with truthful biting irony.
By Margarethe Von Trotta, Volker Schlonderff; NYF.

FREEDOM TO LOVE (90m   C   1970)
A film about the irrationality of common sexual prejudices and
traditional sex laws, Freedom to Love advances the point of view
that sexual freedom is not inimical to the interests of society.   The
film suggests that official and unofficial suppression of sexuality and
the resultant sexual frustrations are actually a contributing factor in
social ills.   It makes an impassioned plea for a more open-minded
and tolerant attitude toward sex for greater personal happiness and
a healthier society.   By Drs. Phyllis and Eberhard Kronhausen;
GP.

FRENCH CHEF, THE (Series) (26/29m ea.   C   1973   VIDEO)
French chef, Julia Child, presents detailed cooking instructions
for a variety of French dishes.   Information about equipment, sea-
soning and serving included.   Write to PTL for individual program
titles.   WGBHTV; PTL.

FRENCH LUNCH (15m   C   1971)
A fast-paced look at the midday meal in New York's expensive
and famous La Caravelle Restaurant.   By Nell Cox; PF; TWY.

FRESH SEEDS IN THE BIG APPLE (25m   C   1975)
Some fundamental questions are asked in this film: Why is day
care available to only six percent of the preschoolers in the cities?
Are the children learning in these day care centers or only kept busy
until they are picked up?   What are these children learning?   With
increasing numbers of women looking for work in this time of economic depression, the lack of this vital service puts a brake on
their reaching the job market.   Finally, the film shows the 1974
city-wide demonstration for more and better quality day care.   Made
in cooperation with parents and workers of two publicly funded day
care centers in Manhattan and Brooklyn.   SFN, TWN.

FROG PRINCE, THE (10m   B   1950)
A fairy tale in silhouette animation based on live shadow play.
A princess drops her golden ball into a well.   It is saved by a
frog who becomes her companion and then turns into a prince.   By
Lotte Reiniger; BBCTV; MGH, CEA.

FROM EVERY SHIRES ENDE: THE WORLD OF CHAUCER'S PIL-
    GRIMS (38m   C   n. d.)
Shows churches and chapels, thatched houses, wooden carvings,
illuminated manuscripts, and medieval music that depicts life during
Chaucer's time.   By Naomi Diamond, Mary Kirby; PFMP; IFB.

FROM HERE TO THERE (9m   C   1964)
Relates the story of a United jet en route from Los Angeles to
the East Coast in order to portray the human experience of travel,
pointing out the excitement and the poignancy of partings and greetings and the unique visual experience of flying.   By Elaine Bass,
Saul Bass; BASSS; PF.

FROM THE BATHROOM (7m   C   1970)
"A young man, concerned with growing up, tries on a beard.
His fantasy takes him to an enchanting Oriental garden where he
meets a girl. "--YFD.   By Angela Deitrich; YFD.

FROM THE FIRST PEOPLE (45m   C   1977)
A community produced film which presents the Eskimo village of
Shungnak through early winter subsistence activities in temperatures
of minus 47 and short three-hour days.   d. Sarah Elder, Leonard
Kamerling; p. Leonard Kamerling; ANHFP.

FROM THE INSIDE OUT (13m   B   1967)
Six 15-year-olds express their thoughts and feelings through
·movement in creative dance, defined as "the exercise of body and
imagination in order to bring the whole being into play. "   The filmmaker is an innovator in finding new ways to stimulate creativity in
both children and adults, in developing ways in dance that help people gain command of their bodies without dance mannerisms, and
in relating dance and movement to other fields.   By Carolyn Bilderback; FIM.

FROM 3 A. M. TO 10 P. M. (15m   B   1969)
This Yugoslav documentary is a tribute to the working housewife.   It follows a woman through her never-ending workday from
dawn to dusk,   p. Kreso Golik, ZAGREB; MGH; UM.

FROM ZERO TO 16 (7m   C   n. d.)
"An autobiographical attempt both visually and audibly ... including shots of the sixth Rite of Opposite Forces and family album
snapshots. "--N. L. C.   By Naomi Levine; NLC.

FRONTIER EXPERIENCE, THE (25m   C   n. d.)
The Westward Movement--and a woman's perspective of that
movement--emerge in the dramatic story of Delilah Fowler's first
year on the Kansas frontier in 1869.   Based on diaries of the period, this film reveals the cruel violence, and even crueller loneliness, of frontier life.   Delilah left the "pretty" ways of Pennsylvania behind her when she began her trek in a covered wagon with
her husband and four children.   She lost her husband in frontier
violence soon after their arrival.   She painfully parts with her

oldest to earn money so they could go back to the East. When
spring comes and she is reunited with her son, she realizes that
she has indeed survived the frontier and done so unaided. She
writes in her diary: "with God's help, I do believe we shall make
Kansas our home. " By Barbara Loden; LCA.

FULL CIRCLE: THE WORK OF DORIS CHASE, A (10m C 1974)
     The artist traces her own growth as she explores all art forms
including sculpture and dance. Some of her sculptures weigh tons;
but others, created for dancers, are light enough to move with a
gentle touch. Her sculpture forms for children were created specifically for pulling, rocking, and crawling through. By Elizabeth
Wood; PERSPECTIVE; EMC, IU, UC, UM, UU, VFL

FULL LIFE, A (108m B 1962 Scope)
     A rich Japanese film in which a woman leaves her "pig" husband
and learns to take care of herself in a hostile world. It seems as
if she's moving in a political and conscious direction, especially with
her involvement in the 1960 anti-America riots. The end is a dis-
appointment--she falls in love with a man who's made the political
commitment. The last shot shows her sewing his buttons on con-
tentedly while he discusses politics from the hospital bed. By
Susumu Hami; NYF.

FUN ON MARS (5m C 1971)
     Everything is coming up ducky on Mars, the land of a thousand
Miamis, where the Great American Tourist migrates for a quacka-
thon of delight and relaxation. Here the Martians are ducks who
dance, surf and party all night. Reflections on growing old in a
land of eternal youth. By Sally Cruikshank; SB.

FUNCTIONAL ANATOMY OF THE AORTIC VALVE (32m C 1969)
     Correlates anatomy and function of the left ventricle and aortic
valve in health and disease with physical findings. Observes the motion of the heart and the intracardic pressures. Demonstrates the
clinical manifestations of pure aortic regurgitation. By Jean L.
Williams for AHA; AHA.

FUNNY GIRL (161m C 1968 Scope)
     Marvelous musical biography of the legendary Ziegfeld girl,
Fanny Brice, played by Barbra Streisand. d. William Wyler;
COLUMBIA; SWANK.

FUR COAT CLUB, THE (18m C 1973)
     Depicts the adventures of two nine-year-old girls who have in-
vented a secret game of touching fur coats without the wearer
realizing it. While playing this game, they inadvertently become
trapped in a vault of a fur store. Describes their surprise when
the vault door opens, two thieves appear and the girls manage to
trap them and become heroines. By Linda Gottlieb, Joan Silvers;
LCA.

FUSES (19m C si 1968)
     "The notorious masterpiece ... a silent celebration in color of

heterosexual lovemaking.   The film unifies human elements with the
natural environment through cutting and superimposition and layering
on abstract impressions by scratching and blotching of celluloid itself. ...   The film succeeds perhaps more than any other in objec-
tifying the sexual streamings of the body's mind. "--The Guardian.
By Carolee Schneeman; GP, FCOOP, SB.

G. E. SLIDE SHOW (n. d.   SLIDES (50))
     General Electric's promotional material combined with slides
and narrative investigation of G. E. 's manipulation of women, Third
World and poor people through consumer indoctrination and economic
politics.   Shows the connection between sexist socialization, racism
and profit without abstraction or rhetoric--using mostly the company's own ads.   Script included.   WRP.

GALATHEA (12m B 1934)
     An animated film based on live shadow play.   A nude statue
comes to life in classical Athens, driving men frantic and the wom-
en mad.   By Lotte Reiniger; CEA.

GALAXIES (5m C 1974)
     "Computer-simulated disk galaxies that are superimposed and
twirled through space in beautiful colors at different speeds. "--Dr.
Frank Hohl, NASA.   By Lillian Schwartz; LPI.

GALINA ULANOVA (38m B 1964)
     Documents the life and art of Russia's most famous dancer,
Galina Ulanova, from her beginnings with the Leningrad Kirov Bal-
let to her present role as teacher at the Bolshoi Ballet School in
Moscow.   Dance sequences from Ulanova's famous roles include
Gisell, Swan Lake, Romeo and Juliet, Chopiniana, and the Fountains
of Bakhchisarai.   CDFS; ABFI, UILL, USC.

GALLANT LITTLE TAILOR (10m B 1930's)
     A fairy tale in silhouette animation based on live shadow play.
A cunning little tailor first kills flies and then by using his wits
kills giants.   By Lotte Reiniger; BBCTV; CEA, MGH.

GALS, GUYS AND DOLLS (4m C n. d.)
     Satire on sex roles in marriage.   Shows how children playing
with dolls perceive those sex roles as models to follow when they
grow up.   "Busy Becky, " a housewife doll, cleans and vacuums
while chatting with friend, "Shopping Cheryl, " who has just returned
from buying brand name products.   "G. I. Joe, " adventurer and
hero, who is married to "Busy Becky" returns from far-off exotic
places only to quickly change equipment and clothes and abruptly depart again.   "Does he always behave that way?" asks "Shopping
Cheryl" in astonishment.   BM.

GAME, THE (39m B 1972)
     Cinéma-vérité portrait of a Black prostitute and her pimp.   The

filmmakers accomplished a rare achievement in approaching a delicate and sensational subject with empathy. Both the prostitute and
the pimp come across as real human beings who deserve our understanding as well as our interest. They are capable of analyzing
their subculture, providing fascinating insights into the psychological,
economic, social and sexist aspects of "the game. " By Abigail
Child, Jonathan Child; FIM; EMC.

GAME, THE (17m B 1967)
    A film of a New York City ghetto, acted by Black and Puerto
Rican teen-agers who relive their lives in the shadows of their tenement homes. Neither sentimental nor overtly angry, the film has
an impact of unadorned realism. p. /d. Roberta Hodes; MOBY; GP.

GAMEEL GAMAL (OH, BEAUTIFUL DANCER) (24m C 1976)
    Belly dancing is a serious if entertaining ritual of the Far East.
It is also good exercise and many American women are adding the
study of this dance to their regular exercise. The film shows two
beginning belly dancers, a class by the world-famous male belly-
dance teacher Roman Ballardine and a performance by Amina. It
also deals with some of the social problems American belly dancers
must face. p. /d. Gordon Inkeles; PHOENIX, VFI.

GARDEN PARTY (24m C 1974)
    Adaptation and dramatization of the short story (by Katherine
Mansfield) about a young girl's first encounter with death. Her
family does not permit a neighborhood death to interfere with their
lavish garden party. GURSHP; PARACO; OSU, UM.

GARFIELD RIDGE (30m C n. d.)
    "I see it (Garfield Ridge) as middle America ... the vast ma-
jority of people are ... like the people in Garfield Ridge and they
are powerless because they have no organization and because they
are not respected. "--interviewee. By Martha Stuart, David Ruskin;
STUARTM.

GARMENT WORKERS IN SOUTHERN CALIFORNIA (20m C 1975)
    Examines the exploitation of Latino sewing machine operators
in Southern California clothing factories. The piece work system
is in violation of minimum wage laws and industrial homework is
another labor law violation which permeates the industry. The U. S.
Dept. of Industrial Relations says 995 out of every 1000 garment
workers in Los Angeles are not paid a proper wage. The term
"sweatshop" is still very applicable today. In Southern California
90 percent of all garment workers remain without union representation. By Susan Racho, Realidades/N. E. T. ; SFN.

GASLIGHT (114m B 1944)
    A study in Victorian villainy: Ingrid Bergman plays the role of
the distraught wife and Charles Boyer her wicked spouse. Boyer,
in his best deadpan hypnotic style drives Miss Bergman to pieces
while the flames flicker strangely in the gas jets. Adapted from the
play Angel Street by Patrick Hamilton. d. George Cukor; MGM; FI.

GAY DAY, A (3m   C   1973)
"A satire on lesbian monogamy. "--B. H.   By Barbara Hammer;
HAMMER.

GAY VIEW/MALE, A (17m   C   n. d.)
In an intense and personal discussion, three gay men share
their first sexual attitudes and experiences.   They discuss their
feelings about men, women, children, labeling, intimacy, and about
becoming proud of being gay.   They urge the freeing of all people
from labels and compulsive sex.   By Laird Sutton; MMRC.

GENERATION (3m   C   n. d.)
Presents examples of movements by filmmaker, bringing into
play the rhythms and interplay of the kaleidoscope.   By Hilary Harris; FIM.

GENERATIONS OF THE LAND (27m   C   1976)
Traces the development of U. S. agriculture and describes the
challenges facing today's farmers as their operations change from
labor-intensive to capital-intensive.   Gives viewers an appreciation
and respect for the land and for the efforts that family-farm agriculture is making to the plentiful production of food.   d. Harold M.
Weiner; p. Marilyn Weiner, H. Weiner; SSCOPE.

GENESIS 3:16 (17m   B   1971)
A film about the women's movement in Boston.   A good treatment of alternative life-styles, communes, self-defense, women's
images and gay women.   The interviews are very good with two
women and their children who live together as a unit.   They express their expectations of their being a continuing family.   By
Maureen McCue, Lois Ann Tupper; WFC; IRISF.

GENETIC CHANCE, THE (60m   C   1976)
Suppose you were told that your unborn male child stood an
even chance of being born with a crippling disease?   You had the
choice of terminating the pregnancy or allowing it to continue.
Would you run the risk of aborting a healthy fetus or of bringing
into the world a child crippled with a painful disease for the whole
of its life?   This is the very real choice of prospective mothers
who are carriers of the disease hemophilia, since the technique of
diagnosing the sex of the fetus has become a routine procedure.
The film looks at the disease hemophilia in which a genetic error
diminishes the ability of the blood to clot.   Fifty percent of male
children born to carriers of the disease are affected.   The medical
and ethnical issues raised by the possibility of preventing the disease by abortion are stark and complex.   They will become increasingly common as prenatal diagnosis of genetic diseases becomes further developed.   BBCTV; WGBHTV; TL.

GENETICS: MAN THE CREATOR; Towards the Year 2000 Series
(24m   C   1971)
Noted doctors and scientists discuss a science-fiction world of
genetic engineering.   They predict that, in the future, human repro-

duction can be completely separated from sexual intercourse.   One
possibility mentioned is the human sperm bank where famous people
could donate their sperm or eggs to be listed in a kind of human
catalog.   The film investigates the moral implications behind genetic
engineering: Who will decide what is good and what is bad.   By
Susan Murgatroyd; CTV; DA; UILL.

GENTLE BIRTH (15m   C   1976)
   Shows the interaction of mother, father and obstetrician during
a Lamaze-Leboyer delivery.   Actually a synthesis of the birth experiences of two families, the film illustrates "family-centered maternity practice. "   Delivery and commentary is by Dr. John Grover,
Fellow of the American College of Obstetricians and Gynecologists
and Ass't. Clinical Professor of Obstetrics-Gynecology at Harvard
Medical School. d. /p. Alvin Fiering; POLYMORPH.

GENTLEMEN PREFER BLONDES (91m   C   1953)
   Two showgirls embark on the luxurious "ile de France" seeking
rich husbands, or at any rate the diamonds which are "a girl's best
friend. "   d. Howard Hawks; FOX; FI

GEORGIA, GEORGIA (91m   C   1971)
   Presents a penetrating and powerful story that reveals the soul
of the American Black woman.   Diane Sands portrays Georgia
Martin, an international singing star who is confused about her
life and her identity.   "The greatest statement for Blacks that
we've ever seen. "--Ebony/Jet.   d. Stig Bjorknam; CINERAMA;
SWANK.

GEORGY GIRL (100m   B   1966)
   Lynn Redgrave plays a plain-Jane type who decides to break out
of her not-very-interesting mold and winds up with two very off-
beat relationships with James Mason and Alan Bates.   The plot revolves around Lynn's jealousy of her swinging roommate's life-style
and how she can emulate it.   d. Silvio Narizzano; BF, CINE, CWF,
FC, ROA, SELECT, TWY, WHOLFC.

GERMANY'S AGRICULTURE AND INDUSTRY (15m   C   1968)
   Germany's new farms, mines and factories.   For elementary
and junior high school.   By Geraldine Byers, Justin Byers; BFA.

GERMANY'S EVER-CHANGING FACE (19m   C   1967)
   Political and geographical changes in Germany in the past 2000
years.   For junior and senior high school.   By Geraldine Byers,
Justin Byers; BFA.

GERTRUD (115m   B   1964   Danish/subtitled)
   Gertrud is a woman alone.   Misunderstood by the men she has
loved, she has given of herself and received nothing in return.   Her
husband sees her as an ornament, something to be shown off in
public.   Accepting this, Gertrud has an affair with a young composer, Jansson.   But Jansson is too young, and not yet ready for
Gertrud's kind of love.   He boasts publicly of the affair.   For

Gertrud, it is the last straw; she is through giving herself to men
who are, in the end, vain and uncaring. Her husband, after finding
out about the affair, still wants her to remain but she is through
being an ornament. She arranges to go to Paris and devote the
rest of her life to quiet study, removing herself completely from
the world of heartless men. From a play by Hjalamar Soderberg.
d. Carl T. Dreyer; MGH.

GERTRUDE STEIN--THE ROSE THAT IS A ROSE (29m B n. d.
    VIDEO)
    Dr. Herman Harvey, professor at University of Southern Cali-
fornia presents a psychological study of the American author, analyzing Miss Stein's life, works and personal motivation. USC.

GERTRUDE STEIN: WHEN THIS YOU SEE REMEMBER ME (89m
    C 1972)
    Filmed biography of a remarkable woman who influenced 20th-
century art. It is noteworthy that she was not locked into any of
the conventional female roles. She did not conform in her relationships to men, nor did she conform in her writing. A montage
of the author's personality is shown using still photographs, old
film clips, selections from productions of her work, interviews
with old friends and shots of the famous Stein collection of modern
art. The film also documents the major theoretical interchange between Stein's experimental writing and the Cubists' new art. d.
Perry Miller Adato; ed. Aviva Slesin; MGH; EMC, IU, MSU, PAS,
USC, UM, WAYSU.

GESTALT ART EXPERIENCE WITH JANIE RHYNE (27m C 1977)
    Presents a dynamic and affecting experience in group art thera-
py. Led with great insight and vitality by Janie Rhyne, a gestalt
art therapist and teacher at University of California, Santa Cruz.
Her approach encourages natural expressiveness, group interaction,
and perceptive recognition of the participant's personality. The se-
quential experiences are depicted: the first is "finding your own
rhythm vocabulary, " the second is "creating yourself in clay, " and
the third is "building a world together. " In a brief introduction
Rhyne explains the principles and concepts of gestalt art therapy.
EMC.

GESTALT SERIES see MARRIAGE

GETTING ANGRY (10m C 1966)
    Film examines the reaction of children when a child's favorite
birthday present is broken at school. By Sue Stinson, Jim Stinson;
BFA.

GETTING CLOSER (15m C 1975)
    Film helps teenagers to understand their feelings of anxiety
and concern about interacting with people of the other sex. Greg,
shy and self-conscious, really wants to ask Laura to the dance at
school but can't quite bring himself to ask. His friend Louie, outgoing self-styled "lover, " doesn't help matters by kidding Greg
about his reticence. d. Ruth Pollack, Robert Gardner; AIT.

GETTING MARRIED (45m C 1976)
A special look at weddings and marriages that runs the gamut of emotions from solemn to ebullient, humorous to touching. From New York to Hawaii, one thing seems evident--a basic faith in the idea of marriage as a pretty durable institution. Narrated by Cloris Leachman. By Charles Braverman; PF; IU.

GETTING MARRIED (18m C 1975)
Explores why people marry--past and present. Uses an entertaining mixture of dramatic scenes, real-life interviews and silent film movie clips. The film encourages viewers to explore their own attitudes and expectations about getting married before marriage vows are taken instead of afterwards. CREEDMAN; BFA.

GETTING TOGETHER SERIES see PARENTAL ROLES: DON AND
    MAE; TEEN-AGE RELATIONSHIPS: VANESSA AND HER
    FRIENDS

GIBBOUS MOON, THE (22m B 1970)
Film journal of a vulnerable young girl's pregnancy and its poignant conclusion. By Nancy Ellen Dowd; SB, NLC.

GIFT FOR MUSIC (89m B 1975 Russian/subtitled)
A young war orphan is befriended by a conductor and enters the Moscow Conservatory. Eventually, he is chosen to perform solo with the orchestra in place of the conductor's son. A lively glimpse into both Moscow life and the world of music. d. Maria Fyodorva; ABFL

GIFT OF CHOICE; Population Problem Series (60m B 1965)
Reports on experiments carried out to determine factors controlling pregnancies, both to aid those who want children and to control fertility for those who want to limit family size. Details scientific research on why the egg is released, the ovulation process, passage of the egg through the Fallopian tubes, and chemical changes that occur to make conception and implantation possible. IU; EMC.

GIMME SHELTER (90m C 1970)
Begins with footage of the Rolling Stones' concert in Madison Square Garden, including Mick Jagger's exhilarating performance of "Sympathy for the Devil," but moves quickly to the free concert at Altamont, California. Attended by 300,000 people, Altamont became virtually a city for a day. What began as a great party turned into tragedy. The Altamont concert became a milestone in the history of a generation. By Charlotte Zwerin, David Maysles, Albert Maysles; FOX; CIV.

GIRL IN WHITE (93m B 1952)
Story of Dr. Emily Dunning Barringer, who, at the turn of the century, became the first woman to serve on the staff of a municipal hospital in New York City. Based on the book, Bowery to Bellevue by Dr. Barringer. d. John Sturges; s.w. Helen Vincent, Von Cube; MGM; FI.

GIRL OF MY PARENTS (8m   C   n. d.)
What is universal about the teen-age years?   How does growing
up on a kibbutz affect adolescence?   Hagit is a vibrant, mature 17-
year-old who has been raised on a kibbutz in Israel.   In this film,
she shares some of her thoughts and feelings about responsibility,
love, trust, marriage, home, friends, family, and herself.   EDC.

GIRL TO WOMAN (18m   C   1965)
Presents the changes of adolescence.   Moves from the superficial changes of growth, skin, body hair, and body contour to the
more complicated phenomena of glandular changes, sexual matura-
tion and the reproductive function.   The importance of sound habits
of personal hygiene highlighted.   CF; UC.

GIRL WHO WEARS THE CROWN, THE (25m   C   1967)
Describes the Junior Miss Pageant as a scholarship program
for senior high school girls.   Points out that a girl must demonstrate a high degree of character, scholarship, ambition, leadership, religious interest, ladylike poise and demeanor to be chosen.
AMJMP; GM; MTP.

GIRL, YOU NEED A CHANGE OF MIND (8m   B   1973)
Girls who are suffering incredible boredom as long as they hang
around their boyfriends, abruptly change their mood when they start
building a coffee shop in their youth center.   By Fatou N'Jie;
WMM.

GIRLS, THE (FLICKORNA) (100m   B   1971   Swedish/subtitled)
A beautiful, controversial and intricate film, it lucidly articu-
lates the dissatisfaction of three unhappy women whose identities
have always been defined in terms of their men.   On tour with
"Lysistrata, " the actresses find out that they are a catalyst.   As
they become immersed in their roles, they confront the truth about
their own personal oppression.   Finally, at a dinner party, Bibi
Anderson makes her own pathetic gesture at liberation.   A culmina-
tion of Zetterling's own personal war against the existing marital
and social order.   By Mai Zetterling; NLC.

GIRLS AND WOMEN SERIES   see   ADAM'S RIB; EVE'S MIND;
GIRLS IN SCHOOL; HOW THE WORLD SEES WOMEN; NEW
FREEDOM FOR WOMEN; WHAT EVERY WOMAN KNOWS;
WOMAN'S PLACE, A; WOMAN'S WORK, A WOMAN'S LIFE, A;
WOMEN IN THE FAMILY OF MAN; WOMEN, LAW AND POLI-
TICS

GIRLS AT 12; Roles of Women in American Society Series (30m   C
1975)
An unstaged documentary of three friends growing up in a small
industrial city adjacent to Boston, this film examines the complex
influences that are shaping the girls' expectations for themselves.
The first in a series of films that will comprise a high school
course on the role of women in American society.   By Joyce
Chopra; EDC.

GIRLS BEWARE! (10m C 1961)
Explains the problems of young girls falling prey to the molester in four case histories.   Covers do's and don'ts in the babysitting situation.   Develops the problem of the "Pickup" and the girls who go with boys that are too old.   DAVP; UW.

GIRLS' CORNER: TEXTBOOKS AND OPTIONS see IMAGES OF
    MALES AND FEMALES IN ELEMENTARY SCHOOL TEXTBOOKS

GIRLS IN DANGER; History of the Motion Picture Series (18m   B
    1962)
Role of the heroine in silent films.   Excerpts, with commentary, from films starring Jetta Goudal, Gloria Swanson, Mae Marsh, and Lillian Gish.   SEF; PAS.

GIRLS IN SCHOOL; Girls and Women Series (30m   B   1971)
Panel discusses stereotypes of male-female roles as presented in textbooks, teachers' attitudes, and standardized tests.   UMITV; PAS.

GIRLS OF MOUNTAIN STREET (10m   C   1970)
Presents interviews with Montreal fashion models to portray them as feeling individuals rather than lifeless mannequins.   NFBC.

GIRLS' SPORTS: ON THE RIGHT TRACK (17m   C   n. d.)
Shows the experiences of three high school girls--a cross-country runner, a shot putter, and a long jumper.   The first film to summarize the recent changes in girls' sports.   Narrated by Katherine Switzer; p. /d. Ellen Freyer; VFI; BF.

GLASS (5m   B   n. d.)
Tells about a woman glassblower living on the marine coast and the inter-relationship between the natural environment--sun, ocean and rocks--the artist and her work.   By Vicki Polon; POLON.

GLASS MENAGERIE (104m   C   1973)
Katharine Hepburn stars as Amanda Wingfield, an aging Southern belle who clings to memories of her carefree past.   She desperately tries to recreate for her children the gaiety and romance of the life she once knew before her husband deserted her.   Amanda is portrayed as a powerhouse of a woman--irascible and calculating, but full of humor, courage, drive and overwhelming charm.   d. Anthony Harvey; p. David Susskind; TALPAR; CIV.

GLIMPSE OF THE GARDEN (5m   C   1957)
A lyric, tender, intensely subjective exploration of a flower garden, with extreme magnification and flashing color harmonies. By Marie Menken; GP, FCOOP.

GLOOSCAP COUNTRY (4m   C   1961)
Depicts a Micmac Indian legend about Glooscap, a god believed to have lived in the mountains near Cape Blomidon, Nova Scotia. Includes scenery of Nova Scotia.   By Margaret Perry; CORNELL.

GO ASK ALICE (74m   C   1973)
A true story based on the diary of a teen-age girl caught in the
vicious web of drug addiction.   Alice suffers from shyness and a
weight problem.   She desires to be popular.   Her father, a teacher,
should have a better understanding of her, but can't quite reach her.
Starting in a new school, Alice finds loneliness unbearable.   She is
invited to a party and finds herself propelled head-first into drug
culture.   d. John Korty; METROM; SWANK.

GO GO GO (12m   C   si   1964)
"Tour-de-Force on man's activities, taken from a moving ve-
hicle and some stationary shots. "--M. M.   By Marie Menken;
FCOOP.

GO WEST YOUNG MAN (80m   B   1936)
Mae West portrays screen star Mavis Haden who goes on tour
to plug her latest film, Drifting Lady.   She ends up stranded in the
sticks, surrounded by men, but bound by her studio contract to avoid
entangling alliances for five years.   d. Henry Hathaway; s. w. , Mae
West; PARAMOUNT; UNIVE.

GODDESS, THE (105m   B   1958)
The story is of an unloved girl who rises to become one of
Hollywood's most prominent stars.   To appease her ravaged ego
and compensate for a grim, loveless childhood, Emily Ann Faulkner
(Kim Stanley) lets nothing interfere with her rise to fame.   The in-
evitable disillusionment that she must face at the top of her pro-
fession results in tragedy.   d. John Cromwell; p. Milton Perlman;
COLUMBIA; ABFI.

GOIN' TO TOWN (74m   B   1935)
As Cleo Moore, dance hall hostess, Mae West starts out by
winning a husband at dice and ends up standing in for an opera star
in a rendition of Saint-Saëns' Samson and Delilah that rivals the
last scene of A Night at the Opera for sheer hilarity.   She also
practices judo, draws like Wyatt Earp, and appears in pants for
the first time.   d. Alexander Hall; s. w. , Mae West; PARAMOUNT;
UNIVE.

GOING BACK; Whatcha Gonna Do? Series (15m   C   1973)
Dramatizes the specialized role of the rural visiting nurse and
one person's reasons for selecting this career.   Portrays the need
for rural visiting nurses and the training that is necessary to enter
this field.   Stresses that one should consider the needs of people,
affection for home regions, and desire for self-supervision before
deciding upon this career field.   WNVT; EBEC; IU.

GOING HOME (60m   C   1972)
In August, 1971, Adolph Mekas and his brother Jonas returned
to their birthplace in the village of Semeniskiai, Lithuania, and to
their family.   They left Lithuania as young men, destined for German labor camp from which they escaped in the last days of World
War II.   Going Home is less of a picture of life in Lithuania today

than it is a search for memories made real; its strength is in expressing feelings about personal and national identity.   d. Pola Chapelle, Adolfas Mekas; NYF.

GOING HOME SKETCHBOOK (3m   C   1975)
    A cine-poem to the filmmaker's family, based on a reunion with them.   The film begins with largely representational images and transforms into an abstract mood in which the mysterious quality of familial relations is explored.   By Mary Beams; SB.

GOLD DIGGERS OF 1933 (98m   B   1933)
    The opening number "We're in the Money," with Ginger Rogers and the chorus girls attired in nothing other than gigantic coins was a Depression-exorcising masterpiece.   It sets the tone for the rest of the film.   Dick Powell using a can opener to get into Ruby Keeler's metal dress is an explicit example of Busby Berkeley's (Hollywood director/choreographer between 1930-1954) mechanistic view of sex.   d. Mervyn LeRoy; WSA; UAS.

GOLD DIGGERS OF 1937 (101m   B   1937)
    The plot is about an insurance convention and a group of salesmen who, after meeting some Broadway chorus girls; suddenly are taken with an irresistible urge to back a show.   d. Lloyd Bacon; WSA; UAS.

GOLDA MEIR (52m   C   1972)
    Revealing interview with Israel's prime-minister, covering the milestones of her political career and the highlights of her people's struggle to create a new nation-state.   BBCTV; TL, UM.

GOLDA MEIR OF ISRAEL   see   GOLDA MEIR

GOLDEN AGE OF THE AUTOMOBILE, THE (30m   C   1971)
    Presents the people, places and ideas that put four wheels under the pedestrian and changed the pace of the world.   By Helen Jean Rogers, John Secondari; LCA.

GOLDEN EARRINGS (95m   B   1947)
    A steamy romantic melodrama in which Marlene Dietrich plays with talented abandon a voluptuous and uninhibited Gypsy who snares very-properly British Ray Milland in her sensual net.   d. Mitchell Leisen; s. w. Helen Deutsch, Abraham Polonsky, Frank Butler; PARAMOUNT; TWY.

GOOD EARTH, THE (42m   B   1937)
    An abridged version of the feature film which emphasizes the agricultural philosophy of the Chinese people and their dependence on the land for subsistence.   Points out that farming is a family project in China.   d. Sidney Franklin; ed. TFCS; MGM; IU, FL

GOOD EARTH: WOMAN SEQUENCE, THE (18m   B   1943)
    Excerpt from 1937 feature film.   Shows status of women in China before 1940, when they were chattels of their husbands and per-

formed the most menial and laborious tasks in the household and on the farm.   MGM; PAS.

GOOD GUYS ARE FASTER, THE (14m   C   1968)
Demonstrates how modern Bell System communications are being used in the nationwide fight against crime.   Shows how the law enforcement officer is backed up by men and machines to keep the "Good Guys" a step ahead.   By Susan Wayne for ATAT; BELSYS.

GOOD LIFE, THE (14m   B   1972)
Exploration of the Nearing family who farm organically in Harborside, Maine.   The husband is 91, an economist and lecturer, who was not permitted to teach in the early 1900's because of his opposition to World War I and to child labor.   Helen Nearing, 71, is a musician and also lectures with her husband.   Each summer many people visit the farm to learn about their farming methods.   p. Gisela Hoeld; DAYF.

GOODBYE, THE (3m   B   1975)
"Story of a man and a woman separated by war, rendered in hundreds of delicate line drawings using an Oxberry disc and registration bar."--YFD.   By Kathi Slather; YFD.

GOODBYE IN THE MIRROR (80m   B   1964   Italian/subtitled)
A dramatic feature filmed on location in Rome.   The film is centered around the adventures and illusions of three girls living abroad.   It explores the restless nature of these girls and their involvements in assuming the role of woman as hunter.   d. Storm De Hirsch; FCOOP; IMPF.

GOODBYE LYNN (22m   C   1972)
The story of Lynn is related visually in chronological order, from her first date with Ted to the late stages of pregnancy.   The sound track presents Lynn's highly personal, stream-of-consciousness comments about her dilemma, her emotional state, her indecision, her abandonment by Ted, the hostile reaction of her parents and the ambivalent feelings of her friends.   Near the end of the film, visual and audio threads of the story merge, revealing that Lynn has been recounting her story to the high school counselor.   She decides to enter a special school for unwed pregnant girls, but makes no long range decisions.   Lynn's future is still in doubt.   CENTRON; UILL, UMIS, USC.

GOODMAN (12m   B   n. d.)
Using mime, this film explores two women's capacities for laughter.   By Barbara Linkevitch; CCC.

GOOGOLPLEX (6m   B   1972)
A black and white film printed only in black and white.   It visually presents pictures consisting of grey shades of varying degrees.   A very definite program of editing based on well-known but little understood psychological experiments produces subjective color. At times the positive and negative images are adjacent.   In other

sequences they are interspersed with as many as six black frames
which are undetected by the viewer but which allow for dynamic
visual response.   The editing is so arranged as to allow the viewer
to superimpose images.   African music from Ghana.   "This viewer
also found Googolplex the six-minute computer-made compilation of
swiftly-moving patterns ... to be inventive, eye-catching examples
of technical professionalism. "--A. H. Weiler, New York Times.
By Lillian Schwartz, Ken Knowlton; LPL

GOT TO PUSH (11m B 1973)
     A film about garment workers in Boston, their perceptions about
themselves and their work, their struggle with internal racism and
their realizations about the system in which they live.   Good animated photography.   The sound track is simply women speaking without other analysis.   By Ellen Calmus, Liss Jeffrey; WFC; IRISF.

GOT TO TELL IT: A TRIBUTE TO MAHALIA JACKSON (34m   C
     1974)
     Studs Terkel provides the commentary to this portrait of the
late gospel singer, Mahalia Jackson.   The film covers her life
from her childhood in New Orleans, through the highlights of her
career, to her funeral in 1972 that was attended by more than
40, 000 people.   p. /d. Jules Victor Sherwin; PHOENIX, VFL

GOTHIC NOVEL: JANE EYRE AND WUTHERING HEIGHTS, THE
     (2/18-20m ea.   C n. d.   SFS)
     This program explores how the devices of the Gothic tradition
were incorporated by the Brontë sisters into their dramatic tales of
love, loyalty, and mystery.   EDC.

GRACE KELLY; Biography Series (26m B 1963)
     Views the life and deeds of Grace Kelly, the actress who mar-
ried Prince Rainier of Monaco in 1956.   WOLPER; SEF.

GRAND CONCERT, THE (102m C 1951 Russian/subtitled)
     Presents some of U. S. S. R. 's outstanding artists of opera and
ballet.   Features ballerinas Galina Ulanova, Olga Lepeshinskaya,
and others; opera stars Maria Masakova, Vera Davova, Alexander
Pirogov, Ivan Koslovsky; conductors Leonid Lavrovsky, R. Zasharov.
d. Vera Stroyeva; ABFL

GRAND HOTEL (112m B 1932)
     Story about a cross-section of life in an upper-crust hotel.
John Barrymore is a baron who gets involved in the lives of several
guests.   Chief among them is a Russian dancer (Greta Garbo), a
lonely inscrutable woman.   Other episodes feature Joan Crawford,
a secretary, who accepts her bosses' advances as a part of her job.
Based on a novel, Menschen im Hotel by Vicki Baum.   d. Edmund
Goulding; MGM; FL

GRANDMA MOSES (22m C 1950)
     America's best known primitive painter at age 99.   Scenes from
her busy, simple life on her farm in Upper New York State, the

special preparation given her painting boards and the artist at work.
Includes many of her paintings. FALCON; FIM; EMC, IU, PUR,
UILL, UM.

GRANDMOTHER FILM, THE (15m B n. d.)
    This film (which combines old-silent footage from the 20's, 30's,
and 40's with present day sync-sound footage) is a compassionate,
unsentimental portrait celebrating the strength, resilience and creative resourcefulness of an older woman. Her upper middle class
background is obvious in this film. By Ann Popkin; POPKIN.

GRASS ROOTS (54m C 1975)
    An illustration and analysis of a number of American communes,
including Twin Oaks Community in Virginia founded in 1966 and initially based on B. F. Skinner's book, Walden Two and the theories
of behaviorism. The film analyzes the process of continuous change
as practiced there, both in individual behavior and social organization.
Economy, division of work, sex roles, the individual relating to the
collective and the upbringing of children are given ample space.
Next shown is a community of anarchists in Maryland, then the network of loosely-connected communities in Mendocino County, California. Finally the Lama Foundation, a community based on various
religious disciplines, is viewed through the experience of a boy not
integrated into the lifestyle of the community. p. /d. Luciano Mar-
tinengo, Thomas Wahlberg; PHOENIX.

GRASSHOPPER AND THE ANT, THE (10m B 1930's)
    A fairy tale in silhouette animation based on live shadow play.
The story of foolish Mr. Grasshopper and wise Mrs. Ant, based on
fable by La Fontaine. BBCTV; by Lotte Reiniger; CEA, MGH.

GREASER'S PALACE (91m C 1972)
    Scatological Passion Play done in the form of an anti-western
western, with a hip messiah coming out of the desert. p. Cyma
Rubin; d. Robert Downey; HERALD; CIV.

GREAT ADVENTURE SERIES see HARRIET TUBMAN AND THE
    UNDERGROUND RAILROAD

GREAT BALLERINA (6m B 1950)
    Features the great Russian ballerina Galina Ulanova dancing a
portion of Tschaikowsky's Swan Lake. ABFI; UILL.

GREAT BATTLE OF THE VOLGA (75m B 1945 English narration)
    A documentary, filmed on the spot by 150 army cameramen, of
the defense of Stalingrad and the routing of the Nazis. By Maria
Slavinskaya; ABFI.

GREAT CATHERINE (99m C 1968)
    Presents Catherine the Great, the notorious Russian empress of
much character but few morals. Portrays the stuffy English officer
who is the object of her amorous advances. d. Gordon Fleming;
WSA; ABFI, BF.

GREAT EXPECTATIONS (24m   C   1975)
Emphasizes the importance of good nutrition during pregnancy and while breast feeding.   Through narration and comments, experts and young women describe and demonstrate how they make good nutrition a part of their lives.   d. /p. Jamil Simon; SFNE; UW; UMIS.

GREAT GODDESS, THE (17m   C   1972)
History of matriarchies.   Uses images found in art works from 5000-500 B. C. in Anatolia, Crete and Etruria.   By Anne Shellabarger; SHELLABARGER.

GREAT GRAND MOTHER (29m   C   1975)
Depicts the lives of the pioneer women who settled Western Canada in the 1800's.   Includes re-enactments of diaries, letters, books, and newspaper accounts, as well as interviews with women who recall those days.   NFBC; EMC.

GREAT RADIO COMEDIANS, THE (90m   C   1972)
"The lost art of radio comedy remembered by George Burns, Edgar Bergen and Charlie McCarthy, Jack Benny, Jim Jordan (Fibber McGee), Bing Crosby and the original Allen's Alley cast from the Fred Allen program; with classic examples of their art. "-- P. M. A.   By Perry Miller Adato; ed. Slesin Aviva; MGH.

GREAT THEMES OF LITERATURE SERIES   see   MAN AND WOMAN

GREEKS: IN SEARCH OF MEANING; Western Civilization: Majesty and Madness Series, The (26m   C   1971)
Recreates the concerns and achievements of the Greeks of Athens in the 5th century B. C.   Reveals the universal struggle with the problems of freedom and the meaning of life.   By Helen Jean Rogers, John Secondari; LCA.

GREENE VALLEY GRANDPARENTS (10m   B   1972)
Greene Valley is a state institution for the mentally retarded in Tennessee.   The grandparents' program is one which provides money to pay old people in the community to act as aides at the facility. The program provides a useful and rewarding job for the grandparents, relief for the over-burdened regular staff and a warm relationship for the inmates.   CFSF.

GREENSLEEVES (4m   C   n. d.)
"Pure color forms float lyrically across the screen in this abstract film exercise to music of 'Greensleeves. ' "--CFS.   By Lynn Fayman; CFS.

GREY GARDENS (94m   B   1975)
A filmed account of the life of two women, Edith Bouvier Beale, now 79, and her daughter, Little Edie, 56.   The aristocratic mother and daughter lock out the world and spend two-and-a-half decades in a dilapidated seaside mansion stoking lost fantasies, momentary glories, and mutual antagonism.   They flutter in and out of reality,

playing with elusive memories like children hammering clay while
the horrors of misspent beauty and intelligence--of misspent lives--
thunder home at us.   By David Maysles, Albert Maysles, Ellen
Hovde, Muffie Meyer; MAYSLES; PRI.

GRIEF THERAPY (19m   C   1976)
     Gripping and remarkably powerful document of the work of Dr.
Donald Ramsey, University of Amsterdam, in treating a woman
whose grief at the death of her 12-year-old daughter finds her in a
suicidal state more than two years later.   Particularly interesting
is his probing into and later use of certain signals--such as a
familiar song--that trigger the patient's grief.   CBSTV from "60
Minutes. " CAROUSEL; EMC.

GROWING PAINS (13m   C   1973)
     Adolescents ask questions about sexuality, masturbation, dating
and love.   The physiological aspects of puberty, menstruation and
reproduction are also discussed.   A gentle film to help ease young
people through the critical years of adolescent growth.   By Noel
Nosseck.   PF.

GROWING UP FEMALE: AS SIX BECOME ONE (60m   B   1971)
     Describes the socialization of the American woman through a
personal look into the lives of six females.   Their ages range from
four to 35, and the backgrounds vary from poor Black to upper
middle-class white.   Many forces shape them: their parents, teachers, guidance counselors, the media, pop music and the institution
of marriage.   By Julia Reichert, James Klein; NDF; MSU, PUR,
UM, UW.

GROWING UP TOGETHER: FOUR TEEN MOTHERS AND THEIR
     BABIES (55m   C   1974)
     A documentary in four segments featuring four teen-age mothers
who are raising their children as single parents.   With no script and
no rehearsal, the young women talk about their lives and experiences
in their own words.   A good discussion film on the realities of being
a single parent and the developmental needs of children.   CROMMIE;
UM, UW, UMIS.

GUACAMOLE (10m   C   1976)
     "A short cine-poem whose meter is in the tragic rather than
celebratory mode.   It focuses on the life/death polarity of fiesta
and bullfight, rendered in a deeply painterly texture, where slow-
motion and blue tones give it a lyrical melancholia. "--Anthony
Reveaux, Artweek.   By Chick Strand; SB.

GUALE (59m   C   1976)
     The story of the Georgia coast, its natural history, its people
and its future.   d. Albert Scardino; p. Marjorie M. Scardino, Albert Scardino; SCHRON.

GUERRILLA COMMERCIAL, THE (1m   C   1973)
     "A studio production employing an all-woman crew.   About

discrimination faced by women filmmakers. "--A. R. K.   By Alexis
Rafael Krasilovsky; RAFAEL.

GUIDE FOR THE MARRIED MAN, A (91m   C   1967   Reg. /Scope)
     A philanderer appoints himself teacher to educate a reluctant hus-
band in the art of deception.   Based on the idea that a married man
should have extra-marital activity to keep his wife happy.   d. Gene
Kelly; FOX; FL

GUN CRAZY (DEADLY IS THE FEMALE) (87m   B   1950)
     Gun Crazy is an exhilarating tribute to reckless love and non-
stop action.   There are no excuses given for gun craziness--it's
just crazy.   In no film has the American mania for youth, action,
sex and crime been so immediately portrayed.   Gun Crazy does not
offer much reflection or perspective, but, unlike anything else, it
puts you in the driver's seat.   d. John Lewis; UAS; HCW.

GWENDOLYN BROOKS (30m   B   1967)
     Introduction to the poetry and personality of Gwendolyn Brooks,
a Pulitzer Prize winning Black poet.   A view of Chicago, the city
that provides the source for most of her material.   She describes
her method of working, how she approaches poetry, and the things
in life she finds most pleasant.   IU; EMC.

GYMNASTICS U. S. A. (27m   C   1977)
     Shows the best men and women gymnasts in the U. S. performing
in the qualifying competition for membership on the 1976 Olympic
team, and also shows some younger athletes who may be champions
in the future.   Illustrates, often in lyrical slow motion, numerous
routines for each of the principal men's and women's events.   Close-
ups show many of the techniques of individual athletes in detail.
EMC.

GYNECOLOGICAL SELF-HELP
     A lecture given by Lolly and Jeanne Hirsch on gynecological
self-examination.   Talk includes slides, film, a demonstration of
examination, and a discussion of menstrual extraction.   NFTL

HAD YOU LIVED THEN: LIFE IN A GOLD MINING CAMP 1850's
     (17m   C   1976)
     An old man reminisces about what his father told him about his
greatest adventure--the California gold rush.   Old photos, recreated
scenes taken in the area, views of ghost towns and scenes of deserted mines are combined with music of that time.   Gives a factual
picture of an era in U. S. history.   d. Maria Moraites, Dean Lyras;
PARACO.

HAIRY KARI (11m   C   n. d.)
     "A non-descript member of a sunworshippers' cult sacrifices
his long hair ... for the pot of gold.   The end of the rainbow is in
the Big City where he finds strange employment.   A comical-tragical-

political-pastoral-satirical epic of the absurd. "--CCC.   By Christine Pihl, Richard Harkness; CCC.

HALF OF HEAVEN (29m   C   n. d.   VIDEO)
   Two short original dramas performed in Cantonese about women's issues in Chinatown, San Francisco.   KQEDTV.

HAND TINTING (6m   C   si   1967)
   "A study of poor Black and white girls at a job corps center; brought from rural areas to be educated in typing.   Here you see displaced children. "--J. W.   By Joyce Wieland; FCOOP.

HANDLING MARITAL CONFLICTS (14m   C   1965)
   Explains that some conflict is inevitable in marriage and demonstrates constructive ways to handle it.   Shows two types of conflict. MGH;   USC.

HANDS (2m   B   1971)
   "A thumb, a finger, two fingers, a hand all move in a fascinating way, impelling the audience to take part. "--Programme, Women and Film Festival, Toronto.   By Karen Johnson; SB.

HANDSTRINGS (5m   C   n. d.)
   "The immensity of all landscape is reduced in the mind to the scale of the human body. ...   Contemplates the mystery of similarities. "--CCC.   By Barbara Scharres; CCC.

HANSEL AND GRETEL (10m   B   1930's)
   A fairy tale in silhouette animation based on live shadow play. A classic tale by the Brothers Grimm, gracefully brought to life. By Lotte Reiniger, BBCTV; CEA, MGH.

HAPPY BIRTHDAY I'M FORTY (45m   C   1974)
   A woman looks back on her 40-year evolution into a self-sufficient artist and a free individual.   Surreal imagery.   By Alida Walsh; PHOENIX.

HAPPY BIRTHDAY NORA (6m   B   n. d.)
   "Girl on her 20th birthday wanting something to happen--her fantasies. "--L. F.   By Linda Feferman; FEFERMAN.

HAPPY MOTHER'S DAY, A (26m   B   1964)
   Documents in cinéma-vérité style how Mary Ann Fischer, a quiet housewife and mother in Aberdeen, South Dakota, is suddenly swept up in a whirlwind of commercial, civic, and media exploitation after she gives birth to quintuplets.   A telling comment on commercialism and American society's notion of a woman's greatest achievement.   Sparse and ironic narration.   By Joyce Chopra, Richard Leacock; PENBAK; EMC.

HARD, FAST AND BEAUTIFUL (60m   B   1951)
   The conflict between a young tennis player and her domineering mother is visually paralleled by spectacular tennis court battles.

For the young woman, marriage and career are irreconcilable.
Tension builds between the two, finally erupting in a violent and
powerful confrontation. Lupino brings her feminine perspective to
realistic films of American life in the 50's.   d. Ida Lupino; RKO;
IVY.

HARDMAN QUILT: PORTRAIT OF AN AGE, THE (10m C 1975)
    Tells the story of the creation of the famous Hardman quilt
which reflects life 100 years ago and is now considered a masterpiece
of American folk art.   This quilt is on exhibit at the Pioneer Museum and Haggin Galleries in Stockton, California.   Mrs. Edwin Hardman spent months of planning this quilt in addition to the time spent
making it.   By Hans Halberstadt; LP.

HARLAN COUNTY, U. S. A. (103m C 1976)
    Chronicles the efforts of 180 coal mining families to win a
United Mine Workers contract at the Brookside Mine in Harlan
County, Kentucky.   The strike began in 1974.   This was the first
major confrontation in this county since the bloody union organizing
battles in the 1930's when five men were killed.   p. /d. Barbara
Kopple; a. d. Anne Lewis; CIV.

HARLEM WEDNESDAY (10m C 1959)
    Uses paintings of Gregorio Prestopino (and a jazz band musical
background composed by Benny Carter) to suggest activities of an
ordinary mid-week Harlem day.   By Faith Hubley, John Hubley;
MGH, FI.

HARLEQUIN (24m B 1931)
    An animated film based on live shadow play by the filmmaker.
The amorous escapades of a Casanova harlequin set to 17th-century
music.   By Lotte Reiniger; CEA.

HARMONY (8m C n. d.)
    A witty animated film that describes a few of the ways men and
women take on sex roles to help them achieve "harmony. "   VFI,
WOMBAT.

HARRIET TUBMAN AND THE UNDERGROUND RAILROAD; You Are
    There Series (21m C 1972)
    Harriet Tubman stands out as a woman of rare courage and
abilities among the thousands of anonymous men and women who
helped runaway slaves to safety.   The film follows one of her most
dangerous trips leading a group of four slaves out of Maryland.
Also explored is the Fugitive Slave Law and the pro and con slavery
arguments.   CBSTV; BFA; UILL.

HARRIET TUBMAN AND THE UNDERGROUND RAILROAD; Great
    Adventure Series (54m B r1964)
    Dramatic portrayal of the first 19 trips into the South before
the Civil War, between 1850-60, by Harriet Tubman to lead runaway slaves along the underground railway to freedom in the North.
Excellent depiction of a strong and important Black woman and her

leading role in the struggle against slavery.   Explores the Fugitive
Slave Law and arguments for and against slavery.   CBSTV; MGH,
BFA; BF, EMC, FSU, PAS, UC, UM.

HAT: IS THIS WAR NECESSARY?, THE (18m C 1964)
    Explores in animation the need for a world legal authority to
establish disarmament and settle international disputes peaceably.
While animals move freely across the border, the two border guards
suspiciously guard their ground.   A dispute over a hat accidentally
dropped across the border leads them into conversation, and each
soldier begins to identify with the needs, loves, memories, and
ideas of the other.   By Faith Hubley, John Hubley; MGH; CWU,
EMC, IU, OSU, PAS, SCC, UILL, WSU.

HATTIE (9m B 1975)
    Because she had a life full of activity and many interests, Hat-
tie, at 76, finds her life intolerably lonely and useless.   In an interview, she speaks with much nostalgia of her family, now dead,
and her involvement in productive community activities.   Now, she
can't afford to join clubs.   She spends her time with trivial housework and spending long hours walking around town.   p. Film Australia; AUIS.

HAVE A HEALTHY BABY (19m C 1969)
    Presents the development and needs of an unborn baby, im-
pressing upon young women and mothers-to-be the importance of
good prenatal care.   Animation depicts fertilization of the egg, development of the embryo, and growth of the fetus.   Special emphasis
is placed upon good nutrition and the first 12 weeks as the critical
period in infant development.   CF; UILL.

HAVING A SECTION IS HAVING A BABY (35m C 1977 SFS)
    Provides information about all aspects of Caesarean childbirth,
which is much more than a surgical procedure--it is the birth of a
child which can be shared and enjoyed.   Topics covered are indications for having a section, determining fetal maturity, hospital admitting procedures, preoperative procedures, incision, birth, removal of placenta, suturing, examination of new born, presence of
father in the operating room, contact of parents with newborn, postpartum recovery and parents' feelings before and after birth.   CSEC;
POLYMORPH.

HEAD OF THE FAMILY (105m C 1968 dubbed)
    This somber Italian film depicts the hazards of devotion to the
concepts of "family," as a woman dedicated to helping others sacrifices, and ultimately wears herself down.   The heroism of her al-
legiance to her man and children goes unappreciated until she is
finally separated from them by her nervous breakdown.   d. Nanny
Loy; IVY, ROA, UNF.

HEALTHCARING FROM OUR END OF THE SPECULUM (32m B
    1976)
    The history of women's health care, up through the growing

movement toward self-help, is interwoven with the stories of women who are still experiencing poor, insensitive care.   d. Denise Bostrom, Jane Warrenbrand; WMM.

HEARTBREAK KID, THE (104m   C   1973)
     A story of a Jewish boy from New York who falls in love with Cybil Shepherd, a perfect shicksa, during his honeymoon in Miami, while his new wife is suffering from sun poisoning.   d. Elaine May; FOX; FL

HEARTS AN' SOLES (5m   C   1956)
     A charming and rollicking little film which tells a romantic story with shoes dancing all by themselves.   A pair of bright tan oxfords meets a pert pair of red pumps; mutual attraction is the result, etc.   The tale concludes happily.   Accompanied by a lilting tune.   By Alma Duncan, Audrey McLaren; FIM.

HEAT'S ON, THE (79m   B   1943)
     Sashaying and purring, Mae West plays the turbulent musical comedy star caught in the intrigues of two rival crooked producers. d. Gregory Ratoff; s. w. Fitzroy Davis; COLUMBIA; SWANK.

HEIRESS, THE (115m   B   1949)
     This widely acclaimed version of Henry James' Washington Square is by far the best version of the novelist's work to appear on the screen.   The story deals with a spinster courted by a glib fortune-hunter under the observing eye of her very protective father. d. William Wyler; PARAMOUNT; UNIVE.

HELEN HAYES--PORTRAIT OF AN AMERICAN ACTRESS (90m   C   1973)
     Helen Hayes started her career at the age of six and here re-lives her achievements and trials.   She provides an insight into the American theatre and screen from the early 1900's until the present. Included are many scenes from her plays and films.   By Nathan Kroll; PHOENIX, VFL

HELEN KELLER (15m   C   1969)
     The famous story of a child, left both blind and deaf by a child-hood disease, who grew from an unruly, frightened phantom--"living in a no-world"--into a sensitive human being.   Her writings and work for the blind and handicapped are known the world over. Helen Keller and Anne Sullivan explore what it is to be a person and express the belief that no one is unworthy or incapable of being helped.   MGH; OKSU, UILL.

HELEN KELLER; Biography Series (26m   B   1965)
     Tells the story of Helen Keller, left totally blind and deaf by a childhood disease, who became a well-known author, lecturer and humanitarian.   WOLPER; MMA, OKSU, SEF.

HELEN KELLER AND HER TEACHER (27m   C   1969)
     Explores the amazing and beautiful relationship between Helen

Keller and Anne Sullivan. With touch as their only avenue of communication, Anne and Helen learned together the joy of realizing
one's self as a feeling and thinking entity able to communicate and
to love others. An expanded version of an earlier film. MGH;
EMC, OKSU, UILL.

HELEN KELLER IN HER STORY (45m B 1956)
    The inspirational story of Helen Keller from birth until death--
how she overcame the tremendous handicap of being blind, deaf, and
mute. Includes reminiscences, newsreel, and interview footage.
Narrated by Katherine Cornell. By Nancy Hamilton; DEROACH;
MMA, PHOENIX; PAS, UILL, UM, UU.

HELEN TAMIRIS IN HER NEGRO SPIRITUALS (17m B 1959)
    Records the American dance pioneer, Helen Tamiris, as she
performs some of her early choreography of modern dance, a suite
of five solo dances created from the Negro spirituals "Go Down
Moses," "Swing Low," "Git on Board," "Crucifixion," and "Joshua
Fit the Battle of Jericho." Introduction by John Martin, dance critic
of the New York Times. NAGTAM; MGH; IU, UILL.

HELL NO CUTS (25m B 1973)
    A documentary on why women get caught up in the welfare sys-
tem and what it means to be a welfare mother. Although a local
issue film, the locale being Chicago, scarcity of any films about people organizing against welfare makes this film relevant for audiences
in most cities. By Margie Keller; KELLER.

HELP WANTED--WOMEN NEED APPLY (61 slides with script)
    Shows and describes women in a variety of jobs--flood control
engineer, attorney, chemist, accountant, radio equipment installer
and repairer, photographer and others. By Jim Farron; Civil Service Commission, Dallas, Texas.

HELPING FROGS AVOID THEIR DEATH (3m C n. d.)
    "Italian nostalgia."--CCC. By Dorothy Wiley; CCC.

HERSTORY (9m C 1971)
    Through the use of dramatic colorful drawings on hand-turned
paper film, songs, rhythm, music and narration, the San Francisco
Women's Street Theatre gives a short history of women's struggles
from pre-history to the present. SFN.

HESTER STREET (91m B 1975)
    Tells the story of a Russian Jew who comes to America ahead
of his wife. He is quickly assimilated and in the process becomes
enchanted with another, more modern, woman. Finally his wife
arrives, steeped in the customs of the old country, and a charming
story unfolds as the couple resolve their problems. d. Joan Mick-
lin Silvers; CIV.

HEY DOC (25m C 1971)
    Story of Dr. Ethel Allen, a Black physician, who serves the

people of North Philadelphia's ghetto.   Determined and strong, she
fills the roles of medical advisor, confessor and friend to addicts,
aged and others as she goes through the streets of the slums and
works in her office.   d. Alvin A. Hollander; WCAUTV; CAROUSEL.

HEY! WHAT ABOUT US?; Sex Role Stereotyping in Schools, A
   Series (15m   C   1974)
   Fresh insight into sex-role stereotyping in physical activities in
schools.   Shows four situations for purposes of comparison which
challenge the usual conceptions of "masculinity" and "femininity" by
showing children engaged in activities typical of the opposite sex.
WGBHTV; IU; EMC, UM.

HIDE 'N' SEEK (30m   C   1977)
   A thought-provoking film on peer relationships and pressures.
By Martha Moran; COUNTR.

HIGH ON DRAG (6m   B   1974)
   A comedy of two men in women's clothes acting out their fan-
tasy of being women, including a rape and a hitchhiking scene.   By
Constance Beeson; BEESON.

HIGH SCHOOL (75m   B   1968)
   This documentary looks at a large high school in Philadelphia.
We see teachers oppressing students in a variety of typical situations,
but perhaps the most revealing moments are those that show the differing ways women and men students are programmed.   Look closely
at the home economics and assembly scenes.   Also, watch the male
gynecologist teach the football team "how not to get girls pregnant."
To add a bit of color to his speech, he starts discussing women's
vaginas.   By Frederick Wiseman; ZPH; UW.

HIGH UP DOLL, THE (11m   B   r1962)
   The increased concern over redefining sexual roles in society
is embraced by this symbolic fable.   A mother refuses to buy her
little girl a doll she wants and the girl has fantasies of cruelly being
disinherited.   The girl then sits on her father's lap, playing the seductive little chippie and the father the lecherous filthy-rich man of
the world paying for her charms.   So, she goes on her way and
purchases the doll.   After the purchase of the doll, she does a ballet with it.   The doll diminishes as she runs home.   Her last and
ritual act is to place the doll on a pedestal, not to play house with
it.   p. /d. Val Ginter, Robert Ginter.   MMA.

HIGHWAY (6m   C   1959)
   Captures the power, exhilaration and rhythm of driving along a
modern highway from dawn to night.   By Hilary Harris; FIM.

HIROSHIMA, MON AMOUR (88m   B   1959   French/subtitled)
   This film embodies dialectics between male and female in which
the opposing forces, by the very nature of their opposition, are
fused by a creative understanding into a greater whole.   Adapted
from novel by Margeurite Duras.   d. Alain Resnais; s.w. Margeurite Duras; CORINF, BF, KP.

HIS GIRL FRIDAY (92m B 1940)
Based on Ben Hecht's The Front Page. One of Hawk's best efforts in the Bringing Up Baby tradition of screwball farce. Roz
Russell plays an ace reporter assigned to expose a politically motivated execution. Cary Grant proves his unique talent as virile comic antagonist. d. Howard Hawks; COLUMBIA; SWANK.

HISTORY; American Memoir, The (Series) (29m B 1961)
Mention the 1920's, says Dr. Dodd, and a whole chain of images
is evoked: raucous jazz, champagne baths, John Held flappers, gang
killings--in short, an era of rampant, glamorous decadence. Further, it is only when we view history from many vantage points that
we achieve an undistorted, objective account and gain a perspective
that avoids the pitfalls of our cherished stereotypes. WTTWTV; IU.

HISTORY MAKERS OF THE 20TH CENTURY see WINDSORS, THE

HISTORY MAKERS SERIES see FIRST LADY OF THE WORLD:
ELEANOR ROOSEVELT

HISTORY OF MISS ANNIE ANDERSON, THE (30m C 1976)
At 94 years of age, Annie Anderson is one of America's last
pioneers. For many years, she has been writing a personal history
which has now been made into a film dramatizing the adventure and
struggle experienced by both men and women in their westward push
in the late 19th century. From a life that spans nearly a century,
we get a unique, inside look at the story of a woman who grew up
as the only child in a polygamous Mormon family. Married three
times, the mother of many children, and often the only provider of
the family, Annie Anderson has emerged as a singularly independent
woman of today. By Diane Orr, KUTV; SOHO.

HISTORY OF THE MOTION PICTURE SERIES see GIRLS IN
DANGER

HOARDER, THE (8m C 1972)
A bird-land fantasy by animation. A bluejay takes whatever his
beak can grasp--berries, birds' eggs and nests--into his secret
cache. Even the sun is unsafe from his consuming greed. There
is a moral tucked away, however; bluejay learns his lesson, and
bird-land returns to normal. By Evelyn Lambart; NFBC; MGH.

HOLDING (15m C 1971)
A romantic and impressionistic interpretation of a lesbian relationship. Explores the fantasies and realities of two women falling
in love with each other. The two women relate in a variety of sexual and non-sexual ways. By Constance Beeson; NSF; MMRC, NLC,
IE, GP, SB.

HOLE, THE (16m C 1963)
An animated fantasy about moles, missiles and mankind. The
story of two construction workers, talking deep below the streets of
New York, who interpret the sound of an accident as a bomb explo-

sion.   This film emphasizes the importance of disarmament.   By
Faith Hubley, John Hubley; MGH, FI; EMC.

HOLLY NEAR AND JEFF LANGLEY: SONGWRITER'S NOTEBOOK
  (30m   C   n. d.   VIDEO)
  Holly Near sings and talks about her songs, accompanied on the
piano by Jeff Langley.   KQEDTV.

HOLLYWOOD AND STARS SERIES   see   ODYSSEY OF RITA HAY-
  WORTH

HOMAGE TO MAGRITTE (10m   C   r1975)
  Evokes the image of Magritte through the language of film.
d. /p. Anita Thatcher; THATCHER.

HOMBRE (11m   C   1967   Reg. /Scope)
  A character study of a white man who was raised among the
Apaches and then forced back into the white man's world.   d. Mar-
tin Ritt; co-scripted by Harriet Frank; FOX; FL

HOME BORN BABY (47m   C   n. d.)
  A video-film documenting and de-mystifying childbirth.   The
film graphically presents the tranquility of home birth, including
labor, crowning and birth.   The doctor, midwife, and father all
help just enough, but not too much.   By Sally Pugh, Ralph Diamant;
CCC, IE.

HOME MOVIE (12m   C/B   1973)
  Using a mix of home-movie footage of the filmmaker's childhood
and more recent footage, this autobiographical film makes a political
and personal statement on lesbianism.   Images portray, often comically, the realities and stereotypes of lesbian life.   Also touches on
women's liberation.   By Jan Oxenberg; WFC; MMRC, IRISF.

HOMEFRONT, THE (25m   B   n. d.)
  A powerful documentary about housing and rent strikes around
New York City and what women organizers can do when pushed
against the wall by the system.   These people show gut commitment
to their families and community.   Explores the fear of the people
who can't bring themselves to join the strikes--fear of loss of job
and home, fear of the authorities.   Presented honestly and compas-
sionately.   By Jenny Goldberg, Harvey Schaktman, John Kraus;
GOLDBERG.

HOMESPUN (22m   C   1971)
  Mandelina Oberg is a 70-year-old Minnesota farm wife and an
immigrant from Sweden.   She shows how she works industriously
and happily at the ancient craft of weaving homespun cloth.   Using
handmade tools, many of them brought over from Sweden many years
before, she shears an Angora goat, prepares the wool, and weaves
colorful cloth.   Each step is explained by Mandelina herself.   p.
Elmer Albinson, Harry Webb; IFB.

HOMOSEXUALITY AND LESBIANISM: "GAY OR STRAIGHT--IS
   THERE A CHOICE?" (24m   C   1976)
   A number of personable young people describe their feelings
about their homosexuality and the stereotypes associated with their
way of life.   Well balanced, free of sensationalism.   HL; DA; EMC.

HOMOSEXUALITY IN MEN AND WOMEN (58m   B   1966)
   According to this film, where adverse influences in a person's
childhood experience have caused him to fear the opposite sex, his
need for warm and meaningful relationships may lead him to homosexuality.   One-twentieth of the population of the Western world is
in this category.   Researched in Britain, this study interviews homosexual men and women of all ages in England and Holland, deals
with their circumstances, their attitudes, their problems.   RDFL;
IU; UILL.

HOMOSEXUALITY--WHAT ABOUT McBRIDE (15m   C   1974)
   Presents a discussion by two boys of the possibility of their mutual friend's alleged homosexuality.   Deals with prejudices, beliefs
and feelings about homosexuality.   CRM; MGH.

HOMOSEXUALS, THE (45m   B   1967)
   Views homosexuality as it exists in the U. S.   Presents views
expressed by psychologists, clergy, police and lawyers.   Provides
insight by showing interviews with homosexuals themselves.   CBSTV;
IU.

HOPE IS NOT A METHOD (15m   C   1973)
   Briefly covers seven birth-control techniques: diaphragm, intrauterine device, pill, condom, spermicidal chemicals, withdrawal,
and rhythm.   Lists both their advantages and disadvantages.   Reproductive anatomy and menstrual cycles are explained in animation to
help understand contraception.   PPASYR, CRESSP; BU, UILL, UIO,
UM.

HOT DRY DESERT (16m   C   1964)
   A day in the desert to study its unique eco-system.   For ele-
mentary and junior high school.   By Geraldine Byers, Justin Byers;
BFA.

HOUSE IS NOT A HOME, A (95m   B   1964)
   Examines the life of one of the most fabulous figures of the
world's oldest profession.   Follows Polly Adler's life from an immigrant worker to becoming friend and confidante of not only underworld big wigs, but social leaders, businessmen, politicians, writers
and artists.   More than an account of this most famous brothel-
keeper, the film gives a perceptive and informed look at the most
bizarre eras in American history--the Roaring Twenties and the
Bizarre Thirties.   The story of "Madam" is legendary but her life
was not one of happiness.   d. Russell Rouse; AVCO; ABFI, SELECT,
WHOLFC.

HOW ABOUT YOU?   A FILM ON BIRTH CONTROL AND SEXUALITY
(22m   B   1973)
Factual information about the female body and the major methods of birth control: the pill, the intrauterine device, the diaphragm,
foam and condom.   Teen-age sexuality as expressed by young people
discussing their sexual feelings and experiences.   Deals only with
heterosexuality, with no mention of homosexuality or celibacy as alternatives.   By Bonnie Friedman, Marilyn Mulford, Deborah Shaffer;
FSMP; TEXFM; UM.

HOW BEAVER STOLE FIRE (12m   C   1972)
A re-creation of an American Indian myth on the origin of fire,
using special sand animation technique.   By Caroline Leaf; NFBC;
PARACO.

HOW CLOSE CAN YOU GET? (10m   C   n. d.)
"No matter how close you get to another person, you are still
alone. "   This belief of Ann's leads into an intense discussion of
what people expect from marriage.   Should the wife stay at home
and keep house?   Can you be independent and growing while married?   TELEKETICS; ROA.

HOW LIFE BEGINS (48m   C   1968)
Introduces the concepts of birth by providing a comprehensive
picture of reproduction from the most minute one-celled organisms
to human beings.   Many species of animals, birds and fish are
shown in natural settings, by means of realistic drawings, close-up
photography and microscopic views.   Shows candid scenes of the
birth of a human baby.   A short sequence considers the anatomy of
the cell itself which establishes the definitiveness of genes.   States
that each species has its own unique way of creating life.   Narrated
by Eddie Albert.   ABCTV, JPIP; MGH; UILL, UMIS.

HOW THE WORLD SEES WOMEN; Girls and Women Series (30m
B   1971)
Student group performs a theatre piece entitled "Women Are
Like Elephants, " which spoofs statements about women by writers
as varied as Aristotle, Rousseau, Samuel Johnson and Abbie Hoffman.   Panel discusses children's literature, magazines, advertisements and television, and concludes that the media have been guilty
of presenting stereotypes of women to their disadvantage.   Suggests
how women can escape these negative images and influences.   p.
UMITV; PAS, UM.

HOW TO DO: THE CREATIVE WEAVER SHIRLEY MAREIN (C
n. d.   SFS)
Weaving on and off the loom is discussed and demonstrated by
Shirley Marein, offering a look at a wide variety of tools, techniques, and materials.   Essential for beginners and a source of
new ideas for the advanced student.   Recommended by Booklist,
May 1974.   EDC.

HOW TO DRAW A CAT (3m   C   1973)
Just that: how to draw a cat.   By Pola Chapelle; FCOOP.

HOW TO KEEP FROM CATCHING V. D. (19m   C   1971)
Presents information on venereal disease--its symptoms, effects, treatment and preventive measures.   Dr. Walter H. Smartt,
Chief of the Division of V. D. Control, Los Angeles, talks about
gonorrhea and syphilis with compelling authority and objectivity.
In a straightforward manner, he emphasizes prevention as a critically important means of controlling V. D.   Concludes with Dr.
Smartt answering questions posed by his young audience.   A 44-page
teacher reference guide is available from: Couillard Associates,
142 Paseo de Gracia, Redondo Beach, Cal. 90277.   JACOA; OFF;
UILL, USC.

HOW TO MAKE A LINOLEUM BLOCK PRINT; Creative Craft Series
(13m   C   1955)
Discusses how to make a linoleum block print and shows how to
block print Christmas cards, home furnishings and clothing.   By
Ruby Niebauer; BFA.

HOW TO MAKE A MASK; Creative Craft Series (11m   C   1954)
Four elementary steps in making a mask are shown.   The ways
of creating facial features and expressions are demonstrated.   By
Ruby Niebauer; BFA.

HOW TO MAKE A PUPPET; Creative Craft Series (12m   C   1953)
Describes the steps in creating a puppet and shows the several
kinds of puppets.   By Ruby Niebauer; BFA.

HOW TO MAKE A STENCIL PRINT; Creative Craft Series (12m   C
1961)
Introduces simple ways to cut and print original stencils as an
approach to creative design.   Demonstrates the use of tempera paint
on different textured paper and printing on cloth with permanent textile paints.   By Ruby Niebauer; BFA.

HOW TO MAKE A WOMAN (58m   C   1972)
Adaptation of feminist play that dramatically and symbolically depicts the difficulties facing a woman who tries to create her own
identity in a male-supremist society.   Uses a fast-paced, overtly
propagandistic, "Marat-Sade-like" style to show how two men use
typical manipulative stratagems and put-downs to mold a pair of
women into various submissive roles.   A satirical, penetrating, and
at times shrill statement that will outrage some viewers but will
be revelatory to others.   Excellent for discussion on the reasons
for and the goals of the women's liberation movement.   d. /p. Miriam Weinstein, Alvin Fiering, Bobbi Ausubel; POLYMORPH; EMC.

HOW TO MAKE PAPIER-MACHE ANIMALS; Creative Craft Series
(12m   C   1954)
Demonstrates the steps involved in making papier-mâché animals.
Explains how to decorate the animal forms.   By Ruby Niebauer; BFA.

HOW TO MAKE POTATO PRINTS; Creative Craft Series (12m   C
1955)
Elementary school students demonstrate the steps involved in
making potato prints.   By Ruby Niebauer; BFA.

HOW TO MARRY A MILLIONAIRE (96m   C   1953)
Three luscious models have a simple philosophy: it's just as
easy to love a rich man as a poor one.   To get that rich man, the
trio set themselves up in a luxurious penthouse.   But before the
film and the laughs are over, the trio soon get confused with the
actual choice of male victims.   d. Jean Negulesco; FOX; BF, CVE.

HOW TO SAY NO TO A RAPIST--AND SURVIVE (52m   C   1974)
Focuses on the rape prevention program developed by Frederick
Storaska, Executive Director of the National Organization for the
Prevention of Rape and Assault (NOPRA).   Recorded on the spot
during one of Storaska's public appearances.   Basic to his program
is recognition of the human element and emotional makeup of both
assailant and victim.   Throughout, he puts rape and assault in the
perspective of contemporary society--impersonality, alienation and
violence.   LCA; NIU, SCC, TWY, UILL.

HOW WE GOT THE VOTE (55m   C   1975)
The remarkable saga of how women achieved suffragism.   It is
an epic of determined, organized willpower, of fighting husbands,
clergymen, senators, presidents, and a set of social traditions that
went back generations.   Features the voices of pioneers in the movement, popular songs lampooning women's rights, newsreels, photos
and cartoons.   Includes scenes from feature films that depicted the
plight of women and also some that ridiculed their aspirations.
GOULD; LUC; BF.

HUBERT'S (6m   C   n.d.)
"Defunct freak show on 42nd Street. "--V. P.   By Vicki Polon;
POLON.

HUD (112m   B   1963   Reg. /Scope)
Hud is a fast-driving, hard-drinking woman chaser whose life
is a revolt against the principles of his highly moral father.   Young
Lon, Hud's nephew, is bewildered and torn between love for them
both.   Patricia Neal is the housekeeper old enough to be disillusioned but young enough to be desirable.   Based on the novel Horse-
man.   d. Martin Ritt; co-scripted by Harriet Frank; PARAMOUNT;
FL

HUMAN IMAGE: MASCULINITY/FEMININITY, THE (15m   C   1975)
How do we define ourselves as women?   As men?   How have
these definitions changed in recent years?   Why have they changed?
Some whimsical and serious answers are suggested in this film.
We see dramatization of our dilemmas; we hear opinions from teen-
agers; we hear a theory from an historical perspective; and we are
challenged by a belief in strict sexual roles.   Finally, we are asked
to consider the relationship of being a human to being a man or a
woman.   BFA; UK, USC.

HUMAN RELATIONS FILM SERIES   see   WOMEN'S LIBERATION

HUMAN REPRODUCTION (20m   C   1965)
Uses animation to show the structure and function of the male
and female reproductive systems and the development and birth of a
child.   Emphasizes the importance of and the responsibility involved
in the act of human reproduction.   MGH; UILL.

HUMAN SEXUALITY SERIES   see   INTRODUCTION; SOURCES OF
    INFORMATION; ABORTION AND STERILIZATION; BODY, THE;
    CULTURAL INFLUENCES; FAMILY PLANNING; I AND THOU
    (OBJECT CHOICE); I AND THOU (SEXUAL IDENTITY); IN THE
    BEGINNING; KEEPING YOUR HEALTH; LIFE CHANGES; LOVE
    AND INTIMACY; MARRIEDS, THE; NEW LIFE-STYLES; NON-
    MARRIEDS, THE; NORMALCY: WHAT IS IT?; POPULATION;
    PORNOGRAPHY AND FANTASY; PREGNANCY AND BIRTH;
    PROCESSES; SEX AND ETHICS; SEX AND THE ARTS; SEX
    AND THE LAW; SEX EDUCATION; SEXUAL COMMERCE; SEX-
    UAL DEVELOPMENT; SEXUAL FRINGES; VD TROUBLES;
    WHEN ILLNESS STRIKES; RECAP AND SUMMARY

HUMANITIES SERIES   see   MAGIC PRISON

HUNGER (22m   B   1971)
A woman's aggressive attempt to bring about life through an
idea--a dramatic statement about the power of the human imagination
as it confronts the powers of nature.   By Phyllis B. Pigorsch;
PERENNIAL.

HUNGER KNOWS MY NAME (27m   C   n. d.)
A dramatic appeal for equal distribution of wealth, this film
presents one of the world's most pressing and prevalent socioeconomic problems--starvation.   Questions of responsibilities, priorities and inequities are examined in the context of a family drama
rather than in documentary style.   By Lynn Carlin, William Daniels;
MGH; UILL.

HUNGRY HARBOR ROAD (8m   B   1976)
The security of suburban life is threatened for a young housewife when she is raped in her home.   Her husband's reactions to
the experience gradually lead her to re-evaluate their relationship
and to view herself in a more individualistic light.   By Susan Baskin;
WMM.

HURRY! HURRY! (3m   C   n. d.)
"Daring film ballet danced by human spermatozoa under powerful magnification. ...   Dance of death made from scientific footage,
printed over murky fire. "--Cinema 16.   By Marie Menken; FCOOP.

HUSBANDS (142m   C   1972)
Within every man there is the eternal child, always present, yet
rarely visible.   The conflicts, tensions and tremendous satisfactions
of coming to grips with and mastering the child, is what makes Hus-

<u>bands</u> a comedy about life, death, and freedom.   Three typical
middle-aged suburbanites collide head-on with one of the most fascinating and powerful of life's forces.   In doing so, they shake
themselves to the very roots of their psyches.   Nothing or no one
will ever seem the same to them again.   d. John Cassavetes;
COLUMBIA; SWANK.

HUSH, HUSH SWEET CHARLOTTE (127m B 1965)
   Eccentric spinster (Bette Davis) continues to live on the family
plantation after the unsolved murder of her married lover 37 years
ago.   Now the plantation is to be razed but she refuses to leave.
The arrival of her cousin, Olivia, who has been called to help move
her out, sets macabre complications into action.   d. Robert Aldrich;
FOX; FL

I AM SOMEBODY (28m C 1970)
   Documents the successful 1969 strike by non-professional hospital workers, most of them Black women, in Charleston, South
Carolina.   Reveals the unyielding attitudes of city officials and the
determination of the women backed by civil rights groups and leaders.   Includes newsreel footage.   Narrated by one of the strikers.
d. Madeline Anderson; MGH; EMC, IU, PAS.

I AND THOU (OBJECT CHOICE); Human Sexuality Series (29m C
   1972 VIDEO)
   Two males applying for a marriage license introduce the concept of "object choice" and what it means to people with differing
sexual preferences.   The Kinsey rating scale of sexual partner
choice is explained.   A discussion group of homosexuals, hetero-
sexuals, and bisexuals takes up the problems of "object choice" within their differing life-styles.   KHETTV, UHAWAII; PTL.

I AND THOU (SEXUAL IDENTITY); Human Sexuality Series (28m C
   1972 VIDEO)
   Children reveal their attitudes toward sexual identity during interviews conducted by the host.   In a "game," studio audience members attempt to guess "who is what" in a group of volunteers pro-
fessing different sexual preferences and from the presentation of
an "all-girl impersonator" nightclub act.   KHETTV, UHAWAII; PTL.

I CHANGE, I AM THE SAME (1m B 1969)
   A short, hilarious film of a woman and a man in various stages
of undress--in their own and each other's clothing.   Through stop-
action camera work, they blinkingly exchange positions and clothing
in every possible combination of shorts and bras, private parts and
public parts.   The effect is of very free, playful and open sexuality.
By Anne Severson; SB, CCC.

I DON'T KNOW (27m B 1971)
   A documentary about a woman who wishes she were a man and
a man who wishes he were a woman.   The film traces the develop-

ment (and eventual denouement) of the loving relationship between a lesbian and a pre-operative transsexual male. The cinéma-vérité style of the film allows the touching and complex emotional situation of the characters to develop. At times humorous, the film is a serious study of sexual identity outside the mainstream of hetero-sexual society. By Penelope Spheeris; SB.

"I" IS FOR IMPORTANT; Sex Role Stereotyping in School, A (Series) (12m C 1974)
Focuses on sex role stereotyping in social interactions and emo-tional expression--displayed by teachers and students (kindergarten through the eighth grade). EMC.

I LOVE TO BE HAPPY (30m C 1976)
Presents the dance as a rewarding and spiritually uplifting ex-perience for both young and old alike. From a class in which young children explore body movement and the therapeutic use of dance, jazz dance, mime, the precise training of modern dancers and the dedication of the ballet artist, we see and feel that everyone can dance and have fun. d. Judith Dawn Hallet; p. Diane Orr, KUTV; SOHO.

I LOVE YOU ... GOOD-BYE (74m C 1974)
Contemporary feature-length drama about a married woman with three children who realizes that her self identity is being stifled and leaves her husband and children. Depicts her subsequent transforma-tion from a model wife, chauffeur and maid to a creative, talented, and satisfied businesswoman. Concludes with a brief reunion of the family at a picnic. Some hopeful signs indicate that both husband and wife changed and grew since they parted. Features Hope Lange and Earl Holliman. d. Sam O'Steen. Originally made for TV. LCA; BF, EMC, TWY.

I LOVE YOU, I LOVE YOU see JE T'AIME, JE T'AIME

I MARRIED A WOMAN (84m C 1958)
Presents a comical concoction of marital fumbles, feminine foibles and masculine martyrdom all churned together in the gray flannel ad jungles of Madison Avenue. Explains that an ad agency executive needs his wife to be the showpiece of a promotional stunt to hold his biggest customer. d. Hal Kanter; RKO; AIM, UNF, WCF.

I ONLY WANT YOU TO BE HAPPY; Conflict and Awareness Series (15m C 1975)
Interactions between mother and two daughters provide conflict-ing points of view about "the female role." Presents several ques-tions related to self identity and sex roles in a contemporary soci-ety. CRM, MGH; UILL, UK.

I WALK THE LINE (95m C 1970)
Set in the backwoods of Tennessee, this drama centers around a law officer whose life is ruined by an irresponsible young woman.

Anxious to escape an unhappy marriage, Sheriff Tawes becomes involved with Alma McCain, the beautiful daughter of a moonshiner.
Their brief affair leads him to compromise his professional responsibilities, and eventually to tragedy.   d. John Frankenheimer;
COLUMBIA; ABFI, MTP.

I WAS/I AM (7m B 1973)
    "A woman's fantasy of death from a male chauvinist's gun, inter-
cut with a <u>cinéma-vérité</u> experience of the protagonist who was actually hit by a sniper and the following events of trying to deal with
her injury in a male-dominated world."--B. H.   By Barbara Hammer;
HAMMER.

IF AT FIRST YOU DON'T SUCCEED (15m C 1976)
    Young Edgar is interested in experimentation but is embarrassed
to have his friends see that he couldn't get his kite off the ground.
But then, he learns perseverance after he becomes familiar with the
trials of Thomas Edison and the light bulb.   His diligence is re-
warded with success.   p. Bonnie Crain, William Crain; d. Thomas
Benedek; FFAIR.

IKEBANA (28m C 1971 VIDEO)
    The art of flower arrangement is presented in a historical per-
spective--its origin, as flowers presented to Buddha, and its adaptation into the home.   Flower arrangements for all periods of history
are shown and a demonstration of contemporary arrangements is
given by Koka Mikami.   WNETTV; PTL.

I'LL CRY TOMORROW (117m B 1955)
    Story of Lillian Roth, the singer, who became an alcoholic.
Played by Susan Hayward.   d. Daniel Mann; MGM; FI

I'LL NEVER GET HER BACK (24m B 1965)
    With compassion and understanding, but without preaching, this
film tells the story of the unwed mother.   She relates her experi-
ence--from the time of her arrival at the maternity home through the
birth of her daughter to the signing of the adoption papers, in the
anguished realization that she will never again get her child back.
WKYCTV; FI; BU, CWU, FSU, PAS, TWY, UILL.

ILLEGAL ABORTION (25m B 1966)
    Extremely graphic and shocking dramatization of a young wom-
an's mental and physical suffering before and during an illegal back-
alley abortion.   Also depicts the deterioration of her relationship
with her boyfriend after she becomes pregnant.   Somewhat melo-
dramatic but nevertheless a strong argument for legalized abortion.
NFBC; EMC.

I'M NO ANGEL (88m B 1933)
    Mae West plays the improbable Tira, the Lion-Tamer, in Ed-
ward Arnold's corny show.   She's "been a few things and seen some
places" and collects men like other women dream they could and
never can.   No gold digger, she never asks for jewels, and never

turns them down. Finally, when her romance with Cary Grant
threatens her circus act, Edward Arnold arranges a frame with another man. Grant thinks she's gone sour, she thinks Grant has
jilted her and sues him for breach of promise. Mae acts as her
own attorney blithely leading witnesses, putting on the judge and inviting male jurors to "come up and see me some time." d. Wesley
Ruggles; s. w. Mae West; PARAMOUNT; CINE, TWY, UNIVE.

I'M 17, I'M PREGNANT--AND I DON'T KNOW WHAT TO DO (28m
      C   1970)
      Pam, 17 and pregnant, struggles with alternatives of forced
marriage, abortion, keeping her child, or adoption. Issues come
into focus in group discussions with other girls working out their
solutions to the same problems. Pam decides to keep her child,
then returns to the agency later realizing her son has needs that
are not being met. MENLEE; UM.

"I'M THE PRETTIEST PIECE IN GREECE" (29m   B   1973)
      Billie Haywood was a headliner in the cafe societies of the 30's
and 40's. When her partner was killed, Billie's career soon ended.
A film about an era and about a significant human being. By Richard Wedler; WOMBAT; IU, UILL.

IMAGE AND REALITY: A GESTALT-BIOENERGETICS WORKSHOP
      (60m   B   1974)
      A fresh, powerful document of people learning to trust them-
selves and each other through grappling openly with their deepest
fears and hopes. The tool is Richard C. Olney's Self-Acceptance
Training. Includes strong sequences of women working to experience their full power. d. Paul Shain, Jay Litvin; IE.

IMAGES OF COUNTRY WOMEN: A PATCHWORK QUILT (29m   C
      n. d.)
      Portrait of four country women: a secretary, a dairy farmer,
a housewife, and an artist, all from Virginia and West Virginia,
talking about their life-styles in rural areas. BRF.

IMAGES OF MALES AND FEMALES IN ELEMENTARY SCHOOL
      TEXTBOOKS (39m   n. d.   SLIDES (400))
      Reports the results of a systematic analysis of the most widely
used textbooks in the U. S., grades one through six in science,
mathematics, reading, spelling, and social studies. The differential
treatment of the two sexes is analyzed. The treatment of minorities
is also noted. Packaged in three carousels with carrying case. Includes tape with narration and music. By Lenore J. Weitzman,
Diane M. Rizzo, U. C. at Davis; RCSRE.

IMMIGRANT EXPERIENCE: A LONG, LONG JOURNEY, THE (31m
      C   1973)
      Tells the story of the American dream and the American real-
ity, as it was lived by one family who came to the U. S. from Poland in 1907. d. Joan Silvers; p. Linda Gottlieb; LCA; UM, UMIS.

IMMIGRANT FROM AMERICA; Black America Series (20m C 1970)
Explores the differences between white immigrants to the U. S.
and Black immigrants from other countries to the U. S. Shows how the
opportunities of education, jobs, capital and power obtained by other
groups have been denied to Black Americans by prejudice, discrimination and violence. Presents some of the problems faced by Black Americans. NYT; REPRO; BF.

"IMOGEN CUNNINGHAM AT 93" (13m C 1976)
Charming portrait of the indomitable spirit of Imogen Cunningham at age 93. She was a fiercely independent person who pursued
her career as a photographer from the early 1900's on. This was
a time when women were not even allowed to vote, let alone have a
career as a professional. Throughout her career she maintained
this independence by turning down jobs rather than compromising
her ideals. CBSTV; CAROUSEL.

IMOGEN CUNNINGHAM: NEVER GIVE UP see NEVER GIVE UP

IMOGEN CUNNINGHAM, PHOTOGRAPHER (20m C 1972)
Imaginative portrait of the pioneering photographer in her 90th
year. Includes candid interviews in which she discusses her early
influences, reminisces about her life, and describes her artistic
philosophy. Shows many of her most famous photographs. Also includes scenes of her attending a flower show, printing negatives for
a new exhibit, photographing a nude model, and at her birthday
party. A warm, sympathetic, and humorous production. By John
Korty; EMC, SCC.

IN A SPRING GARDEN (6m C 1967)
Film version of Richard Lewis' haiku poems. By Cynthia Freitag; WESTON.

IN LIKE FLINT (114m C 1967 Reg. /Scope)
Z. O. W. I. learns there is a plot afoot for the world to be taken
over by women. Flint to the rescue! In this derring-do sequel,
the film concentrates more on the dauntless daredevil experiences
of Flint and his cigarette lighter with the 83 uses than on his amorous adventures with the ladies. d. Gordon Douglas; FOX; FL

IN PARIS PARKS (15m C 1955)
"A dance film of children playing in Paris Parks. "--S. C. By
Shirley Clarke; FCOOP.

IN QUEST OF MEAT JOY (7m C 1969)
In the late sixties many artists produced artistic events known
as happenings. This film documents a New York happening entitled
"Meat Joy, " created by Carolee Schneeman. By Bob Giorgio; CCC.

IN SEARCH OF AMELIA EARHART (24m C 1976)
Presents a comprehensive study of the mystery surrounding the
disappearance of Amelia Earhart in 1937 when she vanished without

a trace on the final leg of her global flight. Three men, Captain
Elgen Long, Major Joseph Gervais and Fred Goerner have spent
years attempting to unravel this mystery. These efforts are juxtaposed with newsreel footage of Mrs. Earhart. LNBRG.

IN THE BEGINNING; Human Sexuality Series (28m   C   1972   VIDEO)
    Biologist Milton Diamond, Ph. D., explains sperm and egg pro-
duction and talks with a doctor and social worker about adoption, the
use of fertility pills, artificial insemination and social concerns
about motherhood vs. childlessness.   UHAWAII/KHETTV; PTL.

IN THE NAME OF ALLAH (76m   B   1971)
    Examines culture, vision, history, and scriptures of the Islamic
religion by studying varied aspects of life in the Moslem community
of Fez, Morocco.   Emphasizes importance of teachings of the Koran,
and shows the ceremonies and rituals surrounding such events as
circumcision, bargaining for a wife, confirmation, and marriage.
IU; EMC.

IN THE STREET (16m   B   si   1952)
    Depicts life in New York's East Harlem in the 1940's.   By Janet
Loeb, Helen Levitt, James Agee; MOMA.

IN THIS HOUSE OF BREDE (105m   C   1974 ed.)
    Presents the story of Philippa Talbot, a sophisticated London
widow, who abandons a successful career to enter a Benedictine convent.   Describes her doubts and renewal of faith, and the lives she
touched with her own.   James Costigan's adaptation of the Rumer
Godden novel by the same title.   p. /d. George Schaefer; TOMENT;
LCA.

INCEST: THE VICTIM NOBODY BELIEVES (21m   C   1976)
    Presents the experiences of three women who were victims of
incest in their childhood, and records their suggestions for possibly
helping others.   Three young women speak with candor of their experiences and feelings as victims of incestuous relationship with fathers as well as other relatives.   Severe depressions, chronic drug
abuse and suicidal tendencies plagued these victims of incest, none
of whom could expect comfort from their families.   The film suggests that children be told frankly and honestly exactly what the man
in the car with the bag of candy wants from them and that anybody,
even a relative, can be that man.   All these victims feel that an
incest crises center is badly needed in our society today.   p. Richard Gerhardt; JGMF; CWU, UM.

INCLUDED OUT (2m   C   1973)
    Humorously animated comment on the sexist bias of the English
language and its effect on social values.   A female newcomer listening to a church sermon is told that "man" includes "woman" as well
--until she tries to enter a men's room.   By Sharon Emswiler;
MMA; EMC, IU.

INDIAN CONVERSATION (13m   C   n. d.)
    Two college students, one raised in an Eastern city and one on

a reservation in South Dakota, are talking about being Indian and their hopes for the future.   By Lucy Ann Kerry; BRF.

INDIAN FAMILY OF LONG AGO (14m   C   1957)
Tells the story of the Sioux Indian buffalo hunters of the U. S. of more than 200 years ago.   Shows Red Horn and his family joining the rest of the tribe to prepare for the buffalo hunt.   Depicts the men hunting and the women putting up tepees, cooking, and making clothing.   Pictures the women cutting up the meat and hanging it on poles to dry.   Discusses how the men educate the boys and the women instruct the girls in their skills.   EBEC; IU.

INDIAN FAMILY SERIES see LIFE AROUND LAKE TITICACA; MODERN MAYAN; WOMAN OF CHAMULA

INDIAN HOLY MEN (DARSHAN) (28m   C   n. d.)
Four Indian holy men are presented: one tends a temple garden; another a master of Kundalini Yoga; the third meditates by a mountain stream; while the fourth offers flowers to his guru's picture and body.   By Florence Davey, Satyan Shivan Sandaram; NLC.

INDIRA GANDHI: A HERITAGE OF POWER (21m   C   1976)
Filmed interview of Indira Gandhi, both in her office in New Delhi and at home with her family, with Paul Saltzman in the summer of 1975.   She speaks of her policies and recent political events in India.   Includes various people speaking their feelings about her recent political acts.   d. Paul Saltzman; ECCW; UW.

INDIRA GANDHI OF INDIA (63m   C   1973)
Autobiographical conversations with Indira Gandhi, the political and spiritual leader of 450 million people.   Talks about her relationship with Mahatma Gandhi and her father, Jawaharlal Nehru. BBCTV; WSU.

INFANCY (19m   C   1973)
Babies of different 'ages, in natural home environments and in experimental settings, are shown attempting to put together the concepts needed to cope with their surroundings, to maneuver their environment and to communicate.   p. Barbara Jampel; CRM; MGH.

INFORMATION PROCESSING (28m   C   1971)
This observation of behavior at a cocktail party reveals how humans receive, process, store, and retrieve information.   And why sometimes we have a problem remembering things.   p. Carole Hart; CRM; MGH.

INNOCENCE (3m   B   1973)
Computer-generated music and visuals filmed directly from a color TV monitor.   By Lillian Schwartz. LPI.

INSIDE OPERA WITH GRACE MOORE (28m   B   1934)
An abridged version of "One Night of Love, " with emphasis on the progress of Mary Barrett, a young American singer, from a contest, to European study, to eventual success in the Metropolitan

Opera.   Grace Moore as Mary Barrett, sings seven songs and arias.
COLUMBIA, ed. by TFC; UILL.

INSIDE THE LADIES' HOME JOURNAL (15m B   1970)
   Portrays 200 women from the women's liberation movement entering the offices of the editor-in-chief of the Ladies' Home Journal
on March 18, 1970, demanding day care centers for employees of
the magazine, 125 dollars minimum weekly wages for all employees,
and an end to the orientation of the magazine that sees women only
as related to children, the kitchen and the church.   p. Janet Gardner; AMDOC.

INSIGHT SERIES see ATTENTION MUST BE PAID; CELEBRATION
   IN FRESH POWDER; LAST OF THE GREAT MALE CHAUVIN-
   ISTS; NO TEARS FOR KELSEY; ROOMMATES ON A RAINY DAY;
   SEVENTEEN FOREVER; WAR OF THE EGGS, THE; WELCOME
   HOME

INSIGHT VIGNETTES see DIFFERENT WITH DIGNITY

INTEGRATION REPORT I (24m   1960)
   A documentary showing sit-ins, marches, boycotts and rallies
in 1959 and 1960.   Includes such events as the first mass marches
in Montgomery, Alabama, reactions against police brutality in
Brooklyn and protests against the prejudiced treatment of Negroes
in court.   p. Madeline Anderson; CMC.

INTERCAT '69 (96m C 1969)
   "A cat anthology ... ten films from five hours of films about
cats and by cats shown at the First International Cat Film Festival
(Intercat '69) which took place at the Elgin Theatre, New York City,
on December 20, 1960. "--P. C.   By Pola Chapelle; FCOOP.

INTERFACE SERIES see BETTY CARTER ... WHAT'S NEW;
   CIVIL RIGHTS RETROSPECTIVE AND PROFILE: POLITICAL
   WIFE

INTERLUDE (15m B   1972)
   "An intimate study of a young woman in relation to the world
around her and the process of her self-discovery. "--P. S.   By Pat
Saunders; SAUNDERS.

INTERN: A LONG YEAR; World of Work Series (20m   C   1972)
   Follows a young woman intern in an inner-city hospital to depict the responsibilities and demanding schedule that are part of an
intern's routine: caring for patients, attending staff meetings, making the best of meager medical supplies, exterminating mice, and
voicing the hospital's needs to the public.   Also shows her treating
a helpless old woman, a cancer patient, a chronic alcoholic, and a
drug overdose victim.   EBEC; EMC, UM.

INTERVIEW (7m C 1974)
   "An impression of a friend who lives the dichotomy of discipline

and freedom through his violin experience. "--K. L.   By Kathleen
Laughlin; LAUGHLIN.

INTERVIEW WITH CATHERINE MARSHALL (20m   B   1956)
Arlene Francis interviews Mrs. Peter Marshall, wife of the
Chaplain to the U. S. Senate who died in 1949.   Mrs. Marshall de-
scribes her life since his death and the writing of her book entitled
A Man Called Peter.   NBCTV; FL

INTRODUCTION; Human Sexuality Series (29m   C   1972   VIDEO)
Previews the total series content, illustrates that human sexuality exists all about us in various dimensions.   Goals of the series
are offered and excerpts from various programs in the series are
shown.   UHAWAII/KHETTV; PTL.

INTRODUCTION TO ACUPUNCTURE (22m   C   1973)
Relates the history of acupuncture and shows several operations.
By Vivian Blackstone, Sy Wexler; PF.

INTRODUCTION TO SCULPTURE METHODS (19m   C   1968)
Shows five sculptors in their workshops.   Demonstrates the three
general methods of creating sculpture.   Examines the progress from
beginning to completion of a piece of sculpture.   By Babette Eddleston; BFA.

INTRODUCTION TO THE ENEMY (60m   C   1975)
Portrait of Vietnamese who live in the North--rebuilding their
homes, lives, and society, and preparing a future under the linger-
ing clouds of war as eye-witnessed by Jane Fonda, Tom Hayden and
Haskell Wexler in the spring of 1974.   Narrated by Jane Fonda and
Tom Hayden.   By Christine Burrill, Jane Fonda, Tom Hayden,
Haskell Wexler, and Bill Yahraus; IPCFL.

INTRODUCTION TO THE HUMANITIES (5m   B   1972)
A first-year humanities class at San Francisco Art Institute
steps before the camera and introduces itself one by one.   First the students announce their given names; then, during the second round of
introductions they give themselves silly, but still appropriate names.
By Anne Severson; SB.

INTRUSION (22m   C   1977)
Drama enacted to show the effects of trust and mistrust in the
human equation, and to show the prevalent attitude toward the law
enforcement profession.   By Nancy Greene Fleet; PHOENIX.

INVENTION OF THE ADOLESCENT (28m   B   1968)
Uses paintings and sketches of the past to portray the changes
which have occurred over the last three to four centuries in attitudes toward the transitional period from childhood to adulthood in
Western society.   Traces the development of the adolescent and
shows something of the real problem of this age.   By Patricia Watson; NFBC; PERENNIAL.

IRVINGTON TO NEW YORK (3m C n.d.)
The compacted imagery of a train ride that deals with the visual onslaught of landscape and city images, accompanied by train sounds. By Rosalind Schneider; FCOOP.

IS PERSONAL GROWTH SELFISH?; Choice: Challenge for Modern
Women Series (30m B r1966)
Sister Mary Corita, I.H.M., and Anne Steinmann discuss women's growth throughout life, their dependency upon male and societal attitudes, and opportunities within "the system." EMC.

ISADORA see LOVES OF ISADORA

ISAK DINESEN (29m B 1956)
Interview with famous Danish author of Seven Gothic Tales and Out of Africa. Presents her views on the similarities and differences between poetry and story-telling. NET, IU.

ISLAMIC MYSTICISM--THE SUFI WAY (26m C 1972)
Traces the history of Islam and shows ruins of that empire, which stretches from India to Spain. Presents the rituals, dance, art, music, and philosophy of Sufism, the heart of Islam. By Elda Hartley, Huston Smith; HARTLEY; CWU.

ISLAND, THE (96m B 1961)
The film tells in simple but poetic pictures the story of one family's struggle for survival as the sole inhabitants of a small island. The story concerns a farmer, his wife, and their two sons. The family engages in a day-to-day struggle with soil and time: the fetching of water from the mainland to irrigate their crops; the hot bath at the end of the day; the tragedy of death; and the night on the town. d. Kaneto Shindo; ABFI, CORINF.

ISLAND TIME: GORDON ONSLOW-FORD (25m C 1968)
This West Coast painter is seen where he works in California. The film points up the nature-environment influence on his painting and he discusses his philosophy, the speed of line, and his use of line, circle, dot. By Madeline Tourtelot; GP.

ISSUES IN SEXUAL BEHAVIOR: RAPE, PROSTITUTION, HOMO-
SEXUALITY (C n.d. SLIDES (110))
Through a series of candid interviews with rapists, homosexuals and prostitutes, explosive issues in sexual behavior come alive. Factual information, opinions of medical and legal experts and engrossing case studies are blended together. Instructor's manual and tape included. See individual titles below. HAR.
RAPE. Explores the thoughts and feelings of the victim, the motivation of the rapist and the attitudes toward rape inherent in our society and within its legal system.
PROSTITUTION. Issues delineated and portrayed by law enforcers, psychiatrists, clients, the pimp and the madam as well as the prostitutes themselves.
HOMOSEXUALITY. Explores the biological, psychological and

social aspects of homosexuality.   Parents and homosexuals discuss
their personal experiences and feelings.   The questions of child
custody and the legality of homosexual behavior in a heterosexual
society are fully examined.

ISY BOUKIR (16m   C   1971)
     Nancy Graves shows the way of camels, detail after detail,
shot after shot.   Miss Graves's film is precise and wonderfully particular, and as appreciative of its camels as of the controlled
rhythms of their surges across the screen, the slight shifting of
their legs, the curves of their extended necks.   By Nancy Graves;
FCOOP.

IT CAN BE DONE (30m   B   n. d.   VIDEO)
     How do you, as an individual artist, work collectively with other
artists, and create works that are important and useful to people
struggling to control their lives?   The women of the Chicago Wom-
en's Graphics Collective have worked through this question many
times, on many levels.   This videotape documents the process as
they create a poster for the Farmworkers "Si Se Puede. "   IE.

IT COULDN'T HAPPEN TO ME (28m   C   1975)
     Focusing on the topics of premarital sex, birth control and preg-
nancy, the film consists of an interplay of discussions with professionals and young people.   The most personal discussions are with
young women who have experienced pregnancy, including a group of
pregnant teen-agers, a girl who gave her child up for adoption and
a girl who has had an abortion.   The discussion focuses on the reasons why these young people did not use birth control during their
sexual relations.   Included also is another group of students discussing the sexual attitudes of contemporary youth.   The experts in
the film are three physicians, Dr. Carolyn Pellettier, Dr. Marion
Powell and Dr. M. O. Vincent, who comment on diverse aspects of
adolescent sexuality and pregnancy.   By Edward S. Herold, Ph. D. ;
PERENNIAL.

IT HAPPENED ONE NIGHT (105m   B   1934)
     A wonderfully warm, funny and moving comedy about a fugitive
heiress and a rebellious reporter who sets out to tame her; a runaway romance between a tough guy and a polished jewel.   d. Frank
Capra; COLUMBIA; BF, SWANK.

IT HAPPENS (25m   C   1972)
     A discussion film on teen-age pregnancy in which a young girl
and her boyfriend go through the emotional turmoil of pregnancy out
of wedlock.   Where can she go for tests and counseling without her
parents' knowledge?   Should they marry?   Should the pregnancy be
terminated?   Should she tell her parents?   Open-ended.   By Noel
Nosseck; PF; BU, UM.

IT HAPPENS TO US (30m   C   1973)
     Presents a number of women of different ages, marital status,
and race who candidly describe their abortions in medical and moral

terms. Examines relevant statistics about abortion and birth control, and provides an understanding of the personal effects of abortion on the women involved. By Amalie Rothschild; NDF; EMC, UM.

ITALIAN AMERICAN (26m   C   n. d.)
    Martin Scorsese's interview with his parents in their home; they
talk of the early years of Italian immigrants in New York and of
their life on the Lower East Side.   ABFL

IT'S A MIRACLE (7m   B   1973)
    Story about a nun whose work in a new community hinges upon
winning the trust of a teen-age boy.   By Marie Celene Caulfield;
WMM.

IT'S ALWAYS FAIR WEATHER (101m   C   1955   Reg. /Scope)
    Three ex-G. I. s in a New York bar just after V-J Day make a
pact to return to the same place ten years later.   The clever plot
has an equally clever script and plenty of music and dance.   d. Gene
Kelly, Stanley Donen; s. w. Betty Comden; MGM; FI.

IT'S NOT ENOUGH (16m   C   1974)
    Surveys the economic facts of Canadian life: numbers of women
employed, numbers in top positions, salaries, etc.   The statistics
also tell us that Canadian women do not have enough of the things
that make work rewarding or worthwhile: not enough day care centers, benefits, home help, job opportunities, and psychological support.   d. Kathleen Shannon; NFBC; EDC, EMC.

IT'S NOT ME (26m   C   1975)
    Portrait of Nancy Hohman, a 39-year-old woman, who up until
now has been "other directed. " When 29, she married and moved
to Alaska.   Nancy interspersed bringing up several children and
getting her master's degree.   Then she moved to a remote area of
Alaska where she taught Eskimos.   There she had no time to herself and so headed for an emotional breakdown.   She escapes to a
retreat where she has time for her thoughts and art work and becomes aware of a responsibility to herself as a person.   p. Deborah
Wian; PHOENIX, VFL

IT'S ONLY BOOZE (28m   C   1976)
    April is thirteen.   She's not an alcoholic, not yet, but she
drinks.   So do most of her friends.   Teen-age drinking problem is
on the rise and teen-age alcoholism is becoming almost commonplace.   In ads, in magazines, on TV and in the movies--everywhere
--alcohol is associated with good times, with glamour and sophisti-
cation.   Help is available after the fact but prevention is the ultimate answer.   April thinks there needs to be more dialog between
parents and kids and more strong talk from teachers, church and
government.   d. Larry L. Badger; KNBCTV; FI.

IT'S SNOW (6m   C   1975)
    An animated film to reflect the delicate beauty of winter.   By
Gayle Thomas; IFB.

IT'S WONDERFUL BEING A GIRL (22m   C   1966)
Presents the psychological and physiological aspects of growing
up through the eyes of two twelve-year-olds.   API; CWU.

I'VE GOT A WOMAN BOSS (11m   C   1977)
An animated film showing the fears of a businessman when he
finds out that his new boss is a woman, and how these fears are
dispelled.   A lively and humorous treatment of sexual stereotypes
and business behavior.   BOSUST.

IZY BOUKIR   see   ISY BOUKIR

JACK AND THE BEANSTALK (12m   C   1956)
A fairy tale in silhouette animation based on live shadow play.
Jack's adventures begin when he is sent off to market by his mother
to sell their only pig.   By Lotte Reiniger, BBCTV; CEA, MGH.

JACQUELINE KENNEDY'S ASIAN JOURNEY (30m   C   1963)
A film record of Mrs. John F. Kennedy's trip to India and
Pakistan with her sister, Princess Radziwill, in March 1962.   Includes tours of the Taj Mahal, Jaipur, Khyber Pass, and the Shali-
mar Gardens.   USIA; USOE.

JACQUELINE SUSANN'S ONCE IS NOT ENOUGH (120m   C   1975)
A fading movie producer marries the fifth richest women in the
world for money to lavish on his daughter recovering from a motorcycle accident.   The producer's wife--a lesbian with an aging movie
star lover--tries to pair off her young cousin with her stepdaughter.
But the daughter, deeply attached to her father and jealous of his
new wife, begins an affair with a macho novelist her father's age.
True to the moral code of this kind of melodrama, everyone must
suffer and pay for his sins because in some instances, once is
more than enough.   Based on the novel by Jacqueline Susann.   d.
Guy Green; PARAMOUNT; FI.

JADE SNOW WONG (27m   C   1976)
Tells the story of Jade Snow Wong, fifth daughter of Mr. Wong,
and her struggle to change her destiny amid two conflicting cultures.
Jade Snow becomes an accomplished author and ceramist whose works
currently adorn the collections of major museums.   Traces her childhood, adolescence and early adulthood in San Francisco's Chinatown.
d. Ron Finley; WNETTV; FI

JAMES DAUGHERTY (19m   C   1972)
Filmed biography of the famous author and illustrator of children's books.   By Cynthia Freitag; WESTON.

JAN PEERCE AND NADINE CONNER (14m   B   1953)
Jan Peerce and Nadine Conner perform for the caretaker of a
deserted opera house, and as they sing, the splendor of the opera
setting is seen through the imaginative eyes of the old ex-singer.

Jan Peerce sings "O Paradiso," from Meyerbeer's L'Africaine; Nadine Conner sings "Norina's Aria," from Donizetti's Don Pasquale; and they both join in a duet from Donizetti's Lucia di Lammermoor. WORA; UILL.

JANE; The Living Camera Series 8 (54m   B   1970)
   Follows actress Jane Fonda as she prepares for her Broadway debut by performing in a new play in Baltimore, Wilmington and Philadelphia.   By Hope Ryden; DREW; TL.

JANE BRAKHAGE (10m   B   1974)
   "An expressionistic documentary of the influential and vividly self-reliant woman who combines creation, pioneer spirit, and motherhood in a totally unique individual manner as well as being a nurturing and innovative force in the works of filmmaker Stan Brakhage."
--B. H.   By Barbara Hammer; HAMMER.

JANE EYRE (96m   B   1944)
   Edward Rochester is a moody young squire with a mad wife locked away in his mansion.   Jane Eyre arrives as an orphaned governess.   They later fall in love and are about to be married when Jane discovers he already has a wife.   She leaves him but later returns to marry him after his wife and home have been burned in a fire, and he himself is blinded.   However, he regains sight in one eye later.   Based on Charlotte Brontë's novel.   Starring: Orson Welles, Joan Fontaine, Margaret O'Brien, Agnes Moorehead.   d. Robert Stevenson; FOX; FL.

JANE EYRE (108m   C   1970)
   (See above description.)   d. Delbert Mann; British Lion Films; ABFI, KP, SELECT, TWY, UNF, WHOLFC.

JANE EYRE (70m   B   1934)
   (See above description.)   d. Christy Cabanne; MONOGRAM; HCW.

JANE EYRE (45m   B   1944)
   (See above description.)   TFC; EMC, UILL, UIO, UW.

JANE GOODALL AND THE BABOON TROOP   see   MISS GOODALL
   AND THE BABOON TROOP

JANE KENNEDY--TO BE FREE (27m   C   1974)
   Thought-provoking, humanistic portrait of a Chicago nurse who risked her personal freedom and was imprisoned for participating in civil rights demonstrations and in protests against the Vietnam war. She relates the development of her belief that one must act against immoral and unjust policies of the government and describes her experiences with the U. S. penal system and its dehumanizing effect on prisoners and prison personnel.   By Patricia Barey, Gloria Callaci; IU; EMC.

JANET'S ABORTION (12m   C   1976)
   Camera follows Janet, 23, through an actual abortion in her 14th

week of pregnancy.   The abortion is performed in a doctor's office
using the laminaria procedure, with vacuum and curettage.   Through
narration, the laminaria process is explained as well as what Janet
experiences each step of the abortion.   Sensitive and informative,
the film demystifies the abortion process.   A guide is included.   By
Howard Harrelson; IMEN; MMRC.

JANIE'S JANIE (25m B 1972)
     Documents a white New Jersey welfare mother's struggle to de-
velop her own strength and potential after years of isolation and repression within a working class family.   As she goes about her
housework, Janie tells how the separation from the man she married
at 15 to escape from her childhood home forced her to take responsibility for her own life.   After years of being her Father's Janie,
then her husband's Janie, she is now Janie's Janie--her own person.
d. Geri Asher, Peter Barton; ODEON; UM.

JAPAN: ANSWER IN THE ORIENT; Problem Series (60m C r1965)
     Shows how the Japanese have achieved zero population growth
through legalized abortion, the interest of large industries in fertility
control measures, and the trend among Japanese people to marry at
a later age.   Focuses on a young couple married for two years, who
have remained childless.   p. in Japan; IU; EMC.

JAPAN: PACIFIC NEIGHBOR (16m C 1962)
     Tells how the Japanese have adapted to their environment in
meeting needs in transportation, education, religion, agriculture
and industry.   By Geraldine Byers, Justin Byers; BFA.

JAPANESE FAMILY (23m B 1950)
     Shows life in the home of a Japanese silk weaver before the
war.   Shows the daily life of the family and the celebration of the
New Year.   IFF; OKSU.

JAPAN'S NEW FAMILY PATTERNS; World Changes Series (15m C
1962)
     Contrasts the life of members of the Nakamura family of today
with the typical Japanese family of pre-World War II.   Points out
that the greatest changes have occurred in relation to the role of
girls and women and indicates the difficulty the older women have
in adjusting to the rapid changes.   Shows typical daily life of each
member of the family.   By Hugh Gage; SEF; BF, OKSU, IU.

JASON FILM PORTRAIT SERIES see VERONICA

JASSY (97m C 1948)
     In 18th-century England, women's lib fared poorly.   Outraged
husbands divorced their wives; fathers continually whipped errant
daughters; canes were used not for walking, but for flaying wives
and their inevitable lovers; and soldiers dallied with girls and abandoned them, etc.   Enter Jassy with a backbone of steel, a loyal
heart, a brain in her head as to managing men--all attributes that
were not tolerated in that period.   She marries a villain who, in

fact, settles his estate on her as a marriage gift only to find that "her" idea of marriage is running the house smoothly and never unlocking her door at night. All this enrages Sydney. In the end he is poisoned with rat-bane.... From the novel Jassy by Margaret Lofts. d. Bernard Knowles; KP.

JE T'AIME, JE T'AIME (94m C 1968 French/subtitled)
Film concerns a scientific experiment designed to make a man actually relive a moment of his life. Ridder is an ideal subject, for he has just been unwillingly saved from suicide; therefore, if the experiment fails (and failure means death) little will have been lost. p. Mag Bodard; d. Alain Resnais; NYF.

JEANETTE RANKIN BRIGADE (8m B 1968)
A historic march of 10,000 women in January 1968 against the war in Vietnam. The women discuss the pros and cons of the demonstration. SFN.

JEFFERSON CIRCUS SONGS (19m C 1973)
A musical fantasy of a magical train ride into another world of wild creatures and imaginative ceremonies. Uses both live action pixilation and flat animation. By Suzan Pitt Kraning; SB, CCC.

JENNY (88m C 1970)
Two people meet in Central Park: he, a filmmaker waiting for a summons from the draft board, she an unmarried pregnant girl. They decide on a marriage of convenience--giving him a draft deferment and her a father for her baby. d. George Bloomfield; ABCPC; FL.

JENNY IS A GOOD THING (18m C 1969)
Focuses on food and nutrition of Headstart and Headstart children. p. /d. Joan Horvath; USDHEW; NAVC.

JEREMELU (2m B n. d.)
Visual word poem in white images; shots of varied sexual habits, a baby to be breast-fed, a kiss. By Naomi Levine; FCOOP.

JEWISH WIFE, THE (23m C 1971)
The Jewish wife of an Aryan doctor in Berlin in the late 1930's makes her decision to leave her husband and Germany as the storm of Nazism comes closer. Based on play by Bertolt Brecht. PHOENIX; PAS, UILL.

JEZEBEL (104m B 1938)
Antebellum New Orleans, with its age-ripened atmosphere of mystery and foreboding provides the setting. Bette Davis plays Julie Marston, a woman whose explosive sexuality is repressed by societal constraints. Henry Fonda plays the role of Pres Dillars, a rather inflexible young banker to whom Julie becomes engaged. Even though Julie can create embarrassing situations with her unexpected emotional flareups, Pres is able to manipulate situations for his own ends and humiliate her. Though the two separate when Julie turns

to another man, their paths cross again in New Orleans.   When Pres
is struck down by yellow fever, Julie alone (not his wife) accompanies him to quarantine island, linking forever her own fate to his.
The film fully expresses the Davis persona as we know it.   Based
on play by Owen Davis.   d. William Wyler; WSA; UAS.

JIMMY (15m   B   1970)
    "Priest comes to a realization of his life-style. "--T. S.   By
Terry Sheehy; SHEEHY.

JOAN (11m   B   1975)
    Presents the story of Joan, an alcoholic who at 36 gave birth to
an illegitimate daughter.   She managed to quit drinking and support
her child for 15 years through a variety of jobs.   Now her health is
failing and she has been told to quit work and apply for supporting
mother's benefit.   She feels depressed and useless.   p. Film Australia; AUIS.

JOAN OF ARC (100m   C   1950)
    The trials of Joan, portrayed brilliantly by Ingrid Bergman, en-
compass both the aspiring dedication of the ever-questing Christian
Crusader and the heart-churning confusion of a young girl maturing
to womanhood.   Her ceaseless fight for French unity, whether on
the battlefield or podium, emerges as a struggle for the rights of
all peoples.   Her ultimate execution by her temporal arch-enemies
becomes a victory over Death itself.   p. Walter Wanger; d. Victor
Fleming; RKO; BF, MTP, UNF, WCF, WHOLFC.

JOANJO: A PORTUGUESE TALE (12m   C   1970)
    Presents live action scenes in a Portuguese fishing village which
frame an animated sequence of a little boy's dream of becoming
famous and great.   By Suzanne E. Bauman; PARACO.

JOANNA (107m   C   1968   Scope)
    Feather-brained but beguiling 18-year-old girl (Genevieve Waite)
comes to London to study art and "taste life. "   She is quickly accepted by the artsy-craftsy crowd, and with the help of Beryl (Cal-
vin Lockhart), a Black model, becomes flip and amoral, but still
unsatisfied with her life.   A dying philanthropist and a Black lover
help her find a new reason for being.   p. Michael S. Laughlin;
d. Michael Sarne; FOX; FL

JOB INTERVIEW--THREE YOUNG WOMEN (17m   C   1967)
    Three types of young women interview for a job.   The discussion
centers on the mistakes they make during the interview and how to
correct them.   BEF; BU, BYU, PAS.

JOB SERIES, A see TV TALENT COORDINATOR: SHE'S AL-
    WAYS ON THE MOVE

JOBS FOR WOMEN: WHERE ARE YOU GOING VIRGINIA?; The
    World of Work Series (12m   C   1969)
    Explains, through the experiences of an 18-year-old girl who

lacks a high school education, how to go about getting a job. Emphasizes that one must plan a course of action, develop the needed skills, and ask for help from community and commercial agencies. Uses jobs in retail stores and service-type organizations as examples. The emphasis is very much on slotting women in stereotyped "female" jobs in the economic structure. MGH, VISIONF; MGH; IU, UILL.

JOBS IN THE CITY--WOMEN AT WORK; Real World, The (Series)
    (11m C 1971)
    Each year more and more women enter the work force in an ever-widening variety of jobs. Many young people have the erroneous impression that women are employed in only certain occupations. Portrayed in this film are women at work as newspaper printer, physician, computer keypunch operator, bank teller, pilot, etc. CENTRON; IU, UILL, UK, UM.

JOCKEY (25m C 1973)
    Fascinating cinéma-vérité portrait of Penny Ann Early, the first woman jockey in this country. Shows her in several races, in one of which she finishes second; includes interviews with trainers and with her fellow jockeys, as well as scenes of her with a horse owner, talking with another women jockey, and celebrating her second-finish. Editing somewhat difficult to follow at times. By Gretel Ehrlich; TEXFM; EMC.

JOHN VON NEUMANN; MAA Individual Lecturers Series (59m B
    1966)
    A documentary of the life, work and achievements of John Von Neumann. By Pat Powell; MAA.

JOHNNY BELINDA (103m B 1948)
    Jane Wyman plays a sweet deaf-mute girl, living in austere Nova Scotia, who is brutally raped. Overwhelmed by the problems she must face, she is given essential support by a young doctor. Wyman's character cannot speak, but her emotional articulation is eloquent. d. Jean Negulesco; WSA; UAS.

JOJOLO (12m B 1968)
    Subtle, lyrical study of a graceful young woman of Haitian parentage who works as a fashion and film model in Paris. The city is viewed through her eyes as she walks along its boulevards, streets, and alleyways, and wanders among its people. Excellent cinematography combined with a sound track of Western jazz and African rhythms show how her Haitian background influences her life in the city. GP; EMC.

JOURNALISM--MIRROR, MIRROR ON THE WORLD? (52m B 1968)
    Public Broadcast Library examines the diverse media coverage given to the Jeanette Rankin Brigade demonstration in Washington, D. C. , on January 15, 1968. Led by former Congresswoman Jeanette Rankin who voted against entry into both World Wars. NET, IU.

JOURNEY AROUND A ZERO (3m B 1963)
"A phallic invocation. An abstract occasion of image and sound. "
--S. D. H. By Storm De Hirsch; IMPF; FCOOP.

JOURNEY: THE QUEST FOR SELF-RELIANCE (23m C 1976)
A young man who has studied survival skills sets out to cross
California's Sierra Nevada in late fall, on foot, with no food and
minimal equipment. We see him find food, build shelters, cross a
river, and face deep snow and freezing cold. He tells us what the
experience has taught him about the wilderness and himself. d. /p.
Nina Kleinberg; BFA.

JOURNEY TO THE FAR SIDE OF THE SUN (99m C 1969)
On the theory that another earth, the mirror image of our own,
exists on the far side of the sun, two astronauts are sent out from
the European Space Exploration Center to confirm this. A series of
strange adventures ensues. They eventually return to earth with a
startling new discovery. p. Sylvia Anderson, Jerry Anderson; d.
Robert Parrish; UNIVE; CWF, TWY, UNIVE.

JOURNEY WITH A FRIEND (26m C 1970)
Describes the Lamaze method of natural childbirth and shows a
woman and her husband as they train for the birth of their first
child, then experience the joy and beauty of a painless birth. Includes two sequences from the French film Naissance. POMPOP.

JOYCE AT 34 (28m C 1972)
Joyce at 34 is any woman at any time who faces the conflict of
work versus family. The film shows Joyce caring for her baby while
pursuing her career as filmmaker. It is a sensitive and genuine
portrait of a need for cooperation inside a family in order to acquire
equality without guilt. By Joyce Chopra, Claudia Weill; NDF; UM.

JOYCE CHEN COOKS (25/29m ea. B 1967 VIDEO)
Author-teacher-restaurant manager Joyce Chen shows viewers
how they can cook Chinese dishes in their own kitchens using equipment on hand and ingredients readily available from any supermarket.
Being Chinese by birth and American by adoption, Mrs. Chen brings
to each program glimpses pointing to the similarities and differences
between the two cultures. The history of the recipes, the unique
methods of preparation, and the traditional equipment and acces-
sories used are explained. Write to PTL for individual program
titles. WGBHTV; PTL.

JUDGES (30m C n. d.)
"I sit in criminal court now all the time and I have since I've
been a judge, and looking for the truth is a tough, tough thing. "--
M. S. By Martha Stuart, David Ruskin; STUARTM.

JUDY (29m B n. d.)
Tells of a young woman's decision to leave her small Australian
hometown for an independent life in Sidney. Her pending departure
causes near hysteria among her parents, friends and boyfriend who

view life in the big city as uncertain and look on her decision as a rejection of themselves. What the film never tells is what happened when Judy reaches the city. d. Bruce Heinnart; WOMB.

JUDY CHICAGO AND THE CALIFORNIA GIRLS (27m C r1971)
Judy teaches women at Fresno State College the new consciousness partly by means of exaggerated dramatic role-playing. Her methods are strident--for the purpose of exposing roles as roles-- but her manner is good-humored and her sensibility is pleasantly ebullient. By Judith Dancoff (Judy Chicago); DANCOFF; CFS.

JULES AND JIM (104m B 1961 French/subtitled)
Exquisitely illuminates a modern woman. Catherine, amoral and classically beautiful, loves two fraternal friends and must have them both--even if she must die to do so. For her, no commitment is forever and only death is final. Joyously realized and vitally acted. Adapted from novel by Henri-Pierre Roche. d. Francois Truffaut; JANUS.

JULIET OF THE SPIRITS (137m C 1965 Italian/subtitled)
Juliet is about a universal problem--the role of women in marriage. Giulietta, the wife of a businessman, suspects her husband of having an affair. She employs a detective agency and her fears are confirmed. However, her husband is unembarrassed by her discovery, tells her she is mistaken and leaves on a business trip. Giulietta knows he is going to meet her rival, but at the end faces her position with honesty. Until now, her whole life was centered around her husband, but now she must find another role in life. d. Federico Fellini; ABFL

JUMP CUT (2m C 1972)
An adult take-off on the story of "Goldilocks." A woman's pelvis is being shown as she experiments with vegetables and other things, while a child's voice comments "too big," "too little," etc. Finally a man appears and it's "just right!" By Christine Pihl; ACRAUT; MMRC.

JUNE (8m B 1972-74)
"Slow-paced preparation for an evening out by a 50-year-old woman. Clothes, make-up, hair, all a somber ritual. As June saw the film one year after it was made, her comments were inserted into the film at the points they refer to."--M. H. By Martha Haslanger; HASLANGER.

JUNG SAI: CHINESE AMERICAN (29m C 1976)
A young Chinese American journalist seeks out her ethnic origins, traveling among the West Coast Chinese community. She interviews people on the early immigration, the problems encountered, the work done by their forefathers, and contributions made to American culture. d. Frieda Lee Mock, Terry Sanders; p. Elaine Attias, Saul Rubin; ABFL

JUST BRIEFLY (15m B 1976)
Portrays a young Black woman's search for emotional fulfillment.

Adie is walking through a deserted park on a cold snowy day.   She
recalls the pleasant but brief encounter with a man, and his un-
willingness to commit himself.   He was passive and comfortable in
his illusiveness, offering a few moments of passion.   Adie is not
bitter.   The dreariness and dankness of winter is contrasted to the
vitality and the promise of spring.   p. /d Louise Fleming; PHOENIX.

JUST LOOKING (6m   B   1973)
An older woman's dull morning turns into an adventurous and
unpredictable afternoon.   In creating the story of an older woman
who breaks out of her isolation, the filmmaker involves herself in
a whole neighborhood filled with actors and locations.   The movie
treads a fine line between story and documentary, capturing the
reality of the invisibility of older persons in our society.   By Suzanne Armstrong; WMM.

JUST MARRIED (30m   B   1974)
The myth and reality of marriage combines five speak-outs from
the New York Radical Feminists' Conference on marriage, February
1973, and footage of a traditional wedding.   By Patricia Bertozzi,
Marian Hunter; HERSTORY.

KALI (4m   C   n. d.)
"Four image media, using flowing bodies and female forms, set
to a sensual Indian sound track by Calo Scott and Ahmed Abdul
Malik. "--C. M. G.   By Cassandra M. Gerstein; FCOOP.

KAMOURASKA (119m   C   1973   French/subtitled)
A classic love story written from a woman's point of view.   Its
heroine, Elizabeth, is a tragic victim of a narrow-minded Victorian
age when love was incidental and marriage was to last a lifetime.
When the story begins, she is a worn-out, middle-aged wife waiting
for her husband to die.   In a flashback dream, Jutra reveals the
past--a young girl's marriage to a rapacious, slow-witted hard-
drinking Antoine Tassy, a man she hates; her love affair with a kind
but possessive American doctor; the murder of the oafish husband,
prison, and finally another loveless marriage.   The result--a sweep-
ing, passionate film set in 19th-century Quebec and the story of a
sensuous woman, bedeviled by an unobtainable love in a soul ex-
tinguishing society.   From the novel of the same title by Anne Hebert.   Written by Anne Hebert and Claude Jutra.   d Claude Jutra;
NLC.

KATHY (19m   C   1969)
The presentation, while realistic and frank, is not intended to
induce unwarranted fear.   The film is designed to present the facts
about gonorrhea, and to stress the necessity for teenagers to get
medical checks if they even suspect they might have the disease.
AIMS; UW.

KATIE KELLY (5m   B   1973)
A portrait of Katie Kelly--professional writer, author of Garbage,

Its History and Future in America, environmentalist and active community leader. By Barbara Brown, Nancy Greiner, Lorraine Mc-
Connell, Ann Weiner, and Helen Zaglen; WMM.

KATY (17m C 1974)
    Dramatic portrayal of a young girl's fight to be permitted to de-
liver newspapers along with the boys. When her brother goes to
camp, she takes over his route, despite the jeers of the boys and
the adult manager in the all-male paper shack. Encouraged by an
older feminist, she and two of her friends ask for permanent routes.
Although they are turned down, there is a sense of victory in their
willingness to fight for equality at such a tender age. d. Monica
Dunlap; featuring Jill Haugse; CBSTV; BFA; EMC, ROA, UM.

KEEPING YOUR HEALTH; Human Sexuality Series (29m C 1972
    VIDEO)
    Scenes from a doctor's examining room show what happens dur-
ing male and female exams. Women are given detailed instructions
on breast self-examination. The host talks with several people
about the general reluctance to get periodic health checks and with
several physicians about sexual problems connected with alcoholism,
diabetes and heart problems. UHAWAII, KHETTV; PTL.

KENNETH (3m B si n. d.)
    "Non-narrative, abstract film. "--P. S.   By Patricia Sloane; WAF,
SLOANE.

KENOJUAK see ESKIMO ARTIST: KENOJUAK

KIBBUTZ DAPHNA (26m C 1968)
    Explains how the kibbutz settlements of Israel are organized as
agricultural communities to serve all the people living there. Shows
how the kibbutz society has been brought to fulfillment at Daphna in
northern Galilee. By Virginia Garner, Ray Garner; ALDEN.

KIENHOLZ ON EXHIBIT (21m B 1969)
    Shows Edward Kienholz's controversial exhibit at the Los Angeles
County Museum of Art, with public reactions. By June Steel; MGH.

KILLING OF SISTER GEORGE (138m C 1969)
    Because the ratings on her TV show have been dropping, aging
lesbian "Sister George" is written out of her series. Distraught,
she spends more time with her gin and less time with her roommate lover, Childie, who becomes restless. This film, try as it
does to make lesbians look like perverts, reveals the women as
strong people trapped by their roles and desperately trying to get
out of them. By Robert Aldrich; ABCPC; FL

KILLING TIME (12m C/B n. d.)
    "... in reality and fantasy a female relates ambivalently to the
males around her. "--G. L.   By Gloria Laskowich; FCOOP.

KINESIS (5m C 1975)
    Escher-like images stepping through the frames to the music of

a jazz group. Delightful--shows a depth in the imagery not accomplished by computer before. By Lillian Schwartz: LPL

KIRSA NICHOLINA (16m C 1970)
This deceptively simple film of a child being born to a Woodstock couple in their home is an almost classic manifesto of the new sensibility, a proud affirmation of man amidst technological genocide and ecological destruction. Birth is not presented as an antiseptic "medical" experience but as living-through of a primitive mystery, a spiritual celebration, a rite of passage. Her whole body is seen at times; the continuity between lovepartner and birthgiver is maintained; she remains "erotic." By Gunvor Nelson; MMRC, SB; CCC, FCOOP, GP, MMRC, SB.

KISS, THE (61m B si 1929)
A crime is committed by Madame Guarry and the victim is her husband. The trial ends with Madame Guarry being acquitted as the jury believed it was suicide. Madame Guarry had shot her husband to save a young man from her raging husband who believed she was in love with Pierre. Pierre loves her, there is no doubt there, but she is enamored with an attorney impersonated by Conrad Nagel. It is Nagel who convinces the jury to look upon the death as self-inflicted. Pierre knows M. Guarry had killed her husband, but he believes she did it because she loved him. d. Jacques Feyder; MGM; FL

KISS ME, STUPID (124m B 1964)
Dean Martin, returning from Las Vegas, is forced by accident to detour to Climax, Nevada. There he is pounced upon by a pair of local songwriters who sabotage his car and bring in an accommodating cocktail waitress to seduce him. Based on a play by Anna Bonacci; d. Billy Wilder; UAS.

KISSES FOR MY PRESIDENT (113m B 1964)
Non-partisan, non-political and non-serious, this good-natured comedy explores the possibilities of what could happen were a glamorous and brainy woman elected president of the U.S. and her business tycoon husband became the first male "First Lady" in American history! There are gags and wild complications as the new President, her husband and two children move into the White House. d. Curtis Bernhardt; WSA; ABFI, FC, WEL.

KITTY FOYLE (107m B 1940)
The life and loves of a white-collar girl, viewed in tender retrospect. Kitty Foyle (Ginger Rogers), from the wrong side of the Philadelphia tracks, is briefly married to a weak-willed scion of a Main Line family. Later, she is faced with a decision: a choice between her ex-husband or a steady young actor. Based on a novel by Christopher Morley. p. David Hempstead; d. Sam Wood; RKO; FL

KITTY HAWK TO PARIS--THE HEROIC YEARS (54m C 1970)
Depicts the first chapter in the continuing story of men who fly --their successes, failures and sacrifices which blazed the trail

that leads from Kitty Hawk to Paris. By Helen Jean Rogers, John Secondari; LCA.

KLONDIKE ANNIE (83m B 1936)
Mae West emerges from the thick studio haze of an evil-looking opium den, wearing a candelabra hat, plucking a mandolin, and crooning "I'm an Occidental Woman in an Oriental Mood for Love." Based on her play Frisco Kate, the story tells how the notorious Frisco Doll skedaddles to the Yukon, where she lives incognito as a Salvation Army worker. d. Raoul Walsh; s. w. Mae West; PARAMOUNT; UNIVE.

KLUTE (114m C 1971)
A stunning private eye melodrama with psychological overtones. A corporate big shot from a small Pennsylvania town disappears in the canyon of New York. Klute, a small town detective, tries to track down the executive, and his investigation leads him to Bree, a high-priced call girl--hard on the surface but confused. Bree is the key to the vanished executive. She's being hunted by a psychopathic killer, a man with hatred for prostitutes. A psychiatrist outlines Bree's needs and the mind of the killer for Klute. All ends happily for Klute and Bree at the marriage bureau. D. Alan Pakula; WSA; BF, CINE, CWF, MGH, SELECT, WCF, WEL, WHOLFC.

KNEE AD, A (22m B 1972)
"... a loose take-off on Virgil's Aeneid, but only in the limited sense that both are about journeys, and therefore about motion. Although most of the footage was shot while leaving, entering, or commuting within New York, what appears on the screen is a journey around the environs of the screen itself. Filmmaker says: "I think of the film as a sort of camp mythopoesy reduced to the level of absurdity."--P. S. By Patricia Sloan; FCOOP.

KOAN (2m C n. d.)
A cyclic poem made into a simple theme. Koan is a prayer in animation. By Denise Gallant; CCC.

KUDZU (16m C 1977)
An off-beat, witty, informative documentary about the vine Kudzu, or Pueraria Thunbergiana, that is taking over a large portion of the Southern landscape. Imported from Japan in the 1930's by the Dept. of Agriculture for erosion control, its spreading growth has become a problem of menacing proportions. By Marjie Short; PF.

KUMAK THE SLEEPY HUNTER (13m C 1952)
A charming puppet-film based on an Eskimo legend from the Land of the Long Night where life itself depends on prowess as a hunter. Kumak, the Eskimo, has a problem--he would rather sleep than hunt. One day, he is given magical powers that makes him a great hunter--a secret he's never to disclose. He marries the prettiest girl in the village; eventually, his wife induces him to tell the secret of his success and the magical powers cease. Kumak loses his importance in the eyes of his friends and is back to his sleepy self. By Alma Duncan, Audrey McLaren; NFBC; FIM.

KYPSELI: WOMEN AND MEN APART--A DIVIDED REALITY (40m
   C   1976)
   A tightly constructed essay on a peasant society of Kypseli, a
small isolated Greek village on the island of Thera (Santorini) in the
Cyclades. It depicts how the people divide time, space, material
possessions and activities according to an underlying pattern based
on the separation of the sexes, and how this division, in turn, determines the village social structure. It is one of the rare films
that present an abstract theory in terms concrete enough to aid the
general public in understanding the problems they experience in
everyday life. Susannah M. Hoffman, anthropologist and researcher.
p. Richard Cowan; EMC.

L-SHAPED ROOM, THE (124m   B   1963)
   A lonely, frightened young woman finds romance (and a lot of
trouble) while awaiting the birth of a baby conceived in a loveless
weekend affair. D. Bryan Forbes; COLUMBIA; SWANK.

LABOR (3m   C   1976)
   The birth experience is told from the mother's point of view in
this animated film drawn from the filmmaker's real life experience.
Josie is shown at the mercy of all-powerful doctors who are insensi-
tive to her difficulties in labor. A caesarean is finally performed,
and she nurses her new baby. The father is supportive throughout.
A positive, upbeat affirmation of childbirth. By Josie Ramstad;
SB.

LABOR AND CHILDBIRTH (15m   B   1967)
   Shows the main muscles involved in labor, and the stages of
labor. Birth is shown by diagrams. Shows labor, delivery and
nursery rooms of the hospital. MEDAA; BU.

LABOUR AND DELIVERY; Pregnancy and Childbirth Series (19m
    C 1977)
   Examines the stages of labour and the delivery of the child in
detail. The father's participation is discussed. Hospital care after
the delivery, care of the newborn, and the first few days at home
are included. CRAWLEY; IFB.

LACE OF SUMMER (4m   C   si   1973)
   Cine-sonnet No. 1. Filmed in Venice. By Storm De Hirsch;
FCOOP.

LADY AND THE WATERCOLOR, THE (4m   C   1975)
   Non-narrated story in animation about a woman who did not
have a hobby. One day she decided to remedy this and bought a
water color set and began to paint, paint, paint--only to discover
everything was colored squares. She decided to stop painting altogether and was soon off to the dime store in pursuit of another hobby. By Jeannie Youngson; BULSUSP; FL.

LADY BARBARA WARD JACKSON (23m B 1962)
Lady Barbara Ward Jackson, the author of The Rich and Poor Nations speaks about the disappearance of distinctions of wealth in a world of abundance.   She raises the questions of human solidarity and use of leisure.   She stresses man's moral duty to create the city of God in which the family of man can live.   EBEC; USC.

LADY BEWARE! (16m C 1973)
Demonstrates effective common sense techniques that women can use to protect themselves from the growing menace of personal assault.   Through realistic dramatizations, all the precautions and defense methods that a woman has at her command are reviewed.   Includes details of security for home, car and the phone, precautions for avoiding danger when out at night, the wisdom of flight, and what to do when flight isn't possible.   By Bruce Kerner; JULF; CWU, NIU, PP, UILL.

LADY EVE, THE (97m B 1941)
Barbara Stanwyck plays a distaff card-shark who spots a cast-iron sucker in beer heir "Hopsie" Pike (Henry Fonda).   Hopsie, too engrossed in his lifelong project of writing a book, isn't caring about looking after his millions so the lady's father, Handsome Harry Harrington, sends the lady into action.   d. Preston Sturgis; PARAMOUNT; UAS.

LADY IN THE DARK, THE (100m C 1944)
A successful fashion-magazine editress who has a perplexing subconscious block toward men goes to a psychiatrist and discovers she has a king-sized father complex, and that the men she attracts are weaklings with queen-sized mother complexes.   Most elaborate and excessive Freudian musical.   Adapted from the play by Moss Hart. d. Mitchell Leisen; PARAMOUNT; CVE, UNIVE.

LADY IN THE LINCOLN MEMORIAL (18m C 1969)
Some of us respond militantly to injustice.   Marian Anderson expressed her commitment for change through her art.   The film traces her career from childhood to her early singing days in churches and small concert halls ... through her triumphant concert tours of Europe and America ... to her historic performance at the Lincoln Memorial in 1939 after she had been denied the use of Constitution Hall.   NYT; BF, REPRO; BU, UILL.

LADY NANCY ASTOR (April 15, 1951) (28m B 1951)
Lady Nancy Astor discusses the current socialist government in England with Martha Roundtree, moderator Marshall McNeil, Ruth Cowan, Richard Oulahan, and Lawrence Spivak on "Meet the Press." NBCTV.

LADY SINGS THE BLUES (144m C 1972 Scope)
Billie Holiday, who was born in poverty in 1915 and died of drug addiction at age 44, was the greatest blues singer America ever produced.   This movie biography of her life and Diana Ross's rendition of her personage succeeds not through imitation, but

through a loving evocation of Lady Day, fully realized by a film-making team with a sincere commitment to the subject and a star who in her life has given freely of her own emotions in song. Based on Billie Holiday's autobiography.   p. Jay Weston, James White; d. Sidney Furie; PARAMOUNT; FL

LADY WITH A LAMP, A (110m   B   1952)
Story of Florence Nightingale, founder of the nursing profession. Starring Ann Neagle.   d. Herbert Wilcox; ABFL

LAMENTATION see A MOTION PICTURE STUDY OF MARTHA GRAHAM FROM HER DANCE, "LAMENTATION."

LAMPS IN THE WORK PLACE (28m   C   n. d.)
A case-study approach to the Equal Pay Act covering sex discrimination, child labor, age discrimination, and garnishment. USDL.

LAST OF THE GREAT MALE CHAUVINISTS; Insight Series (27m
C   n. d.)
Shows the necessity for women to develop a sense of their own importance and for men to sustain them in this effort.   Every wife and mother eventually reaches a period in life when she retires from certain duties.   It is essential that these women equip themselves to handle what some call "the non-productive years," which, in fact, can be the happiest and most fulfilling.   By Kim Hunter, Don Porter; MGH.

LAST PATROL (54m   C   n. d.)
Follows a group of Vietnam veterans traveling from Los Angeles to the 1972 Democratic Convention in Miami to present their demands to the delegates.   By Laura Cavastani, Frank Cavastani; IMPF.

LAST PICTURE SHOW, THE (118m   B   1971)
A narrative of a life in a bleak one-horse Texas town in 1951. At its mythic center is Ben Johnson (Sam the Lion) who owns the town's pool room, diner, and the one-aisle show house.   Timothy Bottoms and Jeff Bridges are two high school seniors no longer boys and not yet men.   It is about their affairs with their peers where ritualized petting had its definite limits as well as seduction of and being seduced by older restless women.   An air of suppressed sex broods over the town.   Sam the Lion dies and with him the last vestige of an era also dies.   The movie house closes with the death of Sam.   Bottoms and Bridges attend the last picture, Red River.   Bridges goes to Korea, and Bottoms stays behind to a life equally without point.   d. Peter Bogdanovich; p. Stephen J. Friedman; BBS; RBC, SWANK.

LAST REFLECTIONS ON A WAR; Way It Is, The (Series) (44m
B   1968)
Presents critical comments and views of Asian scholar and war correspondent Bernard B. Fall.   Discusses the nature of the war in

Vietnam, its effect on the people, and the possibility of a practical solution. Includes the comments which Fall was recording when he was killed. By Beryl Fox; PBL/CBCTV; NET, IU.

LAST SUMMER, THE (97m   C   1969)

Four young people discover themselves and each other in a summer at a beach party. Perhaps most appealing is the open and honest relationship they promise each other early in the picture and adhere to with both joyful and devastating effect throughout the story. At the same time, the drama points up the sometimes vicious effects of group pressure that are frequently the dark side of togetherness. d. Frank Perry; s.w. Eleanor Perry; ALLIED ARTISTS; HCW.

LAST WEEK (5m   B   1969)

"Apollo II--down 5-3/4, two shares traded."--CCC. Sound track of the moon landing with images of lovers. By Marjorie Prisadsky; CCC.

LATER THAT NIGHT (4m   C   1976)

Films in animation an exploration of the filmmaker's dream. Most women will recognize their own conflicts about being female. Frank, though innocent, nudity may restrict this film to college-level audiences. By Barbara Bottner; FL.

LATER YEARS OF THE WOODLEYS (30m   B   1969)

About how a social worker can meet some of the needs of older persons who are ill. We see one couple's psychological responses to physical incapacity: changes in the husband-wife relationship, insecurity, tension, depression. Stresses the importance of a consistent relationship with the social worker and continuity of contact. For first-year graduate students and caseworkers inexperienced in working with the elderly. NAVC; EMC.

LATEST PICTURE SHOW, THE (2m   C   1972)

"Beautiful drawings and cut-out animation express a girl's infatuation with movies. Her fantasies turn everyone that she meets into a movie star."--YFD. By Valorie Patrak; YFD.

LAURETTE (20m   B   1969)

A portrayal of the circumstances many young women must face when they find themselves left to cope with family problems alone. Laurette is a young secretary, separated from her husband, with a daughter to bring up. Her thoughts, feelings and fears are shown. As she tries to make sense of the broken reality of her life, she must each day convince herself that life can go on while she provides a home for her child--that living as a "solo" parent can go on. NFBC; EMC.

LAVENDER (13m   C   1972)

Honest and sensitive film dealing with the lives of two young lesbians. The two young women in their mid-twenties are genuinely in love with each other. We see them in their daily lives, in their

apartment, at their jobs, at a gay bar, roaming in their favorite
woods. Dialogue reveals their thoughts and feelings, their realization of their lesbianism, and the position of homosexuality in our
society. By Colleen Monahan, Elaine Jacobs; PERENNIAL; UM.

LAVENDER TROUBADOR (40m B n. d.)
     This original one-woman play is a profoundly moving experi-
ence for actress and audience. It tells with eloquence and simplicity
the story of two out-front lesbians and the way they deal with a society that persecutes them. Beyond the story itself, the play is a
call for action. NOWP; CREOU.

LE PINK GRAPEFRUIT (27m C 1976)
     Shows Salvador Dali in the environment he has created for him-
self in Northern Spain. Gives us a glimpse of this fascinating and
complicated man. Leaves us with a fuller awareness of his art and
a deeper understanding of the reality from which his surreal can-
vasses are created. Also shown is the Salvador Dali Museum built
in Figueras, Spain in 1975 and the celebration of the first anniversary of its opening. p. Sue Yung Li Ikeda; d. Lawrence Halprin;
PHOENIX.

LEADERSHIP: STYLE OR CIRCUMSTANCE? (30m C 1974)
     Examined are two styles of leadership--relationship-oriented and
task-oriented. Rather than claiming either style is better, the film
demonstrates that the effectiveness of each depends upon the specific
situation in which it is used. p. Judith Dancoff; CRM, MGH; CWU,
UW.

LEARNED LADIES (LES FEMMES SAVANTES) (100m B 1965
     French/subtitled)
     A satire on the Women's Liberation Movement in early 17th-
century France. Both men and women were making effort to lead a
more elegant life; intellectual games were played, epigrams and letters in verse were popular, and the art of conversation was developed. Many women from the salons became quite well-known and
respected for their learning and intelligence. There are always
those who respond to any movement by indulging in excesses. It is
these women Moliere attacks and ridicules. Adapted from Moliere's
Les Femmes Savantes. d. Jean Meyer; MGH.

LEARNING (30m C 1971)
     An abbreviated course on the many aspects of learning, this film
uses a variety of cinematic techniques to portray species-specific behavior, sign stimuli, imprinting, behavior shaping, and other types
of learning behaviors. p. Carole Hart; CRM, MGH.

LEARNING THROUGH MOVEMENT (36m B 1968)
     Presents a creative movement program for the elementary
school, developed by Anne Lief Barlin at the Sycamore Elementary
school, Claremont, California. Dance classes in grades one through
six were photographed over an eight month period to illustrate types
of movement activities, goals and philosophy of the program, and

the involvement of growth of the children. By Anne Barlin, Paul
Barlin; SLFP; UILL.

LEATHER BOYS (103m B 1963 (Gr. Br.))
Against a background of lower-middle-class London, drama
probes the relationship among young people of the motorcycle set.
Reggie, a young mechanic, marries Dot, a high school dropout, for
whom marriage represented an escape from Mum, the chance to
read True Romance in bed, and to peroxide her hair. Dot has no
more idea of Reggie's emotional needs than he has of hers. When
Reggie leaves Dot and rooms with Pete, a fellow cyclist, he discovers the homosexual side of the black-leather boys. Based on
the novel by Eliot George. d. Sidney J. Furie; p. Raymond Stross;
ABFI.

LEAVE HER TO HEAVEN (110m B 1946)
Jeanne Crain plays the moody, petulant woman so possessive in
her love for her husband that she kills anyone to whom he devotes
any attention--even destroying herself through trickery when she
learns her husband and sister have fallen in love. d. John Stahl;
FOX; FI.

LEENYA: DAUGHTER OF THE NOBLE BLACKS OF SURINAM (11m
C 1973)
Introduces Leenya, a bush Negro girl of the South American Surinam jungle, explains her people's proud history as escaped African
slaves, her life in a large family and her ideals. GODAJ; IFB; BU.

LEFT SIDE, RIGHT SIDE (7m B 1972)
"Concerns differences between a mirror and monitor in relation
to self-perception. "--Women and Film: A Resource Handbook. By
Joan Jonas; CASTELLI.

LEGACY OF ANNE FRANK (29m C 1967)
A heart-warming treatment of the Anne Frank story visually
traces this young girl's life, and highlights her legacy--the delightful
love of life and beauty which she held. Superb on-location and documentary footage used. NBCTV; MGH; UM.

LEGACY OF ANNE SULLIVAN, THE (30m C 1968)
Demonstrates the work being done today to teach and rehabilitate
deaf-blind children and adults. Describes the pioneering work of
Anne Sullivan with Helen Keller. PERKNS; CAMPF; USC.

LEGAULT'S PLACE (11m B 1965)
A story about a man who wanted from life only to be left in
peace to live with his memories in the familiar comfort of his aging
cabin. Tells how the city began to build around him, how he evaded
eviction and how he eventually became wealthy from the sale of his
cabin. By Susanne Angel; NFBC; FI.

LEGEND OF LYLAH CLARE, THE (130m C 1968)
A melodrama about an actress portraying a sex goddess who

finds herself losing her own identity in the role.   d. Robert Aldrich;
MGM; FL

LEISURE (14m   C   1976)
    Traces the "history" of leisure hours from the caveman's first
moment of play, through the Industrial Revolution's triumph over
scarcity to the present concern for having a good environment for
our leisure hours.   d. Bruce Petty; p. Suzanne Baker; FILM
AUSTRALIA; PF.

LESBIAN FAMILY (28m   C   1973)
    A film about Sandy, Maddy and their families, and their strug-
gle to live as they want despite their differences with society's
definition of what it is to be normal.   Sandy and Maddy are two
Seattle women living together with their children, while their husbands sue them for the children's custody.   The upshot of the trial
was that the women have custody, but only on the condition that they
not live together.   Included are interviews with family members,
doctors, psychiatrists, social workers, and a priest.   MMRC.

LESBIANS (28m   C   1975   VIDEO)
    In this program facts are presented to diminish myths and
stereotyped views about lesbians.   Historical information about individual lesbians, current legislation which affects homosexuals, and
a panel discussion by five lesbians form the core of this program.
An opportunity to view a group of lesbians as they are.   NOWP;
CREOUT.

LESLIE (5m   C/B   1971)
    A seven-year-old girl talks about her life.   By Vicki Polon;
POLON.

LET'S MAKE A FILM (13m   C   1970)
    Documentary of children creating animated films.   By Yvonne
Anderson; YBW; FCOOP.

LET'S TALK ABOUT MEN (93m   C   1978   Italian/subtitled)
    A quartet of bittersweet comedies.   In the first story a husband
is enraged to learn of the shocking way his wife earns money.   As
he reflects on his failures and lack of funds, he becomes less and
less enraged....   Second story focuses on a knife thrower in a circus and his assistant who acts as his target.   She thinks his eyesight is failing and implores him to purchase new glasses.   He
disagrees with her.   Unfortunately she was right....   Third story
is about a husband who considers himself quite superior to his wife
and who is constantly putting her down.   The husband claims to
have uncovered a plot by his wife and her lover to kill him.   He
goads his wife into shooting him, and collapses in a heap.   In the
end, however, love conquers all....   The fourth story concerns a
peasant family.   The husband is unemployed.   He spends his days
drinking at the tavern with the boys, then returns home drunk,
eager to claim his bedroom prerogatives.   The wife, slaving over
chores at home all day, is in no mood.   These telling vignettes

are likely to bring little joy, and perhaps even considerable squirm-
ing to male chauvinists, but there are very few women who won't
recognize one or more (or heaven forbid, perhaps all) of the male
idiosyncrasies projected here. d. Lina Wertmuller; HCW.

LET'S TALK ABOUT WOMEN (108m B 1964 Italian/subtitled)
     Vittorio Gassman plays nine different roles in as many vignettes.
The episodes are satiric comments on contemporary sex problems
and practices. Among other roles, Gassman plays a waiter who
tricks prostitutes into taking him home because there is no other
transportation; a man who is reluctant to leave a young lady's bed,
even though she must dress for her wedding; a rag collector who
is called up five flights of stairs to a lavish apartment, and is in-
dignant when the rich woman offers sex, not rags. d. Ettore Scola;
ABFL

LETTER FROM AN UNKNOWN WOMAN (90m B 1948)
     A lavish, well-acted romance between a beautiful young woman
and a great concert pianist who gives her no more than one night
and a bastard child. She is haunted throughout her life by the image of her unrequited love. d. Max Ophuls; UNIVE; IVY.

LETTER TO AMY, A (7m C 1970)
     Story of a little boy who writes an invitation to his friend Amy.
Adapted from book by same title by Ezra Jack Keats. By Cynthia
Freitag; WESTON.

LETTERS (11m C n. d.)
     Letters are love energy, are valentines. This is a film of four
letters received by the filmmaker. By Dorothy Wiley; CCC.

LIBELED LADY (98m B 1936)
     A sardonic comedy with Jean Harlow, William Powell, Myrna
Loy and Spencer Tracy. The story is about a libel suit resulting
when the Evening Star prints an unfortunate story from London, confusing Connie Allenbury with someone else, thus accusing her of
stealing another woman's husband. So, the wily Mr. Powell sets
about to have the aloof Connie be caught in the act of pilfering someone's husband so the Star will shine again. From a story by Wal-
lace Sullivan. d. Jack Conway; s. w. , Maurine Watkins; MGM; FL

LIEBALALA (SWEETHEART) (58m B r1972)
     Rare ethnographic document of life of the Lozi people of Barot-
seland (now part of Zambia), filmed in 1935. Native actors depict
scenes from their daily lives, portraying all aspects of courtship
and marriage. Other aspects of Lozi culture shown include mining,
smelting, and shaping of iron by miners and craftsmen, and a cooperative fish hunt on the part of several villages. Sound track contains authentic Lozi music. Margaret Hubbard describes her experience and provides insight of then and now. p. Margaret Carson Hubbard; EMC.

LIFE AND DEATH OF FRIDA KAHLO (40m C r1976)
     Documentary of Frida Kahlo, wife of Diego Rivera, Mexico's

most famous woman painter--brilliant, flamboyant and obsessed.
Her fame is legendary. She painted for resurrection; she painted
to plead for rebirth; she painted to plead for miracle. The film
focuses on the events that molded her life. By Karen Crommie,
David Crommie; SB.

LIFE AROUND LAKE TITICACA; Indian Family Series (14m C
  1971)
    Illustrates a day in the life of a typical Indian family living in
the area of Lake Titicaca, which lies between Peru and Bolivia.
Shows how the lake shapes the life of the people, and explains their
dependence on the totora reed growing in its waters. By Elda Hartley; HARTLEY.

LIFE AROUND US SERIES see ROCK-A-BYE-BABY

LIFE CHANGES; Human Sexuality Series (29m C 1972 VIDEO)
    Changes in human sexuality during different life stages (child-
hood to puberty, puberty to adolescence, maturity to senescence)
are illustrated through interviews with people who have reached
these stages. Guests express their concern about sexuality. The
host debunks some of the myths about each life stage. UHAWAII/
KHETTV; PTL.

LIFE OF ELIZABETH; News Magazine of the Screen Series (10m
  B 1953)
    Presents a 1952 Screen News Digest excerpt showing the English
Royal couple's visit to Canada and U.S. in 1952. Shows briefly
Queen Elizabeth's early life. Shows colorful crown jewels in prepa-
ration for the coronation in 1953. Covers the historic coronation
and pageantry. PATHE; HEARST.

LIFE OF MOTHER SETON (45m B 1959)
    Documents the inspiring life of the foundress of the American
Sisters of Charity and the parochial school system in this country.
Her thoughts and feelings are revealed through her own statements
concerning her philosophy and dedication. CATHFC; UM.

LIGHT FANTASTIK (58m C 1974)
    Superlative and detailed retrospective of the contributions made
by artists at the National Film Board of Canada to the development
of the animated film. Includes numerous excerpts and several works
in their entirety, and illustrates and explains animation techniques
such as Norman McLaren's pixilation and drawing-on-film, Evelyn
Lambart's fairy-tale cutouts, Lotte Reiniger's delicate shadow puppets, and Ryan Larkin's visual improvisations. d. Rupert Glover,
Michael Patenaude; p. Wolf Koenig; NFBC; EMC, UW.

LIGHTS (7m C si 1964-66)
    "Made during the brief Christmas-lit season, usually between
midnight and 1 a.m. ... Based on store decorations, window displays, fountains, public promenades, Park Avenue lights, buildings
and church facades."--M.M. By Marie Menken; FCOOP.

LIKE A ROSE (23m B   1975)
    Documentary of two women who are serving 25-year sentences
in the Missouri State Penitentiary. Photographs of long-ago contrast
the bleak reality of the present. Peggy and Carolyn speak of their
day-to-day existence and how inappropriate any of these activities
are for getting along on the outside. They view their time spent in
confinement as a terrible waste. There are no funds available for
furthering their education. Carolyn adds that the depression gets
worse with time. Her sympathetic roommate smiles and tells her,
"Baby, you'll come out smelling like a rose. " A candid film that
will stimulate discussion on prison reform for women. d. Sally
Barrett-Page; TPL

LIKE EVERYBODY ELSE (32m C   1976)
    A documentary which depicts the life of the retarded adult in
the community and illustrates the best model of comprehensive pro-
gramming for the retarded adult in America. d. Biff Boyle; p.
Julie Leavy; STNFLD.

LIKE OTHER PEOPLE (37m C   1973)
    An utterly moving, extraordinary film dealing with the sexual,
emotional and social needs of the mentally or physically handicapped.
The two main characters are cerebral palsy patients who, by using
their own words, make a plea to humanity for the understanding
that they are "real" people. At one point this is a poignant love
story which will help us to understand that physically handicapped
people share our emotions. Because their speech may be affected,
cerebral palsy patients sometimes have a hard time communicating.
There is a tendency to switch off the film because it is sometimes
difficult to understand. This fact reflects the attitude of society--
only then it is people we are switching off and not a film. This
film raises intense questions about the quality of life, about privacy,
and about understanding "other people. " DIDTFL; PERENNIAL.

LIKE THE TREES; Challenge for Change Series (15m C n. d.)
    Rose is a Metis from northern Alberta, a woman who has lifted
herself out of an anguished existence in the city by rediscovering
her roots among the woodland Cree. "I've left everything. ...   I'm
just being myself. ... Like the trees, we belong here. " By Kathleen Shannon, Len Chatwin; NFBC; EMC.

LILLIAN (20m C n. d. VIDEO)
    Computer-controlled video tape presents a story of a primordial
woman who experiences something much like Dorian Gray's disintegration. By Lillian Schwartz; LPL

LINCOLN SERIES see NANCY HANKS

LINDA'S FILM--MENSTRUATION (18m C 1974)
    A story of a 15-year-old girl and her 16-year-old male com-
panion during the week her menstrual period starts. A good sex
education film, vastly funny, communicates information marvelously.
Useable for all ages. Includes an animated segment explaining the

physiological process of menstruation. By Linda Feferman; PHOE-
NIX, VFI; EMC, UM.

LINE (10m B 1969)
A line appears on the film, creating the illusion of film on film.
By Yvonne Rainer; VRL

LINE, THE (10m C 1975)
Computer-generated animation. "Abstract geometry acts out a
Zen-like theme of birth and awakening. Point A to point B is
drawn; their connection is awakening. "--V. C. M. By Vicky Chaet
Meyer; MEYER.

LINES HORIZONTAL (7m C 1965)
A subtle abstract film in which lines, ruled directly on film,
move with precision and grace against a background of changing
colors, in response to music specially composed for the film by
Pete Seeger. See Lines Horizontal and Vertical. By Evelyn Lambart, Norman McLaren; NFBC; CFS.

LINES HORIZONTAL AND VERTICAL (14m C 1961)
See Lines Horizontal and Lines Vertical for separate descriptions. The two films are mounted on one reel and offered as a
single unit at a reduced total rental rate for those who wish to rent
both films simultaneously. By Evelyn Lambart, Norman McLaren;
NFBC; CFS.

LINES VERTICAL (7m C 1961)
A subtle abstract film comparable in technique to Lines Hori-
zontal. Music (electronic piano) by Maurice Blackburn. See Lines
Horizontal and Vertical. By Evelyn Lambart, Norman McLaren;
NFBC; CFS.

LION IN WINTER, THE (132m C 1968 Reg. /Scope)
A 12th-century historical drama recreates the pomp, pageantry
and pride of merry old England during the reign of King Henry II
(Peter O'Toole) with Katharine Hepburn as the silvery-tongued Queen
Eleanor of Aquitaine. d. Anthony Harvey; AVCO; ABFL

LION'S LOVE (110m C 1969)
It's about movies, making movies, life in the 60's in America,
being a superstar, being a woman director, being stoned on life
and participating in a vision of the American dream as seen through
the eyes of its youth. Agnes Varda fell in love with Los Angeles
when she came to America and decided to make a film about her
feelings of the city and the time in which she lived. Enlisting the
help of filmmaker Shirley Clarke, Andy Warhol, star Viva, and the
writers of Hair, she put this together. d. Agnes Varda; EYR; IMA,
TWY.

LITTLE BURGUNDY (30m B 1968)
When an old area of a city is to be demolished to make way for
a new low-rental housing development, is there anything that the

residents can do to protect their own interests?   This film airs
such a situation in the little town of Burgundy, district in Montreal.
It shows how citizens organized themselves into a committee that
made effective representations to city hall and influenced the housing
policy.   By Bonnie Klein; NFBC.

LITTLE CHIMNEY SWEEP (10m   B   1930's)
     A fairy tale in silhouette animation based on live shadow play.
In 18th-century London, a little chimney sweep rescues a rich young
heiress from the clutches of an evil nobleman.   By Lotte Reiniger;
BBCTV; CEA, MGH.

LITTLE DRUMMER BOY, THE (7m   C   1971)
     Story adapted from Ezra Jack Keats' illustrated version of the
Christmas caroL   By Cynthia Freitag; WESTON.

LITTLE FOXES, THE (116m   B   1941)
     This timeless study in avarice revolves around a family of sec-
ond generation Southern carpetbaggers in the early 1900's.   Bette
Davis plays Regina, the greedy and ruthless woman who sacrifices
everything, including her husband's life, in order to attain wealth
and status.   Lillian Hellman wrote this film adaptation of her own
internationally acclaimed play.   d. William Wyler; AIM; ABFL

LITTLE GIRAFFE, THE (8m   C   n. d.)
     Animated puppet film enacted by toys.   A delightful fantasy film
for the youngest audience.   d. Theresa Badzian; MGH.

LITTLE GIRL AND A GUNNY WOLF, A (6m   C   1971)
     Tells of a little girl who, in spite of her mother's warning,
goes to pick flowers in the forest where she encounters a fabulous
animal known as the Big, Bad Gunny Wolf.   By Marion Klein, Steve
Klein; PARACO.

LITTLE JOYS, LITTLE SORROWS (10m   B   1968)
     A little girl happily nurses her doll until a cat appears.   The
doll is cast aside--second best to the cat.   However, the capricious
animal refuses to play.   Disappointed, the little girl returns to the
abandoned doll, her faithful friend, and the confidante of her childish
sorrows.   No narration.   d. Jadwiga Kedzierzawska; Featurette Film
Studio in Lodz; MGH.

LITTLE MEN OF CROMAGNON, THE (9m   C   n. d.)
     An animated introduction to primary colors and their combina-
tions in which little elf-like creatures make all the discoveries.
By Francine Desbiens; NFBC.

LITTLE RED RIDING HOOD (6m   C   1968)
     Through the magic of animation, again the classic story of Lit-
tle Red Riding Hood is told in a delightful way.   By Rhoda Leyer;
NFBC.

LIVES AND LIFE STYLES (20m   C   1972)
     A group of Maine people talk about different ways of life--an

old lady who grows most of her own food, a young couple from a self-supporting commune, a long-time resident who has a Dory boat business. All of them talk about their own life-styles and comment on those of others. POLYMORPH.

LIVES OF PERFORMERS (90m B 1972)
"Autonomous work, deriving from her performance with dancers of the past two years."--Whitney Museum. By Yvonne Rainer; VRL

LIVIA MAKES SOME CHANGES (7m B 1974)
Livia, a middle-aged housewife and mother, gets a job outside the home and returns to face the emphatic opposition of husband and son. She remains determined, however, and her determination is unexpectedly rewarded--a family which has learned to share together. By Kathleen Malanaphy, Anne Sandys, Sheelah Weaver; WMM.

LIVING BETTER (52/13-14m ea. C 1971-73 VIDEO)
This consumer and homemaking series for low income women presents practical advice in the fields of health, education, home furnishings, clothing, money management, food and nutrition, housing and equipment, and child development. Write to PTL for individual program titles. MAETEL; PTL.

LIVING CAMERA SERIES see JANE; SUSAN STARR

LIVING ON THE EDGE (5m C 1974)
"Seattle filmmaker Vetter opens an 'educated' eye on some 'romantic' symbols and cliches of our time."--Freude Bartlett. By Barbara Vetter; SB.

LIVING TOGETHER (28m B 1972)
Three families, living in alternative family groups are shown: a young woman who lives alone with her child; a group of young women, some of whom have children, live together; and several middle-aged couples share a large house. Intended as a discussion provoker, the film has commentary on the styles shown and on the changing family by anthropologist Margaret Mead. p. S. Spence Meighan, M. D. ; GSHDME.

LIVING WITH PETER (22m B 1973)
Cinéma-vérité techniques are put to an interesting autobiographical use in an investigation of a filmmaker's personal dilemma. Miriam and Peter have been living together for some time without the benefit of marriage and with substantial ambivalence over that status. The film explores their attitudes as well as her mother's towards modern living arrangements and the problems it poses for someone with traditional needs. By Miriam Weinstein; SB.

LIZARD MOSAIC (3m C 1971)
"Lush exploration of a chameleon changing color."--K. J. By Karen Johnson; SB.

LIZZY (88m B 1957 German/subtitled)
The film sheds some light on why the Jews fell into disfavor

during the economic dislocations of pre-Nazi Germany.   Recounts
the story of a woman who actually existed--focuses on the human
dimension of the Holocaust.   Based on a novel by F. C. Weiskopf.
d. Konrad Wolf; ABFL

LOGOS (2m   C   n. d.)
A dynamic audio-visual experience which combines non-objective
visuals and electronic music to produce optical illusions and a distortion of time perception.   Electronic music score by Henry Jacobs.
By Jane Belson; CFS.

LOLA MONTES (110m   C   1955   Scope   French/subtitled)
Based on the life of a woman who lived in the 19th century.
Clowns and acrobats dance and ride across the arena floor as the
ringmaster (Peter Ustinov) invites the audience to ask Lola (Martine
Carol) any questions they choose, no matter how personal.   Lola
recalls her romances with Franz Liszt, a student and a king before
she was reduced to poverty and ill fortune to the humiliation of her
present life--a paid spectacle for the masses, a living example of
sin and downfall.   Ophuls suggests that the traditions of elegance
and romance which Lola represents are as necessary to the world
as Lola is to the ringmaster who exploits, yet loves her.   Based
on the novel The Extraordinary Life of Lola Montes by Cecil Saint-
Laurent.   d. Max Ophuls; ABFL

LONELY NIGHT, THE (62m   B   1955)
A detailed account of a young woman's recovery from a severe
emotional disturbance with the help of a skilled psychiatrist.   The
film shows the patient gaining insight which releases her from the
past and gives her hope for the future.   The film also shows a
family in which the children receive from their parents what the
sick girl had to get from the therapist.   d. Irving Jacoby; MHFB;
IFB.

LONG CHAIN, THE (20m   B   1972)
Revealing study of the construction of two buildings for U. S.
companies in Bombay.   Shows how women construction workers
brought to Bombay from Southern India work for starvation wages,
only to be stranded in the city's slums once construction is finished.
Examines the economic and political role of U. S. corporations such
as I. T. T. and Citibank in India, and illustrates the consequences of
foreign investment and foreign aid.   Swedish production; TFC; EMC.

LONG DAY'S JOURNEY INTO NIGHT, A (136m   B   1962)
Playwright Eugene O'Neill wrote this autobiographical play in
early 40's, but stipulated it never be performed until after his
death.   It's a long day's journey for the family of four.   The aging
actor-father's fear of failure drives him to projects beneath him
artistically--and this destroys him.   The convent-reared, Irish-
Catholic mother has become addicted to morphine because her
penurious husband sent her to a quack doctor.   The elder son has
been unable to follow in his father's footsteps and has a life of illusion assuaged by heavy drinking.   The younger son, Edmond, the

would-be-poet, has come home from the sea, gripped by the growing suspicion he is dying from tuberculosis. He is terribly attached to the mother, and is most able to perceive what the family has already become and will yet be. d. Sidney Lumat; EMBASSY; TWY, UNF.

LONG DISTANCE SOFT SHOE, THE (4m   B   n. d.)
"Super light lyrical entertaining quickie film (no sex) of a Golden Gate soft shoe crossing. "--CCC.   By Kit Carson; CCC.

LONG HOT SUMMER, THE (115m   C   1958   Reg. /Scope)
A story of a turbulent relationship between a wealthy aggressive father and his two grown children--one a frustrated, unmarried young woman; and the other a married son who is a weakling.   d. Martin Ritt; co-scripted by Harriet Frank; FOX; FL

LONG TIME COMING, A (30m   B   n. d.   VIDEO)
Shows the progress of Mary, an artist, from a strict upbringing to orgasmic fulfillment.   This graphic presentation of her recent discoveries is an excellent and supportive tool for pre-orgasmic women.   By Constance Beeson; IE.

LONGEST WAR, THE (30m   C   1973)
Wounded Knee--site of the 1890 massacre of the Sioux nation by the U. S. Cavalry--was once again scene of confrontation between the white man and the Indians on March 8, 1973.   The film presents the case of the American Indian Movement (AIM) and focuses on one of its leaders, Dennis Banks.   It covers the events leading up to Wounded Knee, scenes of the Indian people discussing the problems they face, meetings, confrontation with the police, interviews with the white community and with Indians under fire in the compound in their dramatic attempt to bring about corrective changes.   By Dianne Orr; SOHO.

LONGHORNS (6m   B   n. d.)
Stimulates dance with graceful rhythms contrived with the use of longhorns.   By Hilary Harris; FIM.

LOOK OUT GIRLIE, WOMEN'S LIBERATION'S GONNA GET YOUR
    MAMA (n. d.   1968   SLIDE/TAPE)
An introduction to women's liberation produced by the Oberlin College Women's Liberation Group.   UCM.

LOOKING AT TOMORROW ... WHAT WILL YOU CHOOSE? (16m
    C   1974)
Interview sequences depict several job choices for women--a bricklayer, a congresswoman, fashion illustrator, air traffic controller, lawyer, personnel job interviewer, linear computer programmer, one of a few violin makers in the world today, etc.   The film stresses that finding the right job is not simply luck, but the result of a purposeful pursuit of those occupations best suited to one's own interests and skills.   CP.

LOOKING BACK--REMEMBERING VIRGINIA (26m B 1967)
Presents a conversation between Malcolm Muggeridge and Leonard Woolf, husband of the novelist Virginia Woolf. They discuss her life, her writing, the connection between her madness and her genius, and her suicide. BBCTV; BBCL; EMC.

LOOKING FOR ME (29m B 1970)
A film about the delights of experiencing one's body, as well as a document supporting a talented young teacher's belief that movement awareness is essential for all children, and that for psychotic or handicapped children body language is an important means of communication. Shows Jane Adler, a dance or movement therapist, working with normal and emotionally disturbed children and also with a group of therapists and teachers. Powerful sequence shows her working with two autistic girls, aged two and five, trying to enter their world in their terms, reflecting their movements until they recognize her response. Well photographed, with brief and concise narration; a remarkable example of a good film editor's ability to telescope time, make comparisons, and provide quick insights. By Virginia Bartlett, Norris Brock; IMC; UILL.

LOOSE ENDS (108m B 1975)
Loose Ends is about America, the America lived daily by millions of ordinary people who live and work and die with no time to dream or no skills to make their dreams into reality. Eddie and Linda are such ordinary people into whose lives pops Billy. Billy is the catalyst, the match to the fuse that may destroy them all. He's the dreamer of dangerous dreams who in the end is left ground up and defenseless. By Victoria Wozniak, David Burton; TWY.

LOREN MACIVER, PTS. I and II (46m C 1962)
The filmmaker has captured in depth the vibrancy of the artist, her paintings, and her environment. All three emerge as clearly interwoven patterns and constitute the structure of this two-part film, each part of which is a self-contained episode. Appropriately without narration. By Maryette Charlton; FIM.

LORRAINE HANSBERRY: THE BLACK EXPERIENCE IN THE CRE-
ATION OF DRAMA (35m C 1975)
Examines the life and work of our first major Black woman playwright. The film intercuts Ms. Hansberry's spoken words and recollections with scenes from her major plays to present the Black experience in the creation of drama. Narrated by Ms. Hansberry and Claudia McNeil. d. Harold Mantell; FFHI; UILL, CWU, UM.

LOST AND FOUND (5m C n.d.)
"A view from the other side of the counter--an old man looking for a briefcase full of mandolin music, a woman looking for her umbrella..."--Programme, "Women and Film Festival," Toronto. By Claudia Weill, Eliot Noyes, Jr. TEXFM.

LOST HONOR OF KATHARINA BLUM, THE (102m C 1975)
Examines the abusive power of the state and further reveals the

unrelenting pressure of "yellow" exploitive journalism. A young woman's chance affair with a fugitive terrorist results in a reign of terror characterized by a pervasive sexism that victimizes and destroys the heroine. Based on the novel by Heinrich Boll; co-scripted and co-directed by Margarethe Von Trotta; New World; FL

LOTTERY, THE; Short Story Showcase Series (19m C 1969)
A dramatization of Shirley Jackson's masterpiece about the annual lottery ritual in a small American town which culminates in the sacrifice of a human victim. A companion film is titled A Discussion of Shirley Jackson's "The Lottery." EBEC; UILL, UIO, UMIS, WAYSU.

LOUISA MAY ALCOTT (18m B 1950)
Life and works of one of the greatest U. S. women writers. Shows us her childhood and family life, dedication to her family, work as nurse and her resulting illness--all the humor and pathos of her existence which led to her many novels. EBEC; BU, IU, UILL, UKEN, UM, UMIS, USC.

LOUISE NEVELSON (25m C 1971)
Pictures this internationally acclaimed sculptor as an artist and a person. Develops the background of various periods in her work--the period when her sculpture was all painted black and when she regarded herself as "an architect of shadow"; her transition to white, to gold and then to light; her work characterized by structure--in boxes and the juxtaposition of units--and by her intriguing combination of the simple and direct with the unusual and unexpected. SPCTRA; CONNECTICUT; UM.

LOVE (11m B 1962-63)
A poetically erotic avant-garde film with imagery verging on surrealism. Music by Yoko Ono. d. Takahiko Iimura; CCC.

LOVE (11m C 1970)
In discussions with each other, with parents and with friends, a young couple examines the question of love and marriage. Are they ready for real responsibility? Are they in love with each other or with the idea of love? MLP; SEF; UILL.

LOVE AFFAIR, OR THE CASE OF THE MISSING SWITCHBOARD OPERATOR (78m B 1967 Yugoslavian/subtitled)
A bold, bizarre and comic love story between Isabell, a charming young switchboard operator and Ahmed, a rat exterminator. Director Makavejev imaginatively unfolds and brings together events that give view to the cold, intellectual way society views sex and murder. d. Dusan Makavejev; ABFL

LOVE AND ANARCHY (108m C 1973 Italian/subtitled)
Tunin, a shy awkward peasant arrives in Rome from the countryside in the 1930's and goes directly to a luxurious bordello. He is looking for Salome, a bold and most glamorous lady of the house, and his aide in carrying out his plan to assassinate B. Mussolini.

Tunin parades as Salome's cousin while Salome contacts underground anarchists in order to successfully carry out the plot. In the meantime, Tunin falls in love with a young prostitute, and the conflict between "love and anarchy" sparks an explosion of passion that is felt far beyond the bordello.   d. Lina Wertmuller; CIV.

LOVE AND INTIMACY; Human Sexuality Series (29m   C   1972
VIDEO)
     A dance sequence, folk singing and poetry readings are introduced to set a mood of love, warmth and intimacy. The host uses this technique to support his point that love is not synonymous with sex or marriage and defies strict definition.   UHAWAII/KHETV; PTL.

LOVE AND MARRIAGE (106m   B   1966   (dubbed in English))
     This engaging sex farce combines four stories about married couples in various stages of past, present and future infidelity. In "The First Night," a jaded aristocrat offers a million lire to a pair of honeymooners if the bride will spend one night with him. "One Moment Is Enough" portrays a jealous husband who fails to stop his wife's infidelity, even after he drowns her. In "The Last Car," a woman tries to solve her husband's financial problems by offering his services as a gigolo. "Saturday, July 8" depicts a man who discovers the truth about his supposedly faithful wife, while vacationing with her on Capri. Original title: L'Idea Fissa.   d. Gianni Puccini, Mino Guerrini; ABFI.

LOVE GIFT, THE (10m   C   n. d.)
     A young man arrives in San Francisco, briefcased, with a Wall Street Journal. He quickly trades these things for love beads, bright clothes and mysticism. But, rather than finding the liberation and transcendence he seeks, he contracts gonorrhea. Though humorous and ironic, this film examines contemporary values. By Barbara Styman, John Brown; GP.

LOVE GODDESSES, THE (87m   B   1963   1974 rev. ed.)
     A movie about the movies. It is a 60-year history of the treatment of women on the screen and how the movie heroines have always been a reflection of our social behavior, of the customs, manners, and morals of the times.   d. Saul J. Turrell, Graeme Ferguson; CONTINENTAL; JANUS.

LOVE IN THE AFTERNOON (126m   B   1957)
     A romantic comedy about an aging millionaire (Gary Cooper) and a naive young music student (Audrey Hepburn) who loves him and her private-detective father (Chevalier). Based on the novel Ariane by Claude Arnet.   d. Billy Wilder; ALLIED ARTISTS; HCW.

LOVE IS A PLANNED FAMILY; Family Planning and Sex Education--
A Series (19m   C   1972)
     Documents the viewpoints of several men and women to show that their interest in family planning is motivated by love as well as by a very deep concern for their families, including members

yet unborn. Interwoven with the "why" of family planning is a discussion by Dr. Richard Tyson on the effectiveness of birth control methods: the pill, spermidical foam, intrauterine devices, diaphragm, condom, and rhythm. OF; UILL.

LOVER'S QUARREL WITH THE WORLD, A see ROBERT FROST: A LOVER'S QUARREL WITH THE WORLD.

LOVES OF ISADORA, THE (131m C 1969)
A biographical film of Isadora Duncan who could be considered the original "hippie" except she sought wealth as the means to advance her philosophy. Isadora, the high priestess of modern dance (who never wrote Art without capitalizing it) may have been--even with all her lovers, vanities and her muddled philosophy--this century's most innocent, most implacable, most successful revolutionary. Played by Vanessa Redgrave. Based on the books My Life by Isadora Duncan and Isadora Duncan: An Intimate Portrait by Sewell Brooks. d. Karl Reisz; UNIVE; CVE, CWF, TWY, UNIVE.

LOVING COUPLES (113m B 1965 Swedish/subtitled)
Takes place in Sweden during World War I. It's an assault on men's domination of women in a period of changing social structures. Although the film is primarily a social drama, there are outstanding moments of farce and satire. Based on the novel The Misses Von Pahlen. Original title Alksandre Par. d. Mai Zetterling; ABFI.

LUCIA (160m B 1969 Spanish/subtitled)
A three-part epic of the Cuban struggle for liberation shows women participating in the fight against the classically machismo Latin culture. The story centers around Lucia; begins in 1895, with historical progression which emphasizes the changing role of women and shows their increasing participation in all aspects of social and political life. d. Humberto Solas; ICAIC, TFC.

LUCIANO: BOY OF THE PAMPAS (15m C 1972)
. The son of an Argentina cattleman talks about his life. By Sherry Zabriskie, George Zabriskie; PARACO.

LUCY (13m C 1971)
Presents the story of Lucy, a teen-ager, unwed and pregnant. Explains her relationship with her boyfriend, her conflicts and distress when she discovers she is pregnant, her problems with her family and the alternative courses open to her when she decides to bear the baby rather than have an abortion. Open-ended. PIC.

LUKE WAS THERE (32m C 1976)
A young boy runs away from his disillusioning experience with the adult world until he learns the meaning of trust from a perceptive Black counselor. Based on a book by Eleanor Clymer. p. Linda Gottlieb; d. Richard Marquand; LCA.

LUCKILY I NEED LITTLE SLEEP (8m C n. d.)
Kathy worked as a nurse in Greece and then came to Canada.

She and her family live in northern Alberta where they are developing a farm. Kathy nurses, sews for the children, maintains the
house, and helps with the farm work. By Kathleen Shannon; p. Len
Chatwin; NFBC; EMC.

LUTA CONTINUA, A (36m C 1971)
    Presents historical background on Portuguese colonialism in
Africa and analysis of the various economic interests with a description of the status quo in South Africa.   Shows how Mozambique
women have integrated themselves into the daily revolutionary structure. English narration. Discussion guide available.   p. /d. Robert
Van Lierop, Robert Fletcher; TFC.

MACBETH (80m C 1951)
    A dramatization of Macbeth with a gospel introduction by Dr.
Bob Jones, Jr. , president of Bob Jones University, starring Dr.
Jones. Students and faculty make up the cast. p. /d. Katherine
Stenholm; UF.

MADALYN (29m C 1970)
    Camera follows atheist Madalyn O'Hair, a staunch and contro-
versial advocate for the separation of Church and State, while she
explains her beliefs regarding tax laws benefiting church ownership
of property; relates her experiences of having been taken at gun-
point onto a plane when forced to leave Mexico; and gives her views
on women's liberation, "hippies" and other subjects. p. Robert
Elkins; CF; IU.

MADAME BINH (15m C 1971)
    Madame Binh addresses American women about the war and the
shared role Vietnamese and American women have in struggling to
end it. Her first filmed interview, Nov. 1970. KMP.

MADAME BOVARY (102m B 1934 French/subtitled)
    Madame Bovary evokes the mood and feeling of an era (19th
century) that no one could possibly know or remember. Based on
a novel by Gustave Flaubert.   The romance-ridden wife of a stolid,
middle-aged doctor who in rebellion at the provincial life forced
upon her engages in one illicit affair after another. Mlle. Tessier
snugly fills the Flaubert sketching. d. Jean Renoir; MGH.

MADAME BOVARY (106m B 1949)
    (See above description.) d. Vincente Minnelli; MGM; FL

MADAME CHIANG KAI-SHEK (26m B 1965)
    Rare actuality footage used to portray the personal life and
history-making deeds of Madame Chiang Kai-Shek. WOLPER; SEF;
UMIS.

MADAME CURIE (124m B 1944)
    Warmly moving picturization of the lives of Marie and Pierre

Curie, the brilliant scientists who sacrificed their own health and happiness to their discovery of radium that would benefit all mankind. d. Mervyn LeRoy; MGM; FI.

MADAME CURIE (24m B 1950)
Story of the discovery of radium; the long arduous work of the Curies in separating radium from pitchblende; the scientific methodology and processes which they followed in identifying radium. MGM; TFCI; UM.

MADAME ROSINA LHEVINNE: PIANIST AND MASTER TEACHER (40m B r1974)
Portrait of the remarkable pianist and teacher as she works with outstanding young pianists in a master class conducted in 1964 at UCLA.   Probably the sole surviving figure of the great tradition of the 19th-century school of Slavic pianism, Mme. Lhevinne encourages the development of musical individuality--a quality that involves the artist's style, stage presence, and ability to project the mood of a composition.   She encourages her students to acquire a broad education and experience in the arts, to keep their minds open to new interpretations, and to attempt more individual performances.   It is structured to encompass many elements of technique and musicianship.   EMC; PAS.

MADELEINE (11m B 1950 (Gr. Br.))
A once famous Scottish case taken from the files of the Glasgow procurator Fiscal of 1857 is retold here.   Ann Todd plays the introverted, seemingly shy Madeleine Smith.   Her pitilessly Calvinistic father (Leslie Banks) has the charm of a corroding pillory and her secret lover (Ivan Desny as Pierre Emil Langelier) is a cad of the "Gaslight" School of Caddery, who either wants to share in her money and social position, or else expose her passionate love letters to her father.   Her callous lover one day takes poison, the very kind of poison Madeleine used everyday to keep her hands free of liver spots.   Anyway, her father says, scornfully, ... suicide is quite prevalent among that class.   Still, there were those love letters. ...   d. David Lean; KP.

MADSONG (5m C 1976)
Combines live action and animation to convey a sense of conflicting internal and external realities.   A young woman's confusion about her life and personal identity is expressed in a multi-voice sound track, while evocative images reflecting changing seasons and spaces add to the sense of ambiguity and fragmentation.   By Kathleen Laughlin; PHOENIX, SB.

MAEDCHEN IN UNIFORM (90m B 1931 German/subtitled)
A sensitive portrayal of life in a school for daughters of Prussian Army officers in Potsdam, 1913, and the tragic results of authoritarianism.   Based on a play Gestern und Heute (Yesterday and Today) by Christa Winsloe with an all woman cast.   d. Leontine Sagan; FIM, JANUS.

MAGGIE KUHN: WRINKLED RADICAL (27m C 1975)
Focuses on 69-year-old Maggie Kuhn, an assertive, dynamic woman who calls herself a "wrinkled radical" and who organized the Gray Panthers, a group characterized as "age and youth in action." Explains that the Gray Panthers are fighting for the rights of the elderly. Observes Maggie Kuhn being interviewed at home by Studs Terkel, working in the Gray Panther's Philadelphia office, and speaking with several groups concerned about discrimination against the elderly. (Also see Matter of Indifference). IU.

MAGIC HORSE, THE (10m B 1930's)
An animated film based on live shadow play. An "Arabian Nights" story of a prince, a flying horse and a bird princess. By Lotte Reiniger; BBCTV; CEA, MGH.

MAGIC LANTERN MOVIE, THE (9m C 1976)
Using animation and live action, the film traces the history of the Magic Lantern. d. /p. Maxine Haleff; STARR.

MAGIC MACHINES, THE (15m C 1970)
Kinetic sculptor Robert Gilbert describes his own work and style of life. The artist is shown on his trips to the junkyard in the desert where he gathers much of the material for his art. A delightfully zany portrait of a "flower child." d. Joan Keller Stern; p. Bob Curtis; LCA, PF; WCF.

MAGIC MIRROR OF ABYSE, THE (27m C 1966)
Aloyse, a chronic schizophrenic in a Swiss mental hospital, has fascinated the medical world over forty years by the rare, creative qualities of her drawings. This film examines these unusual outpourings not only for their psychiatric interest but for their artistic merit as well. The symbolic nature of her drawings is scrutinized, and thus the viewer is able to share the magic of Aloyse's private microcosm. CMC; EMC.

MAGIC PRISON; Humanities Series (36m C 1969)
In this dramatized exchange of letters and poems, interspersed with beautiful photography of the nature she wrote about, the genius of Emily Dickinson is movingly revealed. Corresponding with a stranger, Col. T. W. Higginson, the shy poet is able to speak her mind and heart almost as freely as she does in her poetry. Readings selected by Archibald MacLeish. EBEC; EMC, PAS, UKEN.

MAI EAST (5m C/B n. d.)
Compares male and female sexuality using four images on the screen simultaneously. By Cassandra M. Gerstein; FCOOP.

MAIS MOI (5m B 1968)
"A lonely girl's fantasy about bold knights fighting for her charms. "--YFD. By Lois Greenfield; YFD.

MAKEOUT (10m B 1970)
Depicts teen-age couple making out on the screen. The sound

track registers her reactions and fantasies which are at odds with
her apparent absorption in sexual pleasure.   As he becomes more
aggressive, the sound track blurs, indicating her boredom with boyfriend and sex.   Clearly brings out the social code that forces a
girl to pretend to enjoy something she dislikes in order to be popular and "normal. "   TWN; SFN.

MAKING IT (11m B n. d.)
     Charlene Imhoff talks about her work as an administrator of
Title I and Title VI Education Programs in rural Virginia, then
more personally about her divorce and life raising four daughters
alone on a farm.   By Lucy Ann Kerry; BRF.

MAKING IT (18m C 1975)
     Presents contemporary, realistic, sexual conflicts and issues to
promote discussion of values and communication in personal relationships.   Janis and Brian's relationship breaks up over differing
sexual values.   Brian experiences sex with magazine writer but discovers sex by itself does not make a relationship fulfilling.   Brian
and Janis get together to talk over their relationship.   d. Pat Cor-
bett; p. John Churchill; MLP.

MAKING IT IN THE WORLD OF WORK (25m C 1972)
     A group of young adults discuss their jobs and why they chose
them: postwoman, teacher, etc.   A good film to open a discussion
on the various possibilities for employment.   FFAIR.

MAKING THINGS WORK SERIES (15/13-15m ea. C 1972 VIDEO)
     A primer on household mini-disasters.   The idea of the series
is to help the ordinary person cope with familiar problems in familiar surroundings with familiar tools, says Thalassa Cruso.   Write
to PTL for individual program titles.   Also available in captioned
versions for the deaf and hearing impaired.   p. WGBHTV; PTL.

MALAWI: THE WOMEN (20m C 1971)
     This southeastern country of Africa exemplifies the contrasting
cultures of a society in transition.   Focuses on the women of a village where Westernization has already left its mark, then on a
secretary in a city office and finally on a housewife who still re-
tains village customs in her suburban tract house.   CF; BU, IU,
UM.

MALE MENOPAUSE: THE PAUSE THAT PERPLEXES (59m C
     1974 VIDEO)
     Actor William Windom is the host of this documentary examin-
ing the problems of the middle-aged male.   It deals in an entertaining way with the reality and the myths surrounding the mid-life
crisis of mind and spirit.   Dramatic and humorous sketches and
original music by folksinger Oscar Brand combine to reflect the
American male's reaction to the middle years.   Windom stars in
several of the vignettes, along with comedienne Anne Meara, et al.
NPACFT; PTL.

MAMMA (30m   C   n. d.)
"Mamma" chronicles the journey and her experiences as one of
the first Italian-Americans in the U. S.   In 1905, at age 19, she
traveled from Sicily to New York just to see the U. S. --the only one
of 12 brothers and sisters never to see Italy again.   She describes
life in Sicily before 1906 and the role of women in a fiercely male-
dominated culture.   She vividly recalls the hard times and the challenges and excitement as old world values overlap and clash with
the new.   Now, at age 89, Mamma reflects on the choices she made
and the changes in her new country, America, over the last 70
years.   By Philip F. Messina; SOHO.

MAN, A (21m   B   n. d.)
Shows a men's consciousness-raising group raising issues about
mourning and death.   Confronted are issues about men and their expression of emotions.   Why do men hold back feelings?   How do
men learn this control?   How does society encourage it?   Why do
men fear touching and giving support to one another even in times
of crisis?   By Len Grossman, Ph. D. , a clinical psychologist.
p. /d.   Len Grossman/Michael Chait; POLYMORPH.

MAN ALIVE: GALE IS DEAD (50m   C   1970)
Documentary of an attractive, intelligent woman who dies a
drug addict at age 19.   By Jenny Barraclough; BBCTV.

MAN AND HIS WORLD SERIES   see   MINERS OF BOLIVIA

MAN AND THE SNAKE, THE (26m   C   1975)
Loosely based on Ambrose Bierce's famous tale of satirical
horror "The Man and the Snake. "   This is a tale of the conflict in
a man's mind, the unsettling struggle between the common sense of
the day and the subtle abduction of the mind by the eerie effects of
nightfall.   By Elizabeth McKay; PF.

MAN AND WOMAN; Great Themes of Literature Series (33m   C
1973)
Edited from Taming of the Shrew, an introduction to the Shakespearean play, this film shows the relationship between the sexes
in literature.   Richard Burton is cast as Petrucchio who woos and
weds with force the flamboyant and resistant Katherine, played by
Liz Taylor.   Almost every famous scene between the two is shown
including the mock trial in which Petrucchio bets others that he has
the most faithful and "tamed" wife.   COLUMBIA; LCA; UILL, USC,
WCF.

MAN AND WOMAN'S GUIDE TO BREAST EXAMINATION (5m   C
1977)
Employs a dramatized situation, in which a couple visits a doctor, to demonstrate proper methods of examining a woman's breasts
for early detection of cancer.   In a flash-forward situation in the
privacy of their bedroom (but with the doctor's voice providing instructions and criticizing incorrect procedures) the man is shown
carrying out the examination.   Animated sequences clarify various

points and concepts.   Concludes with a summary and a plea to women to take greater responsibility for their bodies.   EMC.

MAN WHO LOVED CAT DANCING, THE (114m   C   1973   Scope)
Sarah Miles plays the strong-willed lady riding side-saddle through the old West.   Miles witnesses a train robbery and is kidnapped by the outlaw band headed by Burt Reynolds.   In no time, her stuffy husband (George Hamilton) leads a posse to rescue her for reasons less than romantic.   In the meantime, Miles falls into a passionate love affair with her captor.   d. Richard Serafian; p. Eleanor Perry/Martin Ritt; s. w. Eleanor Perry; MGM; FL

MANDABI (90m   C   1968   Wolof/subtitled)
Acclaimed contemporary African feature about the plight of a traditional Senegalese man who is pushed around, swindled, enraged, and finally robbed while trying to cash a money order sent to him by his nephew in Paris.   A humane yet sharply pointed comment by Ousmane Sembene about burgeoning bureaucracy and Westernization. d. Ousmane Sembene; GP; EMC.

MANHANDLED (50m   B   si   1924)
Tessie, played by Gloria Swanson, a New York department store salesgirl, has a boyfriend Tom Moore, a mechanic, who leaves for Detroit to demonstrate a new carburetor he invented.   During his absence Tessie dresses up as a Russian countess and becomes casually involved with several rich men.   However, she eventually tires of them and returns to her first love who is now a millionaire as a result of his invention.   Based on a story by Arthur Stringer. d. /p. Allan Dwan; PARAMOUNT; ABFL

MANHATTAN STREET BAND (24m   C   1970)
Follows the steel band (Sound Search) that won a city-wide talent hunt sponsored by Mobil Oil Corporation in the disadvantaged neighborhoods of New York City, as they play on Park Avenue, atop the Brooklyn Bridge, and in other unusual places.   By Suzanne E. Bauman; MOBIL: CAROUSEL.

MAPS OF OUR LOCALITY (11m   C   1965)
Aerial land and water views introduce map terminology and use of the grid system.   For elementary use.   By Ruth O. Bradley; BFA.

MAPS OF OUR SCHOOL (8m   C   1965)
Three aspects of map reading: size relationships, symbolic representation and direction.   Children map their classroom and school.   By Ruth O. Bradley; BFA.

MAPS OF OUR WORLD (11m   C   1965)
Typical scenes of various parts of the world show how the land contour influences the activities of the people.   These are followed by models, contour maps, and conventional elevation maps to introduce 3-D reading skills.   By Ruth O. Bradley; BFA.

MARAGOLI (58m   C   1977)
Insightful document on the social and economic problems of village life in the Third World, uses the Maragoli region of Western
Kenya--one of the world's most populated rural areas--as a case
study. In discussion with a sympathetic African interviewer, the
men and women of Maragoli tell their side of the story. A perceptive portrayal of the interlocking problems of high fertility rates,
food shortages, land scarcity, lack of education and employment,
and migration--the elements that must be considered when devising
or evaluating any rural development program. EMC.

MARCO (83m   B   1970)
Cinéma-vérité documentary sharing a young couple's experience:
the birth of their first child by the Lamaze Method. The camera
follows the couple throughout prelabor exercises: their visits with
doctors, and informal talks with friends who offer advice based on
their own experiences. Includes the labor and actual delivery.
Concludes with their coming together as a family unit. FIM.

MARGARET (13m   B   1975)
The story of Margaret, a six-year-old child with disabilities,
and the concern of the parents, two sisters, and three brothers.
The parents speak of the effects Margaret's condition has upon the
other children, and their hopes of a scientific breakthrough in educating the handicapped before it is too late for Margaret. p. Film
Australia; AUIS.

MARGARET MEAD; Wisdom Series (30m   B   1960)
Celebrated anthropologist brings the experience and understanding gained from her study of primitive cultures to a lively discussion of contemporary world problems--marriage and morality, the
place of women in modern life, the education of young people, the
responsibilities of nationhood, the role of the scientific frontiers of
the future. NBCTV; FI; EMC, OKSU, PAS, WISSU.

MARGARET MEAD'S NEW GUINEA JOURNAL, PTS. I, II, III (90m
     C   1967)
Margaret Mead observes the village of Peri on Manus, one of
the Admiralty Islands in the Australian Trust Territory of New
Guinea. Her first visit in 1928 found the village in the Stone Age
but by her second visit in 1953, it had moved into the 20th century.
IU; BU, BYU, UILL, UM.

MARGARET SANGER (15m   B   1972)
Uses still photographs, newsreel footage and other visual sources
to trace the life of Margaret Sanger, who devoted herself to the
struggle to make family planning both legal and practical for women
all over the world. Describes the early influences on her thought,
the development of her conviction that family planning was essential
for the emancipation of women, her persecution by authorities in
the U. S. , her exile to avoid imprisonment, her eventual triumphant
return. Narrated by Katharine Hepburn. MGH; EMC, SCC, USC.

MARGARET SLOAN ON BLACK SISTERHOOD (29m C 1974 VIDEO)
Margaret Sloan, who with a group of friends founded the National
Black Feminist Organization, discusses sexism and feminism and
how they relate to the Black women in the movement. WNEDTV;
PTL.

MARGUERITE (4m C 1974)
Marguerite captures the moment in time which parts a man and
a woman once united. Inspired by the bittersweet prose of Marguerite Duras, the voice of the woman echoes the thoughts and reflections which lead to the relationship's end. A graceful blending
of literature and painting through selective detail, changes of scale
and shiftings of color-value and animation. By Betty Chen; SB.

MARIA OF THE PUEBLOS (15m C 1971)
Traces the career of Maria Martinez, world-famous Indian
artist, showing how she and her family produce their iridescent
black pottery. Explains Maria's impact in helping her people rise
from poverty. Provides an understanding of the culture, philosophy,
art, and economic condition of the Pueblo Indians of San Ildefonso,
New Mexico. CENTRON; NIU, OKSU, UC, UILL, USC.

MARIAN ANDERSON; Concerts on Film Series (27m B 1953)
Presents Marian Anderson as she sings a program of songs in
rehearsal as well as on concert stage. Also provides details of
her life, including her birthplace, friends that have helped her,
her farm home in Connecticut, and the honors bestowed upon her.
WORA; IU, ISU, MSU, UIO, UU.

MARIANA (29m C 1971)
Portrait of a young woman active in the movements for women's
rights and social change in Chile. Shows her at the university,
where she is a student; at work in a day care center for the children of working women; and at a factory where, as a member of
a government commission investigating working conditions for wom-
en, she questions one of the managers. Includes dialogue between
Mariana and several women prominent in Chili's national affairs.
In Spanish with English translation. UN; MGH; EMC.

MARIE AND HENRY (17m B 1966)
Study of two elderly pensioners from rural Midwest. By Barbara Isaacs; ISAACS.

MARIE ANTOINETTE (160m B 1938)
Story of the royal heroine of the French Revolution who later
suffers at the hands of the revolutionaries. d. W. S. Van Dyke;
MGM; FL

MARILYN (83m C 1963 Scope)
The career of the late Marilyn Monroe narrated by Rock Hudson. Includes clips from motion pictures. FOX; FL

MARILYN (10m   B   n. d.)
A biting documentary views the pressures that being a superstar sex symbol brought to Marilyn Monroe. She is shown virtually
mobbed by insensitive fans and reporters during her most emotionally trying real life experiences.   CFS.

MARILYN MONROE--WHY? (28m   B   1962)
Examines the contrast between the bright public image and the
lonely, frightened, private life of motion picture star Marilyn Monroe.   Presents actress Kim Novak, who describes the problems of
being a sex symbol and Lee Strasberg, Jean Negulesco, George
Cukor, and Clifford Odets, who give their assessment of the personality and problems of Miss Monroe.   CBSTV; BF.

MARINE HIGHWAY (20m   C   1968   2nd ed.)
Takes the viewer on a tour of Nova Scotia's seacoast along Highway No. 7.   Visits the Institute of Oceanography at Dartmouth, the
golf courses and the ships at anchor in Bedford Basin.   Includes the
annual regatta and a display of water sports.   By Margaret Perry,
NFBC; CTFL.

MARJOE (88m   C   1972)
From age three until age 28, Marjoe Gortner pursued a highly
lucrative career--a fully ordained fire-and-brimstone preacher in
the Old Time Faith Church.   The film covers the last few months
of his preaching before retirement.   Scenes of him leading his en-
raptured congregations are interspersed with discussions of his life
as a con man on the evangelistic circuit, and of the ethics of his
colleagues in the "religion business. "   d. Sarah Kernochen/Howard
Smith; CIV.

MARKED WOMAN (95m   B   1937)
An underground boss takes over a New York night club and
viciously exploits the "hostesses" in his employ there.   Bette Davis,
playing one of the girls, covers up a murder perpetrated by her
boss, but later determines to expose him when her innocent sister
becomes one of his victims.   Humphrey Bogart, the D. A. , convinces her to turn state's evidence.   d. Lloyd Bacon; WSA; UAS.

MARKETS (10m   C   1974)
"A study of women in the economic marketing situation of buying and selling in Mexico, Guatemala, Telegraph Avenue, Supermarket U. S. A. , and the Alameda Flea Market. "--B. H.   By Barbara Hammer; HAMMER.

MARRIAGE (22m   C   n. d.)
Almost one out of three marriages in the U. S. ends in divorce.
Much of the upheaval is connected with the changing role of women
and man's ever-changing attitude towards her.   Women are no
longer willing to play the role women have played since the beginning of time.   The film says it is essential for the future of marriage that the people involved make a commitment based on their
own needs and not on society's expectations.   CG; FL.

MARRIAGE (17m C 1971)
This animated film is filled with concepts and ideas which will produce a maximum amount of discussion about the subject of marriage--from the wedding to the golden anniversary. It offers a great amount of latitude for the teacher in emphasis, and it opens the way for discussion of a multitude of subjects connected with marriage. Some of the ideas and concepts may be the basis for unconscious learning as well as open discussion. By E. C. Brown; p. WFP; PERENNIAL.

MARRIAGE (25m C 1969)
Using two married couples, Dr. Frederick Perl demonstrates the Gestalt method of achieving a more honest communication in marriage. FI; USC.

MARRIAGE (SVADBA) (44m B n. d. Russian/subtitled)
A sprightly satire on the hypocrisy and petty bargaining that precede a provincial wedding party. Acted by players from the Moscow Art Theatre. Based on Anton Chekhov's play The Wedding. d. Isador Annensky. ARTKNO; ABFI, USC.

MARRIAGE AND FAMILY SERIES see PSYCHOLOGICAL DIFFER-
ENCES BETWEEN THE SEXES

MARRIAGE OF HAMEY AND ADISA, THE; African Heritage Series
(20m C 1976)
The people of the towns Dessa and Niamey, Republic of Niger, Africa reenact a traditional marriage ceremony of two young people of these towns. Begins with the father telling his son, Hamey, that he has chosen Adisa, daughter of a friend in Dessa, a neighboring town, to be Hamey's wife. Depicts the exchanges of dowry, the building of a house for the couple, the dances of the actual ceremony and finally their residence in Hamey's town, Niamey. Narrated in English, the narrator translates the conversation of the people and describes their traditions while the native language is spoken and sung. p. Jacques Vilmont; CAROUSEL, UM.

MARRIAGE OR MIRAGE?; Choice: Challenge for Modern Women
Series (30m B 1966)
Alexander C. Rosen and Gertrude Sackheim discuss individual identity and needs in marriage, as well as differing views of what marriage is, can be, and should be. EMC.

MARRIAGE PROBLEMS (30m B 1963)
Dramatic vignette shows two sisters, one recently married, the other about to have her second child. Neither is happily married: the pregnant one resents her husband; the other sister fears her sterility. Dr. Maria Piers points out that young couples are often the victims of their own unrealistic expectations. She discusses the need for mutuality and independence in a good marriage. EMC; PAS.

MARRIAGE SAVERS, THE (29m C 1974 VIDEO)
Advice on choosing a marriage counselor is offered by Dr.

Catherine S. Chilman of the School of Social Welfare at the University of Wisconsin, Milwaukee, and Dr. David H. Olson of the Family Social Science Department, University of Minnesota. WNEDTV; PTL.

MARRIED LIFE TODAY (19m C 1975)
  Marriage, we are told, is an institution in trouble. Perhaps the truth is that marriage is just more varied and subject to change than in the past, and kids and young adults therefore need to broaden their sense of the options open to them. This film juxtaposes a young couple operating a business together, who see themselves as equal; another couple, more traditional in outlook; and a third couple who, though separated, continue to share the parenting responsibilities of their daughter. As different as they are, all three couples continue to function creatively in their married lives. Designed to draw viewers into examining their own values and expectations of marriage. SSP; BFA; UM.

MARRIED WOMAN, THE (74m C 1965 French/subtitled)
  A story of a young wife and mother in love with both her husband and lover, and finding much the same satisfaction with each. An honest study of what it is to be a woman. Marcha Meril superbly portrays the feminine side of marriage and of love, both romantic and physical. d. Jean-Luc Godard; COLUMBIA; SWANK.

MARRIEDS, THE (29m C 1972 VIDEO)
  Host Milton Diamond, Ph.D., defines a traditional marriage and actors portray several different types of marriages. The host talks with a young "swinging" couple about their sexual activities and interviews two marriage counselors about some of the problems they encounter. Newspaper columnist Ann Landers discusses some of the most common marital questions she is asked. UHAWAII/ KHETTV; PTL.

MARRYING KIND, THE (96m B 1952)
  Florence Keefer (Judy Holliday) and her husband Chet (Aldo Ray) appear before Judge Carroll, seeking a divorce. Each remembers their courtship and marriage in a slightly different way. Both were very much in love, but neither anticipated the disappointments they experienced. Although money was an issue always and Chet was unable to raise backing for his inventions, he would not let Florence accept the large legacy left to her by her boss. Further, their child drowned accidentally. In the end, the judge convinces them how much they still mean to each other and they decide to remain together. d. George Cukor; COLUMBIA; ABFI, ICS.

MARTHA (11m C 1975)
  Martha, a middle-aged suburban woman, has just begun to question some of the values and feelings common to her class and generation. She loves her husband but resents his socially superior role. A devoted mother, she is saddened as her children gradually outgrow their need for her and wonders if she was a good mother. She feels guilty about her material well-being and is sympathetic

toward Blacks and the poor, but she's hesitant to sacrifice her comfort and act on her sympathy.   An intimate portrait of a sensitive
person caught between traditional roles and values and a changing
world, the film speaks to many of the most significant but elusive
conflicts affecting people today.   It offers no solutions, but through
Martha's ability to face her conflicts and consider change, it expresses much hope.   p. Jennifer Mead; PERENNIAL.

MARTHA GRAHAM DANCE THEATRE SERIES see APPALACHIAN
SPRING; DANCER'S WORLD; NIGHT JOURNEY

MARTYRDOM OF MARILYN MONROE (30m   C   1973)
Magaly Alabau plays Marilyn backed by "archetypal sexual
imagery. " By Alida Walsh; WALSH.

MARY CASSATT: AN AMERICAN IMPRESSIONIST (16m   C   n. d.
SFS)
The classic themes of maternity and childhood are expressed in
the delicate, sensitive works of Mary Cassatt.   EDC.

MARY JANE GROWS UP: MARIJUANA IN THE 70'S (52m   C   1976)
No longer the symbol flaunted by young rebels, marijuana is
now used by millions including parents, teachers and professionals.
Its control has become the subject of national political controversy.
The trend is toward decriminalization or, on the other hand, stricter
enforcement of present laws.   Despite extensive research, no con-
clusive evidence of physical harm is available.   What is clear, however, is that marijuana is a fact of life and must be dealt with for
the benefit of society.   d. Joan Konner; NBCTV; FL

MARY KINGSLEY; Ten Who Dared Series (52m   C   1976)
Dramatization spotlighting Mary Kingsley, an adventurous woman
who went to the fever-infested West Coast of Africa as an explorer
and trader in 1893.   Her journey had a lasting impact on white
Europeans, giving them an interpretation of the African that was as new
as it was startling.   d. Lord Anthony Snowdon; BBCTV; TL.

MARY OF SCOTLAND (123m   B   1936)
Mary Stuart's fight with Elizabeth of England for the throne of
Scotland, her love affair with Bothwell, and her tragic failure and
final martyrdom have been beautifully reproduced in this compelling
character study of two monarchs in opposition.   Based on the play
by Maxwell Anderson.   D. John Ford; RKO; FL

MARY PRITCHARD; Artists in America Series (29m   C   1970)
Profile of Mary Pritchard working to preserve part of a culture
before it disappears completely.   She is seen at her home on the
Island of Tutuila, American Samoa, as she searches for the materials, the colors, and the forms she uses in the designing of tapa,
a cloth-like material made from the bark of the mulberry tree.
KVZKTV; BYU, IU.

MARY, QUEEN OF SCOTS (128m   C   1972)
Because Henry VIII annulled his marriage to Anne Boleyn, her

daughter, Elizabeth I, was considered by some to be a pretender to the throne. Her main rival was Mary Stuart, the Catholic Queen of Scotland. The story is of Mary's life after returning from France, but also of the struggle and the relationship between the two queens. Stars Vanessa Redgrave as Mary and Glenda Jackson as Elizabeth. d. Charles Jarrott; UNIVE; CWF, SWANK, TWY, UNIVE.

MARY, QUEEN OF SCOTS, 1542-1587 (30m B 1968)
"I was born a Queen, I will die a Queen." Film begins with these words spoken by Mary, Queen of Scots, before she was beheaded by order of Queen Elizabeth. The tragic life of Mary is told with prints and engravings. It tells of her early life in France and her return to Scotland which she found to be disunited by warring lairds and religious fanaticism. Describes the despair and loneliness that led her to her fateful marriage with Lord Darnley, and the series of complex events which followed. BBCTV; TL.

MARY S. McDOWELL; Profiles in Courage Series (50m B 1966)
Mary McDowell defends her right to teach Latin while keeping her personal beliefs to herself. Because of her refusal, on religious grounds, to sign a voluntary loyalty oath or to engage in any activity which aided the war effort, she is dismissed as a Latin teacher in a New York City high school during the 1918 war hysteria. NBCTV; SAUDEK; IQF; PAS, UILL, UM, WISSU.

MASCULIN-FEMININ (103m B 1966 French/subtitled)
Director Godard has painted a screen canvas which mingles sex and violence with disturbing overtones around the story of a callow young man and a free-wheeling young woman. They have their problems but they are totally absorbed in each other with a freedom and frankness that is engagingly amoral. d. Jean-Luc Godard; SWANK.

MASCULINE OR FEMININE: YOUR ROLE IN SOCIETY (19m C
1971)
Explores the changes in attitude about what constitutes masculinity and femininity in today's society. Prompts students to examine their own roles as men and women, students, parents, workers, and their attitudes toward men and women in jobs, at home, in marriage, athletics and government. Interviews with many people reveal different, sometimes conflicting opinions on masculine and feminine roles. Open-ended. d. J. William Walker; COR; OSU, FSU, UIO, UKEN, UM, UU, UWY, WSU.

MATERNITY HOSPITAL ROUTINE (15m C 1967)
In order to allay fears she may have, a young mother-to-be learns precisely what happens in the hospital maternity ward, labor room, and in pre-delivery tests. Details the work of doctors and nurses during actual delivery, methods of baby identification, and the care given in the recovery room. MLP; SEF; UILL.

MATHOMS (3m B 1970)
A playful concoction of computer-produced images, a few hand-animated scenes and shots of lab equipment. Mathoms is a word

from Tolkien's The Hobbit, which means garbage one saves.   The
film is made largely from leftovers from scientific research.   By
Lillian Schwartz; LPL

MATINA HORNER: PORTRAIT OF A PERSON (17m   B   1974)
Excellent portrait of the noted educator and president of Radcliffe College.   Employs still photographs, old home movies, and
an animated sequence to convey her determined professionalism,
personal warmth, and innovative educational ideas.   Emphasizes
her theories concerning the culturally instilled fear of success often
felt by women, and shows how some of the programs she originated,
such as student-faculty "rap sessions," single-sex classes, and co-
resident dormitories are designed to counter this fear.   p. /d.
Joyce Chopra; co-d. Claudia Weill; PHOENIX; EMC, IU.

MATTER OF BAOBAB, A (1m   B   1967)
"Experiment in compression on film."--P. C.   Features Jonas
and Adolfas Mekas, Storm De Hirsch, and the filmmaker.   By Pola
Chapelle; CHAPELLE.

MATTER OF BAOBAB--WITH ONE GROWTH (3m   C/B   1966-70)
An experimental film starring Jonas and Adolfas Mekas, Storm
De Hirsch and the filmmaker.   Music by the Beatles.   By Pola
Chapelle; CHAPELLE.

MATTER OF INDIFFERENCE (50m   B   1974)
An investigative documentary on the psycho-social, physical, and
emotional problems of aging.   Interviews with Maggie Kuhn, founder
of the Gray Panther Movement, and members of the Bronx Foundation.   A searing indictment of a permissive society which casts
aside its elderly.   It's brought out by these articulate people that
the elderly themselves must take the initiative fighting their own
battles in the political arena.   p. Jack M. Hanick; d. Leonardo
Dacchille.   PHOENIX; BF.

MAUDE IN HER HAT (3m   C   1971)
An old lady collects groovy sounds.   By Jeannie Youngson;
SUSSEX.

MAY SWENSON AND GLORIA C. ODEN see POETRY OF GLORIA
C. ODEN; POETRY OF MAY SWENSON

MAYA HERITAGE, THE (18m   C   1971)
Shows the major Mayan cities in Mexico, Guatemala, and Honduras.   Includes Copan, Tikal, Palenque, Tulum, Bonampak, Uxmal, and Chichen-Itza.   Surveys the art and architecture of the
people.   By Elda Hartley; HARTLEY.

MAYAN (7m   C   1974   VIDEO)
Combines live images filmed in the Yucatan with output from
the Paik Video synthesizer ribboned with computer-generated images.
Made at Channel 13 as part of the Artist-in-Residence program.
By Lillian Schwartz; LPL.

MAYAN MYSTERY, THE (17m C 1970)
Shows the ruins of the major Mayan cities in Mexico, Guatemala, and the Honduras. Lists possible explanations for the decline of the Mayas. By Elda Hartley; HARTLEY; PARACO.

MAYBE TOMORROW (19m B 1969)
A delicate and poignant treatment of an interracial romance between two young people. The film emphasizes the implications of this romance within the Black community and the influence the community has on the couple. The film was made as part of an experimental course in film production at Spring Hill College, a Jesuit liberal arts college, during the academic year 1968-69. p. SHC; NET, IU.

ME AND DAD'S NEW WIFE (33m C 1976)
Twelve-year-old Nina discovers on her first day back to school that her new math teacher is her divorced father's new wife. Provides insight into feelings of guilt, anger and insecurity, while treating a topic of current widespread concern, divorce. d. Larry Elikann; p. Daniel Wilson; ABCTV; TL.

ME, NATALIE (111m C 1969)
The search for "me" of a plain and gawky 18-year-old girl from Brooklyn who lives in a world which rewards beauty. d. Fred Cole; COLUMBIA; BF, ROA, SWANK.

MEDAL FOR MISS WALKER: 1866 (20m B 1954)
Records the efforts of Mary Walker to be commissioned as an Army surgeon for the Union Army, her rejection, and her successful appeal to President Lincoln. Observes Miss Walker being dispatched as a civilian surgeon on contract to the Army of the West, her field hospital being captured by the Confederates, and her remaining with her patients until they had been successfully treated. In 1866, Secretary of War Stanton conferred the Medal of Honor on her for her heroism. FOX; IU.

MEDEA (110m C 1971 Italian/subtitled)
Classic drama about a woman who takes fate into her own hands. Played by Maria Callas. Medea is a creature of ritualistic background who is brought by Jason and the Argonauts to a strange materialistic world. Her struggle is the struggle between these two worlds, between myth and reason, nature and civilization--and this drives Medea to kill Creon's daughter and her two sons by Jason. In the end she leaves Jason, striving for riches and power, with the values of a world in chaos. d. Pier Paolo Pasolini; NLC.

MEDIA: MASSAGING THE MIND; Towards the Year 2000 Series (24m C 1972)
Discusses future media technology, including lasers, satellites, holograms, home information centers, and other advanced electronic devices, and considers social effects of such changes. Includes interviews with William Arthur, a former editor of Look; Arnold Agnew, a former Toronto newspaper editor; Gloria Steinem, publisher

205   Meditation on Violence

of Ms. Magazine and women's lib advocate; and Joe McGinnis, author of The Selling of the Pentagon. They discuss electronic image-making. HL; DA; EMC.

MEDITATION ON VIOLENCE (12m B si 1948)
A poetic dance film which choreographs the movements and rhythms of the Wu-Tang and Shao-Lin schools of Chinese boxing, transforming each into its cinematic equivalent. The accompaniment is by flute and drum. "A challenging commentary on all violence, declaring that in a sense man fights a duel with himself as an elusive opponent."--Parker Tyler. By Maya Deren; GP.

MEET MARGIE (10m C 1976)
Student Margie manages to live on a low income by making creative use of community resources and her own self-reliance. FFAIR; UMIS.

MEMBER OF THE WEDDING (91m B 1952)
Julie Harris portrays Frankie, an awkward, lonely girl of 12 caught between childhood and adolescence and fighting both. Frankie has no friends of her own age. Her companions are her strange six-year-old cousin and her housekeeper. She is anxious to get away from this existence in which she feels rejected. She romanticizes about her brother's forthcoming marriage until she is positive he will take her along on his honeymoon. Julie, the cousin, and the housekeeper who cling together for comfort and companionship are torn apart during the crucial summer in which the film takes place. d. Fred Zinnemann; COLUMBIA; ABFI, BF.

MEMORABILIA (3m C n. d.)
"A Memorial Day in honor of a Memorial Tomorrow."--CCC. By Donna Deitch; CCC.

MEMORIES OF FAMILY (24m C 1977)
We are brought up in families and learn about the world from within the confines of the family. The constellation of our families is the framework through which we see the world and acquire our identity. As we grow up we try to understand our families and then go on to form new families of our own. Ties to family, both as child and as parent, run deeper than other bonds. In a series of six vignettes, the film recreates typical family situations which allow us to recall how we learned about love and trust, disappointment and rejection, being old and being young, being a woman and being a man. It is useful for studying human interaction, child development, or increasing sensitivity to the needs of individuals, or for any group wishing to acquire greater awareness and understanding of the effect of family upon its members. p. /d. Alvin Fiering; POLYMORPH.

MEN AND WOMEN IN MANAGEMENT; Are You Listening Series (29m C 1976)
Reveals some of the fascinating insights into male executives as they explore their growing personal and corporate awareness in relation to their women co-workers. By Martha Stuart; IMPF.

MEN AND WOMEN OF OUR TIMES SERIES see FOR LOVE OF A
WOMAN; MISS POKER FACE

MEN WHO ARE WORKING WITH WOMEN IN MANAGEMENT (29m
C r1975)
Elicits and reinforces understanding between men and women
working together in management. Focuses on a candid conversation
between a group of top level male managers which reveals the way
they feel about their new partners in management--women. p. Martha Stuart; STUART.

MENOPAUSE; Obstetrics and Gynecology Series (10m C 1974)
Examines many of the fears women face when confronted with
menopause and suggests how this period in life can be looked at
realistically. MIFE.

MENOPAUSE: HOW TO COPE; Woman Series (29m C 1974
VIDEO)
Dr. Mary C. Howell of Harvard Medical School, and Paula
Weideger, author of Cycles of Life; Menstruation and Menopause,
discuss ways to prevent acute depression during menopause. WNED-
TV; PTL.

MEN'S LIBERATION; Woman Series (29m C 1974 VIDEO)
Men, as well as women, can be victims of society's stereotyping, according to Warren Farrell, author of Beyond Masculinity.
Commenting on consciousness-raising groups for men which he has
set up in several cities, Farrell says, "The groups aim to make
men aware of how we limit ourselves, and how the respect we need
often comes from our title or our paycheck." WNEDTV; PTL.

MEN'S LIVES (43m C 1975)
A revealing look at what it is like to be a man in America.
Using interviews, the filmmakers explore the lives and feelings of
a male ballet dancer, a factory worker, a barber and others. The
pressures and demands of being male become evident as the men
speak openly. By Josh Hanig, Will Roberts; NDF; CWU, UILL,
UM, UW.

MENSES (3m C 1974)
Women express their rage, chagrin, humor, pathos--whatever
the menses means to them--satirizing Modess, Inc. 's version of
menstruation. By Barbara Hammer; FCOOP.

MENSTRUATION see LINDA'S FILM--MENSTRUATION

MENSTRUATION AND PRE-MENSTRUAL TENSION; Woman Series
(29m C 1974 VIDEO)
Dr. Cynthia Clayton, a pediatrician in Buffalo, New York, and
Leah Cahan Schaefer, psychologist and author of Women and Sex,
discuss the problems surrounding menstruation and premenstrual
tension. Both women emphasize the importance of the role of parents in determining how their daughters will react to menstruation.
WNEDTV; PTL.

MENTAL HEALTH CARE FOR WOMEN, PT. I; Woman Series (29m
C 1975 VIDEO)
Psychologist Naomi Weissten and psychiatrist Anne Seiden discuss the different definitions for "a normal healthy adult" and how
the stereotype tends to affect mental health care for men and wom-
en. WNEDTV; PTL.

MENTAL HEALTH CARE FOR WOMEN, PT. II; Woman Series (29m
C 1975 VIDEO)
Psychiatrist Anne Seiden discusses what qualities to look for in
a therapist. Sympathetic listening, ability to tolerate questions and
disagreement, and sufficient training to recognize medical causes of
depression and psychological problems are some of the characteristics to seek, she says. WNEDTV; PTL.

MEOW, MEOW (8m C 1969)
Animated cutouts--a man finds a cat that turns into a lion, and
the lion turns into a famous singer who is kidnapped by gangsters.
By Yvonne Andersen; YBW; FCOOP.

MERRY-GO-ROUND (90m B n. d.)
A highly sexual update of Max Ophuls' La Ronde set in the
Vienna of 1900. Cast: Marie Schneider, Helmut Berger, Senta
Berger. d. Otto Shenk; NLC.

MERRY-GO-ROUND, THE (23m B 1966)
What are the adolescents saying about sex? To enlarge the discussion, and to indicate some directions that bear examination, the
film invites comments from Ann Landers, columnist; Mary Winspear,
school principal; Albert Ellis, psychotherapist. Between times,
Eric and Jenny, two 17-year-olds whose behavior illustrates what
the discussion is all about, appear. By Tanya Ballantyne; NFBC;
MGH; UIO, USC, WISSU.

MESHES OF THE AFTERNOON (14m B si 1943)
Powerful images of a woman's inner vision. A pioneer sur-
realist film exploring the ambiguities of imaginative and objective
reality. By Maya Deren, Alexander Hammid; GP, MOMA.

METAL DIMENSIONS: BERTOIA (10m C n. d.)
Harry Bertoia, whose welded structures evolve directly from
nature, works in his studio in Pennsylvania as he discusses his
personal philosophy--an intimate insight. By Madeline Tourtelot;
GP.

METAMORPHOSIS (8m C 1974)
"Schwartz's Metamorphosis is a complex study of evolving lines,
planes, and circles, all moving at different speeds and resulting in
subtle color changes. The only computer-generated work on the
program transcends what many of us have come to expect of such
film. It employs subtle variations and significant use of color."--
Catherine Egan, Sight Lines, V. 8, No. 4, Summer 1975. Music:
Symphony in D Major by Saliere. By Lillian Schwartz; LPI.

METATHESIS (3m   C   1974)
"As expert hands in the complex techniques of integrating the
computer and animation, Lillian Schwartz makes fascinating use of
exotic, flowing forms, colors and electronic music in Metathesis. "
--A. H. Weiler.   By Lillian Schwartz; LPL

METHADONE: AN AMERICAN WAY OF DEALING (60m   B   1974)
A documentary showing the abuses of methadone and the falla-
cies in the way government agencies and treatment centers analyze
the "drug problem" in the U. S.   The first reel focuses on the people under treatment at the Dayton Methadone Clinic--with interviews.
The second reel portrays a way to come off drugs entirely--the RAP
family self-help drug program.   The film ends with the warning
that America does not have a drug culture--it "is" the drug culture.
By Julia Reichert, Jim Klein; METHIC.

METHODS OF FAMILY PLANNING; Family Planning and Sex Educa-
tion--A Series (17m   C   1972)
Shown are married couples receiving counseling in family planning from medical authorities.   Through use of diagrams and animation, the film accurately and objectively describes the human reproductive cycle.   All of the presently practiced methods of contraception are illustrated and explained, including the surgical methods
of vasectomy and tubal ligation.   The film recognizes birth control
as a matter of personal choice and decision, and social and moral
considerations are scrupulously avoided.   MLP; OF; UILL.

METROLINER (35m   C   1975)
Explains everything factually important about a train's journey
from New York to Washington, D. C. , while showing what went on in
time before the journey.   Wonderful film for nostalgia buffs.   d.
Victoria Hochberg; HOCHBERG.

MEXICO BEFORE CORTEZ (14m   C   1971)
Uses the art and architecture of the Aztecs, Zapotecs, Mixtecs
and Toltecs, combined with the murals of the modern Mexican artist,
Diego Rivera, to reconstruct a picture of the life of the original inhabitants of the Americas.   By Elda Hartley; HARTLEY; PARACO.

MIAO YEAR (61m   C   1968)
Ethnographic study covering the life of a Miao village in northern Thailand throughout the annual growing cycle.   Shows such activities as planting and harvesting maize and (opium) poppies, marriage customs, a funeral ceremony, healing practices of the shaman,
and making thread from the hemp plant for weaving into clothes and
blankets.   Richly and colorfully detailed, with typical daily scenes.
By Anthropologist William R. Geddes; MGH; EMC.

MIDDLE OF THE NIGHT (118m   B   1959)
A powerful motion picture created from Paddy Chayefsky's stage
story of a young divorcee who in her loneliness finds comfort, companionship and love with her equally lonely middle-aged boss, a
widower.   The opposition of their families, the warnings of their

friends, their own agonizing and conflicting doubts and desires are
skillfully unfolded and illuminatingly portrayed in a sensitive film
drama. Starring Kim Novak, Fredric March. d. Delbert Mann;
COLUMBIA; ABFL

MIDWESTERN COMPOSITIONS (10m   B   n. d.)
"A trip through small midwestern towns ... feeling of lonely
animals. A montage of strikingly desolate places. "--CCC.   By
Julia Allen; CCC.

MILDRED PIERCE (114m   B   1945)
The film charts the rise of a housewife (Joan Crawford) from
waitress to owner of a chain of restaurants on the California coast,
with mayhem along the way. No film has caught so completely the
feel of Southern California, the coast roads, and the plush atmosphere of restaurants; and the endless jostling greeds of the environment are conveyed with an aficionado's knowledge. In their respec-
tive portrayals of ambition, sisterly humor and brainless lust, Joan
Crawford, Eve Arden, and Zachary Scott are in splendid form.
Based on novel by James M. Cain. d. Michael Curtiz; WSA; UAS.

MILL, THE (15m   C   1974)
Two Yugoslav peasant women trek across a rocky landscape.
Their footsteps and the buzz of flies are all we hear. They enter
a mill, sheep "baa, " the old, wrinkled woman smokes--and then the
primitive preparations for an abortion begin. A stick is sharpened,
the young woman is tied down. As the pointed stick is inserted, the
baby's cry is heard. Afterwards, the bloody stick is thrown into the
fire, the old woman washes herself and replaces her black scarf.
Setting and symbols are anti-abortion; however, this is an excellent
film for discussion. d. Zivko Nikolic. WOMBAT.

MIME CONTROL (30m   B   n. d.)
A real mime, Jack Scalice, is directed by the filmmaker in a
computer-controlled video environment to create a beautiful study of
the motions of mime controlled and changed into various grey levels.
By Lillian Schwartz; LPL

MINERS OF BOLIVIA; Man and His World Series (15m   C   1969)
Sensitively exposes the submarginal existence of Indian tin miners
in the highlands of Bolivia. Shows that almost all chew the coca
leaf, from which cocaine is derived, to dull the hardships of life.
Notes that every second a child dies of malnutrition, and that most
miners die before 30. Well portrays the misery and deprivation
found in many Latin American countries. FI; EMC.

MINI MOVIE MAKERS (10m   C   1971)
Presents 7- to 12-year-old filmmakers involved in the film club
at the Henry Street settlement in New York. Describes how these
children make movies. By Dee Dee Halleck, Kirk Smallman;
PARACO.

MINNIE REMEMBERS (5m   C   1976)
Focuses on an old woman who reminisces about the past. It

contrasts the warmth and love which has typified her youth and womanhood with the very evident loneliness and isolation of her present
state.   She yearns to be touched and loved.   Poses many interesting
questions about aging and the poignant situation in which elderly persons find themselves.   A filmed poem from the book Images, Women
in Transition.   p. Kay Henderson; d. Phil Arnold, Kay Henderson,
Wayne Smith; MMM.

MINORITY YOUTH: ANGIE see ANGIE

MINORITY YOUTH: FELICIA see FELICIA

MIRACLE OF BIRTH;   On the Way to Growing Up Series (30m   C
1974)
     An instructor and obstetrician are discussing the psychological
and physical changes that are a part of pregnancies with a group of
prospective parents.   Included in this discussion is a careful analysis of the preparation for childbirth, proper attitudes and expectations and the husband's vital supportive role.   The film then observes three expectant mothers' progress from the first stages of
labor to the actual birth of each child.   BYU.

MIRACLE OF ST. THERESE (90m   C   1959   (dubbed))
     Examines the life of Therese Martin as it emerges from count-
less collected testimonials, from minutely studied facts and from
discussion between the promoter of the faith and lawyers, cardinals
and prelates.   d. George Bernier, ELLIS; ABFI, AIM, IVY.

MIRACLE WORKER, THE (107m   B   1962)
     The real subject of The Miracle Worker is not deafness or blind-
ness but the life principle itself.   Patty Duke plays Helen Keller
and Anne Bancroft plays Anne Sullivan.   The film conveys the ecstasy of sudden breakthrough from the frustrations to the potential fulfillment of the most fundamental of human appetites--the appetite to
know, to express, to communicate--the very principles of creativity.
Based on the play by William Gibson.   d. Arthur Penn; UAS.

MIRAGE (5m   C   1974)
     Filmed directly from color television controlled by computer
programs.   Beautifully flowing shapes that overlap and intertwine.
By Lillian Schwartz; LPL

MIRROR PEOPLE (4m   C   1974)
     A fascinating animated film in which elegantly goon-faced char-
acters cavort with their double images.   By Kathy Rose; CFS; SB.

MIS-TAKES (4m   B   1972)
     A colorful collage, with a subtle ecology theme, made largely
from footage from trial runs of programs used for many of the other films.   By Lillian Schwartz; LPL

MISS AMERIKA (6m   B   n. d.)
     A now historical film about disruption of the Miss America

Pageant of 1968. With raps, guerilla theatre and original songs,
women stress the (mis)use of their sisters as mindless sex objects
by the pageant. KMP; SFN.

MISS ARLEN: HER NEED FOR APPROVAL (20m B n. d.)
    Miss Arlen's overwhelming need for approval is explored. She
has become an actress in search of this affirmation, but her poor
opinion of herself, due to an unhappy childhood, drives her to alienate the very people she would like to have love her. She is unable
to achieve personal success and continues to search for it in therapy. p. Ira Cavrell, Otis Cavrell; PIC.

MISS BAKER: HER LOSS OF FEMININITY (20m B n. d.)
    Miss Baker is a highly successful professional woman, working
as an executive on an important magazine. On the surface her
problem appears to be a dislike of men. As she begins the process
of self-exploration, the realization occurs that in actuality, she is
frightened of women. Miss Baker does not know how to succeed
without being highly competitive; yet she fears a loss of femininity
because of this competitiveness. She does not know how to reconcile her femaleness with her success, and hopes to find the answer
through analysis. p. Ira Cavrell, Otis Cavrell; PIC.

MISS BERNARD: HER LOSS OF IDENTITY (20m B n. d.)
    Miss Bernard suffers from a lack of identity as a grown, at-
tractive woman. She has a mother who, she feels, is brilliant, attractive and talented. Miss Bernard still regards herself as her
mother's little girl and would not strike out for an independent identity. She fears that this will mean competing with her mother, and
that in any such competition she would lose. p. Ira Cavrell, Otis
Cavrell; PIC.

MISS CARLIN: RESULT OF A BROKEN HOME (20m B n. d.)
    Miss Carlin is the product of a broken and unhappy home. In
her desire for security as a child she learned to manipulate her
parents by becoming ill. This controlling, manipulative behavior
has continued into her adulthood and left her unable to form fulfilling, happy relationships with other people, men or women. She
enters therapy in an attempt to change her negative behavior. p.
Ira Cavrell, Otis Cavrell; PIC.

MISS GOODALL AND THE BABOON TROOP (24m C 1975)
    Jane Goodall offers a close-up look at one of the world's most
primitive and fearsome primates, the East African baboon. Ms.
Goodall focuses on inter-group relationships, including mating habits,
child care and leadership rivalries. The result is a fascinating insight into human behavior. Adapted from television special "Miss
Goodall and the Baboons of Gombe. " d. Hugo Van Lawick; METROM;
FI; MSU.

MISS GOODALL AND THE BABOONS OF GOMBE see MISS
    GOODALL AND THE BABOON TROOP

MISS GOODALL AND THE HYENA STORY (52m   C   1975)
The popular view of the hyena as a skulking, cowardly scaven-
ger, is rejected by animal behaviorist Jane Goodall who spent two
years studying the hyena in East Africa's Ngorongoro Crater.   The
film focuses her attention on the Lakeside Clan, its leader and
cubs.   d. Hugo Van Lawick; METROM; FL

MISS GOODALL AND THE LIONS OF SERENGETI (52m   C   1976)
The myths surrounding lions are numerous and contradictory.
Miss Goodall sought the truth on East Africa's Serengeti Plains with
photographer Hugh Van Lawick recording behavior patterns, terri-
torial and social habits, and relationship with other animals.   d.
Hugo Van Lawick; METROM; FL

MISS GOODALL AND THE WILD CHIMPANZEES (51m   C   1965)
Shows Jane Goodall's study of chimpanzees in East Africa, her
observations of their behavior and her discoveries of their use of
tools.   Conveys her feeling that the study of primate behavior can
lead to a better understanding of human behavior.   FI; BU, BYU,
CWU, EMC, IU, WAYSU.

MISS GOODALL AND THE WILD CHIMPS (28m   C   1968)
Presents the story of a 26-year-old English girl and her adventures in the jungles of East Africa, as she observed and lived
with chimpanzees.   Reinforces the anthropological belief that a complete understanding of chimpanzees will lead man to a better understanding of himself.   EBEC; PAS, USC, UU, WAYSU.

MISS GOODALL AND THE WILD DOGS OF AFRICA (52m   C   1973)
Little was known about the wild dogs of Africa until Jane Goodall
led her research party on to the plains of Serengeti.   They were
able to record an intimate film study of a single pack for two years.
She became attached to a young pup, named Solo by the research
team.   Solo gets detached from the pack and many anxious days are
spent while it searches the dry plains for a new family to join.   d.
Hugo Van Lawick; METROM; FL

MISS HAVISHAM (24m   B   1963)
From Dickens' Great Expectations.   Florence Eldridge, as Miss
Havisham, compensates for her own melancholy life by sponsoring
Pip in order to break his heart through her ward, Estella.   COR;
UIO.

MISS JESUS FRIES ON GRILL (12m   C   n. d.)
A newspaper clipping and other images are used to express
grief, pain, curiosity, peace, and how it is just to be alive.   By
Dorothy Wiley; CCC.

MISS JULIE (90m   B . 1950   Swedish/subtitled)
Miss Julie (Anita Bjork), a confused noblewoman, persecutes
herself with the torment of shame and disgrace for allowing her
arrogantly masculine servant to seduce her.   Her mother was a
feminist who refused to marry her father, and who gave all of her

money to a lover. Her mother raised Julie as a boy and endowed her with a hate for men. It is this dutiful hate that proceeds to destroy Julie now that she has allowed herself to give in to a man. Adapted from the play by August Strindberg.   d. Alf Sjoberg; JANUS.

MISS LULU BETT (64m   B   1921)
A drama in which a young woman changes from a self-effacing, drab spinster, to a pretty, assertive woman and leaves her married sister's home to begin a life of her own.   FPFC.

MISS, MRS. , OR MS. --WHAT'S IT ALL ABOUT? (25m   C   1977)
Offers a clear explanation of the term "Ms. ," a simple word which does not identify a woman as married or single, in the same way that "Mr." does not reveal the marital status of a man. CBSTV; CAROUSEL.

MISS POKER FACE; Men and Women of Our Times Series (15m B   n. d.)
Story of Helen Wills, a U. S. tennis champion at age 17. CBSTV; STAR.

MISS ROSSEN: RESULT OF CHILDHOOD REJECTION (20m   B   n. d.)
Miss Rossen had a desperately unhappy childhood. She was physically abused and rejected at a very young age. In her search for love, she turned to men who, like her father, beat her. In her self-hate, she feels she deserves this abuse; at the same time, she resents the world which inflicts it. Miss Rossen is a lonely, angry woman who feels dirty, soiled and unlovable. She has in the past turned to heroin addiction and suicide as means of punishing and degrading herself. She can no longer tolerate her way of life and has turned to therapy as a possible way to stop her self-destructive behavior.   p. Ira Cavrell, Otis Cavrell; PIC.

MISS TOWERS: A CONFUSED TEEN-AGER (20m   B   n. d.)
Miss Towers is a young woman beset by her feelings of inferiority. Born on what she considers "the wrong side of the tracks, " she uses her excellent mind to compensate, but in a destructive manner. She feels she has all the answers to a world which has given her none. She seeks to resolve her problems by gaining attention and approval from her peers by abusing her sexuality.   p. Ira Cavrell, Otis Cavrell; PIC.

MISSING IN RANDOLPH (26m   C   1970)
A visit with the people left behind by a man killed in Vietnam. By Hope Ryden; RYDEN.

MISSION TO MALAYA; Daring American Series (52m   B   1965)
Presents Peace Corps nurse Margery Benning who replaces nurse Rita Franzone on the jungle island of Langkawi. Shows how she proves her worth to the Malayans by arranging to have a critically sick woman ferried across the Straits of Malacca to a hospital. By Hope Ryden, PUREX; ABCTV; DREW.

MISSIONS OF CALIFORNIA: NEW WAYS IN THE NEW WORLD
(22m   C   1968)
Shows the early routes the padres used and the importance of
the missions: for example, "the schools they provided for the Indians. "--BFA.   By Geraldine Byers, Justin Byers; BFA.

MISSISSIPPI RIVER: ITS ROLE IN AMERICAN HISTORY (22m   C
1964)
Tells of the development of the steamboat and early navigation
on the Mississippi, with passages from Mark Twain and actual
footage of steamboat races.   By Geraldine Byers, Justin Byers;
BFA.

MISSISSIPPI RIVER: TRADE ROUTE OF MID-AMERICA (19m   C
1963)
Tells of the Mississippi River System and its far-reaching influence on American lives.   By Geraldine Byers, Justin Byers;
BFA.

MR. AND MRS. WELLS: A PROBLEMED MARRIAGE (40m   B
n. d.)
Mr. and Mrs. Wells find themselves in a marriage totally unac-
ceptable to either.   Mr. Wells is impotent and feels himself to be
inadequate.   He is insecure and most of the time functions passively
and submissively.   When he drinks his behavior reverses and he becomes abusive and overly aggressive.   Mrs. Wells is compulsive
and hyper-critical.   She responds to her husband with nagging and
hysterical behavior.   She considers him a failure as a husband, as
a father and in his profession, and she blames her bad marriage on
him.   Mrs. Wells gains attention through her psychosomatic ills
and feels she is leading an empty, insufficient life.   In a joint session with Mr. and Mrs. Wells, their psychotherapist tries to help
them learn to relate to and understand themselves and each other
so that they can either continue their marriage in a fulfilling way,
or come to a rational, reasoned decision to obtain a divorce.   p.
Ira Cavrell, Otis Cavrell, PIC.

MR. CORELLI: A POWER DRIVEN MAN (20m   B   n. d.)
Mr. Corelli is a power-oriented personality who uses overly aggressive behavior and unsavory business tactics to mask his per-
vading sense of vulnerability.   His unhealthy childhood relationship
with his mother and the overwhelming closeness he felt towards her
have left him afraid of establishing close ties with other women.
He has entered analysis because of his impotency, but continues to
deny the influence of his mother and the reasons for his aggressive
behavior.   p. Ira Cavrell, Otis Cavrell; PIC.

MISTER MIDWIFE (29m   C   1975   VIDEO)
Norman Casserley has been a midwife for 26 years.   He has
assisted at more than 3000 home deliveries and has never had a
death, complication or ambulance case.   He discusses his experiences with moderator Sandra Elkin.   WNEDTV; PTL.

MR. STORY (28m C 1973)
Portrait of 86-year-old Albert Story who repairs cane work on chairs. Shots of his daily life are intercut with sequences in which he discusses society. By Dee Dee Halleck, Anita Thatcher; PHOE-NIX.

MR. TRI-STATE (12m C 1973)
A low-keyed look at a body builders' contest, featuring the contest's winner. By Tom Palazzo, Jeff Kreines; VFI; CCC, PERSPECTIVE.

MISTRESS, THE (106m B 1953 Japanese/subtitled)
Otama, a beautiful young woman, becomes the mistress of a not-too-attractive merchant to support her impoverished father, thinking he will eventually marry her. However, she finds out this man is a disreputable money lender and is already married. Later, Otama meets and becomes attracted to a medical student whom she encourages to call on her. When the money lender finds out, he becomes jealous and ingeniously arranges a loan to enable the student to go abroad to further his studies. Otama's hopes are dashed and her love remains unconsummated. d. Shiro Toyoda; JANUS.

MODERN AMERICAN DRAMA: A RAISIN IN THE SUN (18m C
n. d. SFS)
One of the greatest social protest plays ever written, this classic is a passionate plea for social justice and human understanding. By Lorraine Hansberry; EDC.

MODERN MAYAN; Indian Family Series (14m C 1969)
Shows the life of a Mexican-Indian family in Chiapas, the southern-most state of Mexico, where the Indians live much the same as their Mayan ancestors 1000 years ago. Centers around the father who is a teacher in the local school and who is an important man in the community. By Elda Hartley; HARTLEY.

MODERN OBSTETRICS: NORMAL DELIVERY (26m C 1969)
Shows stages of labor and actual childbirth in incidents of both normal and forced delivery. Shows most recent techniques being used by doctors. For adult and professional audiences only. ORTHO; UNEV.

MODERN WOMEN: THE UNEASY LIFE (60m B 1967)
Examines feelings of college-educated women about the roles available to them--as housewives, mothers, and career women in the U. S. Women interviewed discuss the frustrations and satisfactions of their lives. Men's attitudes toward educated women are also explored. Predates the women's liberation movement. IU; AFC, BU, NIU, PAS, UILL, UK, UM, UIO, PURDUE, WSU.

MOKIL (58m B 1950)
Celebrated ethnographic documentary about the Micronesian atoll of Mokil and the problems caused there by overpopulation and

the shift from a subsistence to a cash economy. Shows many daily
activities, some of which are traditional, such as hut-thatching,
breadfruit harvesting and preparation, fishing, and communal work,
and many which are the result of the recent development of cash
trade, such as copra production, the use of steel tools, and the
making of mats and baskets for export. Also considers the cultural
changes introduced by Christian missionaries. SPF; EMC.

MOMENT IN LOVE, A (8m C 1957)
    "A boy and a girl meet in a romantic wooded glen and with a
leap into space take off into a dance. Multiple images and controlled color turn the lovers into blossoming flowers. "--by Shirley
Clarke; MOMA.

MOMENTS (15m B 1972)
    "Cine-poem: ocean visuals over poetry of Jim Hietter, S. J. "--
T. S. By Terry Sheehy; SHEEHY.

MOMENTS (1m C si 1974)
    "The unblinking stare of a white cat half obscured by darkness
fills the screen ... minimal changes in each hair and texture in
extended time. A quick movement and an enveloping yawn climax
the film. "--R. S. By Rosalind Schneider; SCHNEIDER.

MOMMY-DADDY COMMUNICATION (31m C n. d.)
    Dr. Beryl and Avinoam Chernick meet with a group of expectant
parents to explore some of the normal mixed feelings people have
about being pregnant and about becoming parents. Through role
playing, the importance of sharing of feelings between Mommy and
Daddy to ease the anxiety and enhance the job of the prenatal and
postnatal period is stressed, while some of the myths which burden
sexual functioning during pregnancy are dramatically and humorously
examined. CSP; NIU.

MOOD CONTRASTS (7m C n. d.)
    A pioneer computer abstract film by a pioneer film artist, in
which Rimsky-Korsakov's "Hymn to the Sun" and "Dance of the
Tumblers" are visually interpreted by a multitude of abstract and
surreal visual images, including those created on an oscillograph--
a primitive analog computer. By Mary Ellen Bute; CFS.

MOOD MONDRIAN (7m C si n. d.)
    "Film of a painting of a sound. Piet Mondrian's 'Broadway
Boogie-Woogie' is translated into visual boogie rhythm. "--by Marie
Menken; FCOOP.

MOOD OF ZEN (14m C 1967)
    Alan Watts discusses Zen philosophy. Varied scenes of the
Japanese countryside are set against koto music and the chanting
of. Buddhist monks. By Elda Hartley; HARTLEY.

MOON (2m B si n. d.)
    "Images of the moon--its phases, its astronauts, its dreams. "
--M. A. S. By Mary Ann Spencer; FCOOP.

MOON GATES (15m   C   1973)
"Three five-minute versions of a handsome dance piece.   The
first version is original footage; the second, the same footage optically printed; the third version, the film-video-synthesized . . . for
dance and film study. "--Freude Bartlett.   By Doris Chase; PIC.

MOON GATES (6m   C   1973)
Dance with sculpture filmed in the Avery Court of the Wadsworth Atheneum in Hartford.   By Doris Chase; PIC.

MOON IS MY BALLOON (10m   C   1967-73)
Childhood fantasy.   The filmmaker's daughter at age six creates
a pet from a balloon.   By Constance Beeson; BEESON.

MOON SHOW (2m   C   1969)
A delightful and cleverly animated film.   By Kathy Rose; CFS.

MOONAGE DREAMS OF CHARLENE STARDUST, THE (13m   B
1974)
A portrayal of a teen-ager's experience with the dreams and
expectations of growing up female as projected by the movies, advertising and by magazines.   She dates a young man, has sexual
fantasies, and views marriage gowns in department store windows.
Even washing dishes becomes a dreamy fantasy of married life until the wonder of it fades into the drudgery of her mother's dull
routine.   By Margot Oliver, Jan Carroll, Jan Milne; WMM.

MOONBIRD (10m   C   1959)
One of the most widely praised and beloved animated films ever
made.   In matchless color and drawing and in a sound track composed of their children's own voices, the Hubleys have managed to
capture the magical world of childhood.   The story of two small
boys who set out to capture the mythical moonbird at night, using
candy as bait, is one to delight all ages.   By Faith Hubley, John
Hubley; ABFI; CFS. FI, FIM, GP, VFL

MOONGATES III (5m   C   1974)
A dance film based on kinetic sculpture, with the Mary Staton
Dance Ensemble.   Dancers, each appearing in separate monochromatic images of the primary colors, move through kinetic sculptures
made specifically for the choreographer.   The sculptures move
slightly when touched, taking on the quality of mobiles and setting
up a new dynamic between people and forms in motion.   By Doris
Chase; ABFL

MOONPLAY (5m   B   n. d.)
"Lunar fantasy in animated stop-motion. "--M. M.   By Marie
Menken; FCOOP.

MOON'S POOL (15m   C   1974)
Living bodies, filmed underwater, are interposed with landscapes, creating images which seem to rise from the unconscious,
portraying the search for identity and self-resolution.   By Gunvor
Nelson; CCC, SB.

MORE THAN A SCHOOL (56m C 1974)
Examines the concept used in alternative education carried on
in the Community School in Nassau County on Long Island where
students design their own programs based on their personal interests and career plans.   d. Martha Coolidge; p. Jack Robertson; FI.

MORE THAN NURSERY RHYMES: COORDINATING CHILD CARE
(26m C n. d.)
Describes the work of the Denver Child Care Project, demonstrating both center and home care methods, training techniques for
staff workers, and the role of the coordinators.   Shows how centers
may be organized to resemble home environments more closely, and
the benefits of this environment for the children.   EMC.

MOROCCO (97m B 1930)
Marlene Dietrich plays girl of doubtful past who comes to
Morocco as a cabaret entertainer.   She becomes involved with young
Gary Cooper who serves in the French Foreign Legion.   With each
meeting they become more drawn to each other, each wary of involvement, and each searching for the fatal chink in the other's
armor.   In the days that follow, another suitor (Adolphe Menjou)
vies for her hand.   Many years her senior, but wealthy, he knows
he's no match for the young Cooper, but hopes the security he can
offer will win her over.   When Cooper has to leave with his company for the desert, Dietrich makes her decision and follows him
into the desert.   From the play Amy Jolly.   d. Joseph Von Sternberg; PARAMOUNT; UNIVE, TWY.

MOSAIC (6m C 1965)
An unusual movement in color and sound, created in an unusual
way.   It is an example of "op" art in film, a play on the retina of
the eye.   Basis of the film is a tiny square that divides, eventually
forming a colorful mosaic to the animator's musical orchestration.
By Evelyn Lambart, Norman McLaren; NFBC; IFB.

MOSAICS: THE WORK OF JEANNE REYNAL (18m C n. d.)
Follows the intriguing process of making a mosaic and in so
doing captures the personality of artist Jeanne Reynal at work in
her home environment with her husband, Thomas Sills, a painter,
who assists her.   By Paul Falkenberg; FIM.

MOSORI MONIKA (20m B 1970)
Sensitively observes, through portraits of a Spanish nun and an
old Warao Indian woman, the encounter and subsequent changes of
two cultures in an isolated Venezuelan village.   The words and the
thoughts of the two women are juxtaposed, and scenes of village life
subtly reveal the nun's naive prejudices and condescending attitude,
the simple compliance of the Indian woman, and how each woman
has learned to use the other's culture to ease the difficulties they
both experience in their harsh environment.   A remarkable example
of acculturation from two viewpoints.   p. Chick Strand; MGH; EMC,
SB, UILL.

MOST, THE (27m B 1963)
Scathing documentary on Hugh Hefner, self-styled philosopher
and millionaire creator of Playboy empire. Gordon Sheppard and
Richard Ballentine's cinéma-vérité style reveals Hefner's vision and
provides a yardstick by which to judge current mores and aspirations. PF; PAS.

MOTHER AND THE WHORE, THE (215m B 1973)
Gives the most thorough and insightful analysis of contemporary
sexual mores yet seen on film. The film intently and ironically
surveys the various sexual and conversational permutations of Alex-
andre, Marie, and Veronika. The characters are not young. They
are the products of the cultural revolution of the sixties--30 years
old but still single and uncommitted. They are both the heroes and
the victims of the recent sexual liberation. It is a film of multiple
dimensions so that it not only shows us the contemporary situations
of its characters but also helps us to understand them. Most important, even though Mother and the Whore centers on a male character, it nevertheless shows tremendous respect, understanding--
and even love--for its women. d. Jean Eustache; NYF.

MOTHER-INFANT INTERACTION, NO. I: FORMS OF INTERAC-
TION AT SIX WEEKS (49m B 1967)
Shows variations in mothers' ways of touching, holding, looking
at, and talking to their babies during feeding, and the immediate
effects of differences in handling on the infants. p. Sylvia Brody,
Sidney Axelrad; NYU; EMC.

MOTHER-INFANT INTERACTION, NO. II: FORMS OF INTERAC-
TION AT SIX MONTHS (42m B 1968)
Examines relationship between a baby's feeding experience at
six months and its development of tension tolerance. Shows how an
infant is helped to wait for food, how a mother notes its wish to
take initiative and responds to it, and how the baby can be satisfied
or frustrated by its feeding. p. Sylvia Brody, Sidney Axelrad;
NYU; EMC.

MOTHER LOVE (26m B 1960)
Dr. Harry Marlowe, in his primate laboratory at U. of Wisconsin, tests the reaction of a large colony of newborn rhesus monkeys
to a variety of unusual and inanimate mother substitutes, which he
calls "mother surrogates" in order to find a key to the bond between
mother and child and to understand the effects of the denial of maternal love. He demonstrates that the single most important factor
is body contact and concludes that deprivation of this can cause deep
emotional disturbances, even death. CAROUSEL; AIM, EMC, IU.

MOTHER MARRIES A MAN OF MELLOW MIEN--A LOVE STORY
(7m C 1973)
Warm portrait of filmmaker's mother's second marriage. By
Abigail Child; CHILD.

MOTHER OF THE KENNEDYS: A PORTRAIT OF ROSE FITZGER-
ALD KENNEDY (57m   C   1974)
A filmed portrait of the Mother of the Kennedys, revealing faith
as the motivating force which has shaped her life.   Mrs.
Kennedy, dynamic and attractive at 83, shares some of her attitudes, ideals
and experiences in interviews at her Hyannis home.   Mrs. Kennedy's
role as mother is affectionately sketched in interviews with daughter,
Eunice Shriver Kennedy, and her son, Ted.   p.   RADINC; MMA.

MOTHERS AFTER DIVORCE (20m   C   1976)
Filmed are four women with children of high school age--women
who led protected lives until divorce--talking openly about their new
lives.   By Marilyn Felt, Henry Felt; POLYMORPH.

MOTHERS AND DAUGHTERS (27m   B   1969)
Focuses on two families in which daughters are at odds with
their mothers.   In the first, the mother, a devout Catholic, is out-
raged when her daughter marries a young Jew.   After the daughter
has a baby, she and her mother renew their relationship.   In the
second family, a 19-year-old college student rejects her mother's
values as conventional and security-minded.   The mother is deeply
concerned, but feels powerless to influence her daughter.   CBSTV;
CAROUSEL; AIMS, EMC, PAS.

MOTHERS AND TODDLERS (16m   B   1970)
Presents a unique pre-school program known as the "Toddlers'
Lab, " initiated by the Martin Luther King Family Center of Chicago.
A growth experience not only for the toddlers but for mothers and
staff as well, the lab is based on the fundamental notion that parents
must experience a sense of competence before they can effectively
encourage their children to invest themselves in the risky business
of learning.   JOU; UILL.

MOTHERS ARE PEOPLE; Challenge for Change Series (7m   C
1974)
Joy, a very articulate Jamaican woman, is a research biologist,
a consultant to a large company.   She is also a widow with two
school-age children.   In expressing her own dilemmas she speaks
for many other women.   "The powers-that-be know that women do
work--but they turn a deaf ear. "   Apart from "discrimination
against women, " Joy sees the absence of universal day care as a
loss for children too.   In Canada, day care facilities are "geared
for the bourgeoise, " and are expensive and operate only from 9:00
A. M. to 3:00 P. M.   However, Joy feels changes will come about.
By Kathleen Shannon; NFBC; EDC; EMC.

MOTHERS WHO LEAVE HOME; Woman Series (29m   C   1974
VIDEO)
Judy Sullivan is a wife and mother who walked out on her marriage and wrote about it in her book Mama Doesn't Live Here Anymore.   Here she discusses what marriage became for her, and the
conflicts in having a home, career, and the ambition to write.
WNEDTV; PTL.

MOTION PICTURE STUDY OF MARTHA GRAHAM FROM HER
DANCE "LAMENTATION, " THE (11m C 1943)
Performance by Graham with introductory comments on modern
dance by John Martin, then dance critic of the New York Times.
Musical arrangement and accompaniment by Louis Horst. p. Har-
mon Foundation, and Simon and Gerta Moselsio; UILL, PAS.

MOUCHETTE (90m B 1966 French/subtitled)
Mouchette is a young peasant girl who lives amidst ignorance
and squalor, in the kind of isolated rural community that breeds
depravity. Her father and brothers are bootleggers, her mother is
dying and her classmates are callous and stupid. She, being more
sensitive than those around her, is paradoxically less able to communicate. She is incomplete, proud, stubborn and potentially introspective, but without the spiritual vocabulary to bring thought into
being. She is blocked off not only from external reality but from
her deepest urgings. She is raped by an epileptic poacher, is
further rejected by the village and finally commits suicide. Adapted
from Nouvelle Historie de Mouchette. By George Bernanos. d.
Robert Bresson; NLC.

MOVE IT! (19m C n. d.)
Featuring the Ririe-Woodbury Dance Company as they appear
everywhere from Salt Lake City airport to the feeding corrals of
a hereford breeding ranch. In bizarre costumes, they climb out of
man-holes in the middle of a busy street, pantomime and dance
their way through many parts of scenic Utah. Anything goes. By
Judith Hallet, Stanley Hallet; FIM.

MRS. CASE (14m B 1969)
Stark and provocative portrait of a welfare mother in Montreal
whose husband has deserted her. She is shown to be the victim of
an inadequate and unfeeling welfare system that threatens to take
her children away from her if she complains too strongly about her
inability to manage on her meager budget. Shot in a naturalistic,
cinéma-vérité style; includes an interview with an insensitive welfare agent who denies Mrs. Case money to buy winter shoes for her
children. NFBC; EMC.

MRS. COP (17m C 1973)
Mary Ellen Albrect is a police sergeant on the Washington,
D. C. , force. The film follows her through some typical police
chores: inspecting firearms at the scene of a fire, chairing a de-
partmental meeting, practicing self-defense with another officer.
Includes the reactions of policemen around her. By Sheila Decola,
Joe Decola; ECCW; UILL, VFL

MRS. GRAY: A FRIGID WOMAN (20m B n. d.)
Mrs. Gray is an attractive young woman in her twenties. As
a child, she was traumatized by a sexual overture from her father.
Since that time, Mrs. Gray has experienced an intense, but never
satisfied, need for men. Unable to achieve sexual release because
of her dread of incestuous fantasies, she enters therapy. Mrs.

Gray's fear is symptomized by her nymphomanic behavior.   Until she begins to make connection between her disturbance and her child-hood experience, nothing will penetrate her wall of frigidity.   p. Ira Cavrell, Otis Cavrell; PIC.

MRS. INDIRA GANDHI; 20th Century Series (26m   B   n. d.)
Tells the story of Mrs. Indira Gandhi, prime minister of India. Explains that she is the first woman to hold such a high position in a major country.   CBSTV; ABFL

MRS. JACQUELINE KENNEDY VISITS INDIA (14m   B   1962)
Records the highlights of the nine-day visit of Mrs. Jacqueline Kennedy, wife of the President of the U. S. , to India in March, 1962.   INDIA.

MRS. KAY: HER FAILING MARRIAGE (20m   B   n. d.)
Mrs. Kay's children are grown and married, living far away from her.   Since they left home, her marriage has become more and more unbearable.   She and her husband love each other, but have grown far apart and no longer communicate.   Her husband has become involved with another woman.   Mrs. Kay enters therapy to find out why she and her husband have grown apart and what she can do to make their later years together fulfilling and happy.   p. Ira Cavrell, Otis Cavrell; PIC.

MRS. MIXON (59m   B   1969)
An account of the problems of a middle-aged Black woman from the rural South, her rehabilitation in a Midwestern university hos-pital after diabetes had taken her legs and blinded her, and her un-resolved conflicts with white therapists.   OHSU.

MRS. ROBERT LOUIS STEVENSON (27m   B   n. d.)
An episode in the life of the famed Scottish author, Robert Louis Stevenson, and his devoted wife.   Deals with the dramatic period in their lives during which they searched for a salubrious climate to help the ailing writer win back his health.   IDEAL; UKEN.

MRS. SLATTERY'S STEW (9m   C   1969)
An allegory on women, using abstract images, sacred, profane, biological, antithetical.   Played against the production of a stew. By Phyllis B. Pigorsch; CCC.

MRS. TKACH (11m   C   n. d.)
Portrait of a Ukrainian woman shown as she bakes and talks about her life as a young immigrant.   She explains her satisfaction in baking which, in her hands, becomes an art form.   By Dee Dee Halleck; HALLECK.

MRS. USCHYK (29m   C   1973)
Presents a drama about a Polish American grandmother who struggles to meet the challenges of industrial America, and who hopes for a better life for her grandson.   AFL

MS--THE STRUGGLE FOR WOMEN'S RIGHTS; Screen News Digest
Series (no number given) (21m   C   n. d.)
Presents a pictorial cavalcade of the people, places and events
that have given impetus and leadership to the struggle for women's
rights.   HEARST.

MS--THE STRUGGLE FOR WOMEN'S RIGHTS; Screen News Digest
Series, No. 15 (14m   B   1972)
Depicts the people, places and events that have given impetus
and leadership to the struggle for women's rights.   HEARST.

MUJER DE MILFUEGOS (WOMAN OF A THOUSAND FIRES) (15m
C   1976   Spanish/subtitled)
An expressionistic, surrealistic portrait of a Latin American
woman.   The film depicts in poetic, almost abstract terms the daily
repetitive tasks of Third World Women who spend their entire lives
giving birth, preparing food and tending to household and farm
chores.   Through experiences of ecstasy and madness we are shown
different aspects of the human personality engaged in age-old rituals
of survival.   By Chick Strand; SB; IE.

MUJERES COLOMBIANAS (20m   B   n. d.)
Group of Colombian women discuss (in Spanish) use of birth
control.   "If we had known this before, if that existed in the villages ... we would not have had so many children. "   By Martha
Stuart, David Ruskin; STUARTM.

MURAL ON OUR STREET, THE (18m   C   1965)
Shows children drawing zoo animals for a 70 x 8 foot tile mural
that will be used in a new building for the Henry Street settlement
of New York's Lower East Side.   Follows the making of the tiles
and views the completed mural.   By Dee Dee Halleck, Kirk Smallman; MGH.

MURDER TRIAL (58m   C   n. d.)
The film follows a real murder trial (not a re-enactment) in a
small town in Kentucky.   A man is accused of shooting a young
girl in his apartment.   You are an eye-witness to the selection of
jurors, opening arguments, examination and cross-examination of
witnesses and the final verdict.   A document on the American ju-
dicial system in action.   p. /d. Nell Cox; SOHO.

MURUGA (24m   C   1973)
The god Muruga is worshipped in Ceylon where, each year,
thousands of Hindus attend a festival in his honor.   The sacred
rite lasts 25 days and nights and is a colorful spectacle.   By
Yvonne Hannemann; SB.

MUSIC STUDIO: HARRY PARTCH (18m   C   1959)
An incredible portrayal of one man's life dedication to his
unique art.   He is seen at his studio at the time of his score production of the film "Windsong. "   He explains each of his instru-

ments (43 tones to the octave), and plays excerpts from the film
score.   By Madeline Tourtelot; GP.

MUTATIONS (8m   C   1972)
    An animation that exercises all the possibilities of computer-
generated colors and images in a continually changing pattern of
abstractions.   Also available in video-cassette.   By Lillian Schwartz,
Ken Knowlton; LPL

MY COUNTRY OCCUPIED (30m   B   1971   Spanish/English)
    A documentary about the struggle against United Fruit Co. in
Guatemala, and woman's recognition of her exploitation by the U. S. --
both as rural labor and urban poor.   When after years of poverty
her husband is arrested, she returns to the country and discovers
a group of political women and becomes a guerilla.   Shows us how
our standard of living is based on other people's misery and forced
labor, and gives us an encouraging model of women's resistance.
SFN,   TWN.

MY DAD'S A COP (18m   C   1976)
    Love, pride and respect between father and son, mixes with
problems of having a cop for a dad.   Shows the police officer in
typical day-to-day activities.   Stresses warmth and support of the
family circle.   p. Patricia Brose; d. Bill Brose; WBPL

MY FATHER THE DOCTOR (18m   C   1973)
    A study of the relationship, past and present, between the film-
maker and her father.   Explores the expectations and assumptions
that have guided them; gives some things a chance to be said and
lets some things remain unsaid.   By Miriam Weinstein; WEINSTEIN.

MY LIFE IN ART (1969-73) (30m   C   1974)
    Includes eight films: "Promise Her Anything But Give Her the
Kitchen Sink," "Shooting Star," "Standup and Be Counted," "Adam's
Birth," "Sweet Dreams," "Folly," "Women and Children at Large,"
and "One and the Same."   The above films are available separately,
except for "Adam's Birth."   Freude combines the artifacts of California living with a melange of domestic, maternal, and wholly personal symbols infused with humor, poetry and sensuality.   By
Freude Bartlett; SB.

MY LIFE TO LIVE (VIVRE SA VIE) (83m   B   1962)
    Explores the life of a prostitute by using documentary and
dramatic techniques.   Godard creates both a social and personal
view of prostitution.   With Anna Karina.   d. Jean-Luc Godard;
ACB, CORINF.

MY LITTLE CHICKADEE (91m   B   1940)
    Classic comedy written by W. C. Fields and Mae West.   Mae
plays the seductive Flower Belle Lee, a lady of ill-repute who pretends to marry con artist Fields to fleece him of his oil wells.
Naturally, Fields' oil is for the hair and not from the fields.   When
she discovers this, the fireworks begin.   d. Edward Cline; p. Lester Cowan; s. w. Mae West; UNIVE; CWF, SWANK, TWY, UNIVE.

MY NAME IS OONA (10m B 1970)
"My Name Is Oona captures in haunting, intensely lyrical images, fragments of the coming to consciousness of a child girl. Throughout the entire film, the girl, compulsively and as if in awe, repeats her name, until it becomes a magic incantation of self-realization. "--Amos Vogel, Film As Subversive Art. By Gunvor Nelson; CCC, SB.

MY NAME IS SUSAN YEE (12m C 1976)
Susan is a 10-year-old Chinese Canadian and a victim of urban renewal. Her neighborhood had been torn down and her father heard rumors that Chinatown would be replaced with modern highrises. Her father had to give up his laundry business when all his customers were forced to abandon their homes. d. Beverly Shaffer; NFBC; MG.

MY PEOPLE ARE MY HOME (60m C 1976)
The film draws from the experiences of midwestern women born around 1900--the women, Native American women, the women of the farms and prairies, factory women--to create a documentary of women's history. The words of Meridel Le Sueur act as a narrative thread, weaving a variety of local histories, philosophies, customs and cultures into a whole that gives us a truly personal sense of history. Meridel Le Sueur observed and recorded stories of Midwestern people all her life. A dedicated feminist and socialist, she was blacklisted for years and her writings could not be published. TCWFC; IE.

MY TRIP ABROAD (11m B n. d.)
When Mrs. Roosevelt traveled to Oslo to unveil a statue of her late husband, she visited Norway, Sweden, Finland, Denmark, Holland, France and England, and noted the way the Marshall Plan had been used to aid recovery. AFF; UKEN.

MYRA BRECKINRIDGE (94m C 1970 Reg. /Scope)
Adapted from Gore Vidal's novel. Rex Reed plays the young man who wishes to alter his sex, Raquel Welch stars as the Amazon he becomes, and Mae West is the man-eating talent agent. West wrote her own dialogue and it is ribald as ever. Example: She meets a prospective client, she remarks on how tall he is. "I'm six feet seven inches," he responds. "Never mind about the six feet, son," she answers in that inimitable tone of hers, "tell me about the seven inches." p. Robert Fryer; d. Michael Sarne; s. w. Mae West; FOX; FL

MYRA HESS (11m B n. d.)
Shows Myra Hess, one of the great British pianists, her endurance, flawless technique, and execution of movement as she plays the first movement of Beethoven's "Sonata in F Minor." BIS; UKEN.

MYSTERIANS, THE (6m C 1973)
The animation and bizarre creative imagery is reminiscent of that of Pulse and Street Musique, with its ever-changing fluidic forms. Music score by Larry Stein. By Kathy Rose; CFS, SB.

MYSTERY OF AMELIA EARHART, THE; You Are There Series
(22m   C   1971)
In 1937, in an attempt to be the first woman to fly around the
world at the equator, Amelia Earhart disappeared, presumably over
the Pacific Ocean.   The film dramatically covers the events surrounding her disappearance and the main elements that contribute
to the mystery.   CBSTV; BFA.

MZIMA: PORTRAIT OF A SPRING (53m   C   1971)
Kenya's Mzima Springs, a fascinating ecosystem, demonstrates
the interdependence of animals.   Survival is shown to be dependent
on the success of other species.   By Joan Root, Alan Root; MGH;
UILL, UM.

N. O. W.   NOW; Woman Series (29m   C   1975   VIDEO)
Karen DeCrow, president of the National Organization for Women,
talks about the changes the 40, 000 member group has produced and
the ways in which its goals have altered since its start.   WNEDTV;
PTL.

NADIA BOULANGER (30m   B   1962)
Discusses her early musical training, her association with Igor
Stravinsky and Leonard Bernstein, role of the music teacher in
bringing out the best in a student and her sister Lillis' composition.
NBCTV; PAS.

NADINE GORDIMER (29m   B   1956)
Deals with subjects ranging from effect of South Africa on the
author's work and her attitude towards racial problems to her opinions of C. P. Snow.   Reveals her opinion of America, of herself
and of her writing.   NET, IU; IU.

NADINE VALENTI--PORTRAIT OF A PAINTER (22m   C   1977)
Shown are the techniques, philosophies, and obstacles of an abstract expressionist painter, Nadine Valenti, with emphasis on how
the Women's Movement gave her the strength to rise above fears
and self-doubts and devote her life to painting.   d. /p. Bob Zaslow;
IE.

NAME OF THE GAME (30m   C   n. d.)
"Boy meets girl on a ski weekend. "--R. W.   By Edith Worth,
Robert Worth; FCOOP.

NANA (87m   B   1934)
A moving story of a coquettish Parisian actress who chooses
her lovers unwisely in the days preceding the Franco-Prussian War.
Nana beautifully captures the point of view of a tragic but liberated
19th-century woman.   Adapted from Emile Zola's novel.   d. Dorothy
Arzner; MGM; ABFI.

NANA, MOM AND ME (45m   C   1974)
Prompted by thoughts of bringing her own child into the world,

Amalie Rothschild examines her relationship with her own mother
and grandmother and probes the relationship shared by all three
women in this personal, freewheeling documentary. Rothschild extends this autobiographical exploration and causes viewers to consider their family relationships. By Amalie Rothschild; NDF.

NANCY HANKS; Lincoln Series (28m B 1956)
    Examines the hard life experienced by an American backwoods
family; how young Abe Lincoln was affected by the death of his mother; and how this void in his life was filled by his father's second
wife, Sally Bush Lincoln. MGH; ISU, UIO, UM, UU.

NASHVILLE (159m C 1975 Scope)
    Tells the story of five days in the lives of 24 unforgettable peo-
ple. Altman distributes his interactions among all these actors, using country music milieu as imaginary meeting ground for show
business and politics. He has created a cinematic tapestry that
looks deep and optimistically into the soul of America. Pauline
Kael says "... it's the funniest epic vision of America to ever
reach the screen." d. Robert Altman; s. w. Joan Tewkesbury;
PARAMOUNT; FL

NATURAL MAGIC (4m B n. d.)
    "Witch is in all women, everything. ... Witches have always
been women who dared to be courageous, aggressive, intelligent,
non-conformist, explorative, independent. ... A witch lives and
laughs in every woman. She is a free part of us beneath the shy
smiles. "--The Witch Manifesto. By Clay Colt, Marge Cohen, Larry
Gendron; CCC.

NATURALLY ... A GIRL (14m C 1973)
    Uses vignettes, animation and comments by girls and boys to
explore the medical facts and some personal feelings about menstruation. Also available in Spanish. Free loan. PPC; CINEMK; ASFL

NATURE'S LAST STAND see POINT PELEE

NAVAJO RAIN CHANT (3m C 1971)
    The photograph of an Arizona mesa is transformed into authen-
tic Navajo design patterns through animation techniques, accompanied by a Navajo rain chant on the sound track. An excellent
companion film to Now That the Buffalo's Gone or Home of the
Brave, and a pure cameo of film art as an entirety in itself. By
Susan Dyal; CFS.

NEAR THE BIG CHAKRA (17m C si 1972)
    According to Eastern philosophy, Chakra is an energy center.
The second chakra is in the genital region. This film is a straightforward, unhurried view of 36 women's genitals. The women range
in age from six months to 56 years. This film was created primarily because a woman seldom sees a woman's vagina and clitoris
in detail, least of all the woman herself. For any woman who has
wondered about how her genitals compare with others, this movie

will give some others to compare with.   By Anne Severson; MMRC; NSF; CCC, SB.

NEIGHBORHOOD, THE (18m B 1966)
Captures "the spirit of the classic comedies in a contemporary setting. " An irreverent lampoon of things sacred and profane, amongst the victims of its crossfire are cops, sex, religion, film stereotypes and the wildest seduction scene ever filmed. p. Myrna Changar; d. Myrna Harrison; FCOOP.

NELL AND FRED (30m B 1971)
Nell and Fred are an older couple who are trying to talk them-selves into moving into a senior citizens' project. Humor and sad-ness surround the two as it becomes evident they don't want to leave behind their home, their treasures, and their self-respect. Filmed by Nell's grandson. d. Richard Todd; MGH; IE; MSU, UMIS.

NET JOURNAL SERIES see WELFARE REVOLT, THE

NEVER A BRIDE (20m C 1969)
Dramatic portrayal in which a young woman works at her aunt's dude ranch for a summer in hope of finding romance with the "right man. " A series of unexpected events forces her to re-evaluate her-self and makes her realize that she must become the sort of person the man she is searching for would want.   BYU; EMC.

NEVER FEAR see YOUNG LOVERS

NEVER GIVE UP--IMOGEN CUNNINGHAM (28m C 1975)
Portrait of a 94-year-old woman who has created beautiful pho-tographs since the art began. The film follows Imogen through her day photographing, gardening and, most of all, thinking. A power-ful antidote to the cliches about being old and being a woman. p. /d. Ann M. Hershey; PHOENIX, VFI; UM.

NEVER UNDERESTIMATE THE POWER OF A WOMAN (15m C 1971)
Discusses myths and facts about working women. Looks at horizons of women, employers, unions, and special programs such as Job Corps. Shows women in a variety of non-stereotypical blue-collar jobs. By Norma Briggs with Dept. of Labor grant. MIEVES.

NEW AMERICAN FEMALE FLIES HIGH (5m B n. d.)
This newsreel exemplifies members of Women's Lib of the twenties and early thirties, who defied their role as the weaker sex by performing daredevil stunts aboard high-flying airplanes, swing-ing by their teeth, tap-dancing on the wings. Pathe News for Mile-stones of the Century; CFS.

NEW CAREERS FOR WOMEN (17m C n. d.)
Illustrates the restructuring of the roles between the sexes in a discussion of the new family and the role which the creative work-ing woman will have in the world of the future. Points out that

careers in science, advertising, government and sports are opening up for women at an accelerating pace. AMEDFL.

NEW ENTREPRENEUR; Careers for Now Series (13m C 1974)
     Denise Cobb, an enterprising Black woman, shows what a person with determination and imagination can accomplish in the world of business.   Denise operates a personalized transportation service in San Francisco.   Her early career with a management consultant firm in San Francisco gave her the experience and confidence to launch her own unique business.   First, and most important to her eventual success, she believes, was the packaging of her new idea. She was able to get financial support from the Small Business Bureau.   Denise offers very valuable advice to all prospective entrepreneurs.   p. /d. Paul Feyling; PEFP; PARACO.

NEW FACES (4m B n. d.)
     "Comic, seductive view of two girls growing up. "--Freude Bartlett.   By Noni Reisner; SB.

NEW FREEDOMS FOR WOMEN; Girls and Women Series (30m B 1972)
     Social changes over the past century, particularly as they have affected women, are discussed by university-educated women who conclude that the most significant changes have come about with the development of higher education for women.   UMITV; PAS, UM.

NEW LEAF, A (102m C 1971)
     Fastidious middle-aged bachelor playboy running out of inheritance is forced to go to work (horrors) or to acquire a rich wife. The wealthy source he finds is awkward Miss May, as unsexy as the Alsophipila grahamicus, a new leaf she has created in her role as botanist. d. Elaine May; PARAMOUNT; FL

NEW LIFE OF SANDRA BLAINE, THE (27m C 1977)
     Sandra Blaine has no job, no job skills, no husband, no family, no home.   Shows how Sandra Blaine puts her life together as a recovering alcoholic. d. Jim Tratan; p. Norm Southerby; SOUPRO; EMC, UW.

NEW LIFE-STYLES; Human Sexuality Series (30m C 1972 VIDEO)
     An unmarried couple living together, several members of a commune, representatives from women's lib and gay lib and an unmarried mother discuss sexual ramifications of their differing lifestyles.   Host Milton Diamond, Ph. D. , talks with newspaper columnist Ann Landers and several counselors about the impact of new life-styles on sexual practices.   UHAWAII/KHETTV; PTL.

NEW LOOK--AT PROSTHODONTICS, A (17m C 1976)
     Objective: To overcome the growing shortage of prosthodontists by showing dental students that prosthodontics is an interesting, challenging profession.   Actually students talk about their problems; procedures used to correct these problems are described; patients tell how the work of their prosthodontists has affected their lives. Free loan. d. Helen A. Krupka; p. Joseph G. Betzer; FEPROSO.

NEW ROMANCE (34m   C   1977)
Sensitive exploration of contemporary sexuality and the changing
aspects of sexual roles.   Studies a number of relationships, both
heterosexual and homosexual, among persons of varying backgrounds,
ages, and occupations.   Each is striving in his or her own way to
live as fully and honestly as possible, and each speaks with disarm-
ing candor about his or her most intimate feelings.   Many subjects
are examined: the importance of tenderness, acceptance of self,
fear, the courage required to change oneself, and the sexual miscon-
ceptions and double standards that continue to alienate men and wom-
en.   NFBC; EMC.

NEW SEXUALITY, THE (26m   C   1975)
Explores the changing attitudes about sexual behavior of Americans.   Nude encounter groups, bisexuality, homosexuality, non-
monogamous marriages--unmentionable, even unthinkable, a generation ago--are now discussed openly and openly participated in.   The
possible causes are dealt with: the pervasiveness of sex in the
media, women's liberation movement, and the alienation of youth.
Behavioral experts discuss sex therapy, surrogate sex, counseling
and how the changing patterns of sexual behavior affect individuals
and society.   NBCTV; FI.

NEWS MAGAZINE OF THE SCREEN SERIES   see LIFE OF ELIZA-
BETH

NEWSREEL: JONAS IN THE BRIG (5m   B   si   n. d.)
"A newsreel of Jonas Mekas shooting his version of The Brig
on the set of the Living Theatre Production. "--S. D. H.   By Storm
De Hirsch; CCC, FCOOP.

NIAGARA (89m   C   1953)
Presents an unusual version of Marilyn Monroe as a fifties
femme fatale scheming to drive her weak, neurotic husband to suicide so she can escape with her lover.   p.   Charles Brackett; d.
Henry Hathaway; FOX; FI.

NICE GIRL LIKE ME (91m   C   1969)
A contemporary comedy tells the hilarious tale of Candy, the
fetching unwed young lady with a penchant for pregnancy.   Her adventures begin when she leaves her sheltered boarding school background for Paris.   The result is the birth of Valentine nine months
later.   The escapades are hilarious as she continues to collect
babies.   d. Desmond Davis; AVCO; ABFI.

NIGHT AFTER NIGHT (75m   B   1932)
The story revolves around a wealthy gangster and speakeasy
proprietor (George Raft) and his women.   When he becomes enamored with a Park Avenue girl (Constance Cummings), he pays
Mrs. Jellyman to improve his manner and speech.   But Joe Anton
has two old flames, Iris Dawn and Maudie Triplett (Mae West) who
are vengeful when they realize he has become enamored with the
Park Avenue girl.   In the end Joe Anton wins the Park Avenue girl.

Adapted from Louis Bromfield's story "Single Night. "   d. Archie
Mayo, PARAMOUNT; UNIVE.

NIGHT GAMES (104m 1966 Swedish)
When sexual and emotional inhibitions threaten to destroy his
pending marriage, Jan returns to the manor home of his youth to reflect on the causes of his dilemma.   He recalls his beautiful and ex-
travagant mother giving birth to a stillborn child at an orgiastic
party when he was 12.   He would crawl under her skirt when she
was making love.   He would put on her makeup and jewelry and
parade before her.   He remembers the delight when his mother dried
his body and allowed him to sleep with her.   Then Jan remembers
his mother's death and going to live with his Bible-reading aunt who
taught him to believe in the Resurrection.   But his aunt also dies,
and Jan grows into manhood alone.   Later, Mariana, who bears a
striking resemblance to his mother, stays with Jan at the mansion
offering her love and understanding.   Realizing he will never be free
as long as the mansion remains, Jan invites his mother's parasitic
friends to a party and allows them to carry off any treasures they
can lift.   When they all leave, Jan and Mariana watch the fire destroy the mansion.   By Mai Zetterling; MONDIAL (no U. S. rental
source listed).

NIGHT JOURNEY (29m B 1960)
A superbly photographed film of one of Martha Graham's celebrated Greek dance-dramas, Sophocles' Oedipus Rex.   Sharing Jo-
casta's suffering at the moment of her death, are the blind seer,
the chorus and its leader, Oedipus, who appears as she relives her
destiny.   KROLL; MGH; EMC, PHOENIX, UILL, UM.

NIGHTLIFE (12m C 1976)
Explores the wonders of deep sea at close range.   Filmed in
the Irish Sea.   By Robin Lehman; PHOENIX.

NIGHT'S DARKNESS, A DAY'S SAIL (49m C n. d.)
Biographical portrait of the novelist Virginia Woolf (1881-1941),
with commentary by her friends, acquaintances, and relatives.   Includes readings from her works.   BBCTV; BBCL; EMC.

NIGHTS OF CABIRIA (110m B 1957 Italian/subtitled)
A sad-funny story about a naive prostitute who is continually
duped and betrayed by men.   Her vulnerability lies in the fact that
she thinks of her self as "nothing"--consequently any man who tells
her that she is important or beautiful gives her hope about herself.
In the end, after a near total betrayal, she begins to have respect
for herself.   d. Federico Fellini; ABFL

NINE AND A GIRL (24m B n. d.)
Based on Maxim Gorky's story "Twenty-Six and a Girl. "   It is
a story of nine pretzel bakers and the young girl that came each day
to pick up an order of pretzels.   In their fantasies, she is the pur-
est, kindest, most ideal of women.   Each day, they wait for her arrival, and think about her beauty.   One day, a new baker enters

their lives. He constantly brags about his conquest of women. The
bakers bet the newcomer that they know of one who wouldn't fall victim to his charms, and a tryst is arranged. The newcomer wins,
and the bakers, their ideal destroyed, return to work. VFL

NINE TO FIVE (28m C n. d.)
Of the more than 37, 000, 000 women in the U. S. labor force,
more than one out of three is an office worker. Office workers
are struggling to change their images as appendages to their type-
writers and filing cabinets, and gain respect as human beings and
skilled workers. This documentary illustrates another example of
women organizing together and trying to make this world a better
place to live. WNETTV; UM.

NINE TO GET READY SERIES (12/29m ea. B 1966 VIDEO)
Deals with maternal and child health care, beginning with pre-
conception care, through the nine-months of pregnancy and delivery
(normal vaginal and Caesarean), to current research in reproductive
physiology and family planning. Write to PTL for individual program titles. NEBETV; PTL.

NINE VARIATIONS ON A DANCE THEME (13m B 1966)
Creative filmic exploration of dance. A single female dancer,
an empty dance studio, and a simple dance theme are interpreted in
a surprising number of ways, using the basic elements of film art:
camera angle and camera movement, repetition, filmic time, op-
ticals, and editing. A remarkable tour de force by filmmaker Hilary
Harris, fully integrating the dancing into the film's visual style. The
dancer and camera are partners in the choreography. FIM; EMC,
UILL, USC, UU.

1933 (4m C 1967)
"1933. The year? The number? The title? Was it (the film)
made then? It's a memory (i. e. a Film). No, it's many memories.
It's so sad and funny: the departed, departing people, cars, street!
It hurries, it's gone, it's back! It's the only glimpse we have but
we can have it again. The film (of 1933?) was made in 1967. You
find out, if you didn't already know, how naming tints pure vision. "--
Michael Snow. By Joyce Wieland; CORRF; FCOOP.

NO BED OF ROSES (12m C 1974)
Young girl "finds her identity through sexual experience. "--YFD.
By Peri Muldofsky; YFD.

NO HANDOUTS FOR MRS. HEDGEPETH (27m C 1968)
Poverty seen through the eyes of a domestic whose standard of
living is far below that of her employer. Portrays America's working poor and questions U. S. aid to its disadvantaged. p. North
Carolina Fund, BFA; EMC, PAS.

NO LIES (16m C 1973)
Simulated cinéma-vérité interview in which an insensitive male
camerman questions a young woman who has been raped, and suggests

that a woman may be subject to asexual forms of rape, such as
brutal and unsympathetic questioning by police and friends, and prob-
ings of the documentary camera itself.   Features Shelby Levering-
ton.   p. /d. Mitchell Block; PHOENIX, VFI; BF, EMC, PAS, UIO,
UM.

NO TEARS FOR KELSEY; Insight Series (27m   C   1969)
    Teen-agers today, in the wake of the rebellious sixties, are torn
between their own search for identity and heightened awareness, and
their parents' way of life.   Fourteen-year-old Kathleen Kelsey has
been taken to juvenile hall for truancy.   The parents are warned
Kathleen isn't the same girl who ran away 20 days before.   When
the parents arrive, Kathleen is belligerent and critical.   Each parent reacts to her differently.   The mother screams and accuses her
of filth and ingratitude.   The father is hurt and perplexed, but
tensely controlled.   This is a study of the classic generation gap.
Neither side will give in with any degree of understanding; the suffering is prolonged and the gap widens.   Viewers should watch for
potential turning points--times when either the girl or her parents
might have made some headway and begun a real dialogue toward
reconciliation.   By Geraldine Brooks, Lloyd Bochner; PAULST,
MGH.

NO TEARS FOR RACHEL (27m   C   1974)
    If a woman has been raped, she must cope with the cold legal
process and unpredictable reactions from friends and family.   In
order to prosecute, the rape victim must undergo a physical examination, detailed questioning, and a face-to-face confrontation with
her attacker in court.   One victim discusses the difficulties she had
when she told her friends that she had been raped.   Her psychiatrist
explains the importance of their reactions and the stigma associated
with being raped.   NET, IU; MSU, UILL, UM, UO.

NOBODY EVER DIED OF OLD AGE (58m   C   1977)
    Portrays what it is like to grow old in the U. S. today.   A
young nurse (an actress) plays the part of the book's author, interviewing a number of aging persons in a variety of settings.   The
bulk of the film is made up of character studies and vignettes of the
people she has interviewed.   Some are very funny, and some are
very sad, but all of them say something about aging.   Based on the
book by the same title.   FI, EMC.

NOBODY GOES THERE: ELLIS ISLAND (9m   B   1968)
    Still and live action photography tell the history of Ellis Island,
the point of entry to the U. S. for 30 million European immigrants.
By Joan Horvath; PARACO.

NOBODY'S VICTIM (20m   C   1972)
    Practical suggestions on self-defense for women.   Alerts stu-
dents to growing danger of assault against women, and presents
methods of protection and self-protection.   d. Vaughn Obern; RF;
FILMF; EMC, PAS, UIO, UM.

NOMADS OF BADAKHSHAN, THE (27m   C   n. d.)
    The nomads of Badakhshan in northern Afghanistan live in the
high mountains close to the Russian border in the summer, and then
travel to their winter home in Kunduz, more than 200 miles away.
A small but typical trading group called Atakchai, an offshoot of the
Durrani, one of Afghanistan's important nomadic groups, are shown
as they trade with farmers, and what they trade as they migrate.
A son of a tribal patriarch describes to the filmmakers the family
and possessions, and tells how one of his daughters will soon command a high bride's price because she is strong and pretty, and expects to work hard.   The young sons are already part of the family
work force, responsible for herding and guarding the animals.   Half
the children die young because of smallpox and cholera and the nomads are far from medical facilities.   By Judith Hallet, Stanley Hallet; FIM.

NON-MARRIEDS; Human Sexuality Series (29m   C   1972   VIDEO)
    A widower, a divorced man, two divorced women and two "over-
30" individuals who have never been married join host Milton Diamond, Ph. D. , for a discussion of these different non-married situations.   Newspaper columnist Ann Landers adds her views, and the
manager of a "singles only" apartment complex talks about the advantages and disadvantages of this life-style.   p.   UHAWAII/KHETTV;
PTL.

NORMALCY: WHAT IS IT?; Human Sexuality Series (29m   C   1972
    VIDEO)
    "Man-on-the street" interviews illustrate the dependence of
definitions of "normalcy" on age, sex, attitudes and culture.   Host
Milton Diamond, Ph. D. , discusses general ideas about social norms
applied to partner preferences and sexual practices.   UHAWAII/
KHETTV; PTL.

NORMAN THE DOORMAN (15m   C   1971)
    A satire of the art world.   Adapted from Don Freeman's book
about a mouse who gives tours at the Majestic Museum of Art.   By
Cynthia Freitag; WESTON.

NORTH WITH THE SPRING; We Need Each Other Series (52m   C
    1970)
    Focuses on the world's favorite season--spring.   Follows spring
on a 17, 000 mile journey from the Florida Everglades to the Canadian Arctic.   By Beryl Fox; HL; XEROX.

NOT A PRETTY PICTURE (83m   C   1975)
    Intercutting between past and present, fiction and reality, the
film explores the dynamics and effects of one date-rape involving
the filmmaker while in boarding school.   p. /d.   Martha Coolidge;
FI, UM.

NOT ME ALONE (30m   C   1970)
    The film begins with a father and mother, doctor and nurse,
and the two filmmakers discussing in retrospect the birth they shared.

It then goes back to follow the same couple at natural childbirth (Lamaze) training classes, practicing breathing exercises, sharing labor and delivery and caring for the baby in the hospital. The film reaffirms the value of a supportive, loving relationship between a man and a woman. d. /p. Miriam Weinstein; POLYMORPH.

NOT SO YOUNG NOW AS THEN (18m   C   1974)
A cinéma-vérité film of a 15th high school reunion. It is like all reunions,   you'll recognize the cast of characters.   You can taste the bitter sweet flavor of such events, the inchoate sense of time, youth and innocence slipping away.   Mostly, however, this film is a record of the intermingling of forgotten friends and remembered strangers that prompt one's own memories or expectations rather than analysis or a judgment of people gathered together after 15 years.   By Liane Brandon; NDF.

NOT TOGETHER NOW: END OF A MARRIAGE (25m   C   1975)
A couple that is separated speaks with unusual candor of their reasons for marrying, and what attracted them to each other, the effect of children on their marriage, their years together and leading up to their separation and their lives since. The woman speaks of caring for their three children, her work, her present feelings toward men, marriage and her husband. He speaks of his career, ambition, relations with women and above all his sense of loneliness in being cut off from his wife and children. p. Alvin Fiering; d. Miriam Weinstein; POLYMORPH.

NOTEBOOK (10m   C   si   n. d.)
"A very personal film which she keeps adding to ... a masterpiece of filmic fragments, only shown once, but wow!"--P. Adams Sitney.   By Marie Menken; FCOOP.

NOTES ON AN APPALACHIAN COUNTY: VISITING WITH DARLENE (45m   B   1974)
About Darlene, 28, married, with four children, on welfare and living in a $24 a month house in central Pennsylvania.   But also about a way of living--living in poverty and ignorance in Appalachia. Interview with Darlene as she goes about her household duties. WPSXTV; PAS.

NOTTE, LA (120m   B   1961   Italian/subtitled)
La Notte begins in the afternoon and takes the viewer through a single evening in the lives of an Italian middle-class couple who have forgotten what it is to live and to love.   They are bogged down in a morass of superficiality and aimless wandering.   d. Michelangelo Antonioni; MGH.

NOVA SCOTIA BY-WAYS (14m   C   1963)
Shows the character of Nova Scotia by vagabonding through the natural beauty of sea and shore.   Depicts a ceremonial gathering of Micmac Indians, mysterious happenings in a haunted house and a quiet lily pond.   By Margaret Petty; CTFL.

NOW (5m   B   n. d.)
A short, powerful and emotional reminder of the Civil Rights struggle and its violent repression in the 50's and 60's.   With Lena Horne's song "Now" on the sound track.   By Santiago Alvarez; SFN.

NUER (75m   C   1971)
Depicts with minimum of narration, the harmony and rhythm of the present-day dry season life of the Nuer, a people native to Ethiopia and the Sudan   Shows them caring for their cattle and training their young warriors, and captures the subtle patterns of their collective interaction in work, play, and ritual   p. Robert Gardner; MGH; EMC.

NUN SEQUITOR (6m   C   1973)
"Entering the realm of personal fantasy.   Hamrick portrays a man's sexual desire for a man.   Cinematic rather than explicit. "-- Freude Bartlett.   By Lynn Hamrick; SB.

NUN'S STORY, THE (151m   C   1959)
A young girl (Audrey Hepburn) gives up her worldly possessions to become a nursing nun in Belgian Congo in the thirties.   Later, she leaves the order of her own accord, rather than continue what she believes is her failure to become a good nun.   d. Fred Zinneman; WSA; ABFI, BF, CINE, MOD, ROA, TWY, UNIVE.

NUPTIALS (12m   B   1974)
Opening and closing with "Going to the Chapel of Love, " this is a portrait of a middle-class marriage, with flowers and relatives, white gowns, and all the emptiness of a young bride's attempt to drag all the ego-boosting she can from what's supposed to be her moment   Good film for discussion of values, class and marriage. By Catherine Orentreich; WFC; IRISF.

NURSE EDITH CAVELL (108m   B   1939)
One of history's most exemplary women finally came in for the cinematic praise she so richly deserves.   During World War I Nurse Cavell was operating a nursing home for the indigent, with finances provided from her family trust and Duchess Oliver, whose heart was big as her noblesse oblige.   When she heard of the cries of the wounded when Belgium was invaded by Kaiser's army, she formed a four-woman underground to help nurse men and spirit them out of the country.   The soldiers were Belgian, French, American and British.   Concludes with a mock trial, the sentencing and Cavell's incarceration.   The denouement and later epilogue are deeply moving. Thus, at dawn October 12, 1915, the world lost a lovely human being, who ... never winced or faltered.   d. /p. Herbert Wilcox; RKO; KP.

NURSES TRAINING FILMSTRIP (14m   C   n. d.   SFS)
Nurses show ways they introduce the concept of birth control to appropriate patients.   PP.

OBMARU (4m   C   n. d.)
A mystical, surreal, abstract film recreates a psychedelic experience produced under the influence of hallucinogenic drugs.   Accompanied by a "Voodoo" score by Kaye Dunham.   Photographic assistance by Jordan Belson.   By Patricia Marx; CFS.

OBSTETRICS AND GYNECOLOGY SERIES   see   MENOPAUSE

OCCUPATION: MOTHER; Woman Series (29m   C   1975   VIDEO)
The conflict between women's needs for individual fulfillment
and the demands made on them as mothers of young children is explored by Ruth Armin and Phyllis Brody, both mothers and family
counselors who have been questioning women about what motherhood
means to them.   WNEDTV; PTL.

ODDS AND ENDS (5m   C   1959)
One of the first collage of films ever produced, this film combines painting, out-take of travelogues and bits of animated and live
action TV commercial with a tongue-in-cheek dissertation on poetry-
and-jazz, to create neo-dada fun in the New American Cinema tradition.   Narration by Henry Jacobs.   By Jane Belsen; CFS.

ODYSSEY OF RITA HAYWORTH; Hollywood and Stars Series (26m
B   1964)
Presents a study of the career of Rita Hayworth, using clips
from her films.   Includes scenes of her personal life and her comments on her life and career.   WOLPER.

OF MEN AND DEMONS (10m   C   1969)
An animated parable showing man in his constant quest to better his environment.   Emphasizes the growing threat of pollution of
air, water and natural resources.   By Faith Hubley, John Hubley;
IBMWTC; FI.

OF STARS AND MEN (53m   C   1964)
This film is concerned with man and his place in the universe.
In matchless animation and simple language the nature of space,
time, matter and energy, and how man fits into the complex of
atoms, protoplasms, stars and galaxies is set forth with wit and style
for everyone to understand.   Based on the popular book by Dr. Harlow Shapley, the script was adapted with Dr. Shapley's assistance
and the film is narrated by Dr. Shapley himself.   This is the Hubleys' only animated feature and has been called an astonishing
achievement.   Also available in four parts.   By Faith Hubley, John
Hubley; FIM.

OFFICE CINDERELLA (3m   B   1971)
"In a familiar work situation, a young Black women unexpected-
ly rebels against the oppressive manipulations of her (male) boss. "
--YFD.   By Lauretta Baker; YFD.

OH, FREEDOM!; Black Americans Series (28m   C   1970)
Traces the Black Civil Rights Movement from 1955 when a Black

woman refused to give up her seat on a bus to a white man, to the
cry for Black Power nearly a decade later. Explores the movement
and its impact through the words of the people involved and through
examination of the concept of Black Power. From the NYT--Arno
Press Films. BF.

OIL ON THE BAY (6m   C   1971)
    Records the January 1971 oil spill on San Francisco Bay, the
cleanup and rescue operations, and damage to wildlife. Natural and
"live" sounds without narration. By Sandra Marshall, Ken De Roux;
CCC.

OLD, BLACK AND ALIVE (28m   C   1977)
    A compelling documentary on aging. Aging touches everyone.
Its universality is reflected in this film with candidness and humor.
Seven elderly Blacks share their insight, faith and strength with us.
NEWFLM; UM.

OLD ENOUGH TO KNOW (20m   C   1974)
    Most of the film's action occurs in a city day care center peo-
pled with three- to six-year-olds from many ethnic groups. As they
move appealingly through a routine day--play time, toilet time, rest
time, story time, etc. --their sexual curiosity and expression emerges
as a natural part of their interaction and self-discovery. Overridden
occasionally by spontaneous remarks from the children on the screen,
the sound track consists principally of candid comments from parents
of similar children. They recall their own childhood experiences,
their changing views of sex over the years, their fears, their difficulties and successes. They encourage viewing parents to understand that their own embarrassments and uncertainties are common.
The film makes one point emphatically: the need for a straight
answer to a straight question: "If they're old enough to ask, they
are old enough to know." PPSEA; PERENNIAL; UM.

OLD FASHIONED WOMAN (49m   C   1974)
    Martha Coolidge, in a search for her own past, creates a vi-
brant portrait of her grandmother, 87-year-old Mabel Tilton Coolidge.
The grandmother discusses her philosophy, memories and activities,
and shares her views on abortion and birth control. The bond between the two women is evident, the vitality and strength of the
grandmother refreshing. p. Martha Coolidge; FI.

OLD PEOPLE (28m   B   n. d.)
    Interviews with old people in Central Pennsylvania. Deals with
fear, loneliness for family and friends, change, and what it physically feels like to get old. By Lisa J. Marshall; WPSXTV; PAS.

OLD WOMAN, THE (2m   C   1974)
    Clever animation, without narration, relates a story which could
be an old-folk tale or a modern fable for senior citizens. An old
lady is busy in her home when Death, a skeleton in a sheet, arrives
and beckons her. She tells him to sit down and wait. He tries to
stop the clock, but she starts it again. When she finishes cooking

and eating dinner, he tries again. She gets out a tablecloth and embroiders busily. When he sees how much work she's laid out, he despairs and falls to the ground. She covers him with the tablecloth and weeps cheerful tears over his body. PARACO.

OLGA: A FILM PORTRAIT (47m C r1975)
Portrait of the Russian gymnast Olga Korbut, a teen-age sensation in the 1972 Olympics, showing the tedious vigor of her training schedule and her phenomenal ability in performance. Provides a fascinating insight into the making of an Olympic champion. GRATV; CAROUSEL; EMC, UM.

OLYMPIA I: THE FESTIVAL OF THE PEOPLE (95m B 1938 English narration)
Epic documentary on the Berlin Olympiad of 1936. Despite its underlying Nazi ideology, the film contains some of the finest blending of image, sound and music ever achieved in film. d. Leni Riefenstahl; PHOENIX, MGH; EMC, PAS.

OLYMPIA II: THE FESTIVAL OF BEAUTY (95m B 1938 English narration)
Starts with sequences not covered in Part I--sailing and rowing, field hockey, polo and soccer, equestrian events, bicycling, marathon and decathlon. Riefenstahl's innovations include her use of slow motion to capture bodies in flight, and a sequence of swimmers photographed from below. She made very imaginative use of sound mixing to complement the shots, as she was allowed only one sound camera in the stadium. p. Leni Riefenstahl; PHOENIX, MGH; EMC, PAS.

OLYMPIAD (3m C 1971)
"Figures of computer stylized athletes are seen in brilliant hues chasing each other across the screen. Images are then reversed and run across the screen in the other direction; then images are flopped until athletes are running in countless ways--not unlike a pack of humanity on a football field."--Bob Lehman, Today's Film-Maker Magazine. By Lillian Schwartz, Ken Knowlton; LPI.

ON (5m C 1972)
"Sexuality as a trip."--R. S. By Rosalind Schneider; FCOOP.

ON A QUESTION OF JUSTICE (28m B 1975)
A number of recent court cases and studies have dramatized numerous, unpunished cases of rape and brutalization of women. This film deals with the physical oppression of women and the unjust penalties sometimes faced by women who have been convicted of crimes. The film also concerns the blatant inequities of our present prison system as they apply to both men and women. By Lisa Feiner; GP.

ON MERIT (23m C 1969)
Filmed in a typical American classroom, this film is addressed to the young high school or junior college student facing the question,

"What do I do when I leave school?" Discusses the pros and cons of government employment, and investigates the government's commitment to the "merit system" and its effect upon the employment and promotion of women and minorities. Designed to stimulate discussion. WGPI for U. S. Civil Service Commission. WGPL

ON THAT DAY IN THE EAST BRONX (26m   C   1976)
Documentary of a pageant of a Latin American custom carried out in the East Bronx on Good Friday. Local actors are dressed in Biblical costumes as they reenact the suffering of Christ on the way to Calvary. By Kate Garland; MGH.

ON THE TOWN (97m   C   1949)
Three sailors and their dates on an exuberant romantic spree in New York. d. Gene Kelly, Stanley Donen, s. w. Betty Comden; MGM; FI.

ON THE WAY TO GROWING UP SERIES   see   MIRACLE OF BIRTH

ONCE IS NOT ENOUGH   see   JACQUELINE SUSANN'S ONCE IS NOT ENOUGH

ONCE KITTYHAWK (33m   C   1972)
Filmed documentary, in four movements, features members of the leading experimental theatre company, The Once Group. Shows development of structure, rehearsals, and time elements for their space theatre production "Kittyhawk, " which is re-created in the final sequence. Depicts man's obsession with getting things off the ground, the brutalization of women, and the role of science in the motivations of man. SISO; ABFI; UI.

ONCE UPON A WAR (30m   B   n. d.)
A journalistic report on the condition and treatment of civilian casualties in Quang Nagi, South Vietnam. Focuses on the treatment of amputees and paraplegics, the limbmaking and fitting work of the Quaker Rehabilitation Center and the uncertainty of the future for the thousands of maimed Vietnamese adults and children. Filmed in province hospital. By Patricia Penn; PF.

1. A. 1. a LONDON BRIDGES FALLING DOWN (5m   C   n. d.)
"What it is visually like to be the Waterloo Bridge or the Battersea. "--N. L. By Naomi Levine; FCOOP.

ONE AND THE SAME (4m   C   1973)
"A self-portrait by two women in the process of friendship and filmmaking. "--CCC. By Freude Bartlett, Gunvor Nelson; CCC, SB.

ONE BY ONE (11m   C   n. d.)
A film poem on the theme of passing time. A film of melancholic beauty. The poetry, narration, camera and musical score by Madeline Tourtelot; GP.

ONE DAY I ASKED (9m   B   1970   Spanish/subtitled/Spanish dialog)
A documentary on the religious alienation of exploited people who

look for a miracle as a solution to their daily problems.   A song,
"The Question, " is sung by an Argentine folk-singer Atahualpa
Yupanqu (on same reel with Columbia 70).   By Julia Alvarez; TFC.

108 MOVEMENTS (7m   C   1972)
    A beautiful experimental film in which Tai Chi Chuan exercise
becomes abstracted into hands molding and defining space.   Exceptional use of color.   By Peggy Woolf; WOLPER; CFS, IE.

ONE IS A LONELY NUMBER (97m   C   1972)
    Tender, absorbing drama about one woman's liberation--a social
satire, a judicious blend of wit and compassion, full of perceptive
conservation about contemporary mores.   It evokes the pain of loneliness, yet affirms the precariousness of life.   p. Stan Margulies;
d. Mel Stuart; MGM; FI.

ONE POTATO, TWO POTATO (92m   B   1965)
    An intimate and dramatic look at the problems of interracial
marriage in present-day America.   The prejudices of all races are
implied in the struggle of a man and woman to build a life based on
strong mutual love within a world that rejects their union and attempts to frustrate it in both subtle and overt ways.   d. Larry
Peerce; CIV; BF, EMC, MOD, SWANK, TWF, TWY.

ONE TOUCH OF VENUS (81m   B   1948)
    Adapted from the S. J. Perelman-Ogden Nash-Kurt Weil Broad-
way hit, the film tells the story of a window dresser whose kiss
brings a statue of Venus to life.   d. William A. Seiter; UNIVE; IVY.

ONE WOMAN (25m   C   1973)
    Illuminates all the common elements of women trapped in afflu-
ent contradictions, defined by their fathers and husbands.   The film
does not, however, capture the urgency and desperation of many
women's situations and leaves one hanging.   By Lorna Rasmussen,
Anne Wheeler, and Lorna Jackson; FWAL.

ONSHORE PLANNING FOR OFFSHORE OIL: VOICES FROM SCOT-
    LAND (21m   C   r1976)
    Examines the physical, social, and economic effects that off-
shore oil development has on those who live and work in a coastal
community.   Filmed in Scotland.   Stresses implication for Americans.   d. /p. Janet Mendelsohn; CONSF.

OPENING/CLOSING (5m   B   1972)
    A film about life and opportunities seized or lost.   Rhythmic
opening and closing of washing machine doors conveys the idea of
choices one faces in life, possibilities taken, paths lost or abandoned.   By Kathleen Laughlin; CCC, SB, NLC.

L'OPERA-MOUFFE (14m   B   1959   French/subtitled)
    "An astonishing and haunting film; a poem of the fervors of love,
the gestures of age, the faces of the poor, the symbols of pregnancy and
fertility under the guise of an impressionistic exploration of a Paris
neighborhood, "--Sight and Sound.   By Agnes Varda.   FRANCE.

OPERATION GREENHOUSE (15m   C   n. d.)
Tells the story of how two rural communities worked with state and local agencies to help provide an elderly man with a greenhouse. By Mollie Gregory; TFEL

OPERATION GWAMBA (26m   C   1965)
"Rescue of wild animals in a flooded Surinam jungle. "--H. R. By Hope Ryden; RYDEN.

OPERATOR (15m   C   1969)
A recruitment film produced for AT&T, fast-paced and funny. By Nell Cox; ATAT.

OPPOSITE SEX, THE (116m   C   1956)
A perfume-counter siren schemes to snare a happily married husband with the help of his wife's hypocritical "friends. " Only after the divorce does the wife realize she must herself develop claws to protect her home in the feminine New York jungle.   d. David Miller; MGM; FI.

OPTURED FRAIKEN CHAITRE JOE (3m   B   si   n. d.)
"A dance film.   Joe Chaiken's Open Theatre.   This is a chance film poem.   There are nine shots.   Each shot is cut up X times, X plus 4, X plus 5, X plus 6 frame clips.   They are then rotated from one to ninth, indiscriminately as the X quantity. "--N. L.   By Naomi Levine; FCOOP.

ORAL CONTRACEPTIVES (29m   B   1966)
Dr. Garcia defends the use of oral contraceptives, stressing the superior efficiency of this method.   Dr. Lasagna feels that there are other methods which are clinically more advisable and stresses the now-emerging adverse consequences of contraceptive drugs.   NAVC; FSU.

ORAL LANGUAGE DEVELOPMENT--VIEWS OF FIVE TEACHERS (29m   C   1976)
Through documentary scenes in the classroom and on-camera statements of philosophies, five elementary school teachers demonstrate and discuss the development of oral language skills (listening and speaking) in young children.   d. David Espar; p. Louise Henry; CSDE.

ORANGE (3m   C   1970)
A sensual close-up of the peeling and eating of an orange.   By Karen Johnson; SB; LAFC, CCC.

ORBITAS (10m   C   1972)
"An abstract visual experience using form and color in motion is designed to stimulate for a viewer a journey into the unconscious in which each surrenders to one's own individual interpretation of images seen. "--R. S.   By Rosaline Schneider; FCOOP.

ORDINARY DAYS (24m   B   1974)
Conveys the texture of a woman's life as she struggles to iden-

tify her needs in and apart from her relationship with man. d.
Sally Heckel; NLC.

ORFEO (11m   C   1971)
A personal and compelling animated interpretation of the myth
of Orpheus and Eurydice.   By Caroline Leaf; PF.

ORGANIZING FOR POWER: THE ALINSKY APPROACH SERIES
Produced as a part of the Challenge for Change Program.   The
following five titles examine Saul Alinsky's method of organizing
communities into effective action units based on participatory democ-
racy.   By Bonnie Klein; NFBC.
PEOPLE AND POWER (17m   B   1968).   Conflict and controversy
are integral parts of Alinsky's approach to organizing communities.
Here he talks about his philosophy and the dynamics of organization.
DECIDING TO ORGANIZE (34m   B   1968).   A group of concerned
citizens from Dayton, Ohio, consult Alinsky on the means of creating
an effective organization.
BUILDING AN ORGANIZATION (37m   B   1968).   The obstacles
encountered by a new community action organization in Buffalo,
N. Y. , as it begins to work for recognition.
THROUGH CONFLICT TO NEGOTIATION (46m   B   1968).   A
community action group in Rochester, N. Y. , confronts the community's largest employer on the issue of corporate responsibility
and the employment of minority groups.
A CONTINUING RESPONSIBILITY (43m   B   1968).   As demonstrated in the Woodlawn Organization in Chicago, Alinsky's technique
creates on-going organizations firmly rooted in the community.

ORIGAMI (9m   C   1967)
The Japanese art of folding paper is shown as practiced by
skilled and less adept hands of children.   That anyone can learn
and experiment, and take pleasure from the result, is evident by
the variety of shapes and figures being conjured out of colored
paper.   By Joan Henson; NFBC; PARACO.

ORPHEUS UNDERGROUND (50m   C   1974)
"Legend of the poet and musician who had to go to the underground to bring his wife back.   Shot in New York City and in Washington, D. C. , during the riots, as an allegory of our time. "--S. G.
By Sylvianna Goldsmith; GOLDSMITH.

OTHER HALF OF THE SKY: A CHINA MEMOIR, THE (74m   C
1974)
An account of what Shirley MacLaine and the heterogeneous
group of American women learned about the lives of the Chinese
people on mainland China.   Education, work, child rearing, the
role of women, cultural affairs, political concerns--all are explored
in a genuine effort to comprehend a society which has long been
closed to us.   d. Shirley MacLaine, Claudia Weill; ed. Aviva
Slesin; NDF.

OTHER WOMEN, OTHER WORK (20m   C   r1973)
Shows a number of women who are working in traditionally male

occupations.   On the sound track they discuss the difficulties and
satisfactions of their jobs.   Includes a truckdriver, veterinarian,
roofer, pilot, marine biologist, carpenter and TV news broadcaster.
Emphasizes the positive aspect of increased job opportunities for
women.   By Joan Churchill, James Kennedy; CF; BU, EMC, OSU,
UILL, UM, UMIS.

OTISVILLE SCHOOL FOR BOYS FILMS (60m   C   n. d.)
      Shows program of films made by Ms. Halleck's film classes at
the Otisville School for Boys, a New York reform school.   By Dee
Dee Halleck; HALLECK.

OUR BODIES, OURSELVES; Woman Series (29m   C   1974   VIDEO)
      Sandra Elkin interviews Wilma Diskin and Judy Norsigian, mem-
bers of the Boston Women's Health Book Collective and creators of
the controversial handbook of health care for women entitled Our
Bodies, Ourselves.   WNEDTV; PTL.

OUR CHANGING FAMILY LIFE (20m   B   1957)
      A farm family in 1880 is shown as a closely integrated unit--
economically, culturally and emotionally.   We see that family has
become less important as an economic and social unit.   We are
shown how the roles of husband and wife in the urban family have
shifted and how the companionship of marriage has become even
more important in today's impersonal urban society.   MGH, NIU.

OUR DANCING DAUGHTERS (90m   B   1928)
      A chronicle concerned with the wild young people of this genera-
tion.   Filled with cocktails, flasks, wild dancing and the music
reminiscent of old time singing to lantern slides.   d. Harry Beau-
mont; s. w. Josephine Lovett; MGH; FL

OUR DEAR SISTERS (15m   C   n. d.)
      Alanis is a native North American performer and filmmaker.
In this film she discusses her life and her observations about white
society.   By Kathleen Shannon; p. Len Chatwin; NFBC; EMC.

OUR NORTH AMERICAN FOREMOTHERS (75m   B   n. d.)
      A multimedia documentary of brilliant and moving images from
women's history.   By Ann Grant; GRANTANN.

OUT OF CHAOS: JEAN ERDMAN (13m   B   1967)
      A subjective documentary about the dancer, choreographer, and
play-wright, Jean Erdman, and her ideas on experience and creativity.   Made while Miss Erdman was visiting artist-in-residence at
UCLA.   The film reveals her individual approach through the cumu-
lative effect of scenes of class sessions, her own performances,
conversations in her home, and images from her imagination.   By
Jean V. Cutler; UILL.

OUT OF THE HOME AND INTO THE HOUSE (48m   B   1976)
      Documents an organized effort at influencing legislation in the
U. S. at a state level.   The specific bill being debated is the Equal

Rights Amendment. Lobbying activities are commonplace in a democratic society. With few exceptions, legislators being appealed to are male, both pro and con, and most professional lobbyists are male. Here, the lobbyists, both pro and con, are women. Thus, this film captures an unusual scene in American history: widespread, determined participation in the political process by women. d. Elizabeth Schaal; p. Anne Heinz; FIM.

OUT THERE, A LONE ISLAND (67m   B   1971)
A semi-documentary impression of life on a remote Korean island in the Sea of Japan where the Eastern philosophy of subordination of self to oneness with nature is lived daily. People persist on Ullong-do, no matter what the hardships, as life changes rhythmically with the seasons. The actors are island residents; the story --presented without narration or subtitles and with only incidental dialogue in Korean, accompanied by an original score--is very close to their own lives. One family is featured. Suffering and survival are accompanied by pleasures. Communicates in a purely visual way, the universality of human problems and joys. EMC.

OUTRAGE (75m   B   1950)
The world of Outrage is seen through the eyes of a rape victim who is punished for her "crime" by parents, fiance and gossiping neighbors. She escapes to rural California where she is befriended by a young minister. But the countryside and the minister offer no refuge from insecurity and fears. d. Ida Lupino; RKO; IVY.

OVEN 350 (19m   C   1970)
Presents a story in which a young man and young lady fall in love through a series of comic incidents which occur when the young man cooks dinner for the young lady. p. Doro Bachrach; MATT JEN.

OWL WHO MARRIED A GOOSE, THE (8m   C   1976)
A goose captures the fancy of an owl, and though they are an unlikely match, they set out to share their lives and loves. The owl cannot keep up with the goose and her goslings, and after a series of misadventures, meets with tragic fate. d. Caroline Leaf; NFBC; BOSUST.

P. P. 1. (7m   C   1969)
A story of People's Park in Berkeley, California in spring of 1969. By Donna Deitch; CCC, FCOOP.

PAINTED TRUCK, THE (28m   C   1973)
Features an Afghan multi-colored truck loaded with rice, soap, melons, wheat and seasoned truck travelers making a rugged journey across the 12,700-foot Hajigak Pass from Kabul to Bamian. Views the unusual twists modernity creates in Afghanistan's culture and the inequity of master-servant relationship. By Judith Hallet, Stanley Hallet; FIM.

PAINTER'S JOURNAL, A (10m   C   n. d.)
A subjective documentary in semi-surrealistic style of a painter's approach to her art. While slightly crude technically as a first film, it evokes a mood reminiscent of Kenneth Anger's Inauguration of the Pleasure Dome, in which both Renata Druks and Anaïs Nin co-starred. By Renata Druks; CFS.

PAINTING (2m   C   1974)
Illusions of several types created by computer-manipulated images.   d. Patricia Sloane; NLC.

PANTOMIME FOR THE ACTOR (20m   C   1965)
Earl Lewin, pantomime artist, demonstrates the importance of pantomime to the beginning actor.   He shows how pantomime can be used to convey emotion, action, character, setting and plot.   By Esther Schiller; SB.

PAPA LES PETITS BATEAUX (102m   C   1971   French)
"In Papa I wanted to make a cartoon, to joke against the male way of showing gangsters as 'things of beauty' ... I wanted to show them as the little men they may be: stupid and ugly, thinking that nobody can be stronger and more 'macho' than they.   But one little girl arrives and even she can be stronger and more clever than they, making fun of their virility.   She understands that to survive she has to learn certain things very quickly, and to profit from their prejudices and their stupid vacuity. "--N. K.   By Nelly Kaplan; FFO.

PAPAGENO (11m   B   1935)
An animated film based on live shadow play.   The Bird Catcher from Mozart's "Magic Flute" in an enchanting fantasy.   By Lotte Reiniger; CEA.

PAPILLONS (3m   C   1973)
Mathematical functions resembling butterflies.   Beautiful shapes that are everchanging.   By Lillian Schwartz; LPL

PARADINE CASE, THE (115m   B   1947)
A Hitchcock crime of passion.   A woman is accused and tried for poisoning her husband.   She confesses freely to having done it, but her defense attorney isn't sure.   d. Alfred Hitchcock; s. w. Alma Reville; SELZNICK; ABFI, TWY.

PARADISE LOST (4m   C   1970)
An animated plea without words for the right of all wild creatures to a clean, unpolluted environment.   With style, color and movement sensitive to the subject, the film shows how butterflies, birds, and other woodland creatures succumb to air pollution spread by the inventions of man.   By Evelyn Lambart; BM.

PARALLAX (21m   B/C   1973)
"Enhanced by the technical device of using three screens at once with the same image on each, but projected a-synchronously.   The

use of color, black and white, and the re-elaboration of an image
... fills the eyes ... brings us unconsciously to the most intimately
self-insightful level of intuitiveness. "--R. S.   By Rosalind Schneider;
FCOOP.

PARANOIA BLUES (5m   B   1973)
    What the title suggests: the daily anxiety of city life for wom-
en.   By Jane Warrenbrand; FIM.

PARAPLUIES DE CHERBOURG, LES see   UMBRELLAS OF CHER-
BOURG, THE

PARENTAL ROLES: DON AND MAE (25m   C   1973)
    Reveals some of the problems parents face in coping with grow-
ing children, how they handle the youngsters, and how they react to
each other and to themselves.   Mae, the mother, assumes the more
active role and is seen arguing with the children.   The father, Don,
is more passive, and admits he is too tired or too busy to give the
children much attention.   Focuses on disciplinary problems the
family encounters at the dinner table.   The conflict between Don and
the children draws attention to the expectations various family members may have of this daily event, and the differing values they place
on family togetherness.   EBEC; UILL, IU.

PARENTS; America's Crises Series (59m   B   r1965)
    Report on changing problems of American parents today and
their attempts to find identity, meaning, and purpose in their lives.
Includes candid interviews with parents and children.   Shows effects
of rural-suburban social change and presents interviews with Dr.
Benjamin Spock, Betty Friedan, and Dr. Paul Popenoe.   NET, IU;
EMC.

PARENTS OF DISTURBED CHILDREN (30m   C   n. d.)
    Parents of mentally retarded children discuss problems in car-
ing for them.   By Martha Stuart, David Ruskin; STUARTM.

PARK FILM, THE (2m   B   n. d.)
    "Two girls playing at being boys. "--L. F.   By Linda Feferman;
FEFERMAN.

PARTY (6m   B   1971)
    Dramatizes the effect of loneliness on four women who meet at
an afternoon coffee party.   By Jeffrey Rodman; RODMAN.

PARTY, THE (27m   C   n. d.)
    A forthright look at adolescent sexuality and the multitude of
very real problems it poses for young people in a world that is
rife with adult demands for equal rights and freedom of expression.
By Pam McMyler, Bill Mumy; MGH.

PASSAGES FROM FINNEGANS WAKE see   FINNEGANS WAKE

PASSENGER, THE (119m   C   1975   Italian/subtitled)
    Portrait of a drained journalist whose deliverance is an identity

exchange with a dead man. Accompanied by an equally alienated
girl, he passively embarks on a treacherous journey through Africa,
Germany, England, and Spain. Andrew Sarris (Village Voice) says
"... Maria Schneider expresses a purity of spirit that ennobles the
hero's quest for new identity. " d. Michelangelo Antonioni; MGM;
FI.

PASSENGERS, THE (EL GHORBA) (90m B r1971 French/sub-
titled)
      Exposes the day-to-day reality of the life of an Algerian, an
immigrant to France. Ranchid, a shy immigrant in the beginning,
changes in the two years to a physically tired, knowing, and a tense
young man. There is an unspoken evocation of the price of cross-
cultural conflict. By Annie Tresgot; Centre Algérien de Documenta-
tion et d'Information; TFC.

PASSING QUIETLY THROUGH (26m B 1972)
      This film, about the death of an old man, characterized by
Richard Roud, director, the New York Film Festival, is "one of
the finest American short films I have seen in some time... "--
Dinitia McCarthy. By Martha Coolidge; GP.

PASSION OF ANNA, THE (99m C 1970 Swedish/subtitled)
      A probe into the mysteries of why male and female find it so
hard to reach each other. d. Ingmar Bergman; UAS.

PASSION OF JOAN OF ARC (85m B 1928)
      The events are those of Joan's last five days: the interrogation,
the trial, her imprisonment and execution. One of the most significant displays of the emotional power of photography. The shorn
head and piercing eyes of Maria Falconetti, the unforgiving faces of
her interrogators, the brutal arms of the soldiers, the smoke and
the flames of execution pyres are the visual vehicles through which
Dreyer communicates the pathos and heroism of Joan's passion.
Musical score only. d. Carl T. Dreyer; ABFI, EMC, KP, MGH,
SELECT, UKEN, UW.

PASTEL PUSSIES (3m C 1972)
      "Cats walking, playing, rolling, jumping--warped through wonder-
ful printing techniques, producing mirror images, multiple images,
etc. The sound track is perfectly matched, the cat's meow electronically stretched. By Judith Wardwell. "--Toronto Women and Film.
By Judith Wardwell; CCC, SB.

PAT AND MIKE (95m B 1952)
      Impressed by the athletic prowess of a dignified college physical
education teacher, a seedy promoter takes her on as a client to bill
her as a star all-around professional athlete. d. George Cukor; p.
Lawrence Weingarten; s. w. Ruth Gordon, Garson Kanin; MGM; FL

PAUL REVERE (9m B 1971)
      "A didactic work inspired by the structure of the educational
film using instructional cards ... deals with the nature and limits
of communications systems. "--L. C. G. By Joan Jonas; CASTELLL

PAUL REVERE IS HERE (7m   B   1976)
Shows a rag tag bunch of locals and tourists who have descended
upon a statue of Paul Revere in a Boston park. The filmmakers
have rotoscoped this into patterns of quivering outlines against a
rich blue background, so the material takes on an exciting, impressionistic dimension. By Mary Beams, Susan Rubin; SB.

PAUL'S FILM (10m   C   1971)
About a 24-year-old Black woman in New York City out on bail.
By Amy Taubin; TAUBIN.

PEACE PICKETS ARRESTED FOR DISTURBING THE PEACE (7m
C   1967)
A documentary film of non-violent anti-draft demonstration in
October 1967 at the Oakland, California induction center that led to
the arrest of Joan Baez and 120 pacifists. Singing, clapping, speak-
out by Joan Baez; song text by Bob Dylan. By Leonard Henny;
CFS.

PEACE WOMEN (16m   C   1977)
Shows what the courage and determination of one woman can
accomplish against obstacles and opposition. In August of 1976, a
Belfast housewife, Betty Williams, watched in horror as three small
children were struck and killed by a runaway car driven by a
wounded IRA terrorist. This tragic incident motivated her to organize a "People for Peace" movement which has attracted as many
as 50,000 marchers from all factions to its weekly demonstrations.
Betty Williams and Mairead Corrigan may represent the last hope
for a normal life in Northern Ireland. CBSTV; CAROUSEL; EMC.

PEARL BUCK: THE GOOD EARTH (15m   n.d.   SFS)
A study of Pearl Buck's timeless tale, considered by many
critics to be her greatest work. This program analyzes the story
and gives insights into culture, philosophy, and mystery of China.
EDC.

PEARL S. BUCK; Wisdom Series (30m   B   1960)
Miss Buck describes her childhood in China, points out basic
differences between Western and Oriental approaches to living, dis-
cusses changes under Communist regime, considers ways in which
America may recover good will lost in Asia during recent years.
NBCTV; EBEC; PAS, USC.

PEARL WILLIAMS-JONES (59m   C   1974   VIDEO)
A performance program of gospel music and spirituals, with
singer-pianist Pearl Williams-Jones, percussionist Richard Easley
and Joe Harris on the electric bass. Mrs. Williams-Jones explains the origin of each song and comments on her musical career
and the influences on her style. The trio presents songs of freedom, peace, love and power, including "Kum ba ya," "Rockin' Jeru-
salem," "Sweet Little Jesus Boy," "O, Freedom," "I Tol' Jesus,"
"Amen," "I Heard the Voice of Jesus Say," "It Took a Miracle,"
"Precious Lord, Take My Hand," and "Get in Touch with Heaven."
WKARTV; PTL.

PEASANT WOMEN OF RYAZAN (length not given   1927   Russian)
Concerns two peasant women from the village of Ryazan: Anna and Wassillissa. Born out of expediency in 18th-century Russia when Lenin instituted several decrees which nullified the male prerogative, Anna is fated to be a tragic victim of pre-revolutionary oppression. Wassillissa is strong, independent, supportive--qualities which fate her to be a survivor. This film has been recently reclaimed by modern audiences--providing positive, compelling images of the new world. By Olga Preobrajenskaia; CFI.

PEAU D'ANE see DONKEY SKIN

PEDRO LINARES--FOLK ARTIST (22m   C   1975)
Documents the life and works of Mexican papier-mâché artist, Pedro Linares. Shows the beauty of skill of a popular art in the hands of a master. d. Judith Bronowski, Robert Grant; WORKS.

PEEGE (28m   C   1974)
Extraordinarily sensitive and moving story in which a young man home for Christmas accompanies his family to visit his dying grandmother in a nursing home. After a typically awkward time, the rest of the family leaves, but the young man remains and finally succeeds in communicating his love to the old woman. Beautifully directed and acted, free of mawkishness. d. Randal Kleiser; p. David Knapp, Leonard Berman; KLEKNP; EMC, ISU, PAS, UC, UILL, UM, UU, UW.

PEGGY GUGGENHEIM: ART IN VENICE (44m   C   1976)
Film conducts a tour of the Peggy Guggenheim Museum, alternated with an interview with Peggy Guggenheim. Some of the finest 20th-century paintings are represented here. The interview is poorly recorded, but the rest of the narration is distinct and informative. MONDPRO; FFHI.

PEOPLE AND POWER see ORGANIZING FOR POWER: THE ALINSKY APPROACH SERIES

PEOPLE FIRST (34m   C   1974, r1976)
A documentary on the lives, community and political activities of People First, the first self-advocacy group of disabled citizens. d. James Stanfield; p. Diane Stanfield, James Stanfield; STNFLD.

PEOPLE LIKE MARIA (29m   B   1958)
Describes the work of the World Health Organization, an agency of the United Nations, whose experts work in 88 member nations. Shows Maria, a nurse, working with Andean Indians in Bolivia, and Aung Tan, a medical assistant working on community health in the Union of Burma with local villagers. Dramatizes the work of teaching and fighting disease. WWP; CMC; IU.

PEOPLE OF THE AUSTRALIAN WESTERN DESERT: A MULTI-PART SERIES
This series is the product of a 1965 film expedition sponsored

by The Australian Institute of Aboriginal Studies into the Western Desert, a cultural-linguistic region that is the ancestral home of the nomadic Aborigines. The purpose of the expedition was to document the disappearing Aboriginal culture and community. The resulting ten films record the lives of Djagamara and his family, who were met in the desert; of Djun, one of the film unit guides, who exhibits sacred boards and leads a tour of an ancestral site; and of Minma and his family who, after only a very short stay, returned from civilization to the desert to make the films. The ten films in the series are described below. Part 4 is available for rental only.

PART 1: SEED CAKE MAKING AND GENERAL CAMP ACTIVITY (21m B r1969). The women of Djagamara's family gather wooly-butt grass seed near surface pools and return to camp to thresh and pan the seed, grind it into a gray flour on stones, mix the flour in water and bake it in hot ashes. EMC.

PART 2: GUM PREPARATION, STONE FLAKING: DJAGA-MARA LEAVES BADJAR (19m B r1969). Djagamara sets off into the desert to collect and beat gum from spinifex grass; back in camp, he melts it onto a stick over a bark fire, then turns to making a spear-thrower blade by flaking a discarded fragment of chalcedony with a hammerstone. Finally he sets off again in search of his family, who have left to look for food. EMC.

PART 3: SACRED BOARDS AND AN ANCESTRAL SITE (8m B r1969). At Badjar, a key ancestral site in the desert, the film unit's guide, Djun, brings out and displays the sacred boards he keeps hidden here--ancestral links with the Dreamtime of the legendary past. In the Dreamtime, Badjar was the site of a revenge expedition and of sexual rites; it remains a focus of religious sentiment. EMC.

PART 4: DESERT PEOPLE (51m B r1960). The Aborigines of Australia's Western Desert have almost all migrated to federal campgrounds, into the cities, or to large cattle ranches. When this film was made, only a handful held to their traditional way of life, wandering from water source to water source, gathering food on the way. An eloquent picture of a people, capturing the essence as well as the activities of the Aboriginal culture. Available for rental only. EMC.

PART 5: OLD CAMP SITES AT TIKA TIKA (12m B r1969). Minma and his family are encamped at an ancestral site at Tika Tika well, amid broken artifacts, grindstones and other remains. Janindu, one of Minma's wives, mends a cracked wooden dish, then prepares and demonstrates a headache lotion made from the seeds of the quandong tree. EMC.

PART 6: SPEAR MAKING: BOYS' SPEAR FIGHT (10m B r1969). Minma makes a spear from an acacia tree. Two of his sons play with the toy spear. EMC.

PART 7: SPEAR-THROWER MAKING, INCLUDING STONE FLAK-ING AND GUM PREPARATION (34m B r1969). Minma cuts a lump of wood from an acacia tree, shapes it, then finds and flakes a stone for a knife. He collects spinifex grass gum, melts it, uses it to fasten the knife to a wooden handle, and finally mounts a peg on his spear-thrower to receive the end of the spear shaft. EMC.

PART 8: FIRE MAKING (7m B r1969). Minma's son, Burunjaru, rubs the edge of his spear-thrower across a wooden log, igniting dried kangaroo dung placed in a crack in the log.   EMC.

PART 9: SPINNING HAIR STRING, GETTING WATER FROM WELL, BINDING GIRL'S HAIR (13m B r1969). Minma's two wives spin human hair into string while a girl brings water from one of the wells at Tika Tika.   The girl's hair is then bound with the hair string.   EMC.

PART 10: COOKING KANGAROO (17m B r1969). Minma guts a large kangaroo and carries it to camp, where his sons play with it while he prepares a fire.   The kangaroo is cooked whole in a trench, and Minma divides it into pieces, which he gives to his wives and children.   EMC.

PEOPLE OF THE YUKON DELTA (28m C 1973)
Sensitively documents the effects of the influx of white people on the culture of Alaskan Eskimos.   Narrated by an old Eskimo, who describes the differences between his childhood experiences and his grandchildren's.   Shows many facets of traditional and contemporary Eskimo life, including a seal hunt, berry picking by women, and a village festival.   A colorful but ultimately sad portrait of a vanishing way of life.   AARONP; EMC.

PEOPLE, PEOPLE, PEOPLE (4m C 1976)
A cartoon portraying the waves of American immigration as a frantic, pandemonious stream of "people, people, people. " By Faith Hubley, John Hubley; PF.

PERE NOEL U. S. A. (9m B 1968)
The first film of a French-Canadian girl shot in New York on Thanksgiving Day, with the Bread and Puppet Theatre going down the streets protesting against the war in Vietnam.   By Lise Noiseux; JCLP; CFDC; FCOOP.

PERFECT MOTHER: PARADOX OR POSSIBILITY?, THE; Woman
Series (29m C 1975 VIDEO)
Shirley Radl, author of Mother's Day Is Over and founder of a parental stress hotline to help troubled parents and prevent child abuse, and Angela Barron McBride, a psychiatrist-nurse and author of The Growth and Development of Babies, look at how society pressures women to have children and to meet impossibly high standards in raising them.   WNEDTV; PTL.

PERFORMANCE (110m C 1970 (Gr. Br.))
Set in contemporary London and filmed entirely on location within the environs of the capital, Performance is not only a story of the underworld, it is also an incisive probe into the closely-related emotions of love and hate and their effects on human relationships. d. Donald Cammell, Nicolas Roeg; WSA.

PERIOD PIECE (10m C n. d.)
Period Piece is a clearing of the mythic air.   This film debunks the idea that menstruation must be disruptive of one's life, and contains a no-nonsense self-examination of the bleeding cervix by the filmmaker.   By Emilie Culpepper; IE.

PERON AND EVITA; Twentieth Century Series (30m B 1958)
Documents the rise to power of Argentine dictator Juan Peron
and his actress-wife Evita. Describes methods he used to gain control of the country's economy for his personal profit and indicates
the steps in his ultimate downfall. PICA; CBSTV; ASFI; IU.

PERSON TO PERSON SERIES see CATHERINE WOOD MARSHALL

PERSONA (81m B 1967 Swedish/subtitled)
Elizabeth (Liv Ullman) suffers a nervous breakdown and loses
the ability to speak. She is sent to an isolated coastal spot, where
she is to be cared for by a nurse companion, Alma (Bibi Anderson).
An odd mechanism of mutual identification is set-off, and the actress
comes to rely on the nurse for moral sustenance, a need which becomes almost physical. d. Ingmar Bergman; UAS.

PERU: INCA HERITAGE (18m C 1970)
Compares the culture of the Indians of Peru with that of their
ancestors, the Incas. Discusses such points as the similarities between religious festivals of the two groups. Concludes with an exploration of the Inca citadel of Machu Picchu, which remains a
fitting monument to the stone architecture of the Incas. By Elda
Hartley; HARTLEY; PARACO.

PESCA PICSA (4m C 1968)
"Animated and live. A sensual film of continuous orgasm of
pulsating color and image. "--L. D. By Irene Duga; FCOOP.

PESCADOS VIVOS (20m C n. d.)
Abstract animated film. "A warm and comic vision of life with
the aid of the magical optical printer. "--S. F. By Susan Felter;
CCC.

PETER AND THE WOLF see SAND

PETITE LILIE, LA (15m B 1928)
Tells of the heroine (Mary Pickford) who, while beloved by all
for her face and high spirits, knows you can't eat by living on vir-
tue. She quits her job as a seamstress and becomes a streetwalker.
A tongue-in-cheek look at sentimental moralism of the time. d.
Alberto Calvalcanti; BF.

PETULIA (105m C 1968)
A satiric drama of a modern marriage with George C. Scott
as a successful San Francisco society doctor, divorced from his
wife. At a fund raising party, he meets Petulia, a strange and
impulsive girl (Julie Christie) who is married to the spoiled and
destructive son of the city's most influential hospital administrator.
Her freshness captivates him and as he learns of her background
and need to escape from her sick surroundings, he falls in love
with her. Yet these alienated characters can neither help one another or themselves. d. Richard Lester; p. Raymond Wagner;
s. p. Lawrence B. Marcus; WSA; WHOLFC.

PEYOTE QUEEN (8m C 1965)
Using images drawn directly on the film, the filmmaker takes
the viewer on an abstract and colorful journey through ritual,
thought and sensory derangement. By Storm De Hirsch; CCC,
FCOOP.

PHOEBE--STORY OF A PRE-MARITAL PREGNANCY (29m B 1965)
Explores the state of mind of a teen-age girl when she realizes
she is pregnant. Cinematic language is used in an unconventional
manner to express the girl's fantasies of future confrontations with
her parents, her boy friend, and her school principal. Lyric style
manages to avoid the usual cliches about the subject, vividly conveying the girl's loneliness and the deeply felt sense of wonder in
terms today's middle-class teen-agers can identify with. NFBC;
ASU, BU, EMC, PAS.

PHOTOGRAPHY: DOROTHEA LANGE, THE CLOSER FOR ME see
DOROTHEA LANGE: THE CLOSER FOR ME

PHOTOGRAPHY: DOROTHEA LANGE, UNDER THE TREES see
DOROTHEA LANGE: UNDER THE TREES

PHYLLIS AND TERRY (36m B 1965)
Improvised filming of two teen-age Black girls who have grown
up in the slums of New York's Lower East Side and who face the
prospect of adult life in the ghetto. Phyllis and Terry speak their
own private thoughts to each other as they drift through the ordinary
activities of the day. The negative power of their environment becomes obvious: the unlit halls of rotting tenements, ancient school
yards, the fact that both girls say the only way they have to express
themselves is through dancing or listening to the jukebox. By
Carole Satrina, Eugene Marner; AFBI; CFS, CMC, EMC, FCOOP,
UMIS.

PIANO RUB (3m C 1975)
The keyboard and strings of a piano are transformed into graphic
linear patterns of visual music, as the sounds of "piano rubbing"
rise and fall. By Mary Beams; SB.

PICKING UP THE PIECES: ONE WIDOW SPEAKS; Woman Series
(29m C 1975 VIDEO)
Lynne Caine, author of the best-selling book Widow speaks with
extraordinary frankness about the slow and painful process she was
forced to undergo after her husband's death. She says, ".... I
realized there are many options I never conceived of. Rebirth is
very painful but very rewarding." WNEDTV; PTL.

PICNIC (115m C 1956)
About small town American life. William Holden plays a drifter
who upsets the routine of a sleepy town preparing for a Labor Day
picnic. He makes an impact on a small group as well as the town's
prettiest girl, Madge (Kim Novak) who dreams of finding true love,
and her younger sister Millie (Susan Strasberg) who resents Madge's

beauty.   Also involved is a middle-aged school teacher (Rosalind
Russell) who desperately wants to get married to an unwilling busi-
nessman (Arthur O'Connell).   Based on play by William Inge.   d.
Joshua Logan; p.   Fred Kohlmar; COLUMBIA; ABFI, BF.

PICTURES FROM A GALLERY (length not given   C   1975)
    Picture processed photos from the artist-filmmakers' family.
Faces are abstracted in a divisionistic manner.   By Lillian Schwartz;
LPI.

PIERRE VALLIERES (33m   C   1972   French/subtitled)
    A film about a Quebec revolutionary who spent three years in
jail without a trial.   We do not see Pierre Vallieres.   We see only
his teeth, his lips, as he talks in French.   Among other things,
Pierre is a political writer whose mind seems to be very clear,
his grasp of political facts and history very lucid, and he speaks
slowly.   The filmmaker has eliminated all visual distraction including the speaker's face.   Pierre has written the book White Niggers
of America (on French Canadians) since the film was made.   By
Joyce Wieland; FCOOP.

PIGS VS. FREAKS (15m   C   1975)
    Each fall the alternative-culture at Michigan State University
and the local police do battle.   But instead of hurling tear gas and
rocks, they throw footballs.   A humorous film about one of those
rare times when two conflicting life-styles get together and learn
something about each other.   By Jack Epps; PF.

PILGRIMS: A PARABLE (29m   C   1973)
    To a roadside truck stop in the middle of the night with its in-
viting neon warmth, weary truckdrivers are drawn as moths to a
solitary glow in the darkness.   The film eavesdrops on an amazing
confrontation between two men at the truck stop.   Vernon, a
troubled, withdrawn driver, and Fred, a compulsive talker, each
in his own way is in search of companionship and acceptance.   A
revealing vignette of unsettling characters.   Also a tragi-comic
parable of the possibilities of all human relationships.   p.   Peter
Hoffman; PF.

PIT OF LONELINESS (88m   B   1954   French/subtitled)
    A sensitive examination of the corrosive and tragic effect of
love among women.   Based on the English novel Olivia.   The story
takes place at the end of the 19th-century at a French finishing
school run by Mlles. Julie and Cara.   At this school appears Olivia,
a shy English teen-ager.   At school Olivia blossoms into a happy,
giddy girl and joins her mates in their seemingly harmless rivalry
for the attention and affection of Mlle. Julie, the more commanding
and beautiful of the two head-mistresses.   Mlle. Julie realizes her
own interest in certain of the children is unnatural.   Although she
loves Olivia, who clearly worships her, she doesn't allow herself to
make the relationship an actual affair.   Her concern for the girl's
well-being keeps her from making any definite advances, but her
instincts lead her into tempting Olivia further with little doubt she

could succeed should she decide to indulge her true feelings. Mean-
while, the school falls apart, Cara out of jealousy and hurt commits
suicide, and Julie's grief at this event drives her away from the
school. Olivia is left shattered, to move into adulthood. d. Jacqueline Audrey; FCE.

PIXILLATION (4m   C   1970)
    "With computer-produced images and Moog-synthesized sound,
Lillian Schwartz's Pixillation is in a sense an introduction to the
electronics lab. But its forms are always handsome, its colors
bright and appealing, its rhythms complex and inventive. "--Roger
Greenspun, New York Times. By Lillian Schwartz; LPI; IU.

PLACE FOR AUNT LOIS, A (17m   C   n. d.)
    The separated or divorced woman, often single by choice, repre-
sents a valid life style in our society. But even today, a child may
be led to view her as a failure. Is Aunt Lois a failure? What does
her choice of a way of life mean? WOMBAT, VFI.

PLACE IN THE SUN, A (120m   B   1951)
    A fateful romance involving three young people--a confused, am-
bitious factory worker; the glamorous, wealthy debutante who loves
him and whom he wants to marry; and the simple, unattractive working girl who threatens to tie him to a drab future. A profound exploration of individual values underlying successes--of guilt, justice
and punishment. Based on the novel An American Tragedy, by Theodore Dreiser. d. George Stevens; PARAMOUNT; FI.

PLANET OF MAN SERIES   see   UNEVENTFUL DAY, THE

PLASTIC BLAG (7m   B   n. d.)
    A poke at consumer packaging. By Judy Wardwell; CCC.

PLASTIC BODY (25m   B   1964)
    A group of girl dancers demonstrates a number of basic con-
cepts related to movement as the woman narrator discusses them.
The relation of the body to real or imaginary space, the blending of
time and force into rhythm and the interpretation of emotion are illustrated by various dancers. Also includes a folk dance performed
by a group of young women and men in costume. Produced as a
master's thesis by Jane Yosepian; UILL.

PLEASE KEEP THIS OPENED DOOR CLOSED (3m   C   n. d.)
    "An umbrella and a sewing machine meet on an operating table. "
--P. S. Computer generated sound. By Patricia Sloane; WAF.

PLISETSKAYA DANCES (71m   B   1964)
    Previews the career and biography of Maya Plisetskaya, prima
ballerina of the Bolshoi Theatre Ballet Company, Moscow. Excerpts from ballets, interviews with Maya, and views of the ballerina at work and at leisure capture the whole world of ballet.
Plisetskaya (with distinguished soloists and corps de ballet of the
Bolshoi Ballet) gives performances in scenes from Swan Lake,

Sleeping Beauty, Laurencia, Spartacus, Raymonda, Romeo and Juliet, The Little Humpbacked Horse, Khovanschina, The Stone Flower, Walpurgis Night, and Don Quixote. CDFS; ABFI; UILL.

PLUM PUDDING (22m C 1969)
A collection of animated shorts by children. By Yvonne Andersen and children, ages 11-17, YBW.

POEM AS A PERSONAL STATEMENT: TO A VERY OLD WOMAN, THE; A Sense of Poetry (Series) (10m C 1974)
The camera becomes a gentle observer, following the movements of an elderly woman, frail but serene, as she occupies herself in the simple fulfillment of her life. We see her playing solitaire, feeding the birds, sharing her limited time with a child in the playground. Finally, the camera returns her to her empty room and a now-vacant chair where she once sat dreaming of her past in front of the fire. The film conveys a very real sense of the richness of a life experience which is almost over, and her attitude in greeting death as a natural completion of life. From a poem by Irving Layton. By Paul Quigley; CINMET; LCA.

POETRY IS ALIVE AND WELL AND LIVING IN AMERICA SERIES
see POETRY OF EDWARD FIELD; POETRY OF GLORIA ODEN; POETRY OF MAY SWENSON

POETRY OF EDWARD FIELD (10m C 1969)
Visualization of two poems read by poet. Shows poet in his natural environment discussing his work. By Frances D. Ross; MPLUS.

POETRY OF GLORIA C. ODEN (10m C 1969)
Visualization of two poems read by poet. Shows poet in her natural environment discussing her work. By Frances D. Ross; MPLUS.

POETRY OF MAY SWENSON (10m C 1969)
Visualization of two poems read by poet. Shows poet in her natural environment discussing her work. By Frances D. Ross; MPLUS.

POETRY SERIES see ANNE SEXTON; DENISE LEVERTOV AND CHARLES OLSON

POETS RETURN (20m B 1962)
A young poet's return to the place of his boyhood, a land of farms and fishermen. Each place visited renews his realization of the beauty and simplicity of life on this peaceful island. The gentle mood of the film is sustained by the woodwind score by Paul Severson. By Madeline Tourtelot; GP.

POINT PELEE; Nature's Last Stand Series (20m C 1971)
Describes a spit of Canadian land on Lake Erie that is in danger of having its delicate ecological balance disturbed by a growing population. By Nancy Archibald; CBCTV; FL

POLICEMEN (30m   C   n. d.)
Policemen from Chicago talking about what it's like to be a policeman. By Martha Stuart, David Ruskin; STUARTM.

POLKA GRAPH (6m   C   n. d.)
A spritely abstract film visually interpreting Shostakovich's polkas from the "Age of Gold" ballet suite.   By Mary Ellen Bute; CFS.

POLYGAMY, PROSPERING IN EXILE (57m   C   n. d.)
Despite the threat of prosecution by the State, and excommunication by the Mormon Church, polygamists continue to practice plural marriage.   The film takes a close look at polygamous communities and households in Utah and explores the question of polygamy through first-hand accounts from participants.   It considers the history of plural marriage, the role of women, religious freedom vs. Federal law, community life, delegation of responsibilities and the strong religious belief that binds them to their existence.   p. /d. Lucky Severson for KUTV; SOHO.

POMO SHAMAN (20m   B   1964)
Shows, without comment, the authentic healing ceremony derived from ancient practices of the Kashia group of the Southwest Pomo Indians.   The doctor is the spiritual head of the Kashia community. She and four signers in this ceremony use two banboo canes, decorated with dream designs and haliotis ornaments that have special powers for the Shaman.   EMC; MSU, WSU.

POPULATION; Human Sexuality Series (29m   C   1972   VIDEO)
The effects of population pressures on sex are investigated through a look at how sex and sexuality change according to population density and neighborhood structure.   Clinical experiments are described.   Walter B. Quisenberry, M. D. , Hawaii Dept. of Health, is interviewed about population legislation and control.   UHAWAII/ KHETTV; PTL.

POPULATION AND THE AMERICAN FUTURE, PT. II (30m   C   1973)
Reports the President's Commission on Population Growth and the American Future's findings on the economic, social, political, environmental and ethical aspects of past and present population trends and future population growth in the U. S.   Emphasizes the need for education of the population regarding consequences of unlimited growth and stresses the ideal of family planning.   FFG; UKEN.

POPULATION PROBLEM SERIES   see   GIFT OF CHOICE

PORNOGRAPHY AND FANTASY; Human Sexuality Series (29m   C   1972   VIDEO)
Host Milton Diamond, Ph. D. , leads a field trip through a neighborhood noted for its pornographic shops and theatres.   Movie clips shown by a church society to represent "good" and "bad" sex are

shown. A dance sequence illustrates the relationship of pornography
to sexual expression. UHAWAII/KHETTV; PTL.

PORTRAIT (14m C 1971)
A surrealistic portrait of a man, friend and artist. Made on
a homemade optical printer. By Donna Deitch; CCC.

PORTRAIT OF A DEAF CITY (15m C 1971)
Shows how one person, a woman, started by getting viewpoints
of those in power and those out of power in her city. Presents
provocative insights of the powerful and the powerless as they view
their city. They speak on urban renewal, housing, education, police confrontation, and justice. There are no pat answers--insights
vary according to the situation and the social implications and point
out the different needs of individuals. It will provoke one to examine one's own philosophies. REPRO; BF.

PORTRAIT OF A LOST SOUL (15m B n. d. VIDEO)
Deals with women's search for identity through the media of
dance and music. TCWFC.

PORTRAIT OF A NURSE (27m C 1976)
Nurse practitioner Jean Steel exemplifies the new "expanded
role" of the nurse--no longer doctor's hand-maiden but primary care
provider for her own patients. She shares one of the nation's first
nurse-doctor private practice partnerships. Depicts her relationships with patients, and the role negotiations she and her colleagues
engage in. p. Susan Butler; d. Robert Freedman; BUTFREE.

PORTRAIT OF A SENSEI (30m C 1973)
Presents a portrait of the art of Amanji Inoue, a Japanese sensei
and master porcelain potter. d. /p. Madeline Tourtelot; GP.

PORTRAIT OF HAITI (14m C 1977)
Explores the roots of Haiti's distinctive culture in a blend of
real life scenes with the primitive art of the island. A colorful,
brief look at a unique lifestyle. By Diana Colson; SWAIN; PHOENIX.

PORTRAIT OF JASON (105m B 1967)
An uncensored cinéma-vérité documentary focusing on Jason
Holliday, born Aaron Paine, age 33, Black male prostitute and a
sometime night club performer. Jason does all his numbers for
the camera--hysterical female impersonations, tales of his house-
boy days in San Francisco, wildly funny tales about his sexual adventures. He gets stoned and chokes on the despair beneath his
laughter. His "act" gets more serious, he appears to be disintegrating from the pain of so many remembered traumas. One gets
a terrifying view of a soul laid bare, a naked revelation of what
society can do to a man it doubly rejects as a Black and as a homosexual. By Shirley Clarke; NYF.

PORTRAIT OF MY MOTHER (27m C 1974)
Canadian filmmaker Bonnie Kreps's intimate portrait of her

mother, focusing on her relationship to other women (including Bonnie), and on the pleasures and challenges of a life lived quietly, independently and in harmony with the natural environment of Wyoming's Grand Tetons. p. Bonnie Kreps; ODEON.

POSITIVE/NEGATIVE ABSTRACTION (10m B si 1974)
"To be projected on two blue plexi-glass panels one foot wide suspended in front of the screen bracketing the edge of the frame. Patterns of light formed by piercing the filmed images of body abstraction become a rhythmic structure, bouncing off the reflective surface. "--R. S.   Comes with plexiglass panels.   By Rosalind Schneider; SCHNEIDER.

POSTMAN ALWAYS RINGS TWICE, THE (113m B 1946)
The film stays close to the novel by James M. Cain.   Story is about a young bum and a tempestuous blonde (Lana Turner).   He kills the blonde's husband and finds you can't "monkey with murder" profitably.   d. Tay Garnett; p. Carey Wilson; s. w. Harry Ruskin, Niven Busch; MGM; FL

POTENTIALLY YOURS (30m C 1972)
Visits growth centers, college campuses, human potential institutes and retreats to show their methods for developing the human potential.   By Elda Hartley; HARTLEY.

POW WOW AT DUCK LAKE (15m B 1967)
A discussion at Duck Lake, Saskatchewan, where Indian-Metis problems are openly and strongly presented before a gathering of Indians and whites.   Among matters discussed are the kind of schooling available to Indians and the limitations of education that restrict their opportunities to develop in their own way and in ways best for themselves.   By Bonnie Klein; NFBC.

POWER IN PERPETUITY (20m C 1967)
Shows why and how the world's largest single hydroelectric power project is being built in the wilderness of Labrador.   Indicates that it is capable of producing power sufficient for more than three cities.   By Sally MacDonald; CHCORP; CRAF; MTP.

POWER VERSUS THE PEOPLE (36m C 1969)
A filmed record of the hearings conducted by the Equal Employment Opportunity Commission in Houston, Texas.   Testifying at the hearings were several large national corporations, who through their hiring and promotion practices, violate Title VII of the Civil Rights Act.   Includes series of candid cross-examinations by the EEOC Commissioners of corporate officials, minority workers, women, and community leaders.   Corporate community and unions of America are made dramatically aware of their insensitivity to the plight of America's minorities and women.   WGPL

PREGNANCY AND BIRTH (12m C 1969)
In animation, the phenomena of conception and birth are presented, showing the complete process.   Beginning with the explana-

tion of the functions of the female sex organs, the film continues
with the fertilization of the egg and the development of the fetus.
A live sequence shows the actual birth of a baby.   NFBC; FI; UILL.

PREGNANCY AND BIRTH; Human Sexuality Series (28m   C   1971
    VIDEO)
    A pregnancy test is demonstrated and some of the emotions sur-
rounding the first knowledge of pregnancy are described.   Host
Milton Diamond, Ph. D. , narrates a presentation showing a normal
delivery.   Demonstrations of natural childbirth exercises (LaMaze
method) and breast feeding (La Leche League techniques) are given.
UHAWAII/KHETTV; PTL.

PREGNANCY AND CHILDBIRTH SERIES   see   BEFORE PREGNANCY;
    LABOUR AND DELIVERY; PRENATAL; SPECIAL CASES

PRELUDE TO MEDICAL CARE (13m   C   1968)
    Cooperative effort of labor/management to provide health testing
for cannery workers in Northern California.   Made for Health Training Service, Inc. by Constance Beeson, Ray Anderson; BEESON.

PREMOONPTSS (15m   C   si   n. d.)
    "The name Premoonptss: to put a footmark on the events up
to the time of the first moon landing, on July 4, 1969 . . . photographic images change, grow and dramatize the overall feeling of
Man in the 1960's. "--N. L.   By Naomi Levine; FCOOP.

PRENATAL; Pregnancy and Childbirth Series (20m   C   1977)
    Examines changes in the mother's body and the development of
the fetus during pregnancy.   Proper health care and nutrition, pos-
ture, exercises and breathing techniques are shown.   Also shows
how family and friends can help the pregnant woman feel more comfortable.   CRAF; IFB.

PRENATAL CARE (24m   C   1977)
    Using live action, narration, animation, and graphics, the film
gives up-to-date information on recognizing the signs of pregnancy,
doctor's care, fears and expectations, fetal development, precautions and warning signs, diet, weight gain, minor problems, emotional changes, exercise and activity, hospital arrangements, childbirth classes, indications of labor and when to call the doctor.
English and Spanish versions.   p. Paul Burnford; PF.

PRENATAL CARE: WHILE YOU'RE WAITING (30m   C   1967)
    A young couple awaiting the birth of their first child attend a
prenatal class and discover their anxieties and questions are typical
of expectant parents.   Presents information on prenatal care, childbirth, and emotional stresses of pregnancy.   CENTROL; UILL.

PRENATAL DEVELOPMENT; Developmental Psychology Today
    Series (23m   C   1974)
    Interviews with researchers and footage of the developing fetus
are combined to bring the viewer the latest theories and informa-

tion about biological and psychological growth which occurs during the fetal period.   p. Barbara Jampel; CRM, MGH; IU, UILL, WAYSU.

PRIEST AND THE PILOT, THE (20m B n. d.   VIDEO)
     The "Priest" is a woman in her late 70's who has been working in the Episcopal Church for years with the goal of becoming a Priest --which, as yet, she is still denied.   The "Pilot" is a woman who runs her own helicopter service.   She speaks about the hostility she meets every step of the way.   Interviews with them are interspersed with random street interviews in which people are queried about their concept of women's work.   By Susan Milano; MILANO.

PRIME MINISTER GOLDA MEIR, ISRAEL; Face the Nation Series,
     No. 35, 1970 (30m   C   1970)
     An interview with Golda Meir.   CBSTV; HIS.

PRIME MINISTER GOLDA MEIR'S VISIT TO THE U. S. A. IN 1969
     (13m   B   1969)
     Documents the official visit of the Prime Minister of Israel to the White House, followed by a triumphant tour from coast to coast. ALDEN.

PRIMUM NON NOCERE (18m   C   1977)
     A definitive film on home birth conducted according to the standards of The American College of Home Obstetrics.   Film shows a couple go through natural childbirth with no anesthesia, analgesia, I. V. , fluids, enema, shave, stirrups, episiotomy, forceps, stitches, slapping the baby, or the separation of the baby from the parents. By John Barasa; CINEMED.

PRINCESS MARGARET (27m   B   1965)
     The story of Margaret Rose of Great Britain is told through newsreels and other footage from 1935, when events brought her within one step of the throne, to her ill-fated romance with Peter Townsend and her marriage to Antony Armstrong-Jones.   AIM; MMA, FSU.

PRINCESS YANG KWEI FEI (91m   C   1956)
     A story of China in the 8th century when the empire was in full flower; a story of Yang Kwei Fei, a famous beauty, who was brought to Emperor Huan Tsung to console him in a time of grief. She was given the rank of "most noble lady, " and some of her relatives were appointed to positions of privilege in the court.   This caused a great deal of rancor, and the people rebelled against the influence of the Yang family.   They killed the relatives in the palace and finally demanded her life.   Seeing the Emperor and his reign would be in danger if the rebels were not appeased, the Princess walked out calmly to meet her death.   d. Kenji Mizoguchi; NYF.

PRINCIPLE THAT COUNTS, THE; Choice: Challenge for Modern
     Women Series (30m   B   1966)
     Ethel Alpenfels, Herbert Fingarette, and Joan Lasko discuss be-

havior and decisions, based on what is important to the individual
woman and what is defined by society. EMC; UMIS.

PRINTMAKING--FOUR ARTISTS, FOUR MEDIA (19m C 1968)
Explains that printmaking can be divided into four basic methods
--serigraph, woodcut, lithograph and intaglio. Shows four print-
makers in their workshop. Shows progression of each method from
sketch to the finished print, including the special equipment and
skills required by each method. Contrasts the differences in producing each kind of print and the differences in appearance of the
finished artwork. By Babette Eddleston; BFA.

PRISMATIC (20m C si n. d.)
"A rainbow film ... a visual geometric film using the prism. "--
N. L. By Naomi Levine; FCOOP.

PRISON FILM: STILL LIVING, A (27m C 1971)
Thoughts, feelings and frustrations of inmates of a prison for
women. Raises questions as to what we expect of the detention system in comparison with the role it performs. By James Kennedy;
CF; PAS.

PRISON GUARDS (30m C n. d.)
Guards in the North Carolina prison system talk about their
work and the men in their custody. By Martha Stuart, David Ruskin; STUARTM.

PRISONERS (30m C 1971)
Features white and Black prisoners expressing their views on
morals, self-respect, sex, homosexuality and the prison process
which they feel strips them of their self-esteem. By Martha Stuart,
David Ruskin; IMPF.

PRIVATE LIFE OF HENRY VIII, THE (97m B 1933 (Gr. Br.))
In one of the funniest scenes in this boudoir romp, Henry VIII
prepares to enter the bridal chambers of Anne of Cleves, an ugly,
but supposedly fertile wife. The King sighs: "The things I've done
for England!" The line, spoken by Charles Laughton in his lusty
portrayal of a frustrated King, was prophetic. d. Alexander Korda;
ABFI, BF.

PRIVATE LIVES OF ELIZABETH AND ESSEX, THE (106m C 1939)
Based on Maxwell Anderson's play, features Bette Davis as
Queen Elizabeth and Errol Flynn as Earl of Essex as lovers who at
the same time schemed against each other for political power.
Finally, Essex initiated an open revolt. Elizabeth defeated him and
had him beheaded. d. Michael Curtiz; UAS.

PROBLEM OF ACCEPTANCE; Psychodrama in Group Processes
Series (47m B 1970)
Psychodramatic exploration of a 17-year-old homosexual woman's
feelings of self-rejection. Condensed from two-hour spontaneous
workshop session with psychiatric patients at University of Oregon

Medical School. Introductory and closing comments by psychiatrist
Ira Pauly. Subtitles clarify psychodramatic interventions and identify participants. NYU; EMC.

PROBLEM SERIES see JAPAN: ANSWER IN THE ORIENT

PROCESSES; Human Sexuality Series (29m C 1972 VIDEO)
    A group discussion opens consideration of genital sexuality vs.
love and emotion. Host Milton Diamond, Ph. D., is joined by several college students and a married middle-aged male and female for
conversation about the phase of sexual response, the use of artificial
devices to stimulate sexual interaction and personal interpretations
of the meaning of orgasm. UHAWAII/KHETTV; PTL.

PROCESSION: CONTEMPORARY DIRECTIONS IN AMERICAN DANCE
    (18m B 1966)
    Ann Halprin and the Dancer's Workshop Company of San Fran-
cisco perform selections from "Procession," a dance from their experimental repertoire. In this presentation of "total theatre," the
dancers interact with one another and the elements in their stage
environment--light, electronic' sound, a scaffolding, articles of clothing and other props. Includes commentary by Ann Halprin explaining her unique approach to modern dancing. EMC; UILL.

PRODUCTIVITY AND THE SELF-FULFILLING PROPHECY: THE
    PYGMALION EFFECT; Behavior in Business Film Series (30m
    C 1974)
    The power of expectation alone can influence the behavior of
others. It is a phenomenally powerful tool that managers can learn
to use to benefit both their organization and its individuals. Film
explores both R. K. Merton's concept of "The Self-Fulfilling Prophecy" and its practical application to the issues of modern management. By Joan Owens; CRM, MGH.

PROFILES IN COURAGE see ANNE HUTCHINSON; MARY S. MC-
    DOWELL; PRUDENCE CRANDALL

PROFILES IN POWER SERIES see QUEEN VICTORIA

PROGRESS, PORK BARREL AND PHEASANT FEATHERS (27m B
    1966)
    Shows conservation group fighting politicians to save the Ever-
glades. By Holly Fisher, Roman V. Slezas; MGH.

PROMISE HER ANYTHING BUT GIVE HER THE KITCHEN SINK
    (3m C 1969)
    "... an inter-balancing of opposing emotions, a beautiful love-
poem to her husband, a journey of mind-expansion and woman's
statement of rebellion."--Kirk Tougas, Georgia Straight; by Freude
Bartlett; SB.

PROMISE SHARED: WOMEN IN ISRAELI SOCIETY, A (25m C
    n. d.)
    Focuses on working women in Israel, among them labor union

officials, a kibbutz secretary, an attorney and a newspaper publisher. Takes a long hard look at the legal and social status of women in their country. Divergent opinions based on differences in age, experience and expectation, and their penetrating analysis of the women's movement in the U. S. as it affects Israel, combine for a stimulating half hour which probes the minds of women who share working and fighting responsibilities with Israeli men. WSOUTV; ADL.

PROMISED LANDS (87m C 1973 English narration)
A filmed essay on history, a poem about strong emotions, a group portrait of a subject whose features remain eternally in dispute. Abstract images are interspersed with images of the real; irony alternates with tragedy. Israel lives in a maelstrom of myths as well as of geo-political realities. The film sums up those myths as well as those realities. d. Susan Sontag; p. Nicole Stephane; NYF.

PRUDENCE CRANDALL; Profiles in Courage Series (50m B 1965)
A New England teacher in 1833 declared that girls and Negroes had as much right to education as white boys. She met the opposition of her neighbors and a Connecticut law which she believed to be unconstitutional. Stars Janice Rule. SAUDEK; IQF; PAS.

PSSSHT (6m C 1969)
An amusing comment on contemporary life in which the aerosol can is the constant companion of a couple as they get ready to go to work. By Holly Fisher; FISLEF; CFS.

PSYCHODRAMA IN GROUP PROCESSES SERIES see PROBLEM OF ACCEPTANCE

PSYCHOLOGICAL DIFFERENCES BETWEEN THE SEXES; Marriage and Family, The (Series) (18m C 1965)
Illustrates the psychological, emotional and physical differences between males and females. Dramatizes the diverse reactions to similar situations. MGH; UKEN, USC.

PSYCHOMONTAGE (10m B n. d.)
A witty and at times shocking discovery of sexuality in humans and in the animal world. Utilizes visual puns and startling symbolic juxtapositions to further the effects. Nudity and sexual involvement is treated with unabashed good humor and honesty. p. /d. Phyllis Kronhausen, Eberhard Kronhausen; GP.

PSYCHOSYNTHESIS (8m C 1975)
Using double exposure, Barbara Hammer takes a look into her own mind. Universal images of witch, infant and nurturer unfold from the swirling superimpositions. By Barbara Hammer; IE.

PUMPKIN EATER, THE (110m B 1964)
An incisive exploration of the problems of contemporary marriage in many of its possible ramifications: infidelity, multiple divorce, rearing children, psychiatric sessions, living in the country on a small income, living in town profligately. Pictures the husband-

as-artist, the husband-as-philanderer, the husband-as-stepfather.
Anne Bancroft plays the survivor of three marriages and eight chil-
dren. Based on novel by Penelope Mortimer. d. Jack Clayton; p.
James Woolf; ABFI, CINE, MGH, WHOLFC.

PUPPET PROPOSITION, THE (26m   C   1976)
    Films history of puppetry as well as the development of an act.
The origin of puppetry is not definitely known. The modern puppet
evolved from medieval plays. A present day company is seen performing several routines and creating together another routine from
concept to actual performance. The director choreographs the number, a folk dance. Changes are made and logistical problems worked
out in rehearsal. d. David Visser; p. Margo Lovelace; LOVELACE.

PURPOSES OF FAMILY PLANNING; Family Planning and Sex Educa-
    tion--A Series (15m   C   1973)
    Presents in laymen's language the different reasons why people
choose to practice family planning. Shows people in different situations as they learn about planning a family. Among the motivations
for choosing to practice family planning shown are health, emotional
maturity, economic stability and the need to provide each child with
individual love and attention. MLP; OF; UM.

PURSE, THE (12m   B   1966)
    A provocative film about conscience, or the lack of it. An
elderly woman "finds" a purse on a bus. She takes it home and
discovers it contains some money. The woman who lost the purse
collects insurance. The question the film asks is: Does any circumstance excuse taking what is not ours? By Patricia Watson;
NFBC; IFB.

PUSS IN BOOTS (10m   B   1934)
    A fairy tale in silhouette animation based on live shadow play.
By Lotte Reiniger; MGH.

PUTNEY SCHOOL (15m   C/B   1969)
    "The school has a traditional academic program with strong
emphasis on individual responsibility for work ... a very casual
individual policy on clothes and hair styles, and a complex program
of chores and farming in which all participate."--Alternatives, EFLA.
By Claudia Weill, Eliot Noyes, Jr.; CYCLOPS.

PUZZLE OF A DOWNFALL CHILD (104m   C   1970)
    Faye Dunaway stars in the story about a high fashion model,
whose private life belies her public image. The story of a woman
who has found fame and fortune in her work, only to suffer the
agonies of the damned in her personal life. d. Jerry Schatzberg;
p. Paul Newman; UNIVE; SWANK, TWY, UNIVE.

PYGMALION (85m   B   1938   (Gr. Br.))
    The basis for the smash musical My Fair Lady, Pygmalion
tells the story of Professor Henry Higgins and his transformation of
a cockney girl, Eliza Doolittle, into the toast of society from her

beginnings as a common flower girl. d. Anthony Asquith, Leslie Howard; CIE; BF, JANUS.

QUASI AT THE QUACKADERO (10m C 1976)
Incorporates two traditions of American cartoon art. The cartoon's featured players include a spoiled infantile duck appropriately named Quasi, and his disgruntled girlfriend, Anita. She would like to take up with Rollo, the family robot, and the two of them plot to get rid of the gluttonous duck by luring him into a time hole with a chocolate cake. By Sally Cruikshank; PF.

QUE HACER? (WHAT IS TO BE DONE?) (90m C 1972)
Shot in Chile before the coup and Allende's death. "A fictional story about a Peace Corps girl, a murdered priest and a political kidnapping..."--IMPF. Includes an interview with Allende and music by Country Joe MacDonald. By Nina Serrano, James Beckett, Saul Landau, Raul Ruiz; LOBO; IMPF.

QUEEN, THE (68m C 1967)
Cinéma-vérité documentary of a National Transvestite Pageant in New York's Town Hall in 1967. The film's power lies in men's view of what women are. The film follows these men as they make up, pour themselves into corsets, practice walking in highheels. They show a great sense of "esprit de corp" as outcasts altogether. They discuss their relationships to other men, their views on "girls," and their childhoods. The film moves you in many ways. By Frank Simon; GP.

QUEEN CHRISTINA (100m B 1933)
A historical fiction of Queen Christina, played by Greta Garbo, who had been reared as a boy to succeed to the 17th-century Swedish throne. She finds herself in a wayside inn, sharing her room with the new Spanish envoy who has mistaken her for a Nordic youth. In the midst of palace intrigue, they become lovers and barely avert a tragic separation. Based on a story by Margaret P. Levine and Salka Vierted. p. Walter Wanger; d. Rouben Mamoulian; MGM; FI.

QUEEN ELIZABETH (8m B n.d.)
Shows the coronation of the Queen. Includes her acceptance of a bouquet in the Fiji Islands, and her trip to the hot springs, geysers, and the Glow Worm Cavern in New Zealand. WSA; OKSU.

QUEEN ELIZABETH II; Biography Series (26m B 1962)
Highlights the life of Queen Elizabeth II of England. Includes her life as princess of the royal family, her marriage to Philip Mountbatten and her coronation in 1952. WOLPER; OFF.

QUEEN ELIZABETH II VISITS GHANA (34m C 1961)
A pictorial record of the visit to Ghana of Queen Elizabeth II and the Duke of Edinburgh in November 1961. GHANA.

QUEEN IN CANADA--1964, THE (21m B 1964)
A film record of the visit of Queen Elizabeth to Canada in October 1964, to commemorate the historic meetings which led to the Confederation of the provinces of Canada. Shows views of Queen Elizabeth and the Duke of Edinburgh as they visit Charlottetown, Quebec City and Ottawa. NBCTV.

QUEEN OF APOLLO (12m C 1970)
Cinéma-vérité portrait of the 1970 queen of debutantes at an exclusive New Orleans Mardi Gras ball. Follows her as she preens for hours before entering the ball room where she bestows greetings with the traditional sceptor and frozen smile. Satirical, funny, and ultimately sad. By Richard Leacock; PENBAK; EMC.

QUEEN VICTORIA; Profiles in Power Series (26m C 1976)
A historical drama presented as an interview with Patrick Watson interviewing Queen Victoria (played by Kate Reid). The Queen boasts of her accomplishments, wealth, power, empire, and fine cities, and mourns the faded glory of today's England. When the interviewer presses her regarding the abuses of her empire or the less glorious aspects of the Britain she ruled, the Queen cleverly avoids the issue and reminisces about other happenings. p. McConnell Advertising with cooperation of LCA; LCA.

QUEEN'S DESTINY, THE (27m C 1976)
Examines the circumstances behind Hawaii's move toward Americanization and ultimate statehood, a move many Hawaiians opposed. Dramatizes the downfall of Queen Liliuokalani, who ruled Hawaii as a divine monarch until 1893, when she was overthrown by American businessmen. Focuses on the confrontation between the Queen and her ministers when she demands approval of a new Constitution which will restore much of the monarch's power. d. Don Fouser; WNET-TV; FL

QUESTION OF JUSTICE, A (28m B 1975)
Focuses on the physical oppression of women by men and the unjust penalties faced by women who have been forced to use violence to survive. A number of recent court cases and studies have dramatized numerous cases of rape and brutalization of women that have gone unpunished. d. Lisa Feiner; GP.

QUIET ONE, THE (67m B 1948)
Presents the story of an unloved Negro child lost in loneliness and delinquency, who is rehabilitated at the Wiltwyck School for Boys, Protestant Episcopal Church. By Janet Loeb, Helen Levitt, James Agee; MGH; ABFI.

QUIET REVOLUTION OF MRS. HARRIS, THE (20m C 1976)
Gives a housewife's account of her gradual self-realization in becoming a person. Features Gloria Harris talking about her dissatisfaction with her roles as mother, wife and housekeeper. Follows her efforts to establish her own identity by attending college and becoming a professional. CINELO; PHOENIX; MG.

QUILTING WOMEN (27m   C   1976)
Documents the creation of a work of art and examines an important craft. The entire process from piercing a traditional pattern to the finale of a quilting bee is shown. The film conveys a sense of satisfaction that these women derive from their work. APPALL.

RABBIT SEASON (6m   C   n. d.)
A poignant message is well stated in this animated film based on a poem that focuses on the rabbit as an image of the life force-- a vulnerable prey, whether caged or in the open, exposed to violence, war and death from the moment of birth, yet persisting to remain alive, prolific and serving a purpose in spite of the risks involved. By Nancy Webber; CFS.

RABBITS ARE THE FRIENDS OF TOADS (12m   B   n. d.)
A three-year-old boy is walking through thick undergrowth in a wild place. On his way, he has an experience which could be violent but his child's innocence protects him. As the audience is not quite so innocent, its fears are made manifest in terrifying sounds from the screen. The story's significance is left to the spiritual perception of the audience. By Dorothy Knowles; GP.

RACHEL, RACHEL (101m   C   1968)
Rachel (Joanne Woodward) is a 35-year-old elementary school teacher who has never been able to allow herself a full emotional involvement. At a revival meeting she discovers the intense emotions which she is capable of experiencing. She rejects the overtures of a colleague (Estelle Parsons) and chooses the man (James Olson), prostituting herself to him, building a fantasy of love. When her lover abandons her, Rachel lives with the hope she is pregnant, but once again she is let down. Desperate, she turns out of need to the woman she had previously rejected. Based on a novel, A Jest of God by Margaret Lawrence. d. /p. Paul Newman; WSA; ABFI, CVE, CWF, FC, SELECT, TWY, WHOLFC, WCF.

RADCLIFFE BLUES (23m   B   1968)
"A Radcliffe student discusses the process of her radicalization, both on campus in the early stages of the SDS Movement, and during the anti-poverty work in Atlanta. The crippled condition of women in this country is also discussed. "--Films By and/or About Women. By Claudia Weill, Tony Ganz; CYCLOPS.

RADICAL SEX STYLES (45m   B   1973)
An informative and candid film where six people are interviewed --a beautiful transvestite who passes easily as a woman, the members of a ménage à trois who have lived together for several years, a striking young woman who claims to express her freedom via promiscuity, a bright and perceptive lesbian who discusses the gay life, an articulate bisexual who enjoys masochistic practices, and

an attractive, young, married couple who have appeared in pornographic films and who organize group sexual encounters.   By Ar-
mond Weston; GP.

RAIN (91m B 1932)
Film vividly captures the lives of several very different human
beings thrown together on Pago Pago during a fierce monsoon.
Joan Crawford plays the cynical prostitute, and Walter Huston plays
the minister who tries to reform her.   Based on W. Somerset
Maugham's powerful story of Sadie Thompson.   d. Lewis Milestone;
UAS; ABFI, BF.

RAIN (10m C 1972)
"Live animation, shot from overhead angle and edited in the
camera, of New Yorkers crossing the street during a spring rain.
Music: The Galaxie Dream Band. "--L. E. I.   By Louva Elizabeth
Irvine; FCOOP.

RAIN PEOPLE, THE (102m C 1969)
A deeply moving story about an anxious young woman (Shirley
Knight) who discovers she's pregnant, deserts her husband and picks
up with a hitchhiker (James Caan) with whom she travels across the
U. S. A.   This is a panoramic American Odyssey about the emotional
rehabilitation of a distraught individual who learns to face life and
see herself for what she is.   d. Francis Ford Coppola; WSA; BF,
TWY.

RAINBOW BLACK (31m C 1976)
A warm and inspiring portrait of Sarah Webster Fabio, showing
the many facets of this talented Black woman, while emphasizing
her life and work as a poet.   In her interview, Ms. Fabio discusses
the different approaches in writing poetry, drama, and criticism;
the relationship of the Black experience to her work; and the special sensibility she believes comes from being a Black woman.   She
comments on the importance of colors to her emotions as well as
to her writing, and explains why the kaleidoscope is her favorite
image for her own work.   She also tells about her early influences,
paying particular attention to Langston Hughes.   Several of her poems
are read by Ms. Fabio.   By Cheryl Fabio; EMC.

RAISIN IN THE SUN, A (128m B 1961)
Drama of a Chicago South Side family, with its dreams, ambitions and frustrations is told with compassion, warmth and humor.
The impact of an expected insurance bequest, which each member
sees as the means of realizing long-nurtured dreams and escape
from grinding frustrations, provides an eloquent film portrait that
is sensitively and superbly portrayed by the stars of the original
play.   d. Daniel Petrie; s. w. Lorraine Hansberry; COLUMBIA;
ABFI, CINE, KP, MGH, WCF, WHOLFC.

RAISON AVANT LA PASSION, LA (80m C 1968-69)
A whirlwind view of Canada with an anti-dialectical premise.
By Joyce Wieland; FCOOP.

RAMA (16m   C   1969)
"A cinematic tone poem about a mythological sea goddess who is washed ashore to spend one day on earth. Based on Botticelli's 'Birth of Venus.'"--S. C.   By Sugar Cain; FCOOP.

RAMPARTS OF CLAY (85m   C   1970   Arabic/subtitled)
Drama of a young woman living in an isolated village on the edge of the Sahara who can no longer accept the subservient role that her people's ancient traditions demand of her. Her personal conflict and quiet rebellion parallel the villagers' awakening to their own exploitation.   p. /d. Jean-Louis Bertucelli; CIV.

RAP (8m   B   n. d.)
. The first feminist film made at UCLA. The filmmaker barely survived the full-scale attack from male students and faculty after it was screened. None of the women came to her defense, but several came up afterwards to apologize and lend belated support. An excellent film for not-quite-yet-feminist women's groups. It uses the simplistic approach to role-reversal to get across the woman's feeling about sexist practices. By Sarah Kuhn; SARSAKU.

RAPE (28m   C   1975   VIDEO)
Informative program on the experiences and the after-effects of rape, presented by two rape victims. Services available to rape victims in the Portland, Oregon area are also discussed. NOWP; CREOUT.

RAPE: A PREVENTIVE INQUIRY (18m   C   1974)
The subject of rape is explained from the viewpoint of the victim, the police, as well as convicted rapists. Police emphasize self-defense. To support this theory a karate class is visited (taught by a woman) and the students interviewed. JGMF; UC, UI, WAYSU.

RAPE CULTURE (35m   C   1975)
The film examines popular films, advertising, music, and adult entertainment, and records the insights of rapists, victims, rape crises workers, authors and prisoners. The film seeks to establish, with chilling results, the connections between sex and "normal" patterns of male-female behavior. Rape is skillfully and powerfully redefined for us. CDFI; UM.

RAPE, PT. I: PROBLEMS IN PROOF (30m   C   1975)
The alarming incidences of rape and disturbingly low rate of convictions have prompted this effort to identify the appropriate role of police officers in rape investigation. Explores the courtroom problems involved in proof of rape and how these problems relate to the initial police interview with the victim. Included are fundamental rules and requirements relating to the legal definition of rape and the problem of corroboration. AIMS; UILL, UM.

RAPE, PT. II: PROVIDING THE PROOF (30m   C   1975)
The alarming incidences of rape and the disturbingly low rate of convictions have prompted this effort to identify the appropriate

role of law enforcement officers in rape investigations.   Detailed
aspects of the legal problems are discussed including the law on
claim of possession, showups and in-the-field investigations, gathering evidence from vehicles, kidnapping, and new protections for the
victim.   AIMS; UILL, UM.

RAPE TAPE, THE (35m   n. d.   VIDEO)
     A compelling, intimate documentary about four women who share
their experiences with rape and its after shock.   The film explores
the attitudes of parents, police, courts and doctors, and examines
other factors involved, such as guilt, anger, fear, strength and sex.
A powerful jolt for anyone who doubts (or has forgotten) that the oppression of women is personal and immediate, and a new source
of support for women who have been raped whether or not they
shared their experience with other women before.   By Jenny Goldberg et al. ; GOLDBERG.

RAPE: THE RIGHT TO RESIST (16m   C   1975)
     Succinctly presents the positive options available to women who
are threatened by rape.   Shows how to face the problem, and the
strategies that can be employed in evading and escaping.   AIMS;
OSU, UMIS.

RAPE: THE SAVAGE CRIME (C   n. d.   SFS (2))
     Enlightens on where, when, and by whom women are likely to
be raped, and suggests precautions to be taken against rape.   AVNA.

RAPPORT; Vignettes Series (12m   C   1973)
     Presents three vignettes exploring the dynamics of the man-
woman relationship to encourage reflection on the deeper aspects of
contemporary marriage.   PAULST; MG.

RAT LIFE AND DIET IN NORTH AMERICA (16m   C   1968)
     An allegory of oppression and revolution.   Imprisoned by the
U. S. A.   cat police, the "rats, " led by their hero, Skag Mitchell,
break out of prison and escape to Canada, the land of the free,
where they lead suitably organic and bucolic lives under the shadow
of the final irony--that Canada, too, is under the control of the fat
cats they thought they outwitted.   By Joyce Wieland; FCOOP.

REAL WORLD, THE (SERIES)   see   JOBS IN THE CITY: WOMEN
AT WORK

REARING KIBBUTZ BABIES (29m   C   r1975)
     Observes infant rearing in an Israeli kibbutz, organized around
the weekday activities of a young mother and "metapelet" (care-
giver), who cares for four infants in the Baby House and takes
scheduled breaks to visit her own children in the nearby Children's
Houses.   CFDC; EMC.

REBECCA (115m   B   1940)
     Centers around the bride (Joan Fontaine) of Cornish landowner
Maxim de Winter (Laurence Olivier), whose previous wife, Rebecca,

died under mysterious circumstances. When the new Mrs. de Winter arrives at her husband's estate, she finds that the memory of
Rebecca still dominates the life of everyone at the mansion. She
fears that her husband and servants compare her unfavorably with
Rebecca, and is nearly driven to suicide by the governess who in-
sists that she will never be able to take Rebecca's place.   Based
on novel by Daphne du Maurier.   d. Alfred Hitchcock; s. w. Joan
Harrison; UAS; ABFI, BF, TWY.

RECAP AND SUMMARY; Human Sexuality Series (29m   C   1972
    VIDEO)
    Host Milton Diamond, Ph. D., a biologist at the University of
Hawaii reviews topics covered in the "Human Sexuality Series." He
talks about the importance of good communication in successful sexual relationships.   He concludes by discussing the general future of
sexual expressions and practices.   UHAWAII/KHETTV; PTL.

RECUERDO OF TWO SUNDAYS AND TWO ROADS THAT LEAD TO
    THE SEA (17m   B   1969)
    The story of a fishing village and the rituals surrounding a
death.   By Bisby M. Carballo; FCOOP.

RED DESERT (116m   C   1964   Italian/subtitled)
    The inspiration of this film is locale rather than a plot or char-
acter.   Giuliana (Monica Vitti) seems to have been stripped of purpose and emotions by a stark, dehumanized environment.   Antonioni
contrasts the pale muted colors of the landscapes with Giuliana's
brightly colored clothing to suggest the conflict between the woman
and her surroundings.   The incidents of the film further stress
Giuliana's difficult pursuit of a meaningful life.   When Giuliana's
son becomes temporarily paralyzed (psychosomatic ailment) she tells
him a story of a girl on a remote island who one day hears a beautiful distant singing.   The girl tries to discover where the voices
are coming from and eventually realizes it is "everywhere."   Shortly, thereafter, the child is able to walk again, and his mother
seems to be discovering new values in her environment.   d. Michelangelo Antonioni; p. Antonio Cervi; ABFL

RED DETACHMENT OF WOMEN, THE (110m   C   1971)
    A revolutionary dance drama from China dramatizes both the
political problem and the revolutionary spirit of the Chinese revolution.   Traditional ballet was inadequate, so in order to obtain a
dance style that would reflect the strength and the hope of the
Chinese workers, peasants, and soldiers, a new form of dance was
created.   The dancers are stylized romantic characters, but their
spirit and their development are derived from the reality of the
Chinese Revolution.   SFN.

RED-HEADED WOMAN (73m   B   1932)
    Jean Harlow plays a secretary whose goal is to snare a rich
man and pull herself up into a life of luxury.   Ms. Harlow's vulgar
and irrepressible vitality gives the film its force, as she consistent-
ly overcomes all obstacles in pursuit of her goal.   Her crime, if

it can properly be so called, rests in her refusal to repent her
misdeeds and even in defeat to rise again.   Based on novel by
Katherine Bush.   d. Jack Conway; s. w. Anita Loos; MGM; FI.

RED RUNS THE RIVER (90m   C   1963)
    Presents the story of the American Civil War, giving emphasis
to the Confederates.   Describes how men died in defense of what
they believed was true and right.   Shows how conviction and dedication change history.   p. /d. Katherine Stenholm; UF.

RED SKY AT MORNING (113m   V   1971)
    A timeless story about growing up during the war years.   Rich-
ard Thomas is the young son of a man who goes off to war and
moves his family away from the decadent city in favor of the wide
open spaces of New Mexico.   Here among the majority population of
Indians and Mexican Americans, the young son and the handful of
Anglos experience reverse racism.   d. James Goldstone; s. w. Marguerite Roberts; UNIVE; CINE, SWANK, TWY, UNIVE.

REEXAMINING SEX ROLES: EVOLUTION OR REVOLUTION? (C
    SFS (6)   n. d.)
    A non-judgmental and impartial look at the changing sex roles
which affect virtually every aspect of our culture ... marriage and
family living, economic opportunities, sex distinctions in schools,
church doctrine, media, federal and state laws, the constitution, and
even our language.   Teacher's guide included.   JACSTO; HAR.

REFLECTIONS (15m   C   1973)
    "Explores questions of personal identity, self-image, and fem-
inist consciousness.   The sound track, which includes selections
from Doris Lessing, Marlene Dixon, Marge Piercy, Gwendolyn
Brooks, Janis Joplin and Joni Mitchell, works in contrapuntal relationship with images of women as seen by artists through painting
and photography. "--Filmnotes, "Women in Media Festival, " Berkeley.
By Sandy Flitterman; FLITTERMAN.

REFLECTIONS (5m   C   1958)
    Nature is reflected in a quiet lagoon.   Coordinated with fascinat-
ing patterns of music by Ed Bland.   By Madeline Tourtelot; GP.

REFLECTIONS ON THE MOON (33m   B   1974)
    Shots of more than 200 stills of the moon's surface.   By Nancy
Graves, Linda Leeds; GRAVES.

REHEARSAL (27m   C   n. d.)
    Psychodrama is shown as an effective tool in group therapy and
rehabilitation.   Through role playing one can learn the importance
of facing up to social-emotional problems and stress, rather than
laying the blame elsewhere, getting tough, or getting out.   By Janet
McLachlan, Cliff de Young; MGH.

RELEASE (28m   C   1974)
    Tells the story of a woman who has spent four years in prison.

Getting out means searching for a job, and getting reacquainted with
her three children who had been left in foster homes. With the support from women in a halfway house, and love and understanding of
her family, she tries to find strength to stay off drugs and begin a
new life. ODEON.

REMARRIEDS; Woman Series (29m C 1974 VIDEO)
Dr. Hanna Kapit, who works with remarried couples, discusses
how people who want to remarry can prevent the problems that broke
up their first marriages. WNEDTV; PTL.

RENASCENT (14m C 1964)
Edna St. Vincent Millay's poem concerning a young girl's wish
to die. Gratitude for rebirth is portrayed through dance (Don Red-
lick) against a natural background with music excerpts from Partch's
Dance Percussions. By Madeline Tourtelot; GP.

REPLAY (8m C 1970)
Young people and their elders comment on current fads, dancing,
music, women's liberation, sex in movies and dress styles. Movie
and newsreel footage is shown to illustrate the validity of the claims
of those interviewed. Supports the existence of a generation link
instead of a generation gap. MGH; UK.

REPORT FROM CHINA (90m C 1970)
Portrays the apparent success of Mao Tse-Tung's cultural revolution in China. Explains Mao's philosophy and stresses the vast
economic development that has occurred as the result of educating
peasants and city workers to accept and participate in various degrees of industrialization. IWANMI; Toshie Tokieda; FIM.

REPORT FROM MEXICO CITY: INTERNATIONAL WOMEN'S YEAR
    CONFERENCE (30m C 1975 VIDEO)
Journalist Shana Alexander reports from the historic conference
in Mexico City that brought women from around the globe together
to discuss common problems. She presents an overview of the conference and issues, and interviews feminist authors Germaine Greer
and Betty Friedan; Senator Charles Percy (R-Il); Helvi Sipila, Secre-
tary-General for the Conference; Elizabeth Reid, Chief of the Australian delegation; Rita Hauser, United States alternate delegate;
and Millie Miller, United Kingdom delegate. KVIETV; PTL.

REQUIEM FOR A FAITH (28m C 1968)
Houston Smith tells of the paths that lead to enlightenment
according to Tibetan Buddhism and reveals the secret that is discovered. The film shows Tibetan monks and includes an interview
with Dalai Lama. By Elda Hartley, Huston Smith; HARTLEY.

REQUIEM FOR TINA SANCHEZ (23m C r1976)
Examines the social phenomena of teen-age girls running away
from small towns across the country to large cities. Arriving alone
and broke, they are easy prey for pimps who offer security and affection and introduce them to prostitution. Once "on the street, "

few girls are willing or able to do other types of work. Examines
dire consequences of being at the mercy of pimps and customers,
physical abuse and even, as in the case of Tina Sanchez, murder.
d. Patricia K. Lynch; p. WNBCTV; FI.

RESCUE FROM ISOLATION: THE ROLE OF A PSYCHOGERIATRIC
    DAY HOSPITAL (22m C 1973)
    Uses a series of interviews with old people to establish the need
for some sort of half-way house between total isolation and total in-
stitutionalization.   Points out that one answer to this need is a day
hospital, an out-patient facility connected with a geriatric day hospital.   Documents the activities of one such organization in the areas
of physiotherapy and psychiatry.   TRNSIT.

RESOLUTION OF MOSSIE WAX (89m C 1972 VIDEO)
    A drama illustrating the problems of the welfare system for the
elderly and one woman's struggle for a dignified old age.   Kate Harrington stars as "Mossie Wax, " a widow determined to survive
though faced with the indifference of public officials, with loneliness,
the problem of easy-loan artists and the prospect of increased dependence on the state.   WITFTV; PTL.

RESOLVED: MEDICINE NEEDS MORE WOMEN (18m C n. d.)
    Role of American women in medicine.   By AMA; NFC.

RESPECT 2 (9m C 1971)
    "Social commentary on marriage/divorce. "--Cinema Femina.
By Willette Coleman; COLEMAN.

REST OF YOUR LIFE, THE (28m C 1967)
    Identifies and examines some of the problems related to retire-
ment.   Raises pertinent questions and explains the need of planning
for retirement.   JOU; UMIS.

RETICULATIONS (3m B 1974)
    Film made without a camera.   Hand-produced cracks in a black
surface create an animated mass of web-like surfaces.   d. Patricia
Sloane; NLC.

RETURN (5m B n. d.)
    "Abstract mime on the psychological return of Black people to
themselves. "--Cinema Femina.   By Willette Coleman; COLEMAN.

RETURN, THE (30m C 1976)
    A well-woven Ambrose Bierce suspense trap, this "short story
film" takes place in Edwardian England around the turn of the century.   Rumors of the appearance of a murdered woman's ghost bring
Stephen Royds to a boarded-up country mansion one evening.   Armed
with a gun, he shuts himself in the wedding chamber and waits....
By Elizabeth McKay; PF.

REVOLUTIONISTS (107m B 1936 Russian/subtitled)
    Documentary which is the definitive history of revolutionary ac-
tivity in the Soviet Union before 1905.   d. Vera Stroyeva; ABFL

RHYTHMETIC (9m   C   1956)
A delightful experimental animation film utilizing numerals at play. Excellent both as an entertainment short and as an introduction to basic concepts of arithmetic. By Evelyn Lambert, Norman McLaren; NFBC; IFB; CFS, EMC.

RICHARD'S BATH (14m   B   si   n. d.)
Film depiction of a young man taking a bath. "Calm, sensuous, straightforward. "--Ken Jacobs. By Pearlyn Goodman; FCOOP.

RICHEST LAND, THE (23m   C   1974)
"The issues and people of the San Joaquin Valley, the richest farmland in the history of man [sic] and its implications for all Americans. "--M. S. Study guide available. By Maia Sortor, George Ballis; BALLIS, CCC.

RIGHT NOW, IT'S A LOVE TRIP (15m   C   n. d.   SLIDES w/record)
Focuses on needs and attitudes of young people, filmed at counseling service run by and for teen-agers. PP.

RIGHT TO CHOOSE (29m   C   n. d.)
Basically it is a story of three women faced with unwanted pregnancies. This framework leads into the discussion of medical, legal, social and ethical aspects of abortion. The best part is that the audience never finds out which choice the women make; that knowledge is not important. What is important is that they have the right to choose. p. Association for the Study of Abortion; ASFL

RIGHTS OF AGE, THE (28m   B   1967)
Protective services available for the aging are dramatized in an in-depth study of an elderly widow. The film shows how the co-ordinated efforts of professional personnel attempt to keep older people from accidents and injuries, and from losing touch with the world around them. Also shows them consulting on the best ways to help the widow without taking away her independence. Twenty or 30 older people are examined who are in need of physical, psychological, or legal assistance. d. Irving Jacoby for the Mental Health Film Board; AFP; IFB; UIO, UU.

RIPPLE OF TIME, A (24m   C   n. d.)
Interludes of conversation alternate with leisurely and active lovemaking between a couple, ages 50 and 63. "And the sex they perform is the most natural, loving, ebullient and truly mature activity of this nature I have ever, in many score sex films, witnessed. It is ... sensitive, beautifully photographed, graphic and funny. "--John L. Wasserman (San Francisco Chronicle). By Laird Sutton; MMRC.

RISE OF CATHERINE THE GREAT, THE   see   CATHERINE THE
    GREAT

RITUAL IN TRANSFIGURED TIME (15m   B   si   1946)
A poetic psychological study, achieved by acceleration and de-

celeration of time, relating of unrelated gestures, and repetition of complex patterns unrealizable in actuality.   A tragic picturization of the emotions linked to the intensity of a girl's frustrated search for companionship in the real and unreal world in which she lives.   By Maya Deren; GP.

RIVER CREATES AN INDUSTRY, A (15m   C   1959)
Illustrates the production of hydroelectric power on the Saquenay River in Quebec.   Shows the main steps in aluminum production from the mining of bauxite to the production of the metal, including research and development.   By Sally MacDonald; CRAF; ALCAN.

RIVER-GHOST-HUDSON RIVER DIARY: BOOK IV (9m   C   1973)
"Reflections on a haunted cove along the banks of the Hudson River."--S. D. H.   By Storm De Hirsch; FCOOP.

RIVER OF NO RETURN (90m   C   1954)
In the sprawling Northwest of the 1870's, a widower with his ten-year-old son and a dance hall singer (Marilyn Monroe) travel downriver on a raft, menaced by Indians, rapids, and a sneaky gambler.   d. Otto Preminger; FOX; FI.

RIVERBODY (6m   B   1970)
One figure softly dissolves into the next as Ms. Severson catches the entire staff, faculty and students of the Art Institute in San Francisco (87 in all) unclothed before her camera.   Surreal images seem to appear as bodies fade in, fade out and overlap each other.   By Anne Severson, Shelby Kennedy; CCC, SB.

RIVERS OF SAND (83m   C   1974)
Robert Gardner, producer of "Dead Birds," shows us another primitive people, "the Hamar," who manage to exist in a land that seems to grow only thorns.   Men of this tribe view women not as helpers, mothers or housemaids, but rather as slaves.   This film is an attempt to show the effect on mood and behavior of a life governed by sexual inequality.   p. Robert Gardner; PHOENIX; EMC, VFI.

ROAD, THE (28m   B   n. d.)
Documentary of the Frontier Nursing Service.   Tells the history and a great deal about its dedication.   Examined here is the day-by-day, endless round of work of a group of nurses in Appalachia as they perform duties far beyond those laid upon them at their graduation.   Through the difficult seasons they come by jeep and on foot to the mountains and valley cabins.   There they minister to the aged, infirm, the infant and the mother--to those who have no access to modern clinics or hospitals.   Founded in 1925 by Mary Breckinridge; VA; CAROUSEL.

ROAD TO A MOUSE (7m   C   1974)
On a rainy day, the filmmaker watches fire escapes reflected in a sheet of mylar blowing in the wind.   Computer-generated sound. d. Patricia Sloan; NLC.

ROAD TO INTERDEPENDENCE, THE (29m   C   1976)
Dramatically traces and recreates the history of U. S. foreign
relations from the end of World War II to the present.   p. Marilyn
Weiner, Hal Weiner; d. Harold M. Weiner; SSCOPE.

ROBERT FROST: A LOVER'S QUARREL WITH THE WORLD (47m
B   1963)
Cinéma-vérité film on Robert Frost communicating his thoughts
and philosophy of life through his poetry, and his ruminations while
puttering around his New England farm.   d. Shirley Clarke, Robert
Hughes; WGBHTV; BFA; TWY.

ROBERTA FLACK; Artists in America Series (30m   C   1971)
Portrait of Black singer and pianist, showing several numbers
from her varied repertoire of pop, blues, jazz, spiritual, rock and
folk music.   Includes performances at Newport Jazz Festival and
night clubs as well as sequences in which she discusses her personal life and career.   IU; EMC, PAS, UILL.

ROCK-A-BYE-BABY (30m   C   1971)
Examines some of the techniques psychologists use to weigh and
measure mothering practices around the world.   Reveals the critical
importance of touch and movements in the normal development of
children from birth to three years.   TL; EMC, UMIS, PAS, UC,
UW.

ROCKING ORANGE (4m   C   1973)
Dance with sculpture filmed in the Avery Court of the Wadsworth
Atheneum in Hartford.   By Doris Chase; PIC.

ROLE OF WOMEN IN AMERICAN SOCIETY SERIES   see   GIRLS AT
12; VIGNETTES

ROLL OVER (15m   C   1974)
Depicts women's roles, past, present and future, documenting
the changes from traditional to new ones.   By Marian Hunter;
HERSTORY.

ROMANCE, SEX AND MARRIAGE: "ALL THE GUYS EVER WANT
IS S. E. X. " (26m   C   1976)
Focus on groups and individuals from different environments;
describes their experiences and opinions about the meaning and value
of sexual relationships.   Topics include virginity, birth control,
physical appearance, emotional involvement, acceptance, sexual
abuse, masturbation, and self-confidence.   John Brown, a well-
known therapist and adolescent consultant, comments on some of the
thoughts and feelings revealed.   HL; DA.

ROMANS: LIFE, LAUGHTER, AND LAW, THE (27m   C   1971)
Reveals facets of the Romans' humanity by speaking through
their own writings.   Presents the Romans as patriotic, idealist,
irreverent, satirical, law-giving and human.   By Helen Jean Rogers,
John Secondari; LCA.

ROMANTIC ENGLISHWOMAN, THE (116m   C   1975   (Gr. Br.))
A witty drama of contemporary lives.   The love triangle between a wealthy British suburban couple and a visiting German
gigolo cuts across relationships and continents.   Based on a novel
by Thomas Wiseman.   d. Joseph Losey; New World; FL

ROMANTICISM--THE REVOLT OF THE SPIRIT; Western Civilization:
Majesty and Madness Series, The (27m   C   1971)
Presents the romantic movement as an era much like our own,
an era of spiraling technology and bewildering change.   Dramatizes
excerpts from the works of Hugo, Shelley, Byron, Emily Brontë
and others who spoke out for individuality, freedom, sentiment and
revolt.   By Helen Jean Rogers, John Secondari; LCA.

RONNIE (27m   B   1968)
The life of a young Indian told in his own words.   Ronnie's
journey from the government Indian reservation to the large "White
Man's City" is emphasized.   By Mary Van Stolk; FIM.

ROOKIE OF THE YEAR (47m   C   1973)
Story of Sharon, a female adolescent, who likes to play hardball
and plays it well.   As the result of her playing, she must cope with
the hostility of her brother, her girl friends, and the coaches of
rival teams.   She plays well, but pulls out of the final game to protect her coach from being forced out.   She is asked to rejoin the
team, hits a three-bagger, steals home, and wins the game.   Based
on the book Not Bad for a Girl by Isabella Taves; DWP; TL; UM.

ROOM TO LEARN (22m   C   1968)
"Filmed at a new Montessori School in Stamford, Connecticut,
this film is intended to increase awareness of the role of space and
environment in learning. "--J. C.   By Joyce Chopra; NYU.

ROOMMATES ON A RAINY DAY; Insight Series (27m   C   1973)
A young couple suddenly finds their relationship in crisis when
one of them voices the desire for total commitment.   A realistic
look at the questions and preconceived ideas that people face in
these days of disenchantment with the traditional concepts of marriage.   By Nan Martin, Jerry Houser; PAULST; MG.

ROOTS TO CHERISH (34m   C   1974)
For teachers of Native American students.   Cultural differences
which have a significant impact on school performance are identified, and more meaningful ways of teaching the students are explored.   By Marylin Miles, Don Mahler; NICEP.

ROSE ARGOFF; Bitter Vintage Series (9m   B   1973)
A look into the life of 75-year-old Rose Argoff, a strong willed,
proud resident of New York City, who emigrated from Russia when
she was a girl.   Living on Social Security and a union pension on
the Lower East Side, Rose has been victimized by addicts and is
afraid to go out on the street.   Still, her toughness shows through
when she says, "This city grew rich on my body ... I helped build
it!"   WNETTV; CAROUSEL; PAS, UM.

ROSE KENNEDY REMEMBERS--THE BEST OF TIMES ... THE
WORST OF TIMES (52m   C   1975)
Recorded and filmed interviews with Rose Kennedy are juxta-
posed with television film, newsreel, historic motion pictures, and
stills.   A sensitive film portrait of an extraordinary woman.   By
David Gerard, BBCTV; TL; UMIS.

ROSELAND (12m   C   1973)
This film forces the viewer to look at the body, at the material
nature of life.   About Rose Oliver, a frankly fat, white welfare
mother of four, living in the projects in Chicago.   Rose gives birth
to a child, talks squarely into the camera about her life and being
a mother without a man, makes herself attractive and prepares a
Thanksgiving meal.   Shows Rose and her family at this meal, spread
out before them, her children eating and watching her nurse, de-
terminedly pushing and heaving the wheel of life along.   By Royanne
Rosenberg; IE, SB, VQ.

ROSI (9m   C   1976)
A young woman speaks frankly about trying to integrate her public and private lives, giving most of her attention to satisfying her
creative and sexual needs.   Rosi works aboard a fishing trawler
which traditionally is off-limits to women, but it is apparent that
the catch is more important than the discrimination.   Alone in her
apartment, she expresses emotions of contentment, anger, and in-
trospection.   She speaks frankly and at length about her sexual
needs.   By Rachel Wohl; SB.

ROSIE THE RIVETER (75m   B   1941)
With the coming of war, Hollywood mobilized.   Among the rash
of propaganda movies and war films produced, were light farces,
encouraging the effort on the homefront, and somehow making it all
seem a bit more bearable.   d. Joseph Santley; REPUBLIC; IVY.

ROTATE THE BODY (14m   C   1962)
A gay and fantastic experimental film, with Harry Partch's music, of the seven events of competitive gymnastics.   Filmed at U.
of Illinois, Urbana.   By Madeline Tourtelot; GP.

ROUND FEELING, A (5m   C   1974)
A nostalgic trip to an old country fair.   Through the use of optical printing and color solarization, the photographs of the ferris
wheel, carousels and other old favorites become transformed into a
delightful kaleidoscope of color and pattern.   By Kathleen Laughlin;
ECCW.

ROYAL PROVINCE, THE (21m   C   1967)
Portrays the colorful early history of Nova Scotia from its
earliest colonizers in 1605 through the Struggle of Louisbourg to its
entrance into confederation.   Pictures the many races that settled
in Nova Scotia and the contributions they made through their varied
cultures and customs and social and political achievements.   By
Margaret Perry for NOSIS; CTFL.

RUBY GENTRY (82m B 1952)
Jennifer Jones plays the sultry swamp woman whose thwarted love for the scion of a decaying blueblood clan leads to tragedy. Ruby is a scheming, passionate, high voltage temptress, with a determination to seduce her way to the top of the social ladder. d. King Vidor; FOX; ABFL

RULES OF THE GAME (110m B 1939 French/subtitled)
A film made on the eve of World War II and pulled from release a few days after its showing. Thirty years were to pass before it would surface again. Renoir paints a picture of a social world where pleasure is the prize: where intrigue, guile, and the lack of honesty are part of the "rules" of a dying class. d. Jean Renoir; BF, JANUS.

RUNNER (11m C 1972)
Experimental film of a winter landscape shot in negative with an electronic sound track. By Marlys Skelton; SKELTON.

RUTH AND HARRIET: TWO WOMEN OF THE PEACE (27m C 1974)
Portrays the daily routines, strength, and closeness to nature of two women who live along the Peace River in Western Canada. Ruth, a 35-year-old widow and mother of seven children, is a welder in a small factory; Harriet, who is married to Ruth's brother, is the mother of four boys and lives and works on a farm she and her husband have homesteaded. Exemplifies the relative equality that was characteristic of pioneer women in the past century. d. Barbara Greene; NFBC; EMC.

RUTH ST. DENIS AND TED SHAWN (30m B 1958)
Interviews founders of the modern dance in America, in which they speak of their life and work during the past half century. Three dances which they created and which greatly influenced American choreography are shown. NFBC; FI; UILL, UM, UU.

RUTH SLEEPER STORY, THE (34m B 1968)
The story of the life and nursing career of Ruth Sleeper, former president of the National League for Nursing, and 20 years Director of Nursing Service and Nursing Education, Massachusetts General Hospital. KTCATV; PURDUE.

RUTH STOUT'S GARDEN (23m C 1976)
Born in Canada in 1884, Ruth Stout recalls incidents in her long life. She is still an active and an innovative gardener on a plot of land 45 x 50 feet. Mrs. Stout never weeds, never uses a hoe, plow, or fertilizer, or waters. She just plants and picks. Mrs. Stout at 16 smashed saloons with Cary Nation. In earlier days she liked to garden in the nude. She writes and lectures. IFF; AMP, CWU, EMC, SCC.

RUTHIE GORTON: SONGS OF STRUGGLE AND VICTORY (30m C
n. d. VIDEO)
Ruthie shares her songs of struggle and change with an enthusiastic audience. KQEDTV.

RX FOR MARYANNE (15m   C   1963)
Describes the prescription industry and its role in saving lives and relieving misery.   By Sally MacDonald, CRAF for PMA; MTP.

SABOTAGE (71m   B   1939)
This film deals with sabotage in an airplane factory, with the finger of suspicion pointing to the wrong man.   An old night watchman and his cronies finally crush the ring.   d. Harold Young; s. w. Alice Altschuler, Lionel Houser; REPUBLIC; IVY, WCF.

SABOTEUR (98m   B   1942)
When Robert Cummings learns the identity of saboteurs who blow up a California aircraft plant during World War II, he becomes a marked man.   The saboteurs want his head, and so do the police who mistakenly believe he is a murderer.   In true Hitchcockian style, Cummings takes to his heels in flight from the law and his foreign pursuers.   The final scene is atop the Statue of Liberty. d. Alfred Hitchcock; s. w. Joan Harrison; UNIVE; TWY, UNIVE.

SADLER'S WELLS BALLERINA (12m   C   1952)
Tells the story of a young ballet dancer about to make her debut with Sadler's Wells Ballet in London.   Pictures her strenuous life of study and rehearsal and her home life; then shows her debut in Ravel's "Beauty and the Beast" with the Sadler's Wells Ballet. IFF; UILL.

SAILBOAT (4m   B   1967)
"Sailboat has the simplicity of a child's drawing.   A toy-like image of sailboat sails, without interruption on the water, to the sound of roaring waves, which seems to underline the image to the point of exaggeration, somewhat in the way a child might draw a picture of water and write wordsounds on it to make it as emphatic as possible.   The little image is interrupted at one point by a huge shoulder appearing in the left-hand corner."--Robert Cowan, Take One Magazine.   By Joyce Wieland; FCOOP.

SAILOR DANCE (8m   B   1963)
"In the village of Tania on the Island of Crete, there is a tavern where Greek sailors from a nearby naval base come to dance."--S. R.   By Diane Rochlin, Sheldon Rochlin; FCOOP.

ST. LOUIS BLUES (17m   B   1928)
Documentary on Bessie Smith--singing the blues, chasing after a man who was using her for a fast buck; her knowing it, but not being able to stop herself.   By Dudley Murphy; MMA.

ST. THERESE OF LISIEUX--STORY OF THE LITTLE FLOWER
(90m   B   n. d.   French/subtitled)
Shows Therese Martin from the time she was born.   Shows her life at home with her father and sisters, at school, and as she enters the convent of the Carmelites.   Presents the contrasting story of her close friends.   CATHFC.

SALAMANDRE, LA (125m B 1971 French/subtitled)
A feckless girl (Bulle Ogier) who refuses to be locked into an ordinary life moves in and out of jobs, affairs and adventures with two over-serious writers. Like the salamander, she is not consumed by the fires of her experiences, but emerges still free and unscathed. d. Alain Tanner; NYF.

SALAMOU: YOUNG GIRL OF THE NIGER (20m C n. d.)
Describes the life a 17-year-old girl in a rural village in Nigeria. Salamou is a pottery-maker who must work long hours to help support her family during the severe drought which left the land barren, and threatened her people's existence. By Philippe Jamain; CAROUSEL.

SALESMAN (90m B 1969)
A comic and poignant documentary of four representatives of Mid-American Bible Company. By Charlotte Zwerin, David Maysles, Albert Maysles; MAYSLES.

SALOME (35m B si 1922)
"Exquisite camp treatment of biblical figure Salome, who asks for the head of John the Baptist on a platter. Costume and set designs are based on drawings by Aubrey Beardsley. "--ABFI With music sound track. p. Alla Nazimova; d. Charles Bryant; ABFI.

SALT OF THE EARTH (94m B 1954)
Socially conscious drama about the struggle of Mexican American zinc miners and their wives--the men for equality of working and living conditions with Anglo miners, the women for equality with men. It's the first major American film to deal honestly with the labor struggle and the first to present a minority with dignity and understanding. Made by blacklisted artists during the McCarthy era. d. Herbert J. Biberman, s. w. Michael Wilson, and composer Sol Kaplan; AMDOC; ABFI, EMC.

SALT OF THE EARTH (25m C 1973)
Members of the Charismatic Movement within the Catholic Church talk about the changes in their family life styles since joining the movement. The group is somewhat fundamentalist-oriented and places emphasis on the man as head of the house, instructor of the wife and children. Many viewers will see these changes as regressive rather than progressive, but the film is certain to stimulate a lively discussion of the various family and community roles. p. Bruce Baker; CHARISM.

SAM (20m B 1973)
Explores the themes of culture and class through the portrayal of a Japanese American, whose public persona--as the "Japanese gardener" in a white suburb of Los Angeles--contrasts with glimpses of the private man, his past and his family. Comments by several of Sam's clients reveal genuine affection; yet their understanding of Sam--the private man, not the gardener, is incomplete. By Margaret Bach; EMC.

SAMBIZANGA (102m   C   1972   Portuguese/subtitled)
Focuses on a young Black couple who bask in each other's presence until the husband, a tractor driver, is suddenly arrested as a political prisoner.   His wife, who knows nothing about his politics, walks with their baby on her back from village to village trying to locate him.   Angry and desperate at moments, stoical at others, she struggles through a world that rarely explains anything to women.   In the meantime, he is being tortured by his inquisitors in hopes he will reveal the names of others in the movement.   And even his death is a relief.   Both subtly and simply we are shown how bad things are, and how much better they could be.   The movie doesn't put forth heroes or villains, and it offers a class analysis rather than a racial one.   The emphasis is on the oppression of the poor by the rich--on the system that perpetuates a minority. Throughout, the plight of individuals helps to nail the political point. Based on the novel The True Life of Domingos Xavier by Luandino Vieira.   d. Sarah Maldorer; ISABELLE-FILMS, PARIS; NYF.

SAN JOSE WOMEN REPORT ON THE INTERNATIONAL WOMEN'S YEAR CONFERENCE (30m   C   n. d.   VIDEO)
Maria Monce and five of the over 500 women from San Jose who attended both the governmental conference and The Women's Tribune in Mexico City discuss the value of these events.   KQEDTV.

SAND (10m   B   1969)
An animated story of Peter and the Wolf in a precise study in silhouette, using the medium of sand.   By Caroline Leaf; PHOENIX.

SAND: THE DESERT IN MOTION (11m   C   1969)
Explains where sand comes from and how it affects the land. Elementary and junior high school level.   By Geraldine Byers, Justin Buyers; BFA.

SANDY AND MADELEINE'S FAMILY (30m   C   1974)
A filmed documentary of Sandra Schuster and Madeleine Isaacson who were sued by their husbands on July 18, 1972, in King County, Superior Court, Washington, for divorce and child custody.   In an unusual court decision, the judge granted custody to each of the mothers even though they admitted their homosexual relationship. However, he ordered them to establish separate households.   A number of experts are interviewed on the legal, social, and religious aspects of the custody case.   Psychiatric experts testify as to the current mental health of the six children.   Anthropologist Margaret Mead expresses her view that the welfare of the children will depend on the warmth and love of the family environment and not on sexual orientation.   Includes individual interviews with each of the children about their feelings about lesbianism, the family and their fathers.   By Constance Beeson; NSF; MMRC.

SAVAGE STREETS (28m   C   1973)
Intimate documentary of The Savage Skulls, a South Bronx gang, focusing on Luis Quiles, a murdered gang member.   Produced for the Community Affairs Unit of WNBCTV.   By Abigail Child; CHILD.

SAY HI!   A HOSPITAL BIRTH (25m C 1976)
A natural childbirth film combining documentary footage of a
normal vaginal labor and spontaneous delivery with an animated explanation of the mechanism of childbirth. d. P. Stern, A. Linden;
p. Dr. A. Barnes, P. Stern; LINDSTERN.

SCARLET EMPRESS, THE (109m B 1934)
Marlene Dietrich plays the life of Catherine the Great, who con-
verted political power into sexual capital and vice versa.   Sam Jaffe
gives a bizarre performance as the pop-eyed, moronic Grand Duke,
and the orgy and torture scenes smack of lunacy.   d. Joseph Sternberg; PARAMOUNT; CVE, TWY, UNIVE.

SCARLET LETTER, THE (78m B 1934)
Nathaniel Hawthorne's classic novel of the Puritan era comes
to life as a superb study of guilt and retribution.   This is the story
of Hester Pyrnne, who bore an illegitimate child by the minister of
the village.   Unwilling to reveal the child's father, she is made to
wear a letter "A"--for adultery--on her clothing.   The Scarlet Letter is a portrait of the Puritan period in America's first days.   d.
Robert Vignola; MAJESTIC; BF, CVE.

SCARLET LETTER, THE (79m B 1917)
(See above description.) d. Carl Harbaugh; FOX; FCE.

SCARLET LETTER, THE (86m B si 1926)
(See above description.) d. Victor Seastrom; MGM; FI.

SCARY TIME, A (20m B 1960)
This touching plea for the United Nations Children's Fund "begins as a Halloween celebration and continues to show these nightmares come true in the intercut scenes of children starving... "--
MOMA.   By Shirley Clarke; MOMA.

SCENES FROM A MARRIAGE (163m C 1974 Swedish/subtitled)
"One of the greatest films I've seen in my lifetime.   A masterpiece of intimacy, sensitivity, wisdom and intelligence.   Scenes from
a Marriage asks the question everyone has faced or refused to face:
is it better to hide away in a relationship because it is comfortable
and easy, or is it better to accept growth and change even though it
is painful. "--Rex Reed, New York Daily News.   With Liv Ullman,
Ingmar Bergman.   By Ingmar Bergman; CIV.

SCENES FROM B. ASAFYEV'S BALLET "THE FLAMES OF PARIS"
(22m B 1953)
Asafyev's ballet based on the 1789 revolution in France shows
the nature of life there when the "Marseillaise" was new.   Performers are members of the Bolshoi Ballet of Moscow and the Kirov
State Opera Theatre at Leningrad.   LSP; ABFI; UILL.

SCENES FROM THE BALLET "THE FOUNTAIN OF BAKHCHISARAI"
(27m B 1953)
Scenes from the exotic legend of Pushkin's poem furnish the

substance of this ballet, performed by Galina Ulanova, M. Plisetskaya, and the members of the State Bolshoi Theatre in Moscow.
LSP; ABFI; UILL.

SCHMEERGUNTZ (15m B 1966)
    Celebrated, pioneering women's film anticipating the feminist
movement of the 70's. Contrasts the romantic stereotyped "glamour
girl" ideal with the harsher, seamier aspects of women's commonplace role. A skillfully executed montage of rapid-fire images of
morning sickness, garbage, etc., intercut with the glamour sequences, insipid music, and commentary produces a powerfully sardonic effect. Some may find this film offensive, but many will find
it forthright and honest.   By Gunvor Nelson, Dorothy Wiley;
NELSNG; CCC, EMC, FCOOP, SB.

SCHOOL FOR WIVES (30m C 1974 VIDEO)
    Birgit Cullberg created this chromakey ballet interpretation of
Molière's classic comic-tragedy. His dance troupe "The Cullberg
Balleten" performs the story of an older man who raised a young
girl into womanhood with the idea of training her to be the perfect
wife. However, she falls in love with a man her age and the old
man is forced to accept this reality. WHATV; PTL.

SCRAPS (6m C 1973)
    An untouchable woman of India creates a colorful toy bird from
materials collected from the city streets. An artist and a member
of a community in which the women serve as scavengers, she proves
that a lively imagination may transcend the limitations of even a
destitute people. Accompanied by lyrical flute music.   By Yvonne
Hannemann; SB.

SCRATCH, THE (3m C 1971)
    Explains that there have been scratches on film as long as
there has been film, and yet no one has given the scratch anything
but grudging recognition. Shows that the scratch gets its due
recognition. By Jan Baross, KMLG; ABFI.

SCRATCH THE SOIL (20m C 1975)
    "The dawn of sexual awareness in a young, withdrawn adolescent
girl, whose personality is played off against that of her 35-year-old,
vivacious, kittenish mother ... questions the ability of a young girl
to resist cultural pressures to make her adopt the traditional feminine role."--L. T.   By Lois Tupper, Maureen McCue; WFC; IRISF.

SCREEN NEWS DIGEST SERIES see MS--THE STRUGGLE FOR
    WOMEN'S RIGHTS, (n. d.); MS--THE STRUGGLE FOR WOMEN'S
    RIGHTS, (1972)

SCULPTURE (3m C n. d.)
    Impressions in movement of an aluminum sculpture. By Emiko
Omori; CCC.

SCULPTURE FOR CHILDREN (4m C n. d.)
    "A New York City classroom of children ages 6 to 9 playing

and learning with Chase-designed set of 'Sculpture for Children. ' "--
D. C. By Doris Chase, Laurie Steig, Elizabeth Wood; CHASE.

SEARCH, THE (13m   C   n. d.)
A blending of poetry, sculpture, and music with the sounds and
beauty of a far north river bank in spring. . . . By Anne Curtis
Calagni; FIM.

SEARCH FOR ALTERNATE LIFE-STYLES AND PHILOSOPHIES, THE
(20m   C   1973)
Survey of contemporary efforts to find meaningful alternatives to
traditional religions, family life, etc. Visits a cooperative village
in the Sierras with life-style based on a yoga philosophy. Too many
subjects tackled on a short film. The result is somewhat superficial. Could be used as an introductory tool for a discussion. d.
J. Gary Mitchell, Ron Fisher; FFAIR.

SEARCHING EYE, THE (18m   C   1964)
Views the world under the sea, the world of post geological
formations, the inner world of microscopic creatures, the process
of growth and fruition, the world of outer space and the world of
imagination. By Elaine Bass, Saul Bass; PF.

SEARCHING EYE, THE (11m   C   1960)
Delicate colors weave patterns of light and shade over autumn
leaves, waves over sunlit rocks, grass shadow line patterns on sand:
nature themes as stimuli for ink drawings. By Madeline Tourtelot;
GP.

SEARCHING YEAR, THE (SERIES) see WAIT UNTIL YOUR FATH-
ER GETS HOME

SEASHELL AND THE CLERGYMAN, THE (38m   B   si   1928)
One of the classic examples of the Avant-garde Film Movement,
produced in 1928. While bearing many similarities in its use of
symbolism to Un Chien Andalou, this film marks the transition from
dada surrealism to Freudian surrealism, as it takes us into the
mind of a clergyman to explore, through his conscious vs. subconscious thoughts, his conflict between his normal impulses and the
religious vows which stifle him. By Germaine Dulac; ABFI, CFS,
MMA.

SECOND CHANCE: SEA (10m   C   1976)
An animated film (featuring Dizzy Gillespie) with the natural
sounds of whales and porpoises. Second Chance visualizes the state
of the oceans from the beginning of time to the present condition of
crises. No narration. Designed to evoke an optimistic attitude toward the "planet ocean. " d. Faith Hubley; HUBLEY; PF.

SECRET LIFE OF AN AMERICAN WIFE, THE (92m   C   1968)
Neglected suburban housewife doubts her desirability to her
press agent husband, so when he tells her he "arranges" for female
companionship (at $100 a call) for one of his clients, a well-known

movie star, she decides to become one of the girls to test her sex appeal. d. George Axelrod; FOX; FL

SECRET LOVE OF SANDRA BLAINE (28m B 1971)
Follows the step by step progression into alcoholism of a middle-aged woman. Shows how, in her unrecognized illness, she deceives her husband, her friends, her family, her physician, and herself. Examines extent of alcoholism among women, citing recent statistics indicating that half of nine million alcoholics in the U. S. are female. Considers alcoholism as a disease, and shows facilities and methods available for successful treatment of its victim. AIMS; BF, EMC, PAS, UM, UW, WSU.

SECRET SQUINT, THE (9m C 1964)
A young painter becomes very successful through the magic of the secret squint. "Mirthful little film."--F. L. By Sherry Zabriskie, George Zabriskie; FL

SEDUCED AND ABANDONED (118m B 1964 Italian/subtitled)
A comedy of honor. Seduced by her sister's fiancé, Agnes discovers that she is pregnant. In court, Peppino, the culprit, has two choices: marry Agnes or go to jail. About then, the girl's father has a heart attack which complicates matters further. According to a Sicilian custom, a daughter cannot marry if she is in mourning. Agnes is now mourning for her honor as well as for her father. d. Pietro Germi; MGH; BF.

SEDUCTION OF MIMI, THE (92m C 1972)
A political comedy played by Giancarlo Gianini as Mimi who gets into incredible predicaments in reacting to forces he doesn't understand. Mimi is lead by his friends to vote Communist, for which the Mafia runs him out of town. Having abandoned his wife, he soon marries Mariangela Melato and has a child. He is then forced to return with his new family to his old home where he must lead a double life to keep his two wives separate. His first wife becomes pregnant by another man which drives him into a rage. To redeem his "manhood" and to demonstrate his prowess he seduces the wife of his wife's lover. This tangle of honor finally results in Mimi's being forced to take responsibility for two large families, losing the wife he truly loved and being once again under the thumb of the Mafia. d. Lina Wertmuller; NLC.

SEED REEL (4m B 1975)
A three-part animated fantasy of sensuality in which female and male genitalia have a life of their own and like nothing better than dancing to the tune of "Turkey in the Straw" or engaging in a friendly, graceful minuet. By Mary Beams; SB.

SEEDS OF TOMORROW (27m B n. d.)
Traces the development of the Friend's Center in Dacca, East Pakistan. Shows the process by which neighborhood groups gradually took over responsibility for various center activities. Used by Peace Corp to inform trainees going to underdeveloped countries. By Edith Worth, Robert Worth; AMFSC; FCOOP.

SEEING THROUGH COMMERCIALS (15m   C   1976)
Designed to alert children to the techniques and motivations behind TV commercials aimed at them.   Typical commercials for toys,
candies, and sugar cereals are shown.   Viewers are led through a
point-by-point analysis of the techniques used to make products look
bigger, better, and more fun.   p. /d. Ruth Arens, Larry Stein;
VISIONF.

SELF BREAST EXAMINATION (30m   C   n. d.   VIDEO)
Explicit instructions for women about how to do breast examinations and how to recognize the signs of breast cancer are presented
through discussion and demonstrations.   KQEDTV.

SELF-DEFENSE FOR GIRLS (16m   C   1969)
Bruce Tegner and Alice McGrath demonstrate methods that enable girls to get out of dangerous situations with the least violence
to the attacker and with safety to themselves.   A training film for
building self-confidence in women through teaching self-defense.
BFA; PAS, UC, UK, UILL.

SELF-DEFENSE FOR WOMEN (25m   C   n. d.)
Stresses the importance of women's needs for instruction in
methods of self-defense against hold-up, mugging and rape.   Explains and demonstrates effective defense techniques.   STLCPD.

SELF-HEALTH (23m   C   1974)
Made with the help of San Francisco's Women's Health Center,
the film provides clear instruction in methods of breast and vaginal
self-examination for the purpose of self-discovery and preventative
medical care.   Presented in a warm and caring manner, Self-Health
is based on the concern that no meaningful understanding of self or
sexuality is possible without women having an understanding and acceptance of their own bodies.   By Allie Light, Judy Irola, Joan Musante dba Lighthouse Films.   MMRC; SB.

SELF IDENTITY/SEX ROLES: I ONLY WANT YOU TO BE HAPPY
(16m   C   1975)
The story: Helen is an ambitious college graduate who is
about to enter medical school.   Her sister, Dru, has decided to
remain in their hometown, work in a nursery, and probably marry
the boy next door.   Their mother is a traditional, contented housewife in her mid-forties.   The interaction among these women and
their conflicting points of view about "the female role" creates a
tension as revealing as it is educational.   By Steve Katten; CRM,
MGH.

SELF-PORTRAIT (5m   C   1973)
Using her own drawings, realistic, surrealistic or abstract,
Maria has drawn the moods, fears, thoughts and parts of a life
story.   The self-portrait was done before a mirror.   The film conveys a sense of life, a touching and witty portrait of a woman
whose self-image changes as she herself does.   By Marie Lassnig;
FCOOP.

SELF-PORTRAIT (3m   C   si   n. d.)
"Cyclical self-portrait in which the viewer feels herself to be
inside the lens.   Extremely intense and somewhat sexual, this film
makes audiences uncomfortable. "--CENTER.   By Barbara Scharres;
CENTER.

SEMPRE LIBRA (16m   C   n. d.)
"Misadventures of an astrological Everyman. "--FCOOP.   By
Myrna Changar; FCOOP.

SENSE OF POETRY SERIES   see   POEM AS A PERSONAL STATE-
MENT: TO A VERY OLD WOMAN, THE

SEPARATION/DIVORCE: "IT HAS NOTHING TO DO WITH YOU"
(14m   C   1974)
The story: Larry has just returned home from an overnight
stay at a friend's home.   He finds that his parents have argued
furiously at a party the night before and are continuing their quarrel.   The issues: The film encourages discussion of the changing
role of the family in today's society and explains some of the underlying issues common to most divorces.   It centers on the dilemma
posed upon children of separating parents.   p. Steve Katten; CRM,
MGH.

SEPTEMBER EXPRESS (6m   C   si   1973)
"Layers of visual movement and stationary objects entwine with
memory--trace to structure the shape of motion in time. "--S. D. H.
By Storm De Hirsch; FCOOP.

SERAPHIC DIALOGUE BY MARTHA GRAHAM (27m   C   1969)
A dance drama about Joan of Arc, who, at the moment of her
exaltation, seeks to understand her life and fate, and sees herself
as a maiden, a warrior, and a martyr.   In this film, through the
fusion of dance-action with scenery, properties, modern costumes
and music, Miss Graham creates her own kind of dance, and also
succeeds in achieving her own ideal of total theatre.   By H. R.
Poindexter; PF; UILL.

SERENDIPITY SERIES   see   SPEAK UP; WORLDLY WISE; WRITE
ON

SESAME STREET FILMS (7m   C   n. d.)
Five animated short films from "Sesame Street. "   By Dorothy
Todd; CTW.

SETS, CROWS AND INFINITY (12m   C   n. d.)
Shows mathematical concepts of sets and infinity.   By Katherine
Cornwell, Bruce Cornwell; BFA.

7-1/2 MINUTE FILM, A (7-1/2m   C   1974)
". . . a story of paralysis and waste set in the town of Colfax,
Louisiana.   It is a beautifully shot film of a contemporary Southern
belle packing and leaving home to wait for a man at a bus stop--the

man who never comes. The film is made to the music and lyrics of 'Delta Dawn, ' sung by Jackie De Shannon. "--Siew-Hwa-Beh, Women and Film. By Nedra Deen; SB.

SEVEN BEAUTIES (116m   C   1975   Italian/subtitled)
Seven Beauties is a story of a man in Italy in the 1930's with seven sisters. To protect the honor of one of them, he kills a man. There follows a series of events throughout which the theme is survival, both psychological and physical. He goes to prison, then to a mental hospital, then to war in Mussolini's army, and finally to a concentration camp in Germany.   d. Lina Wertmuller; CIV.

SEVEN LITTLE DUCKS (11m   C   1967   (rev.))
Portrays the life habits of domesticated muscovy ducks. Shows a child can care for pets by feeding, watering and sheltering them. By Marian Evans; BFA.

SEVEN WOMEN (93m   C   1966)
During the turbulent 1930's in China, an isolated missionary post is headed by a straitlaced spinster, eagerly awaiting the new resident doctor.   The staff is shocked when the doctor turns out to be breezy, profane, drinking, chain-smoking Bancroft dressed in riding breeches.   d. John Ford; MGM; FL

SEVENTEEN FOREVER; Insight Series (27m   C   1973)
A revealing look at three people and how they have handled the inevitability of growing older.   Viewers will be shocked to recognize their own prejudices and defenses against growing older.   PAULST; MG; UILL.

SEVENTH YEAR, THE (82m   C   1969   German/subtitled)
There are too few contemporary films in which a woman and her problems occupy a central and pivotal position.   This film is such a film--one week in the seventh year of a marriage between a woman heart surgeon and a successful actor.   Original title: Das Siebento Jahr.   d. Frank Vogel; ABFL

SEWING SKILLS--TAILORING (SERIES) (37/29m ea.   C   1970 VIDEO)
Hostess Ruth Hickman gives lessons in sewing skills.   Write to PTL for individual program topics.   KRMATV; PTL.

SEX AND ETHICS; Human Sexuality Series (29m   C   1972   VIDEO)
A round table conversation with an attorney, a rabbi, a Roman Catholic priest, and a professor of comparative religion concentrates on issues of ethics, morality and sex.   The group discusses cultural values, eccentric sexual practices, adultery, consent, and the distinction between law and ethics.   UHAWAII/KHETTV; PTL.

SEX AND THE LAW; Human Sexuality Series (28m   C   1972   VIDEO)
"Man-on-the-street" interviews illustrate pro and con views on matters of law related to sex.   People are asked to speak about age and consent, prostitution, sex discrimination, pornography and cen-

sorship.   Differences between family law and criminal law are
pointed out by host Milton Diamond, Ph. D.   UHAWAII/KHETTV;
PTL.

SEX AND THE PROFESSIONAL (25m   C   1975)
It is of special importance that men and women in the health
and human service fields understand the diverse sexual needs of patients and clients.   To do so, they must accept their own sexual
feelings and impulses.   The film provides a context for discussion
of the health professional's problem of communication in sexual
counseling.   The film is specifically geared toward health educators
and medical and paramedical professionals.   TEXFM; UIO, UW.

SEX AND VIOLENCE (27m   C   1975)
The Feminist Alliance Against Rape and Women Organized
Against Rape are two national organizations defending women against
out-dated and unjust laws.   Members of these two organizations talk
about the work they do.   An attorney speaks about attitudes of people when a woman reports rape.   Women who have been raped speak
of their experiences.   Rapists serving time speak candidly of their
reasons for their attacks on women.   GRATV; BM.

SEX BIAS IN EDUCATION, PT. I; Woman Series (29m   C   1974
VIDEO)
Judy Wenning, feminist psychotherapist and former president of
New York NOW, and Phyllis Alroy, member of Women on Words
and Images, an organization formed to analyze children's school
readers, discuss their concern about the sex role bias in education.
WNEDTV; PTL.

SEX BIAS IN EDUCATION, PT. II; Woman Series (29m   C   1974
VIDEO)
Two mothers actively working in their own school districts continue the probe into sex bias in schools with a discussion of the
challenge of ridding a school system of sexist textbooks, curriculum
and teaching practices.   WNEDTV; PTL.

SEX DIFFERENCES IN CHILDREN'S PLAY (27m   B   1974)
Preschool and primary school children show sex differences in
play behavior.   Shows size of play groups, rank, style of play, and
precourtship behavior during group sessions on the playground.
UCHI; PAS.

SEX EDUCATION; Human Sexuality Series (29m   C   1972   VIDEO)
Examples of informal and formal sex education are given by
host Milton Diamond, Ph. D.   Parents express their concerns about
sex education for children and a group of senior citizens add their
comments.   UHAWAII/KHETTV; PTL.

SEX EDUCATION: ORGANIZING FOR COMMUNITY ACTION (23m
C   1968)
Frances Breed and Frederick J. Margolis present key factors
in the strong program of community action for sex education.   They

discuss the concept of sexuality and what it means in terms of sex education, how to establish a community council for sex education, and essential steps in an action program.   FLEMRP; MARGOL; WAYSU.

SEX IN TODAY'S WORLD (52m B 1968)
Presents an examination of social forces in the U.S. which have changed public treatment of sex, and the resultant repercussions in private lives.   Features a college girls' talk session at the University of Michigan, a Playboy Club, a rock and roll night club, a sex education class in Flint, Michigan and interviews with clergymen, psychologists and educators.   GITLNI; FOCUSE.

SEX IS A BEAUTIFUL THING (27m C 1970)
A documentary filmed in the Berkeley-San Francisco area. Presents two engaged couples on the campus giving an intimate, behind-the-scenes look at their lives as they confront the problems of sexual morality.   Discusses the new morality, sexual freedom and permissiveness.   FAMF.

SEX ROLE DEVELOPMENT; Developmental Psychology Today, The
(Series) (23m C 1974)
Examines some specific sex role stereotypes, tracing their transmission to children via the socialization process.   Alternate approaches, which allow pre-schoolers to grow up outside of traditional stereotypes, are also explored.   By Barbara Jampel; CRM, MGH; CWU, IU, MSU, OSU, UIO, UK, UILL, WAYSU.

SEX ROLE STEREOTYPING IN SCHOOL SERIES see ANYTHING
THEY WANT TO BE; CHANGING IMAGES: CONFRONTING
CAREER STEREOTYPES; HEY! WHAT ABOUT US?; I IS FOR
IMPORTANT; WOMEN EMERGING: COMPARING CULTURAL
EXPECTATIONS.

SEX-STEREOTYPING IN THE SCHOOLS (18m C n.d. SLIDE/
TAPE)
Written by two high school girls, this presentation covers sex-stereotyping in kindergarten toys, early texts, industrial arts classes, career counseling, sports, etc.   UEUWIS.

SEX SYMBOLS OF HOLLYWOOD, PT. I (22m B n.d.)
Description of the rise of sex in films through the 1930's.   The "glamour girls" are portrayed through their actual film roles. WAYSU.

SEX SYMBOLS OF HOLLYWOOD, PT. II (25m B n.d.)
Description of the rise of sex in films from the 1940's to the 1960's.   WAYSU.

SEXES, THE (17m C 1975)
Dr. William Masters and Virginia Johnson explain categories of sexual malfunction, and something of sex as a branch of medicine. Shows a homosexual marriage ceremony and gives statistics reflect-

ing society's attitudes. Discusses trial marriage as advocated by
Margaret Mead. HL; DA; UILL.

SEXES: BREAKING THE BARRIER, THE; Towards the Year 2000
Series (22m C 1971)
Surveys recent attempts to study and solve sexual problems.
Dr. William Masters and Virginia Johnson discuss their research
and treatment programs, and express hope that more freedom of
sexual expression will result from their work. Includes a nude encounter and therapy group in which participants discuss their sexual
and emotional problems. A group of New York college students talk
about their attitudes toward sex, marriage, and monogamy. Includes scenes of a homosexual wedding of two men, and a brief description of gay liberation movement activities. DA; EMC.

SEXISM IN RELIGION--ANOTHER VIEW; Woman Series (29m C
1974 VIDEO)
Rabbi Robert Alper of Temple Beth Zion, Buffalo, and Dr. William Marra, professor of philosophy at Fordham University, discuss
recent charges of sex bias in religious organizations. WNEDTV;
PTL.

SEXUAL COMMERCE; Human Sexuality Series (29m C 1972
VIDEO)
Commercial sex items are shown and explained by the host
Milton Diamond, Ph. D. Commercial aspects of sex are discussed
by a prostitute, an advertising executive, a massage parlor owner,
and others who use sex as a sales approach or a product. UHAWAII/
KHETTV; PTL.

SEXUAL DEVELOPMENT; Human Sexuality Series (29m C 1972
VIDEO)
Theories of sexual development (Freudian, role-modeling, social
learning, cognitive and interactional) are presented. Detailed ana-
tomical drawings are used to illustrate prenatal physiological events
which affect sexual development. Questions regarding homosexuality
and heterosexuality are raised. UHAWAII/KHETTV; PTL.

SEXUAL FRINGES; Human Sexuality Series (28m C 1972 VIDEO)
Aspects of human sexuality not often discussed are considered.
Topics covered include sexual abstention (discussed by several
prisoners and a Hare Krishna devotee), nudism (discussed by the
director of a nudist colony), and inter-sexuality and hermaphroditism
(explained through descriptions of clinical cases). UHAWAII/
KHETTV; PTL.

SEXUAL IDENTITIES: A BIO-HISTORICAL APPROACH (SERIES)
(5 Sets C n. d. SLIDE/TAPE (110) w/manual)
Beginning with early civilizations, this program probes the
many aspects of sexual identities. Viewers will question their feelings, thoughts and culturally accepted prejudices as they learn how
the thinking of the past has influenced their own point of view. For
individual program descriptions, see the next five titles. HAR.

PART I: BIOLOGICAL BEGINNINGS AND ANTHROPOLOGICAL
PERSPECTIVES. Focusing on the issue of sexual identity, this program looks at the traits which are absolutely determined genetically
and those which are conditioned by the pressures of our culture and
our own needs.
PART II: A HISTORICAL OVERVIEW. Explores the dynamics
of history and sexual identities by focusing on such questions as:
Where does the history of our identities begin? Are there exceptions to the male dominant, female submissive mode? How were
roles defined throughout the major eras in history? Where did feminism begin? Is stable identity possible in our swiftly changing
world?
PART III: RELIGIOUS ASPECTS. An in-depth discussion of the
multi-faceted religious aspects of sexual identities. Is God male?
How did the symbols of sexuality and fertility change? Why were
nuns able to wield immense power during the Middle Ages? How
did religious views of sexual identities develop? What transitions
are taking place today?
PART IV: MYTHS AND ARCHETYPES. Focuses on such questions as what are the basic sexual archetypes in mythology and literature and how have they changed through the ages? How did the
advent of the novel influence sexual archetypes? How has film
changed myth-making? Does television perpetuate myths?
PART V: SOCIOCULTURAL FACTS AND TRENDS. Examines,
in detail, such thought provoking questions as: Why the present
women's rights movement? Are significant changes in the ways men
and women relate to each other socially, professionally and sexually
possible ... and at what costs? What effect will the large growth
in world population play in our roles and sexual identities? How
will the sexes respond to each other when life can be reproduced
outside the uterus?

SEXUAL SUICIDE; Woman Series (29m   C   1975   VIDEO)
George Gilder, who has aroused the wrath of feminists with his
books, Sexual Suicide and Naked Nomads--in which he maintains that
marriage and family are society's most indispensable institutions--
discusses single men and women and freedom, independence, and
sexual diversity. WNEDTV; PTL.

SEXUALITY AND CRIME; Criminal Man Series (30m   B   1957)
Explains three categories of sex crimes: offense motivated by
sexual desire, profit from sex, and sex deviation. Contrasts American and British attitudes towards this problem. IU; EMC.

SEXUALITY AND THE TEEN-AGER, PT. I (28m   C   1968)
Uses a combination of vignettes, classroom sequences, and a
round-table discussion to consider individual differences in the maturing process. Discusses the differences in male and female responses,
the need for open communication between parents and children, and
the need to love and be loved. FLEMRP; MARGOL; PERENNIAL,
WAYSU.

SEXUALITY AND THE TEEN-AGER, PT. II (22m   C   1968)
Two high school students describe such common concerns of the

teen period as the physical changes that take place, the sexual feelings that develop, the influence of the peer group and the pressures
exerted by the family.   FLEMRP; MARGOL; PERENNIAL, WAYSU.

SEXUALITY AND THE TEEN-AGER, PT. III (19m C 1968)
    A round-table discussion group considers the need all young per-
sons have for successful social relationships.   Explains the difference between infatuation and mature love.   FLEMRP; MARGOL;
PERENNIAL, WAYSU.

SEXUALITY: THE HUMAN HERITAGE; Thin Edge, The (Series)
(59m C 1975)
    Traces the development of human sexual identity from the in-
fluence of prenatal sex hormones in the uterus to the external influence of family and society which help to shape perceptions of
what is feminine and what is masculine.   Professor Jerome Kagan
discusses how these sexual identities develop from children through
their teen years.   Homosexuals explain how they view themselves
in relation to the standards of society.   Explores man/woman role
in marriage, menopause, sex, and old age.   NET, IU; EMC.

SEXUALLY MATURE ADULT, THE (16m C 1973)
    Covers the physiology and emotions involved in mature sexual
behavior during the four stages of sexual response in intercourse.
The film uses live photography to show responses of individual
couples in each stage of lovemaking.   Animated diagrams illustrate
internal response.   This material is explicit and should be pre-
viewed before showing to a group.   WILEY; SCC.

SHADOW OF A DOUBT (108m B 1943)
    "Vintage Hitchcock" describes this thriller about the dashing man-
about-town (Joseph Cotton) who comes to visit his normal, middle
class, small town American relatives.   All is well until his niece
(Teresa Wright) begins to suspect her uncle is a psychopathic murderer underneath his veneer of charm and confidence.   Teresa is
torn between affection for her uncle and fear for her life at his
hands.   d. Alfred Hitchcock; s.w. Alma Reville; UNIVE; TWY,
UNIVE.

SHADOW OVER ITALY (30m C n.d.)
    Projects the contemporary religious situation in Italy against the
background of natural beauty, ancient history and Renaissance culture.   Describes the rise of communism and the rebellion against
ecclesiastical pressure.   Narrated by Dr. Bob Jones, Jr.   p. /d.
Katherine Stenholm; UF.

SHAKERS, THE (9m B 1967)
    The Ohio State University Dance Company performs a Doris
Humphrey dance based upon the Shaker religious ceremony.   This
sect, which flourished in the U.S. in the 19th century, believed they
could shake away their sins in the fervor of dance and song.   OHSU;
UILL, WAYSU.

SHAKESPEARE--A MIRROR TO MAN; Western Civilization: Majesty
and Madness Series, The (26m C 1971)
   Presents scenes from Taming of the Shrew, Othello, and Macbeth, in an attempt to reveal the universality of England's greatest
playwright, Shakespeare. Provides background on Elizabethan Theatre and introduces each scene with appropriate background information. By Helen Jean Rogers, John Secondari; LCA.

SHAMAN, A TAPESTRY FOR SORCERERS (12m C 1967)
   "Dedicated to all the magic makers of the world who weave a
talisman for man's rebirth in his house of breath."--S. D. H.   By
Storm De Hirsch; FCOOP.

SHAMELESS OLD LADY, THE (95m B 1966 French/subtitled)
   After 60 years of servitude as dutiful daughter, wife, and mother, a 70-year-old woman cuts loose--to the consternation of her
stuffy children. Madame Bertini becomes a veritable whirlwind of
activity in the final 18 months of her life. She rides around town
in a hansom cab; consorts with questionable people; drives her new
car at breakneck speed and helps put a Communist cobbler in business.   Based on a story by Bertolt Brecht. d. Rene Allio; KP,
MGH, TWY, WRS.

SHARED BEGINNING, A (25m C 1971)
   A young couple shares together every phase of the birth of
their baby. Scenes from preparatory breathing technique and training classes are interspersed with the filmed record of the labor
period and the birth itself, with post-natal discussions in which the
parents evaluate the experience. PERENNIAL; UILL.

SHAW AND WOMEN (46m B 1969)
   Examines Irish playwright George Bernard Shaw's relationship
with ten women and their influences on his life and works. Shows
how many of the women Shaw became acquainted with became characters in his plays. Dramatizes scenes from Candida, Man and
Superman, and Pygmalion to illustrate his constant theme of the
male's attempting to escape a pursuing female and the rejection of
romantic love. BBCTV; TL; BF, IU.

SHE DONE HIM WRONG (68m B 1933)
   This film based on Mae West's "Diamond Lil" has her singing
and holding court in a Bowery saloon. Next door is the Salvation
Army with Cary Grant in command. He's collecting souls and she's
collecting diamonds. The two meet and comedic lightening strikes.
d. Lowell Sherman; s. w. Mae West; PARAMOUNT, rel. by UNIVE;
MMA, TWY, UNIVE.

SHE SHALL BE CALLED WOMAN (14m B 1954 English narration
   (Belgium))
   "A muted, fluent depiction of woman's place in primitive society
through selected Belgian Congo sculpture."--Howard Thompson, New
York Times. p. /d. Gerard DeBoe; s. w. Emile Degelin. ABFL

SHE WAS A VISITOR (2m   C   n. d.)
"A lightime journey across the bridge of the midnight color..."
--CCC.   By Donna Deitch; CCC, FCOOP.

SHEILA LEVINE IS DEAD AND LIVING IN NEW YORK (112m   C
1975)
Sheila's goal in life is to get a man, not to satisfy herself but
her mother.   While Portnoy projected his guilt outward onto his
mother, Sheila, in true feminine fashion, introverts hers in an endless, comically coruscating litany of self-deprecation.   Acerbetically
witty and realistically contemporary.   Based on novel by Gail Parent.   d. Sidney F. Furie; PARAMOUNT; FL

SHELL BUILDER, THE (1977)
The concrete shell buildings of Mexican designer-architect, Felix Candela.   By Madeline Tourtelot; GP.

SHELTER (23m   B   1973)
An inside look at a woman's overnight shelter and the women--
mostly Indian and Metis--who live and work there.   Poorly edited.
FWAL.

SHE'S BEAUTIFUL WHEN SHE'S ANGRY (17m   B   1969)
A filmed skit, presented at an outdoor abortion rally, in which
a beauty contestant is primed by her mother, her teacher, her boyfriend, and a capitalist for the roles she must play to be a successful "sinner. "   SFN, TWN.

SHOOTING STAR (5m   C   1970)
"Shooting Star is about love, about men, and, in particular,
about the mysterious capacity which lets us treasure and respect
our lovers, knowing all the while that they're flawed, foolish, even
a little ridiculous.   A kind of sweet irony runs throughout the film,
underscored by Bonnie Bramlett singing in the background, 'tough as
nails, for a man to hold my trembling hand. ' "--Francine Prose,
Canyon Cinema News; by Freude Bartlett; SB.

SHOP STEWARDS (30m   C   n. d.)
"If you would treat a man a little better, you wouldn't have to
give him better machines. "--M. S.   By Martha Stuart, David Ruskin;
IMPF.

SHOPPING BAG LADY, THE (21m   C   1975)
Emily and her friends are teen-agers who have a great deal of
vitality and not much patience with anything beyond their sphere of
interest.   Among those things is a disregard for old people.   The
story is an encounter between Emily, her friends and one elderly
and lonely woman.   Raises awareness that one day we will be
middle-aged and old.   SALZB; LCA; IU, UILL, UMIS, UU.

SHORES (14m   C   n. d.)
"Poetic documentary about the West Coast artist, Ken Shores,

and his new work in clay and feathers. "--M. G.   By Mollie Gregory;
SB.

SHORT AND SUITE (5m   C   r1960)
A color cocktail translates into moving patterns of color and
lights the moods of music written for jazz ensemble by Eldon Rath-
burn. Inscribed and colored on film.   By Evelyn Lambart, Norman
McLaren; NFBC; IFB; BU.

SHORT STORY SHOWCASE SERIES see LOTTERY, THE

SHOUT IT OUT ALPHABET, THE (12m   C   1969)
Film game in which children try to see as many letters as
possible in the animated collage.   By Lynn Smith; PHOENIX.

SHRIKE, THE (88m   B   1955)
Under observation resulting from mental depression, a Broadway
director unfolds a tale of escape from his estranged wife who has
robbed him of his individuality.   d. Jose Ferrer; UNIVE; CVE,
UNIVE.

SHULIE (29m   C   1967)
Women's Liberation spokeswoman and author of The Dialectics
of Sex, Shulamith Firestone, is the subject of an intimate study,
made while she was a student at the Art Institute in Chicago.   Her
individualistic attitudes and extraordinary articulateness about her
own independent life become a fascinating account of what preceded
her current involvement.   NWUFL; VFL

SHUNKA'S STORY (20m   C   1977)
Sensitive and intimate portrait of a Tzotzil Maya woman of Zin-
acantan, in Chiapas, Mexico, conveying her thoughts and feelings
about her life, her culture, and her children, living and dead.
Quietly observed, full of everyday detail, and built around a story
line concerning the death of one of her children--a girl named Petu
--the film records with almost painful awareness the daily tribulations faced by many women such as Shunka.   The narration consists of the voice-over comments (in English) of Shunka herself.
EMC.

SHUSHA (27m   C   1973)
Persian folk singer Shusha Guppy sings the songs of her native
land, against the backdrop of the Zagros Mountains in Southern Iran.
Her emotional and spiritual commitment to her homeland and her
people is evident in her songs, with the camera providing its own
commentary.   By Anthony Howarth, David Koff; FL

SI SE PUEDE (IT CAN BE DONE) (40m   B   n. d.)
How does an individual artist work collectively with other artists in creating works useful to people struggling for control of their
lives?   The women of the Graphics Collective have worked through
this question many times, and show that process as they make a
poster for the United Farmworkers Union.   By Shirley Blumenthal,
Barbara Bejna; CWGC; IE.

SIDEWALKS (7m   B   si   1966)
"Looking down instead of around while walking, finding the magic patterns in pavements of a city. "--John Hawkins, photographer.   By Marie Menken; FCOOP.

SIGABOY (52m   C   1971)
Presents a study of a small village on the island of Mindanao and its people, who are caught in a social, cultural and political revolution.   By Pat Powell; MARYFA; WORLDH.

SIGHTS AND SOUNDS OF THE SEASONS (22m   C   1976)
People move from place to place because of family needs. Birds and animals migrate for the same reason.   Naturalist Elizabeth Terwilliger teaches the children to use their senses to develop an awareness of sights and sounds of the seasons.   p. Joan Linn Bekin; d. Wm. Cohen; TERWILLIGER.

SIGN ON THE DOTTED LINE (30m   C   n. d.   VIDEO)
At present, retired Americans are struggling along on incomes less than $5, 000 a year.   And of the older women living alone, three-quarters scrape by on less than $2, 000 annually.   The film presents a practical look at three basic types of financial planning available for women: life insurance, social security, and the newly-created Individual Retirement Account.   Discussed are special needs of women and what they should look for ... and look out for ... when considering their future security.   WNETTV.

SILENCE (10m   C   1956)
A sensitive and beautifully composed film rendering of the immortal fable by Edgar Allan Poe.   By Madeline Tourtelot; GP.

SILENCE, THE (95m   B   1963   Swedish/subtitled)
United since childhood in lesbian incest, two sisters, Ester the oldest, and Anna the younger, struggle and part as the younger seeks her freedom in a heterosexual affair.   Bergman's sober view of modern man's condition, wherein human relations are grotesquely ego-centric and perversely sexual, is shattering, yet a plea for hope from man himself.   d. Ingmar Bergman; JANUS.

SILENCED MAJORITY, THE (75m   C   1971   SFS)
Five part program narrated by Arlene Francis surveys women's struggle for equal rights from both a historical and a present-day point of view, and pinpoints the position of women today in relation to the home, employment, law, education, and media.   (1) Liberation Now; (2) Women, Jobs and the Law; (3) Women and Education; (4) This Ad Insults Women; (5) Rapping with the Feminists.   MPLUS.

SILENT SPRING OF RACHEL CARSON (55m   B   1963)
Presents an authoritative discussion, with opposite points of view, on the book which created such a controversy about the misuse and dangers of insecticides.   Contains interviews with Rachel Carson, the author of the book; Secretary of Agriculture Freeman; Surgeon-General Terry; authorities from the chemical industry; Food

and Drug Administration; and the U. S. Public Health Service.   CBS-TV; MGH; ASU, BU, EMC, IU, UMIS, UW.

SILVER LINING (24m   C   1977)
    Examines the scope and accomplishments of the W. P. A. Federal Art Project during President Franklin D. Roosevelt's administration.   This project enabled states to hire painters and sculptors to decorate public buildings at workman's wages with localities paying only for paint, brushes and material.   Shows sequence of stills of the breadlines as well as a great variety of murals and sculptures over comments of artists (women and men) who participated in this great art movement.   Narrator E. G. Marshall concludes that the Federal Art Project was a "silver lining to the black cloud of the depression."   By Barbara Bernstein; MAR/CHUCK.

SILVER POINT (25m   C   1974)
    "Silverpoint, about a woman who loves another woman and loses her to a third, is an intense study of jealousy and loneliness when love is no longer returned.   One of the women involved is a dancer and the film merges identities and memories in a balletic betrayal."
--Linda Gross, Los Angeles Times.   By Barbara Linkevitch; SB.

SIMPLEMENTE JENNY (33m   C   1977)
    A filmed documentary about women in Latin America and the cultural values that shape their lives.   It is a film about image and reality, the models of society and the facts of poverty and violence.   Shot in Argentina, Bolivia, Brazil, Ecuador, Mexico and Puerto Rico.   Jenny speaks of women's sufferings and fantasizes about being rich, but ultimately she says, "I want to be simply Jenny," in an eloquent plea for a social order in which human values come first.   d. Helena Solberg-Ladd; ed. Christine Burrill; IWFPI; CINEINC.

SING LOTUS (14m   C   1966)
    "18th-century Indian miniatures enact a traditional wedding ceremony of a Hindu Prince and Princess.   An exotic landscape of the mind; fable-fantasy of childhood-manhood."--S. D. H.   By Storm De Hirsch; FCOOP.

SINGIN' IN THE RAIN (101m   C   1952)
    Fun-filled charming musical which combines nostalgia and sentiment is a gentle spoof on the styles and manners of the late 20's.   d. Gene Kelly, Stanley Donen; s. w. Betty Comden; MGM; FL

SINGLE PARENT, THE (42m   C   1975)
    A filmed portrait of Colleen and her three small children.   The contained wrath and bitterness of Colleen, her alternation of almost brutal anger and devotion with the children, the burdens of running the house alone and her efforts to find a new relationship are done with economy and illumination.   Richard Elder (New York Times) says, "Single Parent makes Alice Doesn't Live Here Anymore look like soap opera."   p. Hubert Smith; MGH; MG, UILL, UIO, UM.

SINGLE PARENT EXPERIENCE, THE; Woman Series (29m   C   1975
VIDEO)
Marjorie Margolies, a reporter with NBC News in New York,
who has adopted two daughters of Oriental background, talks about
the joys and pitfalls of the single parent experience.   One advantage
she has over a divorced or widowed mother is that her children
have never known her to be anything other than a working mother.
WNETTV; PTL.

SINGLE ROOM FURNISHED (102m   C   n. d.)
Jayne Mansfield portrays an innocent but voluptuous teen-ager, a
deserted pregnant wife, a waitress and a demented streetwalker.   p.
Michael Musto; d. Matteo Ottaviano; Uniform Productions; Crown;
ABFI.

SIR (7m   C   1973)
"Psychic struggle, ghetto escape featuring a Black dancer, Sir
Lawrence Washington. "--C. B.   By Constance Beeson; BEESON.

SISTER KENNY (119m   B   1946)
Story of the Australian nurse and her struggles against medical
conservatism while trying to develop a method to treat infantile
paralysis.   d. Dudley Nichols; REPUBLIC; FL

SISTERS (21m   C   1971)
Two sisters on a symbolic journey which begins on the younger
one's birthday party.   The older sister takes the younger from her
mother and leads her through a series of incidents representing the
emptiness of female roles.   At the end, the older sister is confronted by her own image, and she realizes for the first time that
she is involved in some of the patterns she wants to warn her sister
against.   Film limited by its middle class reference.   By Jill Forman Hultin; WFC; IRISF.

SISTERS! (12m   C/B   1973)
"A celebration of lesbian women including footage of the Women's
International Day march in San Francisco and joyous dancing from
the last night of the lesbian conference at UCLA when 'Family of
Women' played. "--B. H.   By Barbara Hammer; WFC; IRISF.

SIX FILM-MAKERS IN SEARCH OF A WEDDING (13m   C   1971)
A fascinating, provocative film in which six filmmakers present
their personal views of a conventional wedding, utilizing collage/
animation, pixilation, home movies, cinéma-vérité, and official
wedding photographer's still photos.   The ritual and meeting of
courtship, the wedding ceremony and marriage itself are magnified
and clarified by repetition of the marriage ritual seen through different eyes.   ENVIC; POLYMORPH, PF; BU.

SIX SILLIES, THE (10m   C   1970)
Animated medieval fable.   An eccentric flying family tries to

find a suitor for their daughter.   Because of their wacky behavior, the suitors leave.   One suitor finally arrives, falls in love and ultimately flies.   By Maureen Cellwood; SFD.

SKI TOURING (30m   C   1970)
Shows the attraction of cross-country skiing in beautiful wild country.   Includes an instruction sequence for beginners.   By Virginia Duncan; FW.

SKIPPER'S LADY: DUTY FIRST; Cavalcade of America Series (20m B 1965)
Dramatization of the historic incident of the courage and skill of a captain's wife who was forced to take command of the ship, while sailing from New York to San Francisco in 1840, with the annual government allotment of supplies for the Indians of Oregon and California.   Excerpt from a TV film by same title.   TFC; OSU.

SKYEBOAT FOR BISCUIT (3m   C   n. d.)
Prompted by the death of the filmmaker's dog, Biscuit, this film is a short and unsentimental addition to the ranks of experimental film.   By Beverly O'Neill; SB.

SKYSCRAPER (20m   C/B   1959)
Musical salute to the collaborative effort of building a skyscraper. By Shirley Clarke; MOMA.

SLEEPING BEAUTY (10m   B   1930's)
A fairy tale in silhouette animation based on live shadow play. By Lotte Reiniger; BBCTV; MGH.

SLOWSILVER BUBBLES (4m   B   si   n. d.)
Study of air bubbles in transparent viscous liquid.   By Athena Tacha; VRL

SMATTERING OF SPOTS, A (11m   B   n. d.)
The Hubley TV commercials are famous for their wit and imagination in design, drawing, and musical scores.   Here are 14 of these TV "spots, " including five award winners.   By Faith Hubley, John Hubley; FIM.

SMILING MADAME BEUDET, THE (35m   B   si   1922   French)
An early feminist film of a woman haunted by her patriarchal husband.   Trick photography expresses pictorially her psychological conflict.   By Germaine Dulac; MOMA.

SMOKESCREEN (5m   C   1970)
A highly imaginative anti-smoking film designed for elementary and secondary school students.   By Mimi Warshaw, Michael Warshaw; PF.

SNOW WHITE AND ROSE RED (10m   B   1953)
A fairy tale in silhouette animation based on live shadow play. By Lotte Reiniger; MGH.

SNOWBOUND (33m   C   1978)
Depicts two young people whose hazardous experiences when
stranded in the midst of a blizzard bring them to a new understanding of themselves and each other.   Popular high school teen-ager
offers a lift to not-so-attractive classmate Cindy to spite his girlfriend.   Then, his car is wrecked in a snowstorm.   Although unhurt,
they are totally lost in the snowbound wilderness.   For days they
are forced to survive on their own, encountering terrors that test
their courage to the breaking point.   When Tony's initial confidence
wanes, Cindy reveals unsuspected strength and resourcefulness and
it is she who, in a final desperate effort, sets fire to the car and
attracts the helicopter that rescues them.   d. Robert M. Young;
p. Linda Gottlief; LCA.

SOCIAL CHANGE AND THE AMERICAN WOMAN (19m   B   1967)
Surveys the changes in the American woman from the innocent
years of the Gibson girl to the often puzzling role she fills today.
Examines changes occurring in the larger fabric of American life--
legal emancipation, widening economic opportunities, changing social
conditions, expansion of education and the impact of technology.
WOLPER; FI; IU, UKEN, USC, WISSU.

SOCIAL PSYCHOLOGY (33m   C   1971)
A recent busing incident involving elementary school children
is used to demonstrate the social comparison theory.   It provides
an illustration of attitude formation and change, and is a revealing
study of the nature of racial prejudice.   By Carole Hart; CRM, MGH.

SOCIAL SEMINAR SERIES see BUNNY; CHANGING; FAMILY, THE

SOCIOBIOLOGY: DOING WHAT COMES NATURALLY; Towards the
Year 2000 Series (22m   C   1972)
Surveys research on the biological origins of human behavior.
Several biologists and anthropologists explain--citing their work with
monkeys, rats, fish, insects, etc. --their theories about male competitiveness and aggression, whether female "sexual reticence" is
social or biological, the origins of warfare, and reasons for the
current rebellion by young people.   DA; EMC, PAS.

SOCIOLOGY SERIES see OUR CHANGING FAMILY LIFE

SOLIDARITY (10m   B   1950)
Tells about the industry-wide strike of the United Mine Workers
Union in January 1950 in which women are involved.   This story is
told in a very different way.   By Joyce Wieland; FCOOP.

SOLO (2m   B   1975)
Abstract film--images include windows opening, water dripping,
and a naked lady--all developed from a game of animation solitaire
based on cycles.   By Mary Beams; SB.

SOME LIKE IT HOT (121m   B   1959)
A slapstick comedy about two Chicago musicians, Tony Curtis

and Jack Lemmon, on the lam, and how they get mixed up with an
all-girl band and its ukulele-playing vocalist, Marilyn Monroe.
Based on a story by R. Thornton and M. Logan. d. Billy Wilder;
UAS.

SOME OF THESE DAYS (30m   B   1972)
     A group of men and women in a nursing home in Boston are
rehearsing an original revue, directed by a psychologist, Dr. Martha
Nobel. Her care and commitment provide a spark for people who
have been forgotten. d. Dr. Martha Nobel; p. Martin Ostrow;
ODEON; WFF.

SOME OF YOUR BEST FRIENDS (40m   C   1972)
     Documents the Gay Liberation Movement. Contains articulate
gay civil rights leaders, with various parades and demonstrations.
Presents the case for homosexuality as an alternate life style.
USC; UW.

SOME WILL BE APPLES (15m   C   1975)
     Some Will Be Apples is a prose-poem, a beautiful melange of
lyrical material recreating in expressionistic terms the look and
feel of the Victorian period in middle-America. The film focuses
upon the socio-political facts of life which have led to the present
day movement for women's rights. Based on the writings of Zona
Gale, a popular novelist and playwright (1870-1938), the film brings
to life the thoughts, expectations, and childhood conditioning of pre-
suffrage women. By Kathleen Laughlin, Phyllis Poulette MacDougal;
SB; UIO.

SOMEBODY CRUSHED YOU, ROSEMARIE (6m   C   1972)
     "Deals with the growth of one woman's consciousness as seen
through her childhood memories (growing up in the 30's), her dreams
and nightmares, and her paintings. Made about the filmmaker's
mother, Gladys Golden. "--L. G.   By Nancy Golden, Laura Golden;
GOLDEN.

SOMETHING DIFFERENT (65m   B   1968   Czech/subtitled)
     Compares a quest for meaning of life as it evolves in the lives
of two very different women. Vera, a harried housewife, and Eva,
a champion gymnast, reflect complementary aspects of modern woman's role. The film is commended for its objectivity and its re-
straint from moralizing. d. Vera Chitylova; GP.

SOMETHING TO BUILD ON (29m   C   1971)
     Uses animation and interviews with minority students to analyze
motivations and persuade viewers that higher education is both necessary and possible for them. p. St. Clair Bourne; CEEB.

SOMETIMES I WONDER WHO I AM (10m   B   1970)
     A brief, succinct study of the conflict felt by a young housewife
who dreams of a career she could have had. As she works, we
hear her thoughts about her husband and baby, and how she views
her life. By Liane Brandon; NDF.

SONG DELAY (18m   B   1973)
A dream-like sequence of people playing with wood, their voices creating the sound track.   By Joan Jonas; CASTELLI; VRL

SONG FOR DEAD WARRIORS, A (25m   C   1973)
Recounts the history of Indian struggles with the U. S. Government and the Bureau of Indian Affairs--the long history of divide-and-rule tactics which have created the present inter-tribal rivalries.   Also explores the conflict between traditional Indian ways and the demands of the modern world.   Several sequences of Indian music are featured, including the "Song for Dead Warriors," in which an old woman mourns those who fell in 1891 and 1973, at Wounded Knee.   By Norma Allen, Michael Anderson, Larry Janss, Saul Landau, Rebecca Switzer, and Bill Vaharas; TFC.

SONG OF INNOCENTS (12m   C   1971)
Studies the nature of violence by following a group of racially-mixed poor children in New York as they make a motion picture. Shows the children's films in which they play symbolic roles and are innocently moved to violence.   By Dee Dee Halleck; ECCW.

SONG TO REMEMBER, A (112m   C   1945)
Stars Paul Muni, Merle Oberon and Cornell Wilde in the emotional story of composer-pianist Frederic Chopin.   Depicts the bitter struggle between Chopin's music master and Madame George Sand, famous novelist, for supremacy over the will and genius of the great composer.   Includes the numerous melodies which brought Chopin immortality.   d. Charles Vidor; COLUMBIA; ABFI, BF, CWF, ROA, WEL.

SONG TO THEE, DIVINE ANDROGYNE (30m   C   n. d.)
"Abstract, free-flowing film induces a meditative state in the viewer so the universe within can be experienced.   Takes you through the energy centers of the body. "--Freude Bartlett.   By Rowena Pattee; SB.

SONGS OF HELENE ATTIA (30m   C   n. d.   VIDEO)
Helene Attia, a California song writer, performs some of her own songs, as well as some popular French songs.   KQEDTV.

SONGWRITER AT WORK: MALVINA REYNOLDS (30m   C   n. d.
VIDEO)
The famous Bay Area protest songwriter performs old as well as new songs, including "Little Boxes. "   KQEDTV.

SOON THERE WILL BE NO MORE OF ME (10m   C   1972)
Intensely moving legacy of a young, fatally ill mother to her baby daughter.   Compiled from her husband's still photographs and her own last writings.   Sensitive treatment of the value and meaning of one individual's life.   ALSKOG; CF; EMC, UC.

SOPHISTICATED VAMP (4m   C   n. d.)
"Pure color forms glide across the screen to the music of a vamp in this abstract exercise. "--CFS.   By Lynn Fayman; CFS.

SOUND AND THE FURY, THE (115m   C   1959   Reg. /Scope)
A degenerate Southern family caught in a whirlwind of seething emotions and ensnaring alcoholism.   Joanne Woodward's portrayal of the lonely teen-age girl just beginning to experience passion is exceptional, as is Yul Brynner's interpretation of her uncle, the tyrannical master of the old mansion, who tries to retain some semblance of respect and honor even when the girl's promiscuous mother returns after having deserted her as a baby.   Based on novel by William Faulkner.   Co-scripted by Harriet Frank; d. Martin Ritt; FOX; FL

SOUND OF MY OWN NAME (28m   C   1974)
Four vignettes depict adult basic education programs involving students of widely varying backgrounds: a 33-year-old Black woman enrolled in an urban adult learning center; a mother of eight being tutored in her Appalachian home by a paraprofessional; a middle-aged couple enrolled in evening classes in the local public school; a young Cuban participating in an ESL program conducted in the industrial plant where he works.   p. Center for Adult Education; NAVC.

SOURCES OF ART (11m   C   1966)
Uses examples from nature, professional artists and students to show that no two artists ever see the same world in the same way. Demonstrates the four basic elements of art--line, color, shape and texture.   By Marie Larkin; BFA.

SOURCES OF INFORMATION; Human Sexuality Series (29m   C   1972   VIDEO)
An exploration of where and how people get information about sex, and a discussion of the implications of the sources.   Host Milton Diamond, Ph. D. , distinguishes between fact and fiction in sexual information and talks about "direct" and "indirect" sources. UHAWAII/KHETTV; PTL.

SOVIET UNION: FACES OF TODAY (26m   C   1972)
Overview of the Soviet Union, focusing on selected facets of economic activity and the people who participate in them.   Discusses the size and regional variety of the U. S. S. R. , and contrasts city and country life in different areas.   Interviews a farmer and a dairy truck driver on a collective farm in European Russia, a farmworker on a state farm in Central Asia, an engineer in Leningrad, a woman physician in Tbilisi, and a young industrial worker in Bratsk. Sound track includes traditional songs of areas shown.   EBEC; EMC.

SOVIET WOMAN, THE (53m   B   1963)
Discusses the role of women in Russia, considering their equal status with men.   Uses interviews and candid pictures to point out the activities and attitudes of Soviet women.   Shows Madame Khrushchev, students, a mother heroine with eleven offspring, models and others.   Entitled Soviet Women in some catalogs.   ABCTV; MGH; ASU, BU, OSU, PAS, USC, UW.

SOVIET WOMEN, THE see SOVIET WOMAN, THE

SPACE BETWEEN, THE (7m B n. d.)
   Impressions of the Marin County, California, Civic Center building designed by Frank Lloyd Wright. By Emiko Omori; CCC.

SPACE TO BE ME, A (30m C 1973)
   Interviews several women who have overcome obstacles and developed in unique ways. The second half analyzes the need for day
care in terms of the positive effects on children and the possibilities
it creates for women to develop in roles other than housewife and
mother. By Maureen Sherlock, David Weinkauf; SFN, TWN.

SPACESHIP (3m B si n. d.)
   "Dream, in which a young boy is recalled to the planet of his
origin by flashes of light and troubling half-memories. In the end,
he is both consumed and transported by fire. "--CENTER. By Barbara Scharres; CENTER.

SPEAK UP; Serendipity Series (15m C 1976)
   Demonstrates how students can be helped to expand their ability
to use language as a medium of communication to enrich their social, intellectual, and emotional involvement in the world. Numerous speaking activities are shown--games, songs, etc. Students are
encouraged to speak up. By Suzanne Bauman; MGH.

SPEAKER: A FILM ABOUT FREEDOM, THE (42m C 1977)
   Through dramatization, the film addresses one of the most sensitive, but doubtless one of the most important, aspects of freedom of
expression: toleration of ideas we find offensive or repugnant. It
portrays the potential we face each day for the gradual suffocation
of the sacred fire of liberty granted to us in the First Amendment,
specifically, the Freedom of Speech. A powerful film that will re-
mind us all that there is a need for constant reeducation and rededi-
cation or this liberty will be lost. By Judith F. Krug, Florence
McMullin, Lee R. Bobker of VA; ALA.

SPEAKING OF MEN (20m C 1977)
   Three young, professional women talk about men: their attitudes toward men, their relationships with men, and how men are
important to them. Further, they also reveal much about their
conceptions of themselves and the world about them. The film
should promote discussion among both men and women about the expectations people have for relationships, and about the roles men
and women play in each other's lives. p. /d. Christine M. Herbes,
Ann-Carol Grossman; POLYMORPH.

SPECIAL CASES; Pregnancy and Childbirth Series (12m C 1977)
   Depicts modern techniques that can assure safe childbirth.
Shows special cases such as Caesarean section, forceps delivery,
induced labor, epidural anesthesia, and midwife delivery. CRAF;
IFB.

SPECTRUM IN WHITE (11m   C   1971)
    Graphic images are scratched directly on film.   By Lois Siegal;
SIEGALL.

SPIEGELEI (7m   C   1969)
    An abstract play of natural reflections in the lagoons of Venice
and the Lake of Zurich without any photographic manipulation.   By
Isa Hesse; HESSE.

SPIRIT OF THE PEOPLE IS GREATER THAN THE MAN'S TECH-
    NOLOGY, THE (3m   C   1970)
    Animation in clay figures in which man emerges from a stream
bed and builds a fire in the forest.   Technology strikes.   A chase
to the sea, then a battle ensues, and man triumphs over technology
and returns to earth.   By Patricia Amlin; CCC.

SPOOK SPORT (9m   C   n. d.)
    A stylized semi-abstract cartoon interpretation of Saint-Saëns'
"Danse Macabre. "   By Mary Ellen Bute (animation by Norman Mc-
Laren); NFBC; CFS.

SPRING AND FALL OF NINA POLANSKI (8m   C   n. d.)
    An animated and open-ended film looks at a woman's life with
sensitivity and humor.   It shows what she thinks of her husband and
children, and how they perceive her.   Then it touches on an old issue many women in today's society are facing--the dilemma of what
to do after the children are grown and gone.   MG.

SPRING THING (7m   C   1974)
    "The tightly closed buds of dormancy and the full flowering of
peace blossoms sucked by bees, is contrasted by the slow hunting
rhythms of animals. "--R. S.   By Rosalind Schneider; SCHNEIDER.

SPY BY MARRIAGE, A   (C   n. d.)
    Features Mrs. Wolfgang Lotz, wife of one of Israel's most ef-
fective spies, who tells how she shared her husband's three-year
espionage assignment in Cairo until they were caught and sent to
prison.   ADL.

SQUARES (7m   C   1973)
    "Computer-generated abstract film in which multi-images of
squares in both positive and negative colors float gracefully in
space. "--CFS.   By Doris Chase; PIC.

STAGE DOOR (83m   B   1937)
    Stage-struck maidens (played by Ginger Rogers, Katharine Hep-
burn and Gail Patrick) nurse their disappointments and sharpen their
claws (on whatever victim is handy) and fight a triangular sham battle over the leering, black-mustached Adolphe Menjou.   Adapted
from a play by Edna Ferber, George S. Kaufman.   d. Gregory
La Cava; p. Pandra S. Berman; RKO; FL

STAGE TO THREE, THE (28m   B   1964)
    In this film are three portraits of renowned performers: Katina

Paxinou, Greece's leading interpreter of classical and modern drama, illustrates her involvement in theatre as both actress and teacher; Chatuporn, the foremost demon dancer in Thailand, exhibits the
discipline and technical virtuosity required for an art that is a blend
of history, religion, drama and ballet; and Bruno Gerussi, who talks
about acting in Canada and how he personally advanced from little
theatre to television, and finally to Shakespearean repertory at Canada's Stratford.   NFBC; CMC.

STAMEN (6m   C   1972)
     A sensitive interpretation of a male homosexual relationship.
Fantasies and realities are explored in flashbacks, overlays, and
unusual visual effects as the two young men meet and make love.
By Constance Beeson; NSF; IE, SB.

STAND UP AND BE COUNTED (90m   C   1972)
     A women's liberation comedy.   d. Jackie Cooper; p. M. J.
Frankovich; COLUMBIA; SWANK.

STAND UP AND BE COUNTED (3m   C   1969)
     A continuous dissolve into a series of happy nude couples in
various configurations: female/male, female/female, male/male,
as the Rolling Stones sing "We Love You. " By Freude Bartlett,
Scott Bartlett; SB.

STANDING BUFFALO (22m   C   1968)
     Gives an account of a rug-making cooperative organized by
Sioux women on the Standing Buffalo Reserve in southern Saskatchewan.   Explains that the Indians of this tribe are descended from a
tribe that migrated from Minnesota during armed clashes 100
years ago.   By Joan Henson; NFBC.

STANDING WATER (7m   B   n. d.)
     Film of a horse trained by the filmmaker in the hills of Marin
County, California.   By Sandra Marshall; CCC.

STAR, THE (98m   B   1953)
     Bette Davis plays a washed-up movie queen, a studio has-been,
too old to play glamour-girl roles and too vain and publicity de-
luded to surrender her laurels gracefully.   Violently, she represents the fury and the vengeance of an actress whose career has
come to a point of grim transition while she herself will not ac-
knowledge change.   d. Stuart Heisler; s. w. Katherine Albert, Dale
Eunson; FOX; MOD.

STAR OF BETHLEHEM, THE (20m   C   1956)
     The traditional Nativity story performed as a Medieval Miracle
Play, with music specially composed by Peter Gellhorn, and sung by
the famous Glyndebourne Chorus.   By Lotte Reiniger; CEA.

STARS OF THE RUSSIAN BALLET: SWAN LAKE (33m   C   1953
     Russian/subtitled)
     Tschaikowsky's Swan Lake is danced by Galina Ulanova and

and performers of the State Bolshoi Theatre in Moscow, assisted by the chorus and orchestra of the Kirov State Opera and Ballet Theatre, Leningrad LSP; ABFI; UILL.

STEELYARD BLUES (92m C 1973)
Jane Fonda, Peter Boyle and Donald Sutherland sail through this wild comedy about a group of outrageous misfits who take on society, the establishment, rules, pettiness, stupidity and superficiality. It's kooky yet striking satire with an imperishable cast. p. Julia Miller; d. Alan Myerson; ass't. d. Daisy Gerber; WSA; ABFI, ICS, TWY, WCF.

STEP ASIDE, STEP DOWN (20m C 1971)
Produced for the White House Conference on Aging, this film presents some of the man-made situations of the aged as they face the problems of income, housing and nutrition. ELIP; NAVC; UIO.

STEPPARENTING: NEW FAMILIES, OLD TIES (25m C n. d.)
Interviews Dixie de Vienne, families, professionals, and a support group telling about some of the problems of stepparenting and the ways families deal with this. By Marilyn Felt, Henry Felt; POLYMORPH.

STEPS OF AGE, THE (25m B 1951)
Shows the necessity of preparing for retirement and old age during the younger years. Contrasts the emotional weakness of a man who goes into a depression and dies soon after his retirement with the strength of his wife. By Helen Levitt; MHFB; IFB.

STERILE CUCKOO, THE (107m C 1969)
Moving story of a young girl's desperate search for love, or what she thinks is love and what we, for a long while, do too. The girl, Pookie, is played by Liza Minnelli as a female Holden Caulfield: a solitary child, daunted and daunting, hilariously gabby, wearing her heart on her lips, blessed with intelligence, not beautiful, young beyond her years and setting off for her first year at college where she pursues, at first, a disinterested college freshman. Pookie eventually wins his love, only to be left behind when he emotionally outgrows her. Based on a novel by John Nichols. p. /d. Alan J. Pakula; PARAMOUNT; FI.

STILL LIFE (7m C 1971)
"Surrealistic view of organic objects."--YFD. By Lauri Robertson; YFD.

STILL LIFE (5m C 1972)
"A voyage into red cabbage and shells. Shells transform themselves into orange canyons. Cabbage is the universe!"--R. S. By Rosalind Schneider; FCOOP.

STOCKYARDS: END OF AN ERA (59m C 1973)
Traces history and death of the famed Chicago stockyards. Includes interviews with leaders of the Amalgamated Meatcutters and

Butcher Workmen of North America, meat company officials, and
many men and women who worked in the stockyards--even some old-
timers who worked under the conditions described by Upton Sinclair
in The Jungle. Reviews the history of the struggle for unionization,
a story of broken strikes and company harassment. Reveals the
role of women and racial minorities in reinvigorating the union
leadership. WTTWTV; IU; EMC.

STOLEN HEART, THE (10m B 1934)
    Martin, a poor woodcutter, frees a fairy trapped in a tree and
is given a magic ring that will grant him three wishes. In animation. By Lotte Reiniger; CEA.

STORE ON TELEGRAPH, THE (18m C n. d.)
    A look at a store on Telegraph Avenue in Berkeley, California,
on its last day. The first light shows were done at the store,
which was an early counter-culture answer to ordinary stores on
Telegraph. Music is the juke-box in the store. By Patricia Ober-
haus; CCC.

STORY OF A DOT, A (2m C si n. d.)
    Animated doodling of a dot changing. By Naomi Levine; FCOOP.

STORY OF ADELE H. , THE (97m C 1975 English or French/
    subtitled)
    Truffaut compassionately relates the true story of Adele Hugo,
the younger daughter of Victor Hugo, and her unrequited and unrelenting love for a British lieutenant--an unrestrained passion of
immoderateness, self-preoccupation and inclination toward destruction. It is a story of an obsession, but Truffaut gives it cleanli-
ness, clarity and power. The result is an esthetic purity that becomes a moral force. d. Francois Truffaut; NEW WORLD. Reviews by Vincent Canby, Pauline Kael, Judith Crist, and Molly
Haskell are excellent. FL

STORY OF CHRISTMAS, THE (8m C 1977)
    "Evelyn Lambart, a long-time close assistant of Norman Mc-
Laren and a gifted animation artist in her own right, deserves super-
latives for this cinematic re-telling of the story of the Annunciation
and birth of Christ. ... The film's individual components--artwork,
music and animation, each outstanding on its own--form a harmoni-
ous whole, radiating the aura and the mystery inherent in the story
of Christ's birth. ... It is a measure of Ms. Lambart's consummate
artistry that she does not need a single spoken word to tell it most
eloquently. "--Milena Pribramska, Film News (Sept. /Oct. 1976).
By Evelyn Lambart; NFBC; FL

STORY OF ERIC (35m C 1971)
    Shows classes in the Lamaze method of childbirth and a labor
delivery which utilizes the Lamaze method. Includes techniques of
relaxation and breathing and the role of the husband in labor delivery; the second stage of labor; an epistiotomy; delivery; and
breast feeding of the newborn child. Stresses close relationship of

the couple and the importance of their cooperation.   By David Seltzer; CENTRE; UM.

STORY OF SOLO   see   MISS GOODALL AND THE WILD DOGS OF AFRICA

STORY OF THE ST. LAWRENCE SEAWAY, THE (29m C/B 1959)
Describes the Seaway Project from conception to completion, from the early fur trade to June 1959, when her majesty Queen Elizabeth and President Dwight D. Eisenhower declared the seaway open.   Animated drawings show the profile of the waterways.   By Isobel Kehoe; NFBC; MGH.

STRADA, LA (107m B 1954 Italian/subtitled)
Because of her family's poverty, Gelsomina is sold to Zampano, who tours the countryside with his strongman acts.   She is a pathetic, impressionable little person who is willing to abase herself for Zampano.   In time, she learns to love this caffone, but he repays her with cruelty.   While on tour, they meet Il Matto (The Fool), an acrobat with the soul of a philosopher, upon whom Gelsomina begins to dote.   Il Matto's philosophizing continually irritates Zampano to the point where he finally kills him in a fight.   Gelsomina, in her remorse over Il Matto's death, becomes useless to Zampano after that and one night, he abandons her.   With the passage of time, however, he awakens to the realization that he really loves her.   But it is too late--he learns she has died, and Zampano is left alone weeping by the sea.   d. Federico Fellini; JANUS.

STRAIGHT AND NARROW (10m B 1970)
"... A study in subjective color and visual rhythm.   The hypnotic poetry of the images will cause viewers to experience a programmed gamut of hallucinatory color effects. "--BC/TC.   By Beverly Conrad, Tony Conrad; FCOOP.

STRANGE LANDS (7m B n. d.)
"An erotic audio homage to Ingmar Bergman. "--C. M. G.   By Cassandra M. Gerstein; FCOOP.

STRANGE WOMAN (101m B 1946)
Beautiful strong-willed woman (Hedy Lamarr) marries a ruthless man (Louis Hayward) and events begin to take a strange turn.   d. Edgar G. Ulmer; UAS; BF.

STREET, THE (10m C 1976)
In soft, simple washes of watercolor and ink, the filmmaker captures the reality of family reactions to a dying grandmother from a child's point of view.   From a short story by Mordecai Richler.   d. Caroline Leaf; p. Guy Glover; NFBC; EMC.

STREET OF SHAME (AKASEN CHITAI) (88m B 1956 Japanese/ subtitled)
A filmed indictment of a society that legally exploits women.   The Japanese Diet is considering legislation that would ban legalized

prostitution in Tokyo red light district. The brothel owners are protesting because it would mean closing of their business. They claim that they provide employment for women who otherwise would be destitute. Shown are prostitutes and the various reasons why they are involved in this profession, and the social and psychological impact the profession has on these women. The film remains a penetrating social analysis ... it is a summing-up of Mizoguchi's attitudes to society and women. d. Kenzo Mizoguchi; JANUS.

STREET OF THE SARDINE (21m C 1971)
A testimony to man's mismanagement of natural resources. Shows the abandoned docks of Steinbeck's Cannery Row. By Eva Lothar; PF.

STRING BEAN (17m B r1964)
Wistful portrait of an old Parisian woman and her devotion to a string bean plant, which she plants in a row of blossoming white shrubs in the Jardin des Tuileries and visits daily. The string bean's ultimate fate, and the woman's act of faith and optimism, form the basis of the story. No dialogue or narration. By Edmond Sechan; MGH; EMC, PAS.

STRONGER, THE (17m C 1969)
Film based on the one-act play by Swedish playwright August Strindberg. Features Swedish-born actress Viveka Lindfors in a dual role. Shows an actress sitting alone in a cafe; an old acquaintance, also an actress, approaches, joins her and begins to speak. The first woman never speaks, but her silence compels the other to continue talking compulsively and finally expressing a long-harboured suspicion that the silent woman has been having an affair with her husband. The silent woman is stunned; her adversary goes home to husband and children. Both are profoundly affected by the encounter. Young Productions; PHOENIX.

STRUGGLE FOR LOS TRABAJOS (35m C 1976)
What happens when a complaint of job discrimination is lodged by an individual with the Equal Employment Opportunity Commission. This film illustrates the investigation and conciliation process used by the E. E. O. C. in following through on such a complaint. Also discussed is reverse discrimination against non-minority group workers. Constructed in dramatic form, using role-playing techniques. WGPI.

STRUGGLE OF THE MEAT (3m C 1974)
A rhythmic sonnet of wildlife footage celebrating life on Earth, which conveys the struggle for survival with abstract clarity. By Anne Severson; SB.

STUDIES IN INTERVIEWING SERIES see AID TO FAMILIES WITH
DEPENDENT CHILDREN, INTAKE INTERVIEW; UNMARRIED
MOTHER INTERVIEW

STUDY IN CHOREOGRAPHY FOR CAMERA, A (4m B si 1945)
"Classic experiment in film-dance. Through an exploitation of

cinematic technique, camera creates its own space and time. "--GP. By Maya Deren; GP.

SUGAR (1m   C   1973)
"Animated reptilian analogy to a woman's life. "--T. S.   By Terry Sheehy; SHEEHY.

SUGAR AND SPICE (32m   C   1974)
Sex-role socialization and what the people are doing in three different schools to develop a program that opens up options for both boys and girls.   Shows ways that sex role divisions in our society are reflected in children's play at school, and how the non-sexist curriculum developed by the women's action alliance is implemented in a New York City day care center.   Examines the relationship of staff to Children's Center in Brookline, Massachusetts, and focuses on parents' ideas regarding sex role discrimination at the Woodward School in Brooklyn.   Vicki Breitbart, Eric Breitbart, Alan Jacobs; ODEON; UM.

SUGAR 'N SPIKES (30m   C/B   n. d.   VIDEO)
Presents a variety of viewpoints on the controversial issues surrounding women athletes, including several interviews with school children.   The tape covers the image of the female athlete, attitudes toward sexually-mixed teams, sportscasting and, most importantly, unequal funding for female sports by high schools.   An excellent organizing tool for implementing recent Congressional actions regarding equality for women in sports.   By Carol Cole, Rosemary Wiesner, Tom Klinkostein; IE.

SUICIDE (25m   C   1975   r1976)
Interviews and discussions with attempted suicide victims reveal some of the reasons for this final and desperate act.   The common denominator of suicides is aloneness, a sense of being worthless and unloved, a feeling that "there is no way out."   Professional counselors, clergy and police discuss the causes of suicide and how they respond to cries for help.   d. /s. w.   Dinitia McCarthy; WNBCTV; FI.

SUICIDE: IT DOESN'T HAVE TO HAPPEN (24m   C   1976)
Presents a teen-age girl who has attempted suicide as she is directed to group therapy by a high school teacher.   There she explores the group therapy approach to intervention in suicide.   Shows the girl's parents dealing with the situation and observes group sessions where members discuss problem-solving techniques and symptoms of suicide.   Adds the perspective of time as the high school teacher comments on his own teen-age suicide attempt and his healing process.   BFA; IU.

SUMLEO (8m   B   si   n. d.)
"Lithuanian music, destruction of our Capitol ... Japanese androgyne ... shots of Vietnam... "--Piero Heliczer.   By Patti-Lee Chenis; FCOOP.

SUMMER (20m   B   n. d.)
    Three girls on a beach daydream.... There is symbolic pan-
tomime in this light-humored film.   By Madeline Tourtelot; GP.

SUMMER OF '42 (102m   C   1971)
    Hermie (Gary Grimes) relives the summer of 1942 when he was
15, on the threshold of manhood, as he strolls on a lonely beach
among the sandpipers.   The story is one of growing up--of three
boys spending the summer with their families on an island, of their
adolescent yearnings and fumblings, their adventures and the hesitant
forays into the mysteries of the opposite sex.   Jennifer O'Neill plays
the "older woman" in this story.   d. Robert Mulligan; WSA; CWF,
SWANK.

SUMMER WE MOVED TO ELM STREET: ALCOHOLISM AND THE
    FAMILY, THE (28m   C   1966)
    In today's mobile society some families move a lot, and chil-
dren have to make new friends just when they are becoming comfortable with the ones they have.   This film tries to show what goes
on in the mind of a nine-year-old girl who finds happiness disturbed
by a move to another street and by her father's increasing drunken-
ness.   NFBC; MGH.

SUMMER WISHES, WINTER DREAMS (95m   C   1973)
    An intense, sensitive story about a woman trying to regain the
lost happiness of her youth.   A piercing commentary on middle-
aged women in America.   d. Gilbert Cates, COLUMBIA; SELECT,
SWANK.

SUNDAY, BLOODY SUNDAY (110m   C   1971)
    A love story concerning one woman (Glenda Jackson), one bi-
sexual man (Murray Head) and a homosexual man (Peter Finch).
The rivalry, though strongly felt, is not bitterly fought out in the
open, but at a more subliminal level.   The relationships are very
sensitively portrayed.   At times they are very funny.   d. John
Schlessinger; s. w. Penelope Gilliatt; UAS.

SUNDOWNERS, THE (133m   C   1960)
    A story of a family of itinerant sheep herders and their search
for permanence in a land of change.   This film of frontier Australia
in the 1920's breathes with humanity, honesty and respect for the
characters as human beings attempting to know themselves, each
other, and the meaning of life.   d. Fred Zinnemann; s. w. Isobel
Lennart; WSA; ABFI, BF, CWF, TWY, WIL.

SUNSET BOULEVARD (108m   B   1950)
    A forgotten star of silent film lives surrounded by her past in
a decaying mansion attended by the man who launched her career.
She lives only for her return to the screen in her own adaptation of
"Salome. " With Gloria Swanson.   d. Billy Wilder; PARAMOUNT; FL

SURE, I CAN DANCE (25m   C   n. d.)
    Film shows how an enlightened dance troupe can introduce an

entire community to the fun of dancing.   The Ririe-Woodbury Dance
Company conducted an Artists-in-the-Schools Residency in Mesa,
Arizona, under the auspices of the National Endowment for the Arts,
and invited teachers, parents, and children to participate.   Everyone came away with a whole new awareness of dancing, teaching,
learning, and of themselves.   By Judith Hallet, Stanley Hallet; FIM.

SUSAN, APRIL TO JUNE (25m   C   1975)
    This cinéma-vérité portrait shows three months in the life of
Susan, a 23-year-old white woman trying to extricate herself from
the vicious cycle of poverty-drugs-prostitution-imprisonment.   The
film ends with a glimmer of hope expressed when the filmmaker
confronts her with a symbol of strength from her past.   d. Linda
Jassim; IE.

SUSAN B. ANTHONY (20m   B   1951)
    Susan B. Anthony's work in building the foundation of women's
suffrage.   Her activities in organizing women's temperance movement; obtaining property rights for women; campaigning for voting
privileges.   Dramatizes her trial, in which she heroically states her
case.   EBEC; ASU, BU, BYU, IU, OKSU, UILL, UM, USC, UU.

SUSAN B. ANTHONY IS TRIED FOR VOTING; You Are There Series
    (25m   C   1955)
    Depicts the second day of legal proceedings in which Susan B.
Anthony is being prosecuted for voting.   CBSTV; OKSU, PAS.

SUSAN STARR; Living Camera Series (54m   B   1970)
    Follows three days in the life of Susan Starr, competitor in the
finals of Dimitri Mitropoulos' international piano competition.   Shows
her during the competition at the Metropolitan Opera House, back-
stage as her rivals perform and onstage as she performs.   DREW.

SUSAN THROUGH CORN (2m   C   1975)
    A short, simple film giving an exhilarating sense of a young
woman entering a large corn field (being followed with a single-
frame camera), emerging on the other side, then disappearing.   It
begins slow and soft, and becomes sharper, faster, louder--climax-
ing when the corn tassles dance with the sky-brightness to a triple
flute sound track.   Susan's unresisting face, her red and yellow
dress, and the green, green shapes interwoven all around her, form
a momentary portrait of the cornfield and a sunlit day in August, as
well as Susan of herself.   By Kathleen Laughlin; SB.

SUSPICION (99m   B   1941)
    Somber thriller involving a young woman (Joan Fontaine) who fears
that her husband (Cary Grant), jealous of her wealth, is trying to poison
her.   Shy Fontaine is immediately attracted to unprincipled charmer
Grant, but the honeymoon is over when Grant's behavior becomes
quirky.   Death strikes down Fontaine's father and a family friend.
Then sudden threats are made against her.   d. Alfred Hitchcock;
RKO; FI.

SWAMP (6m C 1971)
Exploration of a swamp--weeds, reeds and marsh. By Nancy
Holt, Robert Smithson; VRL

SWAN LAKE--LE LAC DES CYGNES (23m B 1949)
Gives excerpts from Tschaikowsky's classical ballet, performed
in a real woodland setting. Features the ballerina Genevieve Moulin.
DBASIL; USC.

SWEET BANANAS (30m C 1972)
A colorful documentary which tangles the separate working lives
and ambitions of a weaver, a dancer, and a writer. As the heroines are introduced to each other and get into a house full of women,
their love/hate feelings surface and collide unpredictably. By Ariel
Dougherty; WMM.

SWEET DREAMS (3m C 1971)
Sweet Dreams was initially inspired by an erotic encounter with
a dolphin which took place in a dream during the filmmaker's pregnancy. Later, during nursing, the sensuality inherent in the mother/
child bond gave meaning to the dream. A poetic celebration of
earthy and tender aspects of female sexuality. By Freude Bartlett;
SB.

SWEETHEART see LIEBALALA

SWEPT AWAY (BY AN UNUSUAL DESTINY IN THE BLUE SEA OF
AUGUST) (116m C 1975 Italian/subtitled)
Raffaella, a rich, beautiful, sharp-tongued Milanese who has
chartered a yacht, and Gennarino, a swarthy Sicilian deckhand, become marooned on an island in the Mediterranean. She is a capitalist for whom the system has paid off; he is a dedicated communist. This is the story of their tumultuous courtship. d. Lina
Wertmuller; CIV.

SWISS GRAFFITI (6m C 1976)
The creation of the world looked at and corrected by two women.
The story of the creation of the world has been found on walls
throughout the world--told through primitive graffiti. The symbols
used are always those of masculine supremacy, feminine inferiority.
One day Eve gets tired of her role and revolts--and the symbols
are changed. p./d. Jacqueline Veuve, Monique Renault; PHOENIX.

SWITCHBOARD (30m C n.d.)
"The problem is that the law deals with the supply of drugs,
not the demand."--Interviewee. By Martha Stuart, David Ruskin;
STUARTM.

SYLVIA, FRAN AND JOY (25m B 1973)
Provides portraits of three women who represent typical options
presently open to white middle-class women. One woman pursues a
career while her husband takes care of the house and children; the

Sylvia Scarlett 320

second is divorced and participates in a number of activities of interest to her, including dance and photography; and the third is an apparently satisfied housewife. Subtle depiction of the ironies and insecurities in each woman's life. By Joan Churchill; CF; BU, EMC, IU, OSU, PAS, SCC, UILL, UKEN, UM, UMIS.

SYLVIA SCARLETT (97m B 1935)
The film collects some odd characters and sends them on an odd sort of vagabond odyssey. When Sylvia's father commits larceny and is forced to flee France, Sylvia joins him and becomes a boy for the occasion so as not to be a bother during their flight. Finally, Sylvia's secret passion for a handsome artist causes her to abandon the disguise. From the novel by Compton Mackenzie. d. George Cukor; p. Pandra S. Berman; s. w. Gladys Unger, John Collier, Mortimer Offner; RKO; FL

TAKE HER SHE'S MAD (30m C n. d. VIDEO)
A one-act play dealing with the retrospection of a middle-aged woman. Presented by Femedia III, a Mission District women's group in San Francisco. KQEDTV.

TAKE-OFF (10m B 1973)
A dance, a documentary, a metaphysical striptease: animation and live action combine to create a cosmic joke on the science of stripping, female sexual identity and the art of taking off to outer space. By Gunvor Nelson; CCC, FCOOP, GP, SB.

TAKE THIS WOMAN (25m C 1971)
Shows a number of women who have fought to obtain unusual or prestigious jobs and examines discrimination against women at the workplace, and in schooling and training facilities. Particularly emphasizes cases of women who have been involved in legal actions over job discrimination. Includes interviews with the women in question as well as their employers and others. Judge Joan Dempsey Klein, Aileen Hernandez (NOW), and California Assemblywoman Yvonne Braithwaite relate the general question of employment equality to the overall aims of the women's movement. Narrated by Marsha Hunt. p. Michael Fox, KNBCTV, NBCTV; FI, EMC, UILL.

TAKING OUR BODIES BACK: THE WOMEN'S HEALTH MOVEMENT (30m C 1974)
This film documents a growing movement of women to regain control of their bodies. It shows women learning about their bodies, and teaching other women. It also shows women becoming aware of their rights in dealing with medicine, an industry which can no longer expect women to be grateful, passive and ignorant. Explores ten critical areas of the women's health movement, from the revolutionary concept of self-help to the issue of informed surgical consent. By Margaret Lazarus; CDFI; UM, UIO.

TALE OF TODAY, A (10m C 1972)
A fast-paced survey of the search for alternative life-styles.

Somewhat overly romantic view of contemporary young adults. d.
Phyllis and Fred Gebauer; GEBAUER.

TALES (70m B 1969)
An unusual modern-day Decameron in which a group of young
men and women have a cinéma-vérité confessional about their most
bizarre and secret sexual experiences. The atmosphere of revelation builds to a most surprising conclusion in this documentary created by an all-women filmmaking crew. d. Cassandra M. Gerstein; NLC.

TALK WITH IMOGEN CUNNINGHAM (30m C n. d. VIDEO)
Imogen Cunningham, a photographer for over 50 years, talks
about her life and work with Ann Hershey, the maker of a recent
film Never Give Up. Included in the program is a selection of
Imogen's photographs. KQEDTV.

TALKING ABOUT BREAST FEEDING (17m C 1971)
Affirms the values of breast-feeding as the simplest, safest,
and most nutritious way to feed an infant. Helps allay common
fears, featuring a number of nursing mothers who have overcome
medical problems and social pressures concerning breast-feeding.
p. /d. Alvin Fiering; POLYMORPH.

TALL ARCHES III (6m C 1974)
The Mary Staton Dance Ensemble interacts with nesting arches.
Their mobility enables them to coordinate dance movements with
lyrical ease. Simple motions are multiplied in visual echoes of the
primary colors as the dancers reach, glide and gesture, their images
finally resolving into one. Music by George Kleinsinger. By Doris
Chase; ABFL

TAMING OF THE SHREW (95m B 1929)
A screen adaptation of William Shakespeare's comedy set in
15th-century Padua in which the swaggering, handsome Petruchio attempts to tame the vile-tempered but lovely Katherine. PICKFO;
UAS.

TAOS (6m C 1973)
"Dance fantasy in nature with Daria Halprin. "--C. B. By Constance Beeson; BEESON.

TARASCAN ARTISANS (40m C n. d.)
Documents the Indians living by their crafts around Lake Patz-
cuaro, Michoacan, Mexico. The crafts produced are taken to the
Patzcuaro market by dug-out canoe. The beauty of the region and
some of the customs of the Tarascans add much interest to the film.
By Madeline Tourtelot; GP.

TARGET FIVE, PTS. I & II (26m, 22m C n. d.)
Virginia Satir, an eminent family therapist, in cooperation with
Dr. Everett L. Shostrom, Director of the Institute of Therapeutic
Psychology, demonstrate the four manipulative response forms in
Part L In Part II, Mrs. Satir and Dr. Shostrom combine to de-

scribe the three essential qualities of an actualizing relationship. The first of these is hearing and listening, the second is understanding, and the third is mutual meaning.   Each of these is discussed and demonstrated.   PFI.

TASTE OF HONEY, A (100m   B   1962   (Gr. Br.))
   Portrays a lonely British schoolgirl whose self-centered mother forces her out of the nest.   Ill-equipped to find a life of her own, she makes a number of errors, but learns from her experiences only to find, after she has achieved some measure of maturity, that her mother wants to move back in with her as if nothing has happened. An interesting statement about the problems of youth and their attraction to alternative life-styles.   d. Tony Richardson; KP, TWY, WRS.

TATTOOED MAN, THE (35m   C   1969)
   Sensual color and imagery; abbreviated dream-like sequences. Produced on a grant from American Film Institute.   By Storm De Hirsch; CCC, FCOOP.

TEACH YOUR CHILDREN WELL (30m   C   n. d.)
   Documentary about three women: a Black, a Chicano, and a white, and a comparison of the ways their parents educated them. Shows the consequences of their differing educations.   By Marta Ashley, Nina Janowsky, Marty Coe; FEMEDIA.

TEACHER'S PET (120m   B   1958)
   Clark Gable plays the tough, brash, admittedly unlettered city editor of the New York Chronicle, who has come up the hard way and passionately hates education and the educated, especially journalism schools and their faculties.   All this is undermined when he makes an appearance in a journalism class of a local college and the instructor turns out to be none other than the blonde, shapely Doris Day.   And passion and true love, in that order, finally make the twain meet.   d. George Seaton; p. William Perlberg; s. w. Fay Kanin, Michael Kanin; PARAMOUNT; FI.

TEATRO CAMPESINO, EL (61m   B   1971)
   Shows the origins, progress and purpose of El Teatro Campesino from its beginnings in the fields, where its intent was to boost the morale of striking Mexican American farmworkers, to its present role as a theatre committed to social change.   By Victoria Hochberg, Janet Sternberg; IU.

TECHNIQUES OF CONTEMPORARY DANCE (11m   C   1954)
   A contemporary dance group demonstrates Harriet Ann Gray's techniques to develop flexibility, flowing movement, and elevation. Also shows ways of stimulating the imagination to develop dramatic character and to find fresh ways of moving.   PORTMAN; UILL.

TEEN-SCENE (37m   C   1972)
   A documentary depicting the operations of Planned Parenthood of Chicago.   Nearly every modern teen-ager is confronted with the

problem of obtaining proper information on sex education and birth
control. Unfortunately, many learn too little, too late. Shown are
group "rap session" and individual counseling sessions about pregnancy tests, related medical examinations, V. D. tests, and birth
control services. Not limited to clinical aspects. Other such sensitive issues as dating, relationships, and the problems of parental
misunderstanding are discussed openly and freely. PPFA; WSA.

TEEN SEXUALITY: WHAT'S RIGHT FOR YOU? (28m C 1975)
Informs and helps teens to understand human sexual values.
Shows teens on class trip to New York City reacting to a "scare
pregnancy." Includes birth control counseling interview. In a rap
session, Dr. Calderwood provides information on sexuality and
values clarification. d. Maureen McGuire; BB; PERENNIAL; UMIS.

TEENAGE MOTHER: A BROKEN DREAM (15m C 1977)
Examines the relationship of Mary Levandoski, a 15-year-old
girl from Grand Rapids, Michigan, who is part of an ever-growing
statistic in this country--the unwed teen-age mother. Over 900, 000
teen-agers become pregnant each year--the reason why girls drop
out of high school. Only a third have abortions. Half of those who
marry are divorced within five years. These mothers are unable
to find jobs to support their children, ending up on welfare. In an
attempt to break this cycle, the Grand Rapids Board of Education
has created The Park School for pregnant girls. Here, an attempt
is made to keep these women in school and to give them an education so that they will be able to find employment and not become a
burden on the state. Mary's case, like so many others, has not
worked out as she had imagined: her boyfriend decided not to marry her, her baby is in a foster home, and she is now in a detention
home. The film presents the stark reality of teen-age pregnancy
and motherhood for those who cannot visualize it for themselves.
CBSTV; CAROUSEL; EMC, UIO.

TEENAGE PREGNANCY; Family Living Program Series (17m C
1969)
The discovery that 16-year-old Betty is pregnant brings emotional and psychological upheaval to her entire family. A frantic
mother seeks advice and comfort from a doctor, and tries to restore unity to her family. No solutions are given, and the film is
left open-ended for discussion. MLP; SAF; UILL.

TEENAGE RELATIONSHIPS: VANESSA AND HER FRIENDS; Getting
Together Series (18m C 1973)
Presents a cinéma-vérité portrait of Vanessa, a 10th grade stu-
dent, exploring many relationships and events in her life. Includes
Vanessa's comments on her relationships with friends and dates,
and her future expectations. Interviews with many of those close to
Vanessa accompany her commentary. EBEC; IU, UILL, USC.

TEENAGERS TALK: GETTING THROUGH ADOLESCENCE (12m C
1975)
Identifies and discusses many problems, such as weight, physical

size, and emotions, that are associated with puberty and adolescence.   Examines the pressures and joys of relationships with parents and friends and decisions about freedom, sex, and drugs.
BFA; IU.

TELL ME WHERE IT HURTS (78m   C   1974)
Warm and human drama about a middle-aged working-class
housewife groping for recognition and identity as a person. At the
suggestion of her college-age daughter, the woman organizes a discussion group with her friends. She begins to understand the limitations in the complacent routine of caring for her children and for
her husband who takes her for granted. When her daughter leaves
home, she goes to an employment agency and gets a job. Her husband, terrified of losing her, rushes to her when she calls him,
and they are united as equals.   Emmy award-winning script by Fay
Kanin. Originally made for TV. TOMENT: LCA; BF, EMC, TWY,
UM.

TEN WHO DARED SERIES   see   MARY KINGSLEY

TEN YEARS ALIVE ON THE INFINITE PLAIN (20 to 200m   B   1972)
Three or more projectors are used with some visual material on
each projector (vertical or horizontal stripes).   With live music.
Requires personal direction by the filmmakers.   By Beverly Conrad,
Tony Conrad; FCOOP.

TENDER GAME (6m   C   1958)
To the tune of "Tenderly," sung by Ella Fitzgerald and played
by Oscar Peterson Trio, this animated short describes how two
semi-abstract representations of a girl and a fellow fall in love.
By Faith Hubley, John Hubley; MGH; ABFI, FL

TENEMENT, THE (40m   B   1967)
Presents a sharp portrayal of a Chicago slum dwelling and the
people who live there.   Some of the residents of "The Tenement"
are ground down, worn to dull stupefaction; others are poignantly
articulate as they express their dreams of a "richer, sweeter life
out there--beyond reach--beyond hope." In a few there is a streak
of nobility--these are the mothers who war daily against despair and
strive fiercely to keep their children in school.   CBSTV; CAROUSEL;
EMC.

TENNIS MOTHERS (14m   C   n. d.)
The 30's gave us stage mothers; the 50's and 60's saw the rise
of Little League fathers.   Now the world must brace itself against
the newest power--tennis mothers.   Tennis Mothers is a perceptive
and humorous view of this latest type of parental pressure.   We are
shown a typical day in the life of Ilyse Wilpon, a 12-year-old girl
whose mother is a self-appointed tennis coach.   Margie Wilpon's
approach to the game is simple: "If you don't have competitive spirit you're not a winner, and you might as well just play for fun. "
CBSTV; CAROUSEL.

TERRITORIAL WEAPONRY IN ASSERTIVENESS TRAINING (32m   B
1976   VIDEO)
The following weaponry are skillfully played by Chris Story and
Charlotte Booth: "It's for Your Own Good," "No Fight," "Collusion,"
"Definitions," "Seduction," "Guilt Induction," "Illness," and "Psycho-
analysis." Defense against these weapons are shown. Based on
Bakker's No Trespassing. By Jim Parks, University of Washington
School of Social Work Media.   UW.

TESTING, TESTING, HOW DO YOU DO? (4m   C   1969)
Filmed at the 1969 Miss America Pageant held at Atlantic City,
Testing ... contains an interview with Miss Virginia, footage of the
pageant rehearsal and of the Women's Liberation demonstration taking place outside Convention Hall.   By Sheila Paige; WMM; CCC.

TEXTURE STUDY (15m   B   si   n. d.)
"A visual game of Destruction Sites. "--P. L. C.   By Patti-Lee
Chenis; FCOOP.

THAT FORSYTE WOMAN (112m   C   1949)
Rebellion against the Victorian taboos of society changes a man
(Errol Flynn) who had believed that money and position can buy any-
thing, including a good wife.   d. Compton Bennett; MGM; FL

THAT HAMILTON WOMAN (128m   B   1941   (Gr. Br.))
Alexander Korda teams with Laurence Olivier in the story of
Admiral Nelson and his mistress.   A careful, sympathetic and touching drama tracing the life of Nelson from his victory on the Nile to
his death in Trafalgar.   d. Alexander Korda; IVY.

THAT'S OUR BABY (23m   C   1975)
A 28-year-old woman in her first pregnancy tells of the routine
she and her husband adopted to prepare for the birth of their child.
Emphasizes the methods related to natural childbirth.   Scenes of the
pre-birth are juxtaposed with scenes of the delivery at the hospital
to show the result of advance planning.   Conversations between the
mother and other women who have practiced natural childbirth provide additional insight into the psychological and medical aspects of
this method of childbirth.   p. Carrie Agins, Jack Agins; SB; LP.

THEATRE OF SOCIAL PROBLEMS: IBSEN, HEDDA GABLER (59m
C   n. d.)
Shows how the emerging feminist consciousness in modern times
is exemplified in the theatre by Henrik Ibsen's heroine Hedda Gabler.   FFHL

THENOW (16m   C/B   1970)
An erotic, interracial sexual fantasy, in which a Black woman
experiences many selves and lovers.   By Constance Beeson; IE.

THERE HE GOES (22m   B   1971   r1975)
Short term "theraplay" with an overactive aggressive boy.

Shows actual psychotherapy sessions and includes a segment showing how theraplay therapists are trained. Ends up with a follow-up on child, three years after termination of theraplay. d. Ann M. Jernberg; p. Theodore W. Hurst; THERAPL.

THERMOMETERS: HOW WE USE THEM (11m C 1964)
    The thermometer revealed. By Geraldine Byers, Justin Byers; BFA.

THESE ITEMS ON SALE (20m C 1971)
    At the funeral of their old, beloved teacher, three women meet. The film reviews their ideas and feelings about themselves as children and as teen-agers and how, by using the teacher's moral prescriptions literally, they sell their potentials as humans to concepts of what they should be. They find themselves in the present as a manipulative executive, a loveless call girl, and a lonely wife and mother. UG.

THEY APPRECIATE YOU MORE; Challenge for Change Series (15m C n. d.)
    Aliette lives in Montreal with her husband and three children. Since both Aliette and Pierre work outside their homes "full time, " they share household responsibilities. This development has changed them as individuals and, they think, has affected the dynamics of their family--for the better. d. Kathleen Shannon; p. Len Chatwin; NFBC; EDC; EMC.

THIEF OF BAGDAD, THE (143m B si 1924)
    A tale of the Arabian nights in which Douglas Fairbanks finds a magic chest and saves the princess and the city from the Mongols. d. Raoul Walsh; s. w. Lotta Woods; UAS; ABFI, EMG, KP, SELECT, TWY, UNF.

THIN EDGE SERIES, THE see SEXUALITY: THE HUMAN HERITAGE

THIN MAN, THE (93m B 1934)
    Series of delightfully unpretentious screwball comedies and murder mysteries based on a story by Dashiell Hammett. William Powell and Myrna Loy starred as a perfectly happy, sophisticated couple whose marriage never stood in the way of their having fun and going off on detective capers. d. W. S. Van Dyke; Co-scripted by Frances Goodrich; MGM; FL

THINGS I CANNOT CHANGE, THE (55m B 1966)
    A look at a family in trouble, seen from the inside. There is trouble with the police, the begging for stale bread at a convent, and the birth of another child. The father explains his father's predicament. Although filmed in Montreal, this is an anatomy of poverty as it occurs in North America, seen by a camera that became part of family life for several weeks. By Tanya Ballantyne; NFBC; FL

THINGS IN THEIR SEASON (63m   C   1975)
Presents a story of a Wisconsin dairy farming family forced to deal with their interrelationships in the face of death. Mrs. Gerlach is a wife who feels her love was never returned by her husband. Her son is planning to marry and leave home to escape tensions with his father. When Mrs. Gerlach learns she has leukemia, she asks her son to delay his departure in order to help his father adjust and to keep the farm running smoothly after her death. Mr. Gerlach, realizing he has never been a loving husband, decides to take his wife on a vacation that has always been their dream. A series of painful and touching confrontations brings all members of the family to the realization that their lives have been full and, therefore, that they need not change their plans drastically in order to continue a fulfilling life. d. James Goldstone; TOMENT: LCA.

THINGS TO COME (3m   C   1954)
A sprightly abstract animation film in which the basic visual images were created by painter Marx and then animated by Jordan Belson. Music by Dizzy Gillespie. By Patricia Marx; CSF.

THIRD EYE BUTTERFLY (10m   C   1968)
Color patterns change and vibrate, creating an exciting abstract "painting" on film. By Storm De Hirsch; CCC, FCOOP.

THIS DECADE SERIES see LADY BARBARA WARD JACKSON

THIS IS NO TIME FOR ROMANCE (28m   C   1968   French/dubbed)
Dramatic portrayal of a day of low-keyed marital crises in the life of an upper-middle-class Canadian woman who is bored by domestic tranquility, beautiful children, a luxurious lakeside summer home, and seemingly endless leisure time. Shot in the style of the French "New Wave. "   d. Fernand Dansereau; NFBC; EMC, OSU, PAS, UM.

THIS IS THE HOME OF MRS. LEVANT GRAHAM (15m   B   1970)
Documents a Black family, living noisily and gregariously, in the Shaw area of Washington, D. C.   A bittersweet encounter that leaves one saddened by the oppressiveness of the physical situation but elated by the seemingly limitless potential of the human spirit to transcend its environment. Useful for discussion on poverty, marriage, values, what makes for happiness and whether cinéma-vérité can really be objective. By Claudia Weill, Topper Carew, Eliot Noyes, Jr. ; NTFC; PF; UILL, UM, USC.

THIS TIME LET'S TALK ABOUT MEN see LET'S TALK ABOUT MEN

THOROUGHLY MODERN MILLIE (138m   C   1967)
A light-hearted musical spoof of the 1920's with Julie Andrews as the "thoroughly modern" maiden, who, in true 1922 fashion, bobs her hair, smokes cigarettes, and is on a dedicated search for a millionaire husband. Mary Tyler Moore as Millie's constant companion,

a scatterbrained girl of incredible naiveté, innocently steals all the fellows from poor Millie.   d. George Roy Hill; p. Ross Hunter; s. w. Richard Morris; UNIVE; ABFI, CWF, FC, ROA, SWANK, TWY, UNIVE, WHOLFC.

THESE MEMORY YEARS (9m   C   1972)
"Autobiographical trivia.   A short musical film which recreates in full color, the longings and dreams of a woman of the past, replete with trembling blue mornings and the anxieties of a woman in search of ful-film-ment. "--P. C.   By Pola Chapelle; CHAPELLE.

THOUGHT DREAMS (3m   B   1972)
A surreal study of human and animal textures turns into an abstract game of hide and seek in which psychic states of being are momentarily revealed. "Four incongruous images compose Linkevitch's stark, yet alluring exploration into the area between conscious and unconscious thought. "--Karen Cooper, Film Forum.   By Barbara Linkevitch; SB.

THREE (18m   C   r1975)
Examines bisexuality in women.   Through a series of interviews a number of women offer candid views of what they expect from their own femininity, and their assessment of women's role in contemporary society.   d. Lisa Feiner; p. WNETTV; GP.

THREE BY MARTHA GRAHAM   see   ACROBATS OF GOD; CORTEGE OF EAGLES; SERAPHIC DIALOG

THREE FACES OF EVE (91m   C   1957   Scope)
Based on a true case history, this is the provocative story of a woman whose psychosis causes her to take on one personality, then a second, and finally a third: a drab spiritless housewife, a loose-living beauty, and a combination of the two.   Played with superlative power by Joanne Woodward.   d. Nunnally Johnson; FXO; FI.

THREE GRANDMOTHERS, THE; Comparison Series (28m   B   1963)
A glimpse into the lives of three grandmothers--a Nigerian (Muslim), a Canadian (Protestant), and a Brazilian (Catholic).   Shows that despite the great differences in the patterns of family life, the grandmothers have similar functions: to protect the young, guide the newlyweds, and enjoy the freedom to help.   NFBC; MGH; BU, BYU, EMC, FSU, PAS, UIO, USC, UW.

THREE GUESSES (29m   C   1973)
A film study of Ms. Jackie Burroughs of Toronto and the many roles she assumes during the course of a day--actress, mother, daughter, woman and estranged wife.   d. Joan Henson; NFBC; PHOENIX; VFI, UILL.

THREE IN A PARK (7m   C   1971)
"Girlfriends out for a day in the park meet a young man who creates an awkward triangle with racial overtones ... pastoral set-

ting helps smooth over the strong and disturbing under-currents. "
--YFD. By Bernadette Beekman; YFD.

THREE ISLAND WOMEN; Face of Change Series (17m   C   r1975)
Observes the role of three women--one young, one middle-aged,
and one old--on a small island in Hong Kong territory; shows that
they participate in the island's decision-making processes and share
with men the rigors of manual labor.   By Judith Von Daler, Nancy
Dupree; AUFS; WER; EMC, IU, MSU, UK.

THREE LIVES (70m   C/B   1971)
Focuses on three women: a middle-aged woman, a divorcee,
and a young lesbian.   First feature length, collectively made, wom-
en's liberation documentary.   By Louva Elizabeth Irvine, Susan
Kleckner. Robin Mide, Kate Millett; IMPF.

THREE LOOMS WAITING (50m   C   r1972)
Dorothy Heathcote, drama teacher at University of Newcastle,
England, explains her innovative teaching theories and methods,
demonstrating how serious improvisational drama can stimulate the
creative talents of children of various age and intelligence levels.
Shows her working with youngsters at a residential boy's school,
with ten-year-olds at a primary school, with a teen-age theatre
group, and with both children and drama education students at a
school for the mentally retarded.   TL; EMC, IU, UILL.

THREE MAGICAL METHODS (13m   C   1972)
Designed to teach children storytelling skills.   By Pat Sauer,
John Sauer; ECCW.

THREE WISHES (11m   B   1950)
Animated story of a peasant who receives three wishes for aid-
ing two gnomes, but wastes them due to his own greed and his wife's
spitefulness.   By Lotte Reiniger; CEA; MGH.

3:10 TO YUMA (38m   B   n. d.)
Perceptive analysis of the Western as morality play and myth
by New Statesman editor, John Freeman.   It uses excerpts from the
classic American film with special emphasis on its psychological
overtones.   d. Hazel Wilkenson; GP.

THROUGH CONFLICT TO NEGOTIATION   see   ORGANIZING FOR
POWER: THE ALINSKY APPROACH

THUMBELINA (10m   B   1930's)
Presents in animation the fairy tale, Thumbelina, based on the
live shadow play.   By Lotte Reiniger; BBCTV; MGH, CEA.

TICKY TACKY SONGBOOK: "MALVINA REYNOLDS" (30m   C   n. d.
VIDEO)
Bay Area songwriter Malvina Reynolds performs new songs to
an enthusiastic audience.   She sings "The Whales, " "Backyard Blues, "
"Plutonium, " "If You Love Me, " "World in Their Pocket, " and oth-
ers.   KQEDTV.

TIGER MAKES OUT, THE (95m C 1967)
A New York postman and self-taught intellectual confronts a suburban matron who is trying to re-enter college. The film deals with an unconcerned society which hinders and limits their needs and aspirations. d. Arthur Hiller; COLUMBIA; ABFI, CWF, ROA, SWANK.

TIGER ON A TIGHT LEASH; Challenge for Change Series (8m C n. d.)
Cathy, mother of three, is a university department head in a maritime city. She speaks of the insecurity she experiences because of unpredictable day care arrangements--and of the reflection of the same difficulty in the work of her married students. "They don't work as creatively as they could. " d. Kathleen Shannon; p. P. Len Chatwin; NFBC; EMC.

TILLIE'S PUNCTURED ROMANCE (44m B si 1914)
A takeoff on the old melodramas about country girls and city slickers, based on the musical comedy, "Tillie's Nightmare. " Healthy, vulgar, and full of earthy American humor. With Marie Dressler, Charlie Chaplin, Mabel Normand. d. Mack Sennett; KEYSTONE; ASFI, BF, FIM.

TIME AND NO TIME (5m B 1976)
Takes us into the loft of a young artist/writer, Barbara Bottner, and lets us see the unique surroundings in which she lives and works. As Barbara speaks of her involvement with her work and her aspirations, one begins to understand the compelling nature of creativity. By Rita Xanthoudakis; FL.

TIME FOR BURNING, A (58m B 1966)
Films in cinéma-vérité an actual drama of real people caught in the conflict between doubt and conviction. The individuals in the film are the members of Omaha's Augustan Lutheran Church (an all-white, middle-class congregation), their young spiritual leader, Pastor William Youngdahl, and members of the city's Negro ghetto. The film affords insight into all the cruelties and hazards of segregation. By Barbara Connell, William C. Jersey. MGH; EMC, UILL.

TIME HAS NO SYMPATHY (28m C 1975)
A humanistic portrait of women in prison. Made by a woman. Without special emphasis on political or expository material, Time Has No Sympathy conveys strong emotion through detailed coverage of daily prison life and the unfolding character of LaRue, a committed spokeswoman for social change. By Kristine Samuelson; SB, IE.

TIME OF YOUR LIFE, THE; Choice--Challenge for Modern Women
  Series (30m B 1966)
Presents Eva Schindler-Raiman and Paul Sheats discussing volunteer activities, ways of self-fulfillment and community benefit, and abuses and uses of discretionary time. Provides information about continuing education, employment and volunteer service. Offers perspective on the issue of employment for married women and encourages the development of attitudes that increase women's effectiveness in their chosen roles. EMC; UCLA.

TO A GOOD, LONG LIFE (23m C 1976)
Visits four old people who have varied, interesting life-styles and who enjoy the advantages of age. Presents Walt Stack, 67, who works as a hod carrier; Mitsu Yashima who teaches painting to older people; Jack Collins who meets with people who write and read and discuss their works. Explores Jack's relationship with Marie Rexroth, another member of the group. They both explain how they enjoy independence. CBSTV; BFA; IU.

TO BE A MAN; Circle of Life Series (14m C 1970)
Opens up all the central questions of masculinity, using the voices and opinions of young men: pressure to conform ... phoniness and heroism ... showing affection ... fatherhood ... alcohol and drugs ... sex before marriage ... male chauvinism. Directed to both sexes. A good opener for discussion. BBF; ASFI; UILL.

TO BE A PARENT; Circle of Life Series (16m C 1972)
Young people are taking a hard look at their parents and themselves. Both surprising and encouraging are their reactions to using children as weapons ... using children as shields ... overprotection ... prolonged dependence ... open communication ... formation and information on human sexuality. Primary relationships in the family are discussed. BBF; ASFI; UILL, UMIS.

TO BE A PERSON; Circle of Life Series (20m C 1972)
Examines what goes into a healthy personality growth that a young person can identify with in seeking his/her place in the sun. BBF; ASFI; UILL

TO BE A WOMAN; Circle of Life Series (15m C 1970)
Women and girls were interviewed regarding girlhood, personhood, anti-stereotypes, femininity, sexuality, and idealism. The best statements about themselves, their self-images, their attitudes, and their convictions were transferred to film. BBF; ASFI; CWU, UILL.

TO BE A WOMAN AND A WRITER (1976 SFS (2))
Explores past and present opportunities for women writers. Focuses on women writers as feminist voices, as a creative force in 20th-century American culture, and on women protagonists in fiction and poetry. Features excerpts from the writings of 17th-century New England poet Anne Bradstreet, the Brontës, George Eliot, Jane Austen, Mary Wollstonecraft, Louisa May Alcott, Anne Sexton, Lorraine Hansberry, Doris Lessing, Virginia Woolf, Anaïs Nin, Joyce Carol Oates, Gwendolyn Brooks. GA.

TO BE GROWING OLDER; Circle of Life Series (16m C 1972)
Examines the indifference and cruelty of society towards old people, and attempts to create an awareness of society's indifference. Describes how the young can bridge this chasm. BBF; ASFI; UILL.

TO BE IN LOVE; Circle of Life Series (14m C 1971)
Both male and female are speaking in this film, touching areas

of love for people themselves, first love, flower-child love, love and friendship, love and sex. Thoughts of Aristotle, Ovid, Jesus, Mohammed, Chaucer, Shakespeare, and Disraeli can be found among the young today. BBF; ASFI; UILL.

TO BE MARRIED; Circle of Life Series (15m   C   1971)
Themes treated by youth and adults with candor in this film are marriage and communication ... signs of affection ... divorce ... building together ... wedding day ... living together ... friendship. BBF; ASFI; UILL.

TO BE SOMEBODY (29m   C   1974)
Unrehearsed and unstaged documentary on the progress of a young Mexican American woman who is searching for work in an unfamiliar Anglo-dominated world. Frustrated and desperate after several unsuccessful efforts, she seeks aid at a local training program for youths, where a warm relationship gradually develops between the woman and her counselor, also a woman. Concludes with a description of conflicts that have occurred within the Mexican American woman's close family, and the counselor's own reflections about the meaning of her own job to her life. AP; BU, EMC.

TO BE YOUNG, GIFTED AND BLACK (90m   C   1972)
Sensitive adaptation of the stage production depicting the life and works of Black playwright Lorraine Hansberry who died of cancer in 1965 at age 34. Ms. Hansberry's most famous play, A Raisin in the Sun, made her the youngest American and the first Black playwright ever to win the New York Drama Critics Circle Award. Many scenes filmed on location capture such episodes as her first visit to the South, her response to the streets of Harlem, and her bittersweet memories of a high school English teacher. Conceived in a complex, free-flowing style, much of the script by her husband, Robert Nemiroff, is drawn from her plays, letters, and diaries. A moving and inspiring dramatic experience. d. Victoria Hochberg, Michael A. Shultz; NET, IU; EMC, TWY, UILL.

TO DIE TODAY (50m   B   r1972)
Dr. Elizabeth Kubler-Ross, Professor of Psychiatry, University of Chicago, discusses reasons why contemporary Americans fear death more than earlier generations. Discusses needs of dying people, and her theory of the five emotional stages through which dying persons pass. She interviews a young man, recently told he has Hodgkin's disease, who apparently has reached an acceptance of death. She then discusses his case in a seminar with resident interns. FL; EMC, UM.

TO EACH HIS OWN (122m   B   1946)
A mother (Olivia De Havilland), whose son (John Lund) was born out of wedlock, gives him up for adoption. Years later she meets him again and poses as his aunt. d. Mitchell Leisen; PARAMOUNT; CVE, UNIVE.

TO LOVE A CHILD (26m   C   1969)
"ABC documentary on adoption."--H. R.   By Hope Ryden; RYDEN.

TO PLAN YOUR FAMILY (13m   C   1967)
    Presents the techniques and advantages--to both the individual
and society--of family planning.   Includes diagrams of the female
reproductive organs and illustrations of several popular contraceptive
techniques.   Provides interviews to point out the ease and effectiveness of various birth control methods.   CF; EMC, IU, UILL.

TO SANDY (17m   C   1972)
    "Relationship between LSD and schizophrenia in an experimental
fiction sense."--J. F.   By Janet Foreman; FOREMAN.

TOGETHER (52m   B   1956)
    Classic documentary of two London dock workers who are deaf
mutes.   Views their world as one of anxiety, helplessness and solitude.   By Lorenza Mazzetti; MGH.

TOGETHER SWEETLY (15m   C   1972)
    This short version of How to Make a Woman deals with a wom-
an choosing between two men who represent her conflicting desires:
one offering adventure and sex without commitment, the other marriage, and a family.   She chooses marriage and the film shows what
can happen when a woman derives her identity through devoting herself to caring for her husband's needs while denying her own feelings.
p. Alvin Fiering; d. Alvin Fiering, Bobbi Ausubel; POLYMORPH.

TOILETTE (7m   C   1976)
    A clay animation film which explores a woman seeking her iden-
tity.   Arising in the morning, the woman steps before a mirror.
Disliking what she sees, she begins changing her clothes and then
rearranging her body--new eyebrows, smaller hips, etc.   She tries
several combinations with no success and decides to return to bed.
d. /p. Joan Freeman; FL

TOKEN GESTURE, A (8m   C   1976)
    An animated introduction to the problems of women in today's
society which pokes gentle fun at the traditional stereotypes and re-
strictive attitudes.   p. Julie McGregor, Don Arioli; NFBC.

TOM TIT TOT (13m   C   1955)
    This is the English version of Rumplestiltskin, narrated by
Margaret Lott.   Beautifully costumed actors perform the story in
silhouette and pantomime against colorful stylized backgrounds to
music appropriate to the 13th-century setting of the story.   Music
by Pro Musica Antigua.   By Flora Clar Mock; CFS.

TOMORROW'S CHILDREN (17m   C   1971)
    One of the most vital questions of our time, population growth,
is answered by this compelling, well-photographed film.   The viewer
sees the relationship between man and nature as it evolved from
give-and-take to control.   He feels the effects of the sheer number
of humans and the incredible quantity of their needs.   He perceives
the problem of over-population--and the need for birth control and
education.   He confronts that great responsibility--having a child--

for each child is a part of the earth, and tomorrow's small child affects the whole planet.   By Henry Mayer, M. D. ; PERENNIAL.

TOM'S FILM (1m   B   1973)
Made from four still photos.   "A funny little quirky work ... the importance of sound moving to image.   A gem of anti-sense. "-- Stan Vanderbeek.   By Linda Klosky; KLOSKY.

TORMENT OF JOAN OF ARC, THE; You Are There Series (22m C   1972)
In the turbulent France of the 15th century a young peasant girl, Joan of Arc, is on trial for heresy and treason.   Having been captured and betrayed by her enemies, Joan is imprisoned at the castle of Rouen, where she is tormented by the British and prosecuted by Bishop Cauchon.   By refusing to deny the charges against her, Joan faces the penalty of being burned at the stake.   CBSTV; BFA; OKSU.

TOUGHEST GAME IN TOWN (79m   B   1970)
A community corporation in Santa Fe, New Mexico, tells how the Chicano board of directors (four women and three men) successfully confront the power structure.   By Maia Sortor, George Ballis; CCC.

TOUR OF THE WHITE HOUSE WITH MRS. JOHN F. KENNEDY (58m   B   1962)
Presents a tour of the White House conducted and narrated by Mrs. John F. Kennedy in the company of Charles Collingwood. Emphasizes the history, traditions, and current status of the White House.   Traces the historical development of the White House and the changes made in it throughout the years, using old prints and photographs for illustration.   Additionally, shows the seldom-viewed Lincoln Room and Monroe Room.   Closes with President Kennedy in brief discussion of the impact and significance of the White House. CBSTV; MGH; BU, IU.

TOWARDS A NEW PAINTING: FORD
Based on a book, by Gordon Onslow-Ford, that explains the onset of the surrealism movement in art in Paris through to the 1947 San Francisco Art Museum showing of Ford works.   Not yet released at the time of this typing.   By Madeline Tourtelot; GP.

TOWARDS THE YEAR 2000 SERIES   see   FASHION: THE SECOND SKIN; GENETICS: MAN THE CREATOR; MEDIA: MASSAGING THE MIND; SEXES: BREAKING THE BARRIER, THE; SOCIO-BIOLOGY: DOING WHAT COMES NATURALLY; WOMEN: THE HAND THAT CRADLES THE ROCK

TRACES (12m   C   1973)
This film is multi-layered.   Color, sound, people, objects (both inside and outside the frame), motions, emotions, light, and haze all combine and are manipulated through editing to capture the conscious and unconscious impressions of the transition from child to woman.   "Traces and explores the fragile boundaries between the freedom and the responsibilities and demands of being an adult. "-- Linda Gross, Los Angeles Times.   By Barbara Linkevitch; SB.

TRANSACTIONAL ANALYSIS; Behavior in Business Film Series (30m
C 1974)
Using interviews, animation and live action scenes, this film reveals the TA approach to management to be clearly job-oriented and
pragmatic. It is a simplified approach to understanding why people
act the way they do. Provides guidelines for promoting more productive employee behavior. p. Joan Owens; CRM, MGH; EMC, UILL.

TRANSFORMATION OF MABEL WELLS, THE (12m C 1975)
Mabel Wells lived alone in the same house where she was born
for 79 years. Living alone so long in the big house made her can-
tankerous, disliking everybody and everything. One day while out
for a walk, she was knocked over by a boy on a bicycle. This
caused her to spend time in the hospital. While there, unexpected
things happened to her--people sent flowers and cards. Despite
having shut people out of her life, she had not been forgotten. This
changed Mabel's whole outlook on people and life. p. /d. Peter
Ketchum; GA.

TRANSFORMATION OF PERSEPHONE (10m C n.d.)
Erotic flashback of Persephone's abduction and rape. By Sylvianna Goldsmith; GOLDSMITH.

TRANSPORT (6m C 1970-71)
"An exploration of one movement cycle: a man, then a woman
is lifted from the ground and carried through space. The man and
woman never meet. Their relationship is made entirely through the
way the film is edited; the man and woman move (are moved) between ground and sky with an increasing violence which is an attempt to be transported, lifted out of oneself. "--A. G. By Amy
Greenfield; GREENFIELD.

TRANSPORTATION REVOLUTION: STORY OF AMERICA'S GROWTH,
THE (21m C 1970)
Traces the development of transportation from the horse and
buggy to the airplane, highlighting the important stages in the development of more rapid, comfortable and efficient means of travel
in America. Covers today's problems of congestion and pollution
that mobility has brought with it. By Helen Jean Rogers, John
Secondari; LCA.

TRAP DANCE (2m B 1968)
"An angry Arts 'protest film' with Black and White visuals. "--
S. D. H. By Storm De Hirsch; FCOOP.

TREASURE OF JAMAICA REEF, THE (94m C 1975 Scope)
Adventure and suspense as three men and a girl set out to find
a treasure in gold. Filmed 200 to 240 feet under water in the
Caribbean near the island of Jamaica. d. Virginia Stone; PRU; BF.

TREE GROWS IN BROOKLYN, A (128m B 1945)
The story centers around 12-year-old Francie Nolan (Peggy Ann
Garner) and her poignant struggle for a meaningful life amid an en-
vironment of urban poverty. A tree which Francie can see from her

window is symbolic of the girl herself, growing out of an atmosphere of pavements and rubbish, made strong through adversity.
The relationship between Francie and her weak, gallant father
(James Dunn) is very moving.   Although she depends on him, he is
unable to give her support.   When he dies, she realizes she has
grown up, and is no longer a child.   And, across the courtyard, the
tree has grown tall as well.   An adaptation of Betty Smith's autobiographical novel set in a Brooklyn tenement several decades ago.
The film is a timeless account of the period between childhood and
maturity.   d. Elia Kazan; s. w. Tess Slesinger; FOX; ABFI, CWF,
FI, SELECT, TWY, UNF, WHOLFC.

TREES (10m B 1972)
   "Highway imagery shot between New York and Maryland. "--P. S.
By Patricia Sloane; WAF.

TREMBLING CARTOON BAND (20m B. n. d.)
   A collection of nine shorts created by Ms. Anderson's students.
By Yvonne Anderson; YBW.

TRENDSETTER, THE (6m C 1971)
   A cartoon showing a man with original ideas who succumbs to
the flattery of imitation.   By Vera Linnecare; PF.

TRESTLE, THE (3m C n. d.)
   "Deserted railroad trestle on the edge of town, with clouds
floating unconcernedly over it and several buildings ... marvelously
intuitive first effort. "--Wheeler Dixon.   By Raika Terebey; FCOOP.

TRIAL (54m C 1974)
   "Documentary of an actual (and exceedingly interesting) murder
trial, complete from empaneling the jury, questioning the witnesses,
to rendering the verdict. "--N. C.   Made for the Kentucky Crime
Commission.   By Nell Cox; COX.

TRIAL MARRIAGE (180m B 1929)
   Constance Bannister enters into a trial marriage contract with
Dr. Thorvald Ware and finds happiness with him.   She defies his
wishes by dancing at a charity ball in a revealing costume, however,
and he dissolves the contract not knowing she is with child.   A
year passes.   Constance marries Mowbray, Thorvald marries Constance's sister.   Both couples are unhappy and later obtain divorces.
Oliver and Grace remarry, as do Constance and Thorvald, united by
their love for one another and their child.   p. Harry Cohn; d. Erle
C. Kenton; PARAMOUNT; FCE.

TRIAL OF JOAN OF ARC (65m B 1962 French/subtitled)
   Robert Bresson relying solely on the transcript of the trial of
Joan of Arc, discloses all the drama, mystery and glory that has
lain buried beneath the more conventional images of Joan.   This
portrait is at once engrossing, believable, deeply compassionate
and moving.   d. Robert Bresson; MGH.

TRIAL OF SUSAN B. ANTHONY, THE; You Are There Series (22m
C 1972)
Susan B. Anthony is on trial for the "crime" of having voted in
the last national election. The trial itself and people's reactions to
Susan and her fight for women's suffrage reflect the public opinion
of the time; and in fact, have interesting parallels today. Although
Susan did not win this battle, her courage has inspired others since
to organize and battle for equal rights. CBSTV; BFA; UKEN.

TRIALS OF ALICE CRIMMINS, THE (6m B 1971)
Cooperatively made by women who feel that Alice Crimmins was
convicted on the basis of her life-style. This is a dramatic re-
enactment based on the trials of the divorced mother who was convicted in 1971 for the murder of her two children, a verdict which
is being appealed. Although well motivated, this film doesn't really
make the issues clear because of the editing and brevity. WMM.

TRIBAL EYE SERIES, THE see WOVEN GARDENS

TRIBUTE TO MALCOLM X, A (15m B 1969)
Reports the influence of Malcolm X upon the present Black liberation movement. Reviews his life through an interview with his wife,
Betty Shabass. Tells of his mother's commitment to a mental institution when he was a child and his father's being killed. Shows
how Malcolm X became a Black Moslem minister and a leader of
the Black struggle until his assassination. By Madeline Anderson;
IU; EMC.

TRIO AT NINETEEN (10m B 1970)
"A young woman's alienation and struggle for identity triggers
tension between her and her two friends--both boys. "--YFD. By Judith
Kurtz; YFD.

TRIP TO AWARENESS, A (30m C 1976)
Explores the ancient Jain religion founded in 6th century B. C.
Camera follows the journey of an Indian spiritual leader and 18 of
his American students on a pilgrimage to a number of Jainist shrines
and holy places in India. Some of the basic precepts and practices
of Jain philosophy are presented. Meditation, vegetarianism, and
physical fitness are all a part of the daily regimen. Self-examination
and the concept of God being within the individual are also basic directions. Other Jain concepts and doctrines presented include equality of the sexes, reverence for life, ahimsa or nonviolence, and re-
incarnation. By Elda Hartley; HARTLEY.

TRIUMPH OF THE WILL (120m B 1934-36 German/subtitled)
A two-hour expression of a fanatical devotion to the "Fuehrer"
principle is a unique historical record which perhaps more than any
other document of the time exposes the psychology of the Third
Reich. Commissioned by Hitler himself, this is a record of the
Sixth Annual Party Congress in Nuremberg which involved the efforts
of thousands of people. d. Leni Riefenstahl; ABFI, MGH. MMA
(no subtitle).

TROLLSTENEN (125m   C   1976)
An autobiographical film on the filmmaker, her family, and her past using old photographs, live-action footage and occasional home movies photographed in Sweden.   Medieval music, voice-over narration, sync-sound, childhood songs and rhymes are woven throughout. By Gunvor Nelson; SB.

TROUBLE WITH ANGELS, THE (112m   C   1966)
An outrageously funny comedy with Rosalind Russell playing Mother Superior of a quiet, sedate convent school--that is, until Hayley Mills arrives at the convent.   Hayley keeps Mother Superior in a constant state of panic.   Through it all, Mother Superior is determined to salvage something of worth from the youthful clay and in the end, Hayley graduates, determined to be a nun.   Based on My Life with Mother Superior by Jane Trahey.   d. Ida Lupino; s. w. Blanche Hanalis; COLUMBIA; ABFI, DB, TWY.

TROUBLE WITH WOMEN, THE (110m   B   1963)
A man is murdered during an elegant soiree, and circumstantial evidence points to a dashing playboy (Jacques Charriers) as the killer. When a jealous girl friend (Jill Haworth), whom he has jilted, claims she saw him committing the crime, he tries to hunt out the real killer before the police close in on him.   Filmed on the back streets of Paris.   d. Michele Deville; PARAMOUNT; ABFL

TRUE HEART SUSIE (93m   B   si   1919)
Susie is a country girl who, unbeknownst to him, sacrifices all for a country boy she loves.   She helps him to realize his ambitions until he is out of her reach, and he marries another.   With Lillian Gish and Robert Harron.   d. D. W. Griffith; ARTCRAFT; BF, EMG, MMA.

TRUE LIGHT BEAVER FILM--AFTER THE REVOLUTION (20m   C   1970)
A home-movie exploration of the life-style of an upstate New York commune.   Primarily of interest to those studying communes as a social phenomenon.   p. /d. TLB.

TRYING TIME, THE (20m   C   1974)
Young teen-agers are people groping for independence, awkward about physical and emotional development, experimenting with boy-girl relationships.   They are also looking for guidance based on love, respect, and open communication.   This film is designed to help parents be more sensitive to these needs....   Some emphasis is placed on discussion of sexual values.   Comments of the parents in the film are an excellent springboard for discussion among viewing parents.   More concerned with attitudes than answers, the film strongly encourages the possibility of empathy between parents and teens.   PPSEA.

TUB FILM (2m   B   1973)
Tells the story of a woman and her sweet-voiced kitten.   Shows how both are playful and carefree, but one is in for a surprise.   By Mary Beams; BFA.

TUESDAY (3m B 1972)
"Mercer Street and Environs. "--P. S.   By Patricia Sloane; WAF.

TULIP (5m C 1973)
Male body studied in relation to flower forms in strong red.
By Rosalind Schneider; VRL

TURTLE SOUP (6m C 1967)
"Animated and live ... dream experience of childhood, youth,
old age; past, present, future; child, parent, grandparent; beauty,
vanity, despair; dream, reality, illusion. "--L D.   By Irene Duga;
FCOOP.

TV TALENT COORDINATOR: SHE'S ALWAYS ON THE MOVE, A;
Job Series, A (12m C 1969)
Viewers share the experience of a satisfying job and learn the
educational requirements it demands, as the camera follows Alice
Hill, television talent coordinator, during a typical day of work.
A brief biography at the end of film summarizes Alice's background
and training.   MGH; UILL.

TWELVE LIKE YOU (25m C 1976)
A candid discussion about the career opportunities for women
by women.   Twelve career women share their experiences, ideas
and frustrations, to assist working women reach their potential.
DRUKER; CCCD; ROA, UIO.

20TH CENTURY SERIES see MRS. INDIRA GANDHI; PERON AND
EVITA; WOMAN DOCTOR IN VIETNAM

TWO (11m C 1970)
A riotous spoof on love scenes in Italian movies, complete
with tongue-in-cheek English subtitles.   Written by and starring
Renee Taylor.   WYLDE; ABFI, CFS.

TWO CATS--ONE CHICK (20m B n. d.)
Two young men are interested in the same young girl.   She is
indifferent.   The film amusingly follows them to a final duel between the gents.   Swingy score by Paul Severson.   By Madeline
Tourtelot; GP.

TWO CENTURIES OF BLACK AMERICAN ART (26m C 1976)
Presents 200-year history of Black American art.   Included are
painters, sculptors, cabinet makers, potters, builders and artisans.
Earlier artists included are: Joshua Johnson, Robert S. Duncanson,
Edward M. Bannister, Edmonia Lewis, Patrick Reason, Aaron
Douglas, and Henry D. Tanner.   Later artists presented are: Ro-
mare Beardon, Charles H. Alston, Selma Burke, John Rhoden,
Charles White, John Biggers, et al.   d. Carlton Moss; PF.

TWO DAUGHTERS (TVA DOTTRAR) (22m C 1974 Swedish/sub-
titled)
The title Two Daughters refers to the continuity of generations.
The illness and death of her daughter makes the woman remember

the troubled relationship she had with her own mother. She sees
herself as a daughter, as well as a mother. The theme of motherhood is beautifully handled. This August Strindberg story on which
the film is based is Half a Sheet of Paper written in 1903. Made
with a grant from Swedish Broadcasting Corporation and The
Swedish Film Institute. p. /d. Paul Mareth (an American); EMC.

TWO FACES OF GROUP LEADERSHIP (30m   C   n. d.)
    The film captures the dynamics of group process under the di-
rection of Dr. Marilyn Bates, co-author of Group Leadership: A
Manual for Group Leaders, and a major contributor to the development of group leadership technique and skills. Start with the pre-
group interview and moves quickly through the various stages of
group counseling. Gives a clear view of two basic functions of mo-
bilizing and managing. PFL

TWO FACES OF CHINA, THE (50m   C   r1972)
    Overview of various facets of life in modern China, emphasizing
intermingling of old and new in Chinese culture. Briefly touches on
such issues as family, the role of women, rural communes, education, medicine, Chinese cuisine. Considers the many aspects of
party life as well as the change from protest of submission to abso-
lute party authority. Fails to elucidate the political issues behind
China's modern transformations. BBCTV; PIC; EMC.

TWO FOR THE ROAD (111m   C   1967   Scope)
    In this elegantly mounted comedy, an English couple's year old
marriage, straining at the seams, is recounted in a highly unorthodox, unchronological manner. With Audrey Hepburn, Albert Finney,
Eleanor Bron, William Daniel. d. Stanley Donen; FOX; FL

TWO MINUTES (2m   C   1969   VIDEO)
    Presents the history of Israel from Theodore Herzl to Golda
Meir in rapid-paced survey using 500 still photographs. By Dalia
Steinitz, Dan Israely, and Gabriel Steinitz. SLFP.

TWO OR THREE THINGS I KNOW ABOUT HER (85m   C   1966
Scope)
    A filmed sociological essay on how many of the women residing
in the low-cost high-rise housing complexes resort to casual prostitution in order to make ends meet. The practice has become so
common, apparently, that there is even a name for them: "Shooting
Stars. " The film begins one evening and ends the next, during
which time the young housewife (Marina Vlady) has spent the day in
Paris. d. Jean-Luc Godard; NYF.

TWO PHOTOGRAPHERS: WYNN BULLOCK, IMOGEN CUNNINGHAM
(29m   B   n. d.)
    A humorous and revealing dialogue between two unique artists.
Much of their work is included in the film, along with candid and
personal discussions with each of the artists about experiences,
philosophy, and work. By Fred Padula; CCC.

TWO-PROFESSION MARRIAGE, THE; Woman Series (29m C 1974
VIDEO)
A successful two-profession couple discuss their feelings about
their situation and how other people react to it. Gail Parker, Bennington College's 32-year-old president, and her husband, Tom Parker, the College's vice president, find that most of the problems in
their marriage involve "trying to find time to cook, clean, or shine
shoes. " WNEDTV; PTL.

TWO SPACE TRIPS (14m B si n. d.)
Unusual optical effects achieved by photographing a sprinkler
and water from it dripping on a glass.   By Athena Tacha; VRL

TWO WOMEN (105m B 1961 Italian/subtitled)
A story of a mother (Sophia Loren) and daughter (Eleanora
Brown) struggling to survive in Italy during World War II.   The
two retreat on foot from Rome during the bombings and seek sanctuary in a small mountain village to begin life anew with the peasants.   Cesira, the mother, falls in love with a disillusioned school
teacher, but her life becomes complicated by her daughter's attraction to him.   Then one day the school teacher is forced to guide a
group of retreating Germans across the mountains.   Cesira decides
to return with her daughter to Rome.   On the way, both mother and
daughter are brutally raped by Moroccan soldiers.   The shock and
horror of this experience and the war itself is powerfully etched on
the face of the daughter by the camera.   This and the news of the
death of the school teacher change her.   In the end, she and her
mother are united by a bond of grief and suffering.   Original title
La Ciociara.   Based on novel by Alberto Moravia.   d. Vittorio De
Sica; p. Carlo Ponti; ABFL

U. F. O. 'S (3m C 1971)
"U. F. O. 's proves that computer animation ... once a rickety
and gimmicky device ... is now progressing to the state of an art.
The complexity of design and movement, the speed and rhythm, the
richness of form and motion, coupled with stroboscopic effects, is
unsettling.   Even more ominously, while design and action are programmed by humans, the 'result' in any particular sequence is not
entirely predictable ... being created at a rate faster and in con-
catenations more complex than eye and mind can follow or initiate. "
--Amos Vogel, Village Voice.   By Lillian Schwartz; LPI.

U. S. A. --A SERIES see DANCE--ANNA SOKOLOW'S "ROOMS";
DANCE--ECHOES OF JAZZ; DANCE--FOUR PIONEERS;
DANCE--IN SEARCH OF LOVERS; DANCE--NEW YORK CITY
BALLET

U. S. HIGHBALL (30m C 1963)
An important work by Harry Partch, first composed for guitar
and voice, narrating his experience as a hobo riding the freights

from San Francisco to Chicago in the 30's.   Later, Partch rewrote his music for chorus and full instrumentation.   This film interlocks the musical performance with freight movement across the U. S. landscape.   By Madeline Tourtelot; GP.

UKRAINE IN FLAMES (56m   B   1945   (dubbed))
     A powerful documentary depicting Russia's battle for liberation of the Ukraine.   Yulia Solntseva and Yakov Avdyenko edited the re-markable footage taken by 24 cameramen who advanced with Red Army troops during the actual offensive.   Also shown are captured Nazi newsreels which recorded the thousand-day battle that broke the Nazis' grip on Russia.   Narrated by Bill Downs, CBS corres-pondent.   d. Yulia Solntseva, Yalov Avdyenko; p. /s. w. Alexander Dovzhenko; ABFI.

UMATILLA '68 (37m   B   1968)
     This anthropological film centers on the life and work of the Umatilla Indians.   The reservation lands, located near Pendleton, Oregon, are rich wheat country, yet they are farmed almost com-pletely by whites.   The film explores the relationship of the Uma-tillas to the land.   It looks into their lives, at their jobs, their celebrations, disclosing the nature of their problems, concerns and interests.   Narrated by the Umatilla Indians.   By Anne Kish; CCC.

UMBRELLAS OF CHERBOURG, THE (90m   C   1964   French/sub-
     titled)
     A bittersweet romance, entirely in song, in which absence tragically severs the relationship between two lovers, but never destroys their love.   With Catherine Deneuve and Nino Castelnuovo. d. /s. w. Jacques Demy; p. Mag Bodard; ABFI.

UNDALA (28m   C   r1968)
     Portrays, without narration, village life in the Thar desert in northwest India during hot, windy months before monsoon rains. Shows farmers making repairs and at leisure, women carrying water, and craftsmen going about their daily routine.   Includes view of Rajasthani life such as pottery making, spinning, leatherwork, rope making, and the important task of drawing water.   Original score in Hindustani classical and folk styles.   By Allison Jablonko, Marek Jablonko; CMC; EMC.

UNDER THE COVERS: AMERICAN QUILTS (11m   C   1976)
     People find great satisfaction in creating one of the most popu-lar crafts, quilting.   Started out of necessity quilting today is recog-nized as an art form.   The film survey of patterns and stitches, colors and shapes, focuses on the historical importance and home-spun vitality of American quilts.   A toe-tapping banjo and guitar sound track augments the narration and adds to the authentic feeling. By Millie Paul; PF.

UNDER THE TREES   see   PHOTOGRAPHY: DOROTHEA LANGE--
     UNDER THE TREES

UNDERGROUND (85m C r1976)
Uses interviews with members of the Weather Underground and
footage of the turbulent '60's to give a historical perspective to
those protest years. The members of the Weather Underground express themselves on the subject of revolution as well as on social
and economic change in America. d. /p. Emile D'Antonio, Mary
Lampson, Haskell Wexler; RBC.

UNDERGROUND FILM, THE (23m C 1971)
An in-depth documentary profile of award-winning New American
film-artist Chick Strand. The film shows Chick at home and on location, as she explains her interest in film-art and demonstrates her
techniques. Included in its entirety is the well-known example of
her work "Anselmo." d. Paul Marshall; PARACO; CFS, EMC, VFL

UNDINE (5m C/B 1966)
Depicts the myth of the water spirit that played the violin at
night and drowned his listeners when he finished. Calo Scott's music. By Cassandra M. Gerstein; FCOOP.

UNEVENTFUL DAY, THE; Planet of Man, The (Series) (29m C
1976)
Examines the process of weathering: the physical and chemical
forces that produce the variety and the beauty of our planet's geo-
rama. p. /d. Penny Crompton; FL

UNFOLDING (17m B 1969)
Suggests universal awareness, including aloneness, fantasies,
searching, touching and loving. Blends ocean, hill, sun, woman
and man to portray subterranean feelings. Emphasizes a value-
oriented view of sexuality, and expresses the woman's point of view.
By Constance Beeson; MMRC.

UNION MAIDS (45m B r1976)
A documentary about three remarkable women who became organizers in the 1930's. They give personal accounts of the changes
they and their co-workers went through as they became aware of the
working class oppression, second-class status of women and minorities, and the clear need for collective action to win change. A
realistic sense of the period is fleshed out through a great deal of
archival footage, stills, and labor music of the 1930's and 40's. A
tribute to the courage and power of the working class women everywhere. d. Julia Reichert, James Klein; Miles Mogulescu; NDF; UW.

UNLIKELY ADDICTS: MIDDLE-CLASS WOMEN; Woman Series (29m
C 1974 VIDEO)
Journalist Barbara Kerr discusses private and public addicts.
Private addicts are often the housewives who try to live out the
myth of middle-class women. Quite often their lives are not ful-
filling, not happy. ... They attempt to keep their addictions secret
and usually become dependent on alcohol and/or barbiturates.
WNEDTV; PTL.

UNLONELY WOMAN, THE; Choice: Challenge for Modern Woman
Series (30m   B   r1966)
Richard Farson and Eve Merriam discuss emotional and practical
aspects of being alone; loneliness versus the pleasure of solitude.
UCLA; EMC.

UNMARRIED MOTHER INTERVIEW;   PETERS-BROWNING (68m   B
1965)
Consists of four studies, each on a 17-minute reel.   Interview
situations show how the interviewer's skills and attitudes affect the
interviewee and determine the success of the interview.   USC; FSU.

UNSINKABLE BETTE DAVIS, THE (26m   B   1963)
Describes major events in the life and career of Bette Davis.
Illustrates her acting versatility by showing scenes from several of
her films.   WOLPER.

UNTIL I DIE (30m   C   r1970)
Concise presentation of the work of Dr. Elizabeth Kubler-Ross,
noted researcher and writer in the field of psychological reaction and
adjustment to the process of dying.   Appropriate for specialists and
layman.   WTTWTV; AJN; EMC, IU, PAS.

UNTITLED (17m   C   1972)
"Norman Corwin's classic anti-war radio drama filmed exactly
as it would have been rehearsed and acted on radio in the 40's, in
a special performance for this film by a distinguished cast of famous
radio actors including Loreen Tuttle.   William Shatner plays the
leading role. "--PORTMAN.   By Perry Miller Adato; ADATO.

UP IS DOWN (6m   C   1970)
An animated film about a boy who walks on his hands.   He not
only looks different but also sees things differently.   By Mildred
Goldsholl; PF.

UP, OVER, AND BANG (10m   B   1971)
An objective look at the girls' signal corps of St. Patrick's
Imperial High School.   When viewed ironically, however, this makes
an extraordinary statement about our culture.   The girls are shown
in various stages of preparation for a competitive drill, involving
rote marching with flags and rifles in paramilitary fashion.   d.
Angela Varela; MARQU.

UPKEEP (10m   C   1973)
History of the world as lived by the repair person.   We learn
that maintenance can be more than a corrective maintenance; it can
also be creative.   By Faith Hubley, John Hubley; MTP.

UPPERVILLE SHOW, THE (9m   B   1971)
Presents a documentary of the oldest horse show in America in
Upperville, Virginia.   Views pedigreed people and thoroughbred
horses in a spring festival.   By Rebecca Davenport, Tom Davenport;
NLC.

UPRISING OF THE 20, 000 (30m   B   n. d.   VIDEO)
A drama based on the historic strike of the women garment workers in New York City, 1909.   Performed by students from A. C. T. , with original photographs of the strike.   Music by Prairie Fire.   Produced by the Women's History Project.   KQEDTV.

URBANISSIMO (6m   V   1968)
Features a humorous commentary on modern urban civilization. Deals with city growth and development.   By Faith Hubley; John Hubley; MGH; FL

URINARY TRACT INFECTION (16m   C   1976)
Live action and animation are combined to show the cause and effects of urinary tract infection.   Myths about the origins of infections are examined along with current effective guidelines for treatment.   Emphasis is placed on the patient's role in long-term care and prevention.   d. Marilyn Katz, Dan Bessie; p. R. J. Sternberg, M. D. ; PRORE.

VD (26m   C   1972)
Filmed cinéma-vérité style at an information center, a school, and venereal-disease clinics, the film emphasizes a person's responsibility to seek aid for oneself and others involved if there is a possibility of infection.   BFA.

VD: A CALL TO ACTION (27m   C   n. d.)
A revealing film emphasizing action and presenting positive procedures which can be adopted by every community in combating venereal disease.   The action takes place in Fall River, Massachusetts--but it could be your town.   The camera follows Diane Champagne, R. N. , tracking down VD carriers through teen-agers, police files, doctors, nurses and bartenders.   PORTSP; AFI; UWY.

VD: EPIDEMIC (27m   B   1965)
Discusses the epidemic proportions of venereal disease and its high cost to the nation.   Stresses the need for early treatment and for follow-up of contacts of infected persons.   ABCTV; MGH; USC, UILL.

VD: EVERY THIRTY SECONDS (17m   C   1971)
Dramatizes the seriousness of venereal disease.   The physiological aspects of syphilis and gonorrhea are discussed; and, of equal importance, the effects of untreated VD are carefully explained. p. HIGGINS; PERENNIAL; UMIS, USC.

VD: HANDLE WITH CARE (18m   C   1973)
Documentary dealing with venereal disease on a "feeling" level rather than emphasizing the organic and physical manifestation.   A candid communication of feelings from people who are open and honest about their sexual experiences and what they have learned about VD and human relationships.   CINCON; OF; PARACO, UM.

VD: PREVENT IT (11m   C   1972)
VD is the easiest of all communicable diseases to prevent.
How?   Prevent the VD germs of one person from infecting another.
The precautions are simple: soap and water, urinating after contact,
a bacteria-killing douche, a properly employed condom, germ-killing
medications, periodic physical examinations, no promiscuity.   p.
HIGGINS; PERENNIAL; USC, UILL.

VD QUESTIONS, VD ANSWERS (15m   C   1972)
Venereal diseases are "silent."   A person, particularly a girl,
might not be aware of the disease until too late.   How does one contract VD?   How can we know if we have the disease?   What can be
done about prevention or treatment?   Where does one get help?
With the aid of animation the film helps young people find answers
to the questions they are asking.   A Herbert-Barnard--Harry Robbin
Film; BFA; UMIS, UILL, UWY.

VD--SEE YOUR DOCTOR (22m   C   n. d.)
Through a chain of circumstances, Linda and John have con-
tracted gonorrhea.   Both saw their doctors in the early stages of
infection and cooperated with the health department.   The film explains the causes and symptoms of syphilis and gonorrhea and clearly states the serious consequences of untreated VD.   AFI; UMIS.

VD: THE SILENT EPIDEMIC SERIES (C   n. d.   SFS   (3))
Describes symptoms of gonorrhea and syphilis; presents vignettes dealing with emotional and physical damage done by VD; traces
history and treatment of VD.   Series titles: The Physical Attack;
The Emotional Attack; Crises and Counter Attack.   AVNA.

VD TROUBLES; Human Sexuality Series (29m   C   1972   VIDEO)
A discussion of the difficulty of identifying, treating and con-
trolling venereal disease.   An educational film designed to provide
VD information to high school students is shown during the program.
UHAWAII/KHETTV; PTL.

VALERIE (15m   C   1975)
Explores some of the attitudes and insights of an extremely
gifted sculptor, Valerie Maynard, whose work is acclaimed in America and abroad.   By Monica Freeman; NPI; PHOENIX.

VALERIE (16m   B   1975)
Focuses on the life-style and values of a drag queen, a young
man who assumes the role of a woman.   As the camera follows
"her" through common activities, Valerie discusses her early life
and identification with women; her family's reaction to her first public appearance in women's clothes and her gradual acceptance of female impersonation as a way of life; her techniques as a prostitute
("You have to be concerned..."); her treatment by the law, especially the attempts made to "rehabilitate" her by convincing her that the
life-style she finds comfortable is perverse.   The film may prompt
some initial shock, but its total effect is to promote empathy and
understanding of a socially delicate sexual topic.   By Joseph Horning;
PERENNIAL.

VALI see VALI, THE WITCH OF POSITANO

VALI, THE WITCH OF POSITANO (65m C 1966)
A document of the true life of one of the most far-out witches
in the Western world. The filmmakers have captured a most original woman in this vivid film portrait which literally casts a spell
on viewers, and leaves them in awe of a very powerful personality.
By Diane Rochlin, Sheldon Rochlin; NLC.

VARIETY (57m B si 1925)
Emil Jannings stars as a trapeze artist who finds his wife has
been two-timing him with another member of the circus act. d.
E. A. Dupont; BF, MMA.

VASECTOMIA (20m B 1971)
Listening to a group of men in Bogota, Colombia, who have had
vasectomies. Taped in Spanish with translation. By Martha Stuart;
STUARTM.

VEIL (6m B si (loop) 1971)
"Influenced by Kenneth Anger's Puce Moment (1949) ... the main
intention was to make a film of wipes ... by having layers of
clothes and other materials and pulling them off one at a time ...
erotic designs are shown. "--L. C. G. By Joan Jonas; CASTELLL

VEJEN (THE WAY) (22m C 1969)
Focusing on a young priest and his acolyte as they go about
their daily life, this film sensitively explores the peace and time-
lessness of the Buddhist religion. The patience and suffering of
the people of the East comes into view as the film examines how
they deal with life. d. Elsebet Kjolbye; p. Per Holst Teknisk Com-
pagnie (Denmark); STATNS; CAROUSEL.

VENEREAL DISEASE: THE HIDDEN EPIDEMIC (27m C 1972)
A brief history of venereal disease; people's changing attitude
towards it, the symptoms of syphilis and gonorrhea, and the progression of the diseases. The importance of preventing and treating syphilis and gonorrhea, and the need for developing a personal
attitude toward venereal disease prevention is stressed. EBEC;
UIO, UM, USC.

VENETIAN BLINDS (3m C n. d.)
"Shadow figure of a nude woman in front of a window covered
with venetian blinds. The blinds move constantly, providing an illuminated background for the moving woman, with various filter
changes. "--Freude Bartlett. By D. Samatowicz; SB.

VERA PAINTS IBIZA IN THE SUN (16m C 1974)
Shows how the noted textile designer Vera Newmann is inspired
by the sunny, colorful life on the island of Ibiza, off the coast of
Spain. Later, in New York, shows one of her drawings being transformed into a colorfully printed scarf. Reveals the complexity of
the textile painting and manufacturing process. Often seems to be

a heavy-handed promotional vehicle, but is generally an informative and entertaining production. SCHLAT; PRENTICE; BU, EMC.

VERA SAN PAINTS JAPAN (7m   C   1972)
Shows the American designer Vera developing her Japanese fashion collection, from calligraphic studies done in Japan to the finished designs and prints. VERAIN.

VERONICA; Jason Film Portrait Series (27m   C   r1970)
A cinéma-vérité portrait of Veronica Glover, a Black high school student leader in New Haven, Connecticut, and her struggle to find her own identity in the face of pressures from both Black and white students. Includes sequences of her in school, in a student congress she helped organize, in conversations with friends, and in her private life. Emphasizes her conflicts with militant Black separatists in her school who accuse her of being a "Tom" because she works with white students as well as Blacks. Concludes with Veronica giving the graduation address. By Pat Powell; JASON; EMC, PAS, UM.

VERTICAL ROLL (20m   B   n. d.)
Images of figures on legs and torsos, seen as if on a television set with its "vertical" roll malfunctioning. By Joan Jonas; CASTEL-LL

VERY CURIOUS GIRL, A (LA FIANCEE DU PIRATE) (107m   C
1969   French/subtitled)
A story of a young woman in revolt. "At first Mary lives a serf-like existence, dependent upon a bourgeois landowner, Irene, whom she serves perfunctorily. ... It is during the "wake" of her mother that the stage is set for reversals. Mary leaves Irene's estate and sets up her own business--as village whore. Slowly she reverses existing relations of force in the village by de-mystifying the self-righteous and hypocritical attitudes of the villagers. "--Naomi Gilbert. d. Nelly Kaplan; IE, TWY, UNIVE.

VERY EYE OF NIGHT, THE (15m   B   1959)
A celestial, cinematic ballet filmed entirely in the negative. Choreography by Anthony Tudor. Score by Teiji Ito. p. /d. Maya Deren; GP.

VERY REMARKABLE YAMATO FAMILY, PT. II (59m   C   1975)
Focuses on the contrasts in society and politics in modern Japan. Reports on the change in family structure away from a strong matriarchy; school children being offered individualized instruction while still wearing uniforms; the fading godlike image of the Emperor; a small women's liberation movement; and the growing interdependence of Japan's relationships with China, the Soviet Union and the U. S. IU; EMC.

VESAK (17m   C   1973)
"Vesak is an occasion in India and Ceylon for celebrating Lord Buddha's birthday, his day of enlightenment, and the day he achieved

Nirvana. Vesak is saved from being a nuts-and-bolts travelogue
by the beauty of many of its images. Ms. Hannemann is a smooth
cinematographer. She lovingly photographs the beauty of the lights,
kites, masks, and lanterns used for the celebration of these holy
days. This film is a valid substitute for those who must experience
Vesak by way of a film rather than in person. "--Robert Steele, Previews and Reviews. By Yvonne Hannemann; SB.

VIBRANT NUDES (23m   C   n. d.)
    Psychedelic study of five live nudes intertwined with op art pat-
terns. By Hannah Roman, Joseph Roman; CENTER.

VIBRATIONS ENCORE, PT. I (30m   C   n. d   VIDEO)
    Three women, three styles showcased in performance: Micki
Grant, singer/composer of the Broadway musical Don't Bother Me,
I Can't Cope; Shirley Verratt, concert singer/opera star; and Carol
Hall, singer/composer. All three performers were trained in the
classics, but various musical modes such as gospel, jazz and folk
have influenced each in a different way. The synthesis of these elements into each woman's unique style demonstrates the diverse possibilities of self-expression through music. WNETTV.

VIBRATIONS ENCORE, PT. IV (30m   C   n. d.   VIDEO)
    Portrays Evelyn Lear and Thomas Stewart, singers in the oper-
atic/classical mode. We hear folk songs and observe the process
of profcooional oriticiem. Lear and Stewart stress the need to discuss the various roles and to avoid "cultural racism. " By using
their enormous talents in varied musical forms, they suggest artistic growth and diversity without condescension. Here opera seems
less imposing, but no less grand. WNETTV.

VIBRATIONS ENCORE, PT. V (30m   C   n. d.   VIDEO)
    Portrays soprano Cathy Berberian doing a modern score with
unorthodox notation by composer Luciano Berio who accompanies Cathy.
She also does one of her own scores in this performance. The
emotional reaction of the audience is analyzed. Whether Cathy
Berberian is a super-sophisticate or primitive artisan--this is a
provocative performance. WNETTV.

VIBRATIONS ENCORE, PT. VI (30m   C   n. d.   VIDEO)
    Two in-depth explorations of contemporary personalities in Black
music: Charley Pride and Micki Grant, doing the music they like
best. Charley Pride is an unlikely force in country-and-western
music, which is usually thought of as "white man's music. " Micki
Grant, composer/singer of Don't Bother Me, I Can't Cope, uses
music as the medium for her intense emotional and political statements. With interviewer Robert Sherman, she discusses the rewards and frustrations of being a Black woman composer whose basic
musical idiom is the Broadway style. WNETTV.

VICTORS, THE (22m   C   1972)
    Presents the story of a middle-aged couple's weekend on a
beach. By Doro Bachrach; BACHRACH.

VIE REVEE, LA see DREAM LIFE

VIET FLAKES (15m B 1965)
Animates images such as a Rembrandt drawing and a woman in flames through use of magnifying glasses.   By Carolee Schneemann; FCOOP.

VIETNAMESE WOMEN (C/B n. d. SLIDES (75))
Slides taken over the long course of the Vietnam war include slides from the history of Vietnam.   Juxtaposes slides of life and demonstrations with murder and our "leaders."   The determination of the Vietnamese women is moving and beautiful.   With script. NARMIC; WFC.

VIEW AND DO FILM NO. I (20m B n. d.)
Features three separate creative movement exercises for elementary school children that one can watch, then get up and practice by oneself.   By Anne Barlin, Paul Barlin; SLFP.

VIGNETTES (15m C 1975)
A series of interviews with people who appear in, or are connected with, the film Girls at 12.   Each woman talks about her own life and career decisions and some of the factors affecting her choices.   Provides insight into women's roles and life choices. EDC.

VIRACOCHA; Faces of Change Series (30m C r1975)
Examines rural Bolivian society, showing how mestizos and campesinos are linked by an exploitive economic system that divides them and heightens their mutual contempt.   Scenes from market days and fiestas demonstrate interactions between the two groups. AUFS; WER; EMC, UILL.

VIRGINIA WOOLF: THE MOMENT WHOLE (10m C 1972)
Selected passages from Virginia Woolf's writings convey her concept of women and articulate the problems of being a woman writer.   Visually lyrical sequences that portray scenes of which she wrote alternate in a setting reminiscent of the '30's with scenes of Marian Seldes who reads from Woolf's works.   Seldes reads "A Room of One's Own," "The Waves," and Woolf's diary.   A quiet, evocative introduction to the artist and to her feminist ideas.   d. Janet Sternberg for NET; IE, VFI; EMC, UILL, UM.

VISIT TO THE HSIN HUA SCHOOL IN PEKING, A (16m C 1976)
Shows Chinese children at the 60-year-old Hsin Hua School in Peking.   The 1, 100 students in grades one to six are filmed at work and at play.   They study language, mathematics, physical education, art, music, and labor techniques.   Politics is added in the upper grades.   By Betty McAfee; LP.

VISITANTE, EL (9m B 1975)
Captures the powerful and private emotions of a contemporary woman, her reactions to her own daughter and to her own life.   No narration.   By Arturo Sinclair; TEXFM.

VISITATION, THE see VISITANTE, EL

VISUAL VARIATIONS ON NOGUCHI (4m B n. d.)
    "Sculptures of the famous Japanese American artist, Isamu
Noguchi, are given audacious movement in a controversial art film
experiment. "--Cinema 16. By Marie Menken; FCOOP.

VIVRE SA VIE see MY LIFE TO LIVE

VOICE OF THE KHALAM, THE (28m B 1971)
    Loretta Pauker has been interpreting African poetry through
readings and pantomime for over 20 years. The film presents Miss
Pauker reading the poetry of contemporary African poets: Leopold
Senghor, Okara, Birago Diop, Rubadiri, and Francis Parkes against
a background of African drum and dance. Her expressive movements
lend a unique power to the spoken word. African instruments seen
are kora, shakeree, and khalam--demonstrating the riches of the
African cultural heritage. p. Loretta Pauker; MGH.

VOICES, PTS. I and II (60m C 1975 VIDEO)
    Story of the lives of five women--their dreams, their fears,
their choices. Actors are members of the Lunchbox Theatre. Emmy Award, 1975. By Susan Griffen, Bay Area poet. KQEDTV.

VOLLEYBALL FOR WOMEN (16m B 1966)
    Outstanding women players demonstrate elementary and advanced
skills of volleyball play in regular speed and slow-motion scenes.
Includes game play, fundamentals, drills for learning skills, and
team strategy. AAP; UILL.

VOLLEYBALL--DIG IT (15m C 1974)
    Kathy Gregory, volleyball expert, discusses the skills of the
game as demonstrated by a number of outstanding women players.
Illustrates techniques for serving, the underhand pass, recovery
from the net, the set up, and the spike. BFA; CWU.

VOLUNTEERISM: PRO AND CON; Woman Series (29m C 1975
    VIDEO)
    Both sides of the current controversy over volunteerism, the
traditional bailiwick of educated middle-class housewives currently
under attack by feminist groups, are discussed by Patricia Mc-
Cormick, the national task force coordinator on women and volun-
teering for National Organization for Women; and Ellen Straus,
Chairwoman of Call for Action, a volunteer-run national referral
service. WNEDTV; PTL.

VOTES FOR WOMEN (30m C n. d. VIDEO)
    A dramatic documentary on the women's suffrage movement.
p. Women's History Project. KQEDTV.

VOYAGE TO NEXT (9m C 1973)
    Mother Earth and Father Time are upset at the turn life has
taken on planet Earth. Mother Earth had intended for humans to
share resources and brains; instead they had divided themselves

into a system of nationalistic boxes.   Projecting the future, Father
Time sees disaster.   But there is hope.   People are becoming
aware of each other and choices open to them.   Mother Earth tenta-
tively suggests that they might make it after all.   Father Time is
pessimistic.   By Faith Hubley, John Hubley; FIM; FL

W. O. W. (WOMEN OF THE WORLD) (11m   C   1975)
    Film takes us on an animated journey to view human history
from the feminist perspective.   In prehistory, male and female
hunters and dancers are succeeded by the invention of agriculture
with the goddesses of fertility, art, culture.   War and male domination reduce women to slavery.   Now liberation comes to heal an
alienated world.   Sponsor: World Council of Churches.   By Faith
Hubley; PF; CWU, IU, MMA, ROA.

W. R. : MYSTERIES OF THE ORGANISM (84m   C   1971   Serbo-
    Croatian/subtitled)
    A hilarious, highly erotic political comedy which quite seriously
proposes sex as ideological imperative for liberation--a plea for
Erotic Socialism.   Beneath the film's light-hearted frivolity and
marvelous humor lurks a more serious ideological intent: Opposition to all oppressive social systems, East or West; the removal of
prurience from sex; a final squaring of accounts by the new radicals
with the new reactionary Russian regime.   d. Dusan Makavejev;
NEOPLANTA; CIV.

WAGES OF WORK; Choice: Challenge for Modern Woman Series
    (30m   B   r1966)
    Mary Keyserling and a panel of employment experts discuss why,
when, and where women work, and the effect on family, job, and
community.   UCLA; EMC, UMIS.

WAIT UNTIL YOUR FATHER GETS HOME; Searching Year, The
    (Series) (11m   C   r1971)
    Male vs. female roles are defined as they relate to dominance
and submissiveness.   Boys advocate male supremacy against one
dissenter.   Role-play about a mother and father deciding if their
son may go to San Francisco.   DF; CF; BU, BYU, PAS, ROA.

WAITING (12m   C   1954)
    An experimental collage film utilizing both live action and anima-
tion techniques to illustrate the frustration of individuals who wait
from birth to death for the age of happiness that always seems to be
just around the corner in time, yet never arrives.   By Flora Clar
Mock; CFS.

WAKE DREAM (10m   C   1968)
    "Color and sound combination of collages, posters, varied wall
objects and live action that is imaginative and forceful in making
anti-war statements. "--A. W.   By Alida Walsh; WALSH.

WALK IN THE SPRING RAIN, A (100m C 1966)
This is the love story of an exuberant Tennessee mountain man and an urban sophisticated woman, each married and mature enough to know what they are becoming involved in. Almost as elemental as his world of nature, the Tennesseean is prepared to lose his way of life, as he will his son, because he believes in the kind of miracles which surround him each burgeoning spring. With Anthony Quinn, Ingrid Bergman. d. Guy Green; COLUMBIA; BF, ROA.

WALKING DANCE FOR ANY NUMBER (8m B si n. d.)
Intermedia film projected on dancers dressed in all white. Filmmaker suggests musical improvisation with showings. By Elaine Summers; FCOOP.

WALKING'S TOO SLOW--A FILM ABOUT RUNAWAYS (26m C 1977)
A documentary of six teen-age runaways from cities throughout the U. S. , and their experiences in crisis centers, juvenile courts, youth homes and on the streets of America. The young people provide their own narration and speak about their problems and reasons for running away from home. Includes actual courtroom and prison footage. d. /p. Bill Pace; BANDML

WALLS COME TUMBLING DOWN, THE (29m C 1975)
Examines the resident-management program in public housing projects in St. Louis. Suggests that the program has solved many of the problems of the residents and relieved the atmosphere of confrontation which plagued public housing in the city before the introduction of the program. By Madeline Anderson; FDF; PHOENIX.

WANDA (101m C 1970)
Wanda, divorced, leaves her two children with her ex-husband and drifts off into a relationship with a middle-aged thief. In a world of sleazy landscapes and strange encounters, Wanda emerges as a woman trapped by her environment into paralyzing passivity. The often glamorized image of knight-errant banditry is refocused into reality. By Barbara Loden; FFF.

WANDA LANDOWSKA; Wisdom Series (30m B 1958)
Wanda Landowska, harpsichordist, talks about her life, her career and her philosophy as an artist. She describes her effort to gain public acceptance of the harpsichord as an instrument for which much of the music of Bach and earlier composers was written. She plays several selections from the works of Bach. NBCTV; FI; OKSU, UILL.

WAR OF THE EGGS, THE; Insight Series (27m C 1971)
The film takes a close look at some of the underlying psychological causes of child battering. It offers no solutions. By Elizabeth Ashley, Bill Bixby; s. w. Michael Crichton; PAULST; MG, MGH; UILL.

WASH (11m   C   1971)
"Dance 'happening' on film. "--FIM.   By Judith Hallet, Stanley
Hallet; FIM.

WATCHWORD: CAUTION (27m   C   1974)
The real and present dangers confronting women today and the
importance of maintaining an alert and watchful attitude are discussed.
Dramatized are proper and improper ways of dealing with potential
danger.   Situations include getting into a parked car; being followed
by a strange car; experiencing motor failure on the road; traveling
alone on a bus, elevator, or subway; hitchhiking, and being ap-
proached by suspicious strangers in public.   Advice is also given on
antisocial behavior (peeping Tom), purse snatching, crank phone calls
and physical attacks.   By Ian Stuart; SHILLP; PARACO.

WATER LIGHT/WATER NEEDLE (18m   C   1966)
Outdoor version of an aerial kinetic theatre work.   By Carolee
Schneemann, John Jones; FCOOP.

WATER SARK (14m   C   si   n.d.)
The filmmaker is seen making the film of herself and her magical manipulations of the camera, of mirror, lenses, water, various
objects, and herself.   By Joyce Wieland; FCOOP.

WATERCRESS (9m   C   1972)
"Filmed in the country on communes ... communal togetherness
includes sauna, music, mudbath and a love-in, the touching and
being touched collage of a woman and three men. "--C. B.   Some of
the communes featured are: Wheeler, Arcadia, and Morningstar.
By Constance Beeson; MMRC.

WATERDANCE (10m   C   1972)
"Slowed motion suspension of the play of light on the ocean's
waves, filmed while crossing the Aegean. "--L. E. I.   By Louva Elizabeth Irvine; FCOOP.

WATERFALL (4m   C   1968)
Optically printed, hand developed and solarized, Waterfall incorporates far-flung stock footage in a flowing, floating, and gliding
ode to water.   The sound is Japanese koto music.   By Chick Strand;
SB.

WATERS DREAM (10m   C   1974)
A visual exploration of a stream--from subtle stirrings to
sparkle and rush.   The film moves into the basic patterns of movement, color, and light, and transforms our perceptions of water.
d. Deborah Dickson; NLC.

WATERWHEEL VILLAGE (14m   C   1976)
Story of how two young brothers learn cooperation and respect
for the ability of others, regardless of sex.   Believable performance
and a charming story.   By Peggy Woolf; FFAIR.

WATTS WITH EGGS (2m   C   si   n. d.)
(No commentary provided.)   By Marie Menken; FCOOP.

WAY BACK, THE (29m   B   1964)
A view of the services of the Rehabilitation Institute of Chicago,
organized around the therapy given to one young woman paraplegic.
By Robert Ford; NWUFL.

WAY DOWN EAST (113m   B   1920)
Melodrama of a young girl (Lillian Gish) who leaves her New
England farm to visit rich relatives in Boston.   There she is
charmed by a handsome scoundrel.   The mountebank stages a fake
wedding, and when Lillian announces she is pregnant, he takes
French leave.   From there, it is all downhill for Lillian.   The baby
dies and Lillian humbly accepts work as a servant.   Her employer's
son falls in love with her and hope springs anew.   But not for long,
for her sin is discovered.   Her puritanical employer points to the
door, sending Lillian into a blinding snowstorm.   She is miraculously
rescued by her true love.   Learning the truth, her rich relatives
repent and ask for forgiveness.   d.   D. W. Griffith; UAS; MGH.

WAY IT IS, THE (SERIES)   see   LAST REFLECTIONS ON A WAR
(1968)

WE ARE ASIAN WOMEN (30m   C   n. d.   VIDEO)
The history of stereotyping of Asian women in the U, S, is
shown through a montage of songs, slides, and dramatization.
KQEDTV.

WE ARE OURSELVES (15m   C   1976)
A joyful, entertaining and explicitly sexual film about two thoughtful and independent women who have followed their individual desires
to seek a fulfilling and creative life-style together.   Their discussion
early in the film provides a sense of their individual identities.   By
Ann M. Hershey; MMRC.

WE ARE WOMAN (29m   C   1975)
This film, designed to de-polarize men and women regarding
woman's non-traditional concept of herself, explores traditional sex
roles, the conditioning that perpetuates them, and some alternatives
to them.   Examines women as part of the work force.   Looks at
the possibilities for men and women as equals, without defeminiza-
tion or domination.   Narrated by Helen Reddy.   p. Max Miller;
AVANFI; MM; CWU, OSU, UIO, UMIS.

WE DO!   WE DO! (12m   C   1970)
A vapid stylized takeoff on a wedding ceremony rapidly intercut with vignette offering a pessimistic appraisal of marriage.   The
vignette includes a divorce hearing in a mock courtroom, a boxing
match for marital fights, distorted sexual advice from variety of
wedding guests, etc.   d. Bruce Baker; FCC.

WE DRINK AND DROWN (6m   C   n. d.)
"Stultifying, apparently senseless world of high school is powerfully captured in this picture-sound montage ... one of the most inventive sound tracks ever created by a young filmmaker. "--YFD.
By Mary Lee; YFD.

WE GET MARRIED TWICE (25m   C   1973)
One marriage takes place in the couple's living room with just
a few friends; one in a traditional Jewish ceremony followed by a
large family gathering.   Shows how one couple responds to changing
mores and morals, in terms of marriage and the family, both
nuclear and extended.   By Miriam Weinstein; SB.

WE NEED EACH OTHER SERIES   see   NORTH WITH THE SPRING

WE THE WOMEN; American Parade, The (Series) (35m   C   1974)
The film traces the history of the women's movement from
colonial times to the present day.   Narrated by Mary Tyler Moore.
CBSTV; BFA; IU, OSU, UC, UILL, UIO, UK, UWY.

WE WILL NOT BE BEATEN (50m   C   1977   VIDEO)
Women who have been beaten by their husbands are candidly
speaking of their experiences, and the ways that the legal, social
services, and the medical world deal with these problems.   UPAL

WEAVES (12m   C   n. d.)
A visual and aural impression by a film artist of another artist
--a textile designer-weaver--set to music, no narration.   Shows how
she creates and weaves on the loom, and how her handiwork is made
ready for an exhibition.   p. Homi D. Sethna; IFB.

WEAVING WITH LOOMS YOU CAN MAKE (16m   C   1974)
Shows how to make an open pouch-bag with a simple handmade
loom.   Principles of weaving are demonstrated and terms defined.
By Nancy Belfer; PARACO.

WEENIE WORM OR THE FAT INNKEEPER, THE (10m   C   n. d.)
"I first saw these incredible creatures a couple of years ago at
the Bodega Bay Marine Biology Lab.   I was amazed I could have
lived on this planet so long and not realized I was sharing it with
weenie worms. "--D. W.   By Dorothy Wiley; CCC.

WELCOME HOME; Insight Series (27m   C   1975)
Presents a penetrating look at one of the prime causes of juvenile delinquency, and of one of the most severe problems in re-
habilitating youthful offenders--alienation.   By Nan Martin, Jerry
Houser; PAULST, MGH; UILL.

WELCOME TO THE BELTLESS, PINLESS GENERATION (3m   C
n. d.)
A short animated movie made from cutouts of magazine ads,
focusing on the way women are degraded by most advertisements.
TCWFC.

WELFARE, THE (17m B 1966)
Compiled from the reflections of a new social welfare case-
worker and a young Negro woman receiving aid, this documentary is
designed to stimulate discussion of social rehabilitation. It reflects
the worker's dismay over the mass of paperwork and red tape, and
the welfare recipient's plight when her husband can find no work and
moves out of the home so the family can qualify for aid to needy
children. It is concerned with the area of social work planning that
lies between individual or group interviews and high-level community
organization. EMC.

WELFARE: EXPLODING THE MYTHS (18m C n. d.)
"Rebuttals to six prevalent myths about welfare in American
society today. "--M. G.   Includes a song by Malvina Reynolds.   By
Mollie Gregory; TFEL

WELFARE MOTHERS (30m C n. d.)
"Don't nobody care. "--Interviewee.   By Martha Stuart, David
Ruskin; STUARTM.

WELFARE REVOLT, THE; NET Journal Series (60m B 1968)
Documents how women on welfare in some Northern ghettos
have tried organizing local unions to change what they consider in-
tolerable conditions.   Both Black and white recipients describe their
grievances, and leaders of the movement discuss group pressure
and organized demonstrations as a means of forcing change.   NET,
IU; EMC, PAS, UILL.

WELFARE RIGHTS (30m B 1965)
Documents the four day sit-in and hunger strike in Oakland,
California, by the first welfare rights group.   Conducted primarily
by Black women and their children, the action grew out of the local welfare board's policy of automatically referring all able-bodied
men to five dollars a day farm labor, then dropping their wives and
children from the rolls of Aid to Families with Dependent Children.
AMDOC; IMPF.

WELL-KEPT SECRETS REVEALED (60m B n. d.   VIDEO)
Seven women, most of them now single, all over 50, discuss
what one of them calls "the vagina as a well-kept secret. " The
subjects "you don't talk about"--menstruation, menopause, hyster-
ectomies, and sex--are freely examined by these warm lively women,
all in the context of growing old in a culture that only values youth.
By Sheila de Bretteville; IE.

WELTHY FISHER; Creative Persons Series (30m B 1967)
Introduces educator Welthy Fisher, her philosophy of education,
and the environment in India where she works.   Shows Indian teachers, trained in institutes founded by Mrs. Fisher, teaching in various villages with lectures, books, puppet shows, with opportunities
for pupils to practice agricultural skills.   NET, IU; EMC.

WE'RE ALIVE (45m C/B 1975)
A powerful statement on women's lives in prison, combining fact

and intense emotion. The female prisoners discuss openly their lives, methods of survival, their sexuality, drugs, racism, and the law and punishment in California. Made by the Women's Film Workshop of UCLA and the Video Workshop of California Institution for Women. d. Michie Gleason; IE.

WEST VIRGINIA COLESLAW (14m C 1975)
Documentary about the work of a man who paints signs that advertise chewing tobacco on the sides of barns throughout the Midwest. d. /p. Eleanor Grand; GRAND.

WESTERN CIVILIZATION: MAJESTY AND MADNESS SERIES, THE see ELIZABETH: THE QUEEN WHO SHAPED AN AGE; GREEKS: IN SEARCH OF MEANING, THE; ROMANS: LIFE, LAUGHTER, AND LAW, THE; ROMANTICISM: THE REVOLT OF THE SPIRIT; SHAKESPEARE--A MIRROR TO MAN

WESTWARD THE WOMEN (118m B 1951)
A sometimes humorous adventure experienced by women bent on marriage in California, as they travel westward by wagon train. The women demonstrate their tireless capacity to do anything a man can do--and maybe do it just a little bit better. Based on a story by Frank Capra. d. William A. Wellman; p. Dore Schary; s. w. Charles Schnee; MGM; FI.

WHAT DID YOU LEARN IN SCHOOL TODAY? (48m B 1972)
Newswoman Joan Murray narrates this examination of the alternative educational method--the "open classroom" being used in some schools both here and in England. Focuses on the idea of "satellite" or "mini" high schools to show changes going on in suburban schools. WNETTV; IU.

WHAT DO YOU THINK SERIES see BEING DIFFERENT; CHOOSING A LEADER

WHAT 80 MILLION WOMEN WANT (65m B si 1913)
A political drama showing the suffrage cause in its true light. An absorbing story of love, intrigue, and clever detective work, in which the power of modern Political Boss is challenged by the "Fair Suffragette." After a hard fight in which her lover is involved, she succeeds in defeating the political gang. s. w. Kate Corbally; UNIQUE; FCE, KP.

WHAT EVERY WOMAN KNOWS; Girls and Women Series (30m B 1972)
A panel of women, most of whom are involved in higher education, discusses questions commonly asked by women who are considering a return to the business or educational world after extended absences. Patricia Wulp of the Center for Continuing Education of Women at the University of Michigan demonstrates how she advises prospective students. UMITV; UM, PAS.

WHAT I WANT (10m C 1971)
"A woman is facing the camera; in her hands is a seemingly

endless scroll which she reads throughout this film.   Some of her
desires are universal; others, idiosyncratic fantasy trips.   What
underlies all of them are recognizable emotions--coexisting needs
for power, freedom, escape, dependency, love--spoken with self-
mockery.   Funny and provocative for raising consciousness. "--SB.
By Sharon Hennessey; SB; CCC, GP.

WHAT IS A WOMAN?; Choice: Challenge for Modern Women Series
    (30m   B   1965)
    Keith Berwick and Margaret Mead discuss what is feminine and
masculine, as prescribed by society and confused by changing patterns.   EMC.

WHAT IS THE SHAPE OF TOMORROW?; Choice: Challenge for
    Modern Women Series (30m   B   r1966)
    Jeanne Noble and Rabbi Gottschalk discuss variation in personal
standards, beliefs, and values; spiritual, moral, and interpersonal
sources of strength; and women's power in shaping the world of
tomorrow.   EMC; UMIS.

WHAT IS TO BE DONE?   see   QUE HACER?

WHAT MAKES MILLIE RUN? (14m   C   1976)
    Millie Cooper, the wife of a doctor, speaks about aerobics to
motivate women to exercise.   Interspersed with women who have
found these exercises to be effective both in reducing weight and in
increasing self-confidence.   Mrs. Cooper dispels myths about exercise.   She does, however, caution those over 35 about starting this
program without a medical stress examination.   By Scott Whittaker
for BYU.   BYU; SCC.

WHAT MAKES SALLY RUN? (30m   C   n. d.   VIDEO)
    Marie Hart hosts a program exploring sex discrimination in
sports.   KQEDTV.

WHAT MAN SHALL LIVE AND NOT SEE DEATH? (57m   C   1971)
    Dr. Elizabeth Kubler-Ross interviews a dying mother and talks
about cryogenics, the role of religion, and euthanasia.   By Joan
Konner; WNBCTV; FI; EMC, UILL.

WHAT ON EARTH (10m   C   1966)
    Animated cartoon about Martians who visit earth and are con-
fused about whether the prevailing and most intelligent form of life
on earth is man or the automobile.   By Susan Murgatroyd; NFBC;
MGH; UILL.

WHAT THE DICKENS (15m   C   1973)
    "Backstage, behind-the-scenes look at the annual San Francisco
Dickens Christmas Fair.   Documentary fantasy. "--K. D.   By Karil
Daniels; DANIELS.

WHATCHA GONNA DO? (SERIES) see   GOING BACK

WHAT'S NEW PUSSYCAT? (108m C 1965)
A daffy comedy with Peter O'Toole as the Casanova type who's swinging himself into an early grave. He goes to the psychiatrist, Peter Sellers, whose problem is that he doesn't want to cure O'Toole, he wants to emulate him. With Romy Schneider as a patient fiancee, Capucine as a cool nymphomaniac, Paula Prentiss as a suicidal stripper, and Ursula Andress as an opportunistic parachutist, there's a lot to emulate. d. Clive Donner; UAS.

WHAT'S THE MATTER WITH ALICE? (25m C 1972)
Designed to stimulate thinking by managers and executives about career advancement, upward mobility, and equal opportunity for minorities and women. First part consists of series of interviews with people in various occupations who have had experience in job retraining, affirmative action, and career advancement programs. Second part enacts an office situation in which a bright young Black woman who is an excellent worker decides to quit. Shows how her supervisor learns his own unconscious refusal to advance her to a more challenging and rewarding position caused her to seek work elsewhere. Demonstration of human waste, inefficiency, and loss of profit. NWSUSA; EMC, UW.

WHEAT HEARTS (3m C si n. d. (8mm))
An animated collage. By Stephanie Harvey; CCC.

WHEN A CHILD ENTERS THE HOSPITAL (16m C 1977)
Shows how parent involvement works, chronicling the hospitalization of a young girl undergoing minor surgery. The commentary by Dr. Muriel Sugarman, psychiatric consultant to Boston Hospital for Women and instructor at the Harvard Medical School, explains what is happening to Michele and reveals her feelings and needs. p. Alvin Fiering; d. Miriam Weinstein; POLYMORPH.

WHEN I GROW UP (14m C 1973)
A day in the life of a suburban housewife: children, dogs, shopping, laundry, etc., with no privacy. Intercut with fantasy sequences of escape to freedom and solitude. Could be useful, especially with suburban groups, to raise questions of possible alternative life-styles. d. Roberta London; LWFG.

WHEN ILLNESS STRIKES; Human Sexuality Series (29m C 1972 VIDEO)
Individuals with physical handicaps (paraplegia, polio, myocardic infarction, cerebral palsy and a back problem) discuss their sexual abilities and concerns. They talk freely with host Milton Diamond, Ph. D. , about their feelings and how they have dealt with problems. UHAWAII/KHETTV; PTL.

WHEN LOVE NEEDS CARE (13m C 1975)
In a direct manner, this film portrays the actual experiences of two teen-agers being examined and treated for venereal disease. The boy and girl are nervous but honest; the doctors are frank but supportive. The documentary style allows the audience to identify

with the patients and to learn the importance of detecting VD early and of contacting potentially infected sex partners. By removing the fear surrounding diagnosis and treatment of VD, the film helps the viewer to overcome his/her reluctance in seeking medical attention. p. Leonard C. Schwartz; PERENNIAL.

WHEN THIS YOU SEE REMEMBER ME   see   GERTRUDE STEIN: WHEN THIS YOU SEE REMEMBER ME

WHEN WOMEN GET TO HURTING (18m   C   1975)
    This flim concerns five women from a small Georgia mountain town who lead a wildcat strike against a national sewing factory. When the prolonged strike turns violent and the women lose their case in a court battle, they turn around, and against tremendous odds, establish their own factory.   d. /p. Charlotte Zwerin; WNETTV.

WHERE DOES ALL THE MONEY GO?; Choice: Challenge for Mod-
    ern Women Series (30m   B   r1966)
    Frances Feldman and Bruce McKim discuss the expression of traditions, psychological needs, and cultural attitudes in personal and governmental spending, and the unreality of money.   EMC.

WHERE HER GIFTS ARE RESPECTED (28m   C   1975)
    Demonstrates the pluralism of feminine gifts within the church. It candidly deals with the controversial question of ordination, con-siders the experiences of women in seminaries, and examines the experience of one specific church and its woman pastor.   The film raises questions about a male/female concept of God and takes a new look at some traditional women's roles, as well as some not too traditional roles.   ARCHPORT.

WHERE IS DEAD? (20m   C   r1976)
    Story of the confusion and pain of six-year-old Sarah, mourning the death of her ten-year-old brother, probing her feelings and the feelings of the adults in her life, dealing with the mystery of death, and ultimately, the majesty of life.   d. /p. Jackie Rivett-River; EBEC; IU.

WHERE IS JIM CROW?   A CONVERSATION WITH LENA HORNE
    (30m   B   1967)
    Ms. Horne discusses herself as a symbol of the Black pinup, the representative Black woman, or "this year's Negro, " and tells how she had to conquer this image for her own sake and that of other Black women.   EMC.

WHERE IS JIM CROW?   A CONVERSATION WITH NANCY WILSON
    (30m   B   1967)
    Singer Nancy Wilson discusses civil rights and the Negro in show business.   She says the time for helping the Negro is in early childhood, for by the time the Negro child reaches third grade he has already begun to feel defeated.   Miss Wilson speaks of her own activities in civil rights and her attitudes on discrimination.   She says Americans should study Black history so that the Negro can identify with his past.   EMC.

WHERE MRS. WHALLEY LIVES (28m B 1969)
Study of conflict that can arise between generations, despite the best efforts of everyone to avoid it. Mrs. Whalley, a grandmother, lives with her son and his family, and occasionally it becomes a strain to hide hurt and loneliness for the sake of maintaining harmony in her son's home. NFBC; EMC, PAS.

WHERE TIME IS A RIVER (18m C 1966)
Wordless photographic exploration of works of Rousseau, Gauguin, Chagall and Leger. By Gay Matthaei, Jewell Bjork; VRI; EMC, UILL.

WHITE CALLIGRAPHY (10m B si 1967)
An abstract film, using a Japanese letter in each frame, tells the oldest story in Japan. By Takahiko Iimura; CCC.

WHITE CAT, THE (2m C si n. d.)
"The white cat rolls and tumbles. "--M. A. S.   By Mary Ann Spencer; FCOOP.

WHITE HOUSE RED CARPET WITH JULIA CHILD (49m C 1968; 49m B 1968)
Depicts an official visit as Julia Child, "The French Chef, " documents the event and explains how the White House staff manages such an activity. Covers a visit by the Japanese Prime Minister from the greeting ceremony through the state banquet, and discusses the roles of several White House staff members. Explains the history and importance of such diplomatic affairs. IU; EMC.

WHITE SUSAN (6m B 1971)
"A film on being alone and aroused. "--M. P.   By Marjorie Prisadsky; CCC.

WHITHER WEATHER (11m C 1977)
Using animation, the film visually portrays the earth as one living whole--all parts interrelated. Using the symbolism of a tree and its branches, the film concludes with a message of hope for the future. By Faith Hubley; HUBLEY; PF.

WHITNEY COMMERCIAL (3m C n. d.)
An advertisement commissioned by the Whitney Museum of American Art to promote their film program, "New American Filmmakers Series. " By Suzan Pitt Kraning; CCC.

WHO DO YOU KILL? (51m B 1967)
Frightful and appalling living conditions in the slums of Harlem are examined in this dramatic program from the "East Side/West Side" television series. The rage and grief of a young couple, whose child dies of rat bite, serves to prick the conscience of all who are blind to prejudice, segregation, poverty and ghetto life in our country. p. TALPAR; CBSTV; CAROUSEL; AIMS.

WHO DOES SHE THINK SHE IS? (60m C 1974)
A candid view of novelist, singer, painter and ex-wrestler

Rosalyn Drexler. With a playful poke at her own inhibitions Rosalyn explains the uninhibited content of her dreams, which are improvised by hammy actors on a tacky set saying, "A little repression is interesting, because that's what you build your fantasies on." What makes her lovable is her willingness to assimilate all these elements and her quickness to recognize the comedy when things backfire-- the experience not quite matching up to her imagination and vice versa. d. Patricia Lewis Jaffe, co-d. Gabby Rodgers; NYF.

WHO IS MY SISTER? (88m C 1974 VIDEO)
    A wide-ranging discussion on the women's movement by a panel of women from a variety of backgrounds and ethnic origins. The conversation is spirited, and covers the status of women in the business world and at home. It deals with the special problems of minority women and raises the issues of the solidarity and validity of the entire movement. Participants are: Joan Shigekawa, a television producer; Gloria Steinem, editor of Ms. Magazine; Delores Huerta, Vice-President of the United Farm Workers; Lillian Benbow, President of Delta Sigma Theta, Inc. ; and Clydia Nahwooksy, Director of Indian Awareness for the Smithsonian Institution. Moderator is Jeanne Nobel, Professor of Education at Brooklyn College, New York. WKARTV; PTL.

WHO IS SYLVIA? (27m B 1957)
    Study of the dreams, fears and hopes of a 14-year-old girl, "half child, half woman," and of her relationships with her family, school and friends. The impromptu and unchaperoned get-together of "the gang" after school dramatizes a characteristic lack of communication and understanding between parents and their adolescent children, and the result of the impasse. EMC; BU, UILL, UIO.

WHO IS TRACY WILLIAMS? (28m B 1973 VIDEO)
    Tracy Williams is a Black woman, a mother of two children, and a convicted felon currently serving an indefinite-to-two-year sentence for forgery at the State Correctional Institution at Muncy, Pennsylvania's women's prison. This program focuses on Tracy's problems, frailties and strengths. The discontent of Tracy and her inmate friends becomes evident as they talk about the lack of funds and programs that could aid in their adjustment to society's norms. In their rooms, they also discuss the abnormality of prison life that often leads to homosexuality, and teaches them more about crime. WPSXTV; PTL. Also available in 16mm from PAS.

WHO PAYS THE FIDDLER? (6m C 1971)
    Presents the anxieties and decisions a young and unmarried couple must face concerning abortion. Portrays the couple revealing their uncertainties and rationalizations to each other as they drive to an abortionist in a nearby town. Reviews some of the alternatives to abortion, including marriage, and concludes open-endedly. CENTRON; IU, UILL.

WHO STOLE THE UMBILICAL CORD? (28m C 1975 VIDEO)
    This original play by the Family Circus traces the lives of women from a childhood when they were not allowed to play on monkey

bars, to an old age of being wasted by a society which needs what the older woman has to offer. It covers a wide range of experiences in our lives in a sensitive, moving and thoroughly honest manner. NOWP; CREOUT.

WHO WANTS FREEDOM?; Choice: Challenge for Modern Women
      (30m   B   r1966)
      Elizabeth Mann Borgese and Richard Lichtman discuss the meaning and consequence of "freedom" ... how much is self-determination in what areas of life. Offers perspective on the issue of employment for married women and encourages the development of attitudes that increase women's effectiveness in their chosen roles.   EMC.

WHO WILL TIE MY SHOE? (53m   C   1965)
      Presents unrehearsed and candid discussion groups of both parents and retarded students. Emphasizes the message of hope, for the parent who either did not know or would not admit that his child was afflicted, and for the child himself, who through specialized training, can assume a useful role in the community.   By Pat Powell; AIM.

WHOLE NEW BALL GAME (9m   C   1973)
      Adolescence often is a trying and confusing time, particularly when adolescent roles are redefined with parents, friends, and individuals themselves. Sex roles can pose a perplexing dilemma. Joanne starts this film as a "one of the gang" football player, but ends it as a pensive young person aware that her relationship with boys will now be different. Open-ended. KINGTV; BFA; UM.

WHO'S AFRAID OF VIRGINIA WOOLF? (129m   B   1966)
      A portrait of a marriage in which a middle-aged professor and his wife and a younger faculty couple, invited to the professor's home for drinks, all become involved in the older couple's violent games of verbal assassination, emotional destruction, hatred, and love. Based on play of the same title by Edward Albee. d. Mike Nichols; WSA.

WHY DID GLORIA DIE? (27m   C   1972)
      Examines the problems faced by the growing number of Native Americans who leave the reservation to settle in urban areas. Traces the tragic life of a 27-year-old Chippewa woman who died of hepatitis in Minneapolis. Shows how the problems that contributed to her death--racism, unemployment, inadequate welfare payments, housing discrimination and poor medical care--are faced by most Indians in urban America. From "Bill Moyers' Journal." NET, IU; EMC.

WHY ME? (57m   C   r1975)
      In this sensitive but unflinching probe into breast cancer, ten women who have undergone mastectomies discuss their ordeal, how it has affected their lives, how they have dealt with ensuing problems, and their need for support from friends and family. Includes a demonstration of a self-examination, essential to early detection of cancer. p. CBSTV; CAROUSEL; EMC, UILL.

WHY THE SUN AND THE MOON LIVE IN THE SKY (12m   C   1970)
Filmed animation of a legend of Eastern Nigeria about the sun
and the moon who lived on land until the sea came to visit them,
and the inundation forced them up into the sky.   Based on the book
by Elphinstone Dayrell.   By Suzanne E. Bauman; PARACO; UILL.

WHY WOMEN ARE DISSATISFIED WITH THE GYNECOLOGISTS;
Woman Series (29m   C   1974   VIDEO)
Barbara Seaman, author of Free and Female and The Doctor's
Case Against the Pill, and Ellen Frankfort, Village Voice health
columnist and author of Vaginal Politics, discuss health care from a
consumer point of view.   They maintain that women should work to-
ward demystifying the profession of medicine and its practitioners.
WNEDTV; PTL.

WIDOWS (42m   B   1972)
A moving and evocative presentation on modes of adaptation to
grief by widows.   Death is a traumatic event that produces drastic
changes in almost every aspect of life.   Shows variety of experiences
and types of women as well as the openness of their comments.   The
movie is unpretentious and the interview low-key and unobtrusive.
d. Dr. Edward A. Mason; MHTFP; UW.

WIFE BEATING (27m   C   r1976)
Examines the astonishing incidents of wife beating, the crime of
assault.   Incidents are widespread and know no boundaries of socioeconomic status.   Hard statistics are not available, since many women
do not press charges.   Discusses the cause of wife beating and reveals it as a behavior cycle for most brutal husbands are sons of
brutal fathers.   Interviews beaten wives and professionals trying to
discover repercussions for women and their children, and possible
remedies.   d. Gerald Polikoff; p. Clare Crawford Mason; NBCTV;
FI; IU.

WIFE VS. SECRETARY (85m   B   1926)
The competition is between wife (Myrna Loy) and Clark Gable's
secretary (Jean Harlow).   The competition for the successful publisher (Clark Gable) sounds like a sham battle all the way.   In the
end Miss Loy is convinced that all is over between them, but Miss
Harlow tells her not to be a fool and to go back to her husband
while he still is hers.   From the story by Faith Baldwin.   D. Clar-
ence Brown; p. Hunt Stromberg; s. w. Alice Duer Miller, Norman
Krasna, and John Lee Mahin; MGM; FL

WILD GOOSE, THE (18m   B   1975)
The film satirizes the role that our society assigns to old people, and shows that old people are still as alive as other individuals
and age groups.   By Bruce Cronin; FL

WILD ONES, THE (60m   B   1965)
"Documents the bid for instant success by a young rock group,
Jordan Christopher and The Wild Ones, after Christopher's marriage
to Mrs. Sybil Burton."--J. C.   By Joyce Chopra; CHOPRA.

WILD PARTY, THE (76m B 1929)
Clara Bow plays "the bad girl" in a woman's boarding house.
Despite the insipid hero (Fredric March) gets-her-in-the-end plot,
most of the women are strong, together and loving. Sisterhood in
the middle class, 1929. First talkie for Paramount. d. Dorothy
Arzner; PARAMOUNT; UAS.

WILDLIFE RENDEZVOUS (14m C 1959)
Introduces birds and other animals in the wildlife sanctuary
near Shubenacadie, Nova Scotia. By Margaret Perry; CTFL.

WIND (6m B si 1968)
Choreographed figures interact with wind on a beach. By Joan
Jonas; CASTELLI.

WINDFLOWERS (64m B 1968)
"Elegy for a draft dodger in 20 tableaux. "--A. M. By Pola
Chapell, Adolfas Mekas; FCOOP.

WINDSONG (25m B 1958)
A film in counterpoint: symbolic images of nature against the
story of Daphne and Apollo. Harry Partch's interest in Greek mythology inspired his especially written and self-produced musical score.
By Madeline Tourtelot; GP.

WINDSORS, THE (30m B 1957)
Traces the immediate background of the British royal family and
reviews the activities of the Prince of Wales from World War I to
the time he ascended the throne. Describes the events leading to his
abdicating in 1936 to marry Wallis Warfield Simpson. p. CBSTV.

WINDSORS, THE; History Makers of the 20th Century Series (26m
B 1966)
Story of Duke of Windsor's childhood youth, and his brief period
as King Edward VIII. A portrait of a man who created a world
scandal for the love of a woman, a commoner, Wallis Simpson.
British public favored Edward's marriage and his right to continue
rule; however, political, religious and regal opposition eventually
forced him to abdicate in favor of "the woman I love. " WOLPER;
ASFL.

WINDY DAY (10m C 1967)
An exploration of the child's world of innocence and fantasy,
in which the two girls (the Hubley daughters) muse about romance,
marriage, growing up, and dying as they play-act on a windy day in
the summertime. By Faith Hubley, John Hubley; FIM; GP, VFI,
IRISF.

WINE OF MORNING (120m C 1955)
A story of shipwreck and bloodshed, intrigue and murder, and
of love and redemption. Based on a novel by Dr. Bob Jones, Jr. on
the life of Barabbas. p. /d. Katherine Stenholm; UF.

WINE OF YOUTH (70m B si 1924)
    The narrative was adapted from Rachel Crother's play, Mary
the Third, and deals in a negligible manner with the past and present activities of the younger set, with a fling at incompatible marriages. It's not a bad warm weather show, but the doings of the
young people are a bit exaggerated. With Eleanor Boardman, James
Morrison, Zasu Pitts. d. King Vidor; MGM; FI.

WINNEBAGO TRICKSTER MYTH (8m B n. d.)
    "Animated erotic tale of how it was with the early American
Indians. An authentic story from the past, its message is now. "--
Ray Craig. By Julia Allen; CCC.

WINTERGARDEN--HUDSON RIVER DIARY: BOOK III (5m C 1973)
    "Tonight is a snowbird with heart hung hostage in a water drop,
its iceflaked starfeet remembering the gargoyle's empty threat to
drown in rivulets of melting feather frost. "--S. D. H.   By Storm De
Hirsch; FCOOP.

WISDOM SERIES see EDITH HAMILTON; ELEANOR ROOSEVELT;
    MARGARET MEAD; NADIA BOULANGER; PEARL S. BUCK;
    WANDA LANDOWSKA

WITCH, THE (70m B 1955 Finnish/subtitled)
    The film deals with an archaeologist and his wife, who discover
the remains of a woman, buried 300 years previously, with a stake
driven through her heart. The archaeologist removes the stake,
ignoring the protest of the villagers. A few hours later, the dead
woman returns to life. She is a beautiful femme fatale, and succeeds in placing a number of villagers under her spell before she is
destroyed. d. Roland Hallstrom; s. w. Mika Waltari based on his
play. ABFI.

WITCHES OF SALEM: THE HORROR AND THE HOPE (34m C
    1972)
    Portrays the witchcraft trials of Salem, Massachusetts, in 1692,
based on authentic records. The central characters emerge as the
young girls whose hysterical accusations turn their village into a
witch-hunting ground. Attempts to give an understanding of the political, psychological and religious background, and the consequences
of this episode in American history. By Dennis Azzarella; LCA;
UILL, UMIS.

WITH FABRIC AND THREAD (15m C 1974)
    Creative stitchery is explained and demonstrated, including punch-
hooking and applique methods of creating a picture with thread. By
Nancy Belfer; PARACO; UILL.

WITH JUST A LITTLE TRUST (15m C r1975)
    A story of how a young Black widowed mother of three is
brought out of self-pity by her "gospel-singing" mother who urges
her to trust in the Lord to help her "Meet it, greet it, and defeat
it. " d. Anthony Frangakis; p. Karl Holtsnider; FCC.

WITH NO ONE TO HELP US (19m B 1967)
How the formation of a food-buying club by a group of Newark mothers brought about a necessary change in the community.   USOE; NAVC; UM.

WITH THE CUBAN WOMEN (48m C 1975 Spanish/subtitled)
An inspiring, high-spirited and often funny tribute to the women's liberation movement in Cuba and to their sisters throughout the world.   This documentary on Cuba's "revolution within a revolution" explores the profound transformations in the social status of women (and the changing attitudes of men toward women) in Cuba today. Featured are interviews with women in a wide variety of jobs who speak about the changes in society and in their own lives.   d. Octavio Cortazar; Cuban Film Institute; TFC.

WIVES OF ALCOHOLICS; Woman Series (29m C 1975 VIDEO)
Two suburban housewives and mothers, married to alcoholics and moving in social circles where fairly heavy drinking is common, discuss how alcoholism nearly destroyed their marriages and how they and their husbands successfully sought help.   WNEDTV; PTL.

WIZARD OF OZ, THE (101m C/B 1939)
A Kansas tornado carries Dorothy and Toto, her dog, to the Land of Oz.   Getting back to Kansas is by no means easy but--with the assistance of such unusual friends as a live scarecrow, a tin woodsman, a cowardly lion and the Wizard of Oz himself--Dorothy and Toto do get home.   d. Victor Flemming; s. w. Florence Ryerson, Edgar Allen Woolf, and Noel Langley; MGM; FL

WOMAN SERIES see ANTI-WOMEN'S LIBERATION; BEYOND THE BEAUTY MYTH; CHANGING MOTHERHOOD; CHILDBIRTH, PART I; CHILDBIRTH, PART II; CONGRESSWOMAN BELLA ABZUG; CONSCIOUSNESS RAISING; A CONVERSATION WITH BETTY FRIEDAN; A CONVERSATION WITH VIVECA LINDFORS; COSMETIC SURGERY; THE CREDIT-ABILITY GAP; DIVORCE INSURANCE; ECONOMICS AND THE AMERICAN WOMAN; EQUAL RIGHTS AMENDMENT, PART I; EQUAL RIGHTS AMENDMENT, PART II; FEMALE HOMOSEXUALITY; FEMALE SEXUALITY, PART I; FEMALE SEXUALITY, PART II; FEMINIST THERAPY; FLORENCE LUSCOMB, SUFFRAGIST; FOOD FOR THOUGHT; MARGARET SLOAN ON BLACK SISTERHOOD; THE MARRIAGE SAVERS; MENOPAUSE: HOW TO COPE; MEN'S LIBERATION; MENSTRUATION AND PREMENSTRUAL TENSION; MENTAL HEALTH CARE FOR WOMEN, PART I; MENTAL HEALTH CARE FOR WOMEN, PART II; MISTER MIDWIFE; MOTHERS WHO LEAVE HOME; N. O. W. NOW; OCCUPATION: MOTHER; OUR BODIES, OURSELVES; THE PERFECT MOTHER: PARADOX OR POSSIBILITY; PICKING UP THE PIECES: ONE WIDOW SPEAKS; THE REMARRIEDS; SEX BIAS IN EDUCATION, PART I; SEX BIAS IN EDUCATION, PART II; SEXISM IN RELIGION, ANOTHER VIEW; SEXUAL SUICIDE; THE SINGLE PARENT EXPERIENCE; TOYS FOR CHILDREN; THE TWO-PROFESSION MARRIAGE; UNLIKELY ADDICTS: MIDDLE CLASS WOMEN;

VOLUNTEERISM: PRO AND CON; WHY WOMEN ARE DIS-
SATISFIED WITH THEIR GYNECOLOGISTS; WIVES OF ALCO-
HOLICS; WOMEN AND CHILDREN IN CHINA; WOMEN AND IN-
SURANCE; WOMEN AND INSURANCE: THE INDUSTRY RE-
SPONDS; WOMEN IN POLICING; WOMEN IN PRISON, PART I;
WOMEN IN PRISON, PART II; WOMEN WORKERS; WRITE ON,
WOMEN PLAYWRIGHTS

WOMAN AS PAINTER (29m   C   1971   VIDEO)
Examines the often overlooked feminine artist. Renaissance
portraiturist Sophonisba Anguisciola; 17th-century Italy's Artemisia
Gentileschi; Lisette Vigee-Lebrun, the darling of pre-Revolutionary
French Society; and the neo-classic Swiss painter Angelika Kauff-
mann--are four of the lesser-recognized painters examined. The
program studies in detail the well-known American Impressionists
Mary Cassatt and Berthe Morisot and briefly covers a number of
other artists. The program includes over 200 pieces of art work
and rare slides from the collection of the Metropolitan Museum of
Art. MAETEL; PTL.

WOMAN CANDIDATE: RUNNING FOR OFFICE IS A VICTORY (13m
C   1974)
After working for 20 years behind the scenes for several politicians, Flora Carter decides to run for the office of lieutenant
governor of Virginia. In an interview she discusses the special
problems women face as candidates. By Lucyann Kerry; BRF.

WOMAN DOCTOR IN VIETNAM; 20th Century Series (26m   B   1966)
Tells the story of Dr. Pat Smith of Seattle, who runs a hospital
in Vietnam. CBSTV; ABFL

WOMAN IN THAT JOB?, A (30m   C   1971   SLIDE)
Directed toward employers, their affirmative action plans, show-
ing them how to reengineer positions to encourage women to apply.
USDL/Women's Bureau; USDL.

WOMAN IS (12m   C   1973)
The Biblical account of woman's creation prefaces this cinematic
exploration of the universal roles of women. A collection of primitive sculpture, still photographs and paintings, show woman as
mother both biologically and emotionally. Paintings and pictures
reveal male fascination with the female form. Records women as
exploited employees of the industrial era, and tells how and why
women turned to prostitution then. Women fought for their rights
for generations and contemporary photos show them demonstrating
for solidarity and recognition for their equal rights. p. Sandy Ostertag; PHOENIX, VF.

WOMAN IS A WOMAN, A (88m   C   1961   French/subtitled)
A salute to life, liberty and offbeat movies by Director Jean-
Luc Godard whose joy in his work has never been more apparent.
In this fresh and giddy free-form improvisation, Godard weaves all
the bright idiocy of a Hollywood musical into some very je meme

fische French rounds involving an ecdysiast (Anna Karina) who sheds
her last flimsy inhibition and decides to have a baby with her lover,
or if it happens to work out that way--with her lover's best friend.
d. Jean-Luc Godard; CORINF.

WOMAN IS ... HOMELESS, A (25m C 1976)
    Flophouses and missions exist to take in homeless men. Home-
lessness among women has only recently been noticed. This report
shows women who live in the park and who rummage through garbage cans. Then women at the House of Ruth, Washington, D. C.'s
only shelter for homeless women, talk about their lives. d. Louise
Tiranoff; p. Mary C. Kilday; WRCTV.

WOMAN OF A THOUSAND FIRES see MUJER DE MILFUEGOS

WOMAN OF CHAMULA; Indian Family Series (14m C 1969)
    Shows the life of a Mexican Indian family in Chaipas where the
Indians live in much the same way as did their Mayan ancestors a
thousand years ago. Describes the mother of the family and her
activities in the home. By Elda Hartley; HARTLEY.

WOMAN OF THE GANGES (90m C 1973 French/subtitled)
    Story concerns a middle-aged man who's returned to a seaside
town to kill himself. There, he encounters a woman he loved long
ago. Narration is by two invisible women. A great deal of symbolism with little spoken dialogue and barely any action. d. Marguerite Duras; MOM.

WOMAN OF THE MONTH--INDIRA GANDHI (28m B 1966)
    Surveys the life of Indira Gandhi, prime minister of India.
Shows her childhood, and her later life as the hostess for her father,
Jawaharlal Nehru. Includes an interview in which she discusses her
present hopes and programs for India. CBSTV.

WOMAN OF THE TOUBOU (25m C 1974)
    In the vast Sahara lives a people of pure blood and ancient
race, the Toubou. Toubous are happy and cheerful people, of grace,
elegance and dignity. They are nomadic and prefer to wander through
the Sahara endlessly. They are a strong matriarchy and have re-
sisted all efforts by Turks, French, and now the Black government
to control them. Humans are not their greatest adversary, however;
the last two decades of drought are taking their toll in starvation.
p. Anne Balfour-Fraser; PHOENIX.

WOMAN OF THE YEAR (114m B 1942)
    Hepburn is a distinguished political columnist with a range of
foreign languages and international connections equalled only by her
ignorance of domestic arts. Sportswriter Tracy, her husband, tries
to reconcile her public personality with her private one in order to
introduce intimacy into their home life. p. Joseph L. Mankiewicz;
d. George Stevens; MGM; FI.

WOMAN REBELS, A (88m B 1936)
Strong-willed young woman (Katharine Hepburn) straining at parental ties yearns to try her wings in this film set in 19th-century England. Women's lib gets an early start. d. Mark Sandrich; RKO; FI.

WOMAN TIMES SEVEN (99m C 1967)
Shirley MacLaine stars in seven comic episodes about contemporary Parisian women. The episodes are rich in irony, sly humors, human frailties, the errors of the civilized and the cowardices of the human being. d. Vittorio de Sica; p. Arthur Cohn; AVCO; ABFI.

WOMAN TO WOMAN (48m C r1975)
An enlightening documentary about hookers, housewives, and mothers. Combining interviews, the film reveals many similarities in problems as well as solutions among what are thought to be diverse areas of women's work. A most representative documentary on the current lives of women. Sponsors: AFI/Louis B. Mayer Foundation. By Donna Deitch; SB.

WOMAN, WIFE OR WHAT; Your Marriage Series, No. 3 (29m B n. d.)
Explains that in a modern world many married women have feelings of being trapped, with roles confused. Describes the battle for intellectual recognition and need for creative achievement. KUONTV.

WOMANHOUSE (47m C 1974)
Documents a project created by the Feminist Art Program headed by Judy Chicago and Miriam Shapiro at the California Institute of Arts. Captures the powerful art images (several pieces directed by Judy), moments from the group's consciousness-raising sessions and responses from the public. The camera travels through this "womanhouse"; through rooms of childhood, personal space, sensuality; through minutiae-filled rooms that reveal the focus of women's energies. The theme of women's lives permeates everything. By Johanna Demetrakas; IE, SB.

WOMANHOUSE (12m C n. d.)
Impressionistic film contrasts with Demetrakas' "Womanhouse, " the house developed by feminist artists in Los Angeles. "Objects and decor are seen through filtered lenses, and muted sounds with no visible source echo from walls of empty rooms. "--Art Cinema. By Mako Idemitsu; VRI.

WOMANPOWER: A WOMAN'S PLACE IS... (28m C r1975)
Here Sweden exemplifies the changing life-styles of families in industrial states when both parents have jobs and the traditional woman's work is shared by all. By Elspeth MacDougall; UN.

WOMANPOWER: EQUALITY AND DEVELOPMENT (28m   C   1974)
The film moves back and forth between women speakers at the
three-day United Nations forum on population control and modern
women of Tunisia who are initiating changes in their Moslem-
dominated country, where traditional women still wear veils.   UN.

WOMANPOWER: THE HIDDEN ASSET (17m   C   r1975)
Half of all the manpower in the largely agricultural developing
countries is womanpower, but so far, women's economic contributions have not been counted.   Shows how women of Sri Lanka are
trying to change all this.   d. Yvonne Hannemann; p. UN; SEF.

WOMANPOWER: THE PEOPLE'S CHOICE (28m   C   1974)
Colombian women got the vote little more than 20 years ago
(1957), yet women have entered politics at all levels.   The film
traces the campaigns of three women running for office from the
grassroots level of Bogota city councilwoman to the presidential
race of Maria Eugenia.   Only one woman was successful--she was
re-elected to the Senate--and she is the only woman now serving as
a Senator.   Narrated by Rita Moreno.   UN.

WOMAN'S FACE, A (105m   B   1941)
This film poses the idea that a woman's face can decide her
total personality: the scars on Joan Crawford's face and their subsequent removal cause her personality to be "bisected by the Puritan
Ethic into two mutually exclusive extremes of good and evil"--Molly
Haskell.   Opening in a courtroom with Crawford on trial for murder, the story of her evil connections with the Swedish underworld
unfolds, along with the recounting by surgeon Douglas of his removal
of her hideous scars and the elevation of her morals which followed.
Based on the play Il Etait une Fois by Francois de Croisset.   p.
Victor Saville; d. George Cukor; MGM; FI.

WOMAN'S FILM, THE (50m   B   1971)
A documentary giving real insight into the guts of the Women's
Movement.   We see women of different races, backgrounds and
jobs talk about their real lives and what political action means to
them.   By Louise Alaimo, Judy Smith, Ellen Souin; SFN; UIO.

WOMAN'S GAME, THE (28m   C   n.d.)
Shows six examples of how new opportunities for women are
opening up throughout the U.S.   Shows women from various ethnic
backgrounds at all levels of education.   Free loan.   MTP.

WOMAN'S HISTORY SLIDE SHOW, A (100m   C   n.d.   SLIDE)
Altogether, 450 slides portray average women's lives at different times in history, particularly emphasizing the work women did
and the conditions under which they did it.   The slide show consists
of four sections: Medieval England, 17th and 19th-century England
and a "Women in Revolt" section.   The show is not only descriptive
--it attempts to show why women's lives were the way they were by
analyzing the social and political systems of the times.   Script included.   By Cambridge-Godard Feminist History Project; WFC.

WOMAN'S PLACE, A (52m   C   r1974)
Traces the influences that create and perpetuate the "traditional" role of women, including children's books and toys (called "rehearsals for domesticity"), film clips, and advertising. Offers: a promise that a woman's place is determined by her hormones; a workshop sponsored by the Anti-Defamation League; a class on the status of housewives in the Women's Studies Department at an Eastern university; and a discussion of the problems of older women. Focuses on examples of how women are questioning and attempting to change their roles.   Features Bess Myerson as host and narrator, along with Sheila Tobias of Wesleyan University, Anthropologist Lional Tiger, and Abigail McCarthy.   Covers a broad diversity of women's issues.   Would be appreciated by an audience prepared to deal extensively with the subject.   By Victoria Hochberg, Marlene Sanders; XEROX; ASFI, EMC, IU, UILL, UIO, UM, WSU.

WOMAN'S PLACE, A (25m   C   1977)
Documents notable women who have made contributions to society, with a celebration of the facts that today a woman's place is everywhere.   Based in part on the tremendous volume of material gathered for the Life Special Report, "Remarkable American Women." Narrated by Julie Harris.   FELDD; CCCD; UIO.

WOMAN'S PLACE, A; Girls and Women Series (30m   B   1971)
Although women have ruled countries, waged wars, and led churches, most of recorded history was written by and about men. Using quotations from Livy, Chaucer, and Boswell, a panel discusses woman's role in the three eras--ancient Rome, the Middle Ages, and the 18th century--focusing on class structure, property rights, education, and sexual segregation.   UMITV; PAS, UM.

WOMAN'S PLACE? (30m   B   n. d.)
American Association of University Women panel discussion by six women (including Alice Beeman, General Director of AAUW) deals with the status of women.   Condensation of "Frankly Female" television show, narrated by Betty Grobley.   AAUW.

WOMAN'S PLACE IS IN THE HOUSE: A PORTRAIT OF ELAINE
    NOBLE, A (30m   C   r1975)
Explores the complex personal issues of a gay woman in political life.   The film follows Elaine Noble, a radical lesbian elected to the Massachusetts legislature in 1974, as she goes through a typical day from her Back Bay apartment to the State House.   d. Nancy Porter/Mickey Lemle; WGBHTV.

WOMAN'S ROLE III: IN COMMUNITY AFFAIRS (14m   C   n. d.)
Mrs. Paige Williams, a professional actress, illustrates the excitement of working in a repertory summer theatre and living in the historically beautiful community of Arrow Rock, Missouri.   She discusses her interest in the community with Ruth George, program coordinator for Continuing Education for Women.   UMIS.

WOMAN'S WORK, A (15m   C   1967)
Shows work being done in Alabama by the Cooperative Extension

Service to assist young rural homemakers of low socioeconomic status to become more economically and socially secure. Highlights the work of paid subprofessional program assistants.   UALA.

WOMAN'S WORK: A WOMAN'S LIFE, A; Girls and Women Series (30m   B   1972)
Discussion among women representing various jobs, interests, ages, and family situations is concerned with self-motivation and organization in finding work opportunities outside the home.   UMITV; PAS, UM.

WOMEN (30m   C   1973)
In his life as well as in his plays, George Bernard Shaw was an early advocate of women's liberation, loudly damning the customs that relegated women to an inferior status in marriage and in business.   This dramatic portrayal of Shaw's relationships with many different women gives some insight into how his attitudes were formed. In many ways, Shaw's irrelevance and biting humor uniquely qualified him to be the cutting edge for a new idea--women as outspoken, intelligent, independent human beings.   OECA; FL

WOMEN (15m   C   1975)
A sardonic exploration of the clichés used to describe women. Visuals, including a variety of nude female bodies, are juxtaposed with a multi-voiced sound track that chants a dictionary of terms applied to women.   By Constance Beeson; NSF; IE, MMRC, SB.

WOMEN (3m   C   n. d.)
"Any man you really talk to is either your father, or your husband, or your lover, and pretty soon he's thinking, 'why in hell doesn't she ask me how I feel?' "--Interviewee.   By Martha Stuart, David Ruskin; STUARTM.

WOMEN, THE (134m   B   1939)
An all-female cast interprets the vitriolic play about mischief among the idle, rich and spoiled matrons of New York.   A perfume counter siren schemes to catch a happily married husband with the help of his wife's hypocritical friends.   Only after the divorce does the wife realize that she must sharpen her nails, claw or be clawed to protect her home in the feminine jungle.   p. Hunt Stromberg; d. George Cukor; s. w. Anita Loos, Jane Murfin; MGM; FL

WOMEN AGAINST RAPE (30m   C   n. d.   VIDEO)
Member of the San Francisco Women Against Rape refute myths about rape, talk with two women who have been raped, give information about the criminal justice system and alternatives to that system, and offer ways to prevent rape.   KQEDTV.

WOMEN AGAINST RAPE: SIX PUBLIC SERVICE ANNOUNCEMENTS (3m   C   1976)
These six 30-second public service announcements specifically produced for television provide vital information for rape victims and produce support for rape prevention/crisis centers.   Originally

used by Bay Area Women Against Rape to generate wider community
awareness and donations.   These PSA's are suitable for use in any
community with a rape prevention crisis center.   By Pamela Step-
hens; SB.

WOMEN, AMEN! (15m   C   1973)
    Examines the impact of the women's movement on churches in
the U. S.   Shows a young woman activist who organizes a consciousness-raising group, reforms worship services, and finally enters a
seminary.   Older women lobby for bringing women into decision-
making procedures.   By Mariana Norris, Kaye Henderson; TRAFCO;
MMA; EMC.

WOMEN AND CHILDREN AT LARGE (7m   C   1973)
    A touching and often funny look at the lives and feelings of the
filmmaker and her friends, and the matriarchal circle they constitute.   Includes moving shots of pregnant women dancing naked, and
amusing scenes of children at play.   By Freude Bartlett; SB, CCC.

WOMEN AND CHILDREN IN CHINA; Woman Series (29m   C   1975
    VIDEO)
    Ruth Sidel, a psychiatric social worker who first visited China
in 1971 with her physician husband, tells of the first law passed
after the 1949 revolution which made husbands and wives equal,
abolished arranged marriage, and permitted women to divorce.
WNEDTV; PTL.

WOMEN AND INSURANCE; Woman Series (29m   C   1974   VIDEO)
    Kathleen Peratis, an attorney and director of the Women's
Rights Project at the American Civil Liberties Union, discusses
sex discrimination in insurance.   She believes that discrimination is
practiced in virtually every type of insurance currently available.
WNEDTV; PTL.

WOMEN AND INSURANCE: THE INDUSTRY RESPONDS; Woman
    Series (29m   C   1975   VIDEO)
    Representatives of the insurance industry explain industry prac-
tices and answer charges of discrimination against women.   Robert
Waldron, manager of press relations for the Health Insurance Institute, and Barbara Lautzenheiser, vice president and actuary of
Bankers' Life of Nebraska, discuss changes in attitude toward wom-
en.   WNEDTV; PTL.

WOMEN AND MADNESS (25m   B   n. d.   VIDEO)
    Personal experiences exploring the idea that madness as defined
by society is a political act and results from conflicting ideas of
what accepted behavior is.   TCWFC.

WOMEN AND THEIR HEALTH   see   TAKING OUR BODIES BACK:
    THE WOMAN'S HEALTH MOVEMENT

WOMEN ARTISTS: A HISTORICAL SURVEY: EARLY MIDDLE AGES
    TO 1900 (n. d.   SLIDES   (120))
    Shows many unknown examples of women's art in the styles and

periods most often examined in art history courses. Surveys both
European and American women artists. Some of the artists included
are: Sofonisba Anguissola, Artemisia Gentileschi, Judith Leyster,
Rachel Ruysch, Angelica Kauffmann, Elisabeth Vigee-Lebrun, Ade-
laide Labille-Guiard, Sarah Miriam Peale, Rosa Bonheur, Mary Cassatt, Berthe Morisot, and Suzanne Valadon. Notes included. HAR.

WOMEN ARTISTS: IMAGES--THEMES AND DREAMS (n. d. SLIDES
(80))
    These slides look at women's sense of themselves and sources
of imagery in creating art. The works are open to many interpretations. Some are quite terrifying, or have a satiric bite, while oth-
era joyously affirm the strength and originality of women as individuals. Some of the artists included are: Florine Stettheimer,
Gwen John, Charley Toorop, Frida Kahlo, Leonor Fini, ·Remedios
Varo, Judy Chicago, Niki de Saint Phalle, Joyce Wieland, and Mary
Beth Edelson. Notes included. HAR.

WOMEN ARTISTS SERIES see WOMEN ARTISTS: A HISTORICAL
    SURVEY; WOMEN ARTISTS: IMAGES--THEMES AND DREAMS;
    WOMEN ARTISTS: THIRD WORLD; WOMEN ARTISTS: THE
    TWENTIETH CENTURY. Also see book: Women Artists:
    Recognition and Reappraisal from the Early Middle Ages to the
    Twentieth Century, by Harper Colophon, 1976, Harper and Row.

WOMEN ARTISTS: THE TWENTIETH CENTURY (n. d. SLIDES
(80))
    Examines influential styles and genres of women artists of the
twentieth century. Some of the artists included are: Romaine
Brooks, Gabriele Munter, Paula Modersohn-Becker, Natalia Gon-
charova, Kathe Kollwitz, Barbara Hepworth, Georgia O'Keeffe,
Louise Nevelson, Germaine Richier, Vieira da Silva, Eva Hesse,
and Lee Krasner. Notes included. HAR.

WOMEN ARTISTS: THIRD WORLD (n. d. SLIDES (80))
    Represents individual and collective experiences of Third World
American women. Some of the artists included are: Lois Mailou
Jones, Elizabeth Catlett, Augusta Savage, Consuelo Amezcua, Minnie
Evans, Pablita Velarde, Mine Okubo, Faith Ringgold, Betye Saar,
and Barbara Chase-Riboud. Notes included. HAR.

WOMEN AT LARGE (10m C 1973)
    A comedy about Women's Movement in and out of life and art.
By Freude Bartlett; CCC.

WOMEN EMERGING: COMPARING CULTURAL EXPECTATIONS;
    Sex Role Stereotyping Schools, A (Series) (27m B r1975)
    Documents the experiences of a multicultural women's class at
Agora, an experimental school within Berkeley High School, Berkeley, California. EMC.

WOMEN FOR WOMEN (30m B 1972)
    A documentary of political actions by women in New York, but
relevant to women everywhere. p. Marian Hunter; HERSTORY.

WOMEN GET THE VOTE, THE (27m   B   1962)
The campaign to establish women's right to vote in the U. S. received its first forward movement at Seneca Falls in July 1848,
when a meeting was held to discuss the "social, civil, and religious
rights of women. " Using historic footage, this film covers the difficult years of the campaign and final triumph, and passage of the
19th Amendment.   CBSTV; MGH; AFC, FSU, NIU, OSU, SCC, UILL,
UNH, USC.

WOMEN IN A CHANGING WORLD; Faces of Change Series (48m   C
r1975)
Explores the psychological and technical impact of modernization
on women in four cultures--Bolivia, Northern Kenya, Afghanistan
and Hong Kong territory.   Four women from these cultures are expressing their concern with fundamental rights and human dignity as
it affects their individual lives.   By Nancy Dupree, Judith Von
Daler; AUFS; WER; EMC, UIO, IU, MSU, UK, UM.

WOMEN IN BUSINESS: THREAT OR OPPORTUNITY   see   WOMEN
IN MANAGEMENT: THREAT OR OPPORTUNITY

WOMEN IN CAREERS; Careers in the 70's Series (15m   C   1973)
A floral designer, an assistant social worker, a college physics
professor, a physical education teacher, and a city councilwoman relate why it is important for women to pursue goals and to develop as
people.   p. Richard Siegel; PHOENIX; UILL.

WOMEN IN CHINA (27m   C   n. d.)
Today's China is offering women a new place in society, a new
responsibility, a new pride.   Unlike the old days, today a huge universal educational system exists, available to every child.   Women
are contributing to every aspect of China's new society, are sharing
equally with men the challenge and responsibility of the future.   The
film examines the means by which this tremendous change was possible, through the availability of adequate medical care, food, housing, schools for children, child care and jobs.   By Betty McAfee;
FIM.

WOMEN IN COMMUNICATIONS (15m   C   1975)
Portrays three women who are successfully engaged in careers
in communication, careers traditionally considered to be masculine
fields--reporting, filmmaking, radio announcing.   Describes each
job's requirements and discusses advantages, rewards, and limitations.   FORUMP; BFA; IU.

WOMEN IN CUBA   see   BUENOS DIAS COMPAÑERAS

WOMEN IN DEFENSE (10m   B   1941)
"... Women can do two-thirds of the jobs men can (do) ... " is
one of the sexist statements in this obviously sincere attempt to bol-
ster behind-the-lines sentiment in that it never once refers to women as "girls. " Narrated by Katharine Hepburn.   p. Office for Emergency Management Film Unit;
s. w. Eleanor Roosevelt; NAVC; KP.

WOMEN IN LOVE (132m C 1970)
Two sisters, sexually mature and intellectually active, struggle against the confines of a rural English mining town and its rigidly classed layers of society. Around them D. H. Lawrence weaves one of his best studies of sexual uneasiness and doubt. The story explodes with subtle frustrations, warped joys, and bitter passions. The more placid sister, played by Jennie Linden, becomes engaged to a teacher (Alan Bates), a man who longs for true spiritual companionship. The other sister (Glenda Jackson) has a tangled relationship with Oliver Reed, the son of the mine owner. Based on a story by D. H. Lawrence. d. Ken Russell; UAS.

WOMEN IN MANAGEMENT; Are You Listening Series (29m C 1976)
The opening sentence--"How it feels to be a woman and a manager, how it feels to manage and be managed"--sets the tone for this film that features women from high level management in many fields. Suitable for use in workshop situations. The film is especially valuable to men whether or not they are in management. By Martha Stuart; IMPF.

WOMEN IN MANAGEMENT: THREAT OR OPPORTUNITY? (29m C r1975)
Examines the impact of the women's liberation movement in several business organizations. Reveals the manner in which women are stereotyped into a multitude of roles rather than viewed as capable and talented individuals, and compiles women's attitudes toward these prejudices. p. Barbara Jampel; CRM, MGH; CWU, EMC, UILL, UK, USC, UW.

WOMEN IN MIDDLE MANAGEMENT; Are You Listening Series (29m C 1976)
Many of these women began their work in extremely menial positions. They discuss frankly their conditioning and fear about "coming up from the ranks." By Martha Stuart; IMPF.

WOMEN IN OTHER CULTURES (8m C n. d.)
Hagit is a vibrant, mature 17-year-old, who has been raised on a kibbutz in Israel. In this film, she shares some of her thoughts and feelings about responsibility, love, trust, marriage, home, her friends, her family, and herself. EDC.

WOMEN IN POLICING; Woman Series (29m C 1975 VIDEO)
Catherine Milton of the Police Foundation estimates that five years ago a total of seven policewomen were on patrol in American cities. Today there are about two thousand. Ms. Milton and attorney Margaret Gates explore this dramatic increase and the problems women still face entering police careers. WNEDTV; PTL.

WOMEN IN PRISON (54m C 1974)
When a woman enters prison for the first time, she is stripped and searched. She becomes part of a life-style in which she may be abused, sexually exploited, dehumanized and defeminized. Film

exposes the indignities these women may suffer in prison. Suggests an alternative kind of confinement as in the Des Moines (Iowa) Community Corrections Project. Here a woman convicted of murder is being allowed to live at home with her children, saving taxpayers a great deal of money and providing a way for this woman to be a contributing part of her community. ABCTV; CAROUSEL; EMC, PAS, UIO, UM.

WOMEN IN PRISON, PT. I; Woman Series (29m C 1975 VIDEO)
     A short film, "Like a Rose," focuses on the life in a woman's prison. Nancy Margulies of the production team "Tomato Productions," explains her work on the film. WNEDTV; PTL.

WOMEN IN PRISON, PT. II; Woman Series (29m C 1975 VIDEO)
     Two inmates of the Women's State Correctional Center in Tipton, Missouri (Peggy Russell and Carol Dillard) explore some of the realities of prison life which the film "Like a Rose," touches on. WNEDTV; PTL.

WOMEN IN SPORTS--AN INFORMAL HISTORY (28m C 1976)
     Traces prejudice from the classical period to the present against the physically active woman, the rise of women's participation in sports, the growing awareness of rights and new enthusiasm for sports. d. /p. Dan Klugherz, Dr. Arthur Zitrin; ALTANA; UIO.

WOMEN IN THE FAMILY OF MAN; Girls and Women Series (30m
     B 1971)
     Discussion of old and new life-styles: the traditional, two parent nuclear family; unmarried relationships; communal living; and the trend to more "liberated" families in which women are contributing to the family income. Considers advantages and limitations of each. UMITV; PAS, UM.

WOMEN IN THE OFFICE: CHANGING TIMES (30m C n. d.
     VIDEO)
     A look at the conditions of clerical workers and how they are organizing themselves in the Bay Area. p. Berkeley/Oakland Women's Union; KQEDTV.

WOMEN IN THE PERFORMING ARTS (28m C 1975 VIDEO)
     Portland (Oregon) women artists discuss the work they are doing to create a new culture. Woven through the statements of purpose and feelings are performances of music, theatre, dance, poetry and very powerful songs. The program is a beautiful piece of cultural work. NOWP; CREOUT.

WOMEN IN THE WORLD OF WORK (15m C 1974)
     Looks at a wide variety of young women who have pioneered successfully in non-traditional, normally male-oriented occupations. VOFI; UILL.

WOMEN IN VIETNAM (40m C n. d.)
     Shows Vietnamese women at work, fighting, and relaxing in North Vietnam. IPCFL.

WOMEN IN WAITING (12m B n. d. VIDEO)
An intriguing statement by women becoming aware of the significance of waiting in their lives. TCWFC.

WOMEN, LAW AND POLITICS (30m B 1971)
Panel examines current issues involving freedom and rights of
American women; the change effected by the 1964 Civil Rights bill
which added the words "sex" and "race" to the list of items unlaw-
ful for discrimination; problems of equal pay and equal opportunity
for women; trend toward part-time employment for women; inequities
in the social security system. WMITV; PAS, UM.

WOMEN OF ALL AGES (30m C n. d. VIDEO)
Dramatic readings of literature from antiquity through the present show how the image of women has changed (or not changed)
through the ages. p. Los Altos Branch of the AAUW; KQEDTV.

WOMEN OF ERIN (40m B n. d.)
Irish Catholic women from Belfast and Derry speak about their
day-to-day lives under the control of the British Army, describing
the effects of the Special Powers Act which allows imprisonment
without evidence or trial. Despite some technical difficulties, the
tape offers a profound sense of the strength and power of these wom-
en in their struggle. By Caroline Hatch; IE.

WOMEN OF NEVE UR, THE (29m C n. d.)
Depicts the courage of Israeli women who live in the kibbutz
of Neve Ur and their lack of hostility toward those who have sworn
to destroy them. NET, IU; ADL.

WOMEN OF RUSSIA (12m C 1968)
The juxtaposition of the old and the new reveals the broad spectrum of life-styles in the Soviet Union. Peasant women eating in
the fields are contrasted with elegant women eating in a restaurant;
women working on construction jobs lead into women watching a
fashion show. Explores the large number of careers Russian women
pursue--doctors, gymnasts, housewives, farmers. Nonverbal. p.
Julien Bryan; IFF; PAS, UC, UILL.

WOMEN OF TELECOMMUNICATIONS STATION NO. 6 (20m B
n. d.)
Young North Vietnamese women are learning the skills that enable them to take an active part in all areas of the struggle against
the U. S. aggressors. Here they operate a vital communication and
relay station and defend it against attack. The film touches on the
more personal aspects of the women's lives and their transformation from a role of bondage to one of full participation in their
country's struggle. English sound track. SFN, TWN.

WOMEN OF THE RHONDDA (20m B 1973)
In the Rhondda Valley of Wales, a mining district that was the
site of epic strikes in the '20's, three women share their lives, and
the lives of their mothers, as "slaves of slaves." The women and

filmmakers graphically describe how "women's work" is the underpinning of an entire system of exploitation--neither the miners nor the mines could function without the drudgery of wives, sisters and daughters.   LWFG; IRISF.

WOMEN OF THE TOUBOU (25m   C   1974)
    Within the vast Sahara live a people of pure blood and ancient race.   Toubou are happy people of grace, elegance, and dignity. The women are treated as equals by the men--they share every aspect of life, and are admired and respected as well as loved.   For the past two decades the Sahara has suffered the worst drought in history.   Many are dead and many are dying.   Within a short time, the beautiful Toubou women may cease to exist.   By Anne Balfour-Fraser; VFI, PHOENIX.

WOMEN OF THE WORLD   see   W. O. W.   (WOMEN OF THE WORLD)

WOMEN ON ORGASM: OUT IN THE OPEN (15m   C   1974)
    Women share their feelings about sex and orgasm.   Includes instructions for the pre-orgasmic woman and a short heterosexual lovemaking scene.   d. Patricia Rose Duignan; MMRC.

WOMEN ON THE MARCH, PT. I (29m   B   1958)
    Traces the history of struggle for women's rights in England, Canada, and U. S. --picketing, parading, hunger strikes--from Mary Wollstonecraft in 1792 to 1920.   Film selects a very narrow part of the feminist movement--the fight for suffrage.   The value of this film lies in the historical footage, not in its historical analysis. NFBC; MGH; BU, PAS, SCC, UM, USC.

WOMEN ON THE MARCH, PT. II (29m   B   1958)
    Tells of the story of the role of women in Canadian government. Lacks historical evidence.   Rather dated.   NFBC; MGH; BU, PAS, SCC, UM, USC.

WOMEN TALKING (80m   B   1971)
    Features conversations with leading personalities in the forefront of the Women's Liberation Movement.   Seeking to bring an understanding of the vital problem confronting our society to all women, they relate experiences that contribute to a greater awareness of the social oppression of women.   d. Midge Mackenzie; WLIBCC; IMPF.

WOMEN: THE EMERGING RESOURCE (7 hrs.   C   1972   VIDEO)
    Barbara Boyle, management consultant, and Dr. Frederick Herzberg, Professor of Management at the University of Utah, present this comprehensive program which includes course director's guide and materials for participants.   Program includes role playing, individual participation, group discussions, and team presentations. Ms. Boyle and Dr. Herzberg demonstrate new techniques for counseling women and managers about how to design and implement action programs required by law.   ASL

WOMEN: THE HAND THAT CRADLES THE ROCK; Towards the
Year 2000 Series (22m C 1971)
     Intercuts footage of advertisements that use stereotyped images
of women with brief, occasionally superficial sequences in which
members of the women's liberation movement discuss their ideas.
Includes Dr. Phyllis Chesler, a psychologist, and Anselma Dell
'Olio, director of a feminist theatre.   Shows excerpts of panel dis-
cussion that includes Dr. Albert Ellis, noted sexologist. d. Joan
Fiore; DA; EMC, UILL, WSU.

WOMEN UP IN ARMS (28m B 1966)
     An examination of the evolving position of the Moslem woman
who has been relegated to a peripheral part of her society for centuries.   It contrasts the conflicting life-styles of three generations:
two grandmothers, who regret social change; a mother, caught in the
throes of transition from the traditional; and her modern teen-age
daughter, who wears no veil and dances to Beatles' music.   Lucid
photography and interview tell the changing story of the social development in Tunisia.   UN; MGH.

WOMEN: UP THE CAREER LADDER (30m B 1972)
     Candid discussion of views and experiences of eight women who
hold responsible positions in business, government, and education.
Demonstrates the effects of traditional employment practices and attitudes, and raises new questions for change.   Presented as a continuing workshop, which stimulates a management development course
for women at UCLA Extension.   Intended for awareness-training and
affirmative-action programs at all organizational levels.   UCLA;
EMC, UIO, UMIS, UW.

WOMEN WHO HAVE HAD AN ABORTION (29m C 1972)
     All of the women in this film faced the ordeal of deciding to
have an abortion, subsequently having one, and being willing to talk
about it.   These women, Black and white, represent wide-ranging
and varied socioeconomic backgrounds.   Martha Stuart's theory is
that the real experts on problems are the people who have had the
experience.   The profound dialogue in this film will open the minds
and feelings of others contemplating or waiting to have an abortion.
p. Martha Stuart; IMPF.

WOMEN WITHOUT NAMES (89m B 1951 Italian/subtitled)
     A vivid and accurate portrayal of the way women deal with prob-
lems, emotions and despair.   A neo-realist production filmed on location at a women's displaced person's camp after World War II.
d. Geza Radvany; KP.

WOMEN WORKERS; Woman Series (29m C 1974 VIDEO)
     Barbara Wertheimer, director of trade union women's studies
at the New York State School of Industrial and Labor Relations at
Cornell University, and Margie Albert, union organizer for the Dis-
tributive Workers of America, believe that there is a new consciousness among office workers who are banding together for better wages
and job conditions.   WNEDTV; PTL.

WOMEN'S BASKETBALL--JUMP BALL (15m C 1976)
Stresses the importance of practice and determination in developing the basic skills of the game, while showing how togetherness between teammates and coach can make a difference in winning and losing. We follow a coach and her team through practice drills, game preparation, and actual tournament play. We also see a coach of younger girls teaching them basic stances, shooting styles, and offensive and defensive techniques. By Linda Dobrofsky, Neal Dobrofsky; BFA; IU.

WOMEN'S GYMNASTICS: AN INTRODUCTION (14m C 1968)
Muriel Grossfeld, former Olympic star and one of America's outstanding gymnastics authorities, demonstrates this challenging sport, introducing a number of international competitive events. RYATF; ABFI; UILL.

WOMEN'S GYMNASTICS: BALANCE BEAM FUNDAMENTALS (15m C n. d.)
Performance on the balance beam develops grace and poise. The aim is to create the illusion of space and freedom within the narrow confines of the beam. Basic safety precautions are pointed out, with particular attention to "spotting, " or giving physical support and help to the amateur. A variety of mounts are demonstrated, as well as forward rolls, arabesque, pivot turns, swing turns, and several dismounts. Demonstration by Muriel Grossfeld, head coach of the U. S. Olympics team, with two of her young students. RYATF; ABFL

WOMEN'S GYMNASTICS: FLOOR EXERCISE FUNDAMENTALS (14m C n. d.)
Muriel Grossfeld, head coach of the U. S. Olympics team, puts two novices through their gymnastic paces. Basic movements, such as leaps, cartwheels, jettes, and a variety of turns, are taught. A good instructional film. RYATF; ABFL

WOMEN'S HAPPY TIME COMMUNE (50m C 1972)
A feminist farce set in the old West. A crazy pilgrimage of two frontier ladies from a straitlaced community who run away to be dance-hall girls. They meet up with an ex-preacher's wife turned hooker, a farmgirl, and several others, including a pistol-packin' momma with a vision of the Women's Happy Time Commune. Some great comments about women, men, and the pros and cons of living with either. d. Sheila Paige; WMM; IE.

WOMEN'S HEALTH: A QUESTION OF SURVIVAL (49m C 1977)
Women live longer than men; women visit doctors more often than men. Women have nearly twice as many operations as men. In general, women have more health problems than men and most of these problems are connected with their ability to reproduce. "ABC News Closeup" investigates the care women receive--mostly from men. And they don't like what they see--disinterested doctors, drug manufacturers, government regulators, and legislators. Some women feel it necessary to open self-help clinics to enable women to become

more aware of their bodies and their special problems.   Should be
seen by all women as well as men, particularly physicians and con-
gressmen.   By Marlene Sanders; MGH.

WOMEN'S IMAGES IN ADVERTISING (n. d.   SLIDES   (30))
      A slide show of ads taken mainly from business magazines--
magazines for men.   Women are objectified and identified with
products they're used to sell.   Fear and perversion are documented
as selling techniques.   Script included.   WRP.

WOMEN'S LIB--A LA FRANCAISE (9m   C   1975)
      Short interview with three women who define liberation differ-
ently.   Francoise believes, "If you clean your floor while singing,
you're free. "   Madame Francoise Giroud indicates that most French
women and men are indifferent to the feminist movement, but believes women will eventually share the responsibilities and privileges
men have.   "Women are prisoners of the family, " says Christine,
a career woman.   Press and Information Service of the French Embassy; ASFI.

WOMEN'S LIB--FROM WHAT, FOR WHAT? (30m   C   1975)
      Deals with all the issues making today's headlines: power struc-
ture, job discrimination, child care, the Black woman, the vote.
Marya Mannes, writer and TV personality, is the moderator.   National Board of Young Women's Christian Association; AIM.

WOMEN'S LIBERATION; Human Relations Film Series (25m   C
r1971)
      Examines goals and methods of various groups within the Wom-
en's Liberation Movement, pointing out their similarities and differences.   Shows women of moderate professional organizations as well
as representatives of radical extremist factions.   Features Marlene
Sanders, Senator Birch Bayh and Betty Friedan.   d. Marlene Sanders;
ABCTV; ABCMC; XEROX; MSU, OSU, PAS, UM.

WOMEN'S MOVEMENT, THE (n. d.   SFS   (2))
      Examines psychological aspects of discrimination against women,
goal of National Organization for Women, and consciousness-raising
techniques.   Guide included.   AVNA.

WOMEN'S OLYMPIC INSTRUCTIONAL FILM, 1972 (20m   B   si
1972)
      Shows female athletes in technique-footage, taken during the
1972 Olympic Games in Munich.   Different angles are used to show
the several efforts of the athletes in all field events.   TRACKN;
CWU.

WOMEN'S POLITICAL DANCE (25m   B   n. d.   VIDEO)
      This Vietnamese Dance is a magnificent dancing play which
shows the creative power of the Vietnamese people even while the
U. S. bombed, raped and napalmed them.   In "Manos, " a healing
dance, there is a lovely passage of energy between the two dancers.
"Million-Eyed Woman, " an anti-rape dance, demonstrates a deep
sensitivity to the needs of women and the earth.   NOWP.

WOMEN'S PREJUDICE FILM: MYTHS AND REALITIES (18m   C
1976)
Many myths and clichés are explored in this semi-documentary
approach to contemporary life-styles of women.   Alternate viewpoints
are presented which stimulate the viewer to reappraise his or her
current attitude concerning the equality of roles among women and
men.   The film indicates that women themselves need to explore the
world of work more fully.   Those who have not identified their full
capabilities and potential may well be victims of their own acceptance
of the outdated and outmoded myths and clichés that continue to surround them.   Hosted by Susan Oliver; SANDLER; BARR; UWY.

WOMEN'S RIGHTS IN THE U.S.:   AN INFORMAL HISTORY (27m
C   1974)
Employs excellent period drawings, illustrations, old photographs,
and newsreel footage to provide an amusing and informative history
of the women's movement in America beginning with the 1970's and
going back into the 19th century; the origins of the women's movement in the abolitionist movement; and the long struggle for the vote.
By Dan Klugherz, with Professor Barbara Welter.   ALTANA; EMC,
IU, UILL, UIO.

WOMEN'S RITES (8m   C   1974)
"A joyful dance/full fall film/women in motion ... still/fruition
languor togetherness one."--IE.   By Barbara Hammer; IE.

WOMEN'S SELF DEFENSE (30m   C   n. d.   VIDEO)
A program instructing women on how they can prevent themselves from being crime victim statistics.   KQEDTV.

WOMEN'S SHOW (59m   C   1973   VIDEO)
A report on the issues involved in the debate over the Equal
Rights Amendment.   Guests for a studio question-and-answer session
include Jill Ruckelshaus, an active member of the National Women's
Political Caucus; Gabrielle Burton, author of the book I'm Running
Away from Home, but I'm Not Allowed to Cross the Street; and
Cindy Turner, a 22-year-old bartender in Washington, D.C.   The
program also focuses on the debate in the Indiana State Legislature
over ratification of the Amendment.   Correspondents Robert Mac-
Neil and Jim Lehrer report.   NPACFT; PTL.

WOMEN'S WORK: ENGINEERING (26m   C   n. d.)
Documents both the personal and the professional lives of several
engineering students and working engineers.   Cynthia McCarthy, a
civil engineer, lets us know what her position is really like and how
she feels, being a woman in what was considered a "man's world."
A group of women engineering students, faculty, and engineers discuss what it takes to be an engineer and why they find it meaningful.
Chemical engineer Lita Nelson and her husband point out the problems and benefits of combining a full-time career with the responsibilities of family life.   MIT; EDC.

WOMEN'S WORK: MANAGEMENT (29m   C   n. d.)
What does it mean to be a woman in management?   What skills

are necessary? What are the responsibilities and satisfactions?
Six working women discuss their jobs, their special concerns, and
their management of both a demanding work schedule and their families. They enjoy feeling that they "count, " and that they have an
impact on the society in which they live. MIT; EDC.

WOO WHO? MAY WILSON (33m C 1969)
     Lively and sympathetic portrait of May Wilson, a 63-year-old
former "wife-mother-housekeeper-cook" who, when her husband left
her, moved from the country to New York City and began creating a
new life and identity in which her art, which had been a hobby, became central. Shows her with new, young friends, and at work on
her sculptural assemblages. Her commentary reveals her terrified
lack of confidence when first arriving in Manhattan, and how this has
changed to self-assurance, pride, and a more rewarding life. By
Amalie R. Rothschild; ROTA; NDF; EMC, UM.

WORDS (15m B 1973)
     "Explores within a short period of time the relationship among
three people. "--NTS. By Nadja Tesich-Savage; TESICH.

WORK OF GOMIS (48m C 1973)
     Describes in detail a series of ceremonies used by the doctor
(Gomis), who practices healing in the villages of South Ceylon. He
uses rituals that are 10, 000 years old. It is unlikely he will have a
successor. By Yvonne Hanneman; SB.

WORKING CLASS ON FILM, THE (14m C r1976)
     Back in the 20's John Grierson, documentary filmmaker and
social agitator, had the idea that the lives of working people could
inspire great films. The development of this idea and the beginning
of the documentary movements he fathered in England and Canada are
traced over the last 50 years. d. Susan Schouten; NFBC.

WORKING MOTHERS (30m C 1973)
     Documentary on working mothers. By Abigail Child; CHILD.

WORKING MOTHERS see "... AND THEY LIVED HAPPILY EVER
     AFTER"; EXTENSIONS OF THE FAMILY; IT'S NOT ENOUGH;
     LIKE THE TREES; LUCIKLY I NEED LITTLE SLEEP; MOTH-
     ERS ARE PEOPLE; OUR DEAR SISTERS; THEY APPRECIATE
     YOU MORE; TIGER ON A TIGHT LEASH; WORKING MOTHERS;
     WOULD I EVER LIKE TO WORK

WORKOUT (9m B 1967)
     Impressionistic study of relationship between horse and rider.
By Rhonda Small; AUIS.

WORKS see FULL CIRCLE: THE WORK OF DORIS CHASE, A

WORKS IN SERIES: JOHNS, STELLA, WARHOL (30m C 1973)
     Opening tour of the Art Museum of South Texas. Interviews with
Jasper Johns, Frank Stella, Andy Warhol, and Barbara Rose. By
Barbara Rose; BP.

WORLD CHANGES SERIES see JAPAN'S NEW FAMILY PATTERNS

WORLD OF THE AMERICAN CRAFTSMAN: THE WORLD AND THE
    WORK OF BARBARA SCARPONI, THE (28m   C   1970)
    Presents Barbara Scarponi, American craftswoman in wax and
metal, indicating that her creations lack neatness and organization
because they reflect the personalities of people. Reveals that she
feels people cannot be fully organized because they are influenced
by so many things in their environment. Shows her work and states
that she dislikes completion of objects because she must part with
them. NETRC; IU; BU, EMC.

WORLD OF THE AMERICAN CRAFTSMAN: THE WORLD AND THE
    WORK OF DOROTHY YOUNG, THE (30m   C   1970)
    Surveys life and work of Dorothy Young and her husband, Dr.
Lloyd Young. She describes how she started weaving while in college. Shows her gathering and using natural reeds and grasses,
which she likes to use in her work. Dr. Young also began weaving
after retirement, and the two discuss how weaving has brought them
together with each other and with nature. ETS; IU, BU.

WORLD OF THE AMERICAN CRAFTSMAN: THE WORLD AND THE
    WORK OF VIVIKA HEINO, THE (30m   C   1969)
    Shows how Vivika and Otto Heino express their interpretation of
life through their craft, pottery making. Describes much of their
stimulus for their creation as coming from the setting of their rural
New Hampshire home. Compares the quality of clay to people--
worked too hard the clay breaks down; handled gently, the result is
a self-sustaining work of art. WENHTV; IU; BU.

WORLD OF WORK, THE (SERIES) see INTERN: A LONG YEAR;
    JOBS FOR WOMEN: WHERE ARE YOU GOING VIRGINIA?

WORLDLY WISE; Serendipity Series, The (14m   C   1976)
    Stresses the importance of words in everyday life. Uses music,
verbal play, montage and humor to help students understand the importance and variety of words, and to introduce the dictionary. By
Suzanne Bauman; MGH.

WOULD I EVER LIKE TO WORK; Challenge for Change Series (9m
    C   1974)
    Memorable portrait of a victim of the Canadian Welfare System,
an overburdened mother of seven children who, deserted by her
abusive husband and in poor health, longs for the possibility of a
job outside her home. Particularly poignant is her history of fruit-
less effort to obtain a tubal ligation, which, despite her increasingly
desperate situation, was denied her on the grounds that she was too
young. NFBC; EDC, EMC.

WOULD YOU KISS A NAKED MAN? (20m   C   1975)
    Carefully scripted and staged, the film concerns itself with teen-
age attitudes and behaviors towards sexuality in a non-clinical and
non-scientific manner. The film responds to the questions and moral
issues faced by teen-agers today. Emphasis is focused upon sexual

role playing, values clarification, sexual games people play, the
concept of "love, " the search for commitment, and the pressures
and influences of peer groups and parent-child relationships. The
film especially deals with virginity (of both sexes) and nudity, employing them as exploratory tools, not only in a visual sense but
also as an indication of trust and comfortability. The film contains
a very modest short nude scene.   By Mary E. McLeod; PERENNIAL.

WOUNDED KNEE (45m   B   n. d.   VIDEO)
      Women filmmaker's focus on the events leading up to and emo-
tions surrounding the occupation of Wounded Knee.   Includes interviews with AIM, police, and residents of Rapid City.   TCWFC.

WOVEN GARDENS; Tribal Eye Series, The (52m   C   1976)
      In Iran, nomads continue to wander as they have for centuries.
This film examines the life-style and art of one of these tribes, the
Quashqu'i.   They take great pride in their heritage and strive to
preserve their ways; the men pride themselves on their horseman-
ship; the women on their bright and elaborate clothing, and the ancient art of rug weaving.   As the tribe travels, the women spin
thread from the wool of their own flocks.   When camp is made, the
looms are set up on which elaborately patterned rugs are woven
with threads colored by dyes from pomegranates, henna, vines and
other forms of plant life.   It may take two women working together
as long as five years to complete one small rug.   d. David Collison;
ABCTV/WSA; TL.

WRESTLING (8m   B   n. d.)
      "Crowd-sounds montage sound track.   A TV 'concrete'. "--M. M.
By Marie Menken; FCOOP.

WRITE ON; Serendipity Series, The (15m   C   1976)
      Shows how students can be helped to expand their ability to com-
municate through writing.   Various writing assignments are pursued
by children and they have fun doing the writing.   By Suzanne Bauman; MGH.

WRITE ON, WOMEN PLAYWRIGHTS; Woman Series (29m   C   1974
      VIDEO)
      Playwright Myrna Lamb says "Women playwrights are creating
a new mythology.   They're writing from the point of view of an oppressed majority, about women as subjects rather than objects.   I
call it the view from the other side of the moon. "   WNEDTV; PTL.

WUTHERING HEIGHTS (104m   B   1939)
      The setting is the foreboding, heather-covered, wind-swept
Yorkshire Moors in the early 19th century.   Lovely, impetuous
Cathy (Merle Oberon) is strongly attracted to the handsome, brood-
ing gypsy Heathcliffe (Laurence Olivier), but rejects him for a prop-
er country squire who promises a marriage of comfort and pleasure.
Based on Emily Brontë's novel.   d. William Wyler; GOLDWYN;
ABFI, SELECT, UNF, WHOLFC.

WUTHERING HEIGHTS (29m   C   1976)
    Sets up the novel Wuthering Heights and introduces the main
characters, interweaving the elements of the story with a documentary-style portrayal of Emily Brontë as seen through the eyes
of her sister and her biographer, Mary Robinson.   Shows how the
novelist developed her characters.   OECA; FL

WUTHERING HEIGHTS; Classical Literature Series (13m   C   1967)
    Emily Brontë's impassioned story about the entangled lives of
people who live in the big hilltop mansion, and the secrets they
shared.   Narrated by Geraldine Fitzgerald.   MGH; UC, UILL.

"X" (9m   C   1974)
    "A profound, experimental, personal film of one woman's de-
spair, anger and exhibitionism.   This is my best film to date in the
tradition I most enjoy pursuing in film: honest personal expression
for its own sake. "--B. H.   By Barbara Hammer; HAMMER.

"X" FACTOR: WOMEN AS PEOPLE, THE (60m   B   1970)
    Focuses on the objective status and measurable facts about
women in the U. S. , and a comparison of male and female wages
and opportunities at a wide range of economic levels.   CORNELL.

"Y" (15m   C   1974)
    "An inner psychosynthesis of the sub-personalities of one wom-
an's psyche based upon extended daydream work from gestalt therapy. "--B. H.   By Barbara Hammer; HAMMER.

YANOMAMA: A MULTIDISCIPLINARY STUDY (43m   C   1971)
    A biological-anthropological study of the social structures and
hereditary patterns of the Yanomama, a primitive war-prone people
who live in scattered villages in southern Venezuela and northern
Brazil.   Demonstrates field techniques of a group of specialists--
including a human-geneticist, ethnologist, dentist, doctor, and lin-
guist--as they carry on a unified, multidisciplinary study in a single
Yanomama village.   Shows many details of Yanomama life and culture, and assesses impact of acculturation on social and genetic patterns.   p. Timothy Asch, Napolean Chagnon, James Neel; BRNDSU;
USERD; NAVC; EMC.

YEAR OF THE COMMUNES (50m   C   1971)
    Explores the commune as a way of life, from the drug-centered
commune to communal marriage and the mutual sharing of resources.
Examines the historical foundations of communes in the U. S. in the
18th and 19th centuries, and discusses the positive and negative aspects of 20th-century communes.   d. Nick Chickering; RAWCHL

YEAR OF THE TIGER, THE (62m   C   1974)
    Filmed tour of North Vietnam by anti-war filmmakers, guided

by North Vietnam journalists.   Investigates the lives of the people. Includes visits to schools, day care centers, hospitals, factories and farms, recording Vietnamese cultural life and the process of recon- struction.   By Deidre English, David Davis, Steve Talbot; ODEON.

YEAR OF THE WOMAN, THE (90m C 1973)
      Deals with the antics of a group of women at the Democratic Convention in 1972.   Shots show Shirley Chisholm and Bella Abzug speaking; Art Buchwald taking up a lot of footage; Sandra Hochman reading her poetry; and arguing by women with the news media on how women are covered by the media.   Not much to hold the film together.   Photography well done by Juliana Wang, Claudia Weill; PORTABLE.

YELLOW BALL CACHE, THE (18m C n. d.)
      A set of 13 wonderful short-shorts made by children under the age of 14 years.   By Yvonne Anderson; YBW.

YELLOW LEAF, A (14m B 1973)
      The life of one weary woman in her 70's, who has been reduced to the rhythm of an antique rocking chair, falls into poetic perspec- tive.   Along with spoken rhyme heard off-camera, the woman's withered hopes and bittersweet memories are woven into an intri- cate tapestry with the quaint relics from her past that now decorate her lonely habitation.   She remembers her one-time lover going off to the war, the gunfire that ended that early romance, the cottage- by-the sea she always wanted but never had.   An unopened scrap- book lies nearby.   An unused crib symbolizes a childless marriage. A clock on the wall ticks and chimes.   A cemetery beckons.   A dis- tinctive use of visual repetition and cross-cutting helps this requiem, sung to the lost potential of a woman pathologically enslaved by her past.   p. /d. Ronald W. Rowart; MMA.

YES (23m C/B n. d.)
      "Lyrical and romantic attempt to express joy of being. "--N. L. By Naomi Levine; FCOOP.

YES, WE CAN (30m C n. d.   VIDEO)
      A critical look at how Westinghouse Corporation (WBZ-TV, Bos- ton) and a government agency went about an all-day women's fair and live TV programming.   The women who made this tape were in- volved in a protest of the event which included 38 women's and com- munity groups.   A film important for women to know about since it is intended as model women's programming for all other Westing- house TV stations in the U. S.   A one-hour radio tape is also avail- able which is a more in-depth examination of the event.   By Cam- bridge-Godard; SFVG.

YOGURT CULTURE (12m B si n. d.)
      Animated drawings on various materials: plastic, transparent acetate, etc.   By Patti-Lee Chenis; FCOOP.

YONDER COME DAY (26m C 1975)
      Documents the efforts of 72-year-old Bessie Jones to pass along

to new generations the rich heritage of Black slave songs and culture. Shows how the music, games, songs, and traditions of an earlier time reveal the roots of Black music, its role played in the time of slavery and its significance today.   CAPCC; MGH.

YOU ARE THERE SERIES   see   COLUMBUS AND ISABELLA; FINAL HOURS OF JOAN OF ARC, THE; FINAL PERFORMANCE OF SARA BERNHARDT; HARRIET TUBMAN AND THE UNDERGROUND RAILROAD; MYSTERY OF AMELIA EARHART; SUSAN B. ANTHONY IS TRIED FOR VOTING; TORMENT OF JOAN OF ARC, THE; TRIAL OF SUSAN B. ANTHONY, THE

YOU CAN COMPOSE A DANCE, PT. I (10m B 1970)
Illustrates how young children can create their own dances. Shows how to start an idea.   By Shirley Winters; SLFP.

YOU CAN COMPOSE A DANCE, PT. II (14m B 1970)
Illustrates how young children can create their own dances. Shows dance structure.   By Shirley Winters; SLFP.

YOU DON'T HAVE TO BUY WAR, MRS. SMITH (30m B 1970)
Presents an address by Bess Myerson Grant, commissioner of consumer affairs for New York City.   Shows her impassioned plea before the World Mother's Day assembly of Another Mother for Peace in San Francisco, California in 1970.   She names America's most familiar manufacturers of household goods, accusing them of being war profiteers who make millions on Pentagon contracts. AMDOC; IE, KP, UMIS.

YOU IRRESISTIBLE YOU (11m C r1975)
Shows the sales psychology which lampoons male consumers into purchasing male cosmetics and home furnishings at high prices. Marshall Efron joins the ranks of men willing to pay high prices for products which promise to make them irresistible to women, such as: male grooming and cosmetic aids, and waterbeds with stereo hifi.   d. Jack Sameth; WNETTV; BM; CWU, IU.

YOU MOTHER (10m B 1972)
Examines visually and verbally some of the reasons women give for having children.   Asking "why," the film presents a down-to-earth picture of the realities of motherhood.   Becky Reardon sings "The Mother's Song."   Photography by Douglas Holmes.   By Karen Holmes; FW; CCC.

YOU PACK YOUR OWN CHUTE (30m C 1972)
Dr. Eden Ryl, noted conductor of sales and management motivation seminars, demonstrates with numerous examples that personal responsibility is the keystone of success.   She concludes with a sensational parachute jump to prove her thesis.   Inspirational production designed to motivate achievement in sales and training programs at all levels.   RAMIC; WSU, EMC.

YOUNG BESS (112m C 1953)
Story of Elizabeth I from her childhood to her ascendancy to

the throne. d. George Sidney; MGM; FL

YOUNG LOVE (8m B 1972)
"Traditional rites of courtship and marriage are simply and
beautifully evoked in this lyrical film."--YFD. By Linda Rivera; YFD.

YOUNG LOVERS, THE (110m B 1964)
    Not-very-serious college student (Eddie) and serious student
(Pam) meet on a college campus and she becomes pregnant. Since
he is reluctant to marry her, he suggests she do something illegal.
With Peter Fonda, Sharon Hugueny, Nick Adams. d. Samuel Goldwyn, Jr.; Ida Lupino assisted with production, direction and screenplay. MGM; FL

YOUNG MARRIAGE: WHEN'S THE BIG DAY? (13m C r1975)
    Examines the dilemmas involved in young marriages. Introduces
a young married couple and their engaged friends. Depicts the contrasts between the anticipatory happiness of the engaged couple and
the sullen attitude of the couple whose marriage is already beset
with problems. p. /d. Steve Katten; CRM, MGH.

YOUNG, SINGLE AND PREGNANT (18m C 1973)
    Shows four young women who chose different solutions to the
problem of unwanted pregnancy during their teen-age years. One
married and kept her baby, another chose single parenthood, the
third gave up her child for adoption, and the fourth had an abortion.
Depicts the advantages and disadvantages of each alternative. p.
Leonard C. Schwartz/VARIAF; PERENNIAL; EMC, UM, UMIS.

YOUNG WOMEN IN SPORTS (16m C 1974)
    Cameo sequences show women athletes participating in discus
throwing, diving, sprinting, high jumping, tennis and swimming.
The film explores the feelings and thoughts of four women athletes--
about strength, competition, benefits of participation in sports and
themselves as athletes and as women. Provides the general audience
with an insight into the motivations and rationale that lead young
women into the satisfying and rewarding field of competitive sports.
By Susan Heick, Jaryl Land, and Joseph Shields; SSP; BFA; CWU,
IU, PAS, UK, UM, UWY.

YOUNGEST FILMMAKERS, THE (15m C 1971)
    Documents elementary children making films in a summer school
workshop. Shown are children working on both animated and live-
action filmmaking. Evident is the enthusiasm and creativity of these
children as they work individually and in groups. By Fran Burst
Terranella; CCC.

YOUR HOME IS YOU (15m C 1973)
    "Farcical depiction of interior decoration dicta and wifely life-
styles. How we should live (according to mass advertising myths)."
--M. H. By Martha Haslanger; HASLANGER.

YOUR LIFE AND THE PILL (13m C r1975)
    Explains the ovulatory cycle, how oral contraceptives act in the

body, and answers commonly asked questions about the pill. INTI;
WIL.

YOUR MARRIAGE SERIES see WOMAN, WIFE OR WHAT

YOUR PELVIC AND BREAST EXAMINATION (12m C 1975)
The purpose of this film is to relieve the anxiety many women
feel regarding pelvic and breast examinations. The viewer observes
how a young woman performs a self-examination of her breasts.
Clear, detailed photography shows the cervix, instruments used for
pelvic examination and how a pap smear and gonorrhea culture are
taken. CROMMIE/PPSANM; PERENNIAL; UM, UMIS, WAYSU.

YUDIE (20m B n.d.)
The camera follows Yudie, a sprightly Jewish woman in her
70's, who still walks to work through her beloved streets of New
York City. She underscores the deep sense of neighborliness and
patriotism that existed in the early days. She talks about the family
business, early labor organizing, and life as an independent Jewish
girl who broke some of the expected codes, and who yet represents
the hard work, frugality and outspokenness of her people. By Mirra Bank; NDF; UM.

ZABRISKIE POINT (112m C 1970 Scope/Reg. Italian/subtitled)
The romantic revolutionary is the subject of the first American
film made by Director Michelangelo Antonioni. He delicately explores the world of the young and the uncommitted in a culture
which pressures people and encourages revolution. With a distant
eye Antonioni follows a youth (possibly a revolutionary in a riot) in
his travels as he flees the scene in a stolen plane and meets a
girl in the desert. Their experiences, both sensual and sexual,
liberate their minds and the viewers' senses. Returning to the city,
the boy is shot by the police. The girl goes on to her meeting with
businessman Taylor, and now more aware, explodes his house,
mentally exposing her own increased awareness. One of the few
serious cinematic attempts to deal with the image of America in the
1960's. d. M. Antonioni; MGM; FL

ZANE FORBIDDEN (10m C n.d.)
"I love home movies..."--D.W. By Dorothy Wiley; CCC.

ZAPOTECAN VILLAGE (20m B 1958)
Documents the life of the Zapotecan Indians living today as in
the past. In the mountains of Oaxaca and in the village of Zoogocho
there is candlemaking, market day, women at the fountain fed by
mountain springs, gun powder grinding for fireworks, a "torrito"--
all combine into a pleasant insight into a way of life. By Madeline
Tourtelot; GP.

ZEN, AND THE ART OF BASKETBALL (6m C n.d.)
"An homage of the Hudson River School of Painting. This little

gem is an attempt to cinematize the style of the Hudson River painters of the late 1800's and early 1900's. "--N. L.   By Naomi Levine;
FCOOP.

ZIEGFELD GIRL (131m   B   1941)
Follows the career of a hard working little hoofer with show
business rooted in her bones, and an elevator girl who can't decide
between a rich man and a poor man.   The hoofer rises to the top
and discovers she loves her husband.   The elevator girl finally
finds peace on a duck farm.   d. Robert Leonard; s. w. Marguerite
Roberts/Sonja Levien; MGM; FI.

ZOO (3m   B   1971)
Several people visit animals at the zoo.   By Mary Sparacio
Collins; FS.

ZUCKERKANDL (14m   C   1968)
An animated spoof on academic pomposity, with professor
Zuckerkandl's life's work as the humorous example.   Conceived by
noted educator Robert Hutchins.   By Faith Hubley, John Hubley;
GP; FI, VFL

APPENDIX A:
LIST OF SYMBOLS

AAP	All American Productions & Publishers
AARONP	*Aaron Productions
AAUW	American Association of University Women
ABCMC	ABC Media Concepts
ABCPC	*ABC Pictures Corp.
ABCTV	American Broadcasting Co., Inc.
ABFI	Audio Brandon Films, Inc. (Macmillan Films, Inc.)
ACB	Art Cinema Booking Service
ACRAUT	*A. C. R. Auteur Production
ADATO	Perry Miller Adato
ADL	Anti-Defamation League of B'Nai B'Rith
AFF	Affiliated Film Producers, Inc.
AFI	American Film Institute
AFL/CIO	AFL/CIO Dept. of Education
AHA	American Heart Association
AIM	Association Instructional Materials
AIMS	Instructional Media Services, Inc.
AIT	Agency for Instructional Television
AJN	American Journal of Nursing
ALA	American Library Association
ALCAN	Alcan Aluminum, Ltd.
ALDEN	Alden Films
ALSKOG	*Alskog
ALTANA	Altana Films
AMA	American Medical Association
AMDOC	*American Documentary Films, Inc.
AMEDFL	American Educational Films
AMFSC	American Friends Service Committee
AMJMP	*America's Junior Miss Pageant
AMLIN	*Patricia Amlin
AMP	Arthur Mokin Productions, Inc.
ANHFP	Alaska Native Heritage Film Project
ANIMFC	Animated Films Co.
ANOM	Anomaly Films
ANTHFI	Anthology Films
AP	Atlantis Productions, Inc.
APGA	American Personnel & Guidance Association

---

*Indicates address is unavailable, therefore it is not listed in the Directory.

API	Audio Productions, Inc.
APPALI	Appalshop, Inc.
ARCHPORT	Center of Urban Education & the Radio-TV Commission of the Arch Diocese
ARTKNO	Artkind Pictures, Inc.
ASFI	Association Films, Inc.
ASI	Advanced Systems, Inc.
ASP	Alfred Shands Productions
ASU	Arizona State University
ATAT	American Telephone & Telegraph Co.
ATTICAF	Attica Films, Inc.
AUBU	Auburn University
AUFS	American Universities Field Staff
AUIS	Australian News & Information Bureau
AUSLANDER	Leland Auslander Films
AVANFI	Avanti Films, Inc.
AVCO	AVCO Embassy Pictures Corp.
AVED	AV-ED Films
AVNA	Audio Visual Narrative Arts
BACHRACH	Doro Bachrach
BAILYB	Bob Baily Productions
BALFOUR	*Balfour Films (Anne Balfour-Fraser)
BALLIS	Ballis Associates
BANDMI	Bandanna Media, Inc.
BARR	Barr Films
BASS	Saul Bass and Associates
BAUMSZ	Suzanne Bauman Productions
BB	*Bread and Butter
BBCL	British Broadcasting Corp., London
BBCTV	British Broadcasting Co., TV
BBF	Billy Budd Film Co.
BCGFLM	*B C G Films
BEESON	Constance (Coni) Beeson
BESC	Bilingual Education Service Center
BEF	Business Education Films
BELLE	Anne Belle
BELSYS	Bell System
BESKIND	Dorothy Beskind
BF	Budget Films
BFA	Baily Film Associates Educational Media
BIS	British Information Service
BLFFC	*Berkeley Lesbian Feminist Collective
BLKHF	Blackhawk Films
BM	Benchmark Films, Inc.
BOSUST	Stephen Bosustow Productions
BP	Blackwood Productions, Inc.
BRF	Blue Ridge Films
BRNDSU	Brandeis University
BTF	British Transport Films
BU	Boston University
BULSUSP	*Bulldawg & Sussex Productions

BUTFREE	Butler-Freedom Films
BUTP	Butterick Publishing
BWFC	*Boston Women's Film Cooperative
BYU	Brigham Young University
CABCRF	Cabin Creek Films
CAF	Current Affairs Films
CAMBRIDGE	Cambridge-Goddard
CAMPF	Campbell Films
CANTOR	Arthur Cantor, Inc.
CAPCC	Capital Cities Communications
CAROUSEL	Carousel Films, Inc.
CARTC	The Cartoon Co.
CASTELLI	Leo Galley Castelli
CATFSH	*Catfish Productions, Inc.
CATHFC	Catholic Film Center
CBCTV	Canadian Broadcasting Corporation
CBP	Charles Braverman Productions
CBS	Columbia Broadcasting System
CCC	Canyon Cinema Cooperative
CCCD	Cally Curtis Co.
CCFI	Children's Cultural Foundation, Inc.
CDFI	Cambridge Documentary Films, Inc.
CDFS	Central Documentary Film Studios, Moscow
CEA	Carmen Educational Associates
CECROPIA	Cecropia
CEEB	College Entrance Exam Board
CELLWOOD	Maureen Cellwood
CENTER	Center Cinema Co-op
CENTRE	Centre Films
CF	Churchill Films
CFD	Campus Film Productions, Inc.
CFDC	Canadian Filmmaker's Distribution Center
CFI	Canadian Film Institute
CFP	*Chatsworth Film Production
CFS	Creative Film Society
CFSF	Center for Southern Folklore
CHANGAS	Changas/Loveland
CHAPELLE	Pola Chapelle
CHARISM	*Charis Media
CHASE	Doris Chase
CHCORP	Churchill Falls Corp., Ltd.
CHILD	Abigail Child
CHOPRA	Joyce Chopra
CIE	Cinema Eight/Cinema Concepts
CINCON	Cinematic Concepts
CINE	Cinecraft Productions, Inc.
CINEINC	Cinema Incorporated
CINELO	Cinema Lore Co.
CINEMED	Cinema Medica, Inc.
CINEMK	Cinemakers, Inc.
CINEREL	*Cinerama Releasing

CINESC	*Cine Science
CINE16	Cine 16 Films
CINMET	Cinemetrics
CIV	Cinema V
CMC	Center for Mass Communications
CO	Circle One
COLEMAN	Willette Coleman
COLSON	Diana Colson
CONNEC	Connection, Inc.
CONNECTICUT	Connecticut Films, Inc.
CONSF	The Conservation Foundation
COOLIDGE	Martha Coolidge
COR	Coronet Instructional Films
CORGLW	Corning Glass Works
CORINF	Corinth Films
CORNELL	Cornell University
CORRF	*Corrective Films
COUNTR	Counterpoint Films
COX	Nell Cox Films
CP	Cornerstone Productions
CRAF	Crawley Films, Ltd.
CREEDMAN	Michael Creedman Film
CREOUT	Creative Outlet
CRESSP	*Cressley Productions
CRM	CRM Educational Films
CROMMIE	*Crommie Productions
CRUIKSHANK	Sally Cruikshank
CSDE	California State, Dept. of Education
CSEC	*Caesarean Section, Inc.
CSP	*Caring and Sharing Productions
CSV	*Cinema Service/Vintage Films
CTFL	Canadian Travel Film Library
CTV	C-TV Television Network
CTW	Children's Television Workshop
CUNLIM	Concepts Unlimited, Inc.
CVE	Cousino Visual Education Service
CWF	Clem Williams Films, Inc.
CWGC	*Chicago Women's Graphic Collective
CWU	Central Washington University
CYCLOPS	Cyclops Productions

DA	Document Associates, Inc.
DANCOFF	Judith Dancoff
DANIELS	Karil Daniels
DAVP	Tom Davenport Films
DAVPS	Sid Davis Productions
DAYF	*Daylight Films
DB	Don Bosco Films
DBASIL	De Basil, France
DEROCH	Louis De Rochement Associates
DF	Dimension Films
DICKSON	Deborah Dickson-Macagno

DIDTFL	Didactic Films, Ltd.
DISNEY	Walt Disney Productions
DREW	Robert Drew Associates
DRUCKER	Robert Drucker & Co.
DUNLF	Directions Unlimited Film Corp.
DYAL	Susan Dyal
DWP	Daniel Wilson Productions
EBEC	Encyclopaedia Britannica
ECCW	Eccentric Circle Cinema Workshop
EDC	Educational Development Distribution Center
EDELHEIT	Martha Edelheit
ELIP	*Eli Productions
EMC	University of California, Berkeley
EMG	Em Gee Film Library
ENVIC	Envision Corporation
ETS	Educational Testing Service
ETSPS	Educational Television Service
EYR	EYR
FALCON	Falcon Films
FAMF	Family Films, Inc.
FAROUN	Faroun Films
FARRON	Jim Farron
FC	The Film Center
FCC	Franciscan Communications Center
FCE	Film Classic Exchange
FCHILD	Fairchild Visuals
FCOOP	Film-Makers' Cooperative
FDF	Ford Foundation
FEFERMAN	Linda Feferman
FELDD	Dick Feldman Assoc. , Inc.
FEMEDIA	Femedia
FEPROSO	Federation of Prosthodontic Organizations
FF	Fireweed Films
FFAIR	Filmfair Communications
FFF	Foundation for Filmmakers
FFG	Fisher Film Group
FFHI	Films for the Humanities, Inc.
FFO	French Film Office
FI	Films Incorporated
FIBERC	Fiberglas Canada
FIF	Faces International Films
FIFWF	First International Festival of Women's Films
FILOAG	Films on Aging
FIM	Film Images
FIN	Edward Finney
FISLEF	*Slezas-Fisher Film
FL	Filmmakers Library, Inc.
FLEMRP	Rex Fleming Productions
FLITTERMAN	Sandy Flitterman

FMI	Filmmakers, Inc.
FOCUSE	Focus Education, Inc.
FOREMAN	Janet Foreman
FORUMP	*Forum Productions
FPDB	*Film Play-Data Bureau, Inc.
FPFC	*Famous Players Film Co.
FREDF	*Fredonia Films
FS	The Film School
FSMP	FSM/Pandora Films
FSU	Florida State University
FW	Film Wright
FWAL	Filmwest Associates Limited
FWLERD	Far West Laboratory for Educational Research & Development

GA	Guidance Associates
GATEHC	Gate Hill Co-op
GEBAUER	*Gebauer Productions
GENESIS	Genesis Films, Ltd.
GHANA	Ghana Information Services
GITLNI	Irving Gitlin Producers, Inc.
GM	General Motors Corporation
GOLDBERG	Jenny Goldberg
GOLDEN	Nancy and Laura Golden
GOLDSMITH	Sylvianna Goldsmith
GORDAJ	Alvin J. Gordon
GOTHF	Gotham Films
GOULD	Gould Productions
GP	Grove Press, Inc.
GPI	*Griffin Productions, Inc.
GPN	Great Plains National Instructional Television
GRANTAM	Amy Grant
GRANTANN	Anne Grant
GRATV	Granada TV International Productions Ltd.
GRAVES	Nancy Graves
GREENF	*Greenhouse Films
GREENFIELD	Amy Greenfield
GRPI	*Group I
GSHDME	Good Samaritan Hospital
GURSHP	*Gurion/Shokler Production
GVHOOD	G. V. Hood Films
GWWB	Group W, Westinghouse Broadcasting

HALLECK	Dee Dee Halleck
HALPRO	Halproductions
HAMMER	Barbara Hammer
HANDEL	Handel Film Corporation
HAR	Harper & Row Publishers, Inc.
HARTLEY	Hartley Film Foundation
HASLANGER	Martha Haslanger
HCW	Hurlock Cine World, Inc.

HEARST	Hearst Metrotone News
HERSTORY	Herstory Films
HESSE	Isa Hesse-Rabinovitch
HFHA	Harpers Ferry Historical Association
HIGGINS	Alfred Higgins Productions, Inc.
HIS	Holt Information Systems
HL	Hobel-Leiterman Production
HOBAN	Tanya Hoban
HOCHBERG	Victoria Hochberg
HRAW	Holt, Rinehart and Winston
HSCC	Health Sciences Communication Center
HWP	Holland-Wegman Laboratories, Inc.

IBMWTC	IBM World Trade Corporation
ICAIC	Instituto Cubano del Arte e Industria--Cinema-tograficos
ICS	Institutional Cinema, Inc.
IDEAL	Ideal Pictures, Inc.
IE	Insight Exchange
IFB	International Film Bureau, Inc.
IFF	International Film Foundation
IMA	*Images Motion Picture Rental Library
IMEN	*Image Engineering
IMPF	Impact Films
INDIA	Indian Government Films Division
INSPRO	*Inspirational Production
INTI	Intermedica, Inc.
IP	*Interface Productions
IPCFL	IPC Film Library
IQF	I. Q. Films
IRISF	Iris Films
ISAACS	Brenda Isaacs
ISU	Iowa State University
ITF	*International Television Foundation
IU	Indiana University
IVY	Ivy Films
IWANMI	Iwanami Productions, Inc.
IWFPI	*International Women's Film Project, Inc.

JACF	*Jacoupy Films
JACOA	Jarvis Couillard Associates
JACSTO	Jacoby/Storm Productions
JANUS	Janus Films
JASON	Jason Films
JCLP	*J. C. L. Productions
JGMF	The J. Gary Mitchell Film Co., Inc.
JJ	Joan Jonas
JOU	Journal Films, Inc.
JPIP	Jules Power International Productions, Inc.
JULF	*Julian Films

KART	Kartemquin Films, Ltd.
KAUBOY	Kauffman and Boyce Productions
KDINTV	KDIN-TV
KEEDICK	Keedick Lecture Bureau
KELLER	Margie Keller
KFPC	Kinok Film Production Co.
KHETTV	KHET-TV
KIESER	Ellwood E. Kieser
KINGTV	KING-TV
KLEINW	Walter J. Klein Co., Ltd.
KLEKNP	*Kleiser-Knapp Productions
KLOSKY	Linda Klosky
KMA	Keith Merrill Associates
KMLG	*Kramer, Miller, Lomden, Glassman
KMP	Kansas Media Project
KNBCTV	KNBC-TV
KP	Kit Parker Films
KPI	Keystone Productions, Inc.
KQEDTV	KQED-TV
KRMATV	KRMA-TV
KROLL	Nathan Kroll Productions, Inc.
KTCATV	KTCA-TV
KUONTV	KUON-TV
KUTV	KUTV Documentary Division
KVIETV	KVIE-TV

LAFC	Los Angeles Film Coop
LANDAU	Jack Landau
LASSNIG	Maria Lassnig
LAUGHLIN	Kathleen Laughlin
LCA	Learning Corporation of America
LES	*Irving Lesser Enterprises
LEVINE	Naomi Levine
LEWIS	Susan Lewis
LHF	*Lighthouse Films
LIFESPI	Life-Styles Productions, Inc.
LINDSTERN	A. Lindern/P. Stern
LNDBRG	Alan Landsburg Productions
LOVELACE	Lovelace Theatre
LP	Lawren Productions, Inc.
LPF	*Leon/Pandora Films
LPI	Lilyan Productions, Inc.
LSP	Lenfilm Studios
LUC	Lucerne Films
LURIE	Jane Lurie
LWFG	London Women's Film Group

MAA	Mathematical Association of America
MAETEL	Mississippi Authority for Educational Television
MALIBU	Malibu Films
MAR/CHUCK	Mar/Chuck Film Industries

MARGOL	Frederick J. Margolis, M. D.
MARQU	Marquette University
MARSHALL	Lisa J. Marshall
MARYF	Maryknoll Fathers
MATJEN	*Matt-Jen Entertainments
MAYSLES	Maysles Films, Inc.
MCA	Massachusetts Council on the Arts & Humanities
MCFPB	Maryland Center for Public Broadcasting
MEDAA	*Media Arts Associates
MENLEE	Lee Mendelson Production, Inc.
METHIC	Methadone Information Center
METROM	Metromedia Producers Corporation
MEYER	Vicky Chaet Meyer
MFCF	*Media for Christian Formation
MFLMC	Monument Film Corp.
MG	The Media Guild
MGH	Contemporary Films/McGraw-Hill
MGM	Metro-Goldwyn-Mayer
MHFB	Mental Health Film Board
MHTFP	Mental Health Training Film Program
MIC/FPP	Maternity Infant Care Family Planning Project
MIEVES	Walter Mieves/Jack Lund
MIFE	Milner-Fenwick, Inc.
MILANO	Susan Milano
MIT	Center for Advanced Engineering Study, M. I. T.
MLP	Moreland-Latchford Productions
MM	Motivational Media
MMA	Mass Media Associates
MMM	Mass Media Ministries
MMRC	Multi-Media Resource Center
MOBIL	Mobil Oil Company
MOBY	Mobilization for Youth
MOD	Modern Sound Pictures
MOM	Modern Mass Media
MOMA	Museum of Modern Art
MONDIAL	*Mondial Films
MONDPRO	*Mondadori Productions
MOSHE	*Moshe Duan Productions
MPLUS	Media Plus, Inc.
MS	Mafilm Studios, Budapest
MSU	Michigan State University
MTP	Modern Talking Picture Service
MTROLA	Motorola Teleprograms
NAAJS	The National Academy for Adult Jewish Studies
NAGTAM	*Nagtam Productions, Inc.
NASH	Helen Nash Associates
NAVC	National Audio Visual Center
NBCTV	National Broadcasting Co.
NDF	New Day Films
NEA	National Education Association
NEBETV	Nebraska Educational Television Network

NEDMARP	Nedmar Productions
NELSNG	Gunvor Nelson
NEOPLANTA	*Neoplanta Film
NET	National Educational TV, Inc.
NETI	New Feminist Talent, Inc.
NETRC	National Educational TV & Radio Center
NEWFLM	The New Film Company, Inc.
NFBC	National Film Board of Canada
NFC	Network for Continuing Medical Education
NHMETV	New Hampshire Educational TV
NICEP	Northern Indian California Education Project
NITC	National Instructional TV Center
NIU	Northern Illinois University
NLC	New Line Cinema
NORDSTROM	Kristina Nordstrom
NOSIS	*Nova Scotia Information Service
NOWP	N. O. W. , Portland, Oregon
NOX	Noxell Corporation
NPACFT	National Public Affairs Center for Television
NPI	Nafasi Productions, Inc.
NRW	National Right to Work
NSF	National Sex Forum
NTFC	*New Thing Flick Co.
NTFLMA	National Telefilm Assoc. , Inc.
NTS	N. E. T. Training School
NWSUSA	Newsfilm--U. S. A.
NWUFL	Northwestern University Film Library
NYF	New Yorker Films
NYT	New York Times
NYTC	New York Telephone Co.
NYU	New York University Film Library
NYUCM	New York University, College of Medicine

OCTOPUS	*Octopus, Inc.
ODEON	Odeon Films
OECA	Ontario Educational Communications Authority
OF	Oxford Films, Inc.
OFF	Official Films, Inc.
OHSU	Ohio State University
OKSU	Oklahoma State University
OMORI	Emiko Omori
ONR	Ohio Newsreel
ORETZKY	*Richard Oretzky
ORTHO	*Ortho-Pharmaceutical Corp.
OSU	Oregon State University
OXENBERG	Jan Oxenberg

PARACO	Paramount Communications
PARENTP	Parenting Pictures
PAS	The Pennsylvania State University
PATHE	Pathe News, Inc.

PAULST	Paulist Productions
PEFP	Pelican Films, Inc.
PELGP	Peli-Graphic Productions
PENBAK	Pennebaker, Inc.
PENN	J. C. Penney Co.
PERENNIAL	Perennial Education, Inc.
PERKNS	Perkins School for the Blind
PERSPECTIVE	Perspective Films
PF	Pyramid Films
PFI	Psychological Films, Inc.
PFMP	Pilgrim Film Production
PHOENIX	Phoenix Films, Inc.
PIC	Pictura Films Distribution Corporation
PICA	Prudential Insurance Co. of America
PICKFO	*Pickford (Mary) Co.
PMA	Pharmaceutical Manufacturers Ass'n.
POLON	Vicki Polon
POLYMORPH	Polymorph Films
POMPOP	Pomes and Popcorn
POPKIN	Ann Popkin
PORTABLE	*Portable Productions
PORTMAN	Portia Mansfield Motion Pictures
PORTSP	*Portside Productions
PP	Planned Parenthood World Population
PPASYR	Planned Parenthood Association, Syracuse, N. Y.
PPC	Personal Products Co.
PPFA	Planned Parenthood Federation of America, Inc.
PPSANM	Planned Parenthood of San Mateo
PPSEA	Planned Parenthood of Seattle
PPTUC	Planned Parenthood of Tucson
PRENTICE	Prentice-Hall, Inc.
PRI	Portrait Releasing, Inc.
PRICER	Richard Price Associates
PROART	Professional Arts, Inc.
PRORE	Professional Research, Inc.
PRU	Productions Unlimited
PTL	The Public Television Library
PUR	Purdue University
QP	Quest Productions
RADINC	Radharc, Inc.
RAFAEL	Rafael Film
RAMIC	Ramic Productions
RAMONP	Ramona Productions
RAWCHI	*Rawlings (Chickering) Productions
RBC	RBC Paramount Films
RCSRE	Resource Center on Sex Roles in Education
RDFL	Rediffusion TV Ltd.
REICHERT	Julia Reichert
REPRO	Rediscovery Productions

RF	Ramsgate Films
ROA	Roa Films
RODMAN	Jeffrey Rodman
RONIN	Roninfilm, Inc.
ROTA	Amalie Rothschild
RSP	Stuart Reynolds Production
RYATF	*Ryan Athletic Films
RYDEN	Hope Ryden
SAF	S. A. Films
SALZB	Bert Salzman Films
SANDLER	Sandler Institutional Films, Inc.
SARSAKU	Sarsaku Productions
SAUDEK	Robert Saudek Associates, Inc.
SAUNDERS	Pat Saunders
SB	Serious Business Company
SBI	Storyboard, Inc.
SCC	Shoreline Community College
SCHLAT	Warren Schloat Productions, Inc.
SCHNEIDER	Rosalind Schneider
SCHRON	Southern Chroniclers
SEARS	Sears, Roebuck and Co.
SEESAW	*See Saw Films
SEF	Sterling Educational Films
SEIDELMAN	Susan Seidelman
SELECT	Select Film Library
SFD	Schoenfeld Film Distributing Corp.
SFN	San Francisco Newsreel
SFNE	Society for Nutrition Education
SFVG	*Somerville Feminist Video Gang
SHC	Spring Hill College
SHEEHY	Terry Sheehy
SHELLABARGER	Anne Shellabarger
SHILLP	Summerhill Productions
SIEGALL	Lois Siegal
SIEGELM	Marian Siegel
SISO	*Sight & Sound, Inc.
SIUC	Southern Illinois University at Carbondale
SJDAED	San Jose Unified School District
SKELTON	Marlys Skelton
SLFP	S-L Film Productions
SLOANE	Patricia Sloane
SMILCP	Smiling Cat Productions
SMITHS	Smithsonian Institution
SOHO	Soho Cinema Ltd.
SOUPRO	Southerby Productions, Inc.
SPCTRA	Spectra Pictures
SPF	Special Purpose Films
SSCOPE	Screenscope, Inc.
SSF	Sheldon Satin Films
SSP	*Silver Shadow Productions
STAR	Star Film Co.

STARR	Cecil Starr
STATNS	Statens Filmcentral
STEIGLIZ	*Steigliz Film Market
STERLTV	*Sterling Television
STLCPD	*St. Louis County Police Dept.
STNFLD	Stanfield House
STPL	*Strolling Player, Inc.
STUARTM	Martha Stuart Communications
SUMMERS	Alan A. Summers, M. D.
SUMMRS	Elaine Summers
SURPIN	Shelly Surpin
SUSSEX	Sussex Films
SWAIN	*Hack Swain Productions
SWANK	Swank Motion Pictures
TALPAR	Talent Associates--Paramount, Ltd.
TAUBIN	Amy Taubin
TELEKETICS	Teleketics
TELES	*Tele-Sports, Ltd.
TERWILLIGER	Elizabeth Terwilliger
TESICH	Nadja Tesich-Savage
TEXFM	Texture Films, Inc.
TF	Thunderbird Films
TFC	Tricontinental Film Center
TFCI	Teaching Film Custodians, Inc.
TFCS	*Teaching Film Consultants
TFEI	Thunderbird Film Enterprises, Inc.
THATCHER	Anita Thatcher
THERAPL	Theraplay Institute
THOMSURP	Shera Thompson/Shelly Surpin
TL	Time-Life Multimedia
TLB	*True Light Beavers
TOMENT	Tomorrow Entertainment, Inc.
TPI	Tomato Productions, Inc.
TRACKN	Track and Field News
TRAFCO	TV Radio and Film Commission
TRNKAJ	*Jiri Trnka
TRNSIT	Transit Media, Inc.
TURMOS	Turtletaub and Moss, Inc.
TWCG	Third World Cinema Group
TWF	Trans-World Films, Inc.
TWN	Third World Newsreel
TWY	Twyman Films, Inc.
UAA	United Artists Association
UALA	University of Alabama
UAS	United Artists
UC	University of Colorado
UCHI	University of Chicago
UCLA	University of California at Los Angeles
UCM	University of Christian Movement

UEUWIS	University of Wisconsin
UF	Unusual Films
UG	The University of Georgia
UHAWAII	University of Hawaii
UILL	University of Illinois
UIO	University of Iowa
UK	The University of Kansas
UKEN	University of Kentucky
UM	University of Michigan
UMAINE	University of Maine
UMI	United Methodist Information
UMIS	University of Missouri
UMITV	University of Michigan TV Center
UN	United Nations
UNEBR	University of Nebraska
UNEV	University of Nevada
UNF	United Films
UNH	University of New Hampshire, Durham
UNIQUE	*Unique Film Co.
UNIVE	Universal Films
UPAI	Urban Planning Aid, Inc.
USC	University of Southern California
USDAES	U. S. Dept. of Agriculture
USDHEW	U. S. Dept. of Health, Education & Welfare
USDL	U. S. Dept. of Labor Information
USERD	U. S. Energy Research & Development Agency
USIA	U. S. Information Agency
USOE	U. S. Office of Education
USOWIO	U. S. Office of War Information, Overseas Br.
UU	University of Utah
UW	University of Washington
UWISC	University of Wisconsin
UWY	University of Wyoming

VA	Vision Associates, Inc.
VARIAF	*Variation Films
VERAIN	Vera Industries
VFI	Viewfinders, Inc.
VISIONF	Vision Films
VOFI	Vocational Films
VQ	Vision Quest, Inc.
VRI	Visual Resources, Inc.
VULVA	Vulva Video

WAF	Women/Artist/Filmmakers
WALA	Walter P. Lewisohnn Associates
WALSH	Alida Walsh
WARFB	*F. B. Warren Corp.
WAYSU	Wayne State University
WBPI	William Brose Productions, Inc.
WCAUTV	WCAU-TV

WCF	Westcoast Films
WEBERP	*Lois Weber Productions
WEINSTEIN	Miriam Weinstein
WEL	Welling Motion Picture Service
WENHTV	WENH-TV
WER	Wheelock Educational Resources
WESTEC	Western Electric Co. , Inc.
WESTLC	Westinghouse Learning Corporation
WESTON	Weston-Woods Studio
WFC	The Women's Film Coop
WFF	White Fox Films
WFP	Wexler Film Productions, Inc.
WGBHTV	WGBH-TV Educational Foundation
WGPI	William Greaves Productions, Inc.
WHATV	WHA-TV
WHOLFC	Wholesome Film Center
WIL	Wyeth International Ltd.
WILEY	John Wiley and Sons, Inc.
WISSU	Wisconsin State University at La Crosse
WITFTV	WITF-TV
WKARTV	WKAR-TV
WKYCTV	WKYC-TV
WLIBCC	Women's Liberation Cinema Co.
WMM	Women Make Movies, Inc.
WMVSTV	WMVS-TV
WNBCTV	WNBC-TV
WNEDTV	WNED-TV
WNETTV	WNET-TV
WNVFTV	WNVF-TV
WOLPER	Wolper Productions
WOMB	Wombat Productions
WORA	World Artist, Inc.
WORKS	The Works
WORLDH	World Horizon Films
WOWI	Women on Words and Images
WPSXTV	WPSX-TV
WQEDTV	WQED-TV
WRCTV	WRC-TV
WRP	Women's Research Project
WRS	Walter Reade/16
WSA	Warner Bros. , Inc.
WSU	Washington State University
WSWPTV	WSWP-TV
WTTWTV	WTTW-TV
WWP	World Wide Pictures Ltd.
WYLDE	Wylde Films, Inc.
XEROX	Xerox Films
YBW	Yellow Ball Workshop
YFD	Youth Film Distribution
ZPH	Zipporah Films

ABC MEDIA CONCEPTS
1330 Avenue of the Americas
New York, NY 10019

ACI MEDIA, INC. see
PARAMOUNT COMMUNI-
CATIONS

AFL-CIO, Dept. of Education
Film Division
815 16th St. N. W.
Washington, DC 20006

ADATO, PERRY MILLER
c/o WNET-TV
304 West 58 St.
New York, NY 10019

3 Fraser Rd.
Westport, CT 06880

ADVANCED SYSTEMS, INC.
1701 N. Fort Myer Dr.
Arlington, VA 22209

AFFILIATED FILM PRO-
DUCERS
8 East 93 St.
New York, NY 10028

AGENCY FOR INSTRUCTION-
AL TELEVISION see
NATIONAL INSTRUCTIONAL
TV CENTER

AIMS INSTRUCTIONAL
MEDIA SERVICES, INC.
626 Justin Ave.
Glendale, CA 91201

ALAIMO, LOUISE

11248 Emelita St. , No. 4
N. Hollywood, CA 91601

ALASKA NATIVE HERITAGE
Film Project
Center for Northern Educational
Research
University of Alaska
Fairbanks, AK 99701

ALCAN ALUMINUM, LTD.
620 Fifth Avenue
New York, NY 10020

ALDEN FILMS
7820 20th Ave.
Brooklyn, NY 11214

ALFRED SHANDS PRODUCTIONS
see SHANDS (ALFRED) PRO-
DUCTIONS

ALL AMERICAN PRODUCTIONS
& PUBLISHERS
P. O. Box 91
Greeley, CO 80632

ALTANA FILMS
340 E. 34 St.
New York, NY 10016

AMERICAN ASSOCIATION OF
UNIVERSITY WOMEN
2401 Virginia Ave. N. W.
Washington, DC 20036

AMERICAN BROADCASTING CO. ,
INC.
1330 Avenue of the Americas
New York, NY 10019

410

AMERICAN EDUCATIONAL
FILMS
132 Laskey Dr.
Beverly Hills, CA   90212

AMERICAN FILM INSTITUTE
EFLA, 17 West 60 St.
New York, NY   10023

AMERICAN FRIENDS SER-
VICE COMMITTEE
1501 Cherry St.
Philadelphia, PA   19102

AMERICAN HEART ASSO-
CIATION
c/o Association Films, Inc.
8615 Directors Row
Dallas, TX   75240

AMERICAN JOURNAL OF
NURSING
20 N. Wacker Dr., Suite 1948
Chicago, IL   60606

AMERICAN LIBRARY ASSO-
CIATION
50 E. Huron St.
Chicago, IL   60611

AMERICAN MEDICAL ASSO-
CIATION
535 N. Dearborn St.
Chicago, IL   60610

AMERICAN PERSONNEL &
GUIDANCE ASSN.
1607 New Hampshire Ave.
Washington, DC   20009

AMERICAN TELEPHONE &
TELEGRAPH CO.
195 Broadway, Room 07-1106
New York, NY   10007

AMERICAN UNIVERSITIES
FIELD STAFF
3 Lebanon St.
Hanover, NH   03755

ANIMATED FILMS CO.
907 Sherman Ave.
Evanston, IL   60202

ANOMALY FILMS
135 Hudson
New York, NY   10013

ANTHOLOGY FILMS
P. O. Box 33
Cambridge, MA   02138

ANTI-DEFAMATION LEAGUE
OF B'NAI B'RITH
315 Lexington Ave.
New York, NY   10016

APPALSHOP INC.
P. O. Box 743N
Whitesborg, KY   41858

ARENS, RUTH
1957 Palmerston Pl., No. 3
Los Angeles, CA   90027

ARIZONA STATE UNIVERSITY
Arizona Film Cooperative
Audio Visual Center
Tempe, AZ   85281

ART CINEMA BOOKING SER-
VICE
1501 Broadway
New York, NY   10036

ARTHUR MOKIN PRODUCTIONS,
INC. see MOKIN (ARTHUR)
PRODUCTIONS, INC.

ARTKINO PICTURES, INC.
723 7th Ave.
New York, NY   10019

ASHUR, GERI
33-35 Green St.
New York, NY   10013

ASSOCIATION FILMS, INC.
866 Third Avenue
New York, NY   10022

ASSOCIATION INSTRUCTIONAL
MATERIALS
600 Madison Ave.
New York, NY   10022

ATLANTIS PRODUCTIONS,
INC.
1252 La Granada Dr.
Thousand Oaks, CA 91360

ATTICA FILMS, INC.
789 West End Ave.
New York, NY 10025

AUBURN UNIVERSITY
Cooperative Extension Service
George W. Colburn Labora-
tories
Auburn, AL 36830

AUDIALS AND VISUALS
25 West 43 St.
New York, NY 10036
(formerly TEACHING FILM
CUSTODIANS)

AUDIO BRANDON FILMS, INC.
34 MacQuesten Parkway S.
Mount Vernon, NY 10550

3868 Piedmont Ave.
Oakland, CA 94611

1619 N. Cherokee
Los Angeles, CA 90028

2512 Program Dr.
Dallas, TX 75220

8400 Brookfield Ave.
Brookfield, IL 60513

6420 West Lake Street
Minneapolis, MN 55426

2100 N. Wilmot Road
Tucson, AZ 85710

6200 Market Avenue No.
Canton, OH 44721

AUDIO PRODUCTIONS INC.
103 Park Ave.
New York, NY 10017

AUDIO VISUAL NARRATIVE
ARTS
Box 398
Pleasantville, NY 10570

AUSLANDER, LELAND FILMS

6036 Comey Ave.
Los Angeles, CA 90034

AUSTRALIAN NEWS & INFORMA-
TION BUREAU
636 5th Ave.
New York, NY 10020

AVANTI FILMS, INC.
8271 Melrose Ave.
Los Angeles, CA 90046

AV-ED FILMS
910 N. Citrus Ave.
Hollywood, CA 90038

AVCO EMBASSY PICTURES
CORP.
1301 Avenue of the Americas
New York, NY 10019

BFA Educational Media
2211 Michigan Ave.
P. O. Box 1795
Santa Monica, CA 90406

BACHRACH, DORO
51 E. 93 St.
New York, NY 10028

BAILEY (BOB) PRODUCTIONS
3931 Feagan St.
Houston, TX 77007

BALLIS ASSOCIATES
George Ballis/Maia Sortor
4696 N. Millbrook
Fresno, CA 93726

BANDANNA MEDIA, INC.
572 St. Clair
Grosse Pointe, MI 48230

BANK, MIRRA
108 West 15 St., Apt. 4A
New York, NY 10001

BAREY, PATRICIA
6124 N. Winthrop Ave.
Chicago, IL 60660

BARR FILMS
Arthur Barr Films, Inc.
P. O. Box 7C
Pasadena, CA 91104

BASS (SAUL) AND ASSOCIATES
7039 Sunset Blvd.
Los Angeles, CA 90028

BAUMAN (SUZANNE) PRODUC-
  TIONS
680 5th Ave.
New York, NY 10009

BEAMS, MARY
83 N. Beacon St.
Watertown, MA 02172

BEEKMAN, BERNADETTE
109-65 198 St.
Hollis, NY 11412

BEESON, CONSTANCE (CONI)
99 W. Shore Rd.
Belvedere, CA 94920

BEH, SIEW HWA
2802 Arizona Ave.
Santa Monica, CA 90404

BELL SYSTEM
Telephone Offices
150 West St.
New York, NY 10017

BELLE, ANNE
P. O. Box 5667
Pasadena, CA 91107

Box 413
Remsenberg, NY 11960

BENCHMARK FILMS, INC.
145 Scarborough Rd.
Briarcliff Manor, NY 10510

BERTOZZI, PATRICIA
32 Cooper Square
New York, NY 10003

BESKIND, DOROTHY
475 Park Ave.
New York, NY 10022

BILDERBACK, CAROLYN
26 Grove St.
New York, NY 10014

BILINGUAL EDUCATION SER-
  VICE CENTER
500 S. Dwyer Ave.
Arlington Heights, IL 60005

BILLY BUDD FILM CO.
235 E. 57 St.
New York, NY 10022

BLACKHAWK FILMS
Eastin-Phelan Corporation
1235 W. 5th St.
Davenport, IA 52805

BLACKWOOD PRODUCTIONS,
  INC.
58 W. 58 St.
New York, NY 10019

BLUE RIDGE FILMS
9003 Glenbrook Rd.
Fairfax, VA 22030

BOB BAILEY PRODUCTIONS
  see BAILEY (BOB) PRO-
  DUCTIONS

BOSCO (DON) FILMS
148 Main St.
New Rochelle, NY 10802

BOSTON UNIVERSITY
School of Education
Krasker Memorial Film Library
765 Commonwealth Ave.
Boston, MA 02215

BOSUSTOW (STEPHEN) PRO-
  DUCTIONS
1648 11th St.
Santa Monica, CA 90405

BOTTNER, BARBARA
812 Broadway
New York, NY 10003

BRANDEIS UNIVERSITY
Waltham, MA 02154

BRAVERMAN (CHARLES) PRO-
DUCTIONS
P. O. Box 1048
Santa Monica, CA 90406

BRIGGS, NORMA
c/o Dept. of Labor
Dept. of Apprenticeship Training
310 Price Pl.
Madison, WI 53705

BRIGHAM YOUNG UNIVERSITY
Dept. of Audiovisual Services
290 HRCB
Provo, UT 84602

BRITISH BROADCASTING CO. --
TV
630 Fifth Ave.
New York, NY 10020

BRITISH BROADCASTING
CORP.
London, England

BRITISH INFORMATION SER-
VICE
Film & Publication Division
845 Third Ave.
New York, NY 10020

BRITISH TRANSPORT FILMS
25 Aasville Row
London, W1 England

BROSE (WILLIAM) PRODUC-
TIONS, INC.
3168 Oakshire Dr.
Hollywood, CA 90068

BROWN, BARBARA
413 West 21 St.
New York, NY 10011

BROWN, GWEN
41 King St.
New York, NY 10014

BUDD, BILLY
255 E. 57th St.
New York, NY 10022

BUDGET FILMS
4590 Santa Monica Blvd.
Los Angeles, CA 90029

BURNS, CAROL
4311 Cooper Point Rd., N. W.
Olympia, WA 98502

BURRILL, CHRISTINE
1332 Laurel Way
Beverly Hills, CA 90210

BUSINESS EDUCATION FILMS
5113 16th Ave.
Brooklyn, NY 11204

BUTLER-FREEDMAN FILMS
P. O. Box 454
Cambridge, MA 02138

BUTTERICK PUBLISHING
161 Sixth Avenue
New York, NY 10013

CRM/McGraw-Hill Films
110 15th St.
Del Mar, CA 92014

C-TV TELEVISION NETWORK
48 Charles St. East
Toronto, Ont., Can.
M4Y1T4

CABIN CREEK FILMS
58 East 11 St.
New York, NY 10003

CALAGNI, ANN CURTIS
17 West 60th St.
New York, NY 10023

CALIFORNIA NEWSREEL
630 Natoma St.
San Francisco, CA 94103

CALIFORNIA STATE DEPT.
OF EDUCATION
721 Capitol Mall
Sacramento, CA 95814

CALLACI, GLORIA
561 Stratford Pl.
Chicago, IL 60657

CAMBRIDGE DOCUMENTARY
FILMS, INC.
P. O. Box 385
Cambridge, MA   02139

CAMBRIDGE-GODDARD
Attn: Gail Pellet
6 Upland Rd.
Cambridge, MA   02140

CAMPBELL FILMS
Academy Ave.
Saxtons River, VT   05154

CAMPUS FILM PRODUCTIONS,
INC.
2 Overhill Rd.
Scarsdale, NY   10583

CANADIAN BROADCASTING
CORPORATION
P. O. Box 500, Terminal A
Toronto, Ontario Canada

CANADIAN FILM INSTITUTE
1762 Carling Avenue
Ottawa 13 Ontario Canada

CANADIAN FILMMAKER'S
DISTRIBUTION CENTER
Toronto, Ontario Canada

CANADIAN TRAVEL FILM
LIBRARY
1251 Avenue of the Americas
10th Floor
New York, NY   10020

CANTOR, ARTHUR INC.
234 West 44 St.
New York, NY   10036

CANYON CINEMA COOPERA-
TIVE
Industrial Center Bldg.
Room 220
Sausalito, CA   94965

CAPITAL CITIES COMMUNI-
CATIONS
4100 City Line Ave.
Philadelphia, PA   12901

CARMEN EDUCATIONAL ASSO-
CIATES
Box 205
Youngstown, NY   14174

CAROUSEL FILMS, INC.
Suite 1503
1501 Broadway
New York, NY   10036

CAROUSEL FILMS, INC. (West)
P. O. Box 5240
Santa Monica, CA   90405

CARTOON CO. , THE
1154 Second Ave.
New York, NY   10027

CASTELLI (LEO) GALLERY
420 West Broadway
New York, NY   10012

CATHOLIC FILM CENTER
29 Salem Way
Yonkers, NY   10710

CECROPIA
Suite 108
1100 Spring St. N. W.
Atlanta, GA   30309

CELLWOOD, MAUREEN
1697 Broadway
Room 1401
New York, NY   10019

CENTER CINEMA CO-OP
c/o School of the Art Institute
Michigan at Adams
Chicago, IL   60603

CENTER FOR MASS COMMUNI-
CATIONS
Columbia University Press
562 West 113 St.
New York, NY   10025

CENTER FOR SOUTHERN FOLK-
LORE
1216 Peabody
P. O. Box 4081
Memphis, TN   38104

CENTER OF URBAN EDUCA-
TION AND THE RADIO-TV
COMMISSION OF THE ARCH
DIOCESE OF PORTLAND
2838 East Burnside
Portland, OR 97214

CENTRAL DOCUMENTARY
FILM STUDIOS
Moscow

CENTRAL WASHINGTON UNI-
VERSITY
Audio Visual Library
Victor J. Bouillon Bldg.
Ellensburg, WA 98926

CENTRE FILMS
1103 N. Yale Centron Ave.
Hollywood, CA 90038

CENTRON FILMS
1621 West 9th St.
Lawrence, KS 66044

CHANGAS, ESTELLE
455 Westmount Dr.
Los Angeles, CA 90048

CHANGAS/LOVELAND
2005 Washington Ave.
Santa Monica, CA 90403

CHAPELLE, POLA
29 West 89 St.
New York, NY 10024

CHASE, DORIS
222 West 23 St.
New York, NY 10011

CHILD, ABIGAIL
14 East 13 St.
New York, NY 10003

CHILDREN'S CULTURAL
FOUNDATION, INC.
325 East 57 St.
New York, NY 10022

CHILDREN'S TELEVISION
WORKSHOP
1 Lincoln Plaza

New York, NY 10023

CHOPRA, JOYCE
6 Follen St.
Cambridge, MA 02136

CHURCHILL FALLS CORP.
LTD.
Montreal, Canada

CINE CRAFT FILMS
1720 N. W. Marshall St.
Portland, OR 97208

CHURCHILL FILMS
662 N. Robertson Blvd.
Los Angeles, CA 90069

CINE 16 FILMS
2233 40th Pl. N. W.
Washington, DC 20007

CINEMA EIGHT/CINEMA CON-
CEPTS
91 Main St.
Chester, CT 06412

CINEMA V
595 Madison Ave.
New York, NY 10022

CINEMA INCORPORATED
P. O. Box 315
Franklin Lakes, NJ 07417

CINEMA LORE CO.
650 N. Bronson
Hollywood, CA 90004

CINEMA MEDICA, INC.
664 N. Michigan Ave.
Chicago, IL 60611

CINEMAKERS, INC.
200 West 57 St.
New York, NY 10019

CINEMATIC CONCEPTS
1817 Union
San Francisco, CA 94123

CINEMETRICS
Toronto, Ontario Canada

CIRCLE ONE
2456 E. Magnolia Ave.
St. Paul, MN 55106

CLEM WILLIAMS FILMS, INC.
see WILLIAMS (CLEM)
FILMS, INC.

COLEMAN, WILLETTE
1475 Euclid St. S. W. , Apt.
320
Washington, DC 20029

c/o NET Training School
10 Columbus Circle
Washington, DC 20029

COLLEGE ENTRANCE EXAM
BOARD
888 7th Ave.
New York, NY 10019

COLLINS, MARY SPARACIO
c/o The Film School of Visual
Arts
New York, NY 10010

COLUMBIA BROADCASTING
SYSTEM
383 Madison Ave.
New York, NY 10017

CONCEPTS UNLIMITED, INC.
162 West 56 St.
New York, NY 10019

CONNECTICUT FILMS, INC.
see ITALTOONS CORP.

CONNECTION, INC. see
Marshall, Lisa J.

CONRAD, BEVERLY GRANT
111 West 42 St.
New York, NY 10036

THE CONSERVATION FOUN-
DATION
1717 Massachusetts Ave. N. W.
Washington, DC 20036

COOLIDGE, MARTHA
236 East 19th St.
New York, NY 10003

CORINTH FILMS
410 East 62 St.
New York, NY 10021

CORNELL UNIVERSITY
Ithaca, NY 14853

CORNERSTONE PRODUCTIONS
6087 Sunset Blvd. , Suite 408
Hollywood, CA 90028

CORNING GLASS WORKS
Corning, NY 14803

CORONET INSTRUCTIONAL
FILMS
The Multi Media Co.
65 E. Softwater St.
Chicago, IL 60601

COUNTERPOINT FILMS
14622 Lanark St.
Panorma City, CA 91402

COUSINO VISUAL EDUCATION
SERVICE
1945 Franklin Ave.
Toledo, OH 43624

COX (NELL) FILMS
109 West 11 St. , No. 3
New York, NY 10001

CRAWLEY FILMS, LTD.
19 Fairmont Ave.
Ottawa, Ontario Canada

CREATIVE FILM SOCIETY
7237 Canby Ave.
Reseda, CA 91335

CREATIVE OUTLET
117 N. W. 5th Ave.
Portland, OR 97209

CREEDMAN (MICHAEL) FILM
10 Park Ave.
New York, NY 10016

CRUIKSHANK, SALLY
15 Red Rd.
Chatham, NJ 07928

1890 Arch St.
Berkeley, CA 94709

CURRENT AFFAIRS FILMS
Div. of Keystone Productions,
  Inc.
24 Danbury Rd.
Wilton, CT 06897

CURTIS (CALLY) CO.
1111 N. Las Palmas
Hollywood, CA 90038

CYCLOPS PRODUCTIONS
197 10th Ave.
New York, NY 10011

DANCOFF, JUDITH
1118 10th St.
Santa Monica, CA 90403

c/o California Institute of
  Arts
McBean Parkway
Valencia, CA 91355

DANIELS, KARIL
2477 Folsom St.
San Francisco, CA 94110

DAVENPORT (TOM) FILMS
Pearlstone
Delaplane, VA 22025

DAVIS (SID) PRODUCTIONS
P. O. Box 12
Cary, IL 60013

De Basil
France

DEEN, NEDRA
Nedmar Productions
1265 N. Havenhurst Dr.
Los Angeles, CA 90046

DEES, SYLVIA
6637 Franklin Ave.
Hollywood, CA 90028

DE HIRSCH, STORM
136 West 4 St.
New York, NY 10012

DEITCH, DONNA
413 Howland Canal
Venice, CA 90291

DEMETRAKAS, JOHANNA
6644 Valmont St.
Tujunga, CA 91042

DIAMONT, RUFUS
1730 Carlton St.
Berkeley, CA 94703

DICKSON-MACAGNO, DEBORAH
310 West 88 St.
New York, NY 10024

DIDACTIC FILMS, LTD.
Gatwick House
Horley, Surrey, England

DIMENSION FILMS
666 N. Robertson Blvd.
Los Angeles, CA 90069

DIRECTIONS UNLIMITED LTD.
40 West 55 St.
New York, NY 10019

DISNEY (WALT) PRODUCTIONS
500 S. Buena Vista St.
Burbank, CA 91521

DOCUMENT ASSOCIATES, INC.
211 E. 43rd St.
New York, NY 10017

DOUBLE DAY MULTI MEDIA
  see PHOENIX FILMS, INC.

DOWD, NANCY ELLEN
Box 523
Topanga, CA 90290

DREW (ROBERT) ASSOCIATES
107 West 43 St.
New York, NY 10036

DRUCKER, ROBERT & CO.
10718 Riverside
N. Hollywood, CA 91602

DRUKS, RENATA
16885 Via Linda
Malibu, CA 90265

DUNCAN, VIRGINIA BAUER
Box 18222
San Francisco, CA 94118

DYAL, SUSAN
107 Rose Ave.
Venice, CA 90291

ECCENTRIC CIRCLE CINEMA
WORKSHOP see SPEC-
TRUM ⊕ MOTION PICTURE
LABORATORY

EDELHEIT, MARTHA
1140 Fifth Ave.
New York, NY 10028

EDUCATIONAL DEVELOPMENT
Distribution Center
39 Chapel St.
Newton, MA 02160

EDUCATIONAL TESTING SER-
VICE
Rosedale Rd.
Princeton, NJ 08540

EHRLICH, GRETEL
1780 Twinslope Trail
Topanga, CA 90290

ELDER, SARAH
316 Brookline St.
Cambridge, MA 02139

EM GEE FILM LIBRARY
16024 Ventura Blvd.
Suite 211
Encino, CA 91436

EMBASSY FILMS see AVCO

ENCYCLOPAEDIA BRITANNICA
EDUCATIONAL CORPORA-
TION
425 N. Michigan Ave.
Chicago, IL 60611

ENVISION CORPORATION
51 Sleeper St.
Boston, MA 02116

ERENBERG, ELENA
20812 Hillside Dr.
Topanga, CA 90290

ESPAR, SHERI GILLETTE
1643 Woodland Ave. East
Palo Alto, CA 94303

EXTENSION MEDIA CENTER
see UNIVERSITY OF CALI-
FORNIA, Berkeley

EYR
78 East 56th St.
New York, NY 10022

FSM/Pandora Films
33-35 Greene St.
New York, NY 10013

FACES INTERNATIONAL FILMS
844 Wilshire Blvd.
Beverly Hills, CA 90211

FAIRCHILD VISUALS
7 East 12 St.
New York, NY 10003

FALCON FILMS
9123 Sunset Blvd.
Los Angeles, CA 90069

FAMILY FILMS, INC.
114622 Lanark St.
Panorama City, CA 91402

FAR WEST LABORATORY FOR
EDUCATIONAL RESEARCH
AND DEVELOPMENT
Los Angeles, CA

FAROUN FILMS
Montreal, Quebec, Canada

FARRON, JIM
Civil Service Commission
Dallas Regional Office
Dallas, TX 75250

FEDERATION OF PROSTHO-
DONTIC ORGANIZATIONS
211 E. Chicago Ave., St. 943
Chicago, IL 60611

FEFERMAN, LINDA
42 Grove St., Apt. 25
New York, NY 10014

FELDMAN (DICK) ASSOCIATES,
INC.
205 East 42 St.
New York, NY 10017

FELTER, SUSAN
171 Mt. Vernon Ave.
San Francisco, CA 94112

FEMEDIA
2286 Great Highway
San Francisco, CA 94116

FIBERGLAS CANADA
Toronto, Canada

FILM CENTER, THE
915 12th St. N. W.
Washington, DC 20005

FILM CLASSIC EXCHANGE
1914 S. Vermont Ave.
Los Angeles, CA 90007

FILM IMAGES
A Div. of Radim Films, Inc.
17 West 60 St.
New York, NY 10023

1034 Lake St.
Oak Park, IL 60301

4530 18th St.
San Francisco, CA 94114

FILM-MAKERS' COOPERATIVE
175 Lexington Ave.
New York, NY 10016

FILM SCHOOL, THE
School of Visual Arts
209 E. 23 St.
New York, NY 10010

FILM WRIGHT
4530 18th St.
San Francisco, CA 94114

FILMFAIR COMMUNICATIONS
10900 Ventura Blvd.
Studio City, CA 91604

FILMMAKERS, INC.
1288 W. Long Lake Rd.
Bloomfield Hills, MI 48103

FILMMAKERS LIBRARY, INC.
290 West End Ave.
New York, NY 10023

FILMS FOR THE HUMANITIES,
INC
P. O. Box 2053
Princeton, NJ 08540

FILMS INCORPORATED (also
dist. for 16mm films of
Janus Films)
440 Park Avenue S.
New York, NY 10016

476 Plasamour Dr. N. E.
Atlanta, GA 30341

733 Green Bay Rd.
Wilmette, IL 60091

5625 Hollywood Blvd.
Hollywood, CA 90028

FILMS ON AGING
P. O. Box 315
Franklin Lakes, NJ 07417

FILMWEST ASSOCIATES LIM-
ITED
1081 6A Whyte Ave.
Edmonton, Alberta, T6E 2B3
Canada

FINNEY, EDWARD
1578 Queens Rd.
Hollywood, CA 90069

FIRESTONE, CINDA
c/o Attica Films, Inc.
789 West End Ave.
New York, NY 10025

FIREWEED FILMS
215 West 92 St.
New York, NY 10025

FIRST INTERNATIONAL FESTI-
VAL OF WOMEN'S FILMS
1582 York Ave.
New York, NY 10028

FISHER FILM GROUP
216 E. 49 St.
New York, NY   10017

FLEMING, LOUISE
661 West End Ave.
New York, NY   10025

FLEMING REX PRODUCTIONS
2449 Las Conas Rd.
Santa Barbara, CA   93105

FLITTERMAN, SANDY
2215 Channing Way No. 1
Berkeley, CA   94704

FLORIDA STATE UNIVERSITY
Instructional Media Center
Tallahassee, FL   32306

FOCUS EDUCATION, INC.
3 East 54 St.
New York, NY   10022

FORD FOUNDATION
320 East 43 St.
New York, NY   10017

FOREMAN, JANET
230 East 5 St.
New York, NY   10009

FOUNDATION FOR FILM-
   MAKERS
22 West 68 St.
New York, NY   10023

FRANCISCAN COMMUNICA-
   TIONS CENTER
1229 S. Santee St.
Los Angeles, CA   90015

FRENCH FILM OFFICE
Room 1512
745 5th Ave.
New York, NY   10022

FREYER, ELLEN
112 West 15 St.
New York, NY   10011

FRIEDMAN, BONNIE
200 Riverside Dr.
New York, NY   10025

GATE HILL CO-OP
Stony Point, NY   10980

GENERAL MOTORS CORPORA-
   TION
3044 West Grand Blvd.
Detroit, MI   48238

GENESIS FILMS, LTD.
40 West 55 St.
New York, NY   10019

GERSTEIN, CASSANDRA M.
1227 Quartier le Pioulier
Vence 06 140, France

GHANA INFORMATION SER-
   VICES
U. N. Secretariat
New York, NY   10017

GITLIN (IRVING) PRODUCERS,
   INC.
870 7th Ave.
Tower Suite 30-D
New York, NY   10019

GODMILOW, JILL
480 West Broadway
New York, NY   10012

GOLDBERG, JENNY
c/o Ginsberg
899 Noe St.
San Francisco, CA   94114

GOLDEN, NANCY AND LAURA
1156 Guerrero St.
San Francisco, CA   94110

GOLDSHOLL, MILDRED
420 Frontage Rd.
Northfield, IL   80093

GOLDSMITH, SYLVIANNA
151 West 18 St.
New York, NY   10011

GOOD SAMARITAN HOSPITAL
Dept. of Medical Education
1015 N. W. 22 Ave.
Portland, OR   97210

GORDON, ALVIN J.
1859 Powell
San Francisco, CA 94133

GOTHAM FILMS
11 East 44 St.
New York, NY 10017

GOTTLIEB, LINDA
Omaha Orange
211 Central Park West
New York, NY 10024

GRAHAM, DIANE T.
1936 Aberdeen Dr.
Columbus, OH 43220

GRANADA-TV INTERNATIONAL
Suite 3468
1221 Avenue of the Americas
New York, NY 10020

GRANT, AMY
617 49 St.
Brooklyn, NY 11220

GRANT, ANNE
617 49th St.
Brooklyn, NY 11220

GRAVES, NANCY
164 Mulbery St.
New York, NY 10013

69 Wooster St.
New York, NY 10013

GREAT PLAINS NATIONAL
  INSTRUCTIONAL TELE-
  VISION LIBRARY
Box 80669
Lincoln, NE 68501

GREAVES (WILLIAM) PRO-
  DUCTIONS, INC.
245 West 54 St.
New York, NY 10019

GREENFIELD, AMY
135 East 27 St.
New York, NY 10016

27 Bellis Circle
Cambridge, MA 02140

GREENFIELD, LOIS
c/o Holly Hartley
Children's Cultural Foundation,
  Inc.
325 East 57 St.
New York, NY 10022

GROUP W, WESTINGHOUSE
  BROADCASTING
90 Park Ave.
New York, NY 10016

GROVE PRESS, INC.
196 West Houston St.
New York, NY 10014

GUIDANCE ASSOCIATE
AV Subsidiary
757 Third Ave.
New York, NY 10017

HALEFF, MAXINE
c/o Halproductions
85 Barrow St.
New York, NY 10014

HALLECK, DEE DEE
Maple Shade Movies
Bloomingburg, NY 12721

HALPRODUCTIONS
85 Barrow St.
New York, NY 10014

HAMMER, BARBARA
2824 Harrison
San Francisco, CA 94110

1931 McGee St.
Berkeley, CA 94703

HANDEL FILM CORPORATION
8730 Sunset Blvd.
West Hollywood, CA 90069

HANNEMANN, YVONNE
228 East 22 St.
New York, NY 10010

HARPER & ROW PUBLISHERS,
  INC.
Audiovisual Dept.

70 East 53 St.
New York, NY 10022

HARPERS FERRY HISTOR-
ICAL ASSN.
P. O. Box 147
Harpers Ferry, WV 25425

HARTLEY FILM FOUNDATION
Cat Rock Rd.
Cos Cob, CT 06807

HASLANGER, MARTHA
1200 East University
Ann Arbor, MI 48104

HEALTH SCIENCES COMMUN-
ICATION CENTER
Case Western Reserve Univer-
sity
2119 Abington Rd.
Cleveland, OH 44106

HEARST METROTONE NEWS
235 East 45 St.
New York, NY 10017

HEICK, SUSAN
722 Palms Blvd.
Venice, CA 90291

HEINS, MARJORIE
8 St. Mary's St.
Watertown, MA 02172

HERSTORY FILMS INC. LI-
BRARY
137 East 13 St.
New York, NY 10003

779 Susquehanna Ave.
Franklin Lakes, NJ 07417

HESSE-RABINOVITCH, ISA
8700 Kusnacht
Schiedhaldenstrasse 75
Switzerland

HIGGINS (ALFRED) PRODUC-
TIONS, INC.
9100 Sunset Blvd.
Los Angeles, CA 90069

HOBAN, TANYA
2219 Delancey Pl.
Philadelphia, PA 19103

HOBEL-LEITERMAN PRODUC-
TIONS
880 Third Ave.
New York, NY 10022

HOCHBERG, VICTORIA
184 8th Ave.
New York, NY 10019

HODES, ROBERTA
420 East 23 St.
New York, NY 10021

HOLLAND-WEGMAN LABORA-
TORIES, INC.
207 Delaware Ave.
Buffalo, NY 14202

HOLT INFORMATION SYSTEMS
383 Madison Ave.
New York, NY 10017

HOLT, RINEHART AND WIN-
STON
383 Madison Ave.
New York, NY 10017

HOOD (G. V.) FILMS
P. O. Box 22213
Milwaukie, OR 97222

HULTON, JILL FORMAN
258 Winthrop Rd.
Columbus, OH 43214

HURLOCK CINE WORLD
13 Arcadia Rd.
Old Greenwich, CT 06870

IBM WORLD TRADE CORPORA-
TION
821 United Nations Plaza
New York, NY 10017

IPC Film Library
181 Pier Ave.
Santa Monica, CA 90405

I. Q. Films
P. O. Box 326
Wappingers Falls, NY 12590

IDEAL PICTURES, INC.
915 N. W. 19th Ave.
Portland, OR 97209

IMPACT FILMS
144 Bleecker St.
New York, NY 10012

INDIAN GOVERNMENT FILMS
DIVISION
Ministry of Information and
Broadcasting
24 Peddar Rd.
Bombay 26, India

INDIANA UNIVERSITY
Audio-Visual Center
Bloomington, IN 47401

INSIGHT EXCHANGE see
IRIS FILMS; DIAMONT,
RUFUS

INSTITUTIONAL CINEMA, INC.
915 Broadway
New York, NY 10010

INSTITUTO CUBANO DEL
ARTE & INDUSTRIA--
CINEMATOGRAFICOS
Cuba

INTERMEDICA, INC.
777 Third Ave.
New York, NY 10017

INTERNATIONAL FILM
BUREAU, INC.
332 S. Michigan Ave.
Chicago, IL 60604

INTERNATIONAL FILM FOUN-
DATION
475 Fifth Ave.
Suite 916
New York, NY 10017

IOWA STATE UNIVERSITY
121 Pearson Hall

Ames, IA 50010

IRIS FILMS (also handles some
films of now defunct Insight
Exchange)
2029 Essex St.
Berkeley, CA 94703

IRVINE, LOUVA ELIZABETH
158 East 30 St.
New York, NY 10016

ISAACS, BARBARA
333 East 43 St.
New York, NY 10017

ITALTOONS CORP.
Distribution Sixteen
111 Eighth Ave.
New York, NY 10011

IVY FILMS
165 West 46 St.
New York, NY 10036

IWANAMI PRODUCTIONS, INC.
22-2 Kanda Misakicho
Chiyoda-Ku
Tokyo, Japan

J. C. PENNEY CO.
1301 Avenue of the Americas
New York, NY 10019

JACOBY/STORM PRODUCTIONS
101 East State St.
Westport, CT 06880

JAFFE, PATRICIA LEWIS
1148 Fifth Ave.
New York, NY 10028

JANIS COUILLARD ASSOCIATES
1300 Esplanade
Hollywood Rivera
Redondo Beach, CA 90277

JANUS FILMS (see Films Incorporated for their 16mm
distribution)
745 Fifth Ave.
New York, NY 10022

JASON FILMS
2621 Palisade Ave.
Riverdale, NY   10463

JASPER, SUZANNE
218 Thompson St.
New York, NY   10012

JASSIM, LINDA
921-A Lincoln Blvd.
Santa Monica, CA   90405

JELINEK, MILENA
Adams Rd.
Ossining, NY   10562

JOHNSON, KAREN
10118 Aldea Ave.
Northridge, CA   91324

JONAS, JOAN
66 Grand St.
New York, NY   10013

JOURNAL FILMS, INC.
930 Pitner
Evanston, IL   60202

KDIN-TV
Des Moines, IA   50360

KHET-TV
Honolulu, HI

KING-TV (see BFA Educational Media for their 16mm
distribution)
King Screen Productions
320 Aurora Ave. N.
Seattle, WA   98109

KNBC-TV
3000 West Alameda Ave.
Burbank, CA   91505

KQED-TV
11011 Bryant St.
San Francisco, CA   94103

KRMA-TV
Denver Public Schools
1261 Glenarm Pl.

Denver, CO   80204

KTCA-TV
Twin City Area
Educational Television Corp.
1640 Como Ave.
St. Paul, MN   55108

KUON-TV
University Educational TV Sta-
tion
Box 8311
Lincoln, NB   68501

KUTV--Documentary Division
179 Social Hall Ave.
Salt Lake City, UT   84111

KVIE-TV
Central California
ETV Association
P. O. Box 6
Sacramento, CA   95801

KAARRESALO-KASARI, EILA
134 West 58 St.
New York, NY   10019

KANSAS MEDIA PROJECT
815 Vermont
Lawrence, KS   66044

KARTEMQUIN FILMS, LTD.
1525 East 53 St.
Chicago, IL   60615

KAUFFMANN AND BOYCE PRO-
DUCTIONS
P. O. Box 283
Allston, MA   02134

KEATING, ANNA-LENA
c/o Animated Films Co.
907 Sherman Ave.
Evanston, IL   60202

KEEDICK LECTURE BUREAU
475 Fifth Ave.
New York, NY   10017

KELLER, MARGIE
1610 West Byron St.
Chicago, IL   60613

KENDALL, NANCY LARUE
325 E. Fifth St.
New York, NY 10003

KERANS, BARBARA KAY
260 Vicksburg Dr.
Lansing, MI 48897

KEYSTONE PRODUCTIONS,
INC. see CURRENT AF-
FAIRS FILMS

KIESER, ELLWOOD E.
17575 Pacific Coast Hwy.
Pacific Palisades, CA 90272

KINOK FILM PRODUCTION CO.
455 FDR Dr., No. 706
New York, NY 10002

KIT PARKER FILMS
Carmel Valley, CA 93924

KLECKNER, SUSAN
117 Waverly Pl.
New York, NY 10011

KLEIN (WALTER J.) CO. ,
LTD.
6301 Carmel Rd.
Charlotte, NC 28211

KLOSKY, LINDA
1521 10th Avenue S.
Minneapolis, MN 55404

KRANING, SUZAN PITT
Box 67
Fountain City, WI 54629

KROLL (NATHAN) PRODUC-
TIONS, INC.
390 West End Ave.
New York, NY 10024

LANDAU, JACK
48 West 48 St.
New York, NY 10036

LANDSBURG (ALAN) PRO-
DUCTIONS
Suite 1130 9200 Sunset

Los Angeles, CA 90069

LANDWEBER, ELLEN
11237 Lucerne Ave.
Culver City, CA 90230

LANGHELD, GRETCHEN
c/o DWORKIN
336 East 5th St.
New York, NY 10003

LASSNIG, MARIA
95 Avenue B
New York, NY 10009

LAUGHLIN, KATHLEEN
1521 10th Avenue S.
Minneapolis, MN 55404

LAWREN PRODUCTIONS, INC.
P. O. Box 1542
Burlingame, CA 94010

LEARNING CORPORATION OF
AMERICA
1350 Avenue of the Americas
New York, NY 10019

LENFILM STUDIOS
U. S. S. R.

LEVINE, NAOMI
463 West St., No. 225-G
New York, NY 10014

LEVITT, HELEN
4 East 12th St.
New York, NY 10003

LEWIS, SUSAN
R. R. 1, Box 154
West Branch, IO 52358

LEWISOHNN (WALTER P.)
ASSOCIATES
Box 250, Cruz Bay
1532 Philadelphia National Bank
Bldg.
St. John, VI 00830

LIFE-STYLES PRODUCTIONS,
INC.
709 West Montrose at Marina Dr.
Chicago, IL 60613

LILYAN PRODUCTIONS, INC.
524 Ridge Rd.
Watchung, NJ 07060

LINDERN, A. /P. STERN
43 Fairmount Ave.
Somerville, MA 02144

LINKEVITCH, BARBARA
2523A Polk St.
San Francisco, CA 94109

LLOYD, ROBIN
Wing Farm
Rochester, VT 05767

LOEB, JANET
Alta Lodge
Alta, Utah 94070

LONDON WOMEN'S FILM
GROUP
London, England

LOS ANGELES FILM CO-OP
1843 Canyon Dr.
Los Angeles, CA 90028

LOVELACE THEATER
5888-1/2 Ellsworth Ave.
Pittsburgh, PA 15232

LUCERNE FILMS, INC.
7 Bahama Rd.
Morris Plains, NJ 07950

LURIE, JANE
c/o Labyris Brooks
33 Barrow St.
New York, NY 10014

41 West 16th St.
New York, NY 10011

McCARTHY, DINITIA SMITH
29 West 88 St.
New York, NY 10024

McCUE, MAUREEN
1844 Commonwealth Ave.
Auburndale, MA 02166

McGRAW-HILL/CONTEMPORARY
FILMS
1221 Avenue of the Americas
New York, NY 10020

McGRAW-HILL/CONTEMPORARY
FILMS
Distribution Center
Box 404
Princeton Rd.
Hightstown, NJ 08520

McLAUGHLIN-GILL, FRANCES
49 East 86 St.
New York, NY 10028

MAFILM STUDIOS
Budapest

MALIBU FILMS
P. O. Box 428
Malibu, CA 90265

MANSFIELD, PORTIA MOTION
PICTURES
Box 4026
Carmel, CA 93921

MAPLE SHADE MOVIES see
Halleck, Dee Dee

MAR/CHUCK FILM INDUSTRIES
P. O. Box 61
Mt. Prospect, IL 60056

MARGOLIS, FREDERICK J. ,
M. D.
Sciba Pharmaceutical Co.
2901 Westnedge
Kalamazoo, MI 49001

MARQUETTE UNIVERSITY
College of Journalism
1135 West Kilbourn
Milwaukee, WI 53233

MARSHALL, LISA J.
23 7th St. S. E.
Washington, DC 20003

MARYKNOLL FATHERS
Maryknoll, NY 10545

MARYLAND CENTER FOR
PUBLIC BROADCASTING,
THE
Owing Mills, MD 21117

MASS MEDIA ASSOCIATES
1720 Choutead
St. Louis, MO 63103

MASS MEDIA MINISTRIES
2116 N. Charles St.
Baltimore, MD 21218

MASSACHUSETTS COUNCIL
ON THE ARTS AND HU-
MANITIES
1 Ashburton Pl.
Boston, MA 02108

MASSACHUSETTS INSTITUTE
OF TECHNOLOGY
Center for Advanced Engineer-
ing Study
Room 9-232
Cambridge, MA 02139

MATERNITY INFANT CARE
FAMILY PLANNING PRO-
JECT
377 Broadway
New York, NY 10013

MATHEMATICAL ASSOCIA-
TION OF AMERICA
1225 Connecticut Ave. N. W.
Washington, DC 20036

MAYER, VICKY CHAET
228 Kipling
Palo Alto, CA 54301

MAYSLES FILMS, INC.
250 West 54th St.
New York, NY 10019

MEDIA GUILD, THE
Box 881
Solona Beach, CA 92075

MEDIA PLUS, INC.
60 Riverside Dr. , Suite 11-D
New York, NY 10024

MENDELSON (LEE) PRODUC-

TION, INC.
1408 Chapin Ave.
Burlingame, CA 94010

MENTAL HEALTH FILM BOARD
8 East 93 St.
New York, NY 10028

MENTAL HEALTH TRAINING
FILM PROGRAM
58 Fenwood Rd.
Boston, MA 02155

METHADONE INFORMATION
CENTER
P. O. Box 315
Franklin Lakes, NJ 07417

METROMEDIA PRODUCERS
CORPORATION
8544 Sunset Blvd.
Hollywood, CA 90069

METRO-GOLDWYN-MAYER
1202 W. Washington Blvd.
Culver City, CA 90230

MICHIGAN STATE UNIVERSITY
Instructional Media Center
East Lansing, MI 48824

MIEVES, WALTER/JACK LUND
45 N. Charter
Madison, WI 53715

MILANO, SUSAN
Women's Interart Center
549 W. 52 St.
New York, NY 10019

MILNER-FENWICK, INC.
3800 Liberty Heights Ave.
Bronx, NY 10467

MISSISSIPPI AUTHORITY FOR
EDUCATIONAL TELEVISION
3825 Ridgewood Rd.
Jackson, MI 39205

MITCHELL (THE J. GARY)
FILM CO. , INC.
2000 Bridgeway
Sausalito, CA 94965

MOBIL OIL COMPANY
150 East 42 St.
New York, NY   10017

MOBILIZATION FOR YOUTH
214 East 2nd St.
New York, NY   10009

MOCK, FLORA CLAR
1551 Beverly Dr.
Beverly Hills, CA   94710

MODERN MASS MEDIA
315 Springfield Ave.
Summit, NJ   07901

MODERN SOUND PICTURES
1402 Howard St.
Omaha, NB   68102

MODERN TALKING PICTURE
   SERVICE
5000 Park St. N.
St. Petersburg, FL   33709

MOKIN (ARTHUR) PRODUC-
   TIONS, INC.
17 West 60 St.
New York, NY   10023

MONUMENT FILM CORP.
110 West 14 St.
New York, NY   10011

MORELAND-LATCHFORD
   PRODUCTIONS
299 Queen St. West
Toronto, Ontario M5V 2S6,
   Canada

MOTIVATIONAL MEDIA
8271 Melrose
Los Angeles, CA   90046

MOTOROLA TELEPROGRAMS,
   INC.
4825 N. Scott St.
Suite 23
Schiller Park, IL   60176

MULFORD, MARILYN
33 Greene St.
New York, NY   10013

MULTI-MEDIA RESOURCE CEN-
   TER
1525 Franklin Ave.
San Francisco, CA   94109

MUSANTE, JOAN
1157 Virginia St.
Berkeley, CA   94702

MUSEUM OF MODERN ART
Circulation Dir., Dept. of Film
11 West 53 St.
New York, NY   10019

N. E. T. TRAINING SCHOOL
10 Columbus Circle
New York, NY   10023

N. O. W. , Portland see CRE-
   ATIVE OUTLET

NASH (HELEN) ASSOCIATES,
   INC.
370 Lexington Ave.
New York, NY   10017

NATIONAL ACADEMY FOR
   ADULT JEWISH STUDIES,
   UNITED SYNAGOGUE OF
   AMERICA
155 5th Ave.
New York, NY   10010

NATIONAL AUDIO VISUAL
   CENTER
National Archives and Record
   Service
General Services Administration
Washington, DC   20409

NATIONAL BROADCASTING CO.
   TV
30 Rockefeller Plaza
New York, NY   10020

NATIONAL EDUCATION ASSO-
   CIATION
1201 16th Street N. W.
Washington, DC   20036

NATIONAL EDUCATIONAL TV
   & RADIO CENTER

10 Columbus Circle
New York, NY   10019

NATIONAL EDUCATIONAL TV,
INC.
Indiana University
Bloomington, IN   47401

NATIONAL FILM BOARD OF
CANADA
1251 Avenue of the Americas,
17th Floor
New York, NY   10020

NATIONAL INSTRUCTIONAL
TV CENTER
11 West 17th St., Box A
Bloomington, IN   47401

NATIONAL PUBLIC AFFAIRS
CENTER FOR TELEVISION
Washington, DC

NATIONAL RIGHT TO WORK
1025 Connecticut Avenue N. W.
Washington, DC   20036

NATIONAL SEX FORUM
1523 Franklin St.
San Francisco, CA   94109

NATIONAL TELEFILM ASSO-
CIATION, INC.
12636 Beatrica
Mar Vista, CA   90066

NEBRASKA EDUCATIONAL
TELEVISION NETWORK
Lincoln, NE

NEDMAR PRODUCTIONS
1265 N. Havenhurst Dr.
Los Angeles, CA   90046

NELSON, GUNVOR
Star Route, Box 263
Sausalito, CA   94965

NETWORK FOR CONTINUING
MEDICAL EDUCATION
15 Columbus Circle
New York, NY   10023

NEW DAY FILMS
P. O. Box 315
Franklin Lakes, NJ   07417

NEW FEMINIST TALENT, INC.
25 West 57 St.
New York, NY   10019

NEW FILM COMPANY, INC.
(THE)
331 Newbury St.
Boston, MA   02115

NEW HAMPSHIRE EDUCATIONAL
TV
Box 2
Durham, NH   03824

NEW LINE CINEMA
121 University Pl.
New York, NY   10003

NEW YORK TELEPHONE CO.
100 Church St.
New York, NY   10007

NEW YORK TIMES
2 Kisco Plaza
Times Square
Mt. Kisco, NY   10549

NEW YORK UNIVERSITY
College of Medicine
550 First Ave.
New York, NY   10016

NEW YORK UNIVERSITY FILM
LIBRARY
26 Washington Pl.
New York, NY   10003

NEW YORKER FILMS
16 West 61 St.
New York, NY   10023

NEWSFILM--USA
15 West 46th St.
New York, NY   10036

NORDSTROM, KRISTINA
1582 York Ave.
New York, NY   10028

NORTHERN ILLINOIS UNIVER-
SITY
Division of Communication Ser-
vices
Media Distribution Dept.
Altgeld Hall, Room 114
De Kalb, IL   60115

NORTHERN INDIAN CALIFORNIA
EDUCATION PROJECT
526 "A" St.
Eureka, CA   95501

NORTHWESTERN UNIVERSITY
FILM LIBRARY
P. O. Box 1665
Evanston, IL   60204

NORTON, SUSAN
1050 Newton Rd.
Iowa City, IA   52240

NOXELL CORPORATION
200 Park Ave.
New York, NY   10017

ODEON FILMS
1619 Broadway
New York, NY   10019

OFFICIAL FILMS, INC.
Linden and Grand Avenues
Ridgefield, NJ   07657

OHIO NEWSREEL
Box 19421, Corryville Sta.
Cincinnati, OH   45219

OHIO STATE UNIVERSITY
Motion Picture Division
Film Distribution
156 West 19th St.
Columbus, OH   43210

OKLAHOMA STATE UNIVER-
SITY
Audio-Visual Center
Stillwater, OK   74074

OMORI, EMIKO
24 Bessie St.

San Francisco, CA   94110

ONO, YOKO
1 West 72 St.
New York, NY   10023

ONTARIO EDUCATIONAL COM-
MUNICATIONS AUTHORITY
Toronto, Canada

OREGON STATE UNIVERSITY
(See also Portland State Uni-
versity)
P. O. Box 1491
Film Library
1633 S. W. Park Ave.
Portland, OR   97207

ORENTREICH, CATHERINE
50 East 10th St.
New York, NY   10003

OSTERTAG, SANDY
156 Gray Ave.
Webster Groves, MO   63119

OXENBERG, JAN
24 Breeze Ave.
Venice, CA   90291
Also see IRIS FILMS

OXFORD FILMS, INC. see
PARAMOUNT COMMUNICA-
TIONS

PARAMOUNT COMMUNICATIONS
(Handles distribution of 16mm
educational films)
5451 Marathon St.
Hollywood, CA   90038

PARAMOUNT-OXFORD FILMS
see PARAMOUNT COMMUNI-
CATIONS

PARAMOUNT PICTURES COR-
PORATION (Handles distribution of feature films in
16mm)
5451 Marathon St.
Hollywood, CA   90038

PARENTING PICTURES
R. D. One, Box 355B
Columbus, NJ   07832

PATHE NEWS, INC.
835 Broadway
New York, NY   10003

PAUL, MILLIE
2103 Third St.
Santa Monica, CA   90405

PAULIST PRODUCTIONS
P. O. Box 1057
Pacific Palisades, CA   90272

PEISER, JUDY
3756 Minosa Ave.
Memphis, TN   38111

PELI-GRAPHIC PRODUCTIONS
2104 Hancock St.
San Diego, CA   92110

PELICAN FILMS, INC.
270 Madison Ave.
New York, NY   10016

PENNEBAKER, INC.
56 West 46 St.
New York, NY   10036

PENNSYLVANIA STATE UNI-
   VERSITY, THE
Audio Visual Services
University Park, PA   16802

PERENNIAL EDUCATION, INC.
477 Roger Williams
P. O. Box 855-Ravinia
Highland Park, IL   60035

PERKINS SCHOOL FOR THE
   BLIND
971 Main St.
Watertown, MA   02172

PERRY, ELEANOR
40 Central Park So.
New York, NY   10019

PERRY-MANSFIELD MOTION
   PICTURES see MANS-

FIELD, PORTIA MOTION
   PICTURES

PERSONAL PRODUCTS CO.
Education Dept.
Milltown, NJ   08850

PERSPECTIVE FILMS
369 West Erie St.
Chicago, IL   60610

PHARMACEUTICAL MANUFAC-
   TURERS ASS'N.
1411 'K' St. N. W.
Washington, DC   20006

PHOENIX FILMS, INC.
470 Park Avenue S.
New York, NY   10016

PICTURA FILMS DISTRIBUTION
   CORPORATION
43 West 16 St.
New York, NY   10011

PIGORSCH, PHYLLIS B.
75 Bluehill Park Dr.
Madison, WI   53718

PIHL, CHRISTINE R.
1314 Tarpon
Foster City, CA   94404

PILGRIM FILM SERVICES, INC.
2502 50th Ave. Tuxedo
Hyattsville, MD   20781

PLANNED PARENTHOOD ASSO-
   CIATION
Syracuse, NY   13201

PLANNED PARENTHOOD FED-
   ERATION OF AMERICA, INC.
810 7th Ave.
New York, NY   10019

PLANNED PARENTHOOD OF
   SAN MATEO
San Mateo, CA   94402

PLANNED PARENTHOOD OF
   SEATTLE
202 16th Avenue S.
Seattle, WA   98144

PLANNED PARENTHOOD OF
TUCSON
Tucson, AZ 85726

PLANNED PARENTHOOD
WORLD POPULATION
810 7th Ave.
New York, NY 10019

POLON, VICKI
14 West 10th St.
New York, NY 10011

POLYMORPH FILMS
331 Newbery St.
Boston, MA 02115

POMES AND POPCORN
3795 Mission Blvd.
San Diego, CA 92109

POPKIN, ANN
3 Lamson Pl.
Cambridge, MA 02139

PORTLAND STATE UNIVER-
SITY
Film Library
1633 S. W. Park Ave.
P. O. Box 1383
Portland, OR 97207

PORTRAIT RELEASING, INC.
1697 Broadway
New York, NY 10019

POWELL, PAT
75-1/2 Hoyt St.
Brooklyn, NY 11201

POWER (JULES) INTERNA-
TIONAL PRODUCTIONS,
INC.
25 East 73 St.
New York, NY 10021

PRENTICE-HALL, INC.
Route 9 West
Englewood Cliffs, NJ 07632

PRICE (RICHARD) ASSOCIATES
314 West 56 St.
New York, NY 10019

PRODUCTIONS UNLIMITED
1301 Avenue of the Americas
New York, NY 10019

PROFESSIONAL ARTS, INC.
P. O. Box 8003
Stanford, CA 94305

PROFESSIONAL RESEARCH,
INC.
660 S. Bonnie Brae St.
Los Angeles, CA 90057

PRUDENTIAL INSURANCE CO.
OF AMERICA
Prudential Plaza
P. O. Box 36
Newark, NJ 07101

PSYCHOLOGICAL FILMS, INC.
Distribution Center
1215 East Chapman Ave.
Orange, CA 92669

PUBLIC TELEVISION LIBRARY,
THE
Video Program Service
475 L'Enfant Plaza S. W.
Washington, DC 20024

PURDUE UNIVERSITY
Audio-Visual Center
Steward Center
Lafayette, IN 47907

PYRAMID FILMS
P. O. Box 1048
Santa Monica, CA 90406

QUEST PRODUCTIONS
630 9th Avenue, Room 901
New York, NY 10036

RBC PARAMOUNT/16 see
PARAMOUNT PICTURES
CORPORATION

ROA FILMS
1696 N. Astor
Milwaukee, WI 53202

RAFAEL FILM
426 West 45 St.
New York, NY   10036

RAINER, YVONNE
92 Franklin St.
New York, NY   10013

RAMIC PRODUCTIONS
58 West 58 St.
New York, NY   10019

RAMONA PRODUCTIONS
740 S. W. 17th St.
Corvallis, OR   97330

RAMSGATE FILMS
704 Santa Monica Blvd.
Santa Monica, CA   90401

REDIFFUSION TV LTD.
London, England

REDISCOVERY PRODUCTIONS
2 Halfmile Common
Westport, CT   06880

REICHERT, JULIA
810 Ferndale Ave.
Dayton, OH   45406

RESOURCE CENTER ON SEX
   ROLES IN EDUCATION   see
   UNIVERSITY OF CALIFORNIA
   AT DAVIS

REYNOLDS (STUART) PRODUC-
   TION
9465 Wilshire Blvd.
Beverly Hills, CA   90212

RODMAN, JEFFREY
420 East 64 St.
New York, NY   10021

ROMAN, HANNAH
567 N. Windsor Blvd.
Los Angeles, CA   90004

RONINFILM
43 West 61 St.
New York, NY   10023

ROSENBERG, ROYANNE
243 Elmwood
Evanston, IL   60202

ROTHSCHILD, AMALIE R.
87 East 7th St.
New York, NY   10003

105 Second Ave.
New York, NY   10003

RYDEN, HOPE
345 East 81 St.
New York, NY   10028

S. A. FILMS, INC.
70 H Chestnut Ridge Rd.
Montvale, NJ   07645

S-L FILM PRODUCTIONS
P. O. Box 41108
Los Angeles, CA   90041

SALZMAN, BERT FILMS
117 West 13 St.
New York, NY   10011

SAMATOWICZ, D.
463 W. St.
New York, NY   10014

SAMUELSON, KRISTINE
51 Prosper
San Francisco, CA   94114

SAN FRANCISCO NEWSREEL
   see CALIFORNIA NEWS-
   REEL

SAN JOSE UNIFIED SCHOOL
   DISTRICT
Adult Education Division
San Jose, CA

SANDLER INSTITUTIONAL
   FILMS, INC.
1001 N. Poinsettia Pl
Hollywood, CA   90046
Also See BARR FILMS

SARSAKU PRODUCTIONS
8700 Skyline Dr.
Los Angeles, CA   90046

SATIN, SHELDON FILMS
880 Third Ave.
New York, NY   10022

181 East 73 St.
New York, NY

SAUDEK (ROBERT) ASSOCI-
ATES, INC.
689 Fifth Ave.
New York, NY   10022

SAUNDERS, PAT
685 West End Ave.
New York, NY   10025

SCHLOAT (WARREN) PRO-
DUCTIONS, INC.
150 White Plains Rd.
Tarrytown, NY   10591

SCHNEEMAN, CAROLEE
470 Springtown Rd.
New Paltz, NY   12561

SCHNEIDER, ROSALIND
40 Cottontail Lane
Irving-On-Hudson, NY   10533

301 East 72 St.
New York, NY   10021

SCHOENFELD FILM DIS-
TRIBUTING CORP.
165 West 46 St., Suite 905
New York, NY   10036

SCHWARTZ, LILLIAN
524 Ridge Rd.
Watchung, NJ   07060
Also see LILYAN PRODUC-
TIONS, INC.

SCREENSCOPE, INC.
1022 Wilson Blvd.
Arlington, VA   22209

SEARS, ROEBUCK AND CO.
Sears Tower
Chicago, IL   60684

SEIDELMAN, SUSAN
63 9th St., No. 9B
New York, NY   10003

SELECT FILM LIBRARY
115 West 31 St.
New York, NY   10001

SERIOUS BUSINESS COMPANY
1145 Mandana Blvd.
Oakland, CA   94610

SHAFFER, DEBORAH
33 Greene St.
New York, NY   10013

SHANDS (ALFRED) PRODUCTIONS
334 E. Broadway
Suite 327
Louisville, KY   40202

SHEEHY, TERRY
118 Huntington Dr.
San Francisco, CA   94132

SHELLABARGER, ANNE
Box 286
Tiuron, CA   94920

SHORELINE COMMUNITY COL-
LEGE
16101 Greenwood Avenue N.
Seattle, WA   98133

SIEGAL, LOIS
5028 St. Urbain
Montreal 151 PQ, Canada

SIEGEL, MARIAN
106 Enchanted Hills Rd.
Owing Mills, MD   21117

SKELTON, MARLYS
5336 26th Ave. South
Minneapolis, MN   55417

SLESIN, AVIVA
155 East 77 St.
New York, NY   10021

SLOANE, PATRICIA
79 Mercer St.
New York, NY   10012

SMILING CAT PRODUCTIONS
234 East 5 St.
New York, NY   10003

SMITH, JUDY
532 111 St.
New York, NY   10025

SMITH, LYNN
30 Upland Rd.
Cambridge, MA   02140

SMITHSONIAN INSTITUTION
14th & Constitution Avenue
N. W.
Washington, DC   20560

SOCIETY FOR NUTRITION
EDUCATION
2140 Shattuck Ave., Suite 1110
Berkeley, CA   94704

SOHO CINEMA LTD.
225 Lafayette St.
New York, NY   10012

SOUTHERBY PRODUCTIONS,
INC.
1709 East 28 St.
Long Beach, CA   90806

SOUTHERN CHRONICLERS
P. O. Box 8892
517 Howard St.
Savannah, GA   31401

SOUTHERN ILLINOIS UNI-
VERSITY AT CARBONDALE
Carbondale, IL   62901

SPECIAL PURPOSE FILMS
26740 Latigo Shore Dr.
Malibu, CA   90265

SPECTRA PICTURES see
STANDARD FILM SERVICE

SPECTRUM ⊕ MOTION PIC-
TURE LABORATORY
399 Gunderson Dr.
Carol Stream, IL   60187

SPENCER, MARY ANN
75 Creston
Tenafly, NJ   07670

SPHEERIS, PENELOPE

716 Sunset Ave.
Venice, CA   90291

SPRING HILL COLLEGE
Mobile, AL   36608

STANDARD FILM SERVICE
14710 W. Warren Ave.
Dearborn, MI   41826

STANFIELD HOUSE, THE
12381 Wilshire Blvd.
P. O. Box 3208
Santa Monica, CA   90403

STAR FILM CO.
Div. of Two Star Films, Inc.
79 Bobolink Lane
Levittown, NY   11756

STARR, CECIL
50 West 96 St.
New York, NY   10025

STATENS FILMCENTRAL
Danish Government Film Office
27 Vestergarde
DK 1456 Copenhagen K. Denmark

STEEL, JUNE
2312 Third St.
Santa Monica, CA   90405

STERLING EDUCATIONAL
FILMS
A Div. of the Walter Reade Or-
ganization, Inc.
241 East 34 St.
New York, NY   10016

STERNBERG, JANET
514 West End Ave.
New York, NY   10024

STORYBOARD, INC.
165 East 72 St.
New York, NY   10021

STRAND, CHICK
1834 Canyon Dr.
Los Angeles, CA   90028

STUART (MARTHA) COMMUNI-
CATIONS
66 Bank St.
New York, NY   10014

STYMAN, BARBARA
1219 Taylor St.
San Francisco, CA   94126

SUMMERHILL PRODUCTIONS
Box 156, Stn. Q
Toronto, Canada

SUMMERS, ALAN A., M. D.
309 S. Easton Rd.
Glenside, PA   19038

SUMMERS, ELAINE
c/o Filmmakers Co-op
175 Lexington Ave.
New York, NY   10016

SURPIN, SHELLY   see
THOMPSON/SURPIN

SUSSEX FILMS
29 Washington Square West
New York, NY   10011

SWANK MOTION PICTURES
201 S. Jefferson Ave.
St. Louis, MO   63103

60 Bethpage Rd.
Hicksville, NY   11801

7926 Jones Branch Dr.
McLean, VI   22101

220 Forbes Rd.
Braintree, MA   92184

1200 Roosevelt Rd.
Glen Ellyn, IL   60137

4111 Director's Row
Houston, TX   77092

6767 Forest Lawn Dr.
Hollywood, CA   90068

TALENT ASSOCIATES--
PARAMOUNT, LTD.
1136 N. Las Palmas Ave.
Hollywood, CA   90038

TAUBIN, AMY
141 Wooster St.
New York, NY   10012

TEACHING FILM CUSTODIANS,
INC.   see   AUDIALS AND
VISUALS

TELEKINETICS
276 Riverside Dr.
New York, NY   10025

TEREBEY, RAIKA
43 John E. Busch Ave.
Somerset, NJ   08873

TERWILLIGER, ELIZABETH
Nature Education Foundation
P. O. Box 668
Tiburn, CA   94920

TESICH-SAVAGE, NADJA
855 West End Ave.
Apt. 7A
New York, NY   10025

TEXTURE FILMS, INC.
1600 Broadway
New York, NY   10019

THATCHER, ANITA
33 2nd Ave.
New York, NY   10003

THERAPLAY INSTITUTE
333 N. Michigan Ave.
Chicago, IL   60601

THIRD WORLD CINEMA GROUP
244 West 27 St.
New York, NY   10001

THIRD WORLD NEWSREEL
160 5th Ave.
New York, NY   10010

THOMPSON, SHERA/SURPIN,
SHELLY
467 Hawthorne Ave.
Palo Alto, CA   94301

THUNDERBIRD FILM ENTER-
PRISES, INC.

325 Flint St.
Reno, NV 89501

THUNDERBIRD FILMS
P. O. Box 65157
3501 Eagle Rock Rd.
Los Angeles, CA 90065

TIME-LIFE MULTIMEDIA
Time & Life Bldg.
New York, NY 10020

TIME-LIFE MULTIMEDIA
Distribution Center
100 Eisenhower Dr.
P. O. Box 644
Paramus, NJ 07652

TOMATO PRODUCTIONS, INC.
Box 1952
Evergreen, CO 80439

TOMORROW ENTERTAINMENT,
INC.
570 Lexington Ave.
New York, NY 10022

TRACK AND FIELD NEWS
Box 296
Los Altos, CA 94022

TRANS-WORLD FILMS, INC.
332 S. Michigan Ave.
Chicago, IL 60604

TRANSIT MEDIA, INC.
779 Susquehanna Ave.
Franklin Lakes, NJ 07417

TRICONTINENTAL FILM
    CENTER see UNIFILM

TUPPER, LOIS ANN
60 Chilton St.
Cambridge, MA 02138

TURTLETAUB AND MOSS,
INC.
145 East 49 St.
New York, NY 10017

TV RADIO AND FILM COM-
MISSION

The Methodist Church
1525 McGavock St.
Nashville, TN 37203

TWIN CITIES WOMEN'S FILM
    COLLECTIVE see CIRCLE
    ONE

TWYMAN FILMS, INC.
Box 605
4700 Wadsworth Rd.
Dayton, OH 45401

2321 West Olive
Burbank, CA 91506

Box 794 Cooper Station
New York, NY 10003

U. S. DEPT. OF AGRICULTURE
Extension Service
Independence Ave. between 12th
    & 14th St. S. W.
Washington, DC 20201

U. S. DEPT. OF HEALTH, EDU-
    CATION & WELFARE
330 Independence Ave. S. W.
Washington, DC 20201

U. S. DEPT. OF LABOR
Information Office
Wage and Hour Division
Washington, DC 20210

U. S. ENERGY RESEARCH &
    DEVELOPMENT AGENCY
Audio Visual Branch
Div. of Public Information
Washington, DC 20025

U. S. INFORMATION AGENCY
1776 Pennsylvania Avenue N. W.
Washington, DC 20547

U. S. OFFICE OF EDUCATION
400 Maryland Avenue S. W.
Washington, DC 20202

U. S. OFFICE OF WAR IN-
    FORMATION
Overseas Branch

UNIFILM (merger of Tricontinental Film Center and
Latin American Film Pro-
ject, Inc.)
1550 Bryant St.
Suite 605
San Francisco, CA 94103

UNITED ARTISTS ASSOCIA-
TION
6920 Sunset Blvd.
Los Angeles, CA 90028

UNITED ARTISTS/16
729 7th Ave.
New York, NY 10019

UNITED FILMS
1425 S. Main
Tulsa, OK 74119

UNITED METHODIST COM-
MUNICATIONS
1525 McGavock St.
Nashville, TN 37203

UNITED NATIONS
Films & TV
Distribution Officer
New York, NY 10017

UNIVERSAL 16
205 Walton St. , N. W.
Atlanta, GA 30303

425 N. Michigan Ave.
Chicago, IL 60611

810 S. St. Paul St.
Dallas, TX 75201

8901 Beverly Blvd.
Los Angeles, CA 90048

445 Park Ave.
New York, NY 10022

UNIVERSITY CHRISTIAN
MOVEMENT IN NEW
ENGLAND
11 Garden St.
Cambridge, MA 02138

UNIVERSITY OF ALABAMA
Birmingham, AL 35294

UNIVERSITY OF ALASKA see
ALASKA NATIVE HERITAGE

UNIVERSITY OF CALIFORNIA,
BERKELEY
Extension Media Center
Berkeley, CA 94720

UNIVERSITY OF CALIFORNIA
AT DAVIS
Resource Center on Sex Roles in
Education
Davis, CA 95616

UNIVERSITY OF CALIFORNIA
AT LOS ANGELES
405 Hilgard Ave.
Los Angeles, CA 90024

UNIVERSITY OF CHICAGO
Chicago, IL 60637

UNIVERSITY OF COLORADO
AT BOULDER
Div. of Continuing Education
Educational Media Center
Stadium Bldg.
Boulder, CO 80309

UNIVERSITY OF GEORGIA, THE
Film Library
Georgia Center for Continuing
Education
Athens, GA 30601

UNIVERSITY OF HAWAII
Honolulu, Hawaii 96822

UNIVERSITY OF ILLINOIS
Visual Aid Service
1325 S. Oak
Champaign, IL 61820

UNIVERSITY OF IOWA
Media Library
C-5 East Hall
Iowa City, IA 52242

UNIVERSITY OF KANSAS, THE
746 Massachusetts
Lawrence, KS 66044

UNIVERSITY OF KENTUCKY,
LEXINGTON
Audio-Visual Services
Scott Street Bldg.
Lexington, KY 40506

UNIVERSITY OF MAINE
Portland-Gorham Campus
Gorham, ME 04038

UNIVERSITY OF MICHIGAN
Audio Visual Education Center
416 4th St.
Ann Arbor, MI 48103

UNIVERSITY OF MICHIGAN
TV CENTER
400 S. 4th St.
Ann Arbor, MI 48109

UNIVERSITY OF MISSOURI,
COLUMBIA
Extension Div.
505 East Stewart Rd.
Columbia, MO 65201

UNIVERSITY OF NEBRASKA
Instructional Media Center
Lincoln, NE 68508

UNIVERSITY OF NEVADA
Audiovisual Communication
Center
Reno, NV 89507

UNIVERSITY OF NEW HAMP-
SHIRE, DURHAM
Durham, NH 03824

UNIVERSITY OF SOUTHERN
CALIFORNIA
Dept. of Cinema
University Park
Los Angeles, CA 90007

UNIVERSITY OF UTAH
Educational Media Center
207 Milton Bennion Hall
Salt Lake City, UT 84112

UNIVERSITY OF WASHINGTON
Audio Visual Services
35D Kane Hall, DG-10

Seattle, WA 98195

UNIVERSITY OF WISCONSIN
University Extension
Bureau of A-V Instruction
1327 University Ave.
Madison, WI 53701

UNIVERSITY OF WISCONSIN
Women's Educational Resources
428 Lowell Hall
610 Langton St.
Madison, WI 53706

UNIVERSITY OF WYOMING
Audio Visual Services
Laramie, WY 82070

UNUSUAL FILMS
Bob Jones University
Greenville, SC 29614

URBAN PLANNING AID, INC.
c/o Mary Tiseo
5 Lester Terrace
Somerville, MA 02144

VERA INDUSTRIES INC.
1411 Broadway
New York, NY 10018

417 5th Ave.
New York, NY 10016

VIEWFINDERS, INC.
2550 Green Bay Rd.
Box 1665
Evanston, IL 60204

VISION ASSOCIATES, INC.
680 5th Ave.
New York, NY 10019

VISION FILMS
P. O. Box 48896
Los Angeles, CA 90048

VISION QUEST, INC.
7715 N. Sheridan Rd.
Chicago, IL 60626

VISUAL RESOURCES, INC.
Suite 1219

152 West 42nd St.
New York, NY 10036

VOCATIONAL FILMS
111 Euclid Ave.
Park Ridge, IL 60068

VULVA VIDIO
606 Vanezia Ave.
Venice, CA 90291

WCAU-TV
City Line Monument Ave.
Philadelphia, PA 19131

WENH-TV
University of New Hampshire,
Durham
Durham, NH 03824

WETA-TV
The Greater Washington Educa-
tional TV Ass'n., Inc.
1225 19th St. N. W.
Jefferson Place
Washington, DC 20036

WGBH-TV
Educational Foundation
125 Western Ave.
Boston, MA 02134

WHA-TV
University of Wisconsin
3313 University Ave.
Madison, WI 53705

WITF-TV
S. Central Educational Broad-
casting Council
Box 'Z'
Hershey, PA 17033

WKAR-TV
East Lansing, MI 48901

WKYC-TV
1403 East 6th St.
Cleveland, OH 44114

WMVS-TV
1015 6th St.

Milwaukee, WI 53203

WNBC-TV
Rockefeller Plaza
New York, NY 10020

WNED-TV
Buffalo, NY 14220

WNET-TV
356 West 58 St.
New York, NY 10019

WNVF-TV
N. Virginia Educational Television

WPSX-TV
University Park, PA 16802

WQED-TV
Metropolitan Pittsburgh Educational TV
4802 Fifth Ave.
Pittsburgh, PA 15213

WRC-TV
4001 Nebraska Avenue N. W.
Washington, DC 20016

WSWP-TV
Beckley, WV 25801

WTTW-TV
5400 N. St. Louis
Chicago, IL 60625

WALSH, ALIDA
121 Prince St.
New York, NY 10012

16438 Gilmore St.
Van Nuys, CA 91406

WALTER P. LEWISOHNN
ASSOCIATES see LEWI-
SOHNN (WALTER P.) ASSO-
CIATES

WALTER READE/16
241 East 34 St.
New York, NY 10016

WANG, JULIANA
Smiling Cat Productions
234 East 5 St.
New York, NY 10003

WARDWELL, JUDITH
198 Ely Rd.
Petaluma, CA 94952

WARNER BROS., INC.
Non-Theatrical Division
4000 Warner Blvd.
Burbank, CA 91522
Also see SWANK MOTION
PICTURES, dist.

WASHINGTON STATE UNIVER-
SITY
Audio Visual Center
Pullman, WA 99163

WAYNE, SUSAN
c/o Gotham Films
11 East 44 St.
New York, NY 10017

WAYNE STATE UNIVERSITY
Systems Dist. & Utilization
Dept.
Div. for the Center of Instruc-
tional Technology
5448 Cass Ave.
Detroit, MI 48202

WEINSTEIN, MIRIAM
36 Shepard St.
Cambridge, MA 02138

WELLING MOTION PICTURE
SERVICE
454 Meacham Ave.
Elmont, NY 11003

WESTCOAST FILMS
25 Lusk St.
San Francisco, CA 94107

WESTERN ELECTRIC, INC.
Motion Picture Bureau
Public Relations Division
195 Broadway, Room 1624
New York, NY 10007

WESTINGHOUSE LEARNING
CORPORATION
100 Park Ave.
New York, NY 10017

WESTON-WOODS STUDIO
Weston, CT 06880

WEXLER FILM PRODUCTIONS,
INC.
801 N. Seward St.
Los Angeles, CA 90038

WHEELOCK EDUCATIONAL RE-
SOURCES
P. O. Box 451
Hanover, NH 03755

WHITE FOX FILMS
Davis Westphal
Film Dept.
Brandeis University
Waltham, MA 02154

WHOLESOME FILM CENTER
20 Melrose St.
Boston, MA 02116

WIELAND, JOYCE
c/o Isaacs Gallery
832 Yong St.
Toronto, Ontario M4W2H1,
Canada

WILEY (JOHN) AND SONS, INC.
see MEDIA GUILD for 16mm
distribution

WILLIAMS (CLEM) FILMS, INC.
2240 Noblestown Rd.
Pittsburgh, PA 15205

146 W. Harrison St.
Oak Park, IL 60304

1277 Spring St. N. W.
Atlanta, GA 30309

2170 Portsmouth
Houston, TX 77098

298 Lawrence Ave.
S. San Francisco, CA 94080

WILLIAMS, JEAN L.
c/o The Cartoon Co.
1154 2nd Ave.
New York, NY 10027

General Delivery
Venice, FL 33595

WILSON (DANIEL) PRODUC-
TIONS
300 West 55 St.
New York, NY 10019

WISCONSIN STATE UNIVER-
SITY, LA CROSSE
Audio Visual Center
Florence Wing Communica-
tion Center
1705 State St.
LaCrosse, WI 54601

WOLPER PRODUCTIONS
8489 West 3rd St.
Los Angeles, CA 90048

WOMBAT PRODUCTIONS, INC.
Little Lake
Glendale Rd.
P. O. Box 70
Ossining, NY 10562

WOMEN/ARTISTS/FILM-
MAKERS
c/o Pat Sloane/Alida Walsh
79 Mercer St.
New York, NY 10012

WOMEN MAKE MOVIES, INC.
257 West 19 St.
New York, NY 10011

WOMEN ON WORDS AND
IMAGES
Box 2163
Princeton, NJ 08540

WOMEN'S FILM CO-OP, THE
see IRIS FILMS for 16mm
films
c/o W. I. T. , INC.
P. O. Box 745
Northampton, MA 01060

WOMEN'S LIBERATION CINEMA
CO.
243 West 20 St.
New York, NY 10011

WOMEN'S RESEARCH PROJECT
404 Yale Station
New Haven, CT 06520

WOOD, ELIZABETH M.
102 Western Ave.
Cambridge, MA 02139

WORKS, THE
1659 18th St.
Santa Monica, CA 90404

WORLD ARTISTS, INC. see
LESSER, IRVING ENTER-
PRISES

WORLD HORIZON FILMS
Pinesbridge Rd.
Maryknoll, NY 10545

WORLD WIDE PICTURES LTD.
21-25 St. Anne's Court
London, W1V3AW, England

WYETH INTERNATIONAL LTD.
201 King of Prussia Rd.
Middletown, CT 06457

WYLDE FILMS, INC.
53 East 25 St.
New York, NY 10010

XEROX FILMS
245 Long Hill Rd.
Middletown, CT 06457

YELLOWBALL WORKSHOP
62 Tarbell Ave.
Lexington, MA 02173

YOUNGSON, JEANNIE
29 Washington Square W.
New York, NY 10011

YOUTH FILM DISTRIBUTION
43 West 16th St.
New York, NY   10011

ZIPPORAH FILMS

54 Lewis Wharf
Boston, MA   02110

ZWERIN, CHARLOTTE
43 Morton St.
New York, NY   10014

APPENDIX C:
BIBLIOGRAPHY

Andrew A. Aros (As conceived by Richard B. Dimmitt), A Title
Guide To The Talkies, 1964 Through 1974. Metuchen, N. J. :
The Scarecrow Press, Inc. , 1977.

D. Richard Baer, ed. , The Film Buff's Bible of Motion Pictures
(1915-1972). Hollywood: Hollywood Film Archive, 1972.

Helen W. Cyr, A Filmography of the Third World: An Annotated
List of 16mm Films. Metuchen, N. J. : The Scarecrow Press,
Inc. , 1976.

Bonnie Dawson, Women's Films in Print: An Annotated Guide to
800 16mm Films by Women. San Francisco: Booklegger Press,
1975.

Richard Bertrand Dimmitt, A Title Guide to the Talkies: A Comprehensive Listing of 16, 000 Feature-Length Films From October, 1927 Until December, 1963. 2 vols. Metuchen, N. J. :
The Scarecrow Press, Inc. , 1965.

John C. Gerlach and Lana Gerlach, The Critical Index: A Bibliography of Articles on Film in English, 1946-1973, Arranged
by Names and Topics. New York: Teachers College Press,
1974.

Richard P. Krafsur, exec. ed. , The American Film Institute, The
American Film Institute Catalog of Motion Pictures: Feature
Films 1961-1970, 2 vols. New York and London: R. R.
Bowker Company, 1976.

Landers Associates, "Landers Film Reviews: The Information Guide
to 16mm Films and Multi-Media Materials. " 1967-1978. Los
Angeles: Landers Associates, 1967-1978.

James L. Limbacher, comp. and ed. , Feature Films on 8mm and
16mm, 5th ed. New York and London: R. R. Bowker Company,
1977.

Kenneth W. Munden, exec. ed. , The American Film Institute, The
American Film Institute Catalog of Motion Pictures Produced in
the United States: Feature Films 1921-1930, 2 vols. New York
and London: R. R. Bowker Company, 1971.

445

National Information Center for Educational Media (NICEM), University of Southern California, Index to 16mm Educational Films, 4 vols. Los Angeles: University of Southern California, 1977.

The New York Times. The New York Times Film Reviews, 1913-1968. Index with 8 vols. New York: The New York Times and Arno Press, 1970.

The New York Times. The New York Times Film Reviews, 1975-1976. New York: The New York Times and Arno Press, 1977.

R. A. E. Pickard, Dictionary of 1,000 Best Films. New York: Association Press, 1971.

Sharon Smith, Women Who Make Movies. New York: Hopkinson and Blake, 1975.

University of California, Extension Media Center, "Lifelong Learning: Films 1977-1978." Berkeley: University of California, 1977.

INDEX OF WOMEN FILMMAKERS

FRIEDMAN, Bonnie
Childcare: People's Libera-
tion
Chris and Bernie: A Film
About Single Mothers
Flashettes
How About You? A Film
on Birth Control and
Sexuality

FRIEDMAN, Sonya
Bronze Zoo

FYODORVA, Maria
Gift for Music

GALLANT, Denise
Koan

GARDNER, Janet
Inside the Ladies' Home
Journal

GARLAND, Kate
On That Day in the East
Bronx

GARNER, Virginia
Kibbutz, Daphna

GEBAUER, Phyllis
Tale of Today

GEER, Ellen
Eddie

GERBER, Daisy
Steelyard Blues

GERIMA, Haile
Bush Mama

GERSTEIN, Cassandra M.
Kali
Mai East
Strange Lands
Tales
Undine

GIBBARD, Susan
Centaur

GIFFORD, Ellen
Christo's Valley Curtain
Eggs and Elevators

GILLIATT, Penelope
Sunday, Bloody Sunday

GINTER, Val
High Up Doll

GIRITLIAN, Virginia
Cumulus Nimbus
Eggs and Elevators
81 Bacon
Footlights

GLEASON, Michie
We're Alive

GODMILOW, Jill
Antonia: A Portrait of a
Woman

GOLDBERG, Jenny
Homefront
Rape Tape

GOLDEN, Gloria
Anything They Want to Be
Career Stereotypes
Changing Images: Confronting

GOLDEN, Laura
Somebody Crushed You, Rosemarie

GOLDEN, Nancy
Somebody Crushed You, Rosemarie

GOLDSHOLL, Mildred
Up Is Down

GOLDSMITH, Sylvianna
Coney Island of the Mind
Orpheus Underground
Transformation of Perse-
phone

GOODMAN, Pearlyn
Richard's Bath

GOODRICH, Frances
  Diary of Anne Frank
  Father of the Bride
  Thin Man

GORDON, Ruth
  Actress,
  Adam's Rib
  Ash Wednesday
  Pat and Mike

GORELIK-CARSON, Sonia
  Doll's House

GOTTLIEB, Linda
  Big Henry and the Polka
    Dot Kid
  Case of the Elevator Duck
  Fur Coat Club
  Immigrant Experience: The
    Long Long Journey
  Luke Was There
  Snowbound

GRAHAM, Diane T.
  Act of Contrition
  Barbara

GRAND, Eleanor
  West Virginia Coleslaw

GRANT, Ann
  Our North American Fore-
    mothers

GRAVES, Nancy
  Aves: Magnificent Frigate
    Bird, Great Flamingo
  Isy Boukir
  Reflections on the Moon

GRAYSON, Helen
  Cummington Story

GREENE, Barbara
  Ruth and Harriet: Two
    Women of the Peace

GREENFIELD, Amy
  Dirt
  Element
  Encounter
  Transport

GREENFIELD, Lois
  Mais Moi

GREGORY, Mollie
  Cities Are for People
  ERA and the American Way
  Operation Greenhouse
  Shores

GREINER, Nancy
  Katie Kelly

GREY, Lorraine
  Emerging Woman

GRIFFEN, Susan
  Voices, Pts. I, II

GROSSMAN, Ann-Carol
  Speaking of Men

HABRER, Roberta
  Emerging Woman

HAINES, Juanita
  Batik Rediscovered

HALEFF, Maxine
  Forbidden Playground
  Magic Lantern Movie

HALLECK, Dee Dee
  Children Make Movies
  Mini Movie Makers
  Mr. Story
  Mrs. Tkach
  Mural on Our Street
  Otisville School for Boys
    Films
  Song of Innocents

HALLET, Judith Dwan
  Child of Dance
  Day We Won't Forget
  I Love to Be Happy
  Move It!
  Nomads of Badakhshan
  Painted Truck
  Sure, I Can Dance
  Wash

HAMBURG, Victoria
  Any Empty Space

HELLER, Linda
Album

HELLMAN, Lillian
Little Foxes

HENDERSON, Kay
Minnie Remembers
Women, Amen!

HENNESSEY, Sharon
Bird
What I Want

HENRY, Louise
Oral Language Development--
Views of Five Teachers

HENSON, Joan
Bing Bang Boom
Origami
Standing Buffalo
Three Guesses

HERBERT, Anne
Kamouraska

HERBES, Christine M.
Speaking of Men

HERSHEY, Ann M.
Never Give Up--Imogen Cun-
ningham
We Are Ourselves

HESSE, Isa
About a Tapestry
Spiegelei

HILL, Mary
Barrier Beach

HILL, Pamela
Close-Up--Fire!

HOBAN, Tana
Catsup

HOCHBERG, Victoria
Metroliner
Teatro Campesino
To Be Young, Gifted and
Black

Woman's Place

HODES, Roberta
Game

HOLMES, Karen
You, Mother

HOLT, Nancy
Swamp

HORNISHER, Christina
And on the Sixth Day
4 x 8 equals 16

HORVATH, Joan
Jenny Is a Good Thing
Nobody Goes There: Ellis
Island

HUBBARD, Margaret Carson
Liebalala (Sweetheart)

HUBLEY, Faith
Adventures of an Asterisk
Children of the Sun
Cockaboody
Cruise
Date with Dizzy
Dig: A Journey into Space
Doonesbury Special
Eggs
Everybody Rides the Carou-
sel, Pts. I, II, III
Harlem Wednesday
Hat
Hole
Moonbird
Of Men and Demons
Of Stars and Men
People, People, People
Second Chance: Sea
Smattering of Spots
Tender Game
Upkeep
Urbanissimo
Voyage to Next
W. O. W. Women of the World
Whither Weather
Windy Day
Zuckerkandl

HUDSON, Leonora Pirret
Cry of Pain

Our Dear Sisters
They Appreciate You More
Tiger on a Tight Leash

SHAW, Jean
Fear

SHEEHY, Terry
Athzur
Jimmy
Moments
Sugar

SHELLABARGER, Anne
Great Goddess

SHERLOCK, Maureen
Space to Be Me

SHORT, Marjie
Kudzu

SIEGAL, Lois
Spectrum in White

SILVER, Jody
Birth of the Big Mamoo

SILVERS, Joan
Case of the Elevator Duck
Fur Coat Club
Hester Street
Immigrant Experience: A
Long Long Journey

SKELTON, Marlys
Runner
Terminal Point

SLATHER, Kathi
Goodbye

SLAVINSKAYA, Maria
Great Battle of the Volga

SLESIN, Aviva
"Buenos Dias, Compañeros":
Women in Cuba
Gertrude Stein: When This
You See Remember Me
Great Radio Comedians
Other Half of the Sky: A
China Memoir

SLESINGER, Tess
Bride Wore Red
Dance, Girl, Dance
Tree Grows in Brooklyn

SLOANE, Patricia
Abstract-Expressionist Movie
Aquarians and Antiquarians
Click Clock
Colors: Red, Green, Blue,
Purple
Kenneth
Knee Ad
Painting
Please Keep This Open Door
Closed
Reticulations
Road to a Mouse
Trees
Tuesday

SMALL, Rhonda
Workout

SMITH, Judy
Woman's Film

SMITH, Lynn
Shout It Out Alphabet

SMITH, Mary Jo
Animals Are Crying

SOLBERG-LADD, Helena
Double Day
Emerging Woman
Simplemente Jenny

SOLNTSEVA, Yulia
Ukraine in Flames

SONTAG, Susan
Brother Carl
Duet for Cannibals
Promised Lands

SORTOR, Maia
Dispossessed
Richest Land
Toughest Game in Town

SOUIN, Ellen
Woman's Film

Women Who Have Had an
  Abortion
Woodlawn Sisterhood

STYMAN, Barbara
  Love Gift

SUMMERS, Elaine
  Another Pilgrim
  Walking Dance for Any Num-
    ber

SURPIN, Shelly
  Everything a Woman Could
    Want

SWITZER, Rebecca
  Song for Dead Warriors

TACHA, Athena
  Slowsilver Bubbles
  Two Space Trips

TAUBIN, Amy
  Paul's Film

TAVES, Isabella
  Rookie of the Year

TAYLOR, Renee
  Two

TEREBEY, Raika
  Trestle

TERRANELLA, Fran Burst
  Youngest Film-makers

TESICH-SAVAGE, Nadja
  Film for My Son
  Flickers
  Words

TEWKESBURY, Joan
  Nashville

THATCHER, Anita
  Homage to Magritte
  Mr. Story

THIRD World Newsreel Women
  Women's Film

THOMAS, Gayle
  It's Snow

THOMPSON, Shira
  Everything a Woman Could
    Want

TIRANOFF, Louise
  Woman Is ... Homeless

TODD, Dorothy
  Sesame Street Films

TOKIEDA, Toshie
  Report from China

TOURMARKINE, Doris
  Contemporary Films Itself

TOURTELOT, Madeline
  Ancient Footpath
  Delusion of the Fury
  Folimage
  Island Time: Gordon Onslow-
    Ford
  Metal Dimensions: Bertoia
  Music Studio: Harry Partch
  One by One
  Poet's Return
  Portrait of a Sensei
  Reflections
  Renascent
  Rotate the Body
  Searching Eye
  Shell Builder
  Silence
  Summer
  Tarascan Artisans
  Towards a New Painting:
    Ford
  Two Cats--One Chick
  U. S. Highball
  Windsong
  Zapotecan Village

TREIMAN, JANE
  Families, Alike and Differ-
    ent

TRESGOT, Annie
  Passengers

TUPPER, Lois Ann
  Biofeed Back

ZWERIN, Charlotte
  Gimme Shelter
  Salesman
  When Women Get to Hurt-
    ing

Female Sexuality, Pt. I
Flower Show
Gertrude Stein--The Rose
  That Is a Rose
Gertrude Stein--When This
  You See Remember Me
Helen Keller
Helen Keller and Her Teach-
  er
Helen Keller in Her Story
Interview with Catherine
  Marshall
Isak Dinesen
Jade Snow Wong
Katie Kelly
Lady Barbara Ward Jackson
Looking Back--Remembering
  Virginia
Louisa May Alcott
Nadine Gordimer
Night's Darkness, A Day's
  Sail
Perfect Mother: Paradox or
  Possibility
Shulie
Silent Spring of Rachel Car
  son
Song to Remember
To Be a Woman and a
  Writer
Two Faces of Group Leader-
  ship
Virginia Woolf: The Moment
  Whole
Who Does She Think She Is?
Why Women Are Dissatis-
  fied with Their Gynecolo-
  gists
Write On, Women

BALI
  Bali
  Bali Today
  Balinese Family

BATTERED CHILDREN
  Children of Peril
  Cry of Pain
  Don't Give Up on Me
  Perfect Mother: Paradox
    or Possibility
  War of the Eggs

BATTERED WOMEN
  Battered Women: Violence
    Behind Closed Doors
  Question of Justice
  We Will Not Be Beaten
  Wife Beating

BIOGRAPHY/AUTOBIOGRAPHY/
  PROFILE
  Actress
  Alice Neel, Collector of Souls
  Alice's World
  Alicia
  Amelia Earhart
  America's First Great Lady
  Anaïs Observed
  Angela--Like It Is
  Ann Rutledge
  Anna Karenina
  Anna Rosenberg
  Anne Hutchinson
  Anne of a Thousand Days
  Anne Sexton
  Antonia: A Portrait of a
    Woman
  Aretha Franklin, Soul Singer
  Art of Lotte Reiniger
  Art Profile: Barbara Weis-
    berger
  At 99: A Portrait of Louise
    Tandy Murch
  Aunt Arie
  Aunt Clara
  Autobiography of Miss Jane
    Dubois
  Barbara Hepworth
  Barbara Linden
  Barretts of Wimpole Street
  Bernadette Devlin
  Betty Carter... What's New
  Billy Jean King
  Biography of Susan B. An-
    thony
  Brontë Sisters
  By Themselves
  Carol
  Catechist
  Catherine the Great
  Catherine the Great
  Catherine Wood Marshall
  Chisholm--Pursuing the Dream
  Chris and Bernie: A Film
    About Single Mothers

I

EUROPE--SPAIN
  Columbus and Isabella

EUROPE--YUGOSLAVIA
  From 3 A. M. to 10 P. M.
  Mill

EUTHANASIA see DEATH/
  DYING/EUTHANASIA

FAMILY LIFE--GENERAL
  (also see COURTSHIP/MAR-
  RIAGE/DIVORCE)
  ... and They Lived Happily
    Ever After
  Being in Love
  Bigamist
  ... but What if the Dream
    Comes True
  Cats and Dogs
  Changing
  Divorce, Pt. I
  Divorce, Pt. II
  Doctors' Wives
  Does Anybody Need Me Any-
    more?
  Doll's House
  Doll's House; Pt. I: Destruc-
    tion of Illusion
  Doll's House; Pt. II: Ibsen's
    Themes
  Domestic Tranquility
  Effect of Gamma Rays on
    Man-in-the-Moon Mari-
    golds
  Faces
  Family
  Joyce at 34
  Juliet of the Spirits
  Just Married
  Laurette
  Leather Boys
  Long Day's Journey into
    Night
  Marrying Kind
  Martha
  Mothers After Divorce
  Mothers and Daughters
  Nana, Mom and Me
  No Tears for Kelsey
  Normalcy: What Is It?
  Not Together Now: End
    of a Marriage

Occupation: Mother
Parental Roles: Don and Mae
Pumpkin Eater
Rain People
Replay
Scenes from a Marriage
Sound and the Fury
Tell Me Where It Hurts
Tenement
Things I Cannot Change
This Is the Home of Mrs.
  Levant Graham
To Be a Parent
Tree Grows in Brooklyn
When I Grow Up
Where Mrs. Whalley Lives
Who Is Sylvia?
Young Marriage: When's the
  Big Day?

FAMILY LIFE--ALTERNATIVE
  LIFE-STYLES
  Black Jack's Family
  Changing
  Childcare: People's Liberation
  Dichotomy
  Extensions of the Family
  Family: Life Styles of the
    Future
  Freaks
  Genesis 3:16
  Grass Roots
  Homosexuality in Men and
    Women
  I and Thou
  Jane Brakhage
  Lavender
  Lavender Troubador
  Lesbian Family
  Lesbians
  Lives and Life Styles
  Living Together
  Living with Peter
  Doonesbury Special
  New Life-Styles
  Non-Marrieds
  Polygamy, Prospering in
    Exile
  Roommates on a Rainy Day
  Salt of the Earth
  Search for Alternate Life-
    Styles and Philosophies
  Sexes

Paradise Lost
People, People, People
Pesca Picsa
Pescados Vivos
Pictures from a Gallery
Pixillation
Plum Pudding
Puss in Boots
Quasi at the Quackadero
Rabbit Season
Rain
Rhythmetic
Sand
Scratch
Second Chance: Sea
Seed Reel
Sesame Street Films
Short and Suite
Shout It Out Alphabet
Six Sillies
Sleeping Beauty
Smattering of Spots
Snow White and Red Rose
Spirit of the People Is Great-
  er Than the Man's Tech-
  nology
Spook Sport
Star of Bethlehem
Stolen Heart
Story of a Dot
Story of Christmas
Story of the St. Lawrence
  Seaway
Struggle of the Meat
Sugar
Take-Off
Tender Game
Things to Come
Three Wishes
Thumbelina
Toilette
Token Gesture
Tom Tit Tot
Turtle Soup
U. F. O. 's
Up Is Down
Upkeep
Urbanissimo
Urinary Tract Infection
Viet Flakes
Voyage to Next
W. O. W. Women of the
  World

Waiting
What on Earth
Wheat Hearts
Whither Weather
Why the Sun and the Moon
  Live in the Sky
Windy Day
Winnebago Trickster Myth
Yogurt Culture
Zuckerkandl

FILM--DOCUMENTARY
Ain't Nobody's Business
Americans: 1776
... and Everything Nice
Angela Davis: Portrait of a
  Revolutionary
Antonia: A Portrait of a Wom-
  an
Art in America, Pt. I: The
  Beginnings
Art in America, Pt. II: Hud-
  son River School to Dada
Art in America, Pt. III: The
  20th Century
Art in America, Pt. IV:
  Black Artists of the U. S. A.
As Long as the Rivers Run
Attica
Autopsy of a Queen
Baby Is Born
Balinese Family
Barefoot Doctors of Rural
  China
Baymen--Our Waters Are
  Dying
Behind the Veil
Being a Prisoner
Birth
Birth Film
Buenos Dias Compañeros:
  Women in Cuba
Bush Mamma
Busing: A Rouge Ride in
  Southie
Button, Button
Caesarean Birth Experience
Campaign
Caravan
Celebrating a Century
China Commune
Chris and Bernie: A Film
  About Single Mothers

FILM--EXPERIMENTAL

Nashville
New Leaf
Night Games
Not a Pretty Picture
Olympia I: The Festival of
the People
Olympia II: The Festival of
Beauty
On the Town
Other Half of the Sky: A
China Memoir
Our Dancing Daughters
Outrage
Papa les Petits Bateaux
Paradine Case
Passengers
Pat and Mike
Peasant Women of Ryazan
Pit of Loneliness
Portrait of Jason
Promised Lands
Que Hacer? (What Is to Be
Done?)
Quiet One
Raisin in the Sun
Rebecca
Red Headed Woman
Red Sky at Morning
Red Runs the River
Revolutionists
Sabateur
Sabotage
Sambizanga
Seduction of Mimi
Seven Beauties
Shadow of a Doubt
She Done Him Wrong
Singin' in the Rain
Something Different
Sound and the Fury
Star
Steelyard Blues
Sunday, Bloody Sunday
Sundowners
Swept Away (By an Unusual
Destiny in the Blue Sea
of August)
Sylvia Scarlet
Taming of the Shrew
Teacher's Pet
Tell Me Where It Hurts
Thief of Bagdad
Thin Man

Things I Cannot Change
To Be Young, Gifted and Black
Treasure of Jamaica Reef
Tree Grows in Brooklyn
Triumph of the Will
Trollstenen
Trouble with Angels
Umbrellas of Cherbourg
Underground
Varsity
Very Curious Girl
Wands
What 80 Million Women Want
Wife vs. Secretary
Wild Party
Windflowers
Wine of Morning
Wizard of Oz
Woman of the Ganges
Women
Young Lovers
Ziegfeld Girl

FILM--SHORT
A to B
Abortion
Act of Contrition
Adjusting to Amputation
Admittance
Advertisement
After the Vote
Alexander and the Car with
a Missing Headlight
All Our Voices
All Out
Almira
Amazing Equal Pay
American Myth
Ancient Art of Peru
Ancient Footpath
"And It Is Part of Me"
And on the Sixth Day
And Then There Were...
"...and They Lived Happily
Ever After"
And You Act Like One Too
Andrew Acting Out
Andy Warhol
Andy Warhol: Mencken
Animals Are Crying
Animals of the Desert
Animals Running
Ann: A Portrait

We Get Married Twice
What Is the Shape of Tomor-
    row?
What Man Shall Live and
    Not See Death?
Where Her Gifts Are Re-
    spected
Witches of Salem: The Hor-
    ror and the Hope
With Just a Little Trust
Women, Amen!
World of the American
    Craftsman: The World
    and the Work of Viveka
    Heino

PHOTOGRAPHY / FILMMAKING

Alae
Alice's World
Anselmo
Apotheosis
Art of Marie Cosindas
At Land
Bedroom
Begone Dull Cares
Circles I
Circles I, Variation II
Circles II
Circles II, Variation II
Collage
Dorothea Lange: The Closer
    for Me
Dorothea Lange: Under the
    Trees
Enigma
Film Generation and Dance
Fog Pumas
Full Circle: The Work of
    Doris Chase
Galaxies
Googolplex
Guacamole
Imogen Cunningham, The Pho-
    tographer
Innocence
Isy Boukir
Kinesis
Light Fantastik
Lillian
Lion's Love
Mathoms
Mayan
Meditation on Violence

Meshes of the Afternoon
Metamorphosis
Metathesis
Mime Control
Mirage
Mis-Takes
Moment in Love
Moon Gates
Moon Gates
Mutations
Navajo Rain Chant
Never Give Up--Imogen Cun-
    ningham
Nine Variations on a Dance
    Theme
Olympia I: The Festival of
    the People
Olympia II: The Festival of
    Beauty
Olympiad
Papillons
Pictures from a Gallery
Pixillation
Portrait of Haiti
Squares
Study in Choreography for
    Camera
Talk with Imogen Cunningham
Tall Arches III
Two Photographers: Wynn
    Bullock, Imogen Cunning-
    ham
U. F. O. 's
Underground Film
Very Eye of Night
Waterfall

PHYSIOLOGY

Beginning of Life
Body
Emotions and Physiology of
    the Mature Woman
Girl to Woman
Growing Pains
Have a Healthy Baby
Hope Is Not a Method
How About You? A Film on
    Birth Control and Sexuality
How Life Begins
Human Reproduction
It's Wonderful Being a Girl
Linda's Film--Menstruation
Miracle of Birth

Barnett the Child
Before Pregnancy
Birth
Childbirth, Pts. I, II
Have a Healthy Baby
Marco
Miracle of Birth
Nine to Get Ready
Not Me Alone
Prenatal
Prenatal Care
Prenatal Care: While You're
  Waiting
Prenatal Development
That's Our Baby

PRISON/PENAL SYSTEM
Angela--Like It Is
Being a Prisoner
Chant D'Amour
Cloister
Jane Kennedy--To Be Free
Like a Rose
On a Question of Justice
Prison Film: Still Living
Prisoners
Release
Time Has No Sympathy
We're Alive
Who Is Tracy Williams?
Women in Prison
Women in Prison, Pts. I,
  II

PROFESSION CHANGE see
  CAREER CHANGE

PROFESSIONS see CAREERS

PROSTITUTES/PROSTITUTION
Ain't Nobody's Business
Chinamoon
Game
House Is Not Enough
Issues in Sexual Behavior:
  Rape, Prostitution,
  Homosexuality
My Life to Live (Vivre
  Sa Vie)
Nights of Cabiria
Requiem for Tina Sanchez
Sex and the Law
Street of Shame

Susan: April to June
Two of Three Things I Need
  to Know
Valerie
Very Curious Girl
Woman to Woman

PSYCHOLOGY
Abortion
Abortion
Abortion
Abortion: Public Issue or Pri-
  vate Matter?
Actor
Actor Works
Adam's Rib
Adam's Rib (Girls and Women
  Series)
Adolescence: Crises or Oppor-
  tunity
Aging
Aging: The Search for Eternal
  Youth
Aid to Families with Depend-
  ent Children
All About Eve
All Out
And I Don't Mean Maybe
"...and They Lived Happily
  Ever After"
And Who Are You?
Anna
Any Empty Space
Anything They Want to Be
Anything You Want to Be
Art of Age
Aspiration Abortion Without
  Cervical Dilation
Aspirations
At Land
Attention Must Be Paid
Barbara
Battle of the Villa Fiorita
Being in Love
Being Me
Belle Cerebrale
Between Man and Woman
Bias
Big Bob Kuhn
Big Town
Birth
Bonheur
Breakthrough